February 21–23, 2016
Monterey, CA, USA

**Association for
Computing Machinery**

Advancing Computing as a Science & Profession

FPGA'16

Proceedings of the 2016 ACM/SIGDA International Symposium on
Field-Programmable Gate Arrays

Sponsored by:
ACM SIGDA

Supported by:
*Altera, Baidu, Lattice, Microsemi, Microsoft Research, Xilinx,
Algo-Logic, Atomic Rules, and Trimberger Family Foundation*

Association for
Computing Machinery

Advancing Computing as a Science & Profession

The Association for Computing Machinery
2 Penn Plaza, Suite 701
New York, New York 10121-0701

Notice to Past Authors of ACM-Published Articles
ACM intends to create a complete electronic archive of all articles and/or other material previously published by ACM. If you have written a work that has been previously published by ACM in any journal or conference proceedings prior to 1978, or any SIG Newsletter at any time, and you do NOT want this work to appear in the ACM Digital Library, please inform permissions@acm.org, stating the title of the work, the author(s), and where and when published.

ISBN: 978-1-4503-3856-1

Additional copies may be ordered prepaid from:

ACM Order Department
PO Box 30777
New York, NY 10087-0777, USA

Phone: 1-800-342-6626 (USA and Canada)
+1-212-626-0500 (Global)
Fax: +1-212-944-1318
E-mail: acmhelp@acm.org
Hours of Operation: 8:30 am – 4:30 pm ET

Printed in the USA

FPGA 2016 Chairs' Welcome

It is our great pleasure to welcome you to the 2016 ACM International Symposium on FPGAs (FPGA 2016). Our mission is to serve as the premier forum for presentation of exciting new research on all aspects of the design and use of Field Programmable Gate Arrays. This includes:

- Architecture and circuit design of FPGAs

- Computer-aided design algorithms for synthesis, technology mapping, logic and timing optimization, clustering, placement, and routing of FPGAs

- High-level abstractions and design tools for FPGA users

- FPGA-based and FPGA-like computing engines and accelerators

- Innovative FPGA applications and design studies

In addition, the Symposium is an opportunity for leading FPGA researchers and practitioners from around the world to mingle and share ideas in the relaxed atmosphere of Monterey, California – convenient to Silicon Valley, yet a world apart.

This year we received 111 submissions – an increase of 10 per cent – from 17 countries. The Program Committee accepted 20 full research papers (ten pages), 10 short research papers (six pages), and one tutorial paper, each of which you will find in these proceedings. In addition, 30 other select submissions will be presented as posters at the Symposium; abstracts of these also appear in these proceedings.

This year's evening panel discussion will address the topic "Intel Acquires Altera: How Will the World of FPGAs be Affected?" Bring your tough questions for our expert panelists, concerning either technical or business aspects of this significant change in the FPGA industry landscape.

The Symposium kicks off with the co-located Workshop on Overlay Architectures for FPGAs (OLAF). Overlay architectures (e.g. arrays of special-purpose soft processors) are a potentially powerful way to improve design productivity and virtualize FPGAs. Our Designers' Day sessions will be devoted to tutorials for FPGA users.

We would like to thank the many members of the Program Committee and other reviewers, listed on the following pages, who devoted considerable effort to thoughtfully evaluating all the submissions. Our goal is not only to bring the best work from around the world to the Symposium, but also to provide useful feedback on all submissions. We would also like to thank Stephen Neuendorffer for organizing the Designers' Day sessions, and Hayden So and John Wawrzynek for bringing the second edition of OLAF to our Symposium. Our thanks to Lisa Tolles and John Lateulere for logistical support, and to our sponsors for helping make FPGA 2016 possible.

We look forward to seeing you at FPGA 2016!

Jonathan Greene
Program Chair
Microsemi, USA

Deming Chen
General Chair
University of Illinois Urbana-Champaign, USA

Table of Contents

FPGA 2016 Organization..x

FPGA 2016 Sponsor & Supporters xii

Workshop on Overlay Architectures for FPGAs

- **OLAF'16: Second International Workshop on Overlay Architectures for FPGAs** 1
  Hayden Kwok-Hay So *(University of Hong Kong)*, John Wawrzynek *(University of California, Berkeley)*

Designers' Day Session 1: Hardware Features

- **HyperPipelining of High-Speed Interface Logic**...2
  Gregg Baeckler *(Altera Corporation)*

- **Spatial Debug & Debug without Re-Programming in FPGAs** 3
  Pankaj Shanker *(Microsemi Corporation)*

Designers' Day Session 2: System Level Methodology

- **SDSoC: A Higher-Level Programming Environment for Zynq SoC
  and Ultrascale+ MPSoC** 4
  Vinod Kathail, James Hwang, Welson Sun, Yogesh Chobe, Tom Shui, Jorge Carrillo *(Xilinx)*

- **FCUDA-SoC: Platform Integration for Field-Programmable SoC
  with the CUDA-to-FPGA Compiler**..5
  Tan Nguyen, Swathi Gurumani, Kyle Rupnow *(Advanced Digital Sciences Center)*,
  Deming Chen *(University of Illinois at Urbana-Champaign)*

- **Agile Co-Design for a Reconfigurable Datacenter** 15
  Shlomi Alkalay, Hari Angepat, Adrian Caulfield, Eric Chung, Oren Firestein, Michael Haselman, Stephen Heil,
  Kyle Holohan, Matt Humphrey, Tamas Juhasz, Puneet Kaur, Sitaram Lanka, Daniel Lo, Todd Massengill,
  Kalin Ovtcharov, Michael Papamichael, Andrew Putnam, Raja Seera, Rimon Tadros, Jason Thong, Lisa Woods,
  Derek Chiou, Doug Burger *(Microsoft Corporation)*

Technical Session 1: Neural Networks and OpenCL
Session Chair: Jason H. Anderson *(University of Toronto)*

- **Throughput-Optimized OpenCL-Based FPGA Accelerator for Large-Scale
  Convolutional Neural Networks** 16
  Naveen Suda *(Arizona State University)*, Vikas Chandra, Ganesh Dasika *(ARM Inc.)*,
  Abinash Mohanty, Yufei Ma, Sarma Vrudhula, Jae-sun Seo, Yu Cao *(Arizona State University)*

- **Going Deeper with Embedded FPGA Platform for Convolutional Neural Network**...............26
  Jiantao Qiu, Jie Wang, Song Yao, Kaiyuan Guo, Boxun Liv, Erjin Zhou, Jincheng Yu,
  Tianqi Tang *(Tsinghua University)*, Ningyi Xu *(Microsoft Research Asia)*,
  Sen Song, Yu Wang, Huazhong Yang *(Tsinghua University)*

- **Using Stochastic Computing to Reduce the Hardware Requirements for a Restricted
  Boltzmann Machine Classifier**..36
  Bingzhe Li, M. Hassan Najafi, David J. Lilja *(University of Minnesota, Twin Cities)*

- **A Platform-Oblivious Approach for Heterogeneous Computing:
  A Case Study with Monte Carlo-Based Simulation for Medical Applications**........................42
  Shih-Hao Hung, Min-Yu Tsai, Bo-Yi Huang, Chia-Heng Tu *(National Taiwan University)*

- **A Case for Work-Stealing on FPGAs with OpenCL Atomics** 48
  Nadesh Ramanathan, John Wickerson, Felix Winterstein, George A. Constantinides *(Imperial College)*

Technical Session 2: Cooling and Clocking

Session Chair: Peter Cheung *(Imperial College)*

- **Physical Design of 3D FPGAs Embedded with Micro-Channel-Based Fluidic Cooling** 54
  Zhiyuan Yang, Ankur Srivastava *(University of Maryland, College Park)*

- **Stratix™ 10 High Performance Routable Clock Networks**..................64
  Carl Ebeling, Dana How, David Lewis, Herman Schmit *(Altera Corporation)*

- **Boolean Satisfiability-Based Routing and Its Application to Xilinx Ultrascale Clock Network**..................74
  Henri Fraisse, Abhishek Joshi, Dinesh Gaitonde, Alireza Kaviani *(Xilinx Inc.)*

Technical Session 3: Circuit Design, Graph Processing Applications

Session Chair: Mike Hutton *(Altera)*

- **FPRESSO: Enabling Express Transistor-Level Exploration of FPGA Architectures** 80
  Grace Zgheib, Manana Lortkipanidze, Muhsen Owaida, David Novo,
  Paolo Ienne *(École Polytechnique Fédérale de Lausanne (EPFL))*

- **Towards PVT-Tolerant Glitch-Free Operation in FPGAs**..................90
  Safeen Huda, Jason Anderson *(University of Toronto)*

- **Pitfalls and Tradeoffs in Simultaneous, On-Chip FPGA Delay Measurement** 100
  Timothy A. Linscott, Benjamin Gojman, Raphael Rubin, André DeHon *(University of Pennsylvania)*

- **FPGP: Graph Processing Framework on FPGA: A Case Study of Breadth-First Search** 105
  Guohao Dai, Yuze Chi, Yu Wang, Huazhong Yang *(Tsinghua University)*

- **GraphOps: A Dataflow Library for Graph Analytics Acceleration**..................111
  Tayo Oguntebi, Kunle Olukotun *(Stanford University)*

Technical Session 4: Applications and System-level Tools

Session Chair: James C. Hoe *(Carnegie Mellon University)*

- **High Performance Linkage Disequilibrium: FPGAs Hold the Key**..................118
  Nikolaos Alachiotis, Gabriel Weisz *(Carnegie Mellon University)*

- **LMC: Automatic Resource-Aware Program-Optimized Memory Partitioning**......................128
  Hsin-Jung Yang *(Massachusetts Institute of Technology)*, Kermin Fleming, Michael Adler *(Intel Corporation)*,
  Felix Winterstein *(Imperial College London)*, Joel Emer *(Massachusetts Institute of Technology)*

- **Efficient Memory Partitioning for Parallel Data Access via Data Reuse**..................138
  Jincheng Su, Fan Yang, Xuan Zeng *(Fudan University)*,
  Dian Zhou *(Fudan University & University of Texas at Dallas)*

Evening Panel

Session Chair: Derek Chiou *(Microsoft / University of Texas at Austin)*

- **Intel Acquires Altera: How Will the World of FPGAs be Affected?** 148
  Derek Chiou *(Microsoft/UT Austin)*

Technical Session 5: Architecture and Tools

Session Chair: Jonathan Rose *(University of Toronto)*

- **PRfloor: An Automatic Floorplanner for Partially Reconfigurable FPGA Systems** 149
  Tuan D. A. Nguyen *(National University of Singapore)*, Akash Kumar *(Technische Universität Dresden)*

- **The Stratix™ 10 Highly Pipelined FPGA Architecture**..................159
  David Lewis, Gordon Chiu, Jeffrey Chromczak, David Galloway, Ben Gamsa, Valavan Manohararajah,
  Ian Milton, Tim Vanderhoek, John Van Dyken *(Altera Corporation)*

- **Case for Design-Specific Machine Learning in Timing Closure of FPGA Designs** 169
  Que Yanghua, Chinnakkannu Adaikkala Raj *(Nanyang Technological University)*,
  Harnhua Ng, Kirvy Teo *(Plunify Inc.)*, Nachiket Kapre *(Nanyang Technological University)*

- **Just in Time Assembly of Accelerators** 173

  Sen Ma, Zeyad Aklah, David Andrews *(University of Arkansas)*

- **Cask – Open-Source Custom Architectures for Sparse Kernels** 179

  Paul Grigoras, Pavel Burovskiy, Wayne Luk *(Imperial College London)*

Technical Session 6: System-level Tools
Session Chair: Mingjie Lin *(University of Central Florida)*

- **GPU-Accelerated High-Level Synthesis for Bitwidth Optimization of FPGA Datapaths** ... 185

  Nachiket Kapre, Deheng Ye *(Nanyang Technological University)*

- **Resolve: Generation of High-Performance Sorting Architectures from High-Level Synthesis** 195

  Janarbek Matai, Dustin Richmond, Dajung Lee, Zac Blair, Qiongzhi Wu, Amin Abazari, Ryan Kastner *(University of California, San Diego)*

- **SEU Mitigation and Validation of the LEON3 Soft Processor Using Triple Modular Redundancy for Space Processing** 205

  Michael J. Wirthlin, Andrew M. Keller, Chase McCloskey, Parker Ridd *(Brigham Young University)*, David Lee *(Sandia National Laboratories)*, Jeffrey Draper *(University of Southern California)*

Technical Session 7: High-level Synthesis and Tools
Session Chair: David Biancolin *(University of California, Berkeley)*

- **Optimal Circuits for Streamed Linear Permutations Using RAM** 215

  François Serre, Thomas Holenstein, Markus Püschel *(ETH Zurich)*

- **High Level Synthesis of Complex Applications: An H.264 Video Decoder** 224

  Xinheng Liu *(University of Illinois at Urbana-Champaign)*, Yao Chen *(Nankai University & Advanced Digital Sciences Center)*, Tan Nguyen, Swathi Gurumani, Kyle Rupnow *(Advanced Digital Sciences Center)*, Deming Chen *(University of Illinois at Urbana-Champaign)*

- **Automatically Optimizing the Latency, Area, and Accuracy of C Programs for High-Level Synthesis** 234

  Xitong Gao, John Wickerson, George A. Constantinides *(Imperial College London)*

Technical Session 8: Applications
Session Chair: George Constantinides *(Imperial College London)*

- **Reducing Memory Requirements for High-Performance and Numerically Stable Gaussian Elimination** 244

  David Boland *(Monash University)*

- **FGPU: An SIMT-Architecture for FPGAs** 254

  Muhammed Al Kadi, Benedikt Janssen, Michael Huebner *(Ruhr University of Bochum)*

- **A Study of Pointer-Chasing Performance on Shared-Memory Processor-FPGA Systems** 264

  Gabriel Weisz *(Carnegie Mellon University & University of Southern California)*, Joseph Melber, Yu Wang *(Carnegie Mellon University)*, Kermin Fleming, Eriko Nurvitadhi *(Intel Corporation)*, James C. Hoe *(Carnegie Mellon University)*

Poster Session 1

- **A Low DDR Bandwidth 100FPS 1080p Video 2D Discrete Wavelet Transform Implementation on FPGA** 274

  Mohammed Shaaban Ibraheem, Syed Zahid Ahmed, Khalil Hachicha *(UPMC Paris 06)*, Sylvain Hochberg *(CIRA)*, Patrick Garda *(UPMC Paris 06)*

- **A Scalable Heterogeneous Dataflow Architecture for Big Data Analytics Using FPGAs** 274

  Ehsan Ghasemi, Paul Chow *(University of Toronto)*

- **Accelerating Database Query Processing on OpenCL-Based FPGAs** 274
  Zeke Wang, Huiyan Cheah, Johns Paul, Bingsheng He *(Nanyang Technological University)*,
  Wei Zhang *(HKUST)*

- **An Improved Global Stereo-Matching on FPGA for Real-Time Applications** 274
  Daolu Zha, Xi Jin, Tian Xiang *(University of Science of Technology of China)*

- **ENFIRE: An Energy-Efficient Fine-Grained Spatio-Temporal Reconfigurable Computing Fabric** 275
  Wenchao Qian, Christopher Babecki, Robert Karam, Swarup Bhunia *(Case Western Reserve University)*

- **Floorplanning of Partially Reconfigurable Design on Heterogeneous FPGA** 275
  Pingakshya Goswami, Dinesh Bhatia *(University of Texas at Dallas)*

- **Increasing the Utility of Self-Calibration Methods in High-Precision Time Measurement Systems** 275
  Matthias Hinkfoth, Ralf Salomon *(University of Rostock)*

- **Knowledge is Power: Module-Level Sensing for Runtime Optimisation** 276
  James J. Davis, Eddie Hung, Joshua M. Levine, Edward A. Stott, Peter Y K Cheung,
  George A. Constantinides *(Imperial College London)*

- **Machine-Learning Driven Auto-Tuning of High-Level Synthesis for FPGAs** 276
  Li Ting, Harri Wijaya, Nachiket Kapre *(Nanyang Technological University)*

- **Re-Targeting Optimization Sequences From Scalar Processors to FPGAs in HLS Compilers** 276
  Ronak Kogta, Suresh Purini, Ajit Mathew *(International Institute of Information Technology)*

Poster Session 2

- **A High-Throughput Architecture for Lossless Decompression on FPGA Designed Using HLS** 277
  Jie Lei *(Xidian University & University of California, Los Angeles)*,
  Yuting Chen, Yunsong Li *(Xidian University)*, Jason Cong *(University of California, Los Angeles)*

- **An Activity Aware Placement Approach for 3D FPGAs** 277
  Girish Deshpande, Dinesh Bhatia *(University of Texas at Dallas)*

- **An Extensible Heterogeneous Multi-FPGA Framework for Accelerating N-Body Simulation** 277
  Tianqi Wang, Bo Peng, Xi Jin *(University of Science and Technology of China)*

- **An FPGA-Based Controller for a 77 GHz Mems Tri-Mode Automotive Radar** 278
  Sabrina Zereen *(Invotek Electronics Inc.)*, Sundeep Lal *(VerifEye Technologies)*,
  Mohammed Khalid, Sazzadur Chowdhury *(University of Windsor)*

- **An FPGA-SoC Based Accelerating Solution for N-Body Simulations in MOND** 278
  Bo Peng, Tianqi Wang, Xi Jin, Chuanjun Wang *(University of Chinese Academy of Sciences)*

- **Automated Verification Code Generation in HLS Using Software Execution Traces** 278
  Liwei Yang *(Nanyang Technological University)*, Swathi Gurumani *(Advanced Digital Sciences Center)*,
  Suhaib A. Fahmy *(Nanyang Technological University)*,
  Deming Chen *(University of Illinois at Urbana-Champaign)*, Kyle Rupnow *(Advanced Digital Sciences Center)*

- **DCPUF: Placement and Routing Constraint Based Dynamically Configured Physical Unclonable Function on FPGA** 279
  Jing Ye, Yu Hu, Xiaowei Li *(Chinese Academy of Sciences)*

- **Evaluating the Impact of Environmental Factors on Physically Unclonable Functions** ...279
  Sebastien Bellon *(ALaRI - USI)*, Claudio Favi *(Nagra)*, Miroslaw Malek *(ALaRI - USI)*, Marco Macchetti *(Nagra)*,
  Francesco Regazzoni *(ALaRI - USI)*

- **Stochastic-Based Spin-Programmable Gate Array with Emerging MTJ Device Technology**...279
  Yu Bai, Mingjie Lin *(University of Central Florida)*

- **Testing FPGA Local Interconnects Based on Repeatable Configuration Modules** 280
  Zhen Yang, Jian Wang, Meng Yang, Jinmei Lai *(Fudan University)*

Poster Session 3

- **A 1 GSa/S, Reconfigurable Soft-Core FPGA Adc** 281
  Stefan Visser, Harald Homulle, Edoardo Charbon *(TU Delft)*

- **A Full-Capacity Local Routing Architecture for FPGAs** 281
  Xifan Tang, Pierre-Emmanuel Gaillardon, Giovanni De Micheli *(École Polytechnique Fédérale de Lausanne)*

- **ARAPrototyper: Enabling Rapid Prototyping and Evaluation for Accelerator-Rich Architecture**...281
  Yu-Ting Chen, Jason Cong, Zhenman Fang, Peipei Zhou *(University of California, Los Angeles)*

- **Doubling FPGA Throughput via a Soft SerDes Architecture for Full-Bandwidth Serial Pipelining** 282
  Aaron Landy, Greg Stitt *(University of Florida)*

- **Enhanced TERO-PUF Implementations and Characterization on FPGAs** 282
  Cedric Marchand, Lilian Bossuet *(University of Lyon)*, Abdelkarim Cherkaoui *(TIMA Laboratory)*

- **FPGA Power Estimation Using Automatic Feature Selection** 282
  Yunxuan Yu, Lei He *(University of California, Los Angeles)*

- **HGum: Messaging Framework for Hardware Accelerators**...283
  Sizhuo Zhang *(Massachusetts Institute of Technology)*, Hari Angepat, Derek Chiou *(Microsoft)*

- **Low-Swing Signaling for FPGA Power Reduction** 283
  Sayeh Sharifymoghaddam, Ali Sheikholeslami *(University of Toronto)*

- **Stochastic-Based Convolutional Networks with Reconfigurable Logic Fabric** 283
  Mohammed Alawad, Mingjie Lin *(University of Central Florida)*

- **t-QuadPlace: Timing Driven Quadratic Placement Using Quadrisection Partitioning for FPGAs**...284
  Nimish Agashiwala, Satya Prakash Upadhyay, Kia Bazargan *(University of Minnesota Twin Cities)*

Author Index

Author Index...285

FPGA 2016 Organization

General Chair: Deming Chen *(University of Illinois at Urbana-Champaign, USA)*

Program Chair: Jonathan Greene *(Microsemi, USA)*

Finance Chair: George Constantinides *(Imperial College, UK)*

Publicity Chair: Kia Bazargan *(University of Minnesota, USA)*

Designer's Track Chair: Stephen Neuendorffer *(Xilinx, USA)*

Program Committee: Jason H. Anderson *(University of Toronto, Canada)*
Trevor Bauer *(Xilinx, USA)*
Kia Bazargan *(University of Minnesota, USA)*
Vaughn Betz *(University of Toronto, Canada)*
Philip Brisk *(University of California, Riverside, USA)*
Deming Chen *(University of Illinois at Urbana-Champaign, USA)*
Peter Cheung *(Imperial College, UK)*
Derek Chiou *(Microsoft / University of Texas at Austin, USA)*
Paul Chow *(University of Toronto, Canada)*
Eric Chung *(Microsoft Research, USA)*
Jason Cong *(University of California, Los Angeles, USA)*
George Constantinides *(Imperial College*, UK)
Carl Ebeling *(Altera, USA)*
Wenyi Feng *(Microsemi, USA)*
Haohuan Fu *(Tsinghua University, China)*
Jonathan Greene *(Microsemi, USA)*
Yajun Ha *(Institute for Infocomm Research, Singapore)*
Scott Hauck *(University of Washington, USA)*
James C. Hoe *(Carnegie Mellon University, USA)*
Brad Hutchings *(Brigham Young University, USA)*
Mike Hutton *(Altera, USA)*
Paolo Ienne *(École Polytechnique Fédérale de Lausanne, Switzerland)*
Ryan Kastner *(University of California, San Diego, USA)*
Martin Langhammer *(Altera, UK)*
Miriam Leeser *(Northeastern University, USA)*
Guy Lemieux *(University of British Columbia, Canada)*
Philip Leong *(University of Sydney, Australia)*
David Lewis *(Altera, Canada)*
Mingjie Lin *(University of Central Florida, USA)*
John Lockwood *(Algo-Logic Systems, USA)*
Sundararajarao Mohan *(Xilinx, USA)*
Stephen Neuendorffer *(Xilinx, USA)*
Jonathan Rose *(University of Toronto, Canada)*

Program Committee (continued):

Kyle Rupnow *(Advanced Digital Sciences Center, Singapore)*
David Rutledge *(Lattice Semiconductor, USA)*
Graham Schelle *(Xilinx, USA)*
Herman Schmit *(Altera, USA)*
Lesley Shannon *(Simon Fraser University, Canada)*
Jürgen Teich *(University of Erlangen-Nuremberg, Germany)*
Russ Tessier *(University of Massachusetts, USA)*
Steve Trimberger *(Xilinx, USA)*
Yu Wang *(Tsinghua University, China)*
John Wawrzynek *(University of California, Berkeley, USA)*
Steve Wilton *(University of British Columbia, Canada)*
Michael Wirthlin *(Brigham Young University, USA)*
Zhiru Zhang *(Cornell University, USA)*

Additional Reviewers:

Abdalrahman Arafeh	Hsuan Hsiao	Eric Sather
Andreas Becher	Muhuan Huang	Christian Schmitt
Rafe Camerota	Qijing Huang	David Schultz
Keith Campbell	Safeen Huda	Simon Scott
Fernando Martin del Campo	Mengyao Jin	Ericles Sousa
Charles Chaisson	Dae Hee Kim	Edward Stott
Yao Chen	Jin Hee Kim	Jiang Su
Yu Ting Chen	Choden Königsmark	Welson Sun
Shaoyi Cheng	Vahid Lari	Justin Tai
Young-kyu Choi	Josh Levine	Naif Tarafdar
Jeff Chromczak	Gai Liu	Kosuke Tatsumura
Ron Cline	Jiahe Liu	Tim Vanderhoek
Steve Dai	Xinheng Liu	Jasmina Vasiljevic
Sabya Das	Charles Lo	Jie Wang
James Davis	Chris Madill	Scott Weber
Ashutosh Dhar	Valavan Manohararajah	Aaron Wood
Roberto Dicecco	Joe Mayer	Chang Xu
Xin Fang	Nathaniel McVicar	Liwei Yang
Zhenman Fang	Vincent Mirian	Christopher Yarp
Jeremy Fowers	Kevin Murray	Sadegh Yazdenshenas
Eric Fukuda	Richard Newell	Wang Yi
Brian Gaide	Tan Nguyen	Bai Yu
Dinesh Gaitonde	John O'Dwyer	Bo Yuan
Ilya Ganusov	Bruce Pedersen	Ritchie Zhao
Nithin George	Oliver Reiche	Wenlai Zhao
Udit Gupta	Daniel Rozhko	Weijie Zheng
Swathi Gurumani	Naman Saraf	Daniel Ziener
Dana How		Wei Zuo

FPGA 2016 Sponsor & Supporters

Sponsor:

Corporate Patrons:

Supporters:

Logistics support:

OLAF'16: Second International Workshop on Overlay Architectures for FPGAs

Hayden Kwok-Hay So
Department of Electrical and Electronic
Engineering
University of Hong Kong
Hong Kong
hso@eee.hku.hk

John Wawrzynek
Department of Electrical Engineering and
Computer Sciences
University of California, Berkeley
Berkeley, CA 94720
johnw@eecs.berkeley.com

ABSTRACT

The Second International Workshop on Overlay Architectures for FPGAs is held in Monterey, California, USA, on February 21, 2016 and co-located with FPGA 2016: The 24th ACM/SIGDA International Symposium on Field Programmable Gate Arrays. The main objective of the workshop is to address how overlay architectures can help address the challenges and opportunities provided by FPGA-based reconfigurable computing. The workshop provides a venue for researchers to present and discuss the latest developments in FPGA overlay architecture and related areas. We have assembled a program of six refereed papers and a panel discussion with prominent experts in the field.

CCS Concepts

•Computer systems organization → Reconfigurable computing; *Parallel architectures; Multiple instruction, multiple data; Single instruction, multiple data; Cellular architectures;* •Hardware → Reconfigurable logic and FPGAs;

Keywords

FPGA; Overlay architecture

1. BACKGROUND

The OLAF workshop was started in response to the growing interest in utilizing virtual coarse-grain architectures overlaying fine-grained FPGAs. Despite much work on novel programming models and tools, a huge gap remains in the programming experience on reconfigurable devices versus software processors. Overlay architectures, such as arrays of soft processor cores, and vector processors, originated from academic research to address this challenge of providing familiar programming models and abstractions to users of FPGAs. In a wide variety of applications, these architectures demonstrated their effectiveness to not only supply

FPGA'16 February 21-23, 2016, Monterey, CA, USA

© 2016 Copyright held by the owner/author(s).

ACM ISBN 978-1-4503-3856-1/16/02.

DOI: http://dx.doi.org/10.1145/2847263.2847345

users with convenient programming models and tools but also their ability to take advantage of the inherent computational efficiency of FPGAs. These systems, such as those for supporting openCL, are also now finding use in commercial systems. While originally developed to address design productivity, overlay architectures provide other benefits, such as enhanced debugging, design portability, security, domain specific optimizations, hardware platform independence, support for partial reconfiguration, and user independence from vendor specific tools. As the complexity of FPGA platforms continue to grow exponentially, it is anticipated that the use of overlay architectures on FPGAs will increase and become mainstream practice.

2. SCOPE

Prospective authors were invited to submit original contributions (up to six pages) or extended abstracts describing work-in-progress or position papers (extended abstracts not to exceed two pages). Contributions were sought in, but not limited to, the following topics:

• New overlay architectures • Application of overlay architectures • Tools for designing and generating overlays • Debugging • Design productivity and usability improving tools and practices • FPGA Virtualization • FPGAs in cloud datacenters • Time-multiplexed architectures • Rapid compilation • High-level synthesis • Cross vendor development frameworks.

3. PROGRAM COMMITTEE

We assembled a set of reviewers, drawn from the participants of the first OLAF workshop. All accepted papers received at least three reviews. For this, we would like to thank all the PC members for their time and contributions:

Tarek Abdelrahman (University of Toronto), Jonathan Bachrach (UC Berkeley), Mike Butts (Synopsys), Carl Ebeling (Altera), Jan Gray (Consultant, Gray Research LLC), Brad Hutchings (Brigham Young University), Guy Lemieux (University of British Columbia), Greg Stitt (University of Florida).

4. CONCLUSION

OLAF'16 was a success and we hope it will continue to serve as a venue to advance technologies in FPGA overlays and related areas in the future.

HyperPipelining of High-Speed Interface Logic

Gregg Baeckler
Altera Corporation
101 Innovation Drive
San Jose, CA 95134
gbaeckle@altera.com

ABSTRACT

The throughput needs of networking designs on FPGAs are constantly growing -- from 40Gbps to 100Gbps, 400Gbps and beyond. A 400G Ethernet MAC needs to process wide data at high speeds to meet the throughput needs. Altera recently introduced HyperFlex^{TM} [1][2][3], a change to the fabric architecture aimed to facilitate massive pipelining of FPGA designs -- allowing them to run faster and hence alleviate the congestion that is caused by widening datapaths beyond 512b or 1024b. Though it seems counterintuitive it can be easier to close timing at 781 MHz for a 640b datapath than at 390 MHz for a 1280b datapath when wire congestion is taken into account.

This presentation will discuss some of the practical details in implementing high-throughput protocols such as Ethernet and Interlaken, how we address these traditionally and how the design of the cores is modified with HyperPipelining. We will discuss alternative development styles for control and datapath logic, strategies for wire planning to avoid congestion, the throughput limits of FPGA routing networks, common timing closure issues and how to alleviate them, and how to pipeline intelligently. This presentation is thus partly a tutorial in the issues of making a 400G FPGA design close timing, and partly a case study of using HyperFlex on an FPGA design.

Keywords
FPGA, RTL Design, Pipelining, Performance, HyperFlex

1. REFERENCES

[1] D. Lewis *et. al.*, "The Stratix 10 Highly Pipelined FPGA Architecture", in *Proc. 2016 Int'l Symposium on FPGAs*.

[2] Altera, "WP-01231-1.0 Understanding How the New HyperFlex Architecture Enables Next-Generation High-Performance Systems", https://www.altera.com/en_US/pdfs/literature/wp/wp-01231-understanding-how-hyperflex-architecture-enables-high-performance-systems.pdf.

[3] Altera, "WP-01218-1.0 Using Quartus II Software to Maximize Performance in the HyperFlex Architecture", https://www.altera.com/en_US/pdfs/literature/wp/wp-01218-quartus-ii-software-to-maximize-performance-in-hyperflex-architecture.pdf

FPGA'16, February 21-23, 2016, Monterey, CA, USA
ACM 978-1-4503-3856-1/16/02.
DOI http://dx.doi.org/10.1145/2847263.2847285

Spatial Debug & Debug without Re-programming in FPGAs

Pankaj Shanker
SoC Products Group
Microsemi Corp.
San Jose, CA 95134
(408) 643-6198
pankaj.shanker@microsemi.com

ABSTRACT

SmartFusion2 Family of FPGAs from MicroSemi introduces novel Silicon technology that enables minimally intrusive, spatial debug capabilities. Spatial debug concerns itself with observing and controlling sequential elements in the user's Design Under Test (DUT) at an instant of time, i.e. in a specific clock cycle. This capability is made possible by the in-situ, always available probe network running at 50MHz in Smartfusion2. Observing and controlling DUT is less intrusive than conventional methods. Furthermore, no instrumentation and no re-programming of the FPGA device is required. This reduces the number of debug iterations (test re-runs) and accelerates design bring-up in the lab.

This session showcases a technique to debug pseudo-static signals, i.e. sequential elements that remain static over a duration of time spanning many clock cycles of probe network (50MHz). Partial or entire set of sequential logic in the DUT can be read out via the JTAG or the SPI interface, while the DUT is running. This technique of observation is non-intrusive.

A method to debug DUT using clock halting is presented. In such a method, the clock of the DUT is halted based on a trigger signal that is external or internal to the DUT. The trigger signal can be dynamically chosen without re-programming the device. Once the trigger fires, and clock is halted using a glitchless clock gate, any portion of the sequential logic in the DUT can be written to (altered) and then if required, the user clock can be gated ON to resume normal operation. Though somewhat intrusive, this technique of controlling hard to reach DUT states is invaluable in certain debug situations.

A method based on repetition of controlled sequence of clock halting, stimulus application and clock advancing (i.e. clock-stepping) can be employed to debug synchronous designs to achieve 100% visibility and 100% controllability on-chip, hitherto only achievable via runtime intensive PC-based simulators or costly ASIC/FPGA based emulators. Essentially, it shall be shown that typical capabilities of simulation can be "mimicked" in an on-chip emulation.

Techniques in spatial debug can be applied in hardware-software co-validation for processor based SoC designs, comprising of multitude of SoC peripherals synthesized into the FPGA. This is desirable when one is trying to isolate issues between firmware and hardware. In this technique, firmware instrumented breakpoint can trigger the halt of the DUT, or aternatively, DUT triggered clock freeze and interrupt to firmware can provide a spatial snapshot of the SoC design. The ability to resume execution of the firmware and hardware after peek-poke into firmware state and the DUT state shall be demonstrated.

CCS Concepts

• **General and reference~Validation** • *General and reference~Verification* • **Computer systems organization~System on a chip** • Computer systems organization~Embedded software • **Hardware~Sequential circuits** • **Hardware~Hardware accelerators** • **Hardware~Simulation and emulation** • **Hardware~Bug detection, localization and diagnosis** • **Hardware~Bug fixing (hardware)**

Keywords

FPGA; Debug; On-Chip; Spatial Debug; Emulation; Validation; Hardware Software Co-Validation;

FPGA'16, February 21-23, 2016, Monterey, CA, USA
ACM 978-1-4503-3856-1/16/02.
DOI http://dx.doi.org/10.1145/2847263.2847286

SDSoC: A Higher-level Programming Environment for Zynq SoC and Ultrascale+ MPSoC

Vinod Kathail
Xilinx
2100 Logic Drive
San Jose, CA
vinod.kathail@xilinx.com

James Hwang
Xilinx
2100 Logic Drive
San Jose, CA
jim.hwang@xilinx.com

Welson Sun
Xilinx
2100 Logic Drive
San Jose, CA
welson.sun@xilinx.com

Yogesh Chobe
Xilinx
2100 Logic Drive
San Jose, CA
yogesh.chobe@xilinx.com

Tom Shui
Xilinx
2100 Logic Drive
San Jose, CA
tom.shui@xilinx.com

Jorge Carrillo
Xilinx
2100 Logic Drive
San Jose, CA
jorge.carrillo@xilinx.com

ABSTRACT

Zynq-7000 All Programmable SoC and the new Zynq Ultrascale+ MPSoC provide proven alternatives to traditional domain-specific application SoCs and enable extensive system-level differentiation, integration and flexibility through hardware, software and I/O programmability.

The SDSoC Development Environment is a heterogeneous design environment for implementing embedded systems using the Zynq SoC and MPSoC. It enables the broader community of embedded software developers to leverage the power of hardware and software programmable devices, entirely from a higher-level of abstraction.

The SDSoC environment provides a greatly simplified embedded C/C++ application programming experience including an easy-to-use Eclipse IDE and a comprehensive development platform. SDSoC includes a full-system optimizing C/C++ compiler, system-level profiling and hardware/software event tracing, automated software acceleration in programming logic, automated generation of SW-HW connectivity, and integration with libraries to speed programing. The SDSoC compiler transforms programs into complete hardware/software systems based on user-specified target platform and functions within the program to compile into programmable hardware logic. Hardware accelerators communicate with the CPU and external memory through an automatically-generated, application-specific data motion network comprised of DMAs, interconnects and other standard IP blocks.

The SDSoC Environment also provides flows for customer and 3rd party developers to enable their platforms and integrate RTL IPs as C-callable libraries. It builds upon customer-proven design tools from Xilinx including Vivado Design Suite, Vivado High-level Synthesis and SDK.

In this presentation, we will introduce the motivation and basic concepts behind SDSoC, describe its capabilities and the user-flow, and provide a brief demonstration of the tool using an example.

FPGA'16, February 21-23, 2016, Monterey, CA, USA
ACM 978-1-4503-3856-1/16/02.
http://dx.doi.org/10.1145/2847263.2847284

FCUDA-SoC: Platform Integration for Field-Programmable SoC with the CUDA-to-FPGA Compiler

Tan Nguyen, Swathi Gurumani, Kyle Rupnow, Deming Chen

Advanced Digital Sciences Center
Singapore
{tan.nguyen, swathi.g, k.rupnow}@adsc.com.sg

Electrical and Computer Engineering
University of Illinois at Urbana-Champaign
dchen@illinois.edu

ABSTRACT

Throughput oriented high level synthesis allows efficient design and optimization using parallel input languages. Parallel languages offer the benefit of parallelism extraction at multiple levels of granularity, offering effective design space exploration to select efficient single core implementations, and easy scaling of parallelism through multiple core instantiations. However, study of high level synthesis for parallel languages has concentrated on optimization of core and on-chip communications, while neglecting platform integration, which can have a significant impact on achieved performance. In this paper, we create an automated flow to perform efficient platform integration for an existing CUDA-to-RTL throughput oriented HLS, and we open source the FCUDA tool, platform integration, and benchmark applications. We demonstrate platform integration of 16 benchmarks on two Zynq-based systems in bare-metal and OS mode. We study implementation optimization for platform integration, compare to an embedded GPU (Tegra TK1) and verify designs on a Zedboard Zynq 7020 (bare-metal) and Omnitek Zynq 7045 (OS).

1. INTRODUCTION

High level synthesis (HLS) is increasingly the preferred design method for hardware development due to improved productivity and reduced design effort to effectively explore implementation options. Study of high level synthesis tools initially used serial input languages such as C/C++, C#, SystemC, and Java [5, 8, 23, 26, 29]. HLS of serial languages performs optimization and parallelism extraction with the target of generating a single accelerator core that achieves performance goals. Parallel languages such as CUDA and OpenCL [2, 9, 13, 14, 17, 18, 27] present a throughput-oriented alternative for synthesis; some applications may be 7X or more better with parallel languages than serial languages [13]. Using parallel languages, HLS tools optimize a single accelerator core and increase throughput through multiple instantiations of the core.

Throughput oriented synthesis takes advantage of parallel algorithm representations to allow independent exploration of parallelism within a single accelerator core and parallelism between multiple cores. Thus, in throughput oriented synthesis, platform integration takes even greater importance; accelerator core interconnect and integration with CPUs and memory controllers are critical to producing an overall accelerator system that meets designer goals.

Platform-level integration includes a variety of additional design concerns including HW/SW co-design, core control interfaces, mechanisms for data movement, utilization of internal and external bandwidth, workload distribution, and scalability of core interconnect. The method for CPU to accelerator communication, data transfer, and workload distribution affects both platform design and modeling of incremental benefit of additional accelerator cores. Mechanisms for sharing access to external memory controllers and sharing data among cores affect achievable efficiency of memory bandwidth as well as scaling of bandwidth use. It is important that platform generation is automated; design and interconnection of many-core systems with efficient use of shared resources, efficient mapping for data and workload distribution, and multiple different accelerator core types is a complex and tedious task.

In this paper, we discuss platform integration, optimization, and best-practices for throughput oriented HLS. We develop an automated system for generating optimized platform level designs for a throughput-oriented HLS based on an existing CUDA-to-RTL flow [18], and open-source the CUDA-to-RTL flow and automated platform integration. The automated flow performs integration of the generated HLS cores with the ARM-core of a Xilinx Zynq FPGA platform. We select Zynq platforms for the availability of an on-chip CPU core, and because the existing CUDA-to-RTL flow uses Xilinx Vivado HLS; future Xilinx Ultrascale Zynq products will continue to support ARM-based CPUs.

The automated flow takes in annotated CUDA kernels and host code as inputs and generates an optimized, application-specific platform-level design (bitstream and binary executable) to enable efficient FPGA board-level implementation of CUDA benchmarks. Using the platform integration flow, we map 16 benchmarks to the Zynq platforms, including several simple applications and 12 applications from the Rodinia [6] parallel language benchmarks. In this work, we concentrate on one specific CUDA-to-RTL flow, but this platform integration strategy can be applied to other throughput-oriented languages, such as OpenCL.

This paper contributes to the study of HLS with:

FPGA'16, February 21-23, 2016, Monterey, CA, USA

ⓒ 2016 ACM. ISBN 978-1-4503-3856-1/16/02. . . $15.00

DOI: http://dx.doi.org/10.1145/2847263.2847344

- An open-source academic automated platform generation flow integrated with an HLS tool with complete platform generation, on-chip bus support, and board-level verification.

- Extension of FCUDA to support Field-programmable SoCs.

- Demonstration of platform-level optimization issues in throughput-oriented HLS.

- Discussion of best practices in platform-level design and integration.

The rest of this paper is organized as follows. We discuss related work in interconnection and platform integration in section 2, then introduce the CUDA-to-RTL HLS flow in section 3. In section 4, we discuss features of the Xilinx Zynq platform, and the computation model for throughput-oriented synthesis. In section 5, we discuss platform integration issues, and optimization techniques. Finally, we present results for 16 benchmarks on two Zynq platforms and discuss best-practices in platform integration.

2. RELATED WORK

Platform integration is a common issue in the design and use of FPGA-based accelerators; although design of high-performance cores is common, it remains challenging to integrate those cores with appropriate memory controllers and communications interfaces to make a high performance system. Several recent works have concentrated on this problem by releasing open-source, well-optimized implementations of PCI-Express, DRAM, and Ethernet interfaces [10,15,20,22, 25]. Although these standardized APIs make design and use of FPGA platforms easier, core design, optimization and platform-level optimization are left to the user. System-level linking of hardware and software components [12] has also been explored, but as with the platform interfaces, it concentrates on integration of a small number of cores.

For many core systems, there is extensive prior work on both bus-based [3, 4, 21] and network-on-chip [1, 7, 11] systems. However, these interconnects focus on on-chip communications rather than platform integration, which is a critical part of platform integration.

There are also several industrial throughput HLS tools such as Altera's OpenCL [2] or Xilinx's SDAccel [27] which focus on OpenCL-to-RTL flow for CPU-FPGA systems in data center applications. Similarly, Xilinx's SDSoC [28] builds SoC applications, but does not use throughput oriented languages.

In this paper, we use an existing throughput-oriented CUDA-to-RTL HLS toolflow [17, 18] to design computation cores, and then explore the platform design and optimization using two Xilinx Zynq platforms. On each platform, we explore platform integration optimizations through a fully automated platform integration flow, and present best practices in platform integration for many core, throughput-oriented designs. Our open-source release of the FCUDA-SoC flow also supports NoC communications [7].

3. THROUGHPUT-ORIENTED HLS ON ZYNQ

The Xilinx Zynq platform combines Dual ARM Cortex A9 CPU cores in a processing system (PS) tightly integrated with programmable logic (PL) that can be configured, and

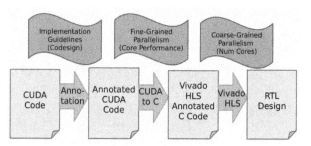

Figure 1: CUDA-to-RTL Flow

controlled by the CPU. We use two platforms: the Zedboard platform contains a Zynq 7020 FPGA with 512MB of DDR2, and the Omnitek platform contains a Zynq 7045 FPGA with 1GB of DDR3. The Zynq 7045 has an identical ARM processor, but substantially more reconfigurable logic: about four times more LUTs, BRAMs and DSPs. The larger platform allows us to specifically concentrate on the scalability of the platform with significant numbers of accelerator cores. On both platforms, the CPU controls the accelerator cores to start computation and monitor completion. We will now briefly discuss the existing CUDA-to-RTL flow that we use in this work, and the on-chip integration.

3.1 CUDA-to-RTL Synthesis Flow

The CUDA programming model is a single program multiple data (SPMD) computation model, where kernels are programs with many threads that operate on independent data with minimal inter-thread communication. In CUDA, each thread follows its own data-dependent control path. The CUDA-to-RTL flow used in this work (Figure 1) translates this SPMD-style code into a core that performs the computation of one or more CUDA threads (typically at least 32 threads). The entire kernel computation is performed by repeated use of the computation core, workload distribution among multiple instantiations of the core, or both.

Starting with CUDA code, the programmer may modify the code to group together data transfers to overlap communication and computation as a performance optimization. The user uses pragmas to identify compute and data transfer code regions as in Figure 2; a transfer pragma translates an assignment into a memcpy(), which Vivado HLS will translate into a burst-mode memory transfer to copy contiguous data with a specified burst length, similar to the memory coalescing access in the CUDA programming model. Transfer pragmas specify burst mode, which variable is the external pointer, the size and direction (input (0) or output (1)) of a data transfer. The compute pragma simply creates a for loop to iterate over the entire computation once for each thread ID. In general, the programmer may specify unrolling, parallelism and memory partitioning in the compute pragma. Note that the CUDA to C translation performs unrolling, parallelisation, and partitioning and does not use the related Vivado HLS-specific pragmas. In this work, we concentrate on scalability issues in the platform integration of cores rather than the performance effects of alternate core designs. Thus, we do not use design space exploration [19], which would examine alternate settings for unrolling, parallelism and data partitioning. We instead concentrate on integrating as many instantiations of a default core design as possible in a single platform.

```
#pragma FCUDA TRANSFER begin type=burst
    pointer=[A] size=[16] dir=[0]
    //Input Data Reading Statement
    As[tIDy][tIDx] = A[a + wA*tIDy + tIDx];
#pragma FCUDA TRANSFER end

#pragma FCUDA COMPUTE begin unroll=4 mpart
    =2 array_split=[As]
    //Kernel code performing computation
#pragma FCUDA COMPUTE end

#pragma FCUDA TRANSFER begin type=burst
    pointer=[C] size=[16] dir=[1]
    //Output Data Writing Statement
    C[c + wB*tIDy + tIDx]=Csub[tIDy][tIDx];
#pragma FCUDA TRANSFER end
```

Figure 2: Data Transfer Pragmas for FCUDA

```
// Control port for parameter wA
#pragma HLS INTERFACE ap_none register
    port=wA
#pragma HLS RESOURCE core=AXI4LiteS
    variable=wA

// Control port of the whole core
#pragma HLS RESOURCE core=AXI4LiteS
    variable=return

// Data port for parameter A
#pragma HLS INTERFACE ap_bus port=A
#pragma HLS RESOURCE variable=A core=
    AXI4M
```

Figure 3: Communications Pragmas for Vivado HLS

After inserting pragmas into the CUDA code, the annotated CUDA is passed into a source-to-source compiler based on MCUDA [24] and the Cetus framework to produce C-code annotated with I/O interface pragmas (Figure 3) that will be processed by Xilinx Vivado HLS to produce RTL. These pragmas specify which variables are in the I/O interface, and the interface type. We will discuss the partitioning of I/O ports and selection of port types in more detail in section 4.

3.2 On-Chip Integration

In a particular application, there may be multiple CUDA kernels; we also support mapping of multiple independent hardware accelerators, each of which may have one or more parallel cores. Our automated flow can instantiate any number of cores. Thus, in applications with multiple CUDA kernels, we simply distribute total FPGA resources evenly between kernels (e.g. two kernels are allowed roughly half of the reconfigurable resources each), unless data-dependence or the number of thread-blocks of the CUDA kernel is the limiting factor (rather than available FPGA area) in number of instantiable cores. We do not explore options for uneven distributions among kernels, but always attempt to find the maximum FPGA utilization that remains feasible for implementation. In section 4.3, we explain the analytical model for determining the number of cores for each kernel.

The cores are integrated together using the ARM-controlled AXI bus. The ARM core signals the cores to begin computation, and the cores will individually perform memory accesses (burst accesses due to the TRANSFER pragma) to read data into each core's local memory. The ARM core

monitors the cores for completion: once all cores are complete, the ARM can continue with other computation or start the cores again on new input data. In the following section, we will discuss optimizations of memory use, data-sharing mechanisms, workload distribution techniques, and core interconnect techniques.

3.3 System Integration

In this paper, we use the Zynq platforms both as a bare-metal platform and as a platform running a Linux-based operating system. At the circuit level, both platform styles are nearly identical. However, there are several specific differences between the integration styles. Most importantly, in the bare-metal platform, the CPU does not use virtual memory, and thus both the CPU and kernel cores can directly use physical memory addresses. The OS-platform uses virtual memory; however, in order to perform parallel accesses without using the ARM core's MMU, the kernel cores must directly access physical memory addresses, and userspace applications are explicitly forbidden from knowing the virtual-to-physical translation. We use a mechanism to maintain our own translation by memory-mapping one or more pages of virtual memory to specific physical addresses, and thus we can always provide the kernel cores with appropriate physical addresses that correspond to the data structures in the userspace application.

In addition, there are a few minor differences in the supporting configuration files. In bare-metal mode, the user must supply a Board Support Package with drivers for the accelerator core and any required peripherals. In OS mode, all periperal drivers are already part of the OS package, so only an accelerator driver is necessary. The OS features simplify development of platform I/O compared to needing to design custom drivers as in a bare-metal platform.

4. PLATFORM INTEGRATION

In this paper, we perform platform integration of HLS-generated cores on a Zedboard with a Zynq 7020 and an Omnitek Zynq 7045 platform. Before we discuss the details of our integration and optimization, we first introduce the features of the Xilinx Zynq chips, particularly, the communications and control for our platform integration. Both platforms contain Xilinx Zynq 7000 series chips with ARM CPUs (667MHz and 800MHz, respectively) and speed grade -1. External memory bandwidth is thus higher on the Omnitek platform, and the Zedboard has less memory (512MB vs. 1GB) The Zynq 7045 also has more reconfigurable resources than the Zynq 7020.

4.1 Xilinx Zynq

The Xilinx Zynq SoC platform consists of a region with a dual-core ARM Cortex A9 processor, together with hard-core implementations of communications interfaces such as USB, Gigabit Ethernet, DDR controllers, and general purpose IOs, and a reconfigurable region. The processor region can be connected to the reconfigurable region via AXI interconnect. There are three types of AXI functional interfaces: a cache-coherent interface (ACP), four high-performance and bandwidth interfaces (HP), and four general purpose interfaces (GP). Although the ACP port provides high-bandwidth and direct connection to the CPU's L1/L2 cache, it only supports up to 8 master devices, limiting the scalability of an approach using this port. Furthermore, the CUDA programming model is explicitly not cache-coherent. Thus, we use the high-performance interfaces for core communications and a general purpose interface for control.

4.2 Computation Model

In our computation model, the accelerator cores operate similar to the CUDA programming model. The ARM cores allocate memory resources for input and output buffers, control the accelerator cores by sending run-time parameters, start computation, and wait for cores to signal completion. However, unlike the CUDA computation model, the CPU is not responsible for moving data from CPU memory into core's local memories: each core will generate streams of memory requests that will fill their local memories and then copy final results into global memory. Due to the TRANS-FER pragmas, each memory request is a burst transfer of multiple data items for efficient bandwidth usage.

4.3 Synthesis and Platform Design Flow

An overview of our automated platform integration flow, depicting the inputs, automated steps and output is shown in Figure 5. In our automated flow, the designer provides the annotated CUDA kernel code, host code, the number of CUDA thread blocks of the kernels, and FPGA device information as input. Through a series of steps, the automated flow generates an optimized platform-level design including the bitstream for the reconfigurable logic, and the binary for software components. We now explain the detailed sequence of steps in our automated flow.

As a first step, our automation script invokes the prior CUDA-to-RTL compiler tool to translate the annotated input CUDA kernels into Vivado-synthesizable C-code (1). This translation step also inserts Vivado communication pragmas as in Figure 3. The annotated C-code is then synthesized with Vivado HLS to create an RTL IP for the kernel. For computational core generation, the core interface is a significant issue. The original CUDA function prototype contains input and output data pointers, and information about the number of threads, thread blocks and their organization is handled by the GPU device driver. Furthermore, the CUDA prototype assumes that function arguments are pointers to data accessible by the GPU (i.e. data that is already copied to GPU memory)[1]

For the FPGA interface, we must both pass references to input and output data buffers ,and call-specific parameters specifying the number of threads, thread-blocks, their organization, memory addresses, and workload distribution among cores. An example showing the difference between the original CUDA prototype and alternate CUDA-to-RTL prototypes is shown in Figure 4. The corresponding set of run-time configurable parameters is shown in Table 1. We will discuss optimizations selecting how to partition and/or merge interface ports in Section 5.

Next, our flow performs system integration using Vivado IP integrator to instantiate the IP core with the ARM CPU, DDR interface, and AXI interconnect (2). This allows the ARM CPU (Zynq processing system (PS)) to control the IP core, and allows the IP core to read and write data to DDR memory. This initial system is only a single core system, but is used to gather post-synthesis area information about

---

[1]CUDA 6 introduced unified memory, which, similar to our model, allows the GPU to read directly from host-memory

---

Table 1: Run-time Configurable Parameters

num_cores	Number of cores used for this kernel call
core_id	Per-Core identifier for the kernel call
wX	Set the scalar value of input scalar wX
gridDim.x	x-dimension value of CUDA grid
gridDim.y	y-dimension value of CUDA grid
gridDim.z	z-dimension value of CUDA grid
blockDim.x	x-dimension value of CUDA thread block
blockDim.y	y-dimension value of CUDA thread block
blockDim.z	z-dimension value of CUDA thread block
X_addr	Set the address of input or output buffer X

```
//Original CUDA function prototype
__global__ void matrixMul(float *A, float
    *B, float *C, int wA, int wB)

//CUDA-to-RTL merged function prototype
void matrixMul(float *memport)

//CUDA-to-RTL parallel function prototype
void matrixMul(float *A, float *B, float *
    C, int wA, int wB, dim3 gridDim, dim3
    blockDim, int A_addr, int B_addr, int
    C_addr, int num_cores, int core_id)
```

Figure 4: Comparison of CUDA vs. CUDA-to-RTL Function Prototypes

the core so that we can automatically estimate the maximal number of core instantiations given an allowed area budget.

The tool flow then synthesizes the design to get an initial estimated resource report (3). In applications with multiple independent kernels, this synthesis is performed once for each kernel. Then, based on the available resources of the target FPGA device (or a proportion thereof), and the number of CUDA threadblocks for the kernel, our flow determines the maximal number of instantiable cores (4). In smaller FPGAs such as the Zynq 7020, the LUT, FF, BRAM or DSP resources are always the limiting factor; however, in larger FPGAs, a large number of cores may not be routable despite small area utilization. We use an analytical model to determine whether a target number of cores (and total I/O ports) is routable [16].

With the updated estimate for the maximal design in number of cores, our flow generates a new C-code wrapper for the required CPU-core control communications. The flow also iterates with Vivado HLS to verify that the integrated system is actually feasibly synthesized as shown in Figure 5 (4). On occasion, the first system design is not actually synthesizable; our analytical model may be aggressive, as it does not attempt to model scaling effects in multiple instantiations other than the loose upper bound on routability. In this case, we simply iteratively remove one core and retry until a design is verified as synthesizable.

Once we have a verified design with the maximum number of cores, the automated flow performs a binary search on the target frequency to find the maximal achievable frequency of the whole design (5). In this work, we do not explore the performance difference of designs with fewer cores but higher achievable frequency; for our purposes, we simply want to demonstrate that our automated flow can find and implement designs with many cores – we do not argue that the maximal number of cores is necessarily the best performing configuration. Similarly, as noted before, we do not compare different core designs; our data simply demonstrates that for any particular core design, we can create an efficient platform-level implementation with many instantiations.

After determining the maximum achievable frequency, the bitstream is generated to configure the Zedboard or Omnitek platform (6), and the corresponding C-code is compiled to an executable for the host ARM CPU. We generate drivers for the ARM cores to interface with the IP, and compile those drivers and the host code to produce a binary (7).

For bare-metal platform implementations, we compile a Board Support Package (BSP) comprising of necessary drivers. The bitstream is downloaded to the board via a JTAG cable using the Xilinx SDK or Xilinx CPU Debugger. For OS mode platform implementations, we do not require a BSP; instead, the FPGA is configured by simply copying the bitstream to the FPGA's device file (via the *cat* command). However, we must also generate a device tree file and include it in the boot image to list all system hardware components and their respective system addresses. When the board boots the OS, it will initialize the hardware components, and the accelerator cores will be available as userspace I/O (uio) devices that will be configured by the core driver.

As discussed earlier, the OS platform also requires additional userspace code in the application to maintain a physical to virtual address mapping, such that we can provide the kernel cores with correct physical addresses. For this, we simply memory map a page-aligned pointer to a physical address and use this memory region for data that needs to be accessible by the kernel cores (for reading or writing). Then, when we need to pass pointers to the kernel cores, we can simply translate a specified physical address to the mapped virtual address.

For functional verification, we generate several related versions of the host code. First, we configure the host code to independently perform the kernel computation and compare CPU-computed and core-computed results. For performance evaluations we generate a version that does not use the core for a CPU-only performance. Then, we also gather the performance using the accelerator cores. In both cases, we measure full application performance including data allocation and transfers. However, we do not measure FPGA configuration time; we are evaluating these platforms as stand-alone platforms, not run-time reconfigurable accelerator boards. If a designer wishes to reconfigure the Zynq platform at runtime, they are responsible for ensuring that each configuration is used sufficiently long to amortize the reconfiguration overhead.

5. PLATFORM OPTIMIZATION

The automated design flow as described produces functionally correct accelerated applications. However, there are many potential design options within this general flow, and performance optimization of the platform characteristics is critical. In this section, we describe performance optimizations in order to generate efficient implementations.

5.1 Core Interfaces

For all core I/Os, we can merge ports together or leave I/Os as multiple parallel ports. Merged interfaces require fewer ports for interconnect at the system level and thus simplify platform integration and the area of system-level interconnects. However, parallel interfaces allow higher performance, and flexible separation of control, input and out-

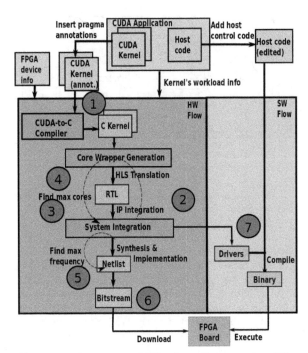

Figure 5: Automated Platform Integration Flow

put data. Although all platform methods must use a unified memory space, both methods can use a unfied address space.

In certain cases, it may be important to partition input and output ports; when all control, input and output data are merged into a single port, we cannot employ ping-pong buffers to pre-fetch the next set of input data because input and output buffers share the same port. Furthermore, merged ports would prevent system-level pipelining between multiple communicating kernels; although we do not implement system-level pipelining in this work, keeping input and output ports separate enables future designs where the output of one kernel fills the input buffer to the next. To prevent large platform-level crossbars, we generally merge multiple ports in the core design using a single memory port with per-array offsets. Although this reduces core parallelism, it also reduces the size of interconnect. When ports have different datatypes, they are left as parallel interfaces to minimize kernel modifications.

For core control signals, we also have the choice of merging ports, but in addition to allowing run-time configurability, we can also assign fixed signals. A fixed num_cores value increases complexity to reuse the cores with multiple input data sizes. Although the number of cores may be fixed, the total amount of work, location of input/output data buffers, and workload distribution may vary at runtime. Thus, we allow run-time control of parameter values for core identification, grid and block dimensions, total number of cores used, and memory offsets for input data.

5.2 Communication Interfaces

The Zynq platform has cache-coherent (ACP), high performance (HP) and general purpose (GP) AXI interfaces. A cache coherent interface is inappropriate – the CUDA programming model explicitly specifies that memory writes by CUDA kernels are not coherent, and the interface is limited to 8 cores on the bus due to the 3-bit identifier field. For data

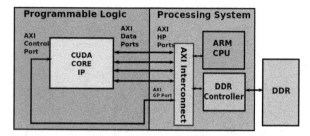

Figure 6: System Integration

```
for (b_index = 0; b_index < gridDim.x;
    b_index += num_cores) {
    bIdx.x = b_index + core_id;
    // Perform computation
}
```

Figure 7: Core computation to determine Workload distribution

ports, the high-performance interface allows high-bandwidth memory accesses. For parameters, a general purpose interface is sufficient; furthermore, partitioning traffic into data and control networks prevents control transactions from affecting efficiency of the high-bandwidth interface. We show an overview of how the programmable logic is connected to the processing system using different ports of the AXI interconnect in Figure 6. The hardware and the processor system communicate with the DDR memory through the DDR controller that is also connected to the AXI interconnect.

To use the high-performance interfaces, we partition cores into four equal groups and, through an AXI interconnect, connect to one of the four HP AXI interfaces. Each AXI interconnect may have up to 16 ports, thus we can support up to 64 cores in a single level of hierarchy. If more cores will be simultaneously active, we can build a hierarchical interconnect to support additional cores. However, in our designs, we did not require more than 64 simultaneously active cores. In platforms with more than 64 total cores, we are able to share ports as we will describe in section 5.6.

As shown in Section 3, the existing source-to-source translation generates Xilinx Vivado-HLS annotations for communications interfaces of the I/O ports. The CUDA to C translation directly performs any unrolling, pipelining, parallelism or partitioning of memory arrays instead of using Vivado HLS pragmas. However, as noted earlier, in this paper we do not perform unrolling, parallelism or partitioning. Depending on the type of interfaces, we specify different annotations; data ports become AXI4 memory-mapped interfaces integrated with a high-performance AXI port for higher bandwidth, and control ports become registers integrated with an AXI4LiteS interface for better scalability and independence from the high-performance ports. An example of the necessary pragmas was shown in Figure 3.

5.3 Workload Distribution

For CUDA kernels, the kernel code is designed so that the number of computation threads and the dimensions of the grid of thread blocks is flexible but directly related to the amount of data to process. During execution, the CUDA driver is responsible for distributing blocks of computation work to the GPU's execution units, assigning a thread-block of work to a single streaming multiprocessor (SM).

In our computation model, the CPU is responsible for setting initial parameters for the core computation, but it is not desirable for the CPU to explicitly handle workload distribution. The extra overhead of the CPU explicitly managing a queue of tasks would eliminate some performance and energy benefits of using FPGA-based acceleration. Thus, it is desirable for the cores to automatically compute which thread blocks of the overall computation will be executed

based on the cores' identifiers and the total number of cores in the designed platform. Figure 7 shows how a core selects a set of thread blocks for computation. Although this is a static workload distribution, it reduces management overhead, and is a reasonable choice when there is little data-dependent variance in core computation latency.

5.4 Shared Control

When instantiating many identical cores, we can assign unique AXI core identifiers in order to make each core individually controllable. However, individual controllability also means that each core must be started individually rather than starting all cores simultaneously. Furthermore, this also requires wiring each AXI4LiteS port through an AXI interconnect block, which consumes additional area. In the CUDA programming model, it is the normal case that we wish to use all cores simultaneously. Thus, we only use one port of the AXI interconnect by wiring all of the control ports together and setting individual identifiers as fixed parameters used only for workload distribution.

5.5 Shared Data

Many CUDA kernels use CUDA constant memory as shared input data; in our processing model, each core would independently generate a stream of external memory requests to copy this identical data into cores' internal BRAMs. To improve the performance of this behavior and reduce external bandwidth demand, we can instead create an AXI stream interface for each core's data port and instantiate AXI DMA engine (configured in simple mode) for each core to stream the constant data to the data port of the cores. However, in a situation where the size of the constant memory is too large to duplicate for all the cores, it is more logical to perform a single memory copy to bring data on-chip by using an AXI central DMA (CDMA); and then, each core can fetch the data from on-chip buffers for their computation instead of performing an expensive off-chip access. The AXI DMA can also be configured in scatter-gather mode to perform a single transaction that distributes data streams to all cores with the multi-channel feature. We show the performance difference between CDMA, multi-DMA versus non-DMA implementation for benchmark coulombic potential (cp) in Figure 8. Each core's memory transactions already use burst-mode requests, so there is little performance benefit with DMA techniques for fewer cores, the area efficiency of the DMAs do not prevent instantiation of additional cores and hence we choose to have CDMA in our design.

5.6 Multiple Core Types

Applications may have multiple computation kernels, each with independent core accelerators. In our system, this is natively handled: each core has independent resource identifiers, so cores can be independently controlled and data ports can inherently share access to external memory over

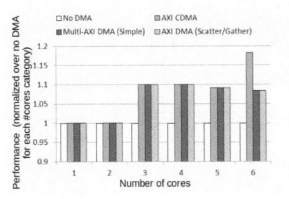

Figure 8: Performance Difference by DMA type of Benchmark cp

the high-performance AXI interconnect. In general, a user should explore the number of cores of each type to instantiate in order to maximize performance; in this work, we distribute resources proportionally based on the CUDA kernels' total workload.

In order to facilitate better organization of kernel instantiations, we create a hierarchy of instantiations. For each kernel, we create a wrapper module that instantiates all copies of the kernel core; then at the system level, we instantiate just the wrapper modules. This has little effect on the area or frequency, but better organizes the instantiations.

However, in applications where the kernels' executions are serialized, we can explicitly share AXI ports when it is statically guaranteed that the two respective cores will never be active at the same time. This technique can substantially reduce area consumption due to the rapid scaling of AXI interconnects. Figure 9 demonstrates a system-level design where kernel 1 and kernel 2 are serialized and can thus share two out of three AXI ports instead of requiring 5 ports.

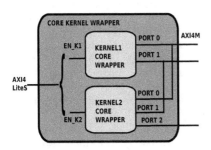

Figure 9: Serialized Kernels Sharing AXI Ports

5.7 Host Control Code

The host control code running on the ARM is a simple set of loops: one to setup core parameters, one to initiate computation of the core, and a third to wait until the core has signaled completion. An example host code containing the three loops is shown in Figure 10. As discussed earlier, in the OS version of the host-control code, the host code must also perform a translation so that it can provide the cores with appropriate physical addresses to access.

In addition, a designer may wish to integrate features to dynamically decide whether to use the kernel cores. For example, if the overhead of kernel calls sets a limitation on

```
// setup core parameters
//One for each input scalar port
XCUDAKern_SetWX(&xcore, wX);

//CUDA Kernel x-Dimension (similar to y, z)
XCUDAKern_SetGriddim_x(&xcore, gridDim.x);
XCUDAKern_SetBlockdim_x(&xcore, blkDim.x);

//One for each input & output buffer port
XCUDAKern_SetX_addr(&xcore,
    (u32)X / sizeof(float));

//Turn on Kernel 1 for execution
XCUDAKern_EnK1(&xcore, 1);

// initiate computation of the core
XCUDAKern_Start(&xcore);

// wait until the core signal completion
while(!XCUDAKern_IsDone(&xcore));
```

Figure 10: Host Control Code

the minimum data size to achieve speedup, the user may wish to use the CPU for smaller data sizes. Similarly, the host code may overlap kernel-core execution with using the CPU for some of the computation. In this work, we concentrate on the hardware platform issues, and do not explore implementation of additional features in the host code.

6. RESULTS AND ANALYSIS

We now present the results of 16 benchmarks running through our automated process, including matrix multiplication (matmul), coulombic potential(cp), discrete wavelet transform (dwt), Fast-Walsh transform (fwt) and 12 benchmarks from the Rodinia benchmark suite [6]. One benchmark from Rodinia is unsupported due to use of computation functions not available from Xilinx Vivado HLS (e.g. floating-point power function). The remaining benchmarks are supported using our flow when provided with a correctly annotated CUDA kernel as input.

The applications are selected to provide a variety of complexity for both the CUDA-to-RTL flow as well as the platform integration demands. As noted earlier, we do not perform unrolling, parallelism, or partitioning. Furthermore, as most of the applications are floating-point, we do not perform datatype bitwidth minimization.

For each benchmark, we use the automated flow to implement the core, select the number of cores to implement, and generate the implementations for both the Zedboard and Omnitek platforms. We present speedup of the maximal number of cores compared to the CPU-only version measured on the respective platform's ARM CPU. In addition, we measure the CPU-only and GPU-accelerated speedup on the NVidia Jetson TK1 platform that contains a Tegra K1 SoC with quad-core ARM Cortex A15 and Kepler GPU with 192 cores. The Jetson TK1 has double the host-accelerator bandwidth of the Zynq platforms. We report the application speedup on the TK1 and will also compare performance per watt on the TK1 with the Zynq platforms. In the case of applications with multiple CUDA kernels, we distribute FPGA resources evenly among the kernels, and then instantiate the maximal number of cores given area, routability, and kernel structure constraints as described in section 4.

Table 2: Platform Performance Results

Benchmark	Tegra K1 Application Speedup over ARM	Zedboard Zynq 7020 Num Cores	Application Speedup over ARM	Execution Freq. (MHz)	Perf./Watt over TK1's	Omnitek Zynq 7045 Num Cores	Application Speedup over ARM	Execution Freq. (MHz)	Perf./Watt over TK1's
Simple CUDA Kernels									
cp	186x	6	3.4x	90	0.02x	20	16.6x	107	0.03x
fwt	6.7x	8,8	9.4x	100	1.05x	36,36	7.7x	97	0.28x
matmul	3.6x	16	4.9x	77	1.74x	64	7.3x	97	1.1x
dwt	2x	14	2.9x	83	2.24x	52	4.4x	87	1.1x
Rodinia CUDA Benchmarks									
backprop	0.4x	6,6	0.5x	90	0.41x	16,16	1.33x	71	0.7x
bfs	1.3x	14,14	0.4x	56	0.33x	48,48	0.96x	71	0.4x
gaussian	6.5x	2,14	1.8x	83	0.26x	2,44	3.8x	71	0.3x
hotspot	6.7x	4	1.3x	77	0.29x	16	7.3x	87	0.47x
lavaMD	17.5	2	1.6x	63	0.16x	8	26.8x	71	0.90x
lud	45.2x	2,3,3	2.3x	77	0.07x	1,14,14	20x	71	0.28x
nn	1x	14	1.4x	59	2.48x	32	0.74x	82	0.54
nw	3.8x	10,10	2.9x	83	1.40x	40,40	4.59x	77	1.01x
particlefilter	0.8x	27	0.6x	56	1.17x	27	0.55	71	1.17x
pathfinder	1.6x	18	1.5x	67	2.75x	32	1.40x	77	1.0x
srad	1.8x	3,3	0.4x	83	0.36x	9,9	1.67x	77	0.62x
streamcluster	2.0x	10	0.6x	67	0.20x	16	1.11x	89	0.14x

Table 2 shows the number of instantiated cores, measured application speedup for each benchmark, and the achieved core execution frequency. When an application has multiple core types, the number of instances is a comma delimited list. We first observe that on the Zedboard platform we have between 2 core instantiations (lavaMD) and 28 cores (bfs), with achievable frequency as high as 100MHz. However, 5 of the 16 benchmarks do not achieve speedup over the ARM CPU. Due to the low total available reconfigurable logic, there is insufficient space to instantiate enough cores to overcome overheads and achieve significant speedup.

This is illustrated by the Omnitek platform results: with 4× more reconfigurable logic, we instantiate roughly 4× as many cores, and achieve sometimes substantially improved speedup. On the Omnitek platform, only 3 benchmarks do not achieve application speedup, including one that does not achieve speedup on the TK1 platform either. These three benchmarks include complex data traversals that may not be inherently well-suited for FPGA acceleration. However, the additional area allows substantially improved performance: sometimes better speedup than the Jetson TK1 (fwt, matmul, dwt, backprop, hotspot, lavaMD, and nw)

It is important to note however, that the Zedboard and Omnitek results are not directly comparable; the ARM core on the Zedboard runs at 667MHz compared to 800MHz on the Omnitek, and we use bare-metal platform integration on the Zedboard vs. OS-based integration on the Omnitek. Speedup results are quoted with respect to each platform's CPU, and are not intended to be directly comparable. Rather, these results simply demonstrate that our automated platform integration flow supports complex applications and many core instantiations, and with sufficient available area, can obtain overall application speedup.

Among the applications that do not achieve speedup on either Zynq platform, the bfs benchmark depends on GPU caching instead of using local storage within the GPU kernel, and thus it is unable to achieve overall speedup. Similarly, particlefilter has complex memory traversals that significantly affect performance without GPU caching. In addition, several benchmarks achieve lower speedup on the Om-

nitek platform than the Zedboard despite the additional resources. It is important to reiterate that the speedup numbers are relative to a higher-performing CPU, and that the OS-based implementation incurs additional overhead, particularly to maintain the physical-to-virtual address translation necessary in OS-mode.

In all applications, a developer can redesign at the CUDA level to improve local data use, access patterns, or required resources. Furthermore, unrolling, parallelism, and data partitioning can further improve the performance of individual core designs, which would correspond to further improvement at the platform level. This work performs efficient, automated platform integration, and prior work has suggested that design space exploration may improve speedup and area per core by over an order of magnitude [19].

In addition to performance, we also estimated the power consumption on both platforms: we use the nominal power reported for Jetson TK1 and the nominal power consumption of the Zynq reported by Vivado Power Estimator. Using this power consumption, we compute the performance per Watt of each platform. Normalizing to the Jetson TK1, we see that the smaller Zedboard platform can have gains of over 2× with several benchmarks that did not achieve significant speedup on the Tegra K1, but both the Zedboard and Omnitek platforms generally have worse performance per Watt. However, this result is expected: most of the applications are floating-point applications with no particular bit-width optimization, which is where FPGAs have particular advantages over GPUs. Nonetheless, performance per Watt demonstrates that our platform integration produces designs that are sometimes more efficient than an embedded GPU and typically within 3× of the GPU efficiency in perf/W despite no particular optimization emphasis.

To demonstrate that customization can further help FPGA results, we also use an integer version of the matrix multiplication benchmark (not presented in Table 2), and compare the performance per Watt of both a 32-bit integer and 16-bit integer version on the Omnitek platform and Jetson TK1. For the 16-bit version, we do not perform design space exploration – we simply pad the integer values to the 32-bit bus width, and keep the same total number of cores in the 16- and 32-bit versions. As expected, performance slightly improves due to efficiency improvements in the 16-bit datapath, and thus performance per Watt gains compared to the Jetson TK1 improve from $1.5\times$ for 32-bit integer to $2.4\times$ for 16-bit integer. In practice, a designer should perform more detailed optimization of the memory bandwidth, and core datapath, as well as perform design space exploration, but this simple experiment demonstrates expected optimization opportunity when using datapath customization.

We also present the area of each integrated platform design in Table 3. As discussed above, we observe that DSP utilization is higher due to the floating-point nature of the benchmarks. We now discuss some best practices in throughput oriented core design and platform integration.

6.1 Automation Flow Performance

Our automation flow includes several steps, and potentially iterative synthesis, place and route. However, these synthesis steps are similar to the iterative optimization and search for achieveable frequency of a typical manual design process. In this article, we use this automation flow with a single, default core design; in deployment, users should either use the flow with a core design previously selected through design space exploration, or, if many full place and route syntheses are acceptable, as part of a design space exploration between multiple alternative core designs.

6.2 Best Practices in Throughput Platforms

Platform integration in throughput oriented designs requires design tradeoffs for scalability throughout the design process. From the selection of core interface, techniques for controlling the cores, the interconnection network, to workload distribution, data sharing, and supporting multiple simultaneous kernels, it is critically important to consider how these decisions will scale to a system with dozens of cores.

The interconnection network is of particular importance, because our decisions and techniques for optimizing the interconnect influence our abilities to optimize all of the other features. Although AXI interconnect IPs are quite efficient, it is still important to apply techniques to share ports and minimize the total amount of interconnect IP blocks needed. Using static information such as cores that cannot execute simultaneously can allow port sharing that may reduce the number of IP cores by $2\times$ or more.

In embedded platforms, it is common to have multiple communications interfaces such as the high-performance and general-purpose AXI interfaces. It is important to partition signals between interfaces so that low-bandwidth signals such as control operations do not compete for bandwidth with high-bandwidth data signals. Using high-performance ports efficiently requires that only high-priority transactions use high-bandwidth. Effective use of available interfaces requires consideration of the frequency of operations on the interface and the relative bandwidth requirements.

Given an efficient interconnect, it remains critical to ensure that cores use the interconnect efficiently. If multiple cores will use the same input data, using DMAs and local buffering to make data movement more efficient can substantially improve performance over identical networks that do not attempt to localize communications and minimize duplication of external memory requests. The interconnect presents an expensive component of the platform, especially

if a core has multiple data ports, the resource consumption will escalate quickly as the design scales with many cores. Therefore, merging data ports reduces the number of interconnect which leaves more area for instantiating more cores in compensation of parallel data communication of a core.

It is also important to consider how the partitioning and interconnect technique affects CPU control. Using shared control signals can effectively start many cores at the same time, significantly reducing management overhead at a cost of lower ability to individually control cores. This tradeoff is typically reasonable for throughput-oriented designs where the common case is to use all cores simultaneously to perform portions of a larger task in parallel.

The input CUDA program must also adopt good programming practices for GPU programming in order to achieve better performance on FPGA. For example, ensuring memory coalescing access is important as it is equivalent to memory bursting which efficiently copies a chunk of data. Using conditional or branching instructions inherently creates dependency which might prevent further parallelism such as unrolling. Exploiting local (shared) memory to cache data helps to reduce memory access latency. In addition, techniques to insert FCUDA pragmas to divide a kernel into multiple sub-tasks which overlaps the execution of those subtasks can potentially improve the core performance.

Having more cores does not always improve performance or performance/Watt. In reality, when an additional core is instantiated into the design, an amount of programmable fabric is spent on implementing interconnect to that core. The cost of this extra logic on area as well as power could outweigh the benefit of adding the core if it provides little benefit to performance. While this work only focuses on building a platform with as many cores as the FPGA can implement (depending on input workload) and the interconnect network, a general design space exploration should include optimizations such as unrolling, array partitioning, pipelining via ping-pong buffers, and bit-width reduction.

7. CONCLUSION

We presented the first academic fully-automated platform generation flow for throughput oriented HLS. Our automated system uses a CUDA-to-RTL flow to generate initial platform designs, estimate maximal core instantiations, and generates optimized platforms for either bare-metal or OS-based platform integration. We demonstrated our automated flow on a Zedboard (Zynq 7020) and Omnitek (Zynq 7045) platform with 16 benchmarks including 4 simple benchmarks and 12 benchmarks from the Rodinia suite. We additionally compared performance and performance-per-Watt to a Jetson TK1 platform. Compared to the ARM CPU, our efficient platform integration achieves speedup in nearly all cases: with sometimes superior performance and performance-per-Watt than the Jetson TK1 despite no particular core optimization effort. Our open-source tool flow can be found at http://dchen.ece.illinois.edu/tools.html.

8. ACKNOWLEDGEMENT

We acknowledge the previous contributors to FCUDA: A. Papakontanstinou, K. Gururaj, J. Stratton, E. Liang, J. Tolar, Y. Chen, Y. Chen, W-M Hwu, and J. Cong.

This study is supported in part by the research grant for the Human-Centered Cyber-physical Systems Programme at the Advanced Digital Sciences Center from Singapore's Agency for Science, Technology and Research (A*STAR).

Table 3: Platform Area Results

Benchmark	Zedboard Zynq 7020				Omnitek Zynq 7045			
	FF (%)	LUT (%)	BRAM (%)	DSP (%)	FF (%)	LUT (%)	BRAM (%)	DSP (%)
Simple CUDA Kernels								
cp	28.7	57.4	72.9	100.0	21.2	40.2	62.4	62.2
fwt	30.0	77.0	40.0	60.0	36.4	90.3	52.8	76
matmul	46.6	86.4	17.0	80.0	41.2	69.0	17.6	78.2
dwt	38.1	82.3	30	97.3	34.0	66.9	28.6	92.4
Rodinia CUDA Benchmarks								
backprop	35.6	73.5	6.4	100	22.0	35.2	4.4	80.0
bfs	41.3	90.9	0.0	38.1	33.2	73.6	0.0	32.0
gaussian	35.4	85.2	0.0	98.2	23.7	49.5	0.0	85.1
hotspot	33.4	61.7	5.7	100.0	23.4	43.4	5.9	97.8
lavaMD	14.1	37.1	10.0	69.9	13.2	36.4	10.3	67.6
lud	39.5	68.7	13.6	93.2	29.9	57.6	13.3	87.6
nn	37.3	87.6	0.0	89.1	19.5	46.7	0.0	49.8
nw	39.7	82.8	21.4	27.3	37.4	75.9	22.0	26.7
particlefilter	42.3	86.2	0.0	36.8	10.5	21.6	0.0	9.0
pathfinder	29.7	70.0	19.3	49.1	22.0	42.4	22.4	21.3
srad	42.0	88.6	29.3	100.0	29.0	60.8	24.8	97
streamcluster	42.4	87.4	10.7	100.0	16.1	33.1	4.4	39.1

9. REFERENCES

[1] M. Abdelfattah and V. Betz. The power of communication: Energy-efficient NOCS for FPGAS. In *FPL*, pages 1–8, Sept 2013.

[2] ALTERA. Altera SDK for OpenCL. http://www.altera.com/products/software/opencl/opencl-index.html.

[3] Altera. Avalon Bus Specification Reference Manual. 2003.

[4] ARM. AMBA AXI and ACE Protocol Specification. http://www.arm.com.

[5] J. Auerbach, D. F. Bacon, P. Cheng, and R. Rabbah. Lime: A Java-compatible and Synthesizable Language for Heterogeneous Architectures. In *OOPSLA*, pages 89–108, 2010.

[6] S. Che, M. Boyer, J. Meng, D. Tarjan, J. Sheaffer, S.-H. Lee, and K. Skadron. Rodinia: A benchmark suite for heterogeneous computing. In *IISWC*, pages 44–54, Oct 2009.

[7] Y. Chen, S. Gurumani, Y. Liang, G. Li, D. Guo, K. Rupnow, and D. Chen. FCUDA-NoC: A Scalable and Efficient Network-on-Chip Implementation for the CUDA-to-FPGA Flow. *IEEE TVLSI*, PP(99):1–14, 2015.

[8] J. Cong, B. Liu, S. Neuendorffer, J. Noguera, K. Vissers, and Z. Zhang. High-Level Synthesis for FPGAs: From Prototyping to Deployment. *IEEE TCAD*, 30(4):473–491, April 2011.

[9] T. Czajkowski, U. Aydonat, D. Denisenko, J. Freeman, M. Kinsner, D. Neto, J. Wong, P. Yiannacouras, and D. Singh. From OpenCL to High-performance Hardware on FPGAS. In *FPL*, pages 531–534, Aug 2012.

[10] K. Eguro. SIRC: An Extensible Reconfigurable Computing Communication API. In *FCCM*, pages 135–138, May 2010.

[11] A. Ehliar and D. Liu. An FPGA Based Open Source Network-on-Chip Architecture. In *FPL*, pages 800–803, 2007.

[12] S. Fleming, D. Thomas, G. Constantinides, and D. Ghica. System-level Linking of Synthesised Hardware and Compiled Software Using a Higher-order Type System. In *FPGA*, FPGA '15, pages 214–217, New York, NY, USA, 2015. ACM.

[13] S. Gurumani, H. Cholakkal, Y. Liang, K. Rupnow, and D. Chen. High-level synthesis of multiple dependent CUDA kernels on FPGA. In *ASP-DAC*, pages 305–312, Jan 2013.

[14] S. T. Gurumani, J. Tolar, Y. Chen, Y. Liang, K. Rupnow, and D. Chen. Integrated CUDA-to-FPGA Synthesis with Network-on-Chip. In *FCCM*, pages 21–24, May 2014.

[15] M. Jacobsen and R. Kastner. RIFFA 2.0: A reusable integration framework for FPGA accelerators. In *FPL*, pages 1–8, Sept 2013.

[16] A. H. Lam. An Analytical Model of Logic Resource Utilization for FPGA Architecture Development. Master's thesis, University of British Columbia, 2010.

[17] A. Papakonstantinou, D. Chen, W.-M. Hwu, J. Cong, and Y. Liang. Throughput-oriented kernel porting onto FPGAs. In *DAC*, pages 1–10, May 2013.

[18] A. Papakonstantinou, K. Gururaj, J. Stratton, D. Chen, J. Cong, and W.-M. Hwu. FCUDA: Enabling efficient compilation of CUDA kernels onto FPGAs. In *SASP*, pages 35–42, July 2009.

[19] A. Papakonstantinou, Y. Liang, J. A. Stratton, K. Gururaj, D. Chen, W.-M. W. Hwu, and J. Cong. Multilevel Granularity Parallelism Synthesis on FPGAs. In *FCCM*, pages 178–185. IEEE Computer Society, 2011.

[20] A. Parashar, M. Adler, K. Fleming, M. Pellauer, and J. Emer. LEAP: A virtual platform architecture for FPGAs. In *CARL*, 2010.

[21] M. Sharma and D. Kumar. Wishbone bus Architecture-A Survey and Comparison. *arXiv preprint arXiv:1205.1860*, 2012.

[22] J. Siegel, S; Kulp. OpenCPI HDL Infrastructure Specification. Tech Rep., 2010.

[23] S. Singh and D. J. Greaves. Kiwi: Synthesis of FPGA Circuits from Parallel Programs. In *FCCM*, pages 3–12. IEEE Computer Society, 2008.

[24] J. Stratton, S. Stone, and W.-m. Hwu. MCUDA: An Efficient Implementation of CUDA Kernels for Multi-core CPUs. In *Languages and Compilers for Parallel Computing*, volume 5335 of *LNCS*, pages 16–30. 2008.

[25] K. Vipin, S. Shreejith, D. Gunasekera, S. Fahmy, and N. Kapre. System-level FPGA device driver with high-level synthesis support. In *FPT*, pages 128–135, Dec 2013.

[26] Xilinx. Vivado High-Level Synthesis. http://www.xilinx.com/products/design-tools/vivado/integration/esl-design.html.

[27] Xilinx. Xilinx SDAccel. http://www.xilinx.com/products/design-tools/software-zone/sdaccel.html.

[28] Xilinx. Xilinx SDSoC. http://www.xilinx.com/products/design-tools/software-zone/sdsoc.html.

[29] H. Zheng, S. T. Gurumani, K. Rupnow, and D. Chen. Fast and Effective Placement and Routing Directed High-level Synthesis for FPGAs. In *FPGA*, pages 1–10, 2014.

Agile Co-Design for a Reconfigurable Datacenter

Shlomi Alkalay   Hari Angepat   Adrian Caulfield   Eric Chung
Oren Firestein   Michael Haselman   Stephen Heil   Kyle Holohan
Matt Humphrey   Tamas Juhasz   Puneet Kaur   Sitaram Lanka
Daniel Lo   Todd Massengill   Kalin Ovtcharov   Michael Papamichael
Andrew Putnam   Raja Seera   Rimon Tadros   Jason Thong
Lisa Woods   Derek Chiou   Doug Burger

Microsoft Corporation
catapult@microsoft.com

ABSTRACT

In 2015, a team of software and hardware developers at Microsoft shipped the world's first commercial search engine accelerated using FPGAs in the datacenter. During the sprint to production, new algorithms in the Bing ranking service were ported into FPGAs and deployed to a production bed within several weeks of conception, leading to significant gains in latency and throughput. The fast turnaround time of new features demanded by an agile software culture would not have been possible without a disciplined and effective approach to co-design in the datacenter. This talk will describe some of the learnings and best practices developed from this unique experience.

Keywords

FPGAs; Reconfigurable Computing; Cloud Computing; Datacenters; Hardware-Software Co-Design

FPGA'16, February 21-23, 2016, Monterey, CA, USA.
ACM 978-1-4503-3856-1/16/02.
http://dx.doi.org/10.1145/2847263.2847287

Throughput-Optimized OpenCL-based FPGA Accelerator for Large-Scale Convolutional Neural Networks

Naveen Suda, Vikas Chandra‡, Ganesh Dasika*, Abinash Mohanty, Yufei Ma,
Sarma Vrudhula†, Jae-sun Seo, Yu Cao

School of Electrical, Computer and Energy Engineering, Arizona State University, Tempe, USA
†School of Computing, Informatics, Decision Systems Engineering, Arizona State University, Tempe, USA
‡ARM Inc., San Jose, USA; *ARM Inc., Austin, USA.
E-mail: {naveen.suda, abinash.mohanty, yufeima, vrudhula, jaesun.seo, yu.cao}@asu.edu,
{vikas.chandra, ganesh.dasika}@arm.com

ABSTRACT

Convolutional Neural Networks (CNNs) have gained popularity in many computer vision applications such as image classification, face detection, and video analysis, because of their ability to train and classify with high accuracy. Due to multiple convolution and fully-connected layers that are compute-/memory-intensive, it is difficult to perform real-time classification with low power consumption on today's computing systems. FPGAs have been widely explored as hardware accelerators for CNNs because of their reconfigurability and energy efficiency, as well as fast turn-around-time, especially with high-level synthesis methodologies. Previous FPGA-based CNN accelerators, however, typically implemented generic accelerators agnostic to the CNN configuration, where the reconfigurable capabilities of FPGAs are not fully leveraged to maximize the overall system throughput. In this work, we present a systematic design space exploration methodology to maximize the throughput of an OpenCL-based FPGA accelerator for a given CNN model, considering the FPGA resource constraints such as on-chip memory, registers, computational resources and external memory bandwidth. The proposed methodology is demonstrated by optimizing two representative large-scale CNNs, AlexNet and VGG, on two Altera Stratix-V FPGA platforms, DE5-Net and P395-D8 boards, which have different hardware resources. We achieve a peak performance of 136.5 GOPS for convolution operation, and 117.8 GOPS for the entire VGG network that performs ImageNet classification on P395-D8 board.

Categories and Subject Descriptors

C.3 [**SPECIAL-PURPOSE AND APPLICATION-BASED SYSTEMS**]: Signal processing systems.

Keywords

FPGA, OpenCL, Convolutional Neural Networks, Optimization.

FPGA '16, February 21–23, 2016, Monterey, CA, USA.
© 2016 ACM. ISBN 978-1-4503-3856-1/16/02…$15.00
DOI: http://dx.doi.org/10.1145/2847263.2847276

1. INTRODUCTION

Convolutional Neural Networks (CNNs), inspired by visual cortex of the brain, are a category of feed-forward artificial neural networks. CNNs, which are primarily employed in computer vision applications such as character recognition [1], image classification [2] [9] [16] [17], video classification [3], face detection [4], gesture recognition [5], etc., are also being used in a wide range of fields including speech recognition [6], natural language processing [7] and text classification [8]. Over the past decade, the accuracy and performance of CNN-based algorithms improved significantly, mainly due to the enhanced network structures enabled by massive training datasets and increased raw computational power aided by CMOS scaling to train the models in a reasonable amount of time.

A typical CNN architecture has multiple convolutional layers that extract features from the input data, followed by classification layers. The operations in CNNs are computationally intensive with over billion operations per input image [9], thus requiring high performance server CPUs and GPUs to train the models. However, they are not energy efficient and hence various hardware accelerators have been proposed based on FPGA [10]-[13], SoC (CPU + FPGA) [14] and ASIC [15]. FPGA based hardware accelerators have gained momentum owing to their reconfigurability and fast development time, especially with the availability of high-level synthesis (HLS) tools from FPGA vendors. Moreover, FPGAs provide flexibility to implement the CNNs with limited data precision which reduces the memory footprint and bandwidth requirements, resulting in a better energy efficiency (e.g. GOPS/Watt).

Previous FPGA-based CNN accelerator designs primarily focused on optimizing the computational resources without considering the impact of the external memory transfers [10] [11] or optimizing the external memory transfers through data reuse [12] [13]. The authors of [13] proposed a design space exploration methodology for CNN accelerator by optimizing both computation resources and external memory accesses, but implemented only convolution layers. In this work, we present a systematic methodology for maximizing the throughput of an FPGA-based accelerator for an entire CNN model consisting of all CNN layers: convolution, normalization, pooling and classification layers.

The key contributions of this work are summarized as follows:

- CNN with fixed-point operations are implemented on FPGA using OpenCL framework. Critical design variables that impact the throughput are identified for optimization.
- Execution time of each CNN layer is analytically modeled as a function of these design variables and validated on FPGA.

Logic utilization is empirically modeled using FPGA synthesis data for each CNN layer as a function of the design variables.

- A systematic methodology is proposed to minimize total execution time of a given CNN algorithm, subject to the FPGA hardware constraints of logic utilization, computational resources, on-chip memory and external memory bandwidth.
- The new methodology is demonstrated by maximizing the throughput of two large-scale CNNs: AlexNet [16] and VGG [17] (which achieved top accuracies in ImageNet challenges 2012 and 2014, respectively), on two Altera FPGA platforms with different hardware resources.

The rest of the paper is organized as follows. Section 2 briefly describes the operations of CNNs using AlexNet as an example. Section 3 presents the challenges in implementing a large-scale CNN on FPGAs. It also studies the impact of precision of the weights on the accuracy of AlexNet and VGG models. Section 4 briefly presents the OpenCL implementation of CNN layers and describes the design variables used for acceleration. Section 5 describes our proposed methodology for design space exploration to maximize the throughput of the CNN accelerator with limited FPGA resources. Section 6 presents the experimental results of two CNNs optimized on two Altera FPGA platforms and compares them with prior work. Section 7 concludes the paper.

2. BASIC OPERATIONS OF CNN

A typical CNN is comprised of multiple convolutional layers, interspersed by normalization, pooling and non-linear activation function. These convolution layers decompose the input image to different features maps varying from low-level features such as edges, lines, curves, etc., in the initial layers to high-level/abstract features in the deeper layers. These extracted features are classified to output classes by fully-connected classification layers that are similar to multi-layer perceptrons. For example, Figure 1 shows the architecture of AlexNet CNN [16], which won the ImageNet challenge in 2012. It consists of 5 convolutional layers each with a Rectified Linear Unit (ReLU) based activation function, interspersed by 2 normalization layers, 3 pooling layers and concluded by 3 fully connected layers which classify the input 224×224 color images to 1,000 output classes. The ImageNet database-based models are characterized by top-1 and top-5 accuracies, which represent whether the input image label matches with top-1 and top-5 predictions, respectively.

2.1 Convolution

Convolution is the most critical operation of CNNs and it constitutes over 90% of the total operations in AlexNet model [13]. It involves 3-dimensional multiply and accumulate operation of N_{if} input features with $K \times K$ convolution filters to get an output feature neuron value as shown in Equation (1).

$$out(f_o, x, y) = \sum_{f_i=0}^{N_{if}} \sum_{k_x=0}^{K} \sum_{k_y=0}^{K} wt(f_o, f_i, k_x, k_y) \times in(f_i, x+k_x, y+k_y) \quad (1)$$

where $out(f_o, x, y)$ and $in(f_i, x, y)$ represent the neurons at location (x,y) in the feature maps f_o and f_i, respectively and $wt(f_o, f_i, k_x, k_y)$ is the weights at position (k_x, k_y) that gets convolved with input feature map f_i to get the output feature map f_o.

2.2 Normalization

Local Response Normalization (LRN) or normalization implements a form of lateral inhibition [16] by normalizing each neuron value by a factor that depends on the neighboring neurons. LRN across neighboring features and within the same feature can be computed as shown in Equations (2) and (3), respectively.

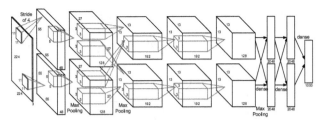

Figure 1: Architecture of AlexNet CNN [16].

$$out(f_o, x, y) = \frac{in(f_o, x, y)}{\left(1 + \frac{\alpha}{K} \sum_{f_i=f_o-K/2}^{f_o+K/2} in^2(f_i, x, y)\right)^{\beta}} \quad (2)$$

$$out(f_o, x, y) = \frac{in(f_o, x, y)}{\left(1 + \frac{\alpha}{K^2} \sum_{k_x=x-K/2}^{x+K/2} \sum_{k_y=y-K/2}^{y+K/2} in^2(f_o, x+k_x, y+k_y)\right)^{\beta}} \quad (3)$$

where K in Equation (2) is the number of feature maps used for LRN computation, K in Equation (3) is the number of neurons in x, y directions in the same feature, while α and β are constants.

2.3 Pooling

Spatial pooling or subsampling is utilized to reduce the feature dimensions as we traverse deeper into the network. As shown in Equation (4), pooling computes the maximum or average of neighboring $K \times K$ neurons in the same feature map, which also provides a form of translational invariance [18]. Although max-pooling is popularly used, average pooling is also used in some CNN models [18]. Reducing the dimensionality of lower-level features while preserving the important information, the pooling layer helps abstracting higher-level features without redundancy.

$$out(f_o, x, y) = \max_{0 \le (k_x, k_y) < K}/average \left(in(f_o, x+k_x, y+k_y)\right) \quad (4)$$

2.4 Activation Functions

The commonly used activation functions in traditional neural networks are non-linear functions such as tanh and sigmoid, which require a longer training time in CNNs [16]. Hence, Rectified Linear Unit (ReLU) defined as $y = max(x,0)$ has become the popular activation function among CNN models as it converges faster in training. Moreover, ReLU has less computational complexity compared to exponent functions in tanh and sigmoid, also aiding hardware design.

2.5 Fully Connected Layer

Fully-connected layer or inner product layer is the classification layer where all the input features (N_{if}) are connected to all of the output features (N_{of}) through synaptic weights (wt). Each output neuron is the weighted summation of all the input neurons as shown in Equation (5).

$$out(f_o) = \sum_{f_i=0}^{N_{if}} wt(f_o, f_i) \times in(f_i) \quad (5)$$

The outputs of the inner-product layer traverse through ReLU based activation function to the next inner-product layer or directly to a Softmax function that converts them to probability in the range (0, 1). The final accuracy layer compares the labels of the top probabilities from softmax layer with the actual label and gives the accuracy of the CNN model.

Table 1. Operations in AlexNet CNN model [16]

Layer	#Features	Feature dimensions		Stride	Kernel/weight dimensions				#Operations
		X	Y		#Output features	#Input features	X	Y	
Input image	3	224	224						
Convolution-1/ReLU-1	96	55	55	5	96	3	11	11	211120800
Normalization-1	96	55	55			5[a]			3194400
Pooling-1	96	27	27	2			3	3[b]	629856
Convolution-2/ReLU-2	256	27	27	1	256	48[c]	5	5	448084224
Normalization-2	256	27	27			5[a]			2052864
Pooling-2	256	13	13	1			3	3[b]	389376
Convolution-3/ReLU-3	384	13	13	1	384	256	3	3	299105664
Convolution-4/ReLU-4	384	13	13	1	384	192[c]			224345472
Convolution-5/ReLU-5	256	13	13	1	384	192[c]			149563648
Pooling-5	256	6	6	2			3	3[b]	82944
Fully connected-6/ReLU-6	4096				4096	9216			75501568
Fully connected-7/ReLU-7	4096				4096	4096			33558528
Fully connected-8	1000				1000	4096			8192000
Total Operations									1455821344

[a] Normalization across 5 neighboring channels.
[b] Max-pooling across 3x3 window.
[c] Convolution performed in 2 groups.

3. CNN MODEL STUDY AND FPGA DESIGN DIRECTIONS

3.1 FPGA Implementation Challenges

While CNNs are proven indispensable in many computer vision applications, they consume significant amount of storage, external memory bandwidth, and computational resources, which makes it difficult to implement on an embedded platform. The challenges in implementation of a large-scale CNN on FPGAs are illustrated using AlexNet model as an example. The different layers in AlexNet along with the number of features in each layer, feature dimensions, number of synaptic weights and the total number of operations in each layer are summarized in Table 1. It has over 60 million model parameters, which needs ~250MB of memory to store the weights using 32-bit floating point representation and hence they cannot be stored in on-chip memory of commercially available FPGAs. They need to be stored in an external memory and transferred to the FPGA during computation, which could become a performance bottleneck. The AlexNet model consists of 5 convolution layers, 2 LRN layers, 3 pooling layers and 3 fully connected layers, where each layer has different number of features and dimensions. If they are implemented independently without resource sharing, it would be either hardware-inefficient or may not fit on the FPGA due to the limited logic resources. The problem gets exacerbated in the state of the art models such as VGG [19] and GoogLeNet [9], which have a larger number of layers. To efficiently share hardware resources, repeated computation (e.g. convolution) should be implemented with a scalable hardware [13], such that the same hardware is reused by iterating the data through them in software.

The performance limitation due to the external memory bandwidth can be alleviated by using reduced precision model weights. Hence we performed a precision study by sweeping model weights and chose the precision values that have minimal impact on the classification accuracy.

3.2 Precision Study for FPGA Primitives

Traditionally CNN models are trained in CPU/GPU environments using 32-bit floating point data. Such high precision is not necessarily required in the testing or classification phase, owing to the redundancy in the over-parameterized CNN models [19]. Reducing data precision of the weights/data without any impact on the accuracy directly reduces the storage requirement as well as the energy for memory transfers.

Using AlexNet and VGG models, we explored the precision requirements of convolution and fully connected layer weights using Caffe tool framework [20]. We obtained the pre-trained models from Caffe, rounded the convolution weights and inner product weights separately, and tested the models using the ImageNet-2012 validation dataset of 50K images. Although data precision is reduced, Caffe tool still performs CNN operations in 32-bit floating point precision using the rounded-off weights. Figure 2 shows the top-1 and top-5 accuracies of the model for a precision sweep of the weights. It shows that the accuracy steeply drops if the weight precision reduces below 8 bits. We use a common precision for the weights in all convolution layers, as the same hardware block will be reused for all the convolution layer iterations. We choose 8-bit precision for the convolution weights and 10-bit precision for inner product weights, which degrades the accuracy by only <1% compared to full precision weights. Similarly, we choose 16-bit precision for the intermediate layer data by performing the precision study.

3.3 FPGA Accelerator Design Directions

In our FPGA design, we first developed computing primitives of CNNs using OpenCL framework. A scalable convolution module is designed based on matrix multiplication operation in OpenCL, so that it can be reused for all convolution layers with different input and output dimensions. Similarly, we developed scalable hardware modules for normalization, pooling, and fully-connected layers. We identified key design variables

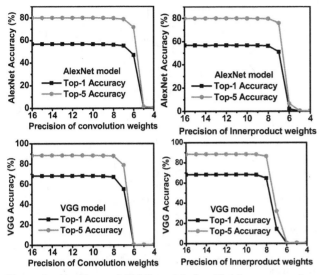

Figure 2: AlexNet and VGG model classification accuracies are shown for different weight precisions of convolution and inner-product layers.

such as loop-unroll factor and SIMD vectorization factor, which determine hardware parallelization and thus directly impact the throughput, external memory bandwidth requirement, and computational resource utilization.

Intuitively, assigning more computational resources to performance-critical operations in convolution and fully connected layers would maximize the overall throughput of the system. However, it may not be a global optimal solution, because each layer has different feature dimensions and the computational resources are limited. Hence, there is a great need for a design space exploration methodology that maximizes the throughput by optimally distributing the FPGA resources among various scalable CNN hardware blocks.

We propose a design space exploration framework based on both analytical and empirical models of CNN layer performance and resource utilization, to find the optimal values of the key design variables that maximize the throughput of a generic CNN model on a given FPGA board with limited computation resources, on-chip memory, and external memory bandwidth.

4. CNN LAYERS IN OPENCL

In this section, we briefly introduce the OpenCL framework, then present the implementation of the CNN layers in OpenCL and explain the key design variables that need to be optimized to maximize the overall throughput of the CNN accelerator.

4.1 OpenCL Framework

High Level Synthesis (HLS) tools are gaining popularity in the FPGA community, as they enable faster hardware development by automatically synthesizing an algorithm in high-level language (e.g. C) to RTL/hardware. There is a recent interest in using OpenCL, a C-based programming language, for FPGAs because of its parallel programming model [21] which matches with the parallel computation capabilities of FPGAs. Moreover, the same OpenCL codes can easily be ported to different platforms: CPUs, GPUs, DSPs or heterogeneous systems consisting of a combination of them. OpenCL compilers not only compile an OpenCL code to RTL, but also integrate it with the interfacing IPs for external memory and for communication between host CPU and FPGA accelerator board. They abstract the

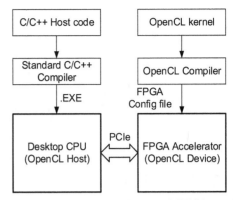

Figure 3: Design flow of OpenCL based FPGA accelerator for CNN.

designer/user from the intricacies of traditional FPGA design flow such as RTL coding, integration with interfacing IPs and timing closure, which considerably reduces the design time, while achieving performance comparable to the traditional flow, but possibly at the expense of higher on-chip memory utilization [22]. The design flow of the OpenCL based FPGA accelerator for CNN used in this work is shown in Figure 3. It consists of an FPGA accelerator board that is integrated into the PCIe slot of a desktop CPU that acts as the OpenCL host. In general, OpenCL framework consists of two components (a) an OpenCL code that is compiled and synthesized to run on the FPGA accelerator and (b) a C/C++ based host code with vendor-specific application program interface (API) to communicate with the FPGA board.

In this work, we use Altera OpenCL software development kit (SDK) for compilation of OpenCL code to RTL, which takes a few minutes for initial compilation, followed by full synthesis which could take hours depending on the size of the design. The tool-kit provides support for emulation, which runs the OpenCL code on host CPU, thus allowing for quick functional verification before going to the full FPGA implementation. The Altera SDK for OpenCL provides different synthesis constructs to enable acceleration of OpenCL kernels such as loop unroll factor and Single-Instruction-Multiple-Data (SIMD) vectorization factor. The details about how these factors improve the performance of the OpenCL kernels and impact the logic utilization are discussed in the following sections.

4.2 3-D Convolution as Matrix Multiplication

Convolutions are the most performance-critical operations in CNNs, involving computationally intensive 3-D multiply and accumulate (MAC) operations of the input features with the convolution weights as given in Equation (1). To maximize the overall throughput of the accelerator and also make the design portable to any other CNN model, a scalable convolution block is needed such that the data can be iterated through it in software.

We implemented the scalable convolution block by mapping the 3-D convolutions as matrix multiplication operations similar to that in [23] by flattening and rearranging the input features. As an example, Figure 4 illustrates how Convolution-1 layer in AlexNet is mapped from 3 input features with dimensions 224×224 to a rearranged matrix with dimensions of $(3 \times 11 \times 11) \times (55 \times 55)$. The input features from the first convolution window of 11×11 are flattened and arranged vertically as shown in Figure 4. Similarly, the entire rearranged matrix can be generated by sliding the 11×11 convolution filter across the input features. After input features are rearranged, the convolution operation transforms to a

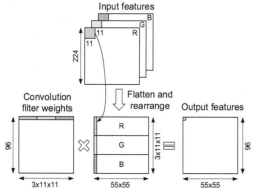

Figure 4: Mapping 3D convolutions to matrix multiplications.

1. Get current work-item/thread identifiers (x, y).
2. For each N_{CONV} elements width-wise in weight matrix:
3.   Compute address locations for input features and weights.
4.   Fetch input features to inputs[x][y] in local memory.
5.   Fetch convolution weights to weights[y][x] in local memory.
6.   Wait till $N_{CONV} \times N_{CONV}$ inputs and weights are loaded.
7.   Do the following N_{CONV} MAC operations in parallel:
8.   convolution output += weight[x][k]*input[y][k].
9.   Wait till all work-items complete computation on fetched data.
10. Save convolution output to output buffer.

Figure 5: Pseudo code for convolution implementation.

generic matrix multiplication operation. Note that we perform the input feature rearrangement on-the-fly by storing them in the FPGA on-chip memory before performing matrix multiplication, which reduces the external memory requirement by eliminating the need to store the entire rearranged input feature matrix.

The pseudo-code for matrix multiplication based convolution implementation in OpenCL is shown in Figure 5. It can be summarized as the following three basic operations which are repeated over each row of the weight matrix.

a) Fetch the convolution weights to the local memory which is implemented using FPGA on-chip memory.
b) Compute the input feature actual address locations before flattening and fetch them to local memory.
c) Compute N_{CONV} multiply and accumulate operations in parallel on the weights and inputs from local memory.

We utilized matrix multiplication OpenCL code from [24] and appended the input feature rearranging operation. Understanding the matrix multiplication OpenCL implementation is critical for acceleration of the convolution operation. The implementation of matrix multiplication operation in OpenCL is illustrated in Figure 6, which consists of convolution weight matrix A (M×N), multiplied by the rearranged input feature matrix B (N×P) to compute the output feature matrix C (M×P). It consists of $N_{CONV} \times N_{CONV}$ threads or OpenCL work-items, which fetch the first $N_{CONV} \times N_{CONV}$ inputs to the local memory where $N_{CONV}=4$ in this example. Each work-item performs N_{CONV} parallel multiply and accumulate (MAC) operations on the local memory data, which is accomplished by loop unrolling that replicates the hardware resources for acceleration. This process is repeated by sliding the $N_{CONV} \times N_{CONV}$ window column-wise in matrix A and row-wise in matrix B and performing the MAC operations to get $N_{CONV} \times N_{CONV}$ elements in the product matrix C.

From Figure 6, we see that the input and output matrix dimensions must be a multiple of N_{CONV}, which might not always be possible because of different number of input and output features and different feature dimensions in different convolution

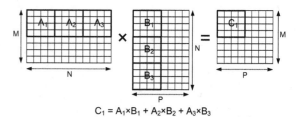

$$C_1 = A_1 \times B_1 + A_2 \times B_2 + A_3 \times B_3$$

Figure 6: Accelerating matrix multiplications in OpenCL.

layers. Hence we use zero padding in the input matrices to make their dimensions a multiple of N_{CONV}. Increasing N_{CONV} boosts the throughput as it fetches larger number of inputs to the local memory and performs computations on them without having to wait for external data. On the other hand, it increases the logic utilization and execution time if the zero-padding is excessive in some layers.

We use SIMD vectorization factor (S_{CONV}), as another design variable to accelerate the convolution operation, which represents the factor by which computational resources are vectorized to execute in a Single-Instruction-Multiple-Data fashion. This factor improves the throughput by a factor of S_{CONV}. Depending on the model configuration parameters such as number of features and their dimensions and the number of CNN layers, choosing an appropriate combination of (N_{CONV}, S_{CONV}) maximizes the overall throughput of the CNN.

4.3 Normalization Layer

Local response normalization (LRN) implementation requires an exponent operation as shown in Equation (2), which is expensive to precisely implement in hardware. Hence we implement the exponent function $f_1(x_o)$ shown in Equation (6) using a piece-wise linear approximation function $pwlf(x_o)$.

$$out(f_o, x, y) = in(f_o, x, y).f_1(x_o) \qquad (6)$$

$$f_1(x_o) = (1 + x_o)^{-\beta}; \; x_o = \frac{\alpha}{K} \sum_{f_i = f_o - K/2}^{f_o + K/2} in^2(f_i, x, y) \qquad (7)$$

Here K represents the number of features used for normalization. Using the AlexNet model data as an example, the exponent function $f_1(x_o)$ is approximated using a piece-wise linear function using 20 points with a maximum error of 1%. Because of the wide dynamic range of values involved in x_i computation, normalization is implemented in 32-bit floating point representation. The exponent function and the piece-wise linear approximate function along with the approximation error are plotted in Figure 7. Normalization is implemented as a single-threaded OpenCL code using loop unroll factor (N_{NORM}), which represents the number of normalization operations it performs in a single cycle. The Altera OpenCL compiler automatically infers pipelining whenever there are no data dependencies between multiple iterations. The pseudo code for normalization is shown in

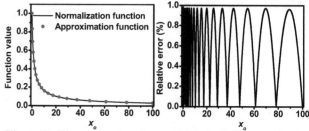

Figure 7: Piece-wise linear approximation of normalization operation kernel with a maximum error of 1%.

1. Compute *sum_of_squares* of first *K*/2 features.
2. For each *input_feature i*:
3.   For each neuron *j* in feature *i*:
4.   Do the following for N_{NORM} neurons in parallel:
5.   Compute *sum_of_squares*[*j*] += *input_feature*[*i*+*K*/2][*j*]
6.   Compute *output_feature*[*i*][*j*] = *input_feature*[*i*][*j*]
7.   **pwlf*(*α*/*K**sum_of_squares*[*j*])
8.   Update *sum_of_squares*[*j*] -= *input_feature*[*i*-*K*/2][*j*]

Figure 8: Pseudo-code for normalization implementation.

Figure 8. It uses local memory to store the sum of squares of a sliding window of *K* input features, while performing the normalization operation on the computed sum of squares using the piece-wise linear approximation function, *pwlf*(x_o).

4.4 Implementation of other Layers

Pooling is implemented using a single work-item kernel where acceleration is achieved by unrolling the loop to generate N_{POOL} parallel outputs in a single cycle. Fully-connected layer or inner-product layer is also implemented as single work-item kernel, where acceleration is achieved by performing N_{FC} parallel multiply and accumulate operations, which accelerates the performance by a factor of N_{FC}. Nonlinear activation function ReLU, which performs the function $y=max(x,0)$ is incorporated at the output of convolution and inner product implementations with a flag to enable or disable it.

5. DESIGN SPACE EXPLORATION

Choosing the best combination of the design variables (N_{CONV}, S_{CONV}, N_{NORM}, N_{POOL}, N_{FC}) that maximizes the performance of the CNN accelerator, while still being able to fit in the limited FPGA resources is a non-trivial task, which emphasizes the need for a systematic design space exploration methodology. Optimization framework that relies on full FPGA synthesis at each design point may not be feasible especially because of the long run time, which could take hours, or potential synthesis failures that occur due to utilization of hardware resources. Hence we model the performance and resource utilization and use them for fast design space exploration.

In this section, we first formulate the optimization problem and present the analytical and empirical modeling of the performance and FPGA resource utilization as a function of the design variables for each CNN layer.

5.1 Problem Formulation

The resource-constrained throughput optimization problem can be formulated as follows.

$$\text{Minimize} \sum_{i=0}^{TL} runtime_i(N_{CONV}, S_{CONV}, N_{NORM}, N_{POOL}, N_{FC}) \quad (8)$$

$$\text{Subject to} \sum_{j=0}^{L} DSP_j \le DSP_{MAX} \quad (9)$$

$$\sum_{j=0}^{L} Memory_j \le Memory_{MAX} \quad (10)$$

$$\sum_{j=0}^{L} Logic_j \le Logic_{MAX} \quad (11)$$

where *TL* represents the total number of CNN layers including the repeated layers, *L* denotes the total number of CNN layer types and *runtime_i* is the execution time of the layer-*i*. DSP_{MAX}, $Memory_{MAX}$, and $Logic_{MAX}$ represent the total DSP, on-chip memory and FPGA logic resources, respectively, available in a given FPGA.

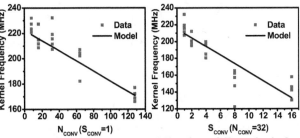

Figure 9: Kernel frequency modeling from full synthesis data at 5 random seeds. RMS error of the fit: 12.57 MHz

5.2 Performance Modeling

The execution time of each CNN layer is analytically modeled as a function of the design variables and validated by performing full synthesis at selective design points and running them on the FPGA accelerator.

5.2.1 Convolution time

The execution time of convolution layer-*i* is modeled as follows.

$$Convolution\ Runtime_i = \frac{No.\ of\ Convolution\ Ops_i}{N_{CONV} \times S_{CONV} \times Frequency} \quad (12)$$

$$No.\ of\ Convolution\ Ops_i$$
$$= PAD_{NCONV}(\text{Conv filter dimensions} \times \text{No. of input features})$$
$$+ PAD_{NCONV}(\text{No. of output features}) \quad (13)$$
$$+ PAD_{NCONV}(\text{output feature dimensions})$$

where PAD_{NCONV} ceils its inputs to the multiple of N_{CONV}. Maximum frequency of the kernel, which is also a function of N_{CONV} and S_{CONV}, is modeled empirically from the synthesis data with different random seeds, as shown in Figure 9. The execution time model and the measured execution time of convolution layers 1-5 of AlexNet implementation for a sweep of N_{CONV} at different S_{CONV} values are compared in Figure 10.

5.2.2 Other layers

Similarly, the execution time of normalization, pooling and fully connected layers are modeled as functions of their respective loop unroll factors used for acceleration as follows.

$$Runtime_i = \frac{\#Operations_i}{Unroll\ factor \times Frequency} \quad (14)$$

The execution time model vs. measured run time of normalization and fully connected classification layers are shown in Figure 11.

5.2.3 Memory Bandwidth

Input data, weights, intermediate data and final output data are stored in the external memory that is present on the FPGA accelerator board. To enable efficient data transfer to and from external memory, Altera OpenCL compiler generates complex load/store units similar to those in GPUs, which combine multiple external memory accesses into a single burst access, known as memory coalescing. This ensures the efficient use of available external memory bandwidth with less contention for memory accesses between multiple computational blocks. On the other hand, this makes it difficult to model the external memory bandwidth usage with respect to the design variables used for acceleration. This problem is aggravated by the reuse of the scalable hardware blocks in multiple iterations of CNN layers

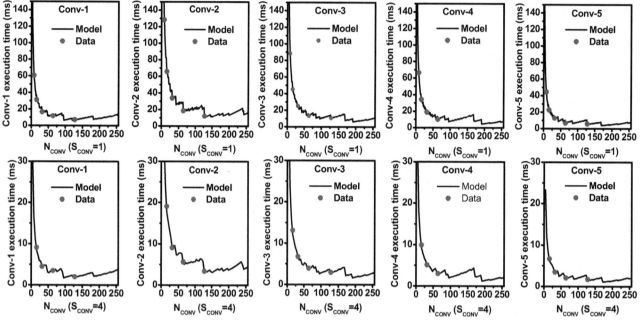

Figure 10: Run time model vs. measured time of convolution layers 1-5 for a sweep of matrix multiplication block size (N_{CONV}) for SIMD vectorization factor, S_{CONV} = 1 and 4.

with different input dimensions, which will have different access patterns. For example, the execution time of fully connected layers 6 and 7 of AlexNet model shown in Figure 11 shows that the model matches well with the measured time till N_{FC}=100. For N_{FC}>100, the measured time increases slightly, but the model still shows a reduction in execution time. This discrepancy is caused by the bandwidth limitation of the FPGA board used for the model validation. Hence we use the bandwidth limitation of the FPGA board to define the upper limits for the design variables in our optimization framework.

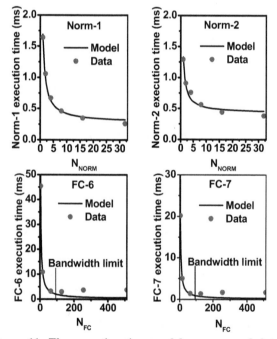

Figure 11: The execution time model vs. measured data of normalization and fully connected layers in AlexNet for sweep of loop unroll factors N_{NORM} and N_{FC}.

5.3 Resource Utilization Modeling

Analytically modeling the FPGA resource utilization of an algorithm in a high-level language such as OpenCL may not be feasible because of the optimizations performed in the HLS tools. Hence, we use synthesis results to empirically model the FPGA resource utilization. DSP block usage, on-chip memory and logic utilization from synthesis results of each CNN layer are fitted to linear regression models as a function of their design variables.

For example, resource utilization models of normalization block are shown in Figure 12. Logic element and DSP utilization from the synthesis data in Figure 12 show a linear increase with the swept design variable N_{NORM}. On the other hand, on-chip memory utilization model shows small discrepancy with the synthesis data at intermediate points because of implementation of coalescing load/store units in which the memory resource utilization depends on whether the external memory data width is an integer multiple of the design variables i.e. N_{NORM}.

5.4 Optimization Framework

From the convolution run time model in Figure 10, we see that it is non-monotonic, because of the differences in dimensions of the CNN layers. Although exhaustive search of all the design variables could be done using the performance and resource utilization models, it may not be feasible if the number of design variables and/or the FPGA resources increase substantially. This

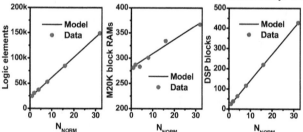

Figure 12: Resource utilization empirical models for normalization block.

calls for global optimization methodologies such as simulated annealing, genetic algorithm or particle swarm optimization with integer variables and multiple inequality constraints. In this work, we use genetic algorithm with integer constraints from the global optimization toolbox in Matlab for the design space exploration.

Genetic algorithm is a stochastic optimization technique that mimics the biological evolution process and is popularly used to find the global minimum of an objective function subject to a set of constraints. It can also handle mixed integer programming problems, where some of the design variables are integers. It iteratively improves the quality of the solution by generating a set of candidate solutions at each iteration or generation from a combination of the best solutions from the previous generation based on a set of genetic rules – selection, crossover and mutation. The solutions that violate the constraints (i.e. Equations (9)-(11)) are penalized with a higher objective function value to ensure convergence of the feasible solutions to a global minimum.

The design space of the OpenCL-based FPGA accelerator design is illustrated in Equation (15).

$$S_{CONV} = 1, 2, 4, 8 \ or \ 16$$
$$N_{CONV} = N \times S_{CONV}, 0 < N < N_{MAX}$$
$$0 < N_{NORM} < N_{NORM(MAX)} \quad (15)$$
$$0 < N_{POOL} < N_{POOL(MAX)}$$
$$0 < N_{FC} < N_{FC(MAX)}$$

where all the design variables are integers, and upper limits of the design space exploration such as N_{MAX}, $N_{NORM(MAX)}$, $N_{POOL(MAX)}$, and $N_{FC(MAX)}$ are determined by the external memory bandwidth of the FPGA board. For example, in a fully connected layer implementation where k bytes are required for each MAC operation, N_{FC} of an accelerator board with external memory bandwidth of M_{BW} is computed as shown in Equation (16).

$$N_{FC(MAX)} = \frac{Memory \ bandwidth \ (M_{BW})}{k \times Frequency} \quad (16)$$

For an FPGA system with 6 GB/s external memory bandwidth, requiring 2 bytes per MAC operation in a fully connected layer with 100MHz kernel frequency, the upper limit for N_{FC} can be computed from Equation (16) as 30. Similarly, the upper limits of other blocks can be computed based on the number of external memory transfers required for each operation.

6. EXPERIMENTAL RESULTS

In this section, we present the validation results of the proposed optimization framework by implementing and accelerating two large-scale CNN models: AlexNet and VGG (16-layer) models on two FPGA boards with different hardware resources. The hardware specifications of the two Altera Stratix-V based boards are summarized in Table 2.

Both networks are implemented in OpenCL with fixed-point operations using 8-bit weights for convolution and fully connected layers as obtained from the precision study in Section

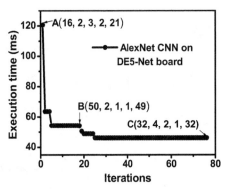

Figure 13: Optimization progress of AlexNet implementation. Design variables (N_{CONV}, S_{CONV}, N_{NORM}, N_{POOL}, N_{FC}) are shown at points A, B and C.

Table 3: Summary of Execution time and Utilization.

	A	B	C
Exec. time (model)	120.6 ms	54.3 ms	46.1 ms
Exec. time (measured)	117.7 ms	52.6 ms	45.7 ms
Logic elements	158k	152k	153k
M20K memory blocks	1,439	1,744	1,673
DSP blocks	164	234	246

3. Although 10-bit precision is chosen for inner product weights, they are still represented using 8-bits as the 2 bits in MSB side are zeros in all the weights. Using the performance and resource utilization models (Sections 5.2 and 5.3) and the maximum hardware resources available in the two boards, optimization framework is run on both AlexNet and VGG models to find the optimal combination of design variables (N_{CONV}, S_{CONV}, N_{NORM}, N_{POOL}, N_{FC}) that maximizes the throughput. For example, Figure 13 shows the execution time of the best solution of each iteration during the optimization of AlexNet implementation on DE5-Net FPGA board. Table 3 shows the execution time from the model, measured execution time on FPGA and the FPGA resource utilization at chosen points A, B and C in Figure 13. The final design variables for both networks optimized for the two FPGA boards are shown in Table 4. VGG model does not include normalization layers, hence the corresponding kernel is removed for the FPGA implementation.

Using Altera OpenCL SDK, the OpenCL kernel codes for AlexNet and VGG models are compiled for the two boards using the corresponding optimized parameters from Table 3. Using the host code APIs, FPGA is programmed and the CNN model is run by queueing the OpenCL implemented CNN kernels with appropriate arguments that consist of input/output buffer address locations and the layer dimensions. The execution time of each kernel and the entire model are measured and throughput is computed as (total number of operations)/(execution time).

Table 2: Comparison of FPGA accelerator boards.

Specification	P395-D8 [25]	DE5-Net [26]
FPGA	Stratix-V GSD8	Stratix-V GXA7
Logic elements	695k	622k
DSP blocks	1,963	256
M20K RAMs	2,567	2,560
External memory	4× 8GB DDR3	2× 2GB DDR3

Table 4: Optimized parameters.

	P395-D8 board		DE5-Net board	
	AlexNet	**VGG**	**AlexNet**	**VGG**
N_{CONV}	64	64	32	64
S_{CONV}	8	8	4	2
N_{NORM}	2	-	2	-
N_{POOL}	1	1	1	1
N_{FC}	71	64	32	30

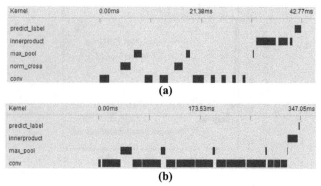

(a)

(b)

Figure 14: The execution time of CNN layers in (a) AlexNet and (b) VGG models on P395-D8 FPGA accelerator.

The execution time of the CNN layers in AlexNet and VGG models implemented on P395-D8 board with kernel profiling support) is shown in Figure 14. The final classification time without kernel profiling will be significantly lower than that shown in Figure 14 because of the delay involved with kernel profiling itself. The execution of fully-connected layers can be overlapped with the initial convolution layers of the next image, which increases the overall throughput of the accelerator (by 27% in AlexNet implementation on P395-D8). The next input image transfer from the OpenCL host to the off-chip memory on the FPGA board is overlapped with current CNN operations, thus not hampering the throughput. The initial model weight transfer from the host to the board, which only occurs once in the beginning, is not included for throughput computation.

The total classification time per image and overall throughput of AlexNet and VGG models on P395-D8 and DE5-Net boards are compared with Caffe tool [20] running on Intel core i5-4590 CPU (3.3 GHz) as shown in Table 5. Although both FPGAs have similar number of logic elements and on-chip memory blocks, the smaller number of DSP blocks in DE5-Net accounts for its lower throughput compared to that of P395-D8. The software implementation in Caffe tool uses libraries optimized for basic vector and matrix operations (i.e., ATLAS [27]) for performing CNN operations. Our OpenCL based FPGA implementations on P395-D8 achieve 9.5x and 5.5x speedups for AlexNet and VGG models, respectively, compared to the CPU implementation in Caffe tool.

The execution time, throughput and the resource utilization of each kernel type of the AlexNet implementation on P395-D8 and DE5-Net FPGA accelerator boards are shown in Figure 15. VGG implementation on P395-D8 achieves a peak throughput of 136.5 GOPS for convolution layers, and 117.8 GOPS including all layers and operations while performing image classification. From the implementation results, we see that throughput of the accelerator is largely proportional to the number of DSP blocks

Table 5: Classification time/image and overall throughput.

	FPGA	**Classification time/image (ms)**	**Throughput (GOPS)**
AlexNet	**P395-D8**	20.1	72.4
	DE5-Net	45.7	31.8
	CPU	191.9	7.6
VGG	**P395-D8**	262.9	117.8
	DE5-Net	651.2	47.5
	CPU	1437.2	21.5

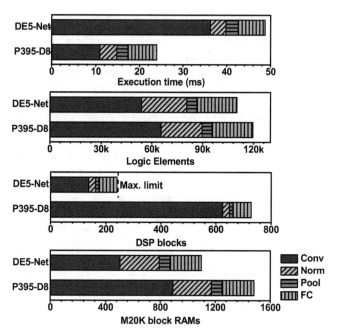

Figure 15: Execution time and resource utilization of each CNN layer type for AlexNet implementation on P395-D8 and DE5-Net FPGA boards.

used in the implementation. AlexNet implementation on P395-D8 board is limited by the number of available M20K block RAMs, while only 727 out of 1963 available DSP blocks are utilized. On the other hand, throughput on DE5-Net FPGA board is limited by the lower number of available DSP blocks, although the on-chip memory resources and logic elements are not fully utilized.

Our optimization framework reports the hardware resource that causes the performance bottleneck, such that the user can choose another FPGA hardware, which has larger number of the specific hardware resources (e.g. DSP blocks). This methodology can also be used to find the ideal specifications of an FPGA suited for CNN, by performing optimization with relaxed constraints for the bottleneck hardware resource. For example, increasing the on-chip memory resources on P395-D8 FPGA by 10% directly increases the throughput of AlexNet implementation by ~10%. This work assumes that MAC operations are implemented using the DSP blocks only. However, we can potentially enhance the throughput further by using the remaining logic elements to implement MAC operations, which will be studied in future work.

The top-1 and top-5 accuracies of FPGA implementation of AlexNet and VGG models compared to those of the full-precision Caffe models are summarized in Table 6. The accuracy degradation due to fixed-point operations in FPGA implementation is <2% for top-1 accuracy and <1% for top-5 accuracy for both AlexNet and VGG models.

Both DE5-Net and P395-D8 boards are connected to a PCIe slot of a desktop computer whose CPU operates as the OpenCL host. Since the FPGA board receives power from external power port as well as PCIe slot, the power measurement of the FPGA

Table 6: Model accuracy comparison.

Accuracy	**Full precision in Caffe tool**		**Fixed-point FPGA implementation**	
	Top-1	**Top-5**	**Top-1**	**Top-5**
AlexNet	56.82%	79.95%	55.41%	78.98%
VGG	68.35%	88.44%	66.58%	87.48%

Table 7: Comparison with previous implementations.

	[12]	[13]	This work
FPGA	Virtex-6 VLX240T	Virtex-7 VX485T	Stratix-V GSD8
Frequency	150 MHz	100 MHz	120 MHz
CNN size	2.74 GMAC	1.33 GOP	30.9 GOP
Precision	fixed	float (32b)	fixed (8-16b)
Throughput	17 GOPS[b]	61.6 GOPS[a]	136.5 GOPS[a] 117.8 GOPS[b]

[a]convolution operation only
[b]all operations for image classification

board itself is not straightforward. We attempted to block the power connection through PCIe and have the FPGA board powered only through the external power port. This way, the average power consumption of DE5-Net board was measured as 24.2W after programming AlexNet configuration, and as 25.8W while performing classification. On the other hand, the same measurement method was not feasible on P395-D8 board as it was designed to use both power supplies. Nonetheless, we measured its power consumption as 19.1W after programming with AlexNet configuration file, using a utility function provided by board manufacturer that measures the steady state power of the board.[1] We compare the performance of VGG model implementation on P395-D8 FPGA board to the existing FPGA based CNN accelerators in Table 7. For the entire VGG model with 30.9 GOP, our FPGA accelerator achieves overall throughput of 117.8 GOPS for ImageNet classification.

7. CONCLUSION

In this work, we implemented scalable CNN layers on FPGA using OpenCL framework and identified the key design variables for hardware acceleration. Further, we proposed a design space exploration methodology based on a combination of analytical and empirical models for performance and resource utilization, to find the optimal design variables that yield maximum acceleration of any CNN model implementation using limited FPGA resources. Using the proposed methodology, we implemented two large-scale CNNs, AlexNet and VGG, on P395-D8 and DE5-Net FPGA boards and achieved superior performance compared to previous work.

8. ACKNOWLEDGEMENTS

This project was partially supported by Samsung Advanced Institute of Technology.

9. REFERENCES

[1] Y. LeCun, et al. Handwritten digit recognition with a back-propagation network. In *Advances in Neural Information Processing Systems*, 396-404, 1990.

[2] O. Russakovsky, et al. ImageNet large-scale visual recognition challenge. In *Int. J. Computer Vision*, 2015.

[3] A. Karpathy, et al. Large-scale video classification with convolutional neural networks. In *CVPR*, 1725-1732, 2014.

[4] H. Li, Z. Lin, X. Shen, J. Brandt and G. Hua. A convolutional neural network cascade for face detection. In *CVPR*, 5325-5334, 2015.

[5] P. Barros, S. Magg, C. Weber and S. Wermter. A multichannel convolutional neural network for hand posture recognition. In *Int. Conf. on Artificial Neural Networks (ICANN)*, 403-410, 2014.

[6] O. Abdel-Hamid, et al. Convolutional neural networks for speech recognition. In *IEEE Trans. on Audio, Speech and Language Processing*, 1533-1545, Oct 2014.

[7] R. Collobert and J. Weston. A unified architecture for natural language processing: deep neural networks with multitask learning. In *Int. Conf. on Machine Learning*, 160-167, 2008.

[8] S. Lai, L. Xu, K. Liu and J. Zhao. Recurrent convolutional neural networks for text classification. In *AAAI Conf. on Artificial Intelligence*, 2267-2273, 2015.

[9] C. Szegedy, et al. Going deeper with convolutions. In *CVPR*, 1-9, 2015.

[10] C. Farabet, et al. Hardware accelerated convolutional neural networks for synthetic vision systems. In *ISCAS*, 257-260, 2010.

[11] S. Chakradhar, et al. A dynamically configurable coprocessor for convolutional neural networks. In *ISCA*, 247-257, 2010.

[12] M. Peemen, et al. Memory-centric accelerator design for convolutional neural networks. In *ICCD*, 13-19, 2013.

[13] C. Zhang, et al. Optimizing FPGA-based accelerator design for deep convolutional neural networks. In *ACM Int. Symp. On Field-Programmable Gate Arrays*, 161-170, 2015.

[14] V. Gokhale, et al. A 240 G-ops/s mobile coprocessor for deep neural networks. In *CVPR Workshops*, 696-701, 2014.

[15] Y. Chen, et al. DaDianNao: A machine-learning supercomputer. In *IEEE/ACM Int. Symp. on Microarchitecture*, 602-622, 2014.

[16] A. Krizhevsky, et al. ImageNet classification with deep convolutional neural networks. In *NIPS*, 1097-1105, 2012.

[17] K. Simonyan and A. Zisserman. Very deep convolutional networks for large-scale image recognition. arXiv:1409.1556.

[18] Y.L. Boureau, et al. A Theoretical Analysis of Feature Pooling in Visual Recognition. In *Int. Conf. on Machine Learning*, 2010.

[19] M. Denil, et al. Predicting parameters in deep learning. In *NIPS*, 2148–2156, 2013.

[20] Y. Jia, et al. Caffe: Convolutional architecture for fast feature embedding. arXiv:1408.5093.

[21] Khronos OpenCL Working Group. The OpenCL Specification, version 1.1.44, 2011.

[22] M. S. Abdelfattah, et al. Gzip on a chip: high performance lossless data compression on FPGAs using OpenCL. In *Int. Workshop on OpenCL 2014*.

[23] K. Chellapilla, S. Puri and P. Simard. High performance convolutional neural networks for document processing. In *Int. Workshop on Frontiers in Handwriting Recognition*, 2006.

[24] Altera OpenCL design examples. Available online at https://www.altera.com/support/support-resources/design-examples/design-software/opencl.html

[25] Nallatech P395-D8 OpenCL FPGA accelerator cards. http://www.nallatech.com/wp-content/uploads/openclcardspb_v1_51.pdf

[26] DE5-Net FPGA kit user manual. Available online at ftp://ftp.altera.com/up/pub/Altera_Material/Boards/DE5/DE5_User_Manual.pdf

[27] R.C. Whaley and J.J. Dongarra. Automatically tuned linear algebra software. In *Proc. SuperComputing 1998: High Performance Networking and Computing*, 2001.

---

[1]The power consumption difference between the desktop computer without FPGA and with FPGA running AlexNet is measured as 26W for DE5-Net and 35W for P395-D8 boards. Note that this difference includes the power consumption of CPU running the OpenCL host code, which could be much smaller with embedded processors in FPGA chips.

Going Deeper with Embedded FPGA Platform for Convolutional Neural Network

Jiantao Qiu[1,2], Jie Wang[1], Song Yao[1,2], Kaiyuan Guo[1,2], Boxun Li[1,2],Erjin Zhou[1],
Jincheng Yu[1,2], Tianqi Tang[1,2], Ningyi Xu[3], Sen Song[2,4], Yu Wang[1,2],
and Huazhong Yang[1,2]
[1]Department of Electronic Engineering, Tsinghua University
[1]Tsinghua National Laboratory for Information Science and Technology
[2]Center for Brain-Inspired Computing Research, Tsinghua University
[3]Hardware Computing Group, Microsoft Research Asia [4]School of Medicine, Tsinghua University
{songyao, yu-wang}@mail.tsinghua.edu.cn

ABSTRACT

In recent years, Convolutional Neural Network (CNN) based methods have achieved great success in a large number of applications and have been among the most powerful and widely used techniques in computer vision. However, CNN-based methods are computational-intensive and resource-consuming, and thus are hard to be integrated into embedded systems such as smart phones, smart glasses, and robots. FPGA is one of the most promising platforms for accelerating CNN, but the limited bandwidth and on-chip memory size limit the performance of FPGA accelerator for CNN.

In this paper, we go deeper with the embedded FPGA platform on accelerating CNNs and propose a CNN accelerator design on embedded FPGA for Image-Net large-scale image classification. We first present an in-depth analysis of state-of-the-art C-NN models and show that Convolutional layers are computational-centric and Fully-Connected layers are memory-centric. Then the dynamic-precision data quantization method and a convolver design that is efficient for all layer types in CNN are proposed to improve the bandwidth and resource utilization. Results show that only 0.4% accuracy loss is introduced by our data quantization flow for the very deep VGG16 model when 8/4-bit quantization is used. A data arrangement method is proposed to further ensure a high utilization of the external memory bandwidth. Finally, a state-of-the-art CNN, VGG16-SVD, is implemented on an embedded FPGA platform as a case study. VGG16-SVD is the largest and most accurate network that has been implemented on FPGA end-to-end so far. The system on Xilinx Zynq ZC706 board achieves a frame rate at 4.45 fps with the top-5 accuracy of 86.66% using 16-bit quantization. The average performance of Convolutional layers and the full CNN is 187.8 GOP/s and 137.0 GOP/s under 150MHz working frequency, which outperforms previous approaches significantly.

This work was supported by 973 project 2013CB329000, National Natural Science Foundation of China (No. 61373026, 61261160501), the Importation and Development of High-Caliber Talents Project of Beijing Municipal Institutions, Microsoft, Xilinx University Program, and Tsinghua University Initiative Scientific Research Program.

Keywords

Embedded FPGA; Convolutional Neural Network (CNN); Dynamic-precision data quantization; Bandwidth utilization

1. INTRODUCTION

Image classification is a basic problem in computer vision (CV). In recent years, Convolutional Neural Network (CNN) has led to great advances in image classification accuracy. In Image-Net Large-Scale Vision Recognition Challenge (ILSVRC) 2012 [1], Krizhevsky et al. showed that CNN had great power by achieving the top-5 accuracy of 84.7% in classification task [2], which was significantly higher than other traditional image classification methods. In the following years, the accuracy has been improved to 88.8% [3], 93.3% [4], and 96.4% [5] in ILSVRC 2013, 2014, and 2015.

While achieving state-of-the-art performance, CNN-based methods demand much more computations and memory resources compared with traditional methods. In this manner, most CNN-based methods have to depend on large servers. However, there has been a non-negligible market for embedded systems which demands capabilities of high-accuracy and real-time object recognition, such as auto-piloted car and robots. But for embedded systems, the limited battery and resources are serious problems.

To address this problem, many researchers have proposed various CNN acceleration techniques from either computing or memory access aspects [6, 7, 8, 9, 10, 11, 12, 13]. However, most of previous techniques only considered small CNN models such as the 5-layer LeNet for simple tasks such as MNIST handwritten digits recognition [14]. State-of-the-art CNN models for large-scale image classification have extremely high complexity, and thus can only be stored in external memory. In this manner, memory bandwidth becomes a serious problem for accelerating CNNs especially for embedded systems. Besides, previous research focused on accelerating Convolutional (CONV) layers, while the Fully-Connected (FC) layers were not well studied. Consequently, we need to go deeper with the embedded FPGA platform to address these problems.

In this paper, we make a deep investigation on how to deploy full CNNs to accelerators on embedded FPGA platform. A CN-N accelerator for Image-Net large-scale classification is proposed, which can execute the very deep VGG16-SVD model at a speed of 4.45 fps. Specifically, this paper makes the following contributions.

- We present an in-depth analysis of state-of-the-art CNN models for large-scale image classification. We show that state-of-the-art CNN models are extremely complex (for example, the VGG16 model has 138 million weights and needs over 30 GOPs), CONV layers are computational-centric, and FC layers are memory-centric.

- For the first time, we present an automatic flow for dynamic-precision data quantization and explore various data quan-

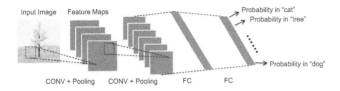

Figure 1: A typical CNN structure from the feature map perspective.

tization configurations. Results show that only a 0.4% accuracy loss is introduced with VGG16 model under 8/4 bit dynamic-precision quantization. Specific hardware is also designed to support dynamic-precision data quantization.

- We show that the performance of FC layers is mainly limited by the memory bandwidth on embedded FPGA platform, which is different from CONV layers. In this manner, we apply SVD to the weight matrix of the first FC layer, which reduces 85.8% memory footprint of this layer, design the convolvers that can compute FC layers to reduce resource consumption, and propose a data arrangement scheme to accelerate FC layers.

- We propose a CNN accelerator design on an embedded FPGA platform for Image-Net large-scale classification. On the Xilinx Zynq platform, our system achieves the performance at 187.8 GOP/s and 137.0 GOP/s for CONV layers and full CNN under 150 MHz frequency respectively. With VGG16-SVD network, our implementation achieves a top-5 accuracy of 86.66% at a 4.45 fps speed.

The rest of paper is organized as follows. In Section 2, the background of CNN is presented. In Section 3, the related work is introduced and discussed. We analyze the complexity distribution of state-of-the-art CNN models in Section 4. In Section 5, the dynamic-precision data quantization flow is proposed. The proposed image classification system design and implementation details are introduced in Section 6. The memory system and data arrangement method for FC layers are introduced in Section 7. The performance of the proposed system is evaluated and discussed in Section 8. We finally conclude this paper in Section 9.

2. BACKGROUND

Deep CNN achieves the state-of-the-art performance on a wide range of vision-related tasks. To help understand the CNN-based image classification algorithms analyzed in this paper, in this section, we introduce the basics of CNN. An introduction to the Image-Net dataset and state-of-the-art CNN models is also presented.

2.1 Primer on CNN

A typical CNN consists of a number of *layers* that run *in sequence*. The parameters of a CNN model are called "*weights*". The first layer of a CNN reads an input image and outputs a series of *feature maps*. The following layers read the feature maps generated by previous layers and output new feature maps. Finally a classifier outputs the probability of each category that the input image might belong to. CONV layer and FC layer are two essential types of layer in CNN. After CONV layers, there are usually pooling layers. A typical CNN example is shown in Figure 1.

In this paper, for a CNN layer, f_j^{in} denotes its j-th input feature map, f_i^{out} denotes the i-th output feature map, and b_i denotes the bias term to the i-th output map. For CONV layers, n_{in} and n_{out} represent the number of input and output feature maps respectively. For FC layers, n_{in} and n_{out} are the length of the input and output feature vector.

CONV layer takes a series of feature maps as input and convolves with convolutional kernels to obtain the output feature maps. A nonlinear layer, which applies nonlinear activation function to

Table 1: # of layers in VGG models.

Model	CONV Group 1	CONV Group 2	CONV Group 3	CONV Group 4	CONV Group 5	FC	Total
VGG11	1	1	2	2	2	3	11
VGG16	2	2	3	3	3	3	16
VGG19	2	2	4	4	4	3	19

each element in the output feature maps is often attached to CONV layers. The CONV layer can be expressed with Equation 1:

$$f_i^{out} = \sum_{j=1}^{n_{in}} f_j^{in} \otimes g_{i,j} + b_i \qquad (1 \le i \le n_{out}), \qquad (1)$$

where $g_{i,j}$ is the convolutional kernel applied to j-th input feature map and i-th output feature map.

FC layer applies a linear transformation on the input feature vector:

$$f^{out} = W f^{in} + b, \qquad (2)$$

where W is an $n_{out} \times n_{in}$ transformation matrix and b is the bias term. It should be noted, for the FC layer, the input is not a combination of several 2-D feature maps but just a feature vector. Consequently, in Equation 2, the parameter n_{in} and n_{out} actually corresponds to the lengths of the input and output feature vector.

Pooling layer, which outputs the maximum or average value of each subarea in each feature maps, is often attached to the CONV layer. Max-pooling can be expressed as Equation 3:

$$f_{i,j}^{out} = \max_{p \times p} \begin{pmatrix} f_{m,n}^{in} & \cdots & f_{m,n+p-1}^{in} \\ \vdots & & \vdots \\ f_{m+p-1,n}^{in} & \cdots & f_{m+p-1,n+p-1}^{in} \end{pmatrix}, \qquad (3)$$

where p is the pooling kernel size. This non-linear "down sampling" not only reduces the feature map size and the computation for later layers, but also provides a form of translation invariance.

CNN can be used to classify images in a forward inference process. But before using the CNN for any task, one should first *train* the CNN on a dataset. Recent research [15] showed that, a CNN model pre-trained on a large dataset for a given task can be used for other tasks and achieved high accuracy with minor adjustment in network weights. This minor adjustment is called "*fine-tune*". The training of the CNN is mostly implemented on large servers. For embedded FPGA platform, we only focus on accelerating the inference process of a CNN.

2.2 Image-Net Dataset

Image-Net [1] dataset is regarded as the standard benchmark to evaluate the performance of image classification and object detection algorithms. So far Image-Net dataset has collected more than 14 million images within more than 21 thousand categories. Image-Net releases a subset with 1.2 million images in 1000 categories for the ILSVRC classification task, which has significantly promoted the development of CV techniques. In this paper, all the CNN models are trained with ILSVRC 2014 training dataset and evaluated with ILSVRC 2014 validation set.

2.3 State-of-the-Art CNN Models

In ILSVRC 2012, the SuperVision team won the first place in image classification task using AlexNet by achieving 84.7% top-5 accuracy [2]. CaffeNet is a replication of AlexNet with minor changes. Both of AlexNet and CaffeNet consist of 5 CONV layers and 3 FC layers.

The Zeiler-and-Fergus (ZF) network achieved 88.8% top-5 accuracy and won the first place in image classification task of ILSVRC 2013 [3]. The ZF network also has 5 CONV layers and 3 FC layers.

The VGG model achieved a top-5 accuracy of 92.6% and won the second place in image classification task of ILSVRC 2014 [16]. VGG model consists of 5 CONV layer groups and 3 FC layers. According to the exact number of layers, there are several versions of the VGG model including VGG11, VGG16, and VGG19, as listed in Table 1.

3. RELATED WORK

To accelerate CNN, a set of techniques from both software and hardware perspectives have been studied. From software perspective, the target is compressing CNN models in order to reduce the memory footprint and the number of operations while minimizing accuracy loss. From the hardware perspective, specific architecture and modules are designed to reuse data, enhance "locality" of data, and accelerate convolution operations. To deploy CNN models on embedded systems, the bit widths of operators and weights are often reduced compared to that on CPU or GPU platform.

3.1 Model Compression

Network pruning and decomposition were widely used to compress CNN models. In early work, network pruning proved to be a valid way to reduce the network complexity and over-fitting [17, 18, 19]. In [20], Han et al. pruned less influential connections in neural networks, and achieved $9\times$ and $13\times$ compression for CaffeNet and VGG16 model without accuracy loss. The Singular Value Decomposition (SVD) [21] is frequently used to reduce memory footprint. In [22], Denton et al. used SVD and filters clustering to speedup the first two FC layers of CNNs. Zhang et al. [23] proposed a method that was tested on a deeper model, which used low rank decomposition on network parameters and took nonlinear units into consideration. Jaderberg et al. [24] used rank-1 filters to approximate the original ones.

3.2 Data Quantization

Implementing fixed-point arithmetic units on ASIC and FPGA is much more efficient compared with floating-point ones. Consequently, most of previous CNN accelerators used fixed-point numbers instead of floating-point numbers [7, 25, 26, 6]. Shorter fixed-point representation of weights and data can also significantly reduce memory footprint and computation resources. For example, Chen et al. showed that the area and power of a 16-bit multiplier is $0.164\times$ and $0.136\times$ compared with that of 32-bit multiplier under 65nm fabrication technology [7].

Most of previous work adopted the 16-bit quantization strategy [27, 25, 7, 8]. In [7], Chen et al. showed that using 16-bit numbers instead of 32-bit ones only introduced 0.26% more error rate on MNIST dataset. In [8], 16-bit numbers were used in the inference process while 32-bit numbers were used in training process, and results on MNIST dataset showed that there was only 0.01% accuracy reduction.

To accelerate large CNN models on the embedded FPGA platform, data quantization is rather important and a shorter representation that introducing negligible accuracy loss is always expected. However, though previous work used data quantization, there is no comprehensive analysis of different quantization strategies.

3.3 CNN Accelerator

Previous CNN accelerator designs can be generally classified into two groups: the first group focuses on the computing engine and the second group aims to optimize the memory system.

CNNs are extremely computational-intensive, and thus powerful computing engines are necessary to accelerate them. Chakaradhar et al. in [11] proposed a dynamically configurable architecture for CNN. They added dedicated switches between the computing modules to enable design space exploration for dynamic configuration across different CNN layers. An associate compiler was also proposed to fully exploit the parallelism among the CNN workloads.

The weights in CONV layers of CNN are used for multiple times in computation, and thus the overall performance can be significantly degraded by frequent memory access. In [7], Chen et al. used the tiling strategy and dedicated buffers for data reuse to reduce the total communication traffic. In their further study [8], a

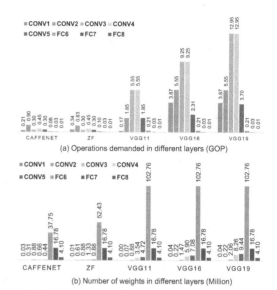

(a) Operations demanded in different layers (GOP)

(b) Number of weights in different layers (Million)

Figure 2: The complexity distribution of state-of-the-art CNN models: (a) Distribution of operations by theoretical estimation; (b) Distribution of weight number.

multi-chip supercomputer was proposed which offered sufficient memory capacity to store all the weights in the CNN on chip. In [10], all the weights of one CNN layer were also stored in on-chip memory. In this manner, the data traffic between on-chip and off-chip memory could be minimized.

3.4 Motivation

State-of-the-art CNN models for large-scale visual recognition are much larger and deeper than early small CNN models. In this case, CNN accelerators such as ShiDianNao [10] which store weights on chip are hard to support those large CNN models. Consequently, state-of-the-art CNN models can only be stored in external memory and the bandwidth problem needs to be considered.

Most of previous studies focused on only accelerating the CONV layers of CNN. For example, in [6], the accelerator design was only applied to several CONV layers rather than the full CNN. In [26] and [11], authors only used models with few CONV layers without any FC layer. In this manner, those accelerators were hard to be used for accelerating full CNNs.

A full CNN model consists of both CONV layers and FC layers, and thus an efficient CNN accelerator for real-life applications need to consider both of them. For CONV layers and FC layers, the encountered problems are rather different. CONV layers are computation-centric: they contain few parameters but need a great deal of operations; FC layers are memory-centric: they usually contain hundreds of million weights, and each weight is used for only once. Consequently, loading weights from the external memory significantly degrades the performance of FC layers. In other words, the bandwidth limits the performance of FC layers. Considering this, we go deeper with the embedded FPGA platform on alleviating the bandwidth problem.

4. COMPLEXITY ANALYSIS OF CNN

Time complexity of a layer in CNN can be evaluated by the number of multiplication operations in the inference process. In a CONV layer, each convolutional kernel is a $k \times k$ filter applied to a $r \times c$ dimension input feature map. The number of kernels equals to $n_{in} \times n_{out}$. Consequently, according to Equation 1, the complexity of this CONV layer is

$$C_{CONV}^{Time} = O(n_{in} \cdot n_{out} \cdot k^2 \cdot r \cdot c). \qquad (4)$$

Table 2: The Memory footprint, Computation Complexities, and Performance of the VGG16 model and its SVD version.

Network	FC6	# of total weights	# of operations	Top-5 accuracy
VGG16	25088×4096	138.36M	30.94G	88.00%
VGG16-SVD	25088×500 + 500×4096	50.18M	30.76G	87.96%

For pooling layers and FC layers, the time complexities are

$$C_{Pooling}^{Time} = O(n_{in} \cdot r \cdot c), \qquad (5)$$

$$C_{FC}^{Time} = O(n_{in} \cdot n_{out}). \qquad (6)$$

For pooling layers, n_{out} equals to n_{in} since each input feature map is pooled to a corresponding output feature map, and thus the complexity is linear to either input or output feature map number.

Space complexity refers to the memory footprint. For a CONV layer, there are $n_{in} \times n_{out}$ convolution kernels, and each kernel has k^2 weights. Consequently, the space complexity for a CONV layer is

$$C_{CONV}^{Space} = O(n_{in} \cdot n_{out} \cdot k^2). \qquad (7)$$

FC layer actually applies a multiplication to the input feature vector, and thus the complexity for FC layer is measure by the size for the parameter matrix, which is shown in Equation 8:

$$C_{FC}^{Space} = O(n_{in} \cdot n_{out}) \qquad (8)$$

No space is needed for pooling layers since it has no weight.

The distribution of demanded operations and weight numbers in the inference process of state-of-the-art CNN models are shown in Figure 2. The measured operations consist of multiplications, adds, and non-linear functions.

As shown in Figure 2 (a), **the operations of CONV layers compose most of the total operations of CNN models**, and thus the time complexity of CONV layers is much higher than that of FC layers. Consequently, for CONV layers, more attention should be paid to accelerate convolution operations.

For space complexity, the situation is quite different. As shown in Figure 2 (b), **FC layers contribute to most of the weights**. Since each weight in FC layers is used only once in one inference process, leaves no chance for reuse, the limited bandwidth can significantly degrade the performance since loading those weights may take quite long time.

Since FC layers contribute to most of memory footprint, it is necessary to reduce weights of FC layers while maintaining comparable accuracy. In this paper, SVD is adopted for accelerating FC layers. Considering an FC layer $f^{out} = W f^{in} + b$, the weight matrix W can be decomposed as $W \approx U_d S_d V_d = W_1 W_2$, in which S_d is a diagonal matrix. By choosing the first d singular values in SVD, i.e. the rank of matrix U_d, S_d, and V_d, both time and space complexity can be reduced to $O(d \cdot n_{in} + d \cdot n_{out})$ from $O(n_{in} \cdot n_{out})$. Since accuracy loss may be minute even when d is much smaller than n_{in} and n_{out}, considerable reduction of time consumption and memory footprint can be achieved.

The effectiveness of SVD is proved by the results in Table 2. By applying SVD to the parameter matrix of the FC6 layer and choosing first 500 singular values, the number of weights in FC6 layers is reduced to 14.6 million from 103 million, which achieves a compression rate at 7.04×. However, the number of operations does not decrease much since the FC layer contributes little to total operations. The SVD only introduces 0.04% accuracy loss.

5. DATA QUANTIZATION

Using short fixed-point numbers instead of long floating-point numbers is efficient for implementations on the FPGA and can significantly reduce memory footprint and bandwidth requirements. A shorter bit width is always wanted, but it may lead to a severe accuracy loss. Though fixed-point numbers have been widely used in CNN accelerator designs, there is no comprehensive investigation

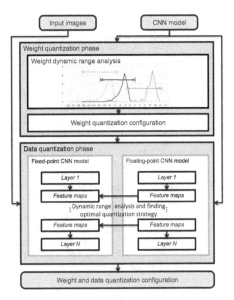

Figure 3: The dynamic-precision data quantization flow.

on different quantization strategies and the trade-off between the bit length of fixed-point numbers and the accuracy. In this section, we propose a dynamic-precision data quantization flow and compare it with widely used static-precision quantization strategies.

5.1 Quantization Flow

For a fixed-point number, its value can be expressed as

$$n = \sum_{i=0}^{bw-1} B_i \cdot 2^{-f_l} \cdot 2^i, \qquad (9)$$

where bw is the bit width and f_l is the fractional length which can be negative. To convert floating-point numbers into fixed-point ones while achieving the highest accuracy, we propose a dynamic-precision data quantization strategy and an automatic workflow, as shown in Figure 3. Unlike previous static-precision quantization strategies, in the proposed data quantization flow, f_l **is dynamic for different layers and feature map sets while static in one layer to minimize the truncation error of each layer**. The proposed quantization flow mainly consists of two phases: the weight quantization phase and the data quantization phase.

The weight quantization phase aims to find the optimal f_l for weights in one layer, as shown in Equation 10:

$$f_l = \underset{f_l}{\arg\min} \sum |W_{float} - W(bw, f_l)|, \qquad (10)$$

where W is a weight and $W(bw, f_l)$ represents the fixed-point format of W under the given bw and f_l. In this phase, the dynamic ranges of weights in each layer is analyzed first. After that, the f_l is initialized to avoid data overflow. Furthermore, we search for the optimal f_l in the adjacent domains of the initial f_l.

The data quantization phase aims to find the optimal f_l for a set of feature maps between two layers. In this phase, the intermediate data of the fixed-point CNN model and the floating-point CNN model are compared layer by layer using a greedy algorithm to reduce the accuracy loss. For each layer, the optimization target is shown in Equation 11:

$$f_l = \underset{f_l}{\arg\min} \sum |x_{float}^+ - x^+(bw, f_l)|. \qquad (11)$$

In Equation 11, x^+ represents the result of a layer when we denote the computation of a layer as $x^+ = A \cdot x$. It should be noted, for either CONV layer or FC layer, the direct result x^+ has longer bit width than the given standard. Consequently, truncation is needed when optimizing f_l selection. Finally, the entire data quantization configuration is generated.

Table 3: Exploration of different data quantization strategies with state-of-the-art CNNs.

Network	CaffeNet			VGG16							VGG16-SVD		
Experiment	Exp 1	Exp 2	Exp 3	Exp 4	Exp 5	Exp 6	Exp 7	Exp 8	Exp 9	Exp 10	Exp 11	Exp 12	Exp 13
Data Bits	Single-float	16	8	Single-float	16	16	8	8	8	8	Single-float	16	8
Weight Bits	Single-float	16	8	Single-float	16	8	8	8	8	8 or 4	Single-float	16	8 or 4
Data Precision	N/A	Dynamic	Dynamic	N/A	2^{-2}	2^{-2}	Not available	2^{-5} or 2^{-1}	Dynamic	Dynamic	N/A	Dynamic	Dynamic
Weight Precision	N/A	Dynamic	Dynamic	N/A	2^{-15}	2^{-7}	Not available	2^{-7}	Dynamic	Dynamic	N/A	Dynamic	Dynamic
Top 1 Accuracy	53.90%	53.90%	53.02%	68.10%	68.02%	62.26%	Not available	28.24%	66.58%	66.96%	68.02%	64.64%	64.14%
Top 5 Accuracy	77.70%	77.12%	76.64%	88.00%	87.94%	85.18%	Not available	49.66%	87.38%	87.60%	87.96%	86.66%	86.30%

[1] The weight bits "8 or 4" in Exp10 and Exp13 means 8 bits for CONV layers and 4 bits for FC layers.
[2] The data precision "2^{-5} or 2^{-1}" in Exp8 means 2^{-5} for feature maps between CONV layers and 2^{-1} for feature maps between FC layers.

5.2 Analysis of Different Strategies

We explore different data quantization strategies with CaffeNet, VGG16, and VGG16-SVD networks and the results are shown in Table 3. All results are obtained under Caffe framework [28].

- For CaffeNet, as shown in Exp 1, the top-5 accuracy is 77.70% when 32-bit floating-point numbers are used. When employing static-precision 16-bit quantization and 8/4-bit dynamic-precision quantization, the top-5 accuracy results are 77.12% and 76.64% respectively.
- VGG16 network with static-precision quantization strategies are tested in Exp 4 to Exp 8. As shown in Exp 4, single-float VGG16 network 88.00% top-5 accuracy. When using the 16-bit quantization configuration, only 0.06% accuracy loss is introduced. However, when employing 8-bit static-precision quantization, no configuration is available since the feature maps between FC layers are quantized to 0. As shown in Exp 8, at least two precisions are needed when using 8-bit quantization and the accuracy degrades greatly in this case.
- Results of VGG16 network with dynamic-precision quantization are shown in Exp 9 and Exp 10. When 8-bit dynamic-precision quantization is used for both data and weights, the top-5 accuracy is 87.38%. Using 8/4-bit dynamic-precision quantization for weights in CONV layers and FC layers respectively even achieves higher accuracy. As shown in Exp 10, in this case, the top-5 accuracy is 87.60%.
- The results of VGG16-SVD network are shown in Exp 11 to Exp 13. Compared with the floating-point VGG16 model, floating-point VGG16-SVD only introduces 0.04% accuracy loss. However, when 16-bit dynamic-precision quantization is adopted, the top-5 accuracy is down to 86.66%. With 8/4-bit dynamic-precision quantization, the top-5 accuracy further drops to 86.30%.

The results show that dynamic-precision quantization is much more favorable compared with static-precision quantization. With dynamic-precision quantization, we can use much shorter representations of operations while still achieving comparable accuracy. For example, compared with 16-bit quantization, 8/4-bit quantization halves the storage space for intermediate data and reduce three-fourths memory footprint of CNN models. Besides, the utilization of bandwidth can also be significantly increased.

6. SYSTEM DESIGN

In this section, we introduce the design of our CNN accelerator. First, the overall architecture is presented. After that, the designs of major modules are introduced. Finally, the implementation details are presented.

6.1 Overall Architecture

In this work, we propose a CPU+FPGA heterogeneous architecture to accelerate CNNs. Figure 4 (a) shows an overview of the proposed system architecture. The whole system can be divided into two parts: the Programmable Logic (PL) and the Processing System (PS).

PL is the FPGA chip, on which we place the *Computing Complex*, *On-chip Buffers*, *Controller*, and *DMAs*. The Computing Complex consists of Processing Elements (PEs) which take charge of the majority of computation tasks in CNN, including CONV layers, Pooling layers, and FC layers. On-chip buffers, including input buffer and output buffer, prepare data to be used by PEs and store the results. Controller fetches instructions from the external memory and decodes them to orchestrate all the modules except DMAs on the PL. DMAs are working for transferring data and instructions between the external memory on the PS side and On-chip Buffers on the PL side.

PS consists of general-purpose processors and the external memory. All the CNN model parameters, data, and instructions are stored in the external memory. Processors run bare-metal programs and help to orchestrate the whole inference phase by configuring the DMAs. We also realize Softmax function on CPU considering that its FPGA implementation will bring inevitable design overhead with little performance improvement since this function is called only in the last layer of the whole CNN.

The complete inference process of an image with the proposed CNN accelerator consists of three steps that are executed in sequence: data preparation, data processing, and result output.

Data Preparation. In this phase, all the data needed in the computation including image data, model data, and control data are stored in the external memory. Control data includes the Buffer Descriptors (BD) used by DMAs and instructions used by Controller. So far the image data is not obtained from the camera.

Data Processing. When all the data are prepared, CPU host starts to configure DMAs with the BDs that are pre-stored in the external memory. The configured DMA loads data and instructions to the controller, triggers a computation process on PL. Each time a DMA interrupt is asserted, CPU host adds up the self-maintained pointer address for each DMA's BD list and configures them with new BDs. This phase works until the last BD has been transferred.

Result Output. After receiving the interrupt of the last BD from DMA, the processor host applies Softmax function to the final results from PEs, and output the results to UART port.

6.2 PE Architecture

Figure 4 (b) shows the architecture of the PE and other modules involved. A PE consists of five parts, including the *Convolver Complex*, the *Adder Tree*, the *Non-Linearity* module, the *Max-Pooling* module, and the *Bias Shift*.

- For **Convolver Complex**, we employ the classical line buffer design [29] as shown in Figure 4 (c). When Input Data goes through the buffer in row-major layout, the line buffer releases a window selection function on the input image. Thus the selected window followed by multipliers and an adder tree will compute the convolution result, one data per cycle. Since the bottleneck of FC layers appears at the bandwidth, we use this module to compute matrix-vector multiplication for FC layers even the efficiency is not good. To realize this function, we set the delay of each line of the line buffer the same as the kernel size by using a MUX at the end of each line. In the proposed implementation, the kernel size is 3. When Input Data goes through the buffer, we get a totally new vector every 9 cycles in the selected window and do a vector inner product. Thus a convolver can do a matrix multiplied by a vector of size 9.

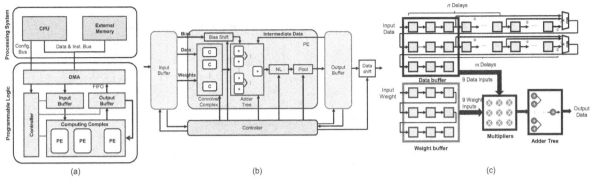

Figure 4: The design of our image classification system: (a) the overall architecture; (b) the processing element; (c) the convolver in the processing element.

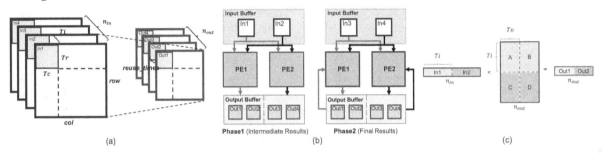

Figure 5: Workload schedule for CONV layers and FC layers: (a) Tiling and reuse of feature maps in CONV layers; (b) two phases in the execution of CONV layers; (c) workload schedule in FC layers.

- **Adder Tree** (AD) sums all the results from convolvers. It can add the intermediate data from Output Buffer or bias data from Input Buffer if needed.
- **Non-Linearity** (NL) module applies non-linear activation function to the input data stream.
- **Max-Pooling** module utilizes the line buffers to apply the specific 2×2 window to the input data stream, and outputs the maximum among them.
- **Bias Shift** module and **Data Shift** module are designed to support dynamic quantization. Input bias will be shifted by Bias Shift according to the layer's quantization result. For a 16-bit implementation, the bias is extended to 32-bit to be added with convolution result. The output data will be shifted by Data Shift and cut back to the original width.

The size of convolutional kernel usually has only several options such as 3×3, 5×5, and 7×7. All the convolutional kernels in the VGG16 model are in 3×3 dimension, and thus in the Convolver Complex, the 2D convolvers are designed for convolution operation only over a 3×3 window.

6.3 Implementation Details

6.3.1 Workloads Schedule

Parallelism. Chakradhar et al. pointed out that there are mainly three types of parallelism in CNN workloads: operator-level (fine-grained) parallelism, intra-output parallelism (multiple input features are combined to create a single output), and inter-output parallelism (multiple independent features are computed simultaneously) [11]. In our implementation, all the three types of parallelism are considered. The operator-level parallelism is realized with 2D convolvers. The intra-output parallelism is realized with multiple convolvers working simultaneously in each PE. The inter-output parallelism is realized by placing multiple PEs.

Tiling and Reuse. Due to limited on-chip memory, tiling is necessary for CNNs. For tiling in CONV layers, we tile each input image by the factor Tr (Tc) in row (column). And we tile the input (output) feature maps n_{in} (n_{out}) by the factor Ti (To). For FC layers, we tile each matrix into tiles of $Ti \times To$. For reuse, the times

Phase 1				Phase n_{in}/T_i		
Data In				Data In		
Data Out	Data Out	......	Data Out	Data Out	Data Out	......	Data Out
Weight In	Weight In	......	Weight In	Weight In	Weight In	......	Weight In
Weight Out	Weight Out	......	Weight Out	Weight Out	Weight Out	......	Weight Out
Result In				Result In		
Result Out				Result Out		

Figure 6: Timing graph. There are totally n_{in}/Ti phases to generate the $reuse\_times \times PE\_num$ tiles in the output layer. In each phase, the next group of data is loaded and the data preloaded in the last phase are output and reused for $reuse\_times$ times. Meanwhile, accompanied weights are loaded and output for $reuse\_times$ times with no reuse. The output buffer works on collecting data in the entire phase, while outputting intermediate data and final data to PEs or the external memory.

of each input tiled block (vector) to be reused is $reuse\_times$. We show how this workload schedule mechanism applies to CONV layers in Figure 5 (a) (b) and FC layers in Figure 5 (c).

6.3.2 Controller System

In each computation phase, the Controller decodes a 16-bit instruction to generate control signals for on-chip buffers and PEs. One instruction is composed with the following signals.

- **Pool Bypass** and **NL Bypass** are used to bypass the Pool and NL module if needed.
- **Zero Switch** is used to select either zero or bias data into added to the result of adder tree, since usually more than one phase is needed to calculate the final result and the bias should be added only once.
- **Result Shift** and **Bias Shift** describe the number of bits and direction for data shifting, for dynamic data quantization.
- **Write En** is used to switch the data from the Output Buffer either to the external memory or to the PEs to be reused.
- **PE En** offers us the flexibility to set several PEs as idle if needed. This can help save energy when computation capacity meet the demand.

31

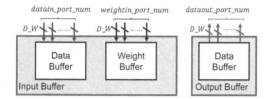

Figure 7: Buffer structure. Image data and weights are stored separately inside Input Buffer, and bias are stored in Data Buffer. The total bandwidth of each buffer is defined by corresponding port numbers multiplied by data width (D_W).

- **Phase Type** helps the Controller to distinguish these phases and send out the corresponding signals.helps the Controller to distinguish these phases and send out the corresponding signals. Several phases need to be specifically taken care of. For example, for the last phase in the last layer an the last output image, no more weights or data should be loaded in, and the input buffers should be configured differently compared to previous phases.
- **Pic Num** and **Tile Size/Layer Type** help the Controller to configure the Input Buffer and Output Buffer.

A compiler is developed on *Matlab* to automatically generate instructions. The compiler takes the fixed-point CNN model as the input and generates instructions as output. Table 4 shows the generated the instructions with the example in Figure 5 (a).

- Instruction 1 commands Input Buffer to load all the needed data, which is distinguished by the Phase Type signal. PE En enables two PEs working in parallel. As $Ti = 2$, Pic Num is set as 2. Tile Size is set as the defined Tr. Layer Type defines the layer type as CONV layer. All the other signals are useless in this phase.
- Instruction 2 starts calculating the four tiled blocks in the output layer. Since they are all intermediate results, Pool and NL modules are bypassed. Bias will be added in this phase only once. And Bias Shift specifies the shift configuration for bias data. Output Buffer will only collect the intermediate data and not write to anywhere.
- In instruction 3, Write En is set as "PE" to command Output Buffer to send the intermediate results back to the PEs. Bias is no longer added, and thus Zero Switch is set to zero. Since all the data generated in this phase is the final results, Pool and NL Bypass are disabled to let data from AD enter these two modules in sequence.
- In the last instruction, supposing this CONV layer is the last layer, then no module is working in PE. Write EN is set as "DDR" to command the Output Buffer to write results back to the external memory. Result Shift is set to shift the results data as we want. This phase is distinguished by Controller by setting Phase Type as last.

7. MEMORY SYSTEM

In this section, we introduce the memory system design which aims to feed the PEs with data efficiently. First the designs of buffers are introduced. After that, the data arrangement mechanisms for CONV and FC layers are presented.

7.1 Buffer Design

As shown in Figure 4 (a), there are two on-chip buffers on the PL side, the Input Buffer and the Output Buffer. The Input Buffer stores the bias, image data, and weights. The Output Buffer saves the results generated from PE and offers intermediate results to the PEs at proper time. For simplicity of illustration, we define three parameters as shown in Figure 7

- *datain_port_num.* The maximum amount of data that can be transferred by DMA each cycle.
- *weightin_port_num.* The maximum amount of weights that can be transferred by DMA each cycle.

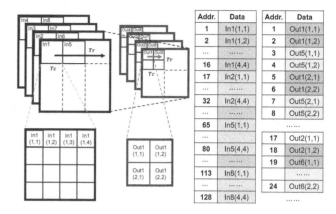

Figure 8: Storage pattern for one CONV layer with max-pooling when the parameter group <Ti, To, $reuse\_times$, PE_num> is set to <2, 4, 2, 2>.

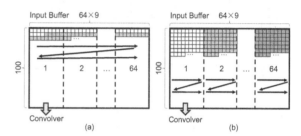

Figure 9: Data arrangement in external memory: (a) Linear arrangement; (b) DMA-oriented arrangement.

- *dataout_port_num.* The maximum amount of results that can be transferred by DMA each cycle.

In CONV layers, the total amount of weights needed in each phase is far less than that of image data, while in FC layers, the amount of weights is far more than the amount of data in input vectors. Therefore, we save the weights of FC layers in data buffer whose capability is larger than weight buffer, and save the input data vector in the weight buffer.

7.2 Data Arrangement for CONV layers

In order to reduce the unnecessary access latency of external memory, we optimize the storage pattern of data in the memory space. The principle is to maximize the burst length of each DMA transaction. Figure 8 shows a brief example of how we organize the input and output data in one CONV layer with max-pooling. We store the tiles which are at the same relative locations in each picture continuously. Therefore, in each phase, we can load all the input tiles for computation continuously. The output feature maps will be the input feature maps of the next layer, therefore, the same storage pattern applies as well.

There is a slight difference between CONV layers with Pooling and other layers. After a 2×2 pooling, the result is only a quarter of a tile. In Figure 8, *Out(2, 1)*, instead of *Out(1,2)*, will be calculated after *Out(1,1)*. This means adjacent result tiles are not stored continuously in external memory. If we write each result tile as soon as it is generated, the burst length will be only $Tr/2$. This will significantly degrade the utilization of the external memory. To solve this problem, we increase the memory budget on chip. We buffer *Out(1,1)* to *Out(4,1)* before generating *Out(1,2)*, then write *Out(1,1)* and *Out(1,2)* together. This strategy increases the burst length to $Tr \times Tc/2$.

7.3 Data Arrangement for FC Layers

The speed of computing FC layers is mainly restricted by the bandwidth. In this manner, using specific hardware to accelerate

Table 4: Instructions for One CONV layer generated by the compiler.

Index	Pool Bypass	NL Bypass	Zero Switch	Result Shift	Bias Shift	Write En	PE En	Phase Type	Pic Num	Tile Size	Layer Type
1	X	X	X	X	X	No	2	First	2	Tr	CONV
2	Yes	Yes	Bias	X	BS	No	2	Cal	2	Tr	CONV
3	No	No	Zero	X	X	PE	2	Cal	2	Tr	CONV
4	X	X	X	RS	X	DDR	2	Last	2	Tr	CONV

Table 5: Parameter configuration and resource utilization.

Param.	tile_size	convolver_num	PE_num	reuse_times
Config.	28	64	2	16
Param.	datain_port_num	weightin_port_num	dataout_port_num	
Config.	8	4	2	

Resource	FF	LUT	DSP	BRAM
Utilization	127653	182616	780	486
Percent(%)	29.2	83.5	89.2	86.7

Figure 10: Testing platform. We use Xilinx Zynq ZC706 for on-board testing. A power meter is used for power analysis.

FC layers is not effective. Considering this, the proposed system uses the Convolver Complex in one of the PEs to do the computation for FC layers. In this case, we need to fully utilize the bandwidth of the external memory with the current PL structure.

In our system, we assign a buffer of length 900, the same as $Tr \times Tr$ to each of the 64 Compute Complex in one PE. The buffers are filled one by one when computing CONV layers. To reduce extra data routing logic for filling buffers while keep a long burst length when fetching data for computing FC layers, we arrange the weight matrix in the external memory. We first divide the whole matrix with blocks of 64×9 columns and 100 rows such that one block can be processed in a phase. In each block, the data is arranged as shown in Figure 9 (b). Without data arrangement for FC layers, as shown in Figure 9 (a), we need **64×100** DMA transactions to load one block while the burst length is just 9. By arranging the data following Figure 9 (b), we need just one DMA transaction to load the whole block and the long burst length ensures a high utilization of the bandwidth of external memory.

8. SYSTEM EVALUATION

In this section, the performance of the implemented system is evaluated. First, we analyze the performance of our system architecture under given design constraints. After that, the performance of the proposed system is presented and compared with other platforms. Finally we compare our system with previous FPGA-based CNN accelerators.

We use 16-bit dynamic-precision quantization and Xilinx Zynq ZC706 for the implementation. Xilinx Zynq platform consists of a Xilinx Kintex-7 FPGA, dual ARM Cortex-A9 Processor, and 1 GB DDR3 memory. It offers a bandwidth of up to 4.2GB/s. All the synthesis results are obtained from Xilinx Vivado 2014.4. We first synthesize each module in Vivado to figure out the resource utilization. Then we choose the optimal parameter group to maximize the throughput with the resource and bandwidth constraints. The parameters and resource utilization are shown in Table 5. We can see that our parameter configuration helps to maximize the resource utilization. Figure 10 shows the hardware platform.

The CPU platform is Intel Xeon E5-2690 CPU@2.90GHz. The GPU platform is Nvidia K40 GPU (2880 CUDA cores with 12GB GDDR5 384-bit memory), and the mGPU platform is the Nvidia TK1 Mobile GPU development kit (192 CUDA cores). For experiments on CPU, GPU, and mGPU, the operating system is Ubuntu 14.04 and the deep learning software framework is Caffe [28].

8.1 Theoretical Estimation

For CONV layer, the number of phases needed in one CONV layer when tiling is adopted can be calculated by the following formula:

$$N_{phase}^{CONV} = \lceil \frac{n_{in}}{Ti} \rceil \times \lceil \frac{n_{out}}{To} \rceil \times \lceil \frac{row}{Tr} \rceil^2,$$

where $To = reuse\_times \times PE\_num$ and $Tc = Tr$. The time of computation and loading data in each phase are:

$$t_{compute\_data}^{CONV} \approx Tr^2 \times reuse\_times,$$

and

$$t_{load\_data}^{CONV} = \frac{Tr^2 \times Ti}{datain\_port\_num}.$$

CONV layers are usually computation-intensive. Consequently, in order to keep ping-pong mechanism working, typically t_{load} is smaller than $t_{compute}$, and thus there should be:

$$datain\_port\_num^{CONV} \geq \frac{Ti}{reuse\_times}.$$

In each phase, data will be reused for $reuse\_times$ times, each accompanied with a new group of weights (9 weights for each kernel as for the model we use). Therefore, for weights, we have:

$$t_{compute\_weight}^{CONV} \approx Tr^2$$
$$t_{load\_weight}^{CONV} = \frac{9 \times Ti \times PE\_num}{weightin\_port\_num}$$
$$weightin\_port\_num^{CONV} \geq \frac{9 \times Ti \times PE\_num}{Tr^2}.$$

According to the workloads schedule shown in Figure 6, the constraint for $dataout\_port\_num$ is:

$$dataout\_port\_num^{CONV} \geq PE\_num.$$

In order to minimize the bandwidth consumption, we consider to choose $weightin\_port\_num$ and $datain\_port\_num$ as fewer as possible. Under the above constraints, we can estimate the computation time for one CONV layer:

$$t_{CONV} = N_{Phase} \times t_{compute}$$
$$= \lceil \frac{n_{in}}{Ti} \rceil \times \lceil \frac{n_{out}}{To} \rceil \times \lceil \frac{row}{Tr} \rceil^2 \times Tr^2 \times reuse\_times.$$

Considering that $Ti = convolver\_num$, $Tr = tile\_size$ and $To = reuse\_times \times PE\_num$ in CONV layers, we further get:

$$t_{CONV} = \lceil \frac{n_{in}}{convolver\_num} \rceil \times \lceil \frac{n_{out}}{reuse\_times \times PE\_num} \rceil$$
$$\times \lceil \frac{row}{tile\_size} \rceil^2 \times tile\_size^2 \times resue\_times.$$
$$\approx \frac{n_{in} \times n_{out} \times row^2}{convolver\_num \times PE\_num}$$

33

Platform	Embedded FPGA				CPU	GPU	mGPU	CPU	GPU	mGPU
Layer (Group)	Theoretical Computation Time (ms)	Real Computation Time (ms)	Total Operations (GOP)	Real Performance (GOP/s)	Real Computation Time (ms)			Real Performance (GOP/s)		
CONV1	21.41	31.29	3.87	123.76	83.43	2.45	59.45	46.42	1578.8	65.15
CONV2	16.06	23.58	5.55	235.29	68.99	3.31	79.73	80.44	1675.5	69.60
CONV3	26.76	39.29	9.25	235.38	76.08	4.25	89.35	151.57	2177.1	103.51
CONV4	26.76	36.30	9.25	254.81	62.53	3.31	107.49	147.91	2791.6	86.04
CONV5	32.11	32.95	2.31	70.16	12.36	2.30	63.75	186.99	1003.5	36.27
CONV Total	**123.10**	**163.42**	**30.69**	**187.80**	**312.36**	**15.45**	**399.77**	**98.26**	**1986.0**	**76.77**
FC6-1	10.45	20.17	0.025	1.24	1.69	0.445	29.35	14.87	56.404	0.86
FC6-2	1.71	3.75	0.0041	1.09	0.26	0.031	5.26	15.65	132.26	0.78
FC7	13.98	30.02	0.034	1.12	1.86	0.19	14.74	18.04	177.78	2.28
FC8	3.413	7.244	0.0082	1.13	0.46	0.96	4.58	17.75	8.56	1.79
FC Total	**29.55**	**61.18**	**0.073**	**1.20**	**4.28**	**1.79**	**53.93**	**17.17**	**40.98**	**1.36**
Total	**152.65**	**224.60**	**30.76**	**136.97**	**316.64**	**17.25**	**453.70**	**97.16**	**1783.9**	**67.81**

For FC layers, the number of phases and the time of different tasks can be estimated with the following equations:

$$N_{phase}^{FC} = \lceil \frac{n_{in}}{Ti} \rceil \times \lceil \frac{n_{out}}{To \times PE\_num} \rceil$$

$$t_{load\_data}^{FC} = \frac{PE\_num \times Ti \times To}{datain\_port\_num}$$

$$t_{load\_weight}^{FC} = \frac{Ti}{weightin\_port\_num}$$

$$t_{compute\_data}^{FC} = t_{compute\_weight}^{FC} = \frac{Ti \times To}{convolver\_num}.$$

Typically, for FC layers, $t_{compute}^{FC}$ is much smaller than t_{load}^{FC}, and thus the total cycles needed by one FC layer can be estimated as:

$$t_{FC} = N_{Phase} \times t_{load}$$
$$= \lceil \frac{n_{in}}{Ti} \rceil \times \lceil \frac{n_{out}}{To \times PE\_num} \rceil \times \frac{PE\_num \times Ti \times To}{datain\_port\_num}$$
$$\approx \frac{n_{in} \times n_{out}}{datain\_port\_num}.$$

In summary, under the given constraints, the runtime of a CONV layer and an FC layer can be estimated through Equation 13 and Equation 12:

$$t_{FC} = \frac{n_{in} \times n_{out}}{datain\_port\_num}, \tag{12}$$

$$t_{CONV} = \frac{n_{in} \cdot n_{out} \cdot row^2}{convolver\_num^2 \times PE\_num}. \tag{13}$$

As shown in Equation 13, CONV layers are bounded both by bandwidth and computation resources. For FC layers, as shown in Equation 12, it is bandwidth-bounded only. Consequently, higher bandwidth can help reduce the runtime of FC layers.

8.2 Performance Analysis

Though the performance of FC layers on FPGA is limited by the bandwidth, it is still higher than ARM processors. Consequently, in our implementation, the FC layer workloads are placed on FPGA.

The performance of our system, CPU, GPU, and mGPU is shown in Table 6. The VGG16-SVD network needs 30.764 GOPs including multiplications, adds, and non-linear functions. Our system achieves an average performance of 187.80 GOP/s for CONV layers and 136.97 GOP/s for the whole network. The frame rate of our system is 4.45 fps, which is 1.4× and 2.0× faster than the CPU and mGPU platform (the power of CPU and mGPU are 135W and 9W respectively). The overall performance of GPU is 13.0× higher than our implementation, but it consumes 26.0× more power compared with embedded FPGA (250W versus 9.63W).

The performance of our system on FC layers is much lower than that of CONV layers even though data arrangement method is adopted due to the limited bandwidth. Consequently, though

Table 7: Comparison with other FPGA accelerators.

	[11]	[30]	[6]	Ours
Year	2010	2014	2015	2015
Platform	Virtex5 SX240t	Zynq XC7Z045	Virtex7 VX485t	Zynq XC7Z045
Clock(MHz)	120	150	100	150
Bandwidth (GB/s)	–	4.2	12.8	4.2
Quantization Strategy	48-bit fixed	16-bit fixed	32-bit float	16-bit fixed
Power (W)	14	8	18.61	9.63
Problem Complexity (GOP)	0.52	0.552	1.33	30.76
Performance (GOP/s)	16	23.18	61.62	187.80 (CONV) 136.97 (Overall)
Resource Efficiency (GOP/s/Slices)	4.30×10^{-4}	–	8.12×10^{-4}	3.58×10^{-3} (CONV) 2.61×10^{-3} (Overall)
Power Efficiency (GOP/s/W)	1.14	2.90	3.31	19.50 (CONV) 14.22 (Overall)

Table 8: Projected frame rates on Zynq/VC707 board using 16-bit and 8/4-bit quantization with VGG16-SVD network.

Platform	Total Resources			16-bit Quantization		8-bit Quantization	
	LUT	FF	Bandwidth	# of PE	FPS	# of PE	FPS
Zynq	218600	437200	4.2GBps	2	**4.45**	4	**8.9**
VC707	303600	607200	4.2GBps	3	**5.88**	6	**11.76**

the number of operations needed by FC layers is only 0.0024× of CONV layers, the runtime of FC layers is 0.374× of CONV layer. The mGPU platform suffers from the same problem due to the limited bandwidth.

Compared with theoretical estimation, there is around 47% performance degradation for on-board test, as shown in the 2nd column and the 3rd column of Table 6. One possible reason is the DDR access latency. The other possible reason is that different DMAs are working asynchronously, since different DMA transactions may affect each other and reduce the total efficiency of bandwidth usage.

8.3 Design Comparison

As shown in Table 7, we compare our CNN accelerator with previous work. In [30], the design was verified on 3 models, including a single CONV layer, a model consisting of 2 CONV layers for face recognition, and a model for street parsing without structure details. Since the first model lacks generality and structure details of the third model were not provided, results of a 2-layer CNN model is adopted for comparison. We also transform the unit $GFLOP$ in [6] into GOP for comparison.

In summary, our accelerator achieved the highest performance, resource efficiency, and power efficiency compared with previous designs. It should be noted, all the performance results of previous designs were obtained from CONV layers only. If we only consider CONV layers, the average performance of our system is 187.80

GOP/s, which is several times higher than previous designs. The performance of our system with the full VGG16-SVD network is 136.97 GOP/s.

8.4 Discussion

At present, our implementation uses 16-bit fixed-point numbers and Zynq board. The projected results with different quantization strategies and platforms are shown in Table 8. Theoretically, when using the 8-bit quantization, $2\times$ PEs can be placed on the FPGA and thus the performance on CONV layers doubles. Besides, $2\times$ weights can be loaded to the system with the same bandwidth compared with the 16-bit quantization, and thus the performance on FC layers also doubles. Further more, when deploying to the VC707 board, one more PE can be placed, and thus the processing capability on CONV layers is expected to be $1.5\times$ higher than that of Zynq platform. For VGG16-SVD network on VC707 with 8-bit dynamic-precision quantization, it is expected to achieve a frame rate at 11.76 fps.

9. CONCLUSION

The limited bandwidth is one of the bottlenecks of accelerating deep CNN models on embedded systems. In this paper, we make an in-depth investigation of the memory footprint and bandwidth problem in order to accelerate state-of-the-art CNN models for Image-Net classification on the embedded FPGA platform. We show that CONV layers are computation-centric and FC layers are memory-centric. A dynamic-precision data quantization flow is proposed to reduce memory footprint and bandwidth requirements while maintaining comparable accuracy. Convolver that can be used for both CONV layers and FC layers is designed to save the resource. A data arrangement scheme for FC layers is also proposed to ensure high bandwidth utilization. Our implementation on Xilinx Zynq with very deep VGG16-SVD model for Image-Net classification achieves a frame rate at 4.45 fps with 86.66% top-5 accuracy with 16-bit quantization. The average performances of CONV layers and the full CNN are 187.8 GOP/s and 137.0 GOP/s under 150MHz working frequency.

10. REFERENCES

[1] O. Russakovsky, J. Deng, H. Su, J. Krause, S. Satheesh, S. Ma, Z. Huang, A. Karpathy, A. Khosla, M. Bernstein, A. C. Berg, and L. Fei-Fei, "ImageNet Large Scale Visual Recognition Challenge," pp. 211–252, 2015.

[2] A. Krizhevsky, I. Sutskever, and G. E. Hinton, "Imagenet classification with deep convolutional neural networks," in *NIPS*, 2012, pp. 1097–1105.

[3] M. D. Zeiler and R. Fergus, "Visualizing and understanding convolutional networks," in *ECCV*, 2014, pp. 818–833.

[4] C. Szegedy, W. Liu, Y. Jia, P. Sermanet, S. Reed, D. Anguelov, D. Erhan, V. Vanhoucke, and A. Rabinovich, "Going deeper with convolutions," *arXiv preprint arXiv:1409.4842*, 2014.

[5] K. He, X. Zhang, S. Ren, and J. Sun, "Deep residual learning for image recognition," *arXiv preprint arXiv:1512.03385*, 2015.

[6] C. Zhang, P. Li, G. Sun, Y. Guan, B. Xiao, and J. Cong, "Optimizing fpga-based accelerator design for deep convolutional neural networks," in *Proceedings of ISFPGA*. ACM, 2015, pp. 161–170.

[7] T. Chen, Z. Du, N. Sun, J. Wang, C. Wu, Y. Chen, and O. Temam, "Diannao: A small-footprint high-throughput accelerator for ubiquitous machine-learning," in *ASPLOS*, vol. 49, no. 4. ACM, 2014, pp. 269–284.

[8] Y. Chen, T. Luo, S. Liu, S. Zhang, L. He, J. Wang, L. Li, T. Chen, Z. Xu, N. Sun *et al.*, "Dadiannao: A machine-learning supercomputer," in *MICRO*. IEEE, 2014, pp. 609–622.

[9] D. Liu, T. Chen, S. Liu, J. Zhou, S. Zhou, O. Teman, X. Feng, X. Zhou, and Y. Chen, "Pudiannao: A polyvalent machine learning accelerator," in *ASPLOS*. ACM, 2015, pp. 369–381.

[10] Z. Du, R. Fasthuber, T. Chen, P. Ienne, L. Li, T. Luo, X. Feng, Y. Chen, and O. Temam, "Shidiannao: shifting vision processing closer to the sensor," in *ISCA*. ACM, 2015, pp. 92–104.

[11] S. Chakradhar, M. Sankaradas, V. Jakkula, and S. Cadambi, "A dynamically configurable coprocessor for convolutional neural networks," in *ISCA*, vol. 38, no. 3. ACM, 2010, pp. 247–257.

[12] C. Farabet, B. Martini, B. Corda, P. Akselrod, E. Culurciello, and Y. LeCun, "Neuflow: A runtime reconfigurable dataflow processor for vision," in *CVPRW*. IEEE, 2011, pp. 109–116.

[13] C. Farabet, C. Poulet, J. Y. Han, and Y. LeCun, "Cnp: An fpga-based processor for convolutional networks," in *FPL*. IEEE, 2009, pp. 32–37.

[14] Y. LeCun, L. Bottou, Y. Bengio, and P. Haffner, "Gradient-based learning applied to document recognition," *Proceedings of the IEEE*, vol. 86, no. 11, pp. 2278–2324, 1998.

[15] A. S. Razavian, H. Azizpour, J. Sullivan, and S. Carlsson, "Cnn features off-the-shelf: an astounding baseline for recognition," in *CVPRW*. IEEE, 2014, pp. 512–519.

[16] K. Simonyan and A. Zisserman, "Very deep convolutional networks for large-scale image recognition," *arXiv preprint arXiv:1409.1556*, 2014.

[17] S. J. Hanson and L. Y. Pratt, "Comparing biases for minimal network construction with back-propagation," in *NIPS*, 1989, pp. 177–185.

[18] Y. LeCun, J. S. Denker, S. A. Solla, R. E. Howard, and L. D. Jackel, "Optimal brain damage," in *NIPS*, vol. 89, 1989.

[19] B. Hassibi and D. G. Stork, *Second order derivatives for network pruning: Optimal brain surgeon*. Morgan Kaufmann, 1993.

[20] S. Han, J. Pool, J. Tran, and W. J. Dally, "Learning both weights and connections for efficient neural networks," *arXiv preprint arXiv:1506.02626*, 2015.

[21] G. H. Golub and C. F. Van Loan, "Matrix computations. 1996," *Johns Hopkins University, Press, Baltimore, MD, USA*, pp. 374–426, 1996.

[22] E. L. Denton, W. Zaremba, J. Bruna, Y. LeCun, and R. Fergus, "Exploiting linear structure within convolutional networks for efficient evaluation," in *NIPS*, 2014, pp. 1269–1277.

[23] X. Zhang, J. Zou, X. Ming, K. He, and J. Sun, "Efficient and accurate approximations of nonlinear convolutional networks," *arXiv preprint arXiv:1411.4229*, 2014.

[24] M. Jaderberg, A. Vedaldi, and A. Zisserman, "Speeding up convolutional neural networks with low rank expansions," *arXiv preprint arXiv:1405.3866*, 2014.

[25] C. Farabet, Y. LeCun, K. Kavukcuoglu, E. Culurciello, B. Martini, P. Akselrod, and S. Talay, "Large-scale fpga-based convolutional networks," *Machine Learning on Very Large Data Sets*, vol. 1, 2011.

[26] M. Sankaradas, V. Jakkula, S. Cadambi, S. Chakradhar, I. Durdanovic, E. Cosatto, and H. Graf, "A massively parallel coprocessor for convolutional neural networks," in *ASAP*, July 2009, pp. 53–60.

[27] D. Larkin, A. Kinane, and N. O'Connor, "Towards hardware acceleration of neuroevolution for multimedia processing applications on mobile devices," in *Neural Information Processing*. Springer, 2006, pp. 1178–1188.

[28] Y. Jia, E. Shelhamer, J. Donahue, S. Karayev, J. Long, R. Girshick, S. Guadarrama, and T. Darrell, "Caffe: Convolutional architecture for fast feature embedding," *arXiv preprint arXiv:1408.5093*, 2014.

[29] B. Bosi, G. Bois, and Y. Savaria, "Reconfigurable pipelined 2-d convolvers for fast digital signal processing," *VLSI*, vol. 7, no. 3, pp. 299–308, 1999.

[30] V. Gokhale, J. Jin, A. Dundar, B. Martini, and E. Culurciello, "A 240 g-ops/s mobile coprocessor for deep neural networks," in *CVPRW*. IEEE, 2014, pp. 696–701.

Using Stochastic Computing to Reduce the Hardware Requirements for a Restricted Boltzmann Machine Classifier

Bingzhe Li, M. Hassan Najafi, and David J. Lilja
Department of Electrical and Computer Engineering
University of Minnesota, Twin Cities, USA
{lixx1743, najaf011, lilja}@umn.edu

ABSTRACT

Artificial neural networks are powerful computational systems with interconnected neurons. Generally, these networks have a very large number of computation nodes which forces the designer to use software-based implementations. However, the software based implementations are offline and not suitable for portable or real-time applications. Experiments show that compared with the software based implementations, FPGA-based systems can greatly speed up the computation time, making them suitable for real-time situations and portable applications. However, the FPGA implementation of neural networks with a large number of nodes is still a challenging task.

In this paper, we exploit stochastic bit streams in the Restricted Boltzmann Machine (RBM) to implement the classification of the RBM handwritten digit recognition application completely on an FPGA. We use finite state machine-based (FSM) stochastic circuits to implement the required sigmoid function and use the novel stochastic computing approach to perform all large matrix multiplications. Experimental results show that the proposed stochastic architecture has much more potential for tolerating faults while requiring much less hardware compared to the currently un-implementable deterministic binary approach when the RBM consists of a large number of neurons. Exploiting the features of stochastic circuits, our implementation achieves much better performance than a software-based approach.

Keywords

Neural network; Restricted Boltzman Machine; FPGA-based implementation; stochastic computing.

1. INTRODUCTION

With growing interest in neural networks, new methods are needed to achieve low-power back-end applications or high performance neural networks rather than being restricted to software implementations running on general-purpose computing systems. However, the capabilities of neural networks

FPGA '16, February 21–23, 2016, Monterey, CA, USA.
© 2016 ACM. ISBN 978-1-4503-3856-1/16/02... $15.00
DOI: http://dx.doi.org/10.1145/2847263.2847340

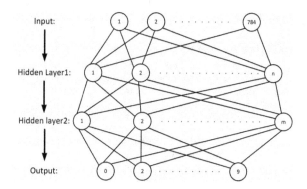

Figure 1: Two-layer RBM structure

highly depend on the size of the network. Power consumption and resource utilization are now considered the main limitations in implementing large neural networks in hardware. The Restricted Boltzmann Machine (RBM) is a type of artificial neural network that is capable of representing and solving difficult problems. Like other machine learning models, the RBM has two process types: learning and testing. During learning, the system is presented with a large number of input examples and desired outputs to generate a suitable RBM structure which learns a general rule to map inputs to outputs. During testing, the RBM produces outputs for new inputs following the general rule obtained in the learning process [6]. The structure presented in Figure 1 is an example of a typical two-layer RBM structure.

Generally, neural networks such as the RBM require enormous and complex computations since parts of their computations, such as the sigmoid function ($Y = 1/(1 + e^{-x})$), do not have a straightforward hardware implementation. Previous work often uses the traditional binary radix encoding to implement parts of the RBM in hardware while other parts are computed on a host processor [11]. However, none of this prior work could implement a large neural network in a single FPGA due to the complexity of the hardware implementation of their methods. In this paper, we exploit the unique characteristics of stochastic computing to implement a large RBM for classifying the most well-known handwriting digit image recognition data set, MNIST [5], completely in one FPGA. The previously proposed structures require substantially more hardware resources than what today's best FPGAs provide. The proposed architecture can reduce the hardware resource requirements significantly to the point that it can be implemented completely on current FPGAs. We extend the work previously presented in [6] by

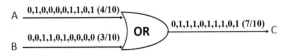

Figure 2: Example of stochastic addition using an OR gate

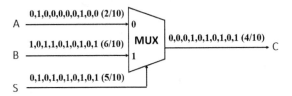

Figure 3: Example of stochastic addition using MUX

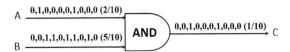

Figure 4: Example of Stochastic multiplications using an AND gate

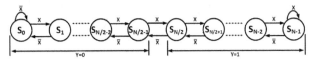

Figure 5: State transition diagram of the FSM-based stochastic tanh function

providing experimental results on the fault tolerant capability of the proposed stochastic RBM. We quantify hardware resource requirement, timing, and classification error rate of the stochastic RBM when shrinking the network size. Comparing with the software-based approach we show that the stochastic implementation achieves much better performance than the software-based MATLAB implementation.

2. STOCHASTIC COMPUTATIONAL ELEMENTS

2.1 Stochastic Bit Streams

A stochastic bit stream is a sequence of binary digits in which the information is contained in the primary statistic of the bit stream or the probability of any given bit in the stream being a logic '1'. The two encoding formats of stochastic bit streams, unipolar and bipolar [1], can express a real number x in the intervals $[0, 1]$ or $[-1, 1]$, respectively. In the unipolar format, the probability of having '1's in a bit stream X is $Pr(X) = x$. In the bipolar format, the probability of seeing '1's in a bit stream X is $Pr(X) = (x+1)/2$ [7]. For the values out of $[-1, 1]$ and $[0, 1]$, the equations shown in (1) could be used to scale the inputs to the required interval using a scaling coefficient of N.

$$Pr(X) = x/N \qquad Pr(X) = (x/N + 1)/2 \qquad (1)$$

2.2 Stochastic Operations

Dickson et al [2], and Qian et al [9] introduced two methods of adding stochastic bit streams. Dickson et al used a standard OR gate to approximate addition as illustrated in Figure 2. As can be seen, the output of the OR gate, 7/10, is the expected output from adding the input values, 4/10 and 3/10. As shown in equation (2), performing an add operation using an OR gate introduces an extra AB term which is an error in the result. The only case that the AB term can be ignored is when $A \ll 1$ and $B \ll 1$.

$$C = A \text{ or } B = A + B - AB \qquad (2)$$

Qian et al implemented scaled addition using a MUX. According to equation (3), when the select line of a MUX is a representation of 0.5 in the stochastic domain, the output is $(A+B)/2$ which scales down the desired result by a factor of two. Figure 3 shows an example of performing scaled addition using the MUX.

$$C = A \cdot S + B \cdot (1 - S) \qquad (3)$$

To generalize the simple two-input adder to a multi-input adder, equations (2) and (3) can be extended to (4) and (5).

$$C = A_1 \text{ or } A_2 \text{ or } A_3 \text{ or } ... \text{ or } A_N \qquad (4)$$

$$C = \frac{1}{N} \sum_{i=1}^{N} A_i \qquad (5)$$

In the stochastic domain, multiplication could be implemented using a standard AND gate for the unipolar (Figure 4) and an XNOR gate for the bipolar representation of bit streams [7]. Brown and Card [1] proposed a stochastic implemention of the hyperbolic tangent (tanh) function using a finite state machine (FSM) (Figure 5). The FSM presented in Figure 5 implements equation (6) where N is the number of states in the FSM, and X and Y are the input and output stochastic streams in bipolar format.

$$Y = tanh(N/2)X \qquad (6)$$

Note that N/2 (N>2) in equation (6) is also the coefficient of the input which increases the value of the input by a factor of N/2 during computation of the tanh function. Since we are looking for the result of tanh(X) rather than tanh(N/2*X), the N/2 coefficient is a potentially unwanted scaling factor. In the next section, we explain how to take advantage of this N/2 coefficient to obtain the desired results.

3. STOCHASTIC IMPLEMENTATION

Handwritten digit recognition is an application of the RBM neural network. In this paper, the RBM coeffcents required for handwritten digit recognition are first generated based on the Hinton et al [3, 10] learning code and then the testing step will be achieved completely on an FPGA-based hardware platform. The selected deep BM structure (Figure 1) is a 2-layer BM in which the inputs to the first layer are thousands of 28×28 pixel images provided by the MNIST data set. The first and the second hidden layers have n and m neural units, respectively. The maximum value produced at the ten units of the output layer determines the final handwritten decimal digit result. Equations (7), (8) and (9) show the functions of the different RBM layers [10].

$$\mathbf{w1p} = 1/(1 + \exp(\mathbf{data} * \mathbf{w1\_vishid} + \mathbf{coef})) \qquad (7)$$

$$\mathbf{w2p} = 1/(1 + \exp(-\mathbf{w1p} * \mathbf{w2} - \mathbf{bias\_pen})) \qquad (8)$$

$$\mathbf{out} = \exp(\mathbf{w2p} * \mathbf{w\_class} + \mathbf{bias\_top}) \qquad (9)$$

where the **data** (1×784) matrix is the handwritten input image and **coef** = **temp_h2** * **w1_penhid** + **bias_hid**. Note that **w1_vishid** ($784 \times n$), **temp_h2** ($1 \times m$), **w1_penhid** ($m \times n$), **w2** ($n \times m$), **bias_hid** ($1 \times n$), **bias_pen** ($1 \times m$), **w_class** ($m \times 10$) and **bias_top** (1×10) are the RBM

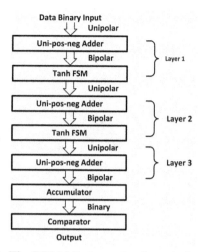

Figure 6: The RBM bit stream implementation data flow

constants computed by the learning process. **w1p** and **w2p** are the probabilities of the first and second hidden layers.

To reduce the complexity of the computations and thereby save FPGA resources, we simplify these equations in two steps. First, we precompute constant coefficients generated by the learning phase For example, **coef = temp_h2 * w1_penhid + bias_hid** is precomputed so that it is necessary to store only the constant value **coef** into the FPGA memory. Secondly, our main goal is to find the maximum value of the 10 outputs produced at the output layer. The purpose of the exponential function in (9) is simply to make finding the maximum value easier by enlarging the differences between the outputs. Thus, the exponential function is actually redundant and we can rewrite equation (9) and convert it to equation (10).

$$out = w2p * w\_class + bias\_top \qquad (10)$$

3.1 RBM Data Flow

As seen in equations (7), (8) and (10), the RBM layers use some similar operations including multiplications and additions. Furthermore, equations (7) and (8) use the same function format, $1/(1 + exp(x))$. However, these similarities do not mean that we can directly connect different layers of the RBM to each other in the stochastic architecture since different stochastic computation elements might use different encoding formats in their inputs and outputs. Figure 6 shows the implementation dataflow of the proposed stochastic RBM. As can be seen in this figure, the input image, which is in unipolar format, comes into a *Uni_pos_neg* adder (see Section 3.3) while its output in bipolar format goes to a bipolar stochastic FSM-based tanh module. The output of the tanh module is in unipolar format which fits with the next layer input and so forth. Although we have used different encoding formats in the structure, each function has been designed in a way that produces its output compatible with the required format for the input of the next level.

Note that we scale down all inputs by an N/2 factor to make sure that all values (inputs, constant coefficients and inter-media results) belong to [-1,1] or [0,1] in order to be able to represent them by stochastic bit streams. This N/2 scaling is canceled automatically by the multiplication with N/2 in equation (6) while it still provides us with the advantage of reducing the errors in equations (2) and (4).

3.2 Matrix Multiplication

A simple presentation of the matrix multiplication performed in the RBM is shown in (11) where each element in the result matrix C is calculated according to equation (12).

$$\mathbf{C} = \begin{bmatrix} A_{11} & \cdots & A_{1m} \\ \vdots & \ddots & \vdots \\ A_{n1} & \cdots & A_{nm} \end{bmatrix} \times \begin{bmatrix} B_{11} & \cdots & B_{1k} \\ \vdots & \ddots & \vdots \\ B_{m1} & \cdots & B_{mk} \end{bmatrix} \qquad (11)$$

$$C_{ij} = \sum_{s=1}^{m} A_{is} \cdot B_{sj} \qquad (12)$$

Based on equation (12), the element C_{ij} of the matrix multiplication result in (11) is the sum of the multiplications of elements A_{is} and B_{sj}. In the stochastic domain, multiplication can be implemented easily by a simple two-input AND gate. However, for the addition operations required in computing each element of the result matrix, **C**, the number of add operations is proportional to the size of the RBM layers.

Taking an example, **data * w1_vishid**, in equation (7), if the input image size is 28×28, a $[1 \times 784] \times [784 \times n]$ matrix multiplication needs to be performed using stochastic circuits, which consists of 784 addition operations. As discussed in Section 2, there are two types of stochastic adders, MUXs and ORs. The N-input scaled adder defined in equation (5) always scales the result down N times and the OR gate introduces an extra error with the term AB in equation (2). Implementing such a large number of additions seems to be a challenge for both the MUX and the OR gates.

For the MUX gate, consider the example presented in Figure 7 in which the expected result of adding 784 input values is 0.8 while we want to use 1024 length bit streams to perform stochastic addition. In the ideal case, when a MUX is being used as the stochastic adder and there is not any correlation between input bit streams, the stochastic result is about 0.8/784=0.00102. This value is too small to be represented even with 1024-bit streams because the output stream will only have a single '1' out of 1024 bits as shown in Figure 7. Representing such small values can make the system vulnerable even to a very small number of errors.

For the OR gate, in order to perform the stochastic addition accurately, we scale the inputs of the OR gate down to properly small values (in our case, scale factor N/2=16) to be able to ignore the effect of the extra AB term in (2) and to avoid the large soft error like MUX adder. For example, if the result of 0.4+0.4 is going to be computed directly using an OR gate, it could introduce about 0.4*0.4/(0.4+0.4)=20% error just from the AB term. However, if we first scale the inputs down 10 times and then scale the result back, the error rate reduces from 20% to 0.04*0.04/(0.04+0.04)=2%. From the soft error point of view, assume that the result of adding 784 input values using the OR gate is 0.08 which contains $1024 * 0.08 \approx 82$ '1's in a 1024-bit stream. If an error causes one bit of the stream to flip from '0' to '1', the output error rate will be just $(83/1024 - 0.08)/0.08 \approx 1.32\%$. Therefore, an OR gate with a proper scaling factor for inputs can be a suitable addition circuit that can help the RBM structure to experience very small error rates.

The default RBM size in our implementations is $500 \times 1000 \times 10$ which means that the first hidden layer of the BM has 500 units, the second hidden layer has 1000 units, and finally the output has 10 units. Selecting this structure, there are three massive matrix multiplications, $[1 \times 784] \times$

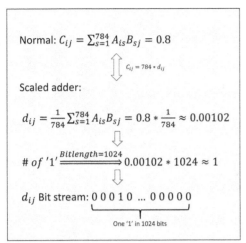

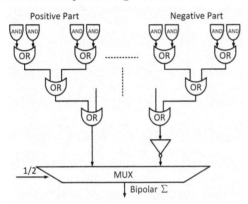

Figure 7: An example of producing outputs vulnerable to soft errors when performing stochastic scaled addition.

Figure 8: *Uni-pos-neg* adder: A large matrix multiplication hardware structure using both positive and negative inputs.

$[784 \times 500]$, $[1 \times 500] \times [500 \times 1000]$, and $[1 \times 1000] \times [1000 \times 10]$ to perform. In order to compute each element of the result matrix using stochastic circuit, we introduce the *Uni_pos_neg adder* (Figure 8).

3.3 Uni_pos_neg adder

The circuits used in the stochastic RBM use both positive and negative values. However, the unipolar representation of stochastic numbers is only suitable for representing pure positive or pure negative values. Since the stochastic tanh function accepts input bit streams in only bipolar format, the output bit streams generated from stochastic matrix multiplication needs to be also in that format. Thus, in this section we propose a *Uni_pos_neg* adder module for implementing the matrix multiplication structure which can automatically handle the format conversion process.

Considering equation (13) as an example, it computes one element of the result matrix of multiplying two matrices. The element C_{ij} in the result matrix equals the sum of the products of $data_{is}$ and $w1\_vishid_{sj}$. Since the products of $data_{is}$ and $w1\_vishid_{sj}$ contain both positive and negative values, we cannot directly use the "OR" gate as the stochastic adder. In the *Uni_pos_neg* adder, the products are first divided into two parts, negative part and positive part, based on the sign bit of the binary value, $w1\_vishid_{sj}$, located in the most significant bit (MSB). Since **data** is the

input image that must be scaled to $[0, 1]$, the sign of the product of $data_{is}$ and $w1\_vishid_{sj}$ only depends on the sign of $w1\_vishid_{sj}$. Finally, those negative and positive parts only contain negative or positive values respectively so we can simply use the stochastic arithmetic elements (AND and OR) with unipolar encoding for both parts.

For the positive part, we directly encode the binary value as a unipolar bit stream, then use AND gates to multiply $data_{is}$ and $w1\_vishid_{sj}$, and OR gates to sum up all of the positive products. For the negative part, at first we consider them as positive values (flipping the MSB to '0') and do the same operations as the positive part. Then, at the final stage of Figure 8, we invert the value computed in the negative part to unify the encoding format. In this way the results of equations (14) and (15) will be obtained after going through the addition tree structure seen in Figure 8.

$$C_{ij} = \sum_{s=1}^{m} data_{is} \cdot w1\_vishid_{sj} \qquad (13)$$

$$A = \sum M_{pos} = \sum_{pos} data_{is} \cdot w1\_vishid_{sj} \qquad (14)$$

$$B = \sum M_{neg} = \sum_{neg} data_{is} \cdot w1\_vishid_{sj} \qquad (15)$$

In equations (14) and (15), A and B are the sums of the positive and the negative products in the matrix multiplication with unipolar encoding. We invert the negative part, B, and use a MUX adder to sum A and the inverted B as seen in Figure 8 to obtain the *sum* variable of equation (16). Comparing this variable with the bipolar expression $Pr(X) = (x+1)/2$, *sum* is the bipolar encoding of C_{ij}. The inverter and MUX automatically transfer two unipolar values, A and B, into the bipolar format version of A-B. Thus, the *Uni_pos_neg* adder produces one element of the output matrix of the matrix multiplication.

$$sum = \frac{A + (1 - B)}{2} = \frac{1 + (A - B)}{2} \qquad (16)$$

For the other BM layers, according to equations (8) and (10), **w1p** and **w2p** are calculated using the sigmoid function and hence their values belong to $[0, 1]$. We repeat the above process for other layers' matrix multiplications by regarding **w1p** and **w2p** as **data** and dividing inputs into the positive and negative parts according to the sign of **w2** and **w_class** the same as is done for **w1_vishid**.

3.4 Sigmoid Function

To implement the sigmoid function, we make some transformations according to equations (17), (18) and (19). Based on these transformations, the sigmoid function could be considered as a bipolar encoding of the tanh function. As seen in Figure 9, both the input and the output of the tanh function are in bipolar format. However, to match with the restrictions of the RBM structure, we obtain the sigmoid function with bipolar inputs and a unipolar output based on (19).

$$tanh(x) = (e^x - e^{-x})/(e^x + e^{-x}) \qquad (17)$$

$$\frac{1}{1 + e^{-x}} = \frac{e^{x/2}}{e^{x/2} + e^{-x/2}} = 1/2(1 + \frac{e^{x/2} - e^{-x/2}}{e^{x/2} + e^{-x/2}}) \qquad (18)$$

$$= (1 + tanh(x/2))/2$$

$$\frac{1}{1 + e^{-Nx}} = \frac{1 + tanh(Nx/2)}{2} \qquad (19)$$

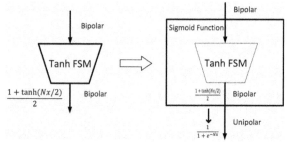

Figure 9: Sigmoid function implementation with bipolar input and unipolar output from tanh function

Table 1: Error rate comparison between the proposed stochastic architecture with different lengths of bit streams and the conventional version.

Sizes	Conventional	Stochastic			
		512	1024	2048	4096
$100 \times 200 \times 10$	1.96%	10.06%	5.72%	3.91%	3.14%
$200 \times 400 \times 10$	1.35%	7.93%	4.24%	3.08%	2.35%
$300 \times 600 \times 10$	1.17%	6.33%	2.92%	1.80%	1.80%
$400 \times 800 \times 10$	1.10%	4.17%	2.37%	1.52%	1.34%
$500 \times 1000 \times 10$	0.98%	5.10%	2.32%	1.64%	1.32%

4. EXPERIMENTAL RESULTS

The proposed stochastic architecture for the RBM has been implemented using the Verilog HDL language, then synthesized, placed and routed using the Xilinx ISE Design Suite 14.7 on the Xilinx Virtex7 xc7v2000t-2flg1925 FPGA. Functional verification of the proposed architecture has been done in Matlab where we implemented both the conventional approach [3] and also our proposed stochastic architecture to work on 10,000 MNIST handwritten test images. Since computation time and the accuracy of stochastic operations are directly proportional to the length of bit streams [9], we ran our simulations for the stochastic architecture on four different lengths of bit streams, 512, 1024, 2048, and 4096 bits, to obtain the trade-off between the output error rate and the required computation time. For converting the deterministic input values into stochastic bit streams we have used the stochastic number generator presented in [9].

4.1 Error Rate Comparison

For the conventional approach we used the MATLAB training method presented in [3] and obtained the output error rates of different RBM sizes as shown in Table 1. The reported error rates are the percentage of miss-classifications in classifying the 10,000 input test images from the MNIST data set. Based on the results presented in Table 1, the stochastic implementations, particularly the ones with the longer bit streams, could compete with the results of the conventional approach with only a little higher error rate. Based on Table 1, the error rates of the stochastic RBM decrease when increasing the length of bit streams for all different sizes of the layers. However, every additional bit in the bit stream needs one extra clock cycle to generate and process the streams. Selecting the optimum length of bit streams is up to the designer based on the application requirements and system limitations.

4.2 Fault Tolerance Comparison

An attractive feature of stochastic architectures is their ability to tolerate faults. The reason is that a single bit flip in a long bit-stream results in only a small change in

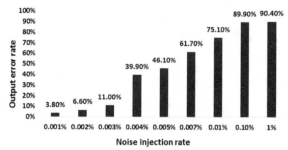

Figure 10: Output error rates obtained from injecting different rates of faults into the conventional architecture

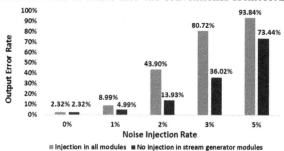

Figure 11: Output error rates obtained from injecting different rates of faults into the stochastic architecture

the value of the stochastic number [8]. To study the fault tolerant capability of the proposed architecture we injected faults into the stochastic and also into the conventional architecture of the RBM, both implemented in the MATLAB tool. For the stochastic case, we injected the faults in the same way as [9], but in two different approaches. In the first approach we do not inject the faults into the stream generator modules whereas in the second approach the fault is injected in both internal computational elements and also the stream generators.

Figure 10 and 11 show the results of injecting faults into the conventional and stochastic implementations of the RBM. Comparing these figures, the stochastic architecture has shown a much better capability to tolerate faults. For example, in the case with 1% fault injection rate, the conventional structure produces a 90.4% error rate whereas for the stochastic implementation, in the first fault injection approach, a 4.99% error rate is reported in recognizing the handwritten digits. Considering this result, if we try to prepare more reliable stochastic stream generators, we can expect the proposed stochastic architecture to gracefully tolerate about a 1%-2% fault rate in its internal computing circuits.

4.3 Hardware Resource Comparison

As mentioned in the introduction section, implementing a fully parallel specially designed hardware implementation of a neural network in an FPGA is expensive, involves extra design overheads, and in most cases is not even possible in today's FPGAs [12]. Recently, for the first time in the literature, a fully pipelined FPGA architecture of a factored RBM has been implemented in [4]. Although the virtualized architecture proposed in [4] could implement a neural network consisting of a maximum 4096 nodes using time multiplex sharing of hardware resources in the largest overall device available at the time of that experiment (Virtex6 LX760), the largest achievable RBM without virtualization on that device is on the order of 256 nodes.

Table 2: Area, timing and error rate results for different RBM sizes.

Size	Area (# of LUTs)	Latency(s)	Output error rate(%) Stream length=1024
$100 \times 200 \times 10$	144,450	$8.561 * 10^{-6}$	5.72%
$200 \times 400 \times 10$	345,710	$9.682 * 10^{-6}$	4.24%
$300 \times 600 \times 10$	603,750	$9.797 * 10^{-6}$	2.92%
$400 \times 800 \times 10$	920,190	$1.025 * 10^{-5}$	2.37%
$500 \times 1000 \times 10$	1,292,310	$1.077 * 10^{-5}$	2.32%

Table 3: Comparing the latency of the software-based and the stochastic FPGA-based implementations of the RBM when the length of bit streams is 1024.

Size	CPU(s)	FPGA(s)	Speedup
$100 \times 200 \times 10$	$6.2 * 10^{-3}$	$8.561 * 10^{-6}$	724.2
$200 \times 400 \times 10$	$7.8 * 10^{-3}$	$9.682 * 10^{-6}$	805.6
$300 \times 600 \times 10$	$9.2 * 10^{-3}$	$9.797 * 10^{-6}$	939.1
$400 \times 800 \times 10$	$1.32 * 10^{-2}$	$1.025 * 10^{-5}$	1287.8
$500 \times 1000 \times 10$	$1.66 * 10^{-2}$	$1.077 * 10^{-5}$	1541.3

Implementation reports from Xilinx give us enough information about the required hardware resources for implementing the proposed stochastic architecture. As shown in Table 2, implementing the stochastic architecture of the RBM with $500 \times 1000 \times 10$ layer size needs an order of one million LUTs and could be placed and routed in Virtex7 2000 Xilinx FPGA.

4.4 Sensitivity to Network size

One solution to fit neural networks on FPGAs with fewer resources is to shrink the size of the layers while still satisfying the application expectations. In this section we explore the effect of shrinking the size of the stochastic RBM layers from the largest size (500*1000*10) that produces the lowest output error rate to smaller sizes and see how reducing the size of the layers changes the output error rate, latency and resource utilization. As shown in Table 2, by shrinking the size of the RBM, the number of LUTs is reduced dramatically while the latency does not experience much change and the error rate increases with a very slow slope.

4.5 Performance Comparison

Since the deterministic architecture of the RBM is not implementable on the current FPGAs, we analyze the performance of the proposed stochastic architecture by comparing the latency of classifying one input test image using the implemented stochastic architecture with the corresponding time for classifying by the software-based MATLAB approach. Running Hinton et al [3] code in MATLAB, we measured the latency of the software-based implementation on a machine with an Intel Core i5 Dual core CPU (3.40GHz) and 16GB DDR3 RAM. Since there are many matrix operations in the RBM application, writing appropriate programs in the MATLAB tool could be a better and more straight-forward way for running these types of applications than writing the program in C. Table 3 shows the execution time of classifying a sample image from the MNIST data set using the software-based implementation and the stochastic FPGA-based implementation for five different sizes of RBMs.

From these results, we can see that the speedup of the proposed stochastic implementation could reach to about 700x for the $100 \times 200 \times 10$ layer size and even to 1500X for the 500x1000x10 neural network size compared to the software-based MATLAB implementation. By increasing the neural

network size, we obtained greater speedup because the layer size did not have much influence on the classification time of an input image in the stochastic RBM (as shown previously in Table 2), whereas larger RBM sizes cost much more computation time in the software-based implementation.

5. CONCLUSION

In this paper, we proposed a stochastic FPGA implementation of a RBM classifier using stochastic logic. In a large RBM network, matrix multiplications and sigmoid functions are the most expensive operations to be implemented. We proposed the Uni_pos_neg adder to implement the stochastic matrix multiplication and used the FSM tanh function to achieve the sigmoid function. Our experimental results show that the proposed stochastic architecture can tolerate 1-2% fault rate in its computing circuits. Performance evaluation results show that the proposed architecture could classify a standard handwritten input image about 700x times faster than the software-based MATLAB implementation when it is implemented on a Virtex 7 xc7v2000 FPGA.

6. ACKNOWLEDGMENTS

This work was supported in part by National Science Foundation grant no. CCF-1408123. Any opinions, findings and conclusions or recommendations expressed in this material are those of the authors and do not necessarily reflect the views of the NSF.

7. REFERENCES

[1] B. D. Brown and H. C. Card. Stochastic neural computation. i. computational elements. *Computers, IEEE Transactions on*, 50(9):891–905, 2001.

[2] J. A. Dickson, R. D. McLeod, and H. Card. Stochastic arithmetic implementations of neural networks with in situ learning. In *Neural Networks, 1993., IEEE International Conference on*, pages 711–716. IEEE, 1993.

[3] G. E. Hinton and R. Salakhutdinov. A better way to pretrain deep boltzmann machines. In *Advances in Neural Information Processing Systems*, pages 2447–2455, 2012.

[4] L.-W. Kim, S. Asaad, and R. Linsker. A fully pipelined FPGA architecture of a factored restricted boltzmann machine artificial neural network. *ACM Transactions on Reconfigurable Technology and Systems (TRETS)*, 7(1):5, 2014.

[5] Y. LeCun and C. Cortes. Mnist handwritten digit database. *AT&T Labs [Online]. Available: http://yann. lecun. com/exdb/mnist*, 2010.

[6] B. Li, M. H. Najafi, and D. J. Lilja. An FPGA implementation of a restricted boltzmann machine classifier using stochastic bit streams. In *Application-specific Systems, Architectures and Processors (ASAP), 2015 IEEE 26th International Conference on*, pages 68–69. IEEE, 2015.

[7] P. Li, D. J. Lilja, W. Qian, M. D. Riedel, and K. Bazargan. Logical computation on stochastic bit streams with linear finite state machines. *IEEE Transactions on Computers*, page 1, 2012.

[8] M. Najafi and M. Salehi. A fast fault-tolerant architecture for Sauvola local image thresholding algorithm using stochastic computing. *Very Large Scale Integration (VLSI) Systems, IEEE Transactions on*, PP(99):1–5, 2015.

[9] W. Qian, X. Li, M. D. Riedel, K. Bazargan, and D. J. Lilja. An architecture for fault-tolerant computation with stochastic logic. *Computers, IEEE Transactions on*, 60(1):93–105, 2011.

[10] R. Salakhutdinov and G. Hinton. An efficient learning procedure for deep boltzmann machines. *Neural computation*, 24(8):1967–2006, 2012.

[11] M. Skubiszewski. An exact hardware implementation of the boltzmann machine. In *Parallel and Distributed Processing, 1992. Proceedings of the Fourth IEEE Symposium on*, pages 107–110. IEEE, 1992.

[12] J. Zhu and P. Sutton. FPGA implementations of neural networks–a survey of a decade of progress. In *Field Programmable Logic and Application*, pages 1062–1066. Springer, 2003.

A Platform-Oblivious Approach for Heterogeneous Computing: a Case Study with Monte Carlo-based Simulation for Medical Applications

Shih-Hao Hung*
National Taiwan University
Taipei 10617, Taiwan
hungsh@csie.ntu.edu.tw

Min-Yu Tsai†
National Taiwan University
Taipei 10617, Taiwan
york.ee88g@gmail.com

Bo-Yi Huang‡
National Taiwan University
Taipei 10617, Taiwan
justfor0223@gmail.com

Chia-Heng Tu§
National Taiwan University
Taipei 10617, Taiwan
chiaheng@gmail.com

ABSTRACT

Light is important and helpful in many medical applications, such as cancer treatment. Computer modeling and simulation of light transport are often adopted to improve the quality of medical treatments. In particular, Monte Carlo-based simulations are considered to deliver accurate results, but require intensive computational resources. While several attempts to accelerate the Monte Carlo-based methods for the simulation of photon transport with platform-specific programming schemes, such as CUDA on GPU and HDL on FPGA, have been proposed, the approach has limited portability and prolongs software updates. In this paper, we parallelize the Monte Carlo modeling of light transport in multi-layered tissues (MCML) program with OpenCL, an open standard supported by a wide range of platforms. We characterize the performance of the parallelized MCML kernel program runs on CPU, GPU and FPGA. Compared to platform-specific programming schemes, our platform-oblivious approach provides a unified, highly portable code and delivers competitive performance and power efficiency.

1. INTRODUCTION

As light plays an important role in many medical applications, light transport through biological tissues is widely studied to help analyze therapeutic effects. Taking cancer treatment for an example, to avoid damaging health cells and maximize the benefit of the treatment, computer modeling and simulation of photon propagation through living tissues is usually performed before the treatment delivery to carefully estimate the outcomes of the treatment. The Monte Carlo modeling of light transport in multi-layered tissues (MCML) [17] program is such an example, and simulation results helps evaluate the candidate configurations.

While the Monte Carlo-based methods for modeling the transports of the photon packets are generally considered to deliver accurate results, it requires intensive computational resources to calculate the interactions between photon packets and the human tissues. To shorten the required computer simulation time, there have been many works proposed to accelerate the Monte Carlo-based simulation with hardware accelerators, such as Graphics Processing Unit (GPU) [7, 9, 1, 12, 15] and Field-Programmable Gate Array (FPGA) [10, 18, 15]. The previous works converted existing programs in platform-specific and low-level programming languages to drive the GPU and FPGA. In other words, the developers had to write Compute Unified Defined Architecture (CUDA) programs for Nvidia graphics cards and Hardware Description Language (HDL) programs for FPGA boards.

While the platform-specific programming schemes may help exploit the computational capability of the underlying GPU and FPGA accelerators, the portability of these schemes is relatively low and raises concerns for medical applications. Particularly for the case of FPGA, it can take a long time for software updates to be converted into HDL, e.g., Verilog, and verified thoroughly. Thus, we are interested in developing a portable, platform-oblivious approach which allows the simulation program to be parallelized and optimized at the high level and executed on a wide range of processing units to harvest heterogeneous computational resources in the system.

As a case study, we choose the high-level programming scheme, OpenCL, and apply it to accelerate the MCML program. As a widely supported open standard, programs written in OpenCL can be executed not only with instruction processors such as CPU and GPU, but also FPGA. In

*Shih-Hao Hung is affiliated with Department of Computer Science and Information Engineering (CSIE), National Taiwan University (NTU).

†Min-Yu Tsai is affiliated with CSIE, NTU.

‡Bo-Yi Huang was affiliated with CSIE, NTU.

§Chia-Heng Tu is affiliated with MEDIATEK-NTU Advanced Research Center, NTU.

FPGA'16, February 21 - 23, 2016, Monterey, CA, USA

© 2016 Copyright held by the owner/author(s). Publication rights licensed to ACM.
ISBN 978-1-4503-3856-1/16/02... $15.00

DOI: http://dx.doi.org/10.1145/2847263.2847335

fact, many CPU/GPU vendors, including Intel, AMD, and NVIDIA, support OpenCL, and FPGA vendors, e.g., Altera and Xilinx, offer compiler toolchains to automatically convert OpenCL programs into Verilog nelists. Hence, for portability, we only need to augment MCML with the parallel constructs provided by OpenCL, and, to be completely platform-oblivious, our scheme does not attempt to apply platform-specific optimization techniques. Instead, generic optimizations are applied on top of the parallelized OpenCL code to improve the simulation efficiency, after observing the performance bottlenecks on GPU and FPGA. We show that the included generic optimizations improve the performance greatly across GPU and FPGA at the same time. Compared to platform-specific programming schemes for MCML [9, 1, 10], our OpenCL-based programs are able to run on various parallel computing platforms with the multicore processor, GPU, and FPGA. Our results show that generic performance optimization can be done at the OpenCL level to improve performance or power efficiency for either GPU or FPGA.

The remainder of the paper is organized as below. Section 2 overviews the MCML program and its workflow. Section 3 introduces the techniques for parallelizing and optimizing the sequential program with OpenCL. Section 4 evaluates the efficiencies of the OpenCL versions across the CPU, GPU, and FPGA, and discusses the trade-offs between our platform-oblivious and platform-optimized schemes. Finally, we conclude this paper in Section 5.

2. MCML OVERVIEW

The MCML [17] was one of the early open source tools available for the simulation of light propagation back in 1995. Although MCML was released two decades ago, it is still popular in the fields [14, 6, 4, 13]. The C-based MCML program simulates the photon propagation in a multi-layered tissue instead of a semi-finite tissue [17]. Its algorithm assumes plane-parallel layers, such as epidermis and dermis of human skins, where each layer is infinitely wide with homogeneous media and has its own set of the parameters for the simulation, including absorption, scattering, anisotropy, and refractive index. With the above assumptions[1], the simulation in the three dimensional space can be reduced into the two dimensional, cylindrical coordinates.

Figure 1(a) shows the four-layer human tissue model[2] used in the MCML photon simulation, where the reflection and absorption data are recorded during the simulation. The simulation outputs are summarized into the absorption array[3], $A[r][z]$, which scores the absorbed photon probability density and is indexed with the radius, r, and depth, z.

Figure 1(b) depicts the workflow of the MCML program, which starts with loading the parameters of the given human skin model. After setting up with its initial random sampled

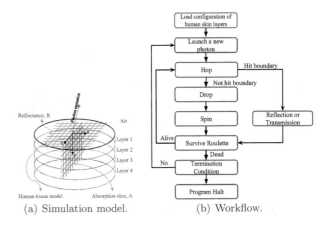

(a) Simulation model.   (b) Workflow.

Figure 1. Simulation model and workflow of MCML.

configuration, e.g., weight, position, direction, and step size, a new photon undergoes the three key operations, *hop*, *drop*, and *spin*, iteratively until it is considered as *dead*.

The hop operation moves the simulated photon from the current position to the next position of interaction, where the step size is calculated by sampling a probability distribution according to the photon's mean free path. The drop operation computes the photon's weight to simulate the energy absorbed by the tissue based on the absorption coefficient at the site of interaction. The spin operation is responsible for deriving the scattering angle.

If the photon weight has reached the pre-determined threshold, the *survival roulette* operation is performed to decide whether the simulation of the current photon should be ended using random numbers. Also, a simulated photon is dead if it exits the modelled tissue through the top or the bottom layer.

3. MCML ACCELERATION

To be specific and without loss of generality, Figure 2 depicts a general system organization for running OpenCL applications, where compute-intensive tasks are programmed with OpenCL *kernels* for acceleration. Usually, the multicore processor acts as the *host* for configuring the parameters of the *kernels*, whereas GPU and FPGA are referred to as the *devices* or *accelerators* for performing the tasks specified by the kernels. Note that the CPU cores on the processor can also be treated as the *device* and used for kernel computation. The *main memory* stores the initial OpenCL program and data. The *device memory*[4] is used to keep the data transferred from/to the *main memory* at the *device* side. The following subsections describe how we parallelize and optimize the MCML program.

3.1 Batch Parallel Execution Model

In the sequential MCML program, the absorbed energy is accumulated in the absorption array. To avoid race condition, the parallelized code should protect the shared re-

---

[1]While the planar layers assumption is oversimplified, it is useful for some applications, e.g., for modeling human skin. However, it would be difficult to model the anatomical structures, such as an irregular buried object within a tissue.

[2]The parameters of the skin model includes the number of skin layers, number of photons involved in the simulation, refractive index, thickness, coefficients for absorption and scattering, etc.

[3]The absorption array is used as an example to illustrate our optimization schemes, and it can be applied to other data structures involved in the simulation, such as reflectance and transmittance data.

[4]The *device memory* refers to the *Global Memory* defined in the OpenCL memory model, whereas the local memory used in the paper refers to either the *Local Memory* or the *Private Memory* in the OpenCL specification.

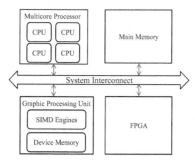

Figure 2. Organization of a typical heterogeneous computing platform.

sources from being accessed concurrently. One known technique is updating the data in the array atomically [9, 1]. However, *atomic update* is a platform-dependent operation and its performance may vary across hardware implementations. In addition, atomic update could serialize the execution of parallel threads when multiple photons visit the same site and this would lead to poor performance.

In our work, a *private* memory region is allocated by the OpenCL kernel for the simulation of a photon to keep the records of the simulated photon, such as the absorption array for photon position and energy of each step. To shorten the latency of the data accesses, when a working thread is initialized to run the kernel code, a piece of per-thread private memory is allocated at the device memory with the OpenCL function call, `clCreateBuffer`. During the parallel simulation of photons, multiple threads estimate the effects of photons, and update the results onto their individual memory region concurrently. Upon the termination of the simulation, the calculated results are then summarized to the absorption array on the system main memory by the OpenCL host program.

As the device memory may not always be large enough to accommodate the needs of the multithreaded execution, we used the *batch parallel execution model* which divides the photons to be simulated into groups according to the size of the device memory. The photon groups are considered sequentially, and photons within the same group are simulated concurrently. Therefore, the actual parallelism delivered by the program, the maximum number of simultaneously running threads, is determined by the size of the device memory.

3.2 Buffering Photon Records

During the simulation, the photon status, such as the absorption array, is stored on the device memory and updated frequently. However, it takes a longer time for computing engines on the device to access the device memory than their local memories. A data buffering mechanism is developed to keep the temporary data in the local memory as long as possible.

According to the profiles of the photon simulations, we observe that the simulated photon usually makes a short distance move, which opens an opportunity for optimization. Figure 3 illustrates the photon steps and the corresponding walking path mapped to the absorption array. The figure shows that the photon records of the i-th and $(i+1)$-th steps fall in the same site of the absorption array, $A[1][0]$, and the records of the $(i+2)$-th and $(i+3)$-th steps should

be updated in $A[0][1]$. As the absorption array only keeps the latest results of the same site, e.g., the $(i+1)$-th step's record for $A[1][0]$, and $(i+3)$-th step's for $A[0][1]$, the data of the consecutive photon steps are updated in the private memory, and only the final version is flushed to the device memory when necessary. The buffering scheme avoids the unnecessary accesses to the device memory.

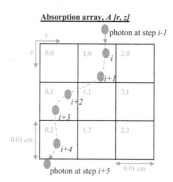

Figure 3. Mapping the photon's travel path to the absorption array.

3.3 Reducing Branch Divergence

Divergent branches are known to degrade the performance of computing devices with *single instruction multiple data* (SIMD) engines. In this work, we apply the branch distribution technique [5] to alleviate the overhead introduced by branch divergence, by identifying and moving the similar code sections from the different code paths to the common place.

3.4 Caching Data with Constant Memory

To reduce the data access latency, the OpenCL standard offers high-level primitives for programmers to arrange their program data at the desired memory region using the keywords, including `__global` for global memory, `__constant` for constant memory, `__local` for local memory, and `__private` for registers. In particular, the keyword, `__constant`, is used to specify that the variable would be placed in the read-only cache if possible to improve the performance of data accesses [3, 11].

As shown in Table 2 [9], the tissue configuration in MCML is important for calculating photon status. Since the tissue configuration is immutable across the entire simulation, we wrap the corresponding parameters into a customized data structure, and place it in the constant memory to reduce data access time during the simulation.

3.5 Sectioning the Thread Execution

The performance of a multithreaded program can be limited by poor utilization of computing resource due to unbalanced loading among threads. Figure 4(a) gives an example to illustrate the phenomenon. The thread synchronization occurs when the longest photon simulation within the group ends at the Step 3, 4, 6, and 8, which makes Thread 1 idle after the simulation of p1, p5 and p7. To improve the resource utilization, one of the common solutions is to use a predetermined synchronization interval for the batch execution. When the simulated steps of the photons are equal to the synchronization interval, the kernel threads running at the device return to the host, and the host program forms a new group of photons for batch execution, where the live photons in the previous run are added to the new group along with the new photons to be simulated. Figure 4(b) illustrate the idea, where the photons are able to perform the simulation as early as possible in Thread 1. Therefore, selecting the photon steps for thread synchronization judiciously is the key to deliver the potential performance. In this paper, empirical experiments are performed to determine the synchronization steps.

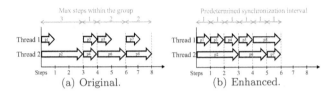

| | (a) Original. | | (b) Enhanced. |

Figure 4. Thread synchronization schemes.

3.6 Fast Relaxed Math

In OpenCL, `-cl-fast-relaxed-math` is a compilation flag which instructs the compiler to: (1) ignore the checking of abnormal input floating-point values, such as not a number or an infinite value, and (2) perform unsafe optimizations which would reduce the accuracy of the computed data, which might violate the IEEE-754/OpenCL standard.

While turning on this flag would increase the risk of abnormal floating-point calculations, error checking mechanisms and standard conformation are often obstacles of performance optimization. We do observe the performance benefit delivered by the optimization. During our code restructuring stage, we carefully examine the MCML code and the outcomes of the floating-point computations to avoid unexpected errors. The validation of the MCML output data is omitted in this paper due to page length limitation.

4. EXPERIMENTAL RESULTS

We have converted the MCML program into the OpenCL versions with the optimizations, and evaluates the efficiency of the OpenCL versions across the three hardware platforms whose specifications are listed in Table 1[5]. Six versions of the converted MCML program are evaluated: *Batch* refers to the OpenCL version described in Section 3.1, and the rest of the optimizations, *Buffering* in Section 3.2, *Branching* in Section 3.3, *Caching* in Section 3.4, *Sectioning* in Section 3.5, and *Fast Math* in Section 3.6, are accumulated optimizations, i.e., the impact of each optimization is added to that of the preceding ones. All the experiments were performed with the properties listed in Table 2 that are identical to the previous work [9] for the comparisons in the following subsections. In the following sections, we present the performance results achieved by the CPU, GPU, and

---

[5]The Intel processor operating at 2.66 GHz runs the operating system with four physical cores, hyper-threading technology, and 32 GB main memory. The NVIDIA GPU, which has 192 cores operating at 1.5 GHz, and the Altera Stratix V 5SGXEA7 FPGA card are attached to the computer via the Peripheral Component Interconnect Express (PCIe) 2.0 x16 slots, respectively.

FPGA in Section 4.1, and the efficiency of the three computing elements in terms of program execution time and power consumption is further discussed in Section 4.2. Finally, the comparison of programming efforts and performance enhancement between our work and the previous studies on the MCML program acceleration [9, 10, 1] is presented in Section 4.3.

4.1 Overall Performance Results

As shown in Figure 5(a), 5(b), and 5(c), *Buffering* and *Sectioning* optimizations contribute to the performance boost significantly across the tested hardware platforms. *Buffering* performs better than *Batch* by merging the potential consecutive photon steps together, so the records of the steps are written to the same buffering data structure whenever necessary, which decreases the number of the data writes to the main memory. On the other hand, by synchronizing the working threads at the pre-determined steps, e.g., thirty steps for GPU, *Sectioning* improves the resource utilization and performs significantly better than *Caching*. As synchronization interval is workload- (the tissue model) and platform-dependent parameter, we profiled the sequential MCML program with the configuration in Table 2 and chose the better configurations for CPU, GPU and FPGA. Overall, up to 14x, 64x, and 21x speedup are achieved against the sequential MCML version by the multicore CPU, GPU, and FPGA, respectively.

4.2 Performance and Energy Efficiency

We compare the performance and power efficiency of the fastest OpenCL version, *FastMath*, on the multicore CPU, GPU, and FPGA. The sequential version is served as the baseline configuration, denoted as *Core i7 (Seq. MCML)*. The power meter is used to estimate the power consumed by each of the computing engines.

We use *Photons per Joule* to give a rough estimate of the efficiency of the three hardware[6]. Table 3 summarizes execution time, power consumption, and processed photons per Joule of the CPU, GPU, and FPGA.. Obviously, the FPGA is the most energy efficient solution among the evaluated hardware platforms, and the GPU offers the fastest simulation. In particular, the FPGA consumes 7.3x less power than the GPU at a cost of being 3x slower than the GPU. Ideally, using multiple or bigger FPGA chips, the FPGA solution can offer similar performance with less power consumption, since the hardware synthesized from our OpenCL code occupies 60% of the resources on the chip.

4.3 Platform-Oblivious vs. Platform-Specific Approaches

Our work is compared with the previous works [9, 10, 1] to measure the tradeoffs between the OpenCL scheme, and the CUDA and Verilog schemes. Figure 6 illustrates the development time for the three programming schemes. As expected, programming with the higher-level API is faster than with the lower-level schemes. The efficiency of the developed simulations is discussed in the following paragraphs.

---

[6]While the Monte Carlo-based simulation has the non-deterministic nature, which implies that the computation power required to simulate a photon's life cycle varies from one run to

Table 1. Experiment environment.

Accelerator	Process (nm)	Memory bandwidth (GB/s)	Last level cache	Board power (W)	OpenCL SDK	Operating system
Intel Core i7-920	45	25.6	8 MB	130	Intel OpenCL 14.2	CentOS 6.5,
NVIDIA GTS 450	40	57.7	256 KB	106	CUDA Toolkit 3.2	kernel 2.6.32-431,
Altera Stratix V	28	25.6	None	25	Altera OpenCL 14.1	gcc/g++ 4.4.7

Table 2. Properties of the five-layer skin tissue at 633nm [16].

Layer	Absorption coefficient (cm^{-1})	Scattering co-efficient (cm^{-1})	Anisotropy factor	Refractive index	Thickness
1st epidermis (top)	4.3	107	0.79	1.5	0.01
2nd dermis	2.7	187	0.82	1.4	0.02
3rd dermis plexus superficialis	3.3	192	0.82	1.4	0.02
4th dermis	2.7	187	0.82	1.4	0.09
5th dermis plexus profundus	3.4	194	0.82	1.4	0.06

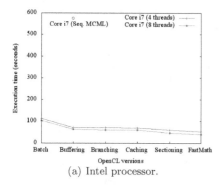

(a) Intel processor.

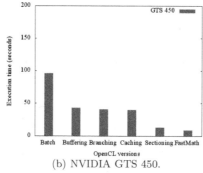

(b) NVIDIA GTS 450.

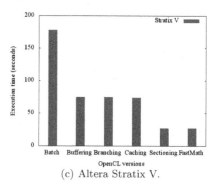

(c) Altera Stratix V.

Figure 5. Execution time of the sequential and parallelized OpenCL programs.

Table 3. Efficiency of the three computing engines.

	Time (s)	Power (W)	Photons/Joule
Core i7 (Seq. MCML)	577	20	867
Core i7 (4 threads)	52	70	2,747
Core i7 (8 threads)	40	110	2,247
GTS 450	9	95	11,103
Stratix V	27	13	28,490

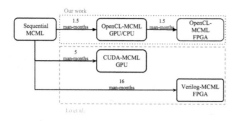

Figure 6. MCML development time w/ OpenCL, CUDA and Verilog.

OpenCL vs. CUDA. We tested the CUDA version of the MCML program [9, 1] on our environment using the same toolchain and configurations, e.g., the hardware platform shown in Table 1, the compilation flags, and the parameters listed in Table 2. Table 5 compares the MCML development and simulation time on the GTS 450.

While OpenCL saves programming efforts across computing platforms by offering the standard API's, it still takes

another, the averaged number, *Photons per Joule*, would still give an idea of the efficiency of the accelerators.

time for programmers to develop architectural specific optimizations to release the computing power of the underlying hardware. The 4.5x performance gap between our work and the CUDA-based MCML, GPUMCML [9, 1], could result from: (1) the different optimizations implemented as listed in Table 4, (2) the differences between the implementation of the underlying OpenCL and CUDA libraries for the GPU, and (3) the different execution models between the two works, which are summarized below.

While a copy of the entire photon information, such as absorption array, is kept in the GPU device memory and accessed by the GPU threads atomically, GPUMCML selectively caches the data with high access rate in the GPU local memory to avoid the contention caused by massive concurrent atomic operations. On the contrary, *Batch* execution model uses the system memory to keep the photon information, device memory for per-thread data, and local memory for buffering temporary data, which avoids the atomic operations. At each synchronization point, the host thread updates the photon status in system memory by referencing the outcomes kept in the thread-private memory regions in the device memory.

As the OpenCL programs will be run on different hardware platforms, we have to judiciously choose the execution model which would deliver the better performance results across platforms. We studied the characteristics of the hardware platforms and evaluated the tradeoffs between the high-level design alternatives. We found that atomic functions are expensive operations on the FPGA boards [2]. Furthermore, if GPUMCML's approach was adopted, the per-

Table 4. Comparison of the optimizations done in our work and Lo et al. [9, 1]

	Batch	Buffering	Branching	Caching	Sectioning	FastMath	Local memory	Atomic operation
Our work	√	√	√	√	√	√		
Lo et al. [9, 1]		√	√	√			√	√

formance of the FPGA board will be limited by the on-board bus frequency due to the bus contention under concurrent accesses. Hence, we chose the *Batch* model for the MCML simulation.

Table 5. Performance and development efforts on GTS 450.

Programming scheme	Exec. time (Seconds)	Dev. time (Months)
OpenCL (Our work)	9	1.5 (1 programmer)
CUDA (Lo et al. [9, 1])	2	2.5 (1-2 programmers)

OpenCL vs. Verilog. We use the FPGA performance data reported by Lo et al. [10, 8] to give a rough estimate of the trade-offs since it is difficult to reproduce their simulation environment without their Verilog source. It is interesting to note that Lo et al. spent a lot of efforts to optimize the Verilog code, i.e., adopting fixed-point point data representation to save the resource utilization, using lookup tables to cache frequent use data, and pipelining the photon simulation to improve parallelism. In particular, they reported to use one hundred of pipeline stages in their design. It took about 16 man-months for the team to develop the platform-specific design.

On the other hand, it took us about 3 man-months from the sequential MCML program to the OpenCL version for FPGA, where several optimizations have also been implemented with less than one fifth of the man-months required by the previous work. As shown in Table 6, the 22% difference of the photon processing rate is very encouraging result, given relatively less resources that we used for the code development. The performance differences would be attribute to the advances in both hardware and software, (1) Altera Stratix III vs. Stratix V, and (2) the toolchains for the hardware platforms.

Table 6. Performance and development efforts for FPGA.

Programming scheme	Processed photons per second	Dev. time (Months)
OpenCL (Our work)	370.3K	3 (1 programmer)
Verilog (Lo et al. [10])	454.5K	4 (2-4 programmers)

5. CONCLUSION

In this paper, we parallelized the sequential MCML program with OpenCL, and several platform-oblivious optimizations have been implemented for the parallel code. We achieve up to 21x and 64x speedups with FPGA and GPU respectively against the sequential version. While the GPU version is faster than the FPGA version, the latter consumes 7.3x less power than the former. Our approach also effectively leads us to trade performance for the short development time, higher software portability and simpler software

maintenance. We believe that such an agile application development and deployment path is desirable as GPU and FPGA both become increasingly popular in the future.

References

[1] E. Alerstam, W. C. Yip Lo, T. D. Han, J. Rose, S. Andersson-Engels, and L. Lilge. Next-generation acceleration and code optimization for light transport in turbid media using gpus. *Biomedical optics express*, 1(2):658–675, 2010.

[2] Altera. Altera SDK for OpenCL Programming Guide. https://www.altera.com/content/dam/altera-www/global/en_US/pdfs/literature/hb/opencl-sdk/aocl_programming_guide.pdf.

[3] AMD. OpenCL. http://developer.amd.com/tools-and-sdks/opencl-zone/amd-accelerated-parallel-processing-app-sdk/opencl-optimization-guide/.

[4] J. Cassidy, L. Lilge, and V. Betz. Fast, Power-Efficient Biophotonic Simulations for Cancer Treatment Using FPGAs. In *2014 IEEE 22nd Annual International Symposium on Field-Programmable Custom Computing Machines (FCCM)*, pages 133–140, 2014.

[5] T. D. Han and T. S. Abdelrahman. Reducing branch divergence in gpu programs. In *Proceedings of the Fourth Workshop on General Purpose Processing on Graphics Processing Units*, 2011.

[6] Y. Kawai and T. Iwai. Hybrid mie-mcml monte carlo simulation of light propagation in skin layers. In *International Conference on Optical Particle Characterization (OPC 2014)*, pages 923206–923209, 2014.

[7] H. Li, J. Tian, F. Zhu, W. Cong, L. V. Wang, E. A. Hoffman, and G. Wang. A mouse optical simulation environment (MOSE) to investigate bioluminescent phenomena in the living mouse with the monte carlo method. *Academic Radiology*, 11(9):1029–1038, 2004.

[8] W. C. Y. Lo. Hardware acceleration of a monte carlo simulation for photodynamic therapy treatment planning. Master's thesis, University of Toronto, Toronto, Canada, 2009.

[9] W. C. Y. Lo, T. D. Han, J. Rose, and L. Lilge. GPU-accelerated Monte Carlo simulation for photodynamic therapy treatment planning. In *European Conferences on Biomedical Optics*, pages 737313–737324, 2009.

[10] W. C. Y. Lo, K. Redmond, J. Luu, P. Chow, J. Rose, and L. Lilge. Hardware acceleration of a Monte Carlo simulation for photodynamic therapy treatment planning. *Journal of biomedical optics*, 14(1):014019–014019, 2009.

[11] Nvidia. OpenCL. http://www.nvidia.com/content/cudazone/CUDABrowser/downloads/papers/NVIDIA_OpenCL_BestPracticesGuide.pdf.

[12] N. Ren, J. Liang, X. Qu, J. Li, B. Lu, and J. Tian. Gpu-based monte carlo simulation for light propagation in complex heterogeneous tissues. *Optics express*, 18(7):6811–6823, 2010.

[13] A. Shahzad, C. M. Tyng, N. Saad, N. Walter, A. S. Malik, and F. Meriaudeau. Subcutaneous veins depth estimation method using Monte Carlo simulations. In *Instrumentation and Measurement Technology Conference (I2MTC), 2015 IEEE International*, pages 376–380, 2015.

[14] H. Shen and G. Wang. A study on tetrahedron-based inhomogeneous Monte Carlo optical simulation. *Biomedical Optics Express*, 2(1):44–57, 2010.

[15] M.-Y. Tsai and S.-H. Hung. Hardware acceleration for proton beam Monte Carlo simulation. In *Proceedings of the 2013 Research in Adaptive and Convergent Systems*, pages 495–496, 2013.

[16] V. V. Tuchin. Light scattering study of tissues. *Physics-Uspekhi*, 40(5):495, 1997.

[17] L. Wang, S. L. Jacques, and L. Zheng. MCML - Monte Carlo modeling of light transport in multi-layered tissues. *Computer methods and programs in biomedicine*, 47(2):131–146, 1995.

[18] B. Zhou, X. S. Hu, D. Z. Chen, and C. X. Yu. Accelerating radiation dose calculation: A multi-FPGA solution. *ACM Trans. Embed. Comput. Syst.*, 13(1s):33:1–33:25, 2013.

A Case for Work-stealing on FPGAs with OpenCL Atomics

Nadesh Ramanathan
Imperial College London, UK
n.ramanathan14@imperial.ac.uk

John Wickerson
Imperial College London, UK
j.wickerson@imperial.ac.uk

Felix Winterstein
Imperial College London, UK
f.winterstein12@imperial.ac.uk

George A. Constantinides
Imperial College London, UK
g.constantinides@imperial.ac.uk

ABSTRACT

We provide a case study of *work-stealing*, a popular method for run-time load balancing, on FPGAs. Following the Cederman–Tsigas implementation for GPUs, we synchronize work-items not with locks, mutexes or critical sections, but instead with the atomic operations provided by Altera's OpenCL SDK. We evaluate work-stealing for FPGAs by synthesizing a K-means clustering algorithm on an Altera P385 D5 board, both with work-stealing and with a statically-partitioned load. When block RAM utilization is maximized in both cases, we find that work-stealing leads to a 1.5× speedup. This demonstrates that the ability to do load balancing at run-time can outweigh the drawback of using 'expensive' atomics on FPGAs. We hope that our case study will stimulate further research into the high-level synthesis of fine-grained, lock-free, concurrent programs.

Keywords

atomic operations, high-level synthesis, K-means clustering, load balancing, lock-free synchronization, parallelism.

1. INTRODUCTION

The central task for high-level synthesis (HLS) tools is mapping the computation and data accesses described by the source program into the FPGA's execution and memory hierarchies. Some computations can be straightforwardly divided among parallel execution units on the FPGA, but it is often the case that partitioning statically (*i.e.*, at compile-time) either is infeasible or leads to inefficient circuits. In this paper, we explore a different approach that involves balancing dynamically (*i.e.*, at run-time) the computational workload across execution units.

Our approach is based on *work-stealing*, a popular paradigm for programming those algorithms that can be phrased in terms of many small tasks, and that have at least one of the following characteristics: 1) data-dependent task execution time, and 2) dynamic sub-task creation. Each parallel

FPGA'16, February 21-23, 2016, Monterey, CA, USA

© 2016 ACM. ISBN 978-1-4503-3856-1/16/02... $15.00

DOI: http://dx.doi.org/10.1145/2847263.2847343

execution unit ('work-item') maintains its own task queue, but can steal from another's queue should its own become empty. We present an implementation of work-stealing that builds on an implementation for GPUs, by Cederman and Tsigas [5], of an algorithm due to Arora *et al.* [3]. It is written in OpenCL (a multi-threaded extension of C for programming heterogeneous systems of CPUs, GPUs, and FPGAs [13]) and automatically compiled to hardware using Altera's software development kit for OpenCL (AOCL) [2]. We describe how we have optimized the OpenCL code for performance and compatibility with the restrictions imposed by AOCL.

Our work-stealing implementation is particularly novel in an FPGA context because we avoid the use of locks and barriers, and rely instead on OpenCL's *atomic operations* (atomics) to synchronize threads. Atomics enable fine-grained concurrency whereby threads can execute without blocking other threads. Although atomics have recently been demonstrated empirically to be the fastest synchronization method for conventional multiprocessors [8], their support on FPGAs is lacking. AOCL supports them for 32-bit integers, but discourages their use, warning that they are 'expensive to implement on FPGAs' and 'might decrease kernel performance or require a large amount of hardware' [1], while Xilinx's OpenCL tool, SDAccel [21], does not support them at all. In this work, we demonstrate that despite these misgivings, atomics can in fact be usefully employed on FPGAs to give overall application speedup.

In our case study, we apply our work-stealing implementation to a K-means clustering (KMC) algorithm [11] with data-dependent task execution time and dynamic sub-task creation. On an Altera P385 D5 board, we compare the performance (a) when the workload is statically determined at compile-time, and (b) when work-stealing is enabled. In both cases, we synthesize sufficiently many work-items to maximize block RAM (BRAM) utilization. We show that our use of dynamic data partitioning for KMC yields a 1.5× overall speedup over an earlier implementation by Winterstein *et al.*, which was already optimized for FPGAs but which relied on static data partitioning [20]. We also show best-case speedup of 1.9× when the number of work-items is fixed. We encourage readers to view our codebase at https://github.com/nadeshr/kmeans-stealing.git.

2. MOTIVATING EXAMPLE

Consider a program that traverses, depth first, binary trees with integer-valued nodes with the help of a stack from/to which pointers to sub-trees yet to be traversed can be popped/pushed. The TRAVERSE program, shown in Algorithm 1, represents a very common class of software programs, yet most HLS tools cannot synthesize it efficiently. Here, POP updates the tree pointer that it is passed by reference, and it returns a Boolean encoding whether the operation succeeded. Each tree node comprises some data (d) and pointers to left and right sub-trees (l and r).

Algorithm 1 Tree traversal

1: **procedure** TRAVERSE(tree* t)
2:    stack $s \leftarrow$ **new** stack
3:    s.PUSH(t)
4:    **while** s.POP($\&t$) **do**
5:        **if** t=NULL **continue**
6:        PROCESS(t->d)
7:        s.PUSH(t->r)
8:        s.PUSH(t->l)
9:    **end while**
10: **end procedure**

The first serious attempt to automatically synthesize FPGA implementations of programs like TRAVERSE was made by Winterstein *et al.* [20]. Under the assumption that the order in which tree nodes are PROCESS'd is immaterial, they divide the tree, at a fixed distance from the root, into a small number (say, P) of disjoint sub-trees that can be traversed in parallel. Applied to our TRAVERSE example, their transformation with $P = 2$ would yield Algorithm 2, in which the vertical line separates parallel threads. The chief shortcoming of their approach is that the static distribution of the workload is optimal only in the case that the input tree is perfectly balanced.

Algorithm 2 Parallel tree traversal (static partitioning)

1: **procedure** TRAVERSE2(tree* t)
2:    **if** t=NULL **return**
3:    PROCESS(t->d)
4:    stack $s_0 \leftarrow$ **new** stack   stack $s_1 \leftarrow$ **new** stack
5:    s_0.PUSH(t->r) s_1.PUSH(t->l)
6:    tree* t_0 tree* t_1
7:    **while** s_0.POP($\&t_0$) **do**   **while** s_1.POP($\&t_1$) **do**
8:        **if** t_0=NULL **continue**   **if** t_1=NULL **continue**
9:        PROCESS(t_0->d)   PROCESS(t_1->d)
10:        s_0.PUSH(t_0->r) s_1.PUSH(t_1->r)
11:        s_0.PUSH(t_0->l) s_1.PUSH(t_1->l)
12:    **end while**   **end while**
13: **end procedure**

In this paper, we present an alternative approach to implementing TRAVERSE-like programs, in which the workload is dynamically distributed at run-time via work-stealing. This overcomes the potential unpredictabilities caused by suboptimal partitioning, data-dependent task execution time, and dynamic sub-task creation. When applied to our TRAVERSE example, again setting $P = 2$, we obtain Algorithm 3. Our approach replaces the stacks with double-ended queues (deques) to enable stealing. Each thread seeks to get work by popping from the local deque ($q[0]$ or $q[1]$), or stealing from the other deque ($q[1]$ or $q[0]$) if popping fails. This implementation uses a *done* array of Boolean flags to ascertain when there is no remaining work in any deque.

Algorithm 3 Parallel tree traversal (dynamic partitioning)

1: **procedure** TRAVERSE3(tree* t)
2:    deque $q[2] = \{$**new** deque, **new** deque$\}$
3:    bool $done[2] = \{0, 0\}$
4:    **while** $done \neq \{1, 1\}$ **do**   **while** $done \neq \{1, 1\}$ **do**
5:        tree* t_0 tree* t_1
6:        $done[0] \leftarrow q[0]$.POP(t) $done[1] \leftarrow q[1]$.POP(t)
7:            $\| q[1]$.STEAL(t) $\| q[0]$.STEAL(t)
8:        **if** t_0=NULL **continue**   **if** t_1=NULL **continue**
9:        PROCESS(t_0->d)   PROCESS(t_1->d)
10:        $q[0]$.PUSH(t_0->r) $q[1]$.PUSH(t_1->r)
11:        $q[0]$.PUSH(t_0->l) $q[1]$.PUSH(t_1->l)
12:    **end while**   **end while**
13: **end procedure**

---

3. DESIGNING THE BASELINE

This section introduces a K-means clustering algorithm, explains why it stands to benefit from work-stealing, and describes how we produced an OpenCL implementation to serve as a baseline for our case study.

K-means clustering (KMC) refers to the problem of partitioning a set of D-dimensional points $X = \{x_1, \ldots, x_N\}$ into a set of clusters $\mathcal{S} = \{S_1, \ldots, S_K\}$ where K is provided as a parameter. A cluster S_i is represented by the geometrical center μ_i of its points. The goal is to assign each point in X to the cluster with the nearest center. In this paper, we consider an efficient algorithm for KMC [11] that uses a *kd-tree* data structure instead of working directly on the point set X. The algorithm begins by choosing a random initial center-set, say $M_0 = \{\mu_1, \ldots, \mu_K\}$. The set $\mathcal{S}$ is iteratively refined until it no longer changes.

In order to assess the potential of work-stealing on the KMC algorithm, we need a baseline OpenCL design for comparison. OpenCL applications are divided into host code that runs on a CPU, and kernel code that runs on an accelerator device (an FPGA in our case). In our application, the host code builds the input tree and partitions it into P sub-trees, each processed by one of P independent work items. Algorithm 4 shows our OpenCL kernel for the KMC algorithm, following Winterstein *et al.*'s implementation in C that was optimized for Vivado HLS [20]. We also provide a graphical representation of the kernel in Figure 2a. The inputs of the KMC kernel are an array of sub-trees t and a center-set M. The kernel uses a heap h that holds the temporary candidate center-sets, a stack whose entries consist of a tree pointer and a heap pointer, and a shared array of center-sets Ms whose elements are reduced to the final center-set result (line 16) after all **while** loops terminate. This result can be then passed to future kernel iterations.

This kernel exhibits some of the features seen in Algorithm 1 that make it a good candidate for acceleration with work-stealing: the processing time of each tree node (line 10) depends on the center-set data, and the decision to traverse a node's children is also data-dependent (line 11 and 12). The effectiveness of parallelization depends on the balancedness of the number of nodes in each sub-tree, which depends on the input data set [20]. It is also known that the heuristics used to generate the *kd-tree* are not optimal [11], which means that even in the best-case the tree is not guaranteed to be perfectly balanced.

Algorithm 4 OpenCL Baseline KMC algorithm

1: **attribute**(REQD_WORK_GROUP_SIZE(P,1,1))
2: **kernel** KMC1(**global** tree *$t[P]$, **local** centerset *M)
3:    **local** stack[P] s
4:    **global** heap[P] h
5:    **local** centerset[P] Ms
6:    $i \leftarrow$ GET_LOCAL_ID(0)
7:    $Ms[i] \leftarrow M$
8:    $s[i]$.PUSH($t[i]$, $h[i]$)
9:    **while** $s[i]$.POP(&$t[i]$, &$h[i]$) **do**
10:      **if** PROCESS($t[i]$, &$h[i]$, &$Ms[i]$) **then**
11:         $s[i]$.PUSH($t[i]$->r, $h[i]$)
12:         $s[i]$.PUSH($t[i]$->l, $h[i]$)
13:      **end if**
14:    **end while**
15:    **barrier**
16:    **if** $i = 0$ **then** $M \leftarrow$ REDUCE(Ms)
17: **end kernel**

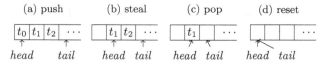

Figure 1: Deque Chronological Sample Execution.

in a fine-grained manner, because multiple work-items can attempt an `atomic_cmpxchg` operation at the same time but only one will succeed. This policy is non-blocking and guarantees that at least one work-item makes progress.

Algorithm 5 presents the KMC algorithm with work-stealing and Figure 2b provides a graphical representation. Compared to the baseline (Algorithm 4), a key change is that the stacks have become deques. We also replaced the POP function with the GET function (line 11), which updates $t[i]$ and $h[i]$ if successful. GET first attempts to pop from the local deque $q[i]$, and then steals from the next deque $q[sid]$ if popping fails. *sid* initially refers to the immediately-following deque, but is updated in a round-robin style if stealing fails. We use a Boolean field *finish* in the deque to keep track of the system's workload: if GET fails to obtain work (line 12), then the work-item is deemed to have finished. When all work-items have finished (line 10), the loop terminates since there is no possibility of new tasks being pushed.

Algorithm 5 OpenCL Work-stealing KMC algorithm

1: **attribute**(REQD_WORK_GROUP_SIZE(P,1,1))
2: **kernel** KMC2(**global** tree *$t[P]$, **local** centerset *M)
3:    **local** deque[P] q
4:    **global** heap[P] h
5:    **local** centerset[P] Ms
6:    $i \leftarrow$ GET_LOCAL_ID(0)
7:    $sid \leftarrow (i+1) \mod P$
8:    $Ms[i] \leftarrow M$
9:    $q[i]$.PUSH($t[i]$, $h[i]$)
10:    **while** $\neg(q[0].finish$ && $\ldots$ && $q[P-1].finish)$ **do**
11:      $success \leftarrow$ GET(&$t[i]$, &$h[i]$, q, i, &sid)
12:      $q[i].finish \leftarrow \neg success$
13:      **if** $success$ **then**
14:         **if** PROCESS($t[i]$, &$h[i]$, &$Ms[i]$) **then**
15:             $q[i]$.PUSH($t[i]$->r, $h[i]$)
16:             $q[i]$.PUSH($t[i]$->l, $h[i]$)
17:         **end if**
18:      **end if**
19:    **end while**
20:    **barrier**
21:    **if** $i = 0$ **then** $M \leftarrow$ REDUCE(Ms)
22: **end kernel**

We found that OpenCL's explicit parallelism simplified our design entry considerably. Where the original C design was a sequential program annotated with special HLS directives to eliminate inferred dependencies between parallel execution units, our OpenCL design could simply define each work-item with a piece of sequential code.

In order to efficiently implement our OpenCL kernel for FPGAs, we need to consider restrictions imposed by AOCL. Firstly, we used OpenCL's `reqd_work_group_size` attribute to ensure that AOCL synthesize only the required number of work-items [1]. Secondly, we have to consider the size of arrays when deciding whether they should be declared in OpenCL private, local or global memory. AOCL implements private memory as registers, local memory as BRAMs, and global memory as DDR memory [2]. Although some arrays could technically be declared private, we actually declare them as local or global memory to save FPGA resources. Based on the size constraints presented by Winterstein *et al.*, we declare the stacks and center-sets in local memory, and the heaps and sub-trees in global memory.

4. ADDING WORK-STEALING

We now describe how we use work-stealing, which we have implemented using OpenCL's atomics, to add dynamic load balancing to the KMC algorithm.

Our implementation of work-stealing follows Cederman and Tsigas [5], who give an implementation for GPUs of an algorithm due to Arora et al. [3]. The implementation is based around a collection of double-ended queues (deques), one per OpenCL work-item in this work. A deque comprises *head* and *tail* pointers to opposite ends of a task array. Each deque provides three main operations: push, pop and steal. Each OpenCL work-item owns a deque to which it has exclusive push and pop access via the *tail* pointer, as seen in Figure 1a and 1c. Since only one work-item can push or pop a deque, the *tail* accesses can be non-atomic. On the other hand, all work-items can steal tasks from any non-empty deque via the *head* pointer (as seen in Figure 1b). Since any work-item can update the *head* pointer, access to the *head* must be atomic (specifically, via OpenCL's `atomic_cmpxchg` function [13]) to eliminate data races. The use of atomics during stealing arbitrates access to the deque

We use a single OpenCL work-group with P work-items to allow our workload to be shared across all work-items. This way, we can characterize the benefits of work-stealing *on-chip* since otherwise work-stealing among multiple work-groups would have to be performed on off-chip global memory.

In adding work-stealing to our design, we expect some resource overhead and clock frequency penalty due to atomics [1]. Figure 2 highlights a further architectural overhead caused by work-stealing. In work-stealing, all the deques,

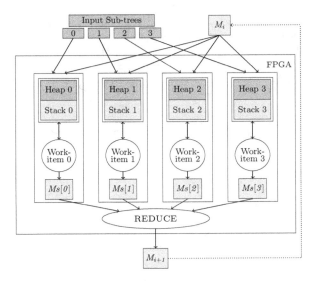

(a) Baseline implementation

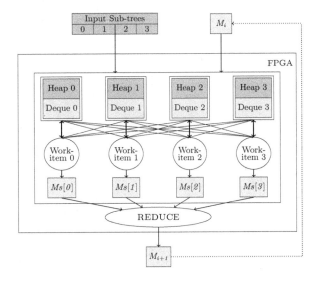

(b) Work-stealing implementation

Figure 2: KMC algorithm for $P = 4$ (dark gray is global memory and light gray is local memory).

heaps and sub-trees are shared between all work-items (as suggested by the crossbar in Figure 2b), where in the baseline these were private to each work-item. Although we introduce sharing in work-stealing, the cycle times of these shared data structures remain comparable since we already have to synthesize larger arrays in OpenCL local or global memory for the baseline.

In addition, we noticed that AOCL replicates local data structures that are accessed many times in a kernel [1]. This replication policy penalizes large structures, since a structure is accessed every time one of its fields is accessed, so we split such structures into individual fields wherever possible. We further reduce the replication effect by manually partitioning the task arrays.

5. EVALUATION

This section evaluates how effectively work-stealing balances the processing load across work-items in the KMC algorithm (Section 5.1). We also evaluate the effect of work-stealing on wall-clock time (Section 5.2) and resource consumption (Section 5.3). We used AOCL (version 15.0.0) for HLS and Quartus (version 15.0.0) for RTL synthesis. All results are taken from fully placed-and-routed designs running on a Nallatech P385 D5 board that includes an Altera Stratix V D5 FPGA and 8GB DDR3 memory.

Our goal is to have as many work-items within a single OpenCL work-group as resource utilization on the FPGA permits. At full capacity of the FPGA, we are able to synthesize 64 work-items for our baseline implementation and 32 work-items for our work-stealing implementation.

The inputs to the KMC algorithm are a tree built from 2^{20} data-points and a 128-element center-set. Each stack and deque holds 128 elements. We run the KMC algorithm for 16 iterations.

5.1 Load Balancing

The goal of our work-stealing approach is to minimize the variation in workload across OpenCL work-items, regardless of the shape of the input tree, to avoid situations where

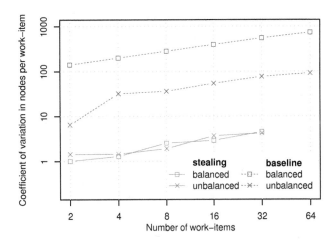

Figure 3: Processing load variation over work items.

the entire kernel has to wait for a single, heavily loaded work-item to complete. The processing load of the KMC algorithm is proportional to the aggregate number of *node-center-pairs*, *i.e.* the cumulative number of candidate centers processed at the visited tree nodes to compute the clustering result. This number depends on the initial choice of centers and, more importantly, on the shape of the input tree. The host code uses heuristics to produce trees that are *fairly balanced*. To push our implementations to their extremes, we also compare with trees that are *perfectly unbalanced*, i.e. trees whose nodes form a single chain with no branching.

Fig. 3 quantifies the variation in the processing load across work-items for each P. It uses the *coefficient of variation*, which is the standard deviation divided by the mean. We make two observations about this graph. Firstly, the variations for the work-stealing cases are much smaller than either of the baseline cases. Work-stealing is able to improve even the best-case input tree because the routine that builds the

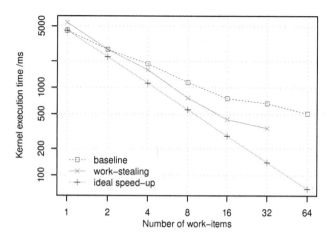

Figure 4: Kernel execution time for the filtering algorithm.

Table 1: Relative resource overhead and relative clock rate penalty due to the work-stealing implementation (negative values indicate increase in clock frequency).

P	1	2	4	8	16	32
Logic overhead	15%	2%	4%	6%	6%	8%
RAM overhead	57%	45%	68%	58%	58%	39%
Clock penalty	10%	1%	16%	7%	0%	−1%
Speedup	0.8×	1.0×	1.2×	1.5×	1.7×	1.9×

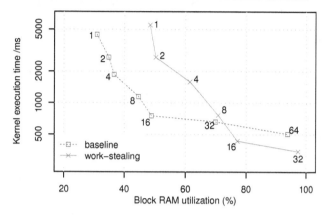

Figure 5: BRAM utilization vs. kernel execution time, for various values of P

tree does not guarantee perfect balance and and the decision to recurse on the children of a node, which in turn spawns more subtasks, is data-dependent. Secondly, work-stealing is immune to the shape of the tree and produce very similar workload variations in both scenarios.

5.2 Execution time

Next, we demonstrate the effect of load balancing on the overall kernel execution time (wall-clock time). The timing results are obtained from the number of clock cycles divided by the minimum achievable clock frequency. The achievable clock frequencies range from 237 MHz ($P = 1$) to 163 MHz ($P = 64$) for the baseline, and from 214 MHz ($P = 1$) to 201 MHz ($P = 32$) with an outlier of 184 MHz at $P = 4$ for the work-stealing implementation.

Fig. 4 shows the kernel execution time (excluding host pre-processing) for both implementations in logarithmic scale with respect to P. We also include the theoretically achievable speed-up, which we obtain by dividing the single work-item baseline by P, to give an indicate to how these implementations could scale. At $P = 1$ in Figure 4, work-stealing performs worse than the baseline implementation because it lowers the clock frequency, as seen in Table 1, and is not applicable to a single work-item. From $P = 4$ onwards, work-stealing is closer to the ideal speed-up trend. The speed-ups for fixed P are shown in the last row of Table 1. At full BRAM capacity on the FPGA, work-stealing achieves an overall speed-up of 1.5× over the baseline. This comparison is made between $P = 64$ for the baseline and $P = 32$ for the work-stealing implementation, showing that the load-balanced version only requires half the number of work-items to achieve better performance.

5.3 Resources

The acceleration gained from load balancing comes at the cost of additional FPGA resources. The total logic utilization (as reported by Quartus II Fitter) for both implementations varies between 47% and 57%. The utilization of DSP blocks is below 3% and remains the same for both the baseline and work-stealing implementations. Table 1 quantifies the resource overheads of work-stealing relative to the baseline for each P in terms of logic utilization, BRAM and clock frequency degradation. Ultimately, BRAM is the resource that limits the scaling of P that is synthesizable for the

FPGA. The work-stealing implementations requires 350 to 550 additional BRAMs for the same P. The BRAM overhead is due to the replication performed by AOCL as discussed in Section 4, which limits work-stealing to $P = 32$ work-items and the baseline to $P = 64$.

Fig. 5 compares the BRAM-time graphs of both implementations. The break-even point occurs at 1500 BRAMs. The work-stealing implementation provides enough speed-up such that, despite its BRAM overhead, it becomes more efficient in terms of BRAM-time product beyond this point. For the two end-points of the BRAM-time graphs ($P = 64$ for the baseline, $P = 32$ for work-stealing), we spend 3.6% more BRAMs (5.6% more logic utilization, no DSP blocks overhead) for a 1.5× improvement of execution time.

6. RELATED WORK

Several authors have investigated the capabilities of OpenCL for FPGAs [6, 14, 16, 10, 17], but their focus has been on highly-uniform, FPGA-friendly benchmarks such as vector addition and matrix multiplication.

Wang *et al.* have studied the problem of data partitioning within an FPGA, but consider only static partitioning [19]; in our work we move towards dynamic partitioning. Wang *et al.*'s work provides the only other case study of OpenCL's atomics of which we are aware; they use atomics to implement locks where we use them in lock-free context. They report that atomics are 'expensive' and that their use is a 'disadvantage'. While our work does not contradict their claims in general, it does provide evidence that atomics can play a vital role in highly-efficient FPGA implementations.

Principles of work-stealing appear in Kestur *et al.*'s FPGA implementation of matrix–vector multiplication [12], but their design is at the register transfer level (RTL). We believe our work to be the first FPGA work-stealing implementation programmed in a high-level language, in the form of OpenCL. Similarly, Nahill *et al.* have investigated implementing non-blocking synchronization on FPGAs [18], but they also work at the RTL level.

The compilation of parallel software threads to hardware has been studied in the context of the Kiwi [9] and LegUp [4] HLS tools, and George *et al.* have looked into mapping parallel computation patterns, such `map`, `reduce`, `zipWith` and `foreach`, into efficient hardware models for FPGAs [7]. All of these tools are limited to lock-based concurrency; our work explores the lock-free case.

Finally, Kumar *et al.* have devised a task-based parallel programming model that involves work-stealing between CPUs and digital signal processors (DSPs) [15]. Our work, on the other hand, implements work-stealing within a single FPGA device.

7. CONCLUSION

We have demonstrated an effective use case of the OpenCL programming language's explicit parallelism constructs to achieve an implementation of work-stealing on FPGAs. Our work is particularly interesting because we are able to describe a work-stealing implementation in a lock-free manner using a state-of-the-art HLS tool (AOCL). Lock-freedom properties require concurrent programs to be non-blocking and synchronized in a fine-grained manner using atomics. Atomics have been deemed 'expensive' in terms of performance and resources by the Altera OpenCL Programming Guide [1]. However, we show an overall speedup $1.5\times$ for the KMC algorithm that incorporates work-stealing (using atomics) to perform dynamic load balancing, compared to a baseline with static partitioning. Our work thereby provides demonstrates that the dynamic load-balancing advantages of work-stealing far outweigh the performance and resource overhead penalties that atomics introduce.

Acknowledgements. We thank David Thomas, Gordon Inggs and our reviewers for their feedback and encouragement. The support of the EPSRC Centre for Doctoral Training in High Performance Embedded and Distributed Systems (HiPEDS, Grant Reference EP/L016796/1) and grants EP/I020357/1 and EP/K015168/1, the Royal Academy of Engineering and Imagination Technologies is gratefully acknowledged.

8. REFERENCES

[1] Altera. *Altera SDK for OpenCL - Best Practices Guide.* OCL003-14.1.0, 2014.

[2] Altera. *Altera SDK for OpenCL - Programming Guide.* OCL002-14.1.0, 2014.

[3] N. S. Arora, R. D. Blumofe, and C. G. Plaxton. Thread scheduling for multiprogrammed multiprocessors. In *SPAA*, 1998.

[4] A. Canis, J. Choi, M. Aldham, V. Zhang, A. Kammoona, J. Anderson, S. Brown, and T. Czajkowski. LegUp: High-level synthesis for FPGA-based processor/accelerator systems. In *FPGA*, 2011.

[5] D. Cederman and P. Tsigas. Dynamic load balancing using work-stealing. In *GPU Computing Gems*. Elsevier, 2012.

[6] T. Czajkowski, U. Aydonat, D. Denisenko, and J. Freeman. From OpenCL to high-performance hardware on FPGAs. In *FPL*, 2012.

[7] N. George, H. Lee, D. Novo, M. Owaida, D. Andrews, K. Olukotun, and P. Ienne. Automatic support for multi-module parallelism from computational patterns. In *FPL*, 2015.

[8] V. Gramoli. More than you ever wanted to know about synchronization. In *PPoPP*, 2015.

[9] D. Greaves and S. Singh. Kiwi: Synthesis of FPGA circuits from parallel programs. In *FCCM*, 2008.

[10] M. Hosseinabady and J. L. Nunez-Yanez. Optimised OpenCL workgroup synthesis for hybrid ARM-FPGA devices. In *FPL*, 2015.

[11] T. Kanungo, D. Mount, N. Netanyahu, C. Piatko, R. Silverman, and A. Wu. An efficient k-means clustering algorithm: Analysis and implementation. *Pattern Matching and Machine Intelligence*, 24(7):881–892, July 2002.

[12] S. Kestur, J. D. Davis, and E. S. Chung. Towards a universal FPGA matrix–vector multiplication architecture. In *FCCM*, 2012.

[13] Khronos Group. *The OpenCL 1.0 Specification*. 2009.

[14] H.-S. Kim, M. Ahn, J. A. Stratton, and W.-m. W. Hwu. Design evaluation of OpenCL compiler framework for coarse-grained reconfigurable arrays. In *FPT*, 2012.

[15] V. Kumar, A. Sbîrlea, A. Jayaraj, Z. Budimlić, D. Majeti, and V. Sarkar. Heterogeneous work-stealing across CPU and DSP cores. In *HPEC*, 2015.

[16] V. Mirian and P. Chow. Using an OpenCL framework to evaluate interconnect implementations on FPGAs. In *FPL*, 2014.

[17] T. T. Mutlugün and S.-D. Wang. OpenCL computing on FPGA using multiported shared memory. In *FPL*, 2015.

[18] B. Nahill, A. Ramdial, H. Zeng, M. Di Natale, and Z. Zilic. An FPGA implementation of wait-free data synchronization protocols. In *ETFA*, 2013.

[19] Z. Wang, B. He, and W. Zhang. A study of data partitioning on OpenCL-based FPGAs. In *FPL*, 2015.

[20] F. Winterstein, S. Bayliss, and G. A. Constantinides. High-level synthesis of dynamic data structures: A case study using Vivado HLS. In *FPT*, 2013.

[21] Xilinx. *SDAccel Development Environment*. UG1023 (v2015.1), 2015.

Physical Design of 3D FPGAs Embedded with Micro-channel-based Fluidic Cooling

Zhiyuan Yang and Ankur Srivastava
University of Maryland, College Park, MD, USA
{zyyang, ankurs}@umd.edu

ABSTRACT

Through Silicon Via (TSV) based 3D integration technology is a promising technology to increase the performance of FPGAs by achieving shorter global wire-length and higher logic density. However, 3D FPGAs also suffer from severe thermal problems due to the increase in power density and thermal resistance. Moreover, past work has shown that leakage power can account for 40% of the total power at current technology nodes and leakage power increases non-linearly with temperature. This intensifies the thermal problem in 3D FPGAs and more aggressive cooling methods such as micro-channel based fluidic cooling are required to fully exploit their benefits. The interaction between micro-channel heat sink design and the performance of a 3D FPGA is very complicated and a comprehensive approach is required to identify the optimal design of 3D FPGAs subject to thermo-electrical constraints. In this work, we propose an analysis framework for 3D FPGAs embedded with micro-channel-based fluidic cooling to study the impact of channel density on cooling and performance. According to our simulation results, we provide guidelines for designing 3D FPGAs embedded with micro-channel cooling and identify the optimal design for each benchmark. Compared to naive 3D FPGA designs which use fixed thermal heat sink, the optimal design identified using our framework can improve the operating frequency and energy efficiency by up to 80.3% and 124.0%.

1. INTRODUCTION AND MOTIVATION

With the continued dimensional scaling, the non-recurring engineering cost in the design of cell-based Application Specific Integrated Circuits (ASICs) escalates enormously. Compared to ASICs, FPGAs have the advantage of higher reusability, simpler design cycle and faster time-to-market. On the other hand, FPGAs suffer from tremendous programming overheads. According to [12], programmable elements can account for 90% total footprint area, 80% total path delay and large portion of power consumption. These overheads enlarge the performance gap between FPGAs and ASICs [9] and become the main limitation to the growth of FPGA market.

3D integration technology provides an opportunity to increase the performance of FPGAs. This emerging technology stacks multiple dies on top of each other and uses

FPGA'16, February 21-23, 2016, Monterey, CA, USA

© 2016 ACM. ISBN 978-1-4503-3856-1/16/02. . . $15.00

DOI: http://dx.doi.org/10.1145/2847263.2847275

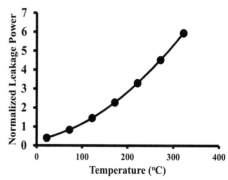

Figure 1: Trend of leakage power with increasing temperature. (Data are normalized to the leakage power at $85°C$)

Through Silicon Vias (TSVs) for inter-die connection which achieves shorter global wire-length and higher transistor density. However, 3D integration is not a panacea and it introduces a number of new challenges: (1) relatively larger TSV dimension will cause the increase in footprint area, (2) switch boxes that provide inter-layer connection will use more transistors resulting in extra power and delay, and (3) stacked structure will exacerbate thermal problem by increasing both the power density and thermal resistance.

Recently, several significant researches have been done to exploit 3D integration in FPGAs. Authors of [6] and [15] studied the design of switch box topology in 3D FPGAs based on the fact that the number of TSVs is limited in 3D ICs. Pangracious et al.[14] proposed to use tree-based interconnect topology to build 3D FPGAs in order to reduce the area overhead and improve logic density. Instead of wafer-stacked 3D FPGAs, people also studied monolithic 3D FPGAs [12, 11] which, according to the results, have better performance. Meanwhile, placement and routing (P&R) tools for 3D FPGAs have also been developed, among which TPR [3] and 3D-Meander [24] are the most popular ones. Unfortunately, despite of the work that has been done, thermal issues are almost unexplored in 3D FPGAs. Conventionally, 2D FPGAs dissipate a small amount of power due to low frequency and low logic density. Therefore, they can be sufficiently cooled by air-based heat sink. With 3D integration technology, power density of 3D FPGAs will increase due to the improvement of frequency and logic density while the heat removal capacity of conventional air-based cooling does not improve accordingly. This will lead to the rise of on-chip temperature. Authors of [6] characterized the temperature of a type of 3D FPGAs based on Virtex-4 architecture and discovered a 2.5x increase in peak temperature when the number of layers increases from one to four. If the on-chip temperature exceeds over the temperature limit, operating frequency should be scaled down to make the design ther-

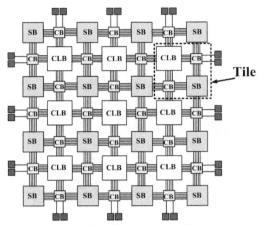

SB: Switch Box   CB: Connection Box
CLB: Configurable Logic Box

Figure 2: Illustration of the architecture of an island-style FPGA

mally feasible, which results in performance degradation in 3D FGPAs.

Thermal problems can be further exacerbated when the leakage power is taken into consideration. With the geometric and supply voltage scaling, leakage power becomes the primary contributor to the total power dissipation in FPGAs. Several researches [4, 26] demonstrate that leakage power can account for as much as 40% of the total power in FPGAs at sub-100nm technology nodes. Moreover, leakage power increases non-linearly with temperature [20] (as illustrated in Figure 1). The positive feedback between temperature and leakage power will lead to thermal runaway if 3D FPGAs are not sufficiently cooled. In order to fix the thermal problem and fully exploit the benefits of 3D FPGAs, more aggressive cooling approaches, such as micro-channel-based fluidic cooling, should be applied.

Micro-Channel-Based Fluidic Cooling (MC Cooling) comprises micro-channels etched into silicon substrate of each layer in 3D ICs. Fluid coolant (usually de-ionized water) is pumped into micro-channels and forms a distributed heat sink. This kind of micro-fluidic cooling is more efficient than air-cooling, because it can directly take heat away from adjacent regions instead of merely removing heat from top of the chip. According to [8, 27], single-phase micro-fluidic cooling can provide heat removal capacity as high as $700W/cm^2$ and two-phase cooling is even more efficient[7]. Recently, researchers built a micro-channel cooling system in the Altera FPGA with 28nm technology node and achieved much lower chip temperature compared to the air cooling [18]. Despite of these benefits, MC Cooling comes with other overheads: (1) TSVs cannot be built through micro-channels which results in a trade-off between micro-channel density and TSV-based vertical bandwidth; (2) extra energy is required to pump the coolant in order to cool the chip even though the pumping power is quite low according to the previous work [28, 16, 13]. For years, the application of micro-channel cooling in 3D ASICs has been widely studied [17, 22] and a 2D FPGA with liquid-cooling was reported recently [18]. However, the design-time optimization of 3D FPGAs with micro-channel cooling has not been investigated.

The scenario of applying MC Cooling in 3D FPGAs is far more complicated than that for 3D ASICs. On one hand, reducing micro-channel density will lead to worsening cooling. And increasing temperature may make 3D FPGAs thermally infeasible. On the other hand, due to the trade-off between channel density and vertical bandwidth, decreasing channel density leads to the increase of vertical bandwidth which may not necessarily reduce the delay of 3D FPGAs. This

is because that although larger vertical bandwidth will improve the latency of 3D nets, it will also cause congestion in 2D routing channels around TSVs due to the restriction of routing resources. This may increase the delay of the whole system in some cases. As for power dissipation, although increasing vertical bandwidth will possibly reduce the use of switch boxes, the average number of transistors per switch box will increase since more transistors are needed to support vertical connection and this will cause the rise of leakage power of a single switch box. Moreover, the dynamic power is determined by the operating frequency which is bounded by the routing delay. Hence the impact of channel density on power dissipation of 3D FPGAs is also nonmonotonic. Therefore, the relationship between cooling, operating frequency and power is very complicated and we cannot find an optimal design based on a simple model.

A comprehensive analysis approach is required to study the impact of the design of micro-channel heat sink on the 3D FPGA performance. Guidelines for designing 3D FPGAs embedded with micro-channel-based fluidic cooling are also necessary.

The contribution of our work is as follows:

(1) We propose an analysis framework to study the impact of micro-channel density on performance and power of 3D FPGAs.

(2) According to the simulation results of our framework, we provide guidelines for designing 3D FPGAs embedded with MC Cooling.

(3) Our framework sweeps different micro-channel densities and identifies the optimal physical design of micro-channel heat sink and 3D FPGAs. Compared to naive designs using fixed micro-channel density, our framework can improve the operating frequency and energy efficiency by up to 80.3% and 124%, respectively.

2. MODELING OF FPGAS

FPGAs are a kind of integrated circuits that can be programmed by customers. Based on different types of global routing architecture, FPGAs can be categorized into hierarchical style and island style[9]. In island-style FPGAs, Configurable Logic Blocks (CLBs) and I/O blocks are arranged in a two dimensional mesh and routing fabrics (including Connection Boxes (CBs), Switch Boxes (SBs) and routing channels) are evenly distributed throughout the mesh. Figure 2 illustrates the architecture of an island-style FPGA. As illustrated by the figure, an island-style FPGA have a regular pattern and can be regarded as the construction of identical tiles[9]. Each tile contains a CLB with its adjacent routing fabrics as illustrated in Figure 2. Due to the regular pattern, island-style FPGAs exhibit a number of desirable properties including efficient connect between CLBs and routing tracks and high scalability. These properties make island-style the most commonly used architecture in modern SRAM-based FPGAs [2]. In this work we will use 2D island-style FPGAs as the baseline and stack several identical FPGA chips vertically to form a 3D FPGA.

2.1 3D FPGA Model

In our work, a 3D FPGA is modeled by vertically stacking a number of identical 2D island-style FPGA chips as illustrated in Figure 3. Some of the switch boxes in 2D FPGAs should be extended to support inter-layer connection and these switch boxes are called 3D switch box (3D-SB) while the others are 2D switch box (2D-SB). Inter-layer connection is realized with TSVs which are fabricated between two 3D-SBs placed on adjacent layers. In our model, we assume that each 3D-SB connects to identical number of TSVs.

A primary concern about 3D FPGAs is the design of switch boxes. In this work, the so-called "subset-style" switch boxes[3,

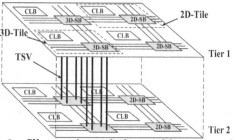

Figure 3: Illustration of the architecture of a 3D stacked FPGA

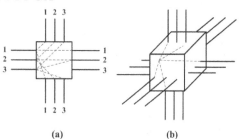

Figure 4: Illustration of the subset topology of (a) 2D-SB and (b) 3D-SB

24] are employed while they can be replaced with any other advanced switch box architectures [6]. The topology of subset-style switch boxes is illustrated in Figure 4. In a switch box, an incoming routing track from one side can connect to routing tracks from other sides with the identical ID number. Therefore, the flexibility (F_s) of a 2D-SB equals three while a 3D-SB has $F_s = 5$ (including two TSVs connecting to the upper and lower layer respectively). Therefore, if both vertical and horizontal routing bandwidth in 3D FGPAs are equal to W_{route}, the number of transistors used in a 2D-SB is $6 \times W_{route}$ while the number of transistors in a 3D-SB is $15 \times W_{route}$. In practice, however, since TSVs occupy much more silicon area compared to 2D routing channels, we have to limit the number of TSVs connected by each 3D-SB (usually the number is smaller than the width of a 2D routing channel).

Another concern is the electrical characterization of TSVs. In this work, we use the following equations [19] to calculate the resistance and capacitance of a TSV:

$$R_{TSV} = \frac{\rho_m H_{TSV}}{\pi r_{via}^2} \qquad (1)$$

$$C_{TSV} = \frac{2\pi\epsilon_r\epsilon_0 H_{TSV}}{ln((r_{via} + t_{ox})/r_{via})} \qquad (2)$$

In the equations, ρ_m is the resistivity of the metal filling in a TSV, r_{via} is the radius of the metal filling region in the TSV, t_{ox} is the sickness of the oxide layer around the TSV and ϵ_r is the relative permittivity of SiO_2.

2.2 Area Model of 3D FPGAs

Calculation of temperature requires accurate modeling of 3D FPGA area. In this work, we follow the methodology introduced in [5] to determine the area of 3D FGPAs. According to [5], FPGA area is modeled as the number of "minimum width transistor areas". The "minimum width transistor area" is the area of the layout of the smallest transistor, plus the minimum spacing to another transistor above it and to its right. In order to calculate the number of minimum width transistor areas, we first determine the number and size of transistors used in each programmable block (i.e. CLB, CB and SB). The schematic of each programmable block in our model is similar to the one described in [5]. For transistors

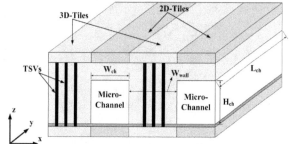

Figure 5: Illustration of a 3D stacked FPGA embedded with micro-channel cooling

with different sizes, their minimum width transistor area (MWTA) is calculated with:

$$\text{MWTA} = 0.5 + \frac{\text{Drive Strength}}{2 \times \text{DSMWT}} \qquad (3)$$

where DSMWT stands for the "Drive Strength of Minimum Width Transistor". Following this, we can calculate the number of minimum width transistor areas for each programmable block and the "real" area is computed by multiplying the number of minimum width transistor areas with the area value of a certain technology node. Note that up to this stage, TSVs are not considered yet. In our model, TSVs are assumed to be built between two 3D-SBs placed on adjacent layers. Therefore, the area of a 3D-SB should be added with the total silicon area occupied by TSVs connected to the 3D-SB.

In order to simplify the analysis, in this work, we extend the "tile" of an island-style FPGA as introduced in Section 2 in the context of 3D FGPAs. By doing this, a tile can be categorized into 3D-tile or 2D-tile based on the different types of switch boxes constituting the tile. This is illustrated in Figure 3 The area of a tile is the total area of all the programmable blocks included in the tile.

2.3 Characterizing The Impact of Micro-Channel Density In 3D FPGAs

The structure of 3D FPGAs embedded with micro-channel-based fluidic cooling is illustrated in Figure 5. Micro-channel structure is characterized by a series of physical parameters: channel width (W_{ch}), silicon thickness between channels (W_{wall}), channel hight (H_{ch}) and channel length (L_{ch}). Usually, the length of the channel is equal to the length of the FPGA chip ($L_{ch} = L_{chip}$). TSVs of 3D FPGAs cannot be built through micro-channels rsultinge in a trade-off between vertical bandwidth and micro-channel density. In this work ,we assume the silicon thickness between channels can only be equal to or be a multiple of channel width ($W_{wall} = \lambda W_{ch}$, $\lambda = 1, 2, 3, ...$). Our work is going to study how the channel density affects cooling capacity and performance of 3D FPGAs.

Because a 3D FPGA is modeled by the array of tiles, we will capture the impact of micro-channel density on the distribution of different types of tiles in the 3D FPGA. In order to do this, we initially set 3D-tile as the default type of tile for all tiles. After this, we change some 3D-tiles to 2D-tiles such that micro-channels can be allocated, since micro-channels can only be allocated below the 2D-tiles due to their conflict with TSVs. It should be noted that, we assume a 2D-tile occupies the same area as a 3D-tile in a single layout even though they may require different areas. After mapping the micro-channel distribution to the 3D FPGA architecture, we can characterize different micro-channel densities by changing the distribution of 3D and 2D tiles in FPGAs. The distribution of different types of tiles will further influence the placement and routing in 3D FPGAs.

56

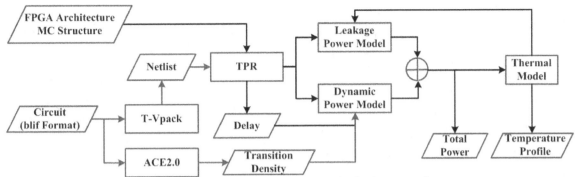

Figure 6: Flow chart of our analysis framework

3. ANALYSIS APPROACH FOR 3D FPGAS WITH MICRO-CHANNEL COOLING

In this section, we will introduce the method we used to study the impact of micro-channel density on the performance, power and energy efficiency of 3D FPGAs. In this work, we use the operating frequency to represent the performance. Energy efficiency is similar to the inverse of energy-delay-product (EDP) and is defined by the following equation:

$$E.E. = Frequency^2/Power \qquad (4)$$

Figure 6 illustrates the flow chart of the framework of our analysis methodology. The kernel of the framework is extended from TPR[3]. A given circuit (in blif format) is fed into T-Vpack (which is part of VPR[5], a P&R tool for 2D FPGA) and ACE2.0[10] (an activity estimation tool) to generate CLB-level netlist and transition density, respectively. Then, CLB-level netlist, FPGA architecture and distribution of micro-channels are fed into TPR for placing and routing. Meanwhile, TPR also calculates the final delay of the circuit based on its embedded delay model. Following this, we take the placement file, routing file as well as the delay and transition density as the inputs to our power model to calculate the power dissipation profile. The power profile is used to calculate temperature profile which is then fed back into power model to update the leakage power. This "power-thermal" loop is necessary because of the positive feedback between leakage power and temperature. The "power-thermal" loop stops when the update of temperature profile is negligible.

3.1 Background of TPR

TPR is one of the most popular P&R tools for 3D FPGAs. Originally, TPR can only support the 3D FPGA architecture with fully-vertical inter-connection. We extend the tool so that it can support different types of switch boxes (i.e. 2D-SB and 3D-SB). In this subsection, we will briefly introduce the principles of TPR. More detailed descriptions can be found in [3].

TPR takes the CLB-level netlist and the 3D FPGA architecture as inputs. In this work, we add micro-channel distribution as another input. In the first stage, the netlist is partitioned into different layers to minimize the total number of TSVs. Following this, TPR performs timing-driven partitioning-based placement successively from the top layer to the bottom layer. After the position of each CLB is determined, the tool uses Pathfinder Negotiated Congestion-delay algorithm [5] to assign routing elements to each net based on the distribution of routing resources. After routing is finished, the delay of the circuit is calculated based on Elmore Delay Model. Finally, TPR will output placement file, routing file and delay which will be used in the following stages.

3.2 Power Model

In order to compute the temperature and evaluate the energy efficiency of 3D FPGAs, we should first calculate the power dissipation profile. Since a 3D FPGA is modeled by an array of 3D and 2D tiles, we assume each tile has the uniform power. Power dissipation profile is characterized by the spacial distribution of tile power. Power dissipation of 3D FPGAs is the sum of dynamic power and static power (leakage power). The methodology of modeling the two types of power is introduced as follows.

3.2.1 Dynamic Power

Dynamic power is generated by transition of signals. Signal transition will cause frequently charging and discharging capacitors and this forms the most significant contribution to the dynamic power in 3D FPGAs. This kind of dynamic power can be modeled using the following equation:

$$P = \sum_i C_i V_i^2 D_i f_i \qquad (5)$$

where C_i, V_i, D_i and f_i are the total capacitance, swing voltage, signal transition density and operating frequency of source i. Another component of dynamic power is the short-circuit power which is caused by signal switching. According to [21], while short-circuit power in CLB accounts for a higher percentage of its total power, it only contributes less than 10% to the power in the interconnect in an FPGA. In order to capture both factors of dynamic power and avoid complex computation, in our work, we model the dynamic power in two independent parts: Interconnect Power and CLB Power.

Interconnect Power: The calculation of interconnect power takes two steps. First, we compute the power for each routing segment (including horizontal routing segments on each layer and TSVs). A segment connects two terminals (a terminal is an input/output pin of a CLB or a pin of an SB). The equation to calculate the capacitor-charging-based dynamic power of segment i is shown as follows:

$$P_i = C_i V_i^2 D_i f_i \qquad (6)$$

where C_i is the sum of input/output capacitance of the two terminals and the distributed capacitance of the segment; D_i is the signal transition density of the net to which the segment belongs and its value is calculated by ACE2.0[10]; f_i is the operating frequency of the system and V_i is simply taken as the supply voltage. Second, we project the power of each segment to the tile because the power of each tile is what really matters. In order to do this, we divide the segment power equally into two parts, and add one part to the tile containing one terminal and add the other part to the tile containing the other terminal. Note that, it is possible that both terminals of a segment reside in one tile. In this case, the whole power of the segment is assigned to this tile.

CLB Power: According to our FPGA model, a CLB contains LUTs, flip-flops, multiplexers, buffers and memory cells. Modeling the dynamic power in a CLB is difficult due to the complex sub-routing within the CLB. In our work, we use a simulation-based method to model the CLB power. First of all, we will calculate the average dynamic power of an active CLB. We use SPICE to simulate each component in a CLB with random input vector pairs at a certain frequency. The simulation gives the dynamic power of each component for all the pairs of input vector. The dynamic power of each component is then taken as the average power for all the input vector pairs of the component, with the assumption that each pair of input vectors has the same probability of occurrence. The dynamic power of a CLB ($Power_{CLB,0}$)is the sum of all the components constituting the CLB. Next, we take $Power_{CLB,0}$ as the input and scale it with the real frequency to get the real dynamic power of an active CLB. Finally, this power is added to the tile which contains the CLB.

3.2.2 Static Power

Static power is caused by the leakage current in FPGAs and can be categorized into two types: gate leakage and source-to-drain leakage. Detailed modeling of the two types of static power is difficult and not accurate at small technology nodes. Therefore, in our work, we take the experiment value from [1] and calculate the leakage power for different temperatures based on an analytical extrapolation function. According to [1], at $85^{o}C$, Typical High-Performance Stratix III has $3W$ static power for 300K logic blocks (similar to the tile in our model). Since the static power is linear to the number of logic blocks, we can calculate the static power for a single logic block, which is around $10\mu W$. This value is then taken as the static power of a 2D-tile at $85^{o}C$ in our 3D FPGA model. The static power of a 3D-tile is $\gamma \times 10\mu W$ where γ is a scaling parameter equal to the ratio of the number of minimum width transistor areas (without considering the area occupied by TSVs) between a 3D-tile and a 2D-tile. Following this, we use the following equation[20] to extrapolate the static power for different temperatures:

$$P_{stat}(T) = P_{stat}(T_0) \times (5.121(\frac{T}{T_0})^2 - 6.013\frac{T}{T_0} + 1.892) \quad (7)$$

Now we get a look-up-table for static power at different temperatures, which is then fed into the simulation framework.

3.3 Thermal Model

The thermal behavior of 3D FPGAs can be characterized with thermal resistance-capacitance (RC) network which resembles the electrical RC network. In order to do this, a 3D FPGA is divided into grids and each grid is represented with a node in the thermal RC network. In this network, the voltage of each node represents the average temperature of the grid while the power of the grid is indicated by the current source connected to the grid. The resistance connecting each adjacent pair of nodes indicates a heat transfer path and the thermal capacitance represents the ability to store heat. In this work, we are mostly interested in steady state thermal behavior. Therefore we will primarily focus on the resistance network. Our resistance network is the same as the one introduced in [23], which is illustrated in Figure 7. The cooling performance of micro-channels is captured by three resistors: R_{cond}, R_{conv} and R_{heat}. R_{cond} and R_{conv} represent the heat transfer between silicon and fluid by conduction and convection respectively. R_{heat} indicates the heat transfer within the fluid. More detailed definition of the resistance network can be found in [23].

After we get the profile of the total power dissipation, we

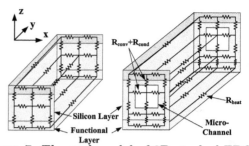

Figure 7: Thermal model of 3D stacked FPGAs

can calculate the temperature with the following equation:

$$GT = P \quad (8)$$

where G is the thermal conductance matrix determined by the thermal resistance network. During the simulation process, when a new temperature profile is calculated, the static power of each tile is updated according to the new temperature. Then the temperature is recalculated based on the updated total power dissipation. This is illustrated in Figure 6. This loop stops until the temperature is converged.

4. SIMULATION AND DISCUSSION

We will describe our simulation and discuss the results in this section. First, we will introduce the setup of the simulation. Next, we use our analysis framework to perform exploration on 12 benchmarks from the Microelectronics Center of North Carolina (MCNC) benchmark suit and study (1) the different characteristics of air-cooling and micro-channel-based fluidic cooling and (2) the impact of micro-channel density in a 3D FPGA embedded with micro-channel-based fluidic cooling.

4.1 Setup of the Simulation

During our design space exploration, we study how the cooling method and the density of micro-channel influence the electrical properties of a 3D FPGA. By "electrical properties", we mean the operating frequency (Freq.), Power per CLB (P_{CLB}) and Energy Efficiency (E.E.), where Energy Efficiency is calculated with Equation 4.

We first run the thermo-electrical simulation on fully-vertical-connected 3D FPGAs (100% of the tiles are 3D-tile) with air-cooling. Following this, we apply micro-channel-based fluidic cooling in 3D FPGAs and sweep the micro-channel density. In our work, we change the micro-channel density by increasing the silicon thickness between channels in multiples of the channel width (Figure 5). We define a new parameter, Micro-Channel Pitch (MC_{pitch}), as $MC_{pitch} = \frac{W_{wall}}{W_{ch}}$ to describe the micro-channel density. The vertical bandwidth is maximized for each micro-channel density. Due to the restriction of the size of benchmarks, we range MC_{pitch} from 1 to 11 with a step of 1, which implies that the percentage of 3D-tiles among all tiles ranges from 50% to 92%. For the fully-vertical-connection, only air-cooling is applied due to the lack of space for micro-channels, while for other cases a hybrid cooling scheme (air-cooling and micro-channel-based fluidic cooling) is used. In this work, we assume the temperature limit is $85^{o}C$ [23]. If the maximum temperature exceeds this limit, the design is regarded as thermally infeasible. In this case, we scale down the operating frequency to fix the thermal problem.

Other simulation variables for 3D FPGAs embedded with micro-channel-based fluidic cooling are summarized as follows:

(1) 3D FGPAs stack up to four functional layers.

(2) Each 3D-SB placed on the ith layer has four TSVs

Table 1: Electrical and thermal variables employed in the simulation

Variable	Value	Unit	Description
T_{amb}	25	^oC	Ambient temperature
T_{ch}	25	^oC	Inlet temperature of micro-channel
v_f	1	m s^{-1}	Fluid velocity
k_{ox}	1.4	W m^{-1}K	Oxide thermal conductivity
k_{si}	149	W m^{-1}K	Silicon thermal conductivity
k_{cu}	401	W m^{-1}K	Copper thermal conductivity
k_f	0.607	W m^{-1}K	Fluid thermal conductivity at 25^oC
R_{seg}	101	Ω	Resistance of one routing segment
C_{seg}	22.1	fF	Capacitance of one routing segment
V_{dd}	0.9	V	Supply voltage

connecting to the $(i-1)^{th}$ layer and $(i+1)^{th}$ layer, respectively.

(3) For each TSV, the diameter is $10\mu m$ and the height is $150\mu m$. The resistance and capacitance of a single TSV is $32m\Omega$ and $223fF$.

(4) According to [25], The dimension of a single micro-channel is set as $50\mu m$ and $100\mu m$ (Width $\times$ Height). This will yield a pressure drop less than $1 \times 10^5 Pa$ and pumping power blow $1W$ according to the model in [23]. Other channel dimensions may have different impact on cooling performance. As illustrated by [23], increasing channel width on one hand reduces the pressure drop hereby leading to smaller thermal resistance, but on the other hand it causes decrease in the coverage of micro-channels hence degrading the heat removal rate. Since the main focus of this paper is the impact of micro-channel density on the performance of 3D FPGAs, we fixed the channel dimension during our simulation although our algorithm works for other channel dimensions as well.

(5) each CLB is composed of a 4-input LUT, a flip-flop and corresponding memory elements. The width of horizontal routing channel is 30.

(6) Table 1 lists the rest of the important electrical and thermal variables employed in this work.

Table 4 and Table 5 show the results of some benchmarks on 3D FPGAs before and after scaling down the operating frequency, respectively. Because of the page limits, only seven out of the twelve benchmarks are shown in the tables. The tables illustrate the peak temperature (MaxT) as well as normalized operating frequency (Freq.) and energy efficiency (E.E.) for each benchmark. In Section 4.2 and 4.3, we will discuss the results in detail.

4.2 Fully-Vertical-Connected 3D FGPAs

In fully-vertical-connected 3D FPGAs, all tiles are 3D-tile, thus micro-channels cannot be allocated under this scenario. Only air-cooling is applied during the simulation. Figure 8(a) shows the maximum peak temperature over all benchmarks as well as normalized operating frequency, power per CLB, and energy efficiency for each number of stacked layers. For each benchmark, operating frequency, power per CLB and energy efficiency are normalized to their counterparts when the benchmark is realized on a 2D FPGA. Then the normalized characters are averaged over all the benchmarks to get the results shown in Figure 8(a). Under this scenario, since there is no room to place micro-channels, we can only use air-cooling to remove heat from top of the 3D FGPA. As illustrated by this figure, the peak temperature of some benchmarks exceeds $T_{limit} = 85^oC$ even when only 2 functional layers are stacked. In addition, the peak temperature increases dramatically by increasing the number of layers in a 3D FPGA. Even though operating frequency and energy efficiency can be improved by stacking more layers in a 3D FPGA, these benefits cannot be realized with a thermally-infeasible design. In order to fix the thermal problem, we scaling down the operating frequency for each

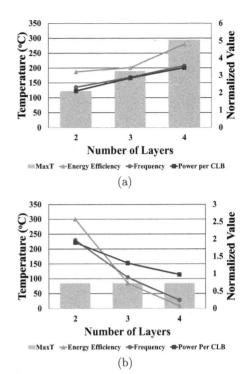

(a)

(b)

Figure 8: Maximum peak temperature (MaxT), normalized frequency, normalized power per CLB and normalized energy efficiency for different number of layers (a) before fixing thermal problem and (b) after fixing the thermal problem

thermally-violated design and the results are shown in Figure 8(b).

According to the results illustrated in Figure 8(b), due to the thermal restriction, increasing number of layers may lead to the degradation of frequency and energy efficiency. Power per CLB also decreases because of the reduction of operating frequency. This degradation can be reduced by using micro-channel-based fluidic cooling. Micro-channel structure imposes new constraints on 3D FPGA design and we will study the impact of micro-channel density on the electrical properties of 3D FPGAs in Section 4.3.

4.3 3D FPGAs with Micro-channel-based Fluidic Cooling

In this scenario, some 3D-tiles are replaced by 2D-tiles, thus a number of micro-channels can be allocated below 2D-tiles. We will discuss the impact of micro-channel density on the cooling and performance of 3D FPGAs in this section.

4.3.1 Before Fixing Thermal Problem

The trend of operating frequency (Freq.), power per CLB (P_{CLB}) and energy efficiency (E.E.) with increasing micro-channel pitch for different number of stacked layers is shown in Figure 9(a)-(c). Note that increasing micro-channel pitch reduces the micro-channel density thereby reducing the cooling capacity. The approach of normalization of each of the three electrical properties is the same as described in Section 4.2. In each figure, we also show the maximum peak temperature over all benchmarks.

According to Figure9(a), as we increase the number of layers in a 3D FPGA, the frequency will increase. However, for a certain number of layers, the change of frequency with reducing micro-channel density is not monotonic. In our work, reducing micro-channel density represents the increase in vertical bandwidth. This nonmonotonic relationship between frequency and vertical bandwidth is also discovered in

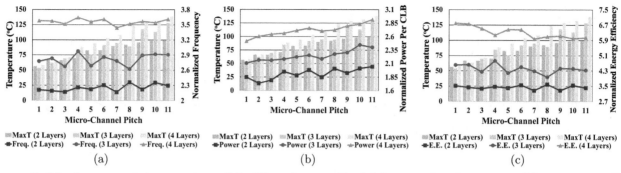

Figure 9: Maximum peak temperature (MaxT) and normalized (a) operating frequency, (b) power per CLB (P_{CLB}), (c) energy efficiency for different number of layers and micro-channel density before fixing the thermal problem

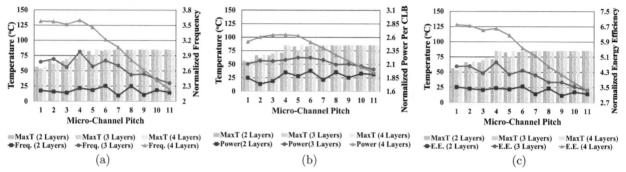

Figure 10: Maximum peak temperature (MaxT) and normalized (a) operating frequency, (b) power per CLB (P_{CLB}), (c) energy efficiency for different number of layers and micro-channel density after fixing the thermal problem

[24]. This phenomenon can be caused by the following two factors:

(1) Although increasing vertical bandwidth will improve the latency in 3D nets, it can also cause congestion in 2D routing channels around the 3D-SB which may lead to the increase in delay of other nets.

(2) The distribution of routing resources changes when we alter the micro-channel density, which forces the router to find completely new paths to connect CLBs. Since each routing channel has tracks of different lengths, these paths may have very significant variations in the RC parameters which are essential in calculating delay.

Since both power density and energy efficiency depend on the operating frequency, they also exhibit nonmonotonic behavior as shown in Figure 9(b)-(c).

Another interesting point that can be made is about power per CLB (P_{CLB}). According to Figure 9(b), for a certain number of layers, power per CLB has an increasing tendency when reducing the micro-channel density. This can be explained as follows: reducing micro-channel density leads to lower mass flow rate of coolant which will reduce the cooling capacity of micro-channel heat sink and increase the on-chip temperature; increased on-chip temperature will in turn cause the rise of leakage power, thus increasing the power dissipation for each CLB. On the other hand, for a fixed micro-channel density, when another functional layer is added, the power dissipation per CLB will increase. This behavior is determined by three factors: (1) operating frequency may increase with the number of layers which leads to the increase of dynamic power per CLB; (2) increasing the number of stacked layers enables us to realize a certain benchmark using smaller number of CLBs; (3) increasing the number of layers causes the rise of on-chip temperature thereby increasing the leakage power per CLB due to the positive feedback between temperature and leakage power.

Since increasing power per CLB may imply larger power dissipation and energy efficiency is inversely related to power, there is a decreasing tendency in energy efficiency by increasing micro-channel pitch. As illustrated in Figure 9(c), this tendency becomes more obvious when the number of layers increases. By increasing the number of layers for a fixed micro-channel density, however, energy efficiency will increase since operating frequency is dominated.

4.3.2 After Fixing Thermal Problem

According to the results shown in Figure 9, although micro-channel-based fluidic cooling can significantly reduce the on-chip temperature. if micro-channel density is too small, thermal violations can still occur. For these cases, we scale down the operating frequency to fix the thermal problem and the results are shown in Figure 10(a)-(c). The figures illustrate that the peak temperatures of all designs are below T_{limit} and the curves of electrical properties are pulled down at the high-micro-channel-pitch end due to the reduction of operating frequency. According to Figure 10(a), the drop of frequency becomes sharper and occurs earlier when more layers are stacked in 3D FPGAs. This is because increasing the number of layers intensifies the thermal problem of 3D FPGAs and frequency should be scaled down to a much lower level in order to fix the thermal problem. The degradation of frequency meanwhile causes the reduction in power dissipation per CLB and energy efficiency. According to the figures, we can get the following guidelines for designing 3D FPGAs embedded with micro-channel-based fluidic cooling: (1) the performance of 3D FPGAs with higher vertical bandwidth will be "locked" due to the thermal restriction; (2) there is an "unlocked window" close to the lower-vertical-bandwidth end where we can find the optimal design of a 3D FPGA; (3) the size of unlocked window shrinks as increasing

Table 2: Comparison to Best Cooling Design

	2 Layers	3 Layers	4 Layers
Freq.	15.0%	20.2%	4.8%
E.E.	15.1%	23.8%	6.0%

Table 3: Comparison to Best Bandwidth Design

	2 Layers	3 Layers	4 Layers
Freq.	24.3%	47.3%	80.3%
E.E.	35.5%	74.0%	124.0%

the number of layers; (4) the architecture of optimal design is different for different number of layers.

Our analysis framework also identifies the optimal physical architecture of 3D FPGAs with different number of stacked layers for each benchmark. In order to evaluate the optimal designs, we compare their operating frequency and energy efficiency against that of the designs with largest microchannel density (Best Cooling) and smallest micro-channel density (Best Bandwidth), respectively. The improvement is averaged over all the benchmarks and the results are shown in Table 2 and Table 3. According to the tables, the improvement with respect to the Best Bandwidth Design is generally larger than that with respect to the Best Cooling Design. This is because that the frequency of the Best Bandwidth Design has already been scaled down to fix the thermal problem, thus leading to the degradation of performance and energy efficiency. It should be noted that optimal design varies for different benchmarks and different number of layers. The optimal design of some benchmarks are shown in bold type in Table 5.

5. CONCLUSION

In this work, we studied the thermo-electrical interaction in 3D FPGAs. Our results demonstrate that micro-channel based fluidic cooling is necessary to realize the true potential of 3D integration technology. We proposed an analysis framework to study the impact of micro-channel density on the performance and identify the optimal 3D FPGA design for each benchmark. According to the simulation results, we proposed guidelines for designing the physical architecture of 3D FPGAs embedded with micro-channel-based fluidic cooling. Comparison with Best Cooling Design and Best Bandwidth Design shows that the optimal design identified by our framework can improve operating frequency and energy efficiency up to 80.3% and 124.0% respectively.

6. ACKNOWLEDGEMENTS

The authors acknowledge that this work has been funded by NSF grant CCF1302375 and DARPA ICECOOL.

7. REFERENCES

[1] Peter Cheung. 2008. Modern FPGA architecutres. (Jun 2008). Retrieved August 30, 2015. from http://www.ee.ic.ac.uk/.

[2] Virtex-4 family overview. (Aug 30 2010) Retrieved September 5, 2015 from http://www.xilinx.com.

[3] C. Ababei, et al. Exploring potential benefits of 3D FPGA integration. In *Field programmable logic and application*, pages 874–880, 2004.

[4] J. H. Anderson and F. N. Najm. Active leakage power optimization for FPGAs. *Computer-Aided Design of Integrated Circuits and Systems, IEEE Transactions on*, 25(3):423–437, 2006.

[5] V. Betz, et al. *Architecture and CAD for deep-submicron FPGAs*, volume 497. 2012.

[6] A. Gayasen, et al. Designing a 3-D FPGA: switch box architecture and thermal issues. *Very Large Scale Integration (VLSI) Systems, IEEE Transactions on*, 16(7):882–893, 2008.

[7] D. H. Kim, et al. A study of Through-Silicon-Via impact on the 3D stacked IC layout. In *ICCAD*, pages 674–680, Nov 2009.

[8] J.-M. Koo, et al. Integrated microchannel cooling for three-dimensional electronic circuit architectures. *Journal of heat transfer*, 127(11):49–58, Jan 2005.

[9] I. Kuon, et al. Fpga architecture: Survey and challenges. *Foundations and Trends in Electronic Design Automation*, 2(2):135–253, 2008.

[10] J. Lamoureux and S. J. Wilton. Activity estimation for field-programmable gate arrays. In *Field Programmable Logic and Applications, 2006. FPL'06. International Conference on*, page 1.

[11] Y. Y. Liauw, et al. Nonvolatile 3D-FPGA with monolithically stacked RRAM-based configuration memory. In *Solid-State Circuits Conference Digest of Technical Papers (ISSCC), 2012 IEEE International*, pages 406–408, 2012.

[12] M. Lin, et al. Performance benefits of monolithically stacked 3-D FPGA. *Computer-Aided Design of Integrated Circuits and Systems, IEEE Transactions on*, 26(2):216–229, 2007.

[13] S. Ndao, et al. Multi-objective thermal design optimization and comparative analysis of electronics cooling technologies. *International Journal of Heat and Mass Transfer*, 52(19):4317–4326, 2009.

[14] V. Pangracious, et al. Designing a 3D tree-based FPGA: Optimization of butterfly programmable interconnect topology using 3D technology. In *3D Systems Integration Conference (3DIC), 2013 IEEE International*, pages 1–8, 2013.

[15] S. A. Razavi, et al. A tileable switch module architecture for homogeneous 3D FPGAs. In *3D System Integration, 2009. 3DIC 2009. IEEE International Conference on*, pages 1–4, 2009.

[16] J. Ryu, et al. Numerical optimization of the thermal performance of a microchannel heat sink. *International Journal of Heat and Mass Transfer*, 45(13):2823–2827, 2002.

[17] M. Sabry, et al. GreenCool: an energy-efficient liquid cooling design technique for 3-D MPSoCs Via channel width modulation. *IEEE Trans. Comput.-Aided Design Integr. Circuits Syst.*, 32(4):524–537, 2013.

[18] T. E. Sarvey, et al. Embedded cooling technologies for densely integrated electronic systems. In *Custom Integrated Circuits Conference (CICC), 2015 IEEE*, pages 1–8, 2015.

[19] I. Savidis, et al. Electrical modeling and characterization of through-silicon vias (TSVs) for 3-D integrated circuits. *Microelectronics Journal*, 41(1):9–16, 2010.

[20] C. Serafy, et al. Continued frequency scaling in 3D ICs through micro-fluidic cooling. In *Thermal and Thermomechanical Phenomena in Electronic Systems (ITherm), 2014 IEEE Intersociety Conference on*, pages 79–85, 2014.

[21] L. Shang, et al. Dynamic power consumption in Virtex-II FPGA family. In *Proceedings of the 2002 ACM/SIGDA tenth international symposium on Field-programmable gate arrays*, pages 157–164, 2002.

[22] B. Shi, et al. Hybrid 3D-IC cooling system using micro-fluidic cooling and thermal TSVs. In *ISVLSI*, pages 33–38, August 2012.

[23] B. Shi, et al. Non-uniform micro-channel design for stacked 3D-ICs. In *DAC*, pages 658–663, June 2011.

[24] K. Siozios, et al. Architecture-level exploration of alternative interconnection schemes targeting 3d fpgas: A software-supported methodology. *International Journal of Reconfigurable Computing*, 2008, 2009.

[25] A. Sridhar, et al. 3D-ICE: Fast compact transient thermal modeling for 3D ICs with inter-tier liquid cooling. In *Proceedings of the International Conference on Computer-Aided Design*, pages 463–470, 2010.

[26] T. Tuan, et al. A 90nm low-power FPGA for battery-powered applications. In *Proceedings of the 2006 ACM/SIGDA 14th international symposium on Field programmable gate arrays*, pages 3–11, 2006.

[27] D. Tuckerman and R. Pease. High-performance heat sinking for VLSI. *IEEE Electron Device Lett.*, 2(5):126–129, May 1981.

[28] X. Wei and Y. Joshi. Stacked microchannel heat sinks for liquid cooling of microelectronic components. *Journal of Electronic Packaging*, 126(1):60–66, 2004.

Table 4: Results of some benchmarks on 3D FPGAs before scaling down the operating frequency (FVC = Fully-Vertical-Connection Scenario, MaxT = Peak Temperature, Freq. = Frequency, E.E. = Energy Efficiency, MC_{pitch} = Micro-channel Pitch. MaxT has the unit of $^{\circ}C$, Freq. and E.E. are normalized to their counterparts on 2D FGPAs. Thermally infeasible designs are shown in bold type.)

									MC_{pitch}					
			FVC	1	2	3	4	5	6	7	8	9	10	11
alu4	2 Layers	maxT	**89.45**	43.27	47.06	50.90	59.55	59.80	61.94	61.00	67.13	74.53	71.91	71.43
		Freq.	**1.72**	1.55	1.50	1.52	1.90	1.62	1.63	1.44	1.70	1.97	1.74	1.63
		E.E.	**1.72**	1.74	1.64	1.70	2.22	1.73	1.79	1.51	1.87	2.22	1.74	1.73
	3 Layers	maxT	**164.42**	42.91	54.93	55.81	63.47	68.34	69.84	75.99	76.30	75.38	**85.59**	**86.67**
		Freq.	**2.34**	1.81	2.57	2.04	2.30	2.31	2.15	2.26	2.15	1.91	**2.15**	**2.18**
		E.E.	**2.16**	2.18	3.35	2.47	2.89	2.86	2.59	2.72	2.60	2.22	**2.46**	**2.57**
	4 Layers	maxT	**237.27**	47.44	54.41	60.53	66.48	71.39	77.74	81.41	84.33	**98.80**	**96.58**	**100.64**
		Freq.	**2.74**	2.79	2.73	2.86	2.81	2.71	2.76	2.74	2.59	**3.05**	**2.74**	**2.74**
		E.E.	**2.79**	3.99	3.82	4.19	4.01	3.78	3.76	3.79	3.44	**4.12**	**3.62**	**3.58**
bigkey	2 Layers	maxT	**121.80**	56.03	66.23	65.94	69.58	82.58	82.89	**89.92**	**92.11**	**95.76**	**98.32**	**98.70**
		Freq.	**3.28**	3.49	3.68	2.98	2.93	3.51	3.26	**3.46**	**3.41**	**3.45**	**3.46**	**3.33**
		E.E.	**5.70**	7.15	7.49	5.82	5.69	6.86	6.30	**6.69**	**6.54**	**6.58**	**6.60**	**6.24**
	3 Layers	maxT	**188.79**	53.44	61.70	69.42	84.60	75.45	**91.49**	**94.67**	89.17	**117.92**	**113.00**	**127.89**
		Freq.	**3.14**	3.10	3.05	3.05	3.68	2.62	**3.26**	**3.14**	2.62	**3.73**	**3.31**	**3.73**
		E.E.	**3.83**	5.07	4.89	4.77	5.95	3.92	**5.03**	**4.78**	3.84	**5.64**	**4.89**	**5.52**
	4 Layers	maxT	**293.59**	57.54	63.19	70.96	**88.38**	**94.29**	**103.15**	**108.02**	**123.98**	**128.61**	**131.79**	**138.32**
		Freq.	**4.45**	4.53	4.02	3.85	**4.64**	**4.43**	**4.49**	**4.24**	**4.78**	**4.68**	**4.45**	**4.45**
		E.E.	**7.05**	9.49	8.17	7.65	**9.30**	**8.76**	**8.77**	**8.06**	**9.09**	**8.86**	**8.25**	**8.16**
des	2 Layers	maxT	**83.45**	44.51	45.30	52.06	56.60	59.71	65.39	59.23	66.77	62.91	69.51	72.23
		Freq.	3.22	3.21	2.50	3.03	3.15	3.21	3.62	2.64	3.26	2.64	3.21	3.31
		E.E.	4.79	5.43	3.92	5.03	5.24	5.31	6.11	4.06	5.27	3.97	5.12	5.26
	3 Layers	maxT	**163.47**	48.79	54.81	60.12	66.65	72.93	76.17	78.47	81.77	**86.21**	**91.77**	86.75
		Freq.	**4.28**	4.78	4.63	4.36	4.61	4.65	4.60	4.32	4.23	**4.34**	**4.56**	3.85
		E.E.	**5.75**	9.49	9.11	8.27	8.87	8.71	8.65	7.88	7.55	**7.76**	**8.13**	6.59
	4 Layers	maxT	**254.74**	50.18	61.36	66.26	72.94	83.57	**90.47**	**87.30**	92.93	102.13	107.66	**113.49**
		Freq.	**5.67**	5.65	6.32	5.76	5.69	6.22	**6.09**	**6.09**	5.29	5.62	5.67	**5.67**
		E.E.	**9.30**	12.75	14.41	12.82	8.87	13.76	**13.01**	**10.87**	11.01	11.62	11.62	**11.43**
diffeq	2 Layers	maxT	**83.10**	44.04	47.54	51.50	57.01	59.73	60.82	64.09	67.20	72.41	72.03	68.64
		Freq.	1.72	1.72	1.58	1.63	1.68	1.72	1.64	1.73	1.73	1.91	1.81	1.59
		E.E.	1.98	2.24	1.99	2.11	2.19	2.20	2.06	2.19	2.14	2.41	2.25	1.93
	3 Layers	maxT	**154.55**	44.30	53.26	54.22	61.72	62.16	73.76	77.32	74.46	**86.30**	**87.74**	**87.77**
		Freq.	**2.46**	2.08	2.42	1.99	2.21	1.95	2.45	2.37	2.04	**2.42**	**2.36**	**2.27**
		E.E.	**2.65**	2.97	3.54	2.75	3.09	2.63	3.44	3.23	2.69	**3.26**	**3.17**	**3.03**
	4 Layers	maxT	**208.64**	44.27	51.52	56.12	61.43	69.00	71.20	81.10	**87.93**	83.42	**98.15**	**98.91**
		Freq.	**2.71**	2.44	2.47	2.43	2.41	2.56	2.44	2.68	**2.92**	2.39	**2.91**	**2.71**
		E.E.	**2.71**	3.53	3.45	3.41	3.30	3.54	3.30	3.64	**4.04**	3.10	**3.90**	**3.52**
dsip	2 Layers	maxT	**107.80**	48.12	54.54	63.37	70.77	68.22	74.19	78.43	80.36	80.43	**88.56**	**87.33**
		Freq.	**2.14**	2.05	2.09	2.37	2.51	2.08	2.24	2.29	2.23	2.12	**2.38**	**2.24**
		E.E.	**3.17**	3.55	3.62	4.12	4.39	3.49	3.79	3.84	3.70	3.46	**3.91**	**3.64**
	3 Layers	maxT	**187.01**	47.86	53.24	57.23	75.21	67.87	78.02	**85.30**	**94.11**	**97.61**	**101.70**	**103.37**
		Freq.	**2.76**	2.47	2.33	2.17	3.02	2.19	2.54	**2.68**	**2.88**	**2.83**	**2.87**	**2.76**
		E.E.	**4.03**	4.77	4.42	4.02	5.82	3.95	4.69	**4.94**	**5.26**	**5.15**	**5.23**	**4.93**
	4 Layers	maxT	**290.81**	55.59	67.26	73.29	83.42	**85.09**	**100.05**	**97.68**	**114.66**	**112.07**	**118.76**	**124.38**
		Freq.	**3.48**	3.85	4.12	3.83	3.88	**3.41**	**3.88**	**3.38**	**3.88**	**3.48**	**3.48**	**3.48**
		E.E.	**5.71**	8.59	9.19	8.34	8.36	**7.07**	**8.11**	**6.89**	**7.90**	**6.94**	**6.84**	**6.78**
ex1010	2 Layers	maxT	**78.46**	45.56	53.45	54.04	58.18	61.40	62.91	64.69	67.81	65.74	68.92	71.77
		Freq.	1.93	1.57	1.95	1.66	1.73	1.78	1.75	1.79	1.90	1.66	1.79	1.85
		E.E.	2.30	1.97	2.62	2.12	2.18	2.26	2.19	2.27	2.45	2.03	2.23	2.30
	3 Layers	maxT	**144.43**	51.86	58.72	65.91	70.12	75.61	81.78	81.81	82.42	87.53	**95.80**	**103.08**
		Freq.	**2.71**	2.68	2.58	2.69	2.54	2.62	2.68	2.46	2.29	2.46	**2.68**	**2.94**
		E.E.	**3.03**	4.14	3.86	4.07	3.71	3.82	3.87	3.47	3.09	3.43	**3.73**	**4.18**
	4 Layers	maxT	**202.35**	50.92	58.65	66.59	72.77	76.34	84.75	**90.46**	**91.81**	**99.10**	**107.15**	**115.23**
		Freq.	**2.91**	2.86	2.81	2.88	2.82	2.65	2.82	**2.87**	**2.61**	**2.80**	**2.96**	**3.10**
		E.E.	**3.08**	4.54	4.36	4.49	4.25	3.88	4.11	**4.17**	**3.62**	**3.97**	**4.17**	**4.34**
frisc	2 Layers	maxT	**77.73**	44.05	49.92	52.92	55.33	54.71	60.62	60.17	68.23	62.64	68.36	69.70
		Freq.	2.20	1.88	2.03	1.98	1.91	1.64	1.99	1.81	2.30	1.78	2.10	2.12
		E.E.	2.74	2.52	2.75	2.66	2.52	2.03	2.61	2.29	3.12	2.21	2.75	2.77
	3 Layers	maxT	**119.51**	46.32	49.95	56.15	61.73	65.31	67.72	69.22	70.69	80.23	81.30	**85.67**
		Freq.	**2.48**	2.50	2.25	2.40	2.47	2.46	2.36	2.24	2.15	2.59	2.49	**2.63**
		E.E.	**2.64**	3.59	3.13	3.35	3.42	3.38	3.17	2.93	2.76	3.47	3.26	**3.49**
	4 Layers	maxT	**191.26**	46.60	50.42	59.96	68.63	70.68	73.30	80.59	78.44	**89.19**	**86.14**	**99.56**
		Freq.	**2.91**	2.93	2.54	3.00	3.26	2.94	2.79	2.96	2.53	**2.95**	**2.57**	**3.11**
		E.E.	**2.94**	4.64	3.86	4.70	5.10	4.43	4.11	4.39	3.53	**4.24**	**3.53**	**4.43**

Table 5: Results of some benchmarks on 3D FPGAs after scaling down the operating frequency (FVC = Fully-Vertical-Connection Scenario, MaxT = Peak Temperature, Freq. = Frequency, E.E. = Energy Efficiency, MC_{pitch} = Micro-channel Pitch. MaxT has the unit of $^{\circ}C$, Freq. and E.E. are normalized to their counterparts on 2D FGPAs. Optimal designs are shown in bold type.)

								MC_{pitch}						
			FVC	1	2	3	4	5	6	7	8	9	10	11
alu4	2 Layers	maxT	84.38	43.27	47.06	50.90	59.55	59.80	61.94	61.00	67.13	**74.53**	71.91	71.43
		Freq.	1.55	1.55	1.50	1.52	1.90	1.62	1.63	1.44	1.70	**1.97**	1.74	1.63
		E.E.	1.52	1.74	1.64	1.70	2.22	1.73	1.79	1.51	1.87	**2.22**	1.89	1.73
	3 Layers	maxT	84.33	42.91	**54.93**	55.81	63.47	68.34	69.84	75.99	76.30	75.38	84.49	84.92
		Freq.	0.69	1.81	**2.57**	2.04	2.30	2.31	2.15	2.26	2.15	1.91	2.10	2.10
		E.E.	0.44	2.18	**3.35**	2.47	2.89	2.86	2.59	2.72	2.60	2.22	2.39	2.46
	4 Layers	maxT	83.80	47.44	54.41	**60.53**	66.48	71.39	77.74	81.41	84.33	84.37	84.29	84.43
		Freq.	0.17	2.79	2.73	**2.86**	2.81	2.71	2.76	2.74	2.59	2.34	2.17	2.03
		E.E.	0.04	3.99	3.82	**4.19**	4.01	3.78	3.76	3.79	3.44	3.03	2.75	2.52
bigkey	2 Layers	maxT	83.96	56.03	**66.23**	65.94	69.58	82.58	82.89	84.12	84.62	84.54	84.58	84.56
		Freq.	1.77	3.49	**3.68**	2.98	2.93	3.51	3.26	3.10	2.97	2.81	2.71	2.58
		E.E.	2.74	7.15	**7.49**	5.82	5.69	6.86	6.30	5.88	5.58	5.19	4.96	4.64
	3 Layers	maxT	84.32	53.44	61.70	69.42	**84.60**	75.45	84.29	84.82	84.42	84.49	84.62	84.59
		Freq.	0.71	3.10	3.05	3.05	**3.68**	2.62	2.84	2.61	2.39	2.19	2.06	1.94
		E.E.	0.54	5.07	4.89	4.77	**5.95**	3.92	4.29	3.86	3.43	3.05	2.81	2.57
	4 Layers	maxT	83.83	**57.54**	63.19	70.96	84.55	84.90	84.76	84.51	84.60	84.75	84.47	84.38
		Freq.	0.19	**4.53**	4.02	3.85	4.32	3.74	3.29	2.87	2.65	2.45	2.23	2.06
		E.E.	0.06	**9.49**	8.17	7.65	8.59	7.24	6.16	5.15	4.63	4.21	3.70	3.35
des	2 Layers	maxT	83.45	44.51	45.30	52.06	56.60	59.71	**65.39**	59.23	66.77	62.91	69.51	72.23
		Freq.	3.22	3.21	2.50	3.03	3.15	3.21	**3.62**	2.64	3.26	2.64	3.21	3.31
		E.E.	4.79	5.43	3.92	5.03	5.13	5.24	**6.11**	4.06	5.27	3.97	5.12	5.26
	3 Layers	maxT	83.87	**48.79**	54.81	60.12	66.65	72.93	76.17	78.47	81.77	84.47	84.36	84.72
		Freq.	1.25	**4.78**	4.63	4.36	4.61	4.65	4.60	4.32	4.23	4.19	3.94	3.69
		E.E.	1.15	**9.49**	9.11	8.27	8.87	8.71	8.65	7.88	7.55	7.43	6.83	6.17
	4 Layers	maxT	83.82	50.18	**61.36**	66.26	72.94	83.57	84.46	84.54	84.39	84.68	84.58	84.46
		Freq.	0.31	5.65	**6.32**	5.76	5.69	6.22	5.44	4.94	4.50	4.13	3.81	3.50
		E.E.	0.11	12.75	**14.41**	12.82	12.56	13.76	11.42	10.21	9.10	8.08	7.29	6.48
diffeq	2 Layers	maxT	83.10	44.04	47.54	51.50	57.01	59.73	60.82	64.09	67.20	**72.41**	72.03	68.64
		Freq.	1.72	1.72	1.58	1.63	1.68	1.72	1.64	1.73	1.73	**1.91**	1.81	1.59
		E.E.	1.98	2.24	1.99	2.11	2.11	2.20	2.06	2.19	2.14	**2.41**	2.25	1.93
	3 Layers	maxT	84.23	44.30	53.26	54.22	61.72	62.16	**73.76**	77.32	74.46	84.82	84.72	84.60
		Freq.	0.84	2.08	2.42	1.99	2.21	1.95	**2.45**	2.37	2.04	2.34	2.22	2.13
		E.E.	0.68	2.97	3.54	2.75	3.09	2.63	**3.44**	3.23	2.69	3.14	2.95	2.80
	4 Layers	maxT	83.89	44.27	51.52	56.12	61.43	69.00	71.20	81.10	**84.88**	83.42	84.40	84.41
		Freq.	0.31	2.44	2.47	2.43	2.41	2.56	2.44	2.68	**2.75**	2.39	2.25	2.06
		E.E.	0.11	3.53	3.45	3.41	3.30	3.54	3.30	3.64	**3.77**	3.10	2.86	2.53
dsip	2 Layers	maxT	84.32	48.12	54.54	63.37	**70.77**	68.22	74.19	78.43	80.36	80.43	84.62	84.88
		Freq.	1.41	2.05	2.09	2.37	**2.51**	2.08	2.24	2.29	2.23	2.12	2.20	2.14
		E.E.	1.93	3.55	3.62	4.12	**4.39**	3.49	3.79	3.84	3.70	3.46	3.59	3.45
	3 Layers	maxT	84.34	47.86	53.24	57.23	**75.21**	67.87	78.02	84.90	84.56	84.98	85.00	84.96
		Freq.	0.64	2.47	2.33	2.17	**3.02**	2.19	2.54	2.66	2.41	2.25	2.14	2.00
		E.E.	0.58	4.77	4.42	4.02	**5.82**	3.95	4.69	4.89	4.28	3.94	3.69	3.37
	4 Layers	maxT	84.07	55.59	**67.26**	73.29	83.42	84.78	84.88	84.97	84.81	84.96	84.62	84.74
		Freq.	0.16	3.85	**4.12**	3.83	3.88	3.39	3.00	2.70	2.43	2.25	2.05	1.91
		E.E.	0.05	8.59	**9.19**	8.34	8.36	7.02	6.07	5.33	4.64	4.21	3.71	3.39
ex1010	2 Layers	maxT	78.46	45.56	**53.45**	54.04	58.18	61.40	62.91	64.69	67.81	65.74	68.92	71.77
		Freq.	1.93	1.57	**1.95**	1.66	1.73	1.78	1.75	1.79	1.90	1.66	1.79	1.85
		E.E.	2.30	1.97	**2.62**	2.12	2.18	2.26	2.19	2.27	2.45	2.03	2.23	2.30
	3 Layers	maxT	84.03	51.86	58.72	**65.91**	70.12	75.61	81.78	81.81	82.42	84.36	84.31	84.94
		Freq.	0.96	2.68	2.58	**2.69**	2.54	2.62	2.68	2.46	2.29	2.30	2.11	2.07
		E.E.	0.77	4.14	3.86	**4.07**	3.71	3.82	3.87	3.47	3.09	3.15	2.77	2.72
	4 Layers	maxT	83.96	50.92	58.65	**66.59**	72.77	76.34	84.75	84.99	84.87	84.97	84.59	84.53
		Freq.	0.26	2.86	2.81	**2.88**	2.82	2.65	2.82	2.56	2.26	2.11	1.93	1.78
		E.E.	0.07	4.54	4.36	**4.49**	4.25	3.88	4.11	3.61	3.02	2.78	2.43	2.16
frisc	2 Layers	maxT	77.73	44.05	49.92	52.92	55.33	54.71	60.62	60.17	**68.23**	62.64	68.36	69.70
		Freq.	2.20	1.88	2.03	1.98	1.91	1.64	1.99	1.81	**2.30**	1.78	2.10	2.12
		E.E.	2.74	2.52	2.75	2.66	2.52	2.03	2.61	2.29	**3.12**	2.21	2.75	2.77
	3 Layers	maxT	83.97	46.32	49.95	56.15	61.73	65.31	67.72	69.22	70.69	**80.23**	81.30	84.99
		Freq.	1.19	2.50	2.25	2.40	2.47	2.46	2.36	2.24	2.15	**2.59**	2.49	2.59
		E.E.	0.97	3.59	3.13	3.35	3.42	3.38	3.17	2.93	2.76	**3.47**	3.26	3.42
	4 Layers	maxT	83.97	46.60	50.42	59.96	**68.63**	70.68	73.30	80.59	78.44	84.49	84.64	84.50
		Freq.	0.30	2.93	2.54	3.00	**3.26**	2.94	2.79	2.96	2.53	2.67	2.48	2.30
		E.E.	0.09	4.64	3.86	4.70	**5.10**	4.43	4.11	4.39	3.53	3.74	3.37	3.02

Stratix™ 10 High Performance Routable Clock Networks

Carl Ebeling
Altera Corporation
101 Innovation Drive
San Jose, CA 95134
cebeling@altera.com

Dana How
Altera Corporation
101 Innovation Drive
San Jose, CA 95134
dhow@altera.com

David Lewis
Altera Corporation
150 Bloor St W., Suite 400
Toronto, ON, Canada
dlewis@altera.com

Herman Schmit
Altera Corporation
101 Innovation Drive
San Jose, CA 95134
hschmit@altera.com

ABSTRACT

We present the clock architecture of the Stratix™10 FPGA, which uses a routable clock network rather than the fixed clock networks of previous generations. We describe the flexibility provided by this routable clock network and how arbitrarily sized clock trees can be synthesized and placed anywhere on the FPGA. We show how this capability to generate customized clock trees can provide better performance through reduced clock loss while maintaining the ability to handle the large number of clock domains that modern systems require. We experimentally demonstrate how a routable clock tree reduces the clock loss of the user design implementation by up to 6% of clock insertion delay.

Keywords

FPGA; clock; configurable; interconnect.

1. INTRODUCTION

FPGAs are frequently used in a system as the nexus where many connections operating at different clock frequencies interact. This use model requires the distribution of many different clocks within the FPGA. Historically, FPGAs have provided a large number of pre-designed, fixed clock networks and each clock region is implemented using one of the fixed clock networks, driven by a selected clock source. The registers in the clock region are then connected via configuration to this fixed clock network. A mix of clock network sizes may be provided since there is typically a range of clock region sizes. For example, clock domains associated with transceivers and IO blocks are usually fairly small and close to the transceivers or IOs. For these domains a small and local fixed clock network is provided by the architecture. Larger fixed clock networks, in addition to global clock networks, may also be provided.

As FPGAs have scaled in size, the number of clocks has grown, driven by the increased number of interfaces. Simultaneously, the performance required of FPGA systems is increasing, which demands clock networks with smaller clock loss caused by skew and variation. Clock loss is most noticeable in global clocks, which have very long divergent clock paths and thus large skew and uncertainty. As the clock period decreases and clock loss increases, the clock period left for useful work shrinks. And yet many clock regions must use global clocks because there is no

appropriately sized fixed clock in the required location on the FPGA.

The primary motivation for the routable clocks in Stratix™10 is to increase performance by replacing fixed clock trees with a routable clock grid that allows arbitrarily sized clock trees to be constructed in arbitrary locations of the FPGA. We show that the ability to construct clock trees that are only as large as necessary can achieve better performance than fixed clock trees. Moreover, the routable clock network can efficiently provide the large number of clock trees that complex FPGA designs require.

2. Background

Historically, conventional configurable routing in SRAM-based FPGAs has been viewed as a poor implementation medium for very low skew signal distribution. Instead, dedicated fixed clock networks have been provided, with configurability limited to the connection of clock sources at the root of a fixed clock tree, and the connection of registers at the leaves of the tree. These dedicated networks have avoided most internal configurability.

Consequently clock distribution in an FPGA consists of a forest of pre-designed and fixed trees, each providing a clock to one part of the FPGA. Source muxes determine which clock sources supply the trees, possibly with upstream dedicated source routing. At the leaves of the fixed trees, a spine-and-rib structure is generally used for local distribution, with clock selection muxes choosing which of the overlapping fixed clock trees is connected to the registers. Since each clock tree is fixed, it provides only one design point in the space of design trade-offs between skew, uncertainty, insertion delay, power, and area. Even though an FPGA may provide a number of differently-sized clock trees, their location and size is fixed by the architecture and thus necessarily less than optimal for most designs.

Academic work uses similar structures; in [1], for example, the "First Stage Network" comprises source routing, source muxing, and the fixed trees, the "Second Stage Network" is the spine-and-rib level, and the "Third Stage Network" is the clock distribution inside the leaf function blocks.

This arrangement of clock resources reduces *clock tree synthesis* to the problem of clock *assignment*, where each clock is assigned to the smallest fixed tree containing all its sinks. If there are too few trees of a certain size and location, then the clock region must be promoted to a larger size tree and unavoidably suffer greater insertion delay and power, along with greater skew and uncertainty. For clock assignment to have a high success rate, clock distribution needs to be over-provisioned, even more so with multiple clock tree sizes.

3. Routable Clock Architecture

For Altera's Stratix™ 10 family we devised a new scheme for clock distribution to respond to the challenges arising from larger and larger, and faster and faster, FPGAs. In essence, the scheme we will now describe relies on routability to provide improvements more significant than the additional overhead.

3.1 Design Objectives

Our first objective was to increase the performance of designs by creating bespoke clock trees, customized in size and location to the clock regions they serve. Besides better performance, such customized clock trees improve area and power and reduce the over-provisioning needed to reliably implement a variety of designs. Thus we would replace clock *assignment* to large fixed trees with clock *routing* using a routable clock grid. A regular clock grid would have the welcome side-effect of greatly decreasing the irregularity and design complexity in the clock distribution system.

Our second objective was to enable new performance trade-offs. Although balanced H-Trees are the default, cheaper skewed distribution is also supported, trading area and power for skew. Alternative H-Tree implementations can include overlap, enabling

the design software to mitigate uncertainty, trading area and power for uncertainty. Finally, since small clock trees can be relocated without changing their topology or uncertainty characteristics, sub-designs can be duplicated or relocated without requiring a new timing closure effort.

Our third objective was to enable the successful co-design and co-assembly of the clock distribution system and the configurable FPGA fabric. In previous families, the global clock network consisted of recursive partial H-trees irregularly embedded in gridded channels that meshed poorly with the array-oriented fabric, and particularly poorly with any obstacles or other floor-plan irregularities in that fabric. The H-trees frequently inherited these irregularities and clock performance suffered. In Stratix™10, we wanted to co-ordinate the design of the fabric and the clocks to avoid these irregularities and provide clock resources optimized for performance.

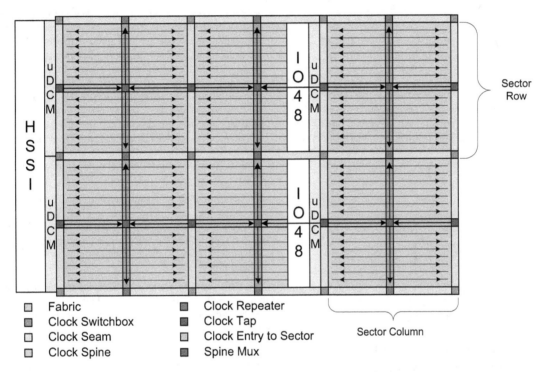

Figure 1 - All clock distribution for fabric and periphery.

3.2 Basic Features

The Stratix™ 10 fabric is constructed as an array of "sectors" primarily to facilitate a "divide and conquer" approach to chip design and assembly. Figure 1 shows a representative 2x3 sector array with one column of transceivers at the left and one column of IOs in the center. Within each sector, the local clock network distributes clocks to all the registers within the sector using a spine-and-rib structure that is very similar to previous generations of FPGAs. The routable global clock network, built into the seams between the sectors, distribute clocks to the sectors. This paper focuses on the routable global clock network since it contains most of the novel features of the Stratix™ 10 clocking subsystem.

The clock grid is shown in green in Figure 1 and is built into the seams between the sectors. At the intersection of the clock seams are clock switchboxes, shown in dark green, which connect the wires in the clock seams to construct clock trees. At the center of the horizontal seams is a clock repeater, shown in light red, and at

the center of the vertical seams is another repeater and a "clock tap", shown in dark red, which taps clocks in the grid for insertion into the sector.

Clocks are distributed by the global network to the center of the sector via the clock tap on either the left or right edge of the sector. Inside the sector, these clocks drive first through the clock entry to the spine mux at the sector's center, then through the sector's vertical local spine to the rib muxes which drive each black rib ("row clock") outward.

Several factors influenced the size of the sectors, each comprising approximately 25K LEs. First was the appropriate size for the leaf-level spine-and-rib local clock distribution. A second factor was the optimal re-buffering length of the clock wires. The length of the clock seam is about twice the optimal re-buffering length and each sector provides a repeater in the middle of each vertical and horizontal seam. Finally, all the other obstacles in the fabric – IO48s (GPIO groups), HSSIs (SERDES groups), processors, and any other hard IP – had to align with and/or allow the clock grid to pass through. This eliminated all irregularities in the clock grid and any clock path built inside it. The result is a uniform clock grid that encompasses the entire fabric.

The clock grid seams contain 32 bi-directional clock wires, labeled 0 through 31. It is convenient to think of all wires labeled the same as a clock plane. That is, if the clock switchboxes only allowed connections between wires with the same label, the clock grid would be partitioned into 32 independent planes. This view of clock planes is important because balanced H-Trees for clock regions of size $2^n \times 2^n$ can be constructed entirely within a single plane as shown in Figure 2.

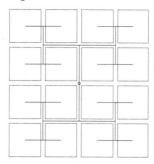

Figure 2 - H-Tree implemented in one clock plane

Figure 3 shows this planar view of the clock grid, with 4 planes represented using different colors. An H-Tree has been constructed in the red plane, and the routing from the clock source to the root of this tree has been done using the green and blue planes.

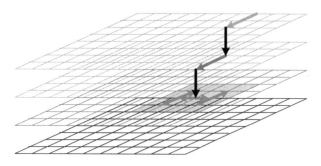

Figure 3 – A planar view of the clock grid

All clock routing is done by the clock switchboxes (CSB). A critical aspect of the routable clock network is the connectivity provided by these switchboxes. The clock network must route clocks with the least amount of delay, and the cost of flexibility in the switchbox inevitably is increased delay. In addition, flexibility also costs area and power. However, too little flexibility may result in a clock network that is unable to implement the large number of clocks in today's complex systems.

It is clear that to implement H-Trees, clock segments should connect to clock segments in the same plane and that these connections should be as low-delay as possible. In addition, we allow clock segments in plane N+1 to connect to segments in plane N. Figure 3 shows the route from the clock source to the H-Tree root implemented using these connections. Moreover, since these "upper-plane" connections are used much less than the same-plane connections, their delay is less important. This leads to the multiplexer structure of Figure 4, shown here driving one output on the east side of the switchbox. The multiplexer closest to the output implements the high-priority same-plane connections. Note there is no **E** input as a segment cannot feed

back on itself. The earlier secondary multiplexer implements the upper-plane connections and includes an input which can be connected to a user signal in the fabric, allowing arbitrary signals to be inserted in the clock network. The **gnd** input on the primary mux is used to force clock nodes to **gnd** during power-up, initialization, and testing.

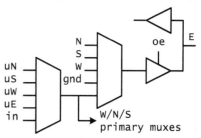

Figure 4 - Muxes driving each of the 4×32 CSB outputs

By construction, path delays in a balanced tree are delay-matched in spite of the unbalanced multiplexer structure of Figure 4. Take any path from root to leaf in a balanced H-Tree. By our construction of the H-Tree, every leaf is on the same plane. Thus every path from the root to a leaf passes through the same number of primary and the same number of secondary multiplexers. As long as the input-output delays for both the primary and secondary multiplexer are balanced within each, then path delays will be balanced. Upon greater inspection, the H-Trees used require even less: it is only necessary to balance paths from an input to two co-planar outputs exiting the CSB in directions 180° from each other. This observation lessens the amount of matched wiring in the CSB.

We also decided to share one secondary mux among all four directions for one plane. This implies that only one output direction can be connected from the next plane. This reduces cost substantially and the reduced wiring results in even better matching of delays in different clock paths, with only a minor loss in flexibility.

The CSB outputs are tri-statable since all grid segment wires are bidirectional. The choice of bidirectional over pairs of unidirectional wires was made in the interest of cost over delay, which is increased slightly by the tri-state driver and extra loading.

Stratix™ 10 and prior products contain columns of HSSIs and IO48s (each containing PLLs) which provide all clocks to the rest of the device. Figure 1 also shows how these are integrated next to or within an array of sectors without disturbing the clock grid. In Stratix™ 10, the HSSIs and IO48s are all pitch-matched to the sectors, and a new "micro" Distributed Clock Mux (μDCM), only one sector tall rather than the entire device height as in previous generations, can connect any external clock into the nearest two clock switchboxes with much less clock delay. This new DCM provides all *source muxing* features into the clock grid, and it also provides clock connections from the clock grid back into the non-fabric blocks.

3.3 Additional Features

Practical clock distribution must include clock gating features. In Stratix™ 10, the IOPLLs and μDCMs include a glitch-free clock gate to shut down a full clock tree. Due to the significant insertion delay downstream from these clock gates, and the synchronizers on their enable pins to tolerate it, they are not for cycle-accurate applications (e.g. "bit slip"). For cycle-accurate clock gating, enable pins are provided at the spine muxes in the center of each sector, as well as inside each leaf block function in the logic fabric. The spine mux also has an extra muxing option to allow gated and ungated versions of the same clock into a sector efficiently.

Since all peripheral clocks enter the FPGA through the μDCMs, they provide a convenient location for test features, like burst counters for at-speed testing.

Given that each plane wire consists of a low-resistance path with a powerful tri-state driver at each end, attention must be paid to properly initializing and configuring the clocks in order to avoid dangerous shorts. Careful selection of low Vt versus high Vt cells in the configuration circuitry ensures that all tri-state drivers respond consistently to the power-on signal. When later configuring the clock grid, the following sequence must be followed:

0. Power-on-reset drives all CSB pins to 0 and tri-states all repeaters in both directions.
1. Configure repeaters to drive in desired direction.
2. Tri-state CSB outputs which should be inputs.
3. Set CSB muxes appropriately.

Reconfiguration requires first undoing this in reverse.

4. Clock Tree Synthesis in Routable Clock Networks

The key advantage of routable clock networks is the ability to construct arbitrarily sized, balanced, and low-skew clock trees at arbitrary locations on the FPGA, where arbitrary means aligned to the sector boundaries in Stratix™ 10. This construction is trivial for symmetric 2^n-size H-trees as described in the previous section, and uses clock resources very efficiently. The construction of H-trees of arbitrary size is more difficult, especially if we want minimum-height H-trees that minimize clock loss. Figure 5 shows a 2x8 clock region. A balanced H-tree can be constructed as shown by overlaying the smallest covering $2^n \times 2^n$ tree, and then deleting those clock segments that are not used. The height of this tree is 7 segments (from root to sector center) while the minimal balanced tree has a height of only 4. Moreover, this tree uses more clock resources than necessary, and if the clock region is at the edge of the chip, some of the segments do not even exist.

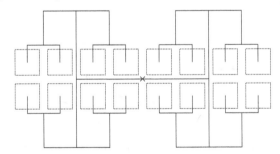

Figure 5 - Non-minimal H-Tree for a 2×8 clock region

We describe how to generate optimal H-trees for arbitrary rectangular clock regions graphically using an example. In summary, we start with the smallest H-Tree that covers the clock region. We then convert this H-Tree iteratively to achieve the minimal-height H-Tree using two complementary transformations. Figure 6 shows the construction of a minimal H-Tree for a 2×5 clock region. To get tree (a), an 8×8 H-Tree has been overlaid on the clock region (aligned arbitrarily at the lower-left), and all unused tree segments have been deleted. Tree (b) is

derived from (a) by simply deleting the segments that lead to the first split in the H-Tree. To transform (b) to (c), two redundant segments have been deleted in the right-hand subtree, reducing the height of the subtree by 2. To compensate, the root has been moved to the left by 1 to re-balance the tree. Tree (c) is transformed to (d) by reducing the height of both top-level subtrees by 1, removing 2 more redundant segments. Tree (d) now has the minimal height of 3. Minimal trees often use overlapping segments in the same track as seen in (d). As shown, the route from the root starts on plane N, as shown in red, and after one segment, switches to plane N-1 for the remainder of the clock tree. Note that if this use of an extra plane causes too much congestion, two segments can be reinserted to move the root up by one segment (stopping earlier at (c)). This increases the tree height by one while reducing the number of planes required.

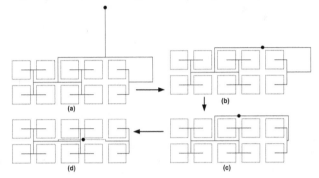

Figure 6 - Constructing the minimal H-Tree for a 2x5 clock region

While space does not allow a detailed description of this algorithm, it should be clear that these transformations are effective for clock regions of any size.

5. Evaluation

There are two key questions we need to ask of the new routable clock architecture. First, can it support very high performance circuits by providing low-skew, low-overhead clock trees? Second, can it provide sufficient clock resources to allow even the most demanding applications to map to the FPGA?

5.1 Performance Analysis

The primary motivation for routable clocks is performance, which is being squeezed from two directions in next generation FPGAs. First, wires are getting slower at smaller dimensions causing the clock insertion delay to increase. This increased delay, along with increased on-chip variation means greater clock skew. Second, applications using FPGAs have increasing demand for high clock frequencies.

As careful as we are at constructing clock networks, there will inevitably be some structural delay differences in different paths through the clock circuits. Even more important in current technology is the role of delay uncertainty, which derives from several sources. First, there is both local and global variation in both transistor characteristics and wire capacitance and resistance (on-chip variation, known as OCV). Variation can also be caused by differences in power supply voltage which can vary depending on local power demands, temperature variation across the die, and differences in coupling to other signals. This variation causes delay skew between different paths through the clock tree that cannot be known a priori. Thus, unlike structural clock skew, which can be estimated from the clock circuit design and compensated for to some extent by the CAD tools, unknown clock skew caused by variation can only be compensated for with increased margins. Both known and unknown clock skew results in what is known as "clock loss", which is the time that must be subtracted from the "useful clock period". As shown in Figure 7, this is the delay allocated to the user critical path delay, and is the clock period with all overheads like register delay, setup time and clock loss subtracted. Clock jitter, both at the PLL source and jitter incurred by power supply noise (PSIJ), also contribute to clock loss. Although we focus here on performance and thus setup timing constraints, hold time constraints are also important, and increased clock skew makes it more difficult for the router to meet hold time constraints.

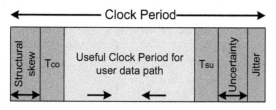

Figure 7 - The clock period available for useful work is reduced by many different overheads

The amount of variation and structural skew incurred increases with the length of the clock path. It is convenient to model the resulting clock loss incurred in a clock network as a linear function of the clock insertion delay. Advanced OCV analysis in fact accumulates delay variation using an RMS model, but for the purposes of our analysis, this is a secondary effect as it applies equally to both routable and fixed trees. The clock loss on the path between two registers at the leaves of the clock tree is $\alpha \cdot l$, where α is a constant and l is the divergent clock path length, which is the length of the path from the root of the smallest subtree containing the two registers. There are two observations we can make. First, the clock loss depends on the size of the clock subtree. Since even large clock trees have many small subtrees, if the clock regions for fast clocks can be restricted to small subtrees, the clock loss can be limited. Unfortunately, this can be very difficult with fixed clock trees and is a primary motivation for the routable clock network. Second, the worst-case clock loss occurs for register transfers between the two largest subtrees. That is, any path between registers across the boundary between these largest subtrees sees the worst-case clock loss.

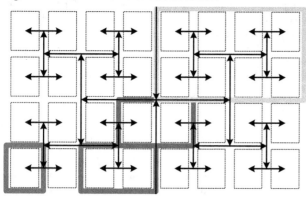

Figure 8 – Example of a fixed clock tree

This is shown for the fixed clock tree in Figure 8. The green and blue clock regions suffer little clock loss since they are aligned to the smallest subtrees. The yellow clock region suffers more simply because it is larger, but the least possible since it is also aligned to a subtree. The red clock region in Figure 8 suffers the worst-case clock loss since is spans the largest subtree boundary,

even though it has the same size as the blue region. Routable clocks by contrast allow the clock tree to be aligned arbitrarily in the grid.

The delay, and thus the clock loss, in routable trees is inevitably greater than that in fixed trees. We will call the delay ratio of a routable tree to a fixed tree p, which is the ratio of a_r to a_f, where a_r and a_f are the α constants for the routable and fixed clocks respectively. Given this linear model for clock loss, we can approximate the crossover point where the clock loss of a configurable correctly sized tree is less than that of a fixed tree as $1/p$. Equivalently, a routable tree whose height is less than $1/p$ that of a fixed clock tree will have less clock loss and thus better performance. We found that p is between 1.3 and 1.4 which means that the crossover point is about 75%. For example, a 6×6 routable clock tree has about the same insertion delay and thus clock loss as an 8×8 fixed clock tree. If in fact a system requires global clock regions, then a fixed clock tree will provide the best performance. But that performance will be less than that attained by the system when partitioned into smaller clock regions that are enabled by a routable clock. This has long been the approach in high-performance ASIC design, and one that FPGA designers will have to adopt for future high-performance systems.

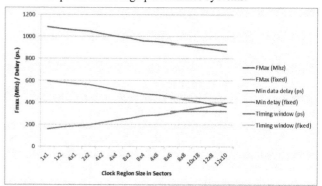

Figure 9 - Performance vs. Clock Region Size for a fixed maximum data delay

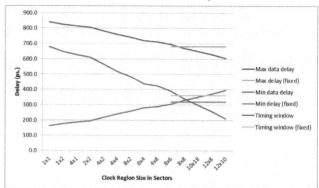

Figure 10 - Performance vs. Clock Region Size for a 1GHz design.

The graphs in Figure 9 and Figure 10 show how performance depends on the clock region size. The data behind these graphs are based on estimates of delays and clock loss in a fabric similar to the Stratix™ 10 FPGA and are used to illustrate the dependence of performance on clock region size. In Figure 9, we assume that the data delay for the paths that cross the worst-case clock tree skew boundary is bounded by some value (let's say 760ps), regardless of how large the clock region is. The clock period is then determined by adding the register delay, the register setup time, and the clock loss to this max delay. As shown, the achievable user frequency decreases with increasing clock region size because of the increasing clock loss. Moreover, the minimum data delay for these paths increases to avoid hold time violations caused by clock skew. The timing window, the difference between the maximum and minimum delay, therefore decreases. The straight lines show the comparative performance of a global fixed tree, assuming the ratio parameter $p=1.4$. This shows that fixed clock trees are better if the design comprises very large clock regions. However, if the design can be partitioned into clock regions smaller than 8×8, the crossover point, then routable clocks will provide better performance.

Figure 10 shows a similar analysis except that we hold user clock frequency constant at 1GHz and show how the available critical path delay decreases with clock region size.

It is clear from these graphs that high performance systems are best comprised of reasonably-sized clock regions. This should not be difficult (a 4×4 clock region in Stratix™ 10 contains over 400,000 LEs), although new system assembly methodologies will need to be used.

5.2 Clock Loss Measurement

To complement the clock performance model developed in Section 5.1, we evaluated the potential benefit of routable clocks using an experimental flow based on the FPGA Modeling Toolkit (FMT) and a separate standalone timing analyzer. The FMT is Altera's version of VPR [1] and has been used to develop all of the Stratix™ and Cyclone™ architectures. However, the FMT timing analyzer uses only nominal delays and is not capable of exploring the effect of clock uncertainty on performance.

To explore the performance effect of routable clocks, we place and route a benchmark set of 59 designs containing 776 clock domains. The FMT performs timing analysis and writes a file containing the XY location of each delay element in the circuit as well as its nominal delay. A separate standalone timing analyzer is used that includes the capability of modeling clock uncertainty using a variety of algorithms as well as modeling on-die delay variation in a variety of methods.

We are interested in the effect of the routable clocks on a modern die. However, the design set is, as usual, composed of designs from the previous generation that are much smaller than the largest die in the next generation. In particular, all of the designs fit into a 7mm×9mm frame, while we adopt a 15mm×15mm core to represent a moderately large FPGA die. To compensate for this effect we move the designs around the die randomly to model the effect of various placements of each design in a larger die.

The relative advantages of clock architecture on clock uncertainty can only be evaluated by a timing analysis that includes some aspects of tracking correlation between clock paths to the source and destination FFs in a path. One experiment uses the algorithm implemented in the Quartus™ software, which tracks the specific buffers and muxes used in each clock path and is able to eliminate uncertainty due to the use of the same element on both source and destination clocks. A simple overview of this is shown in Figure 11. This shows a clock tree in which each buffer has a nominal delay of 100 and variation of ±10, represented by the various y[i] which are constrained to ±1. Each buffer is annotated with a unique identifier and the set of delays used along each path is tracked. The delay to both source and destination is 500±50, so naively the skew is ±100. The source and destination clocks have elements 0 and 1 in common, so it is possible to reduce the skew from ±100 in the uncorrelated case to ±60 by tracking the common elements. This ±60 directly affects both the critical path delay by +60 and the hold time by -60.

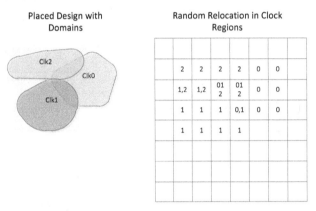

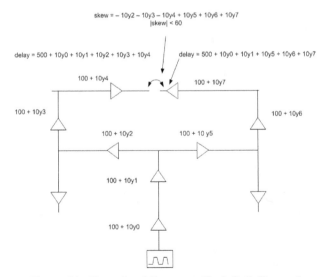

Figure 11 – Example of Common Clock Path Removal

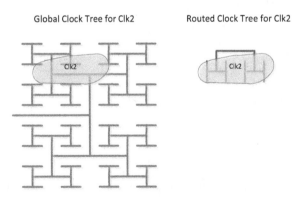

Figure 12 – Illustration of Clock Loss Experiment

Because routable clocks have smaller regions with non-common buffers, we anticipate less clock uncertainty. The experiment used to evaluate this is illustrated in Figure 12. In this experiment, we take all 59 pre-placed designs, and randomly locate them within an 8×8 grid of clock regions. We then perform a timing analysis of the paths within each clock domain in each design using, in one case, a global clock tree, and in a second case, a routed clock tree. The timing analyzer uses Elmore models to calculate the delay to each LAB location, and allows for ±10% variation in the intrinsic delay of the buffer and its drive strength. Wire RC characteristics, which have less variable contribution to delay, are fixed in this experiment. Clock delay is computed to the nearest 40um×40um location. Each design is randomly relocated 25 times.

Table 1 shows the increase in critical path delay, compared to no clock skew, for the global and routable clocks. It shows both the median and extreme values for the 25 different placements of each clock domain. The median case is modestly improved by using routable clocks. This is likely due to the fact that most clock domains are small, and it is unlikely to straddle the worst case skew location on the die. Further, much of the clock network delay is at the lower levels of the tree so there is no common delay to null out. However, there is a substantial reduction in worst case delay increase due to bad placements that have the critical path straddle the worst case location on the die.

It should be noted that the modest improvement in the median performance improvement due to routable clocks may not fully reflect the value of them to the customer. Our design set has an average of 13 clocks per design, and all of them must meet specific performance goals. We expect the user experience is closer to the worst case loss among a set of 13 clocks, which will be somewhere between the median and worst case values shown in the table.

Table 1 – Increase in critical path delay for global vs. routable clocks

%ile	Global Clock Delay Increase	Routable Clock Delay Increase	Difference
Median	5.4%	4.3%	0.9%
Worst Case	11.4%	6.9%	4.3%

This level of analysis is still pessimistic with respect to the maximum possible benefit of routable clocks, for two reasons. First, this assumes that clock buffer delay is completely uncorrelated, regardless of their proximity. In fact, much of the network delay occurs on the low levels of the tree, which being physically small, will in fact have delays that are highly correlated. Thus the source and destination clock delays will vary in a similar manner, cancelling out much of the skew. Second, the worst case skew occurs when the clock path to the source register is slow and the clock path to the destination register is fast. However, in this case, the logic and routing that is near the destination register will also be fast, and mitigate the performance loss. By modeling the correlation between logic delays and clock delays it may be possible to reduce clock loss.

We performed a bounding experiment to investigate this possible upside by more detailed modeling of spatial correlation between logic and clock buffers. This was done by generating 1000 random Monte Carlo delay maps with smooth variation across a specified correlation distance. An example map is shown in Figure 13 with the variation shown in standard deviations. Timing analysis can then be performed on each die by scaling both logic and clock delays by the respective standard deviation using the delay maps. This is not possible to do in general, since timing analyzers do not have die-specific delay information, but the Monte Carlo sweeps provide insight into the best possible result using correlated logic and clock delays, given a timing analyzer that can model spatial correlation.

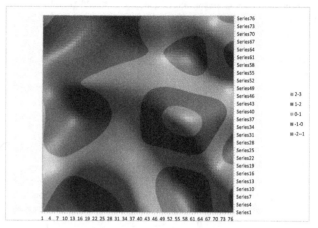

Figure 13 - Monte-Carlo Delay Map of Die, Measured in Std. Dev.

The random delay maps can be used to determine the best possible performance that could be guaranteed by a sufficiently advanced timing analyzer with knowledge of spatial correlation. The delay maps are normalized to a maximum delay of 1, since FPGAs are tested to guarantee that no region on the die is slower than the specified timing. This represents the worst case die that would be sold in a given speed grade, with some region of the die that is the absolute maximum allowed in that speed grade. Using this model, the maximum delay in a region of the die is exactly 1, but the average delay on the die is < 1. In the absence of clock skew, every path will have a delay ≤ 1, and this is the lower bound on delay that can be guaranteed without die-specific knowledge. When clock skew is present, it will sometimes help and sometimes reduce performance. The worst case result is all that can be guaranteed by timing analysis, given a sufficiently advanced algorithm to model spatial variation.

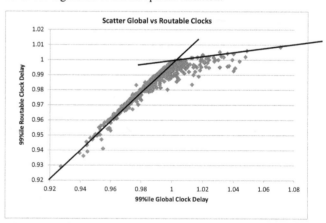

Figure 14 - Scatter Plot of Critical Path Delay for Global and Routable Clocks Using Monte-Carlo Delay Maps

In this experiment we take 1000 random placements and die delay maps for each of the 776 clock domains. Figure 14 shows a scatter plot of the 99th percentile of the critical path delay for global and routable clocks. It can be seen that the majority of critical paths are less than 1, due to average delay being less than 1. In this region there is no substantial difference between routable and global clocks. However when the delay increases beyond 1, which can only be due to clock skew, the trend is for routable clocks to have much lower delay increase due to skew than global clocks. The extreme clock loss for global clocks is 7% delay increase but less than 1% for routable clocks. Thus, the fact that routable clocks confine the non-common part of the clock tree to small physical regions that have good delay correlation can reduce clock loss.

To resolve the tails of the distribution of the clock loss clearly, we plot a quantile plot of critical path delay in Figure 15. The quantile plot shows the CDF of the critical path delay. Instead of simply plotting the CDF, a quantile plot normalizes it using an inverse Gaussian CDF. In this type of plot, a normal distribution will be a straight line with a slope that is the inverse of the standard deviation. Figure 15 shows the CDF of the clock loss for one particular clock domain (using half the delay variation than previously). The Y axis is the inverse Gaussian of the CDF of the number of samples with delay below the X axis; thus, for example, +3 on the Y axis corresponds to the 99.9 percentile. The lines are close to Gaussian except for the tails. When there is no skew the extreme is at 1.0 as expected. Routable clocks have an extreme of 0.6% delay increase vs. 2.4% delay increase for global clocks.

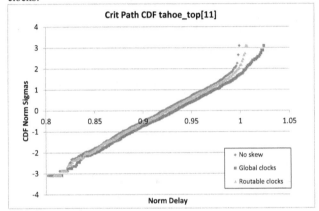

Figure 15 - CDF of Critical Path Delay of One Clock Domain

Altera has developed timing analysis algorithms that can take advantage of this correlation and achieve these lower delay values for routable clocks but these are beyond the scope of this paper.

5.3 Capacity

Ideally, we would map many benchmarks targeting the new FPGA to confirm that the clock architecture provides sufficient clock resources. However, such benchmarks rarely exist for future FPGA generations, and if they do, they are specific to a few applications and do not represent the range of applications that may target the FPGA in the future.

We thus developed a set of benchmarks based on a set of current large designs targeted for the Arria™ 10 family. These designs are mostly large, demanding customer designs, although a small number were large designs developed internally. Since we are benchmarking the clock architecture, we focused on designs with the most demanding clock requirements. We used the following methodology to scale the benchmarks from Arria™ 10 to Stratix™ 10. We first overlaid an 8×8 grid on the Arria™ 10 designs that corresponds to the Arria™ 10 clock spine boundaries.

1. The clock region for each clock was defined as the bounding box in the 8×8 Arria™ 10 clock grid of all registers driven by that clock.

2. Except for smaller peripheral clock regions, the size of each clock region was scaled up by the Stratix™ 10 to Arria™ 10 area ratio. This assumes that clock regions will become larger in the next generation.
3. Peripheral clock regions were not scaled, but instead replicated to reflect the increased number of transceivers and IOs in Stratix™ 10.
4. Finally, all clock regions were sized up to the smallest enclosing Stratix™ 10 sector bounding box to match the Stratix™ 10 sector array and clock grid.

We then extended this set of translated benchmarks to generate a new set of benchmarks to anticipate the clock demands of new, more demanding systems targeting Stratix™ 10. We did this in several ways:

- Expanded: The non-global clock regions were expanded to reflect more complex subsystems and components. Clocks covering more than half the chip were routed to the entire chip. Peripheral clocks were expanded to a minimum of 2 sectors. All other clock regions were expanded by one sector in all directions.
- Merged: To reflect the increased use of many small clock regions, we identified a user benchmark that had 124 1×4 clock regions distributed around the edge of the FPGA, and merged this with each of the other benchmarks.
- 3clocks: To reflect the heavy worst-case use of transceiver modes, we added 3 1×1 peripheral clock regions next to the transceivers.

The result of this process was a total of 101 benchmarks. We mapped these benchmarks using a greedy clock tree synthesis algorithm. For each benchmark, the clock regions were sorted by size, and then clock trees were synthesized for these regions in order from largest to smallest. The clock for a region is generated by first synthesizing a minimal clock tree as described in Section 4. This tree is then embedded in the clock grid at the first clock plane that has no conflicts. The route from the clock source to the root of the clock tree is then performed. If this route fails, the next available clock plane is chosen, and the route repeated. We expect more intelligent production code that tries different trees, different clock region ordering, and makes use of congestion information to do better. To ameliorate the effects of our greedy algorithm, we introduced some randomization: if the clocks fail to route for a design, the order in which planes are considered is changed and the algorithm is tried again. This is repeated several times to try to find a successful mapping. We found in practice this reduced the number of planes used by some designs by one or two planes.

The results of mapping these benchmarks to the routable clock architecture are shown in the graph of Figure 16. Three values are given for each benchmark: the number of clock domains in the benchmark (right axis), the maximum number of clocks used by any sector in the design, and the least number of planes required to successfully route all clock trees. To determine the least number of planes required, we varied the number of clock planes in the clock grid from 16 to 32.

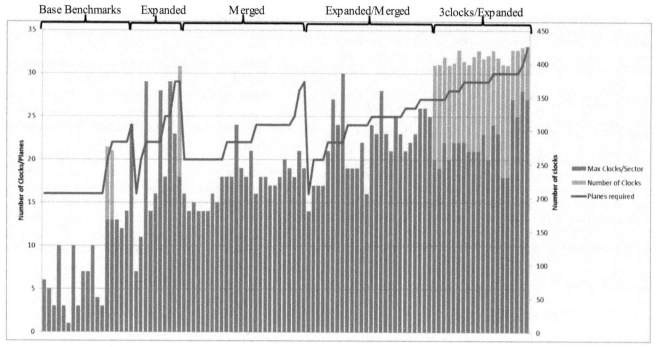

Figure 16 - Benchmark Results

The benchmarks are grouped together in this graph, starting with the base customer benchmarks at the left, and the extended synthetic benchmarks derived from these to the right. Note that there is no exact correlation between the number of clock regions and the number of planes required, since many small clock regions can be routed on a single clock plane, while large clock regions may require more than one plane for minimal height trees.

No customer designs required more than 24 clock planes, and all but one of the largest synthetic benchmarks routed successfully in 32 planes or less, with a majority needing at most 24 planes.

6. The Role of CAD Tools

One of the more exciting outcomes of the routable clock network is the possibility for CAD tools to further optimize performance by taking advantage of the flexibility in generating clock trees. We describe some of these ideas here.

Although balanced trees reduce the maximum skew, this maximum skew is between neighboring registers across the top-level clock tree partition. Fishbone trees, which are easily routed in the routable clock grid, trade increased global skew for reduced local skew, and may be more appropriate for some systems.

Useful skew is an idea that has been around for a long time as a helpful adjunct to retiming. Useful skew can be introduced into the clock network via differential routing. Thus two clocks can be delivered to a sector, one delayed with respect to the other. The CAD tools can then assign clocks to registers to take advantage of the useful skew.

The clock loss that is incurred across the top-level partitions of the clock tree may be reduced by generating trees whose top levels partially overlap. In the overlapping region, registers may select between the two clocks. Thus, the leap from one clock subtree to the other can be done anywhere in the overlapping region, and can be done when there is sufficient slack to compensate for the increased clock loss.

Routable clock networks also open possibilities for closer interaction between clock tree synthesis and system partitioning, placement, and routing. For example, instead of performing clock tree synthesis after place and route, floor-planning can identify the approximate locations of clock regions and clock tree synthesis performed first. Place and route can then make use of timing information of the clock tree to optimize placement for performance. This is a process that may take advantage of an iterative approach, with a fast placement phase performing the floor-planning.

7. Related Work

Very little research has been published on clocking architectures for FPGAs. Lamoureux and Wilton [2] [3] performed a study on the area and power implications of flexibility in the clock network. This work assumed the prevalent approach with fixed clock networks, with configuration in the routing of clock signals to the clock tree roots, and thus did not address general routable clocks.

Xilinx has recently described some details of the Ultrascale clock network [4]. The Ultrascale architecture is based on an array of tiles known as clock regions (CRs), although the array is not completely uniform since there are columns of non-tile structures like I/Os and transceivers. The clock grid comprises 24 "routing tracks" and 24 "distribution tracks", which pass through the centers of the CRs rather than along their edges, as done in Stratix 10. Both the routing and distribution tracks are segmented at the boundaries of the CRs. The routing tracks are used to connect a clock source to a central point, called the clock root, from where it is connected to the clock loads using the distribution tracks. That is, unlike Stratix 10, the Ultrascale clock grid is partitioned into two kinds of clock tracks, where the routing tracks can drive the distribution tracks, but the distribution tracks cannot drive the routing tracks. The distribution tracks are similar to the intra-sector clocking resources in Stratix 10, but with inter-CR segmentation added. However, the distribution tracks alone can implement only higher-skew rib-and-spine structures. Since horizontal and vertical clock tracks bisect the CRs, the clock root for a multi-CR clock region is located at the center of a CR, rather than at a corner of a sector as in Stratix 10. This implies different clock tree constructions for the two architectures. For example, the clock tree constructed for a 2x2 sector clock region will be fundamentally different in the two architectures.

The ability to optimize performance or power via CAD tools that can change how clocks are constructed or configured has been widely studied. An algorithm for retiming by adding intentional skew in the clock tree was first described by Fishburn in 1990 [5]. This idea has been expanded in recent years and incorporated in modern ASIC clock tree synthesis algorithms. It has also been extended to FPGAs [6] [7] and the insertion of programmable delays into FPGA clock networks has been suggested [8]. Even in fixed FPGA clock networks, it has generally been possible to gate clocks within the clock network by disabling clock buffers, effectively turning off the clock to sections of the clock tree. CAD algorithms that optimize power consumption by fully taking advantage of this feature have been described in [9] [10] [11].

There is a large body of published literature on clock synthesis for ASICs. In an ASIC, the degrees of freedom for implementation are much larger, and the requirements are narrower because of the specificity of an ASIC design. The predominant approaches in ASIC clock tree implementations are based on trees, although they might not have a fixed orthogonal topology or be composed of regular resources. Balancing of insertion delay and minimization of clock loss can be performed by relocating buffers, changing buffer sizes, or taking wire detours. A good survey of this broad field can be found in [12].

8. Conclusion and Future Work

The Stratix™10 clock architecture uses a highly configurable, routable approach to customize the clock network based on the user application requirements. This development is inspired by the FPGA philosophy that configurability frequently beats optimized but overly brittle solutions to problems. Our methodology to extend existing designs has provided confidence that our capacity for clocks exceeds almost all customer design demands. Our timing analysis experiments have shown that building a clock tree that is customized for a particular domain can reduce clock loss by up to approximately 6% of clock insertion delay.

This paper sketches the baseline approaches to solving clock problems with a focus on performance improvements. There are numerous software improvements that can leverage this configurable approach. Alternative distribution trees can reduce power at the cost of deterministic clock skew, which can be mitigated and even exploited by particular physical synthesis approaches. Finally, there are numerous causes of timing uncertainty, but many can be mitigated by varying the clock distribution tree built for a system.

9. ACKNOWLEDGMENTS

We are indebted to Jason Peters and his team for the benchmark set used to test the capacity of the routable clock network. Vadim Gutnik performed some of the initial analysis of the routable clock tree area and performance tradeoffs.

10. REFERENCES

[1] V. Betz and J. Rose, "VPR: A New Packing, Placement and Routing Tool for FPGA Research," in *Proceedings of the 7th International Workshop on Field-Programmable Logic and Applications*, 1997.

[2] J. Lamoureux and S. Wilton, "Architecture and CAD for FPGA Clock Networks," in *Field Programmable Logic and Applications*, 2006.

[3] J. Lamoureux and S. Wilton, "On the Trade-off Between Power and Flexibility of FPGA Clock Networks," 2008.

[4] Xilinx, "UltraScale Architecture Clocking Resources," 24 November 2015. [Online]. Available: www.xilinx.com/support/documentation/user_guides/ug572-ultrascale-clocking.pdf.

[5] J. P. Fishburn, "Clock Skew Optimization," *IEEE Transactions on Computers,* vol. 39, no. 7, pp. 945-951, 1990.

[6] D. P. Singh and S. D. Brown, "Constrained Clock Shifting for Field Programmable Gate Arrays," in *Proceedings of the 2002 ACM/SIGDA Tenth International Symposium on Field-programmable Gate Arrays*, 2002.

[7] S. Bae, P. Mangalagiri and N. Vijaykrishnan, "Exploiting Clock Skew Scheduling for FPGA," in *Proceedings of the Conference on Design, Automation and Test in Europe*, 2009.

[8] C.-Y. Yeh and M. Marek-Sadowska, "Skew-programmable Clock Design for FPGA and Skew-aware Placement," in *Proceedings of the 2005 ACM/SIGDA 13th International Symposium on Field-programmable Gate Arrays*, 2005.

[9] J. Lamoureux and S. Wilton, "Clock-Aware Placement for FPGAs," in *International Conference on Field Programmable Logic and Applications FPL 2007*.

[10] S. Huda, M. Mallick and J. Anderson, "Clock gating architectures for FPGA power reduction," in *International Conference on Field Programmable Logic and Applications, FPL 2009*.

[11] A. Rakhshanfar and J. H. Anderson, "An Integer Programming Placement Approach to FPGA Clock Power Reduction," in *Proceedings of the 16th Asia and South Pacific Design Automation Conference*, 2011.

[12] C.-K. Koh, J. Jain and S. F. Cauley, "Synthesis of Clock and Power/Ground Networks," in *Electronic Design Automation: Synthesis, Verification, and Test*, L. Wang, Y. Chang and K. Cheng, Eds., Elsevier Inc., 2009, pp. 751-850.

[13] K. Zhu and D. F. Wong, "Clock Skew Minimization During FPGA Placement," *Transactions on Computer-Aided Design of Integrated Circuits and Systems*, vol. 16, no. 4, pp. 376-385, 2006.

Boolean Satisfiability-Based Routing and Its Application to Xilinx UltraScale Clock Network

Henri Fraisse
Xilinx Inc.
San Jose, CA
henri.fraisse@xilinx.com

Abhishek Joshi
Xilinx Inc.
San Jose, CA
abhishek.joshi@xilinx.com

Dinesh Gaitonde
Xilinx Inc.
San Jose, CA
dinesh.gaitonde@xilinx.com

Alireza Kaviani
Xilinx Inc.
San Jose, CA
alireza.kaviani@xilinx.com

ABSTRACT

Boolean Satisfiability (SAT)-based routing offers a unique advantage over conventional routing algorithms by providing an exhaustive approach to find a solution. Despite that advantage, commercial FPGA CAD tools rarely use SAT-based routers due to scalability issues. In this paper, we revisit SAT-based routing and propose two SAT formulations independent of routing architecture. We then demonstrate that SAT-based routing using either formulation dramatically outperforms conventional routing algorithms in both runtime and robustness for the clock routing of Xilinx UltraScale devices. Finally, we experimentally show that one of the proposed SAT formulations leads to a routing 18x faster and produces formulas 20x more compact than the other. This framework has been implemented into Vivado [21] and is now currently used in production.

CCS Concepts

•Hardware → Software tools for EDA; •Theory of computation → *Routing and network design problems;*

Keywords

Boolean Satisfiability;SAT;routing;clock network;FPGA

1. INTRODUCTION

The Boolean Satisfiability (SAT) Problem consists in determining if there exists an assignment to Boolean variables that satisfies a set of constraints, typically presented in Conjunctive Normal Form (CNF). Since SAT is NP-complete [1], only algorithms with exponential worst case complexity are known to solve it. Despite that, very efficient SAT solvers have been developed over the last two decades [7, 10, 22, 3] and have improved our ability to solve many EDA

FPGA'16, February 21-23, 2016, Monterey, CA, USA

© 2016 ACM. ISBN 978-1-4503-3856-1/16/02. . . $15.00

DOI: http://dx.doi.org/10.1145/2847263.2847342

problems such as logic optimization [9] and formal verification [4].

SAT-based routing consists in encoding a routing problem into a set of Boolean constraints in such a way that any variable assignment satisfying these constraints corresponds to a solution of the routing problem. In other words, the routing problem is translated into an equivalent SAT problem, which is then passed to a SAT solver. If the SAT solver finds a solution, it is translated back into a feasible route. Otherwise, if the SAT solver can prove that no solution exists, it is guaranteed that the routing problem has no feasible route. This last feature confers to SAT-based routing the advantage of being an exhaustive approach, which is a key difference with other conventional routing algorithms.

FPGAs are growing rapidly in complexity and as a result they require a much larger and more complex programmable clocking infrastructure. For example, the largest Xilinx UltraScale device [20] can accommodate more than 600 total clocking buffers. In addition to the abundance of available clocking resources for global and local clocks, FPGAs also need to support programmable clock control signals such as clock enable and reset inputs for a wide variety of applications. All these growing complexities have caused the conventional clock routing heuristics to run out of steam, leading to significant routability issues despite the availability of vast amount of programmable resources. In order to address these emerging clocking challenges, we need new software algorithms that are able to distribute many clock signals over small regions of the device within an acceptable runtime.

This paper presents two SAT formulations for routing problems, the *binary node-based* and *unary node-based* formulations. The former adopts the commonly used log_2 encoding to minimize the number of variables while the later takes advantage of graph traversal techniques to reduce the size of the generated SAT formula. Both formulations use a directed graph to model the network in order to be independent of the underlying routing architecture.

Our first contribution is to demonstrate that SAT-based routing can address almost all unsolved clock routing problems, regardless of which formulation is used. Our second contribution is to provide a detailed study of two SAT formulations and to show that the *unary* formulation outperforms significantly the *binary* formulation for the kind of problems addressed here. In particular, experimental results obtained from almost 2000 hard clock routing problems show that on average, the *unary* formulation is 18X faster then the *binary* formulation.

2. PRELIMINARIES

2.1 Routing and associated terminology

Routing is the final process of FPGA synthesis. It consists in assigning routing resources to each net of the network in order to connect its driver to each of its loads. The routing resources in an FPGA and their connections are represented by the directed graph $G = (V, E)$. The set of vertices V corresponds to the wires in the FPGA architecture and the edges E to the switches that connect these nodes. For example, an FPGA interconnect network made of programmable multiplexers and its abstraction into a directed graph is showed in Figure 1

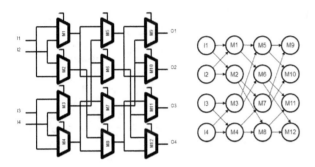

Figure 1: abstraction of a FPGA interconnect network into a directed graph

A routing problem R is represented by a partial map $R : V \rightarrow 2^V$ which associates to each source node its corresponding set of sink nodes. For example, the following routing problem specifies that I_1 must drive M_{10} and M_{12}, that I_2 must drive M_9, and that I_4 must drive M_{11}.

$$R = \{(I_1 \rightarrow M_{10}, M_{12}), (I_2 \rightarrow M_9), (I_4 \rightarrow M_{11})\} \quad (1)$$

The set of source nodes of R is denoted by $Src(R)$ and its set of sink nodes is denoted by $Snk(R)$. In this case, we have:

$$Src(R) = \{I_1, I_2, I_4\}$$
$$Snk(R) = \{M_9, M_{10}, M_{11}, M_{12}\}$$

The **scope** of a source node s with respect to R is the set of nodes that can be used to propagate the signal from s to its sinks $R(s)$. It contains the nodes that are both reachable from s and that can reach at least one of its sinks. For the previous example, we have:

$$scope(I_1, R) = \{M_1, M_2, M_5, M_6, M_7, M_8, M_{10}, M_{12}\}$$
$$scope(I_2, R) = \{M_1, M_2, M_5, M_7, M_9\}$$
$$scope(I_4, R) = \{M_3, M_4, M_6, M_8, M_{11}\}$$

A solution to the routing problem R is a subgraph of G which is composed of disjoint trees so that each tree connect a source to its respective sinks. For example, a routing solution to the previous problem is showed in Figure 2. The sources of the routing problem $\{I_1, I_2, I_4\}$ are expanded into disjoint trees (colored green, red and blue) to connect to their respective sinks. Each tree contains only nodes within the scope of its root.

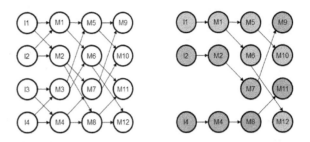

Figure 2: a solution to the routing problem: $R = \{(I_1 \rightarrow M_{10}, M_{12}), (I_2 \rightarrow M_9), (I_4 \rightarrow M_{11})$

2.2 Current approaches to FPGA routing

Conventional FPGA routers use iterative algorithms that try to converge progressively toward a fully routed network. During each iteration, all the nets are typically ripped-up and re-routed one by one. One of the most popular of such routers is PathFinder [8], which attempts to balance the competing goals of eliminating congestion and minimizing delay of critical paths. PathFinder initially allows nets to share routing resources, but subsequently forces them to negotiate with other nets to determine which one needs the shared resources the most. By gradually increasing the cost of shared resources, it forces nets to take alternative paths within permissible timing delay budgets. This heuristics works well in practice and can handle large networks in a reasonable runtime. However, there is no guarantee that it will always converge toward a solution, even if the network is routable, because it does not use an exhaustive strategy to explore the search space. Moreover, if the network is not routable, it will indefinitely loop and execution must be aborted after a suitable time limit. This convergence problem is inherent to all conventional one-net at-a-time routing algorithms: they cannot decide the routability of the given circuit.

In contrast, SAT based routers [19, 13, 11, 18] use an exhaustive approach which considers implicitly all the nets simultaneously. In theory, they are always able to find a route when one exists or else to prove that none exists. This advantage make them particularly attractive for the routing of highly congested networks. However, they cannot handle large networks such as whole FPGA fabrics.

In order to combine the advantages of both approaches, hybrid routers have been proposed [12, 5]. In [5], it is also proposed to change the interconnect of the FPGA architecture to make SAT-based routing more efficient.

3. PROPOSED SAT FORMULATIONS

In this section, we present two SAT formulations for routing problems, the *binary node-based* and the *unary node-based* formulation. The *binary* formulation encode the signal driven by each node in a compact way in order to minimize the number of Boolean variables. The *unary* formulation uses in theory more variables, but has two important advantages. The first one is that the generation of its routing constraints are directly expressed in CNF and the second one is that the actual number of variables can be drastically reduced by filtering those related to nodes outside the scope of the sources.

The main limitation of these formulations is that they do not support cycles in their present form. Therefore, some additional constraints need to be added in order to correctly handle cyclic graphs.

Similar *binary* formulations were proposed by [6] to encode various problems into SAT, and in [13, 11, 18] for detailed routing. Some *unary* formulations were proposed in [2, 16, 18].

3.1 Binary node-based formulation

The source nodes of the routing problem R are indexed from 0 to $\|Src(R)\| - 1$. We note $Index(s)$ the index of source node s and $K_R = \lceil log_2(\|Src(R)\|) \rceil$ the number of bits required to encode in binary format the indices of the source nodes. We first introduce the Boolean variables and then describe the constraints needed to encode the routing problem.

3.1.1 Boolean variables

For each node of the routing graph, a set of K_R Boolean variables is created to encode in binary format the index of the source node that drives it. For convenience, we can always assume that every node is driven by one of the source nodes. The total number of Boolean variables required to encode the problem is therefore $K_R \cdot \|V\|$. They are noted $B_{i,n}$ where $i \in [0, K_R - 1]$ represents the bit number i of the index of the source driving the node n.

3.1.2 Network connectivity constraints

These constraints express that if a node n is driven by a source node s, then one of the direct predecessors of n, noted $FI(n)$, must be driven by s as well.

$$\bigvee_{m \in FI(n)} \left(\bigwedge_{i=0}^{K_R-1} B_{i,n} \Leftrightarrow B_{i,m} \right) \qquad (2)$$

3.1.3 Problem connectivity constraints

These constraints specify which pairs of endpoints need to be connected. For any source node s and any of its sink node t we have:

$$\bigwedge_{i=0}^{K_R-1} B_{i,s} \Leftrightarrow B_{i,t} \qquad (3)$$

3.1.4 Exclusivity constraints

By construction, it is already guaranteed that each node cannot drive more than one signal. The only exclusive constraint required is to assign a distinct signal value to each source node. This is done by forcing the variable $B_{i,s}$ to take the value of the bit number i of its index.

$$B_{i,s} = Bit(i, Index(s)) \qquad (4)$$

3.1.5 Complexity of the formulation

The dominant constraints are by far the network connectivity constraints so we will focus on those. Since SAT

solvers uses CNF formulas, it looks reasonable to use the number of clauses generated from the Boolean formula 2 as our complexity measure. A standard way to translate a Boolean formula into a CNF is to create a new variable at each node of its DAG representation and generate a local CNF expressing the relation between this variable and the ones of its child nodes [17]. This process generates 8 clauses for each node labeled with the $\Leftrightarrow$ operator, so the number of clauses generated from the formula 2 is roughly equal to $8K_R \cdot FI(n)$. Thus, the total number of clauses is approximately:

$$8K_R \cdot \left(\sum_{n \in V} FI(n) \right) = 8K_R \cdot \|E\| = 8\lceil log_2(\|Src(R)\|) \rceil \cdot \|E\| \qquad (5)$$

3.2 Unary node-based formulation

3.2.1 Boolean variables

For each node n of the routing graph, we create a set of $\|Src(R)\|$ Boolean variables to encode which source node it is driving, if any. The Boolean variables are denoted $P_{s,n}$ where $s \in Src(R)$ and $n \in V$. The value of $P_{s,n}$ is set to *true* if and only if the node n is driving the source s, which implies the existence of a conductive path between s and n in the routing graph G. The total number of variables is equal to $\|Src(R)\| \cdot \|V\|$. However, since many of these variables can be constants, the actual number of variables appearing in the formulation can be much lower than that.

3.2.2 Constant variables

The following constant variables can be removed from the formulation:

- For each source node s we have $P_{s,s} = true$

- For two source nodes s_1 and s_2, we have $P_{s_1,s_2} = false$

- If n is not in the scope of s we have $P_{s,n} = false$

The first two cases are easy to handle on the fly. For the third case, we pre-compute the scope (defined in section 2.1) of each source node s by performing a forward / backward graph traversal from s and its sinks.

3.2.3 Network connectivity constraints

These constraints express that if a node n drives a source net s, then one of its direct predecessors must drive s as well. In this case, we restrict the set of predecessors to the ones that are in the scope of s. The direct predecessors of n are noted $FI(n)$.

$$P_{s,n} \Rightarrow \bigvee_{m \in FI(n) \cap scope(s)} P_{s,m} \qquad (6)$$

These Boolean formulas are already in clause form so there is no need to process them in order to have a CNF.

3.2.4 Problem connectivity constraints

These constraints literally specify the routing problem by asserting which pairs of endpoints need to be connected. In this case, they are expressed as unit clauses, which are technically treated as constants by the SAT solver. For any source node s and any of its sink t we have: $P_{s,t} = true$

3.2.5 Exclusivity constraints

They express that each node cannot drive more than one signal. This is a classic *at-most-one* constraint. For each pair of distinct sources nodes s_1 and s_2 and any node n in the scope of both sources we have:

$$\overline{P_{s_1,n}} \vee \overline{P_{s_2,n}} \tag{7}$$

3.2.6 Complexity of the formulation

Let's first look at the exclusivity constraints. For each node n, we note $Src(n, R)$ the set of sources nodes that contains n in their scope. Without any particular optimization, the number of clauses generated for node n is equal to $\frac{1}{2}\|Src(n, R)\| \cdot (\|Src(n, R)\| - 1)$. However, there are well known techniques to optimize the encoding of *at-most-one* constraints by using extra variables [15, 14]. For example, we can reduce the number of clauses to $3\|Src(n, R)\| - 4$, following [15]. Thus, the total number of clauses generated from the exclusivity constraints is bounded by:

$$3 \cdot \left(\sum_{n \in V} \|Src(n, R)\| \right) = 3 \cdot \left(\sum_{s \in Src(R)} \|scope(s)\| \right) \tag{8}$$

Let's look now at the network connectivity constraints. For each source node s, the number of clauses generated is equal to $\|scope(s)\|$. Thus, the total number of clauses for this constraint is equal to:

$$\sum_{s \in Src(R)} \|scope(s)\| \tag{9}$$

The combination of 8 and 9 gives the following upperbound for the number of clauses of the formulation:

$$4 \cdot \left(\sum_{s \in Src(R)} \|scope(s)\| \right) \tag{10}$$

This number is itself bounded by $4\|Src(R)\| \cdot \|V\|$ but can be much lower than that in practice depending on the connectivity of the routing graph.

3.3 Comparison between the two formulations

The equations 5 and 10, give three relevant criterias to choose between the two formulations.

- **The number of source nodes**: a high number favors the *binary* formulation

- **The scope of source nodes**: sources with restricted scopes favors the *unary* formulation

- **The number of edges per node**: a high ratio favors the *unary* formulation

The FPGA local clock networks have typically a low number of sources and a high number of sinks. For example, the local clock network of UltraScale devices has 16 sources and more than two thousand sinks. Moreover, the nodes on intermediate levels can only reach a limited number of sinks, which tend to restrict the scope of sources for clock routing problems.

We should thus expect the *unary* formulation to generate more compact formulas for clock routing problems. Accordingly, our empirical data shows that, on average, the *unary*

formulation uses 10x less variables and 16x less clauses than the *binary* for UltraScale clock routing problems.

The *unary* formulation has another advantage which is independant of the size of the formula and more difficult to quantify. It has the capability to describe many properties about signal propagation as simple clauses. For example, the property *"signal A cannot be routed through node n unless signal B is routed through node m"* can be expressed by the clause $(P_{n,A} \vee P_{m,B})$. In contrast, expressing this property with the *binary formulation* requires $\lceil log_2(\|Src(R)\|) \rceil^2$ binary clauses. We hypothesize that the expressiveness of the *unary formulation* should help the SAT solver to produce more useful conflict clauses during search which, in turn, should help it to converge faster toward a solution or a proof of unsatisfiability.

4. CLOCK ROUTING FOR XILINX ULTRA-SCALE ARCHITECTURE

4.1 Overview of Xilinx UltraScale FPGA devices and their clocking resources

The fabric portion of a Xilinx FPGA device is made of a two dimensional array of Fabric Sub-Regions (FSR). Each FSR is horizontally split into two halves, and each half contains numerous (typically in the range of 30-40) clock leaf columns. We refer to these as Half-columns since they cover half an FSR in the vertical direction. Figure 3 shows a Xilinx device containing 5×4 FSRs.

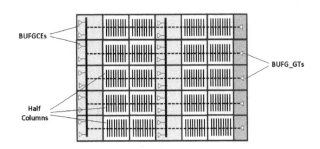

Figure 3: Clock connectivity on a Xilinx UltraScale device

Each Half-column is composed of two columns of 32 Tiles. A Tile is made of an interconnect attached to a Configurable Logic Block (CLB) containing 8 LUTs and 16 registers among other things. Between the two columns of Tiles, there are 16 vertical clock wires, each driven by a clock leaf buffer (GCLK) located at the base of the Half-Column, as shown in Figure 4. These 16 clock leaf buffers drive the load pins in each Tile via a set of 32 global clock nodes (GNodes) located in the interconnect part of the Tile (red oval-shapes seen in Figure 4).

The clocking resources within a Tile are shown in Figure 5. The interconnect of each tile contains 32 GNodes, driven by the clock leaf buffers of its Half-column, and the CLB of the tile contains 18 loads pins.

The connectivity between the leaf clocks and the GNodes and between the GNodes and the loads pins are not full cross-bars. As a result, the detailed clock routing of the Half-column can become a difficult problem for some cases.

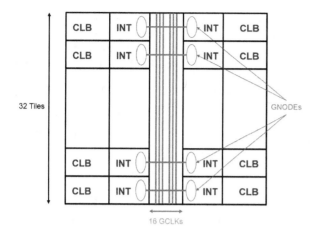

Figure 4: Clock resources within each Half-column

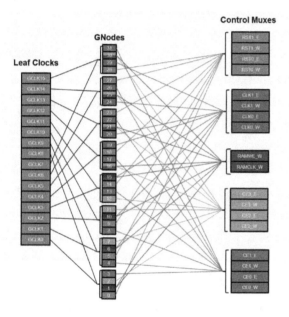

Figure 5: GNode connectivity within a tile

4.2 Clock routing of Xilinx UltraScale devices

The clock routing problem is broken into 2 parts:

- **The global clock routing** generates a partial clock tree that bring the clock signals from the clock sources to the Half-columns.

- **The detailed clock routing** completes the clock tree generated by the global clock routing by assigning clock leaf buffers and GNodes to each clock net within their Half-column. It is composed of many independent sub-problems, one for each Half-column.

Figure 3 illustrates the clock connectivity at the device level. The BUFGCEs and BUFG_GTs are the sources of the global clock nets while the Half-columns are the sinks of the global clock network. Each global net need to use a combination of global clock resources in order to reach any given Half-column.

The detailed clock routing typically takes most of the runtime of the clock routing. In some complicated cases involv-

ing many clock nets, some of the Half-columns might become highly congested and difficult to route. This was our main motivation to investigate SAT-routing as an alternative to solve these cases.

5. EXPERIMENTAL RESULTS

We have experimentally tested the performances of SAT-based routing against the current Vivado router for the UltraScale [20] clock network. First, we have collected the 51 regression tests of the Xilinx database for which Vivado cannot completely route the clock network and extracted all unrouted problems. We have then tested our SAT-based router on all of them using the two proposed SAT formulations. For this experiment, we have used the SAT solver MiniSat2.2 (available at http://www.minisat.se). The results are summarized in the table 1. The SAT-based router is able to fully route more than 82% of the tests and to find a feasible route for about 99% of the problems using any of the two SAT formulations. A test is considered fully routed when all its associated routing problems are routed.

We emphasize that these regression tests were specifically designed to saturate the clock network so it is not surprising that Vivado cannot route 51 of them. However, it is remarkable that the SAT-based router can find a feasible route for 99% of these hard problems.

In this experiment, the SAT router is aborted after one minute since we cannot afford to spend too much time on each problem. This is enough to find a solution when one exists but typically not enough to find a proof of unsatisfiability. However, we have independently verified that among the 17 unsolved problems with the *unary formulation*, 14 are actually unroutable.

	Designs	Routing problems
Total	51	1803
Routed Unary	43 (84.3%)	1786 (99.0%)
Routed Binary	42 (82.3%)	1783 (98.9%)

Table 1: Performances of SAT-based routing on hard clock routing problems

The next table provides a comparison between the two SAT formulations, based on 1783 hard routing problems. In order to avoid any bias, we have excluded from these statistics the routing problems for which the SAT solver was aborted for at least one of the formulations. On average, the *unary formulation* leads to a 18x improvement in runtime, contains 10x less variables, 16.5x less clauses and 20x less literals than the *binary formulation*.

	Unary	Binary	ratio	avg. ratio
Avg. runtime	0.129 sec	1.416 sec	11.0	17.9
Avg. variable count	990.5	10226.6	10.3	10.2
Avg. clause count	3102.4	51493.8	16.6	16.5
Avg. literal count	7500.4	150780.2	20.1	19.9

Table 2: Comparison of various metrics for the two SAT formulations obtained on 1783 routing problems

6. CONCLUSION

In this paper, we have proposed two SAT formulations for routing problems. Using either formulation, we have demonstrated that SAT-based routing clearly outperforms the traditional routing method for the detailed clock routing of the Xilinx UltraScale devices. We have also conducted a comparative analysis between the two formulations and experimentally demonstrated on a large number of test cases that the *unary node-based* formulation outperforms significantly the *binary node-based* formulation. This is interesting because the *binary node-based* formulation uses the mainstream paradigm for SAT encoding and our findings indicate that there are more efficient alternatives.

7. ACKNOWLEDGMENTS

We would like to thank the anonymous reviewers for their constructive feedbacks.

8. REFERENCES

[1] S. A. Cook. The complexity of theorem-proving procedures. In *Proceedings of the Third Annual ACM Symposium on Theory of Computing*, STOC '71, pages 151–158, New York, NY, USA, 1971. ACM.

[2] J. De Kleer. A comparison of atms and csp techniques. In *Proceedings of the 11th International Joint Conference on Artificial Intelligence - Volume 1*, IJCAI'89, pages 290–296, San Francisco, CA, USA, 1989. Morgan Kaufmann Publishers Inc.

[3] N. Eïf¡n and N. Sï£¡rensson. An extensible sat-solver. In E. Giunchiglia and A. Tacchella, editors, *Theory and Applications of Satisfiability Testing*, volume 2919 of *Lecture Notes in Computer Science*, pages 502–518. Springer Berlin Heidelberg, 2004.

[4] E. Goldberg, M. R. Prasad, and R. K. Brayton. Using sat for combinational equivalence checking, 2001.

[5] M. Gort and J. Anderson. Combined architecture/algorithm approach to fast fpga routing. *Very Large Scale Integration (VLSI) Systems, IEEE Transactions on*, 21(6):1067–1079, June 2013.

[6] K. Iwama and S. Miyazaki. Sat-variable complexity of hard combinatorial problems. In *IN PROCEEDINGS OF THE WORLD COMPUTER CONGRESS OF THE IFIP*, pages 253–258. ELSEVIER SCIENCE B.V, 1994.

[7] J. Marques-Silva and K. Sakallah. Grasp: a search algorithm for propositional satisfiability. *Computers, IEEE Transactions on*, 48(5):506–521, May 1999.

[8] L. McMurchie and C. Ebeling. Pathfinder: A negotiation-based performance-driven router for fpgas. In *Field-Programmable Gate Arrays, 1995. FPGA '95. Proceedings of the Third International ACM Symposium on*, pages 111–117, 1995.

[9] A. Mishchenko, R. Brayton, J. hong Roland, and J. S. Jang. Sat-based logic optimization and resynthesis. In *Proc. IWLS '07*, pages 358–364, 2007.

[10] M. W. Moskewicz, C. F. Madigan, Y. Zhao, L. Zhang, and S. Malik. Chaff: Engineering an efficient sat solver. In *Proceedings of the 38th Annual Design Automation Conference*, DAC '01, pages 530–535, New York, NY, USA, 2001. ACM.

[11] G.-J. Nam, F. Aloul, K. Sakallah, and R. Rutenbar. A comparative study of two boolean formulations of fpga detailed routing constraints. *Computers, IEEE Transactions on*, 53(6):688–696, June 2004.

[12] G.-J. Nam, K. Sakallah, and R. Rutenbar. Hybrid routing for fpgas by integrating boolean satisfiability with geometric search. In M. Glesner, P. Zipf, and M. Renovell, editors, *Field-Programmable Logic and Applications: Reconfigurable Computing Is Going Mainstream*, volume 2438 of *Lecture Notes in Computer Science*, pages 360–369. Springer Berlin Heidelberg, 2002.

[13] G.-J. Nam, K. Sakallah, and R. Rutenbar. A new fpga detailed routing approach via search-based boolean satisfiability. *Computer-Aided Design of Integrated Circuits and Systems, IEEE Transactions on*, 21(6):674–684, Jun 2002.

[14] S. Prestwich. Variable dependency in local search: Prevention is better than cure. In J. Marques-Silva and K. Sakallah, editors, *Theory and Applications of Satisfiability Testing ? SAT 2007*, volume 4501 of *Lecture Notes in Computer Science*, pages 107–120. Springer Berlin Heidelberg, 2007.

[15] C. Sinz. Towards an optimal cnf encoding of boolean cardinality constraints. In P. van Beek, editor, *Principles and Practice of Constraint Programming - CP 2005*, volume 3709 of *Lecture Notes in Computer Science*, pages 827–831. Springer Berlin Heidelberg, 2005.

[16] X. Song, W. Hung, A. Mishchenko, M. Chrzanowska-Jeske, A. Kennings, and A. Coppola. Board-level multiterminal net assignment for the partial cross-bar architecture. *Very Large Scale Integration (VLSI) Systems, IEEE Transactions on*, 11(3):511–514, June 2003.

[17] G. Tseitin. On the complexity of derivation in propositional calculus. In J. Siekmann and G. Wrightson, editors, *Automation of Reasoning*, Symbolic Computation, pages 466–483. Springer Berlin Heidelberg, 1983.

[18] M. N. Velev and P. Gao. Comparison of boolean satisfiability encodings on fpga detailed routing problems. In *Proceedings of the Conference on Design, Automation and Test in Europe*, DATE '08, pages 1268–1273, New York, NY, USA, 2008. ACM.

[19] R. Wood and R. Rutenbar. Fpga routing and routability estimation via boolean satisfiability. *Very Large Scale Integration (VLSI) Systems, IEEE Transactions on*, 6(2):222–231, June 1998.

[20] Xilinx. *UltraScale Architecture and Product Overview*.

[21] Xilinx. *Vivado Design Suite User Guide*.

[22] L. Zhang, C. F. Madigan, M. H. Moskewicz, and S. Malik. Efficient conflict driven learning in a boolean satisfiability solver. In *Proceedings of the 2001 IEEE/ACM International Conference on Computer-aided Design*, ICCAD '01, pages 279–285, Piscataway, NJ, USA, 2001. IEEE Press.

FPRESSO: Enabling Express Transistor-Level Exploration of FPGA Architectures

Grace Zgheib
grace.zgheib@epfl.ch

Manana Lortkipanidze
manana.lortkipanidze@epfl.ch

Muhsen Owaida
mohsen.ewaida@epfl.ch

David Novo
david.novobruna@epfl.ch

Paolo Ienne
paolo.ienne@epfl.ch

Ecole Polytechnique Fédérale de Lausanne (EPFL)
School of Computer and Communication Sciences, 1015 Lausanne, Switzerland

ABSTRACT

In theory, tools like VTR—a retargetable toolchain mapping circuits onto easily-described hypothetical FPGA architectures—could play a key role in the development of wildly innovative FPGA architectures. In practice, however, the experiments that one can conduct with these tools are severely limited by the ability of FPGA architects to produce reliable delay and area models—these depend on transistor-level design techniques which require a different set of skills. In this paper, we introduce a novel approach, which we call FPRESSO, to model the delay and area of a wide range of largely different FPGA architectures quickly and with reasonable accuracy. We take inspiration from the way a standard-cell flow performs large scale transistor-size optimization and apply the same concepts to FPGAs, only at a coarser granularity. Skilled users prepare for FPRESSO locally optimized libraries of basic components with a variety of driving strengths. Then, ordinary users specify arbitrary FPGA architectures as interconnects of basic components. This is globally optimized within minutes through an ordinary logic synthesis tool which chooses the most fitting version of each cell and adds buffers wherever appropriate. The resulting delay and area characteristics can be automatically used for VTR. Our results show that FPRESSO provides models that are on average within some 10-20% of those by a state-of-the-art FPGA optimization tool and is orders of magnitude faster. Although the modelling error may appear relatively high, we show that it seldom results in misranking a set of architectures, thus indicating a reasonable modelling faithfulness.

1. EXPLORING FPGA ARCHITECTURES

Better FPGA architectures are of great value. Efforts towards reducing the existing efficiency gap between current FPGAs and dedicated circuits have the potential to bring the many benefits of reconfigurable computing to new domains, such as faster FPGAs for cloud computing or more energy efficient FPGAs for mobile computing.

A software flow able to synthesize circuits onto a wide range of different FPGA architectures is clearly an essential component to enable proper architectural exploration. Fortunately, the *Verilog To Routing (VTR)* project [16] already provides such a retargetable flow supporting a wide variety of easily-described hypothetical FPGA architectures. For example, precursors of VTR have successfully been used in industrially plausible FPGA architectures to explore optimal logic block configurations [2] or to show area and delay tradeoffs [11]. Furthermore, VTR has also been used to explore radically new architectures such as those based on And-Inverter Cones [15] or to assess the feasibility of adding area-efficient hard-logic cells of limited flexibility to reduce the dependence on *Look-Up Tables (LUTs)* [1]. The caveat, however, is that VTR architecture files need reasonable accurate area and delay models if the results are to be meaningful.

Creating a good model of a hypothetical FPGA architecture is difficult because it is hard to predict the effect of transistor-level optimizations on the circuit. We assume that in an FPGA architecture there is not much logic restructuring involved and the transistor-level circuits are generally well known (at least modulo a handful of alternate implementations of some components). Still, two elements change dramatically the area and delay characteristics of an architecture: appropriate transistor sizing and correct signal buffering. Both these elements critically depend on the architecture of the FPGA being explored, such as how many LUTs are connected to a given crossbar or how many crossbar inputs are connected to the output stage of the flip-flop assembly. Implementing the required transistor-level optimizations to obtain a reliable estimate of area and delay is a significant challenge due to the sizes of the circuits at hand.

2. MODELLING CHALLENGES

One possible, slightly wild, idea, would be the use of a semicustom design flow, based on standard cells, to design the hypothetical FPGA from a register-transfer level description. The idea would be to use the results of the semicustom flow as conservative estimates of what good de-

FPGA'16, February 21-23, 2016, Monterey, CA, USA

© 2016 ACM. ISBN 978-1-4503-3856-1/16/02...$15.00

DOI: http://dx.doi.org/10.1145/2847263.2847280

signers could conceive at transistor-level. Actually, the idea is not necessarily that wild since designers have discovered over the years that for many complex components (e.g., fast arithmetic components) semicustom approaches are today even superior to hand-crafted circuits [6]—and thus represent perfect estimates of what is achievable. Unfortunately, for FPGAs, Kim et al. [10] have recently shown that FPGA architectures designed with standard cells still incur severe area and delay overheads when compared to commercial full-custom FPGAs. Furthermore, these overheads largely vary across FPGA components rendering the models hardly faithful and thus unusable to drive realistic FPGA architecture exploration.

The other possibility is the one attempted by Chiasson and Betz with COFFE [4]: reduce the complexity of transistor size optimization in an FPGA by exploiting the structure of the circuit and by building a tool implementing ad hoc but efficient optimization strategies. The result is a reference and parameterizable architecture built at transistor level and a set of scripts implementing programmatically the required optimization for a set of parameters, using appropriate SPICE simulations for measurement. Although this works quite well for the given standard parametric architecture supported by COFFE, the optimization process is quite slow (in the order of hours). More importantly, there is no support for other quite different architectures researchers might want to play with: the optimization strategy is built into the scripts which constitute COFFE and, although in principle adaptable, porting it to wildly different architectures might essentially mean rewriting the tool from scratch, albeit with an excellent starting point. This does not seem in line with the level of generality built in VTR and which we think the research community requires.

In this paper, we address this modelling problem by proposing a novel approach that facilitates proper and quick modelling of FPGA components for users who are not transistor-level circuit designers. Our tool, which we call FPRESSO, is able to model with an acceptable accuracy the delay and area of a wide range of largely different FPGA architectures without requiring the users to understand the issues of transistor sizing. For most users, all it is required is a topological description of the cluster of an FPGA and the automatic results are VTR architecture files annotated with area and timing estimations. We will demonstrate that FPRESSO estimations, when a reference from COFFE is available, are quite close to those produced by a direct transistor-level optimization. We will explain the principles of our optimization strategy in the next section; we defer to the end of it an overview of the rest of the paper.

3. OPTIMIZING LARGE CIRCUITS

Our approach to making sound optimizations of complete FPGA architectures is somehow modelled on the divide and conquer approach used in semicustom design: Firstly, transistor-level designers construct highly-optimized libraries of standard building blocks (the standard cells). Libraries do not only limit the functionality of the cells to a set of basic classes, but contain several replicas of the same cell spanning a wide variety of transistor sizes. Secondly, once a library is available in a given technology, they characterize the cells, measuring in detail their area and delay characteristics. Finally, logic synthesizers, besides logically restructuring the target design and implementing it with the available stan-

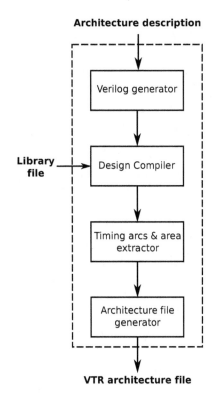

Architecture description

Verilog generator

Library file → Design Compiler

Timing arcs & area extractor

Architecture file generator

VTR architecture file

Figure 1: Tool flow for inexperienced users: Taking only an arbitrary description of the architecture (i.e., how LUTs, crossbars, etc. are interconnected) and a library of precharacterized components, FPRESSO models the timing behaviour of the architecture and returns a VTR-compatible architecture file complete with all required area values and timing arcs.

dard cells, choose the most appropriate functionally equivalent cells and add required buffers to meet detailed high-level delay or area constraints. From the optimization point of view, the key of the semicustom design process is in locally optimizing transistors within cells to display a variety of potentially useful timing behaviours, and then in optimizing the overall circuit at a much higher abstraction than individual transistors and SPICE simulations.

FPRESSO does exactly the same, conceptually, but avoids the unacceptable modelling errors of using standard cells by changing the granularity of the process. In FPRESSO, expert users construct at transistor-level all the usually required components for FPGAs, such as LUTs, crossbars, multiplexers, flip-flop assemblies, etc. In the first step, *Cell Optimization*, an automated procedure generates a variety of implementations in terms of transistor sizes (e.g., drive strengths) and optimizes all versions of the components. In the second step, *Cell Characterization*, SPICE simulations extract the delay characteristics of the cell library. Both steps require a level of expertise that not every user has, but once this is done and as long as no new functional blocks are introduced, a completely automated *Architecture Optimization* step takes from inexperienced users a topological description of the hypothetical FPGA (essentially, a circuit typically composed of a few hundreds of known cells) and optimizes all drive strengths as well as adds buffers to generate a reliable model of the achievable area and delay. It is

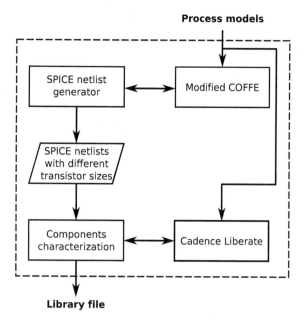

Process models

Library file

Figure 2: Library generation diagram.

important to realize that this last step, shown in Figure 1, demands no more transistor-level knowledge than specifying the cluster topology for VTR and yet is not limited to particular, predefined architectures.

So much this optimization procedure resembles the classic standard-cell design flow, that we strived to use wherever possible widely available off-the-shelf tools. Yet, the fact that our granularity is quite different (LUTs instead of NAND gates, so to speak) creates challenges in every step of this conceptually simple flow. In Sections 4 to 6 we describe in detail these challenges for the three steps mentioned above. In Section 7, we describe how we automated critical steps so that inexperienced users can get ready-made VTR models within minutes for arbitrary architectures. Section 8 compares our modelling results with the only immediately comparable tool, COFFE [4] while Section 10 elaborates on the value of the results. Section 11 discusses related work.

4. CELL OPTIMIZATION

The classes of coarse cells we need is pretty much implicitly determined by the architectures that we need to model: in typical cases, we may want to have LUTs, crossbars (that is, multiplexers with very large number of inputs), flip-flops, and muxes. The challenges of building our library will come from two sides: (1) how to automatically create a variety of versions of each cell with different driving strengths and (2) how to characterize each of these cells to enable a proper optimization. The former challenge is the topic of this section while the latter will be discussed in the next section.

4.1 Cell Transistors Sizing Flow

In a standard cell based ASIC design, a rich library with a wide range of drive strengths is essential to approach full-custom design efficiency [5]. Similarly, for our library of macro component we provide a wide range of different sizes, sweeping from very small components optimized for small loads, up to significantly large ones dimensioned to drive heavy loads.

For simple components such as standard cells, the sizing problem is not a terribly complex optimization problem as most cells are composed of just a handful of transistors. However, for complex components such as LUTs with tens of transistors to size, it becomes quite challenging, even for an expert circuit designer, to decide the optimal transistor sizes and automation of the process is essential. For this optimization, we decided to leverage COFFE [4] which, as mentioned in Section 2, is a tool that optimizes transistor sizes of a parametrized standard FPGA architecture. It uses SPICE simulations to iteratively search a range of transistor sizes to find the optimal combination for a given optimization criteria. COFFE happens to be quite suitable for our purpose since it already contains all the components needed for our cells; we simply modify it in order to isolate and size every component separately.

In the original COFFE flow, a component is sized while considering its context in the cluster, i.e., other components driving its input and connected to its output. We isolate the component from its surroundings and size it for a certain load capacitance C_L. To generate multiple drive strengths per component, we vary the load capacitance over a representative range of values. We use an exponential distribution obeying the following formula:

$$C_L(n) = C_{\text{Inv}} \cdot 2^{\frac{n}{2}}, \tag{1}$$

where C_{Inv} corresponds to the input capacitance for a minimum width inverter and $n = 0, 1, 2, ...N$, with the maximum capacitance defined by N. Accordingly, when substituting $n = 0$ in Equation 1 we obtain a minimum load capacitance equal to the input capacitance of the minimum width inverter in a given process technology. From there, we increment n to a maximum value N for which we obtain adequately large load capacitances. An adequately large load capacitance means that the components so optimized will never be used by the synthesis tool. With this, we would hope to provide a representative set of drive strengths for every component—but there is a catch as we will see in Section 4.2.

COFFE relies on a heuristic and not on the exhaustive exploration of all transistor sizing combinations—which would not be feasible given the very large search space and the need for time-consuming SPICE simulations. Instead, COFFE exploits the symmetries in the transistors netlist of each cell to reduce the number of transistors to be sized. For example, all the paths from one SRAM cell to the output in an LUT are identical, hence, only the transistors of a single path are sized. To further speed up the sizing process, the sizable set of transistors is split into several groups of a controlled number of transistors (5 or 6 transistors). This way, the number of transistor sizing combinations to be explored is further reduced. To compensate for any side effect of this clustering of the transistors, COFFE iteratively sizes the transistor groups until no further improvement is obtained.

To rank the transistor sizing combinations, COFFE uses the following weighted area-delay product as a cost function:

$$Cost = area^a \cdot delay^d, \tag{2}$$

where a and d are user-defined parameters that prioritize area over delay, or vice-versa. The circuit delay for a transistor sizing combination is estimated by a SPICE simulation. The area, however, is calculated by component-dependent formulas that are programmatically encoded in the tool. At

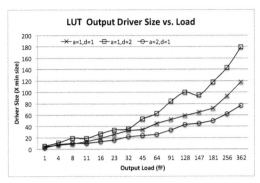

(a) 5-LUT output driver size.

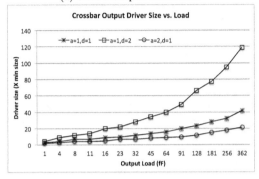

(b) 2-level 25:1 multiplexer output driver size.

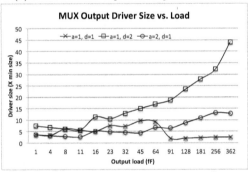

(c) 2:1 multiplexer output driver size.

Figure 3: Analysis of the output driver size for different cells, optimization criteria and output loads.

the end of each sizing iteration, the transistor sizing combination that achieves a minimum cost is selected.

4.2 Generating Variety of Components

We understand that a rich library should include a large variety of driving strengths per component. This variety should be evident from the component output driver, whose size must vary significantly from a minimal size ($\approx 1\times$) to significantly larger sizes ($> 100\times$). This is due to the fact that the output driver is mainly responsible of restoring the output signal and delivering enough drive strength for the component load.

Experimenting with different weight values (a and b) in the optimization cost function (2), we found out that sticking to a certain combination of weight values (e.g., $a = 1, d = 1$) would not produce the type of variety we want in our library. On the other hand, we found that generating a large set of transistor sizings with different optimization

weights coupled with a later pruning creates the desired variety.

Figure 3 shows the size of the output driver of several components, for different loads. A balanced optimization (weight values $a = 1, d = 1$) does not generate enough variety, and in some cases it stops increasing the size of the output driver way too early. This happens when the area increases by a factor that is larger than the delay reduction. Accordingly, an optimization that favours delay but that does not completely ignore area (e.g., weight values $a = 1, d = 2$) will generate larger drive strengths. At the same time, an optimization that gives more weight to area (e.g., weight values $a = 2, d = 1$) will not generate large drive strengths but components that may still be useful to optimize area in non critical paths of the FPGA architecture.

5. CELL CHARACTERIZATION

Cell characterization is a very well understood process: conceptually, tens or hundred of SPICE simulations are run within some simple testbenches with varying driving slopes or load capacitances (and process corner, temperature, and voltage, but this is outside the scope of our goals). EDA tools that perform the task in a completely automated way exist and, of course, they interface very well with any other part of semicustom toolchains. For our purpose, we have decided to use Cadence Virtuoso Liberate: an advanced library characterization tool that creates electrical views, such as timing and power, in standard formats like the Synopsys Liberty format (.lib). To characterize a cell, Liberate takes as input the SPICE netlist along with the foundry device models.

Our components are indeed qualitatively similar to standard cells (and in some cases are practically identical, such as flip-flops or 2-to-1 multiplexers). Unfortunately, many of the critical components, such as LUTs and large multi-level muxes for crossbars, are much bigger (in terms of both transistor count and number of inputs) than the biggest typical standard cells. This implies that, for understandable scalability issues, a tool like Liberate naturally fails to characterize some necessary components. We will discuss in this section how we circumvented the problems.

5.1 LUT Characterization

Liberate is capable of characterizing small size LUTs, such as LUTs with 2 or 3 inputs. However, as the number of inputs increases, the number of SRAMs grows exponentially, making the LUT characterization a major challenge for Liberate. Having a complex functionality and a high number of variables to track, Liberate fails to perform the required task.

In order to simplify the problem, we reduce the LUT complexity for the characterization tool by exploiting the symmetries in the LUT transistor design. As seen in Figure 4, a signal can travel from an input (e.g., in_A) to the output through what seems to be different paths. In practice, however, these paths include transistors of identical sizes because each transistor belonging to a level of the binary tree has the same size. The only actual difference is whether the input inverter is used or not. Thus, it is sufficient to pick a limited number of *representative paths* during the characterization to cover all the different input-to-output timing arcs, which can done by fixing the configurations of the SRAMs

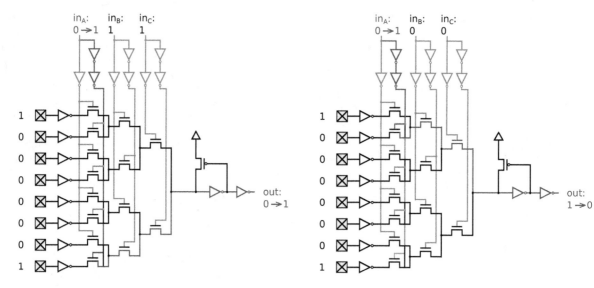

Figure 4: Transistor design of a 3-input LUT. Representative paths that ensure all signal transitions between the inputs and the output are selected to simplify the characterization of an LUT.

(i.e., setting them to '1' or '0'). These representative paths must be selected in a way that guaranties the characterization of both inverted and non-inverted input-to-output paths. Furthermore, these paths must enable all possible signal transitions (rise-fall, rise-rise, fall-fall and fall-rise) between the inputs and the output.For that purpose, we set the configuration bits S_0 and S_7 in the example of Figure 4 to '1' and the remaining ones to '0'. By configuring the 3-LUT in this way, all the input-to-output timing paths, along with their respective rise and fall delays, will exist in the generated library. To configure the LUT, the SRAM cells are connected directly to VDD and GND, reducing the number of variables visible to Liberate.

Once the LUT is characterized for the representative paths, the library is then corrected with the respective Boolean function (logic synthesis tools need the exact function to operate properly) and the SRAMs are added back as input variables. It is important to bring back the complete LUT interface into the library so that it can be directly associated with its circuit description when read into the later stages of FPRESSO.

5.2 MUX Characterization

FPGA crossbars are generally designed as 2-level multiplexers as shown in Figure 5. Each multiplexer is usually connected to all or to a fraction of the crossbar inputs, depending on the desired sparsity. In the Stratix-IV FPGA for instance, the crossbar has 72 inputs and is half populated [12, 13], which means that each 2-level multiplexer has 36 inputs and 12 SRAMs.

So, similar to LUTs, these multiplexers can have a large number of inputs making it impossible for Liberate to characterize. However, to ensure the crossbar functionality, only two SRAMs are set during one configuration (one SRAM in the first level and one in the second) to connect a single input to the output. This property is used to simplify the characterization of the 2-level multiplexers: For each input, the mux is configured to enable the path from that particular input to the output by connecting the two related SRAMs

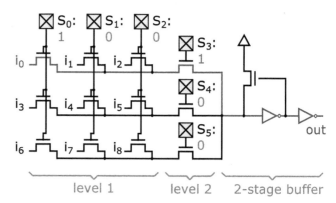

Figure 5: Transistor design and configuration of a 2-level multiplexer.

to VDD and the remaining ones to GND. Figure 5 shows the general structure of a 9:1 mux, where, to connect input i_0 to the output, S_0 and S_3 are set to '1' while the remaining configuration bits are set to '0'. Once an input-to-output path is enabled, the remaining inputs are no longer relevant and can be forced to a logic value ('1' in our case). The mux input is then characterized and the process is repeated for all inputs, which generates multiple library files. Thus, in a final step, all the generated libraries are merged back into one, the Boolean function is corrected and the SRAMS are reintroduced as input variables.

6. ARCHITECTURE OPTIMIZATION

The tasks described in the two previous sections are needed to prepare the library of cells used to construct the architecture. As with standard cells, their development needs to be performed off-line by fairly experienced designers: in case of porting the library from one technology node to another, the process is almost automatic, but the expertise of a transistor-level designer is required if one is to add new components to the library (for instance, non-LUT logic

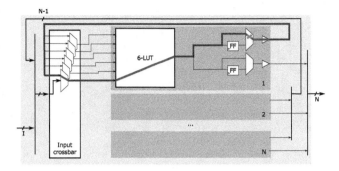

Figure 6: Timing loops within the logic cluster.

blocks). Once the library is available, architects can compose circuits using the defined functional blocks (we will discuss in detail how in Section 7): they define functionally the architecture of the FPGA and completely ignore electric and timing issues. To obtain an area or timing model of the architecture, it is necessary to take the netlist and optimize it for some specific constraints (such as minimizing the delay along some path) in two senses: (i) every functional block can be replaced with another of equal functionality but different characteristics and (ii) buffers can be added wherever it makes sense to. Although this is only a little part of what a logic synthesizer for a semicustom flow does, it does it remarkably well and it is readily available. We thus decided to use *Synopsys Design Compiler* for the global architecture phase—that is, for the optimization that needs to be run for each and every specific architecture a researcher is interested in exploring.

Since Design Compiler is not used within its typical flow as a logic synthesizer but mainly as a driving-strength optimization tool, the FPGA design must be annotated with proper attributes (such as the *set_size_only* attribute for the FPGA cells) indicating that they must only be sized. And, although SRAM cells exist in the FPGA design, Design Compiler has no notion of the reconfigurability of the FPGA and identifies feedbacks as timing loops. For instance, Figure 6 shows one of these timing loops that starts at the feedback multiplexer and continues through the crossbar, the LUT and then back into the feedback multiplexer. This combinatorial loop does not occur in configured FPGAs, but Design Compiler cannot identify this from the design. It can break the timing arcs itself, but for consistency, we decided to specifically tell Design Compiler that the loop does not exist, by breaking the timing path on the feedback multiplexer. Even SRAMs can be seen as a loop of two inverters which is then interpreted by Design Compiler as a timing loop. However, since there is no interest in sizing the SRAMs, Design Compiler must be instructed to ignore them (by assigning the *set_dont_touch* attribute to those inverters) so that it does not try to optimize this part of the circuit.

7. AUTOMATING FPRESSO

Having the main optimization part handled by Design Compiler, the major task of FPRESSO is taken care of. We are just left with the task of abstracting the complexity of the flow from the user and automating the different parts of FPRESSO as shown in Figure 1. This mainly consists of preparing a circuit of the FPGA design for Design Compiler and extracting the static timing analysis data from its tim-

ing reports to produce the VTR architecture file. We discuss in this section how we automate these parts of the tool flow.

7.1 Architecture Generation

To model any FPGA, FPRESSO requires, as input, a description of the architecture, along with the library of cells. The user can either provide a complete VTR architecture file (XML format) or a simplified version of this architecture file. In the simplified version, it is sufficient to specify the different components of the FPGA, their interface (i.e. inputs, outputs and number of instances) and the way they are connected.

Figure 7 gives an example of the user architecture description using our simplified XML format. The example describes the architecture of Figure 8 using 4-input LUTs, 19 cluster inputs, and 6 LUTs per cluster. The description of the architecture is quite simple. Any hierarchical structure can be easily described as a hierarchy of XML elements, similar to the VTR architecture file. The different XML tags allow the user to declare any structural or functional component (e.g., cluster or LUT). The tool flow automatically identifies the hierarchy between the different components and determines which are functional cells and which are container components used only to maintain the hierarchical structure of the architecture. Interconnection blocks such as crossbars can be described simply by their input and output connections as well as they density (i.e. complete, sparse with a user-specified density, etc.) and FPRESSO will automatically translate it into 2-level multiplexer with the appropriate input connectivities. The positions of the switches of the 2-level multiplexer can be specified by the user using elaborate XML specifications. Some default topologies exist also in FPRESSO and can be directly used.

Generally, any FPGA cluster topology that can be expressed in XML format can be modelled by FPRESSO. However, a typical XML description (like the ones used in the VTR flow) can only provide a generic view of the architecture without having to detail accurate architectural specifications. For example, modes of operation can be easily specified using XML (e.g., a 6-LUT can also be configured as two 5-LUTs); however, FPRESSO needs to understand how these modes are translated into hardware components (e.g., the two 5-LUTs are connected through a multiplexer to form the 6-LUT). This kind of information needs to be added by the user to the XML file, providing FPRESSO with a detailed view of the circuit behind the architecture. This gives the user full flexibility and allows for the exploration of a wide range of FPGA architectures. This flexibility is ensured throughout the different stages of the tool flow. FPRESSO takes the architecture description file and translates it into a complete Verilog circuit where all components are instantiated and connected hierarchically the way they are expressed in the input description file.

7.2 Model Extraction

Knowing the different logic blocks and their interconnects, FPRESSO automatically generates the scripts needed to read the FPGA's Verilog description into Design Compiler, constrain it, optimize it, and report the timing arcs of each element. Once the Verilog description of the FPGA design is read into Design Compiler and assigned the right attributes, it is constrained from every cluster input to every cluster

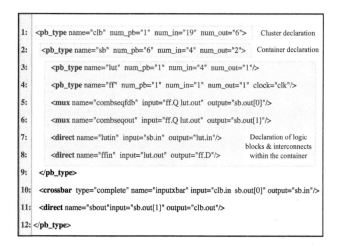

```
1:   <pb_type name="clb" num_pb="1" num_in="19" num_out="6">    Cluster declaration

2:     <pb_type name="sb" num_pb="6" num_in="4" num_out="2">     Container declaration

3:       <pb_type name="lut" num_pb="1" num_in="4" num_out="1"/>

4:       <pb_type name="ff" num_pb="1" num_in="1" num_out="1" clock="clk"/>

5:       <mux name="combseqfdb" input="ff.Q lut.out" output="sb.out[0]"/>

6:       <mux name="combseqout" input="ff.Q lut.out" output="sb.out[1]"/>

7:       <direct name="lutin" input="sb.in" output="lut.in"/>        Declaration of logic
                                                                     blocks & interconnects
8:       <direct name="ffin" input="lut.out" output="ff.D"/>         within the container

9:     </pb_type>

10:    <crossbar type="complete" name="inputxbar" input="clb.in sb.out[0]" output="sb.in"/>

11:    <direct name="sbout" input="sb.out[1]" output="clb.out"/>

12:  </pb_type>
```

Figure 7: Example of the user's architecture description file for the architecture of Figure 8, using 4-inputs LUTs, 19 cluster inputs, and 6 logic blocks per cluster.

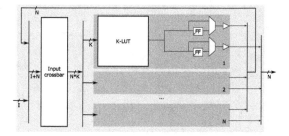

Figure 8: The FPGA architecture used in our experiments, with parameters K, N, and I.

output. However, local feedbacks are a crucial aspect of the FPGA architecture, hence, additional constraints are set on the feedback paths, between the outputs and the inputs of the registers.

During the architecture optimization, FPRESSO targets delay, by default. It starts first by constraining the architecture for a maximum delay of zero, which obviously will not be met. However, at the end of this initial iteration, Design Compiler returns the minimum achievable delay, which is then increased by 10% and set as delay target in a second iteration of the optimization. This time, the timing constraint will be met and the provided extra slack is used by the tool to sensibly reduce the associated area.

Knowing the various cells that compose the FPGA logic cluster and their interconnections, FPRESSO can request the delays of all existing timing arcs from Design Compiler. All the timing reports are then parsed and the cluster cells are back annotated with the delay of every input-to-output timing arc. The overall area of the cluster is also extracted. Having the architecture description, the timing arcs, and the area estimation of the FPGA cluster design, FPRESSO returns a fully annotated architecture file in XML format, compatible with the VTR flow.

8. EXPERIMENTAL SETUP

FPRESSO can read in an architecture description to understand the FPGA cluster design it is modelling, and can thus be used on any architecture topology, as explained in the previous sections. However, in order to benchmark its performance, we restrict our experimental setup to the architectures supported by COFFE, the state-of-the-art modelling tool for FPGA components.

COFFE's architectural exploration is limited to a given FPGA topology customizable through some parameters. Figure 8 shows the cluster architecture supported by COFFE and used in our experiments, along with its three main parameters K, N, and I which represent the number of LUT inputs, total number of LUTs (or BLEs) in a cluster, and number of cluster inputs, respectively. Accordingly, we generate different FPGA clusters by varying K, N, and I and optimize the corresponding components using

the two tool flows: FPRESSO and COFFE. To limit variance in the comparison, all local register feedbacks are disabled in COFFE (and not included in FPRESSO), the crossbar is fully populated and the LUTs are not fracturable. A 65nm UMC technology is used in a typical corner in both flows.

Although *Switch Blocks (SBs)* and *Connection Blocks (CBs)* should be modellable in FPRESSO—they simply are 2-level multiplexers which already exist in the library, we decided to primarily concentrate in modelling the logic cluster components. Thus, the SBs and CBs are not included in the architecture seen by FPRESSO in these experiments. Instead, we properly constrain and size the multiplexers at the outputs of the cluster by specifying a particular load, which is a typical practice in semicustom design flows. This load is computed by taking the channel width assumed in COFFE, the fraction of the channels to which each output is connected (known as f_{Cout}) and the typical load observed for a 2-level multiplexer of that size. The load is then approximated and added before optimizing the cluster in Design Compiler.

FPRESSO is designed to optimize the circuit for delay, by default. So, for a fair comparison, we optimize for delay as well in COFFE by doubling the delay-to-area ratio of the cost function parameters (setting $d = 2$ and $a = 1$).

9. EXPERIMENTAL RESULTS

Multiple cluster architectures are generated (by varying K, N, and I) and optimized in both tools. To represent the delay, we differentiate between two delay paths: (i) the feedback path and (ii) the direct IO path. Using Figure 8 as reference, the feedback path starts at the output of the flip-flop and goes through the feedback multiplexer, the crossbar and the LUT, back to the input of the flip-flop. The direct IO path starts from the cluster inputs and passes through the crossbar, the LUT and the output multiplexer, into the cluster output. Figures 9a and 9b show the relative delay and area measured in FPRESSO with respect to COFFE for the two paths, respectively.

We observe that the differences between COFFE and FPRESSO is around 10% in terms of area and less than 35% in terms of delay—typically, in the 25% range for the feedback path and 10% for the IO path. In general, these results are quite encouraging, since these differences account for both modelling errors due to our library-based approach and differences in the optimization procedure—Design Compiler optimizes for a cost function that is certainly different than the one used in COFFE. However, it is obvious that the optimization of the IO path is closer to the reference than that of the feedback path. One possible explanation could

Table 1: Runtime improvement provided by FPRESSO, when compared to COFFE, for a range of architectures.

Architecture	Speed-up
K5_N6_I19	409
K5_N6_I30	413
K5_N6_I43	347
K6_N6_I19	411
K6_N6_I30	492
K6_N6_I43	278
K4_N6_I19	394
K4_N6_I30	305
K4_N6_I43	308
K5_N8_I41	208
K5_N8_I28	332
K6_N8_I41	267
K6_N8_I28	229
K5_N10_I39	239
K5_N10_I26	193

be the lack of adequate wire load modelling in FPRESSO: given that FPRESSO is not limited to a specific FPGA cluster topology, identifying which wires are longer than others (e.g., long feedback wires) can be a challenge and might require additional physical information from the user. Nevertheless, other factors could have also contributed to these differences, such as the advanced sizing capabilities of Design Compiler or the selective insertion of buffers on the high-fanout feedback path. We intend to further investigate the reasons behind these results and plan to include some wire load modelling capabilities in future versions of FPRESSO.

In a second experiment, we select a single architecture (i.e., $K = 5$, $N = 6$, and $I = 30$) and change the optimization cost functions to vary their relative priority in area vs. delay. Figure 10 shows the resulting Area-Delay Pareto front of the reported solutions. We observe that COFFE is able to cover a wider range of area-delay tradeoffs whereas FPRESSO concentrates in the arguably most interesting regions of that space. We also observe that, within the ranges spanned by our tool, FPRESSO consistently Pareto dominates COFFE. We are not able to conclude whether this is due to a superior optimization of our tool or to the fact that FPRESSO does not yet model intercomponent wire load.

In architecture, usually the relative ranking of some critical delay for various architectures is more important than the absolute delays themselves. To see how faithful FPRESSO is, we ordered many architectures in function of growing delay in COFFE and plotted the delay reported by FPRESSO for the same architectures (see Figure 11). Ideally, the curve should be monotonic and we see that only in four cases it is not. It is worth noticing the scale and the fact that these inversions are relatively modest, in the worst case in the order of 3% and significantly smaller in the others.

Furthermore, COFFE is on average 300 times slower than FPRESSO once all the components are in the library, as seen in Table 1. This is a game-changing difference that can enable far more comprehensive architectural explorations.

10. MODELLING OR DESIGNING

It would be tempting to believe that our tool *designs* optimized transistor-level architectures, instead of simply *mod-*

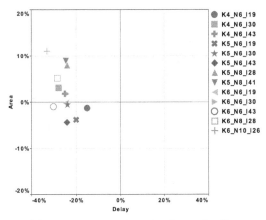

(a) Feedback path: from flip-flop to flip-flop.

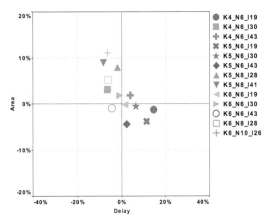

(b) Direct IO path: from cluster inputs to cluster outputs.

Figure 9: Delay and area of the main paths of an FPGA, modelled in FPRESSO with respect to COFFE, for multiple architectural parameters. Figure 9a shows the results for the feedback path, which goes from the feedback multiplexer through the crossbar and the LUT. Figure 9b shows the same results but for the path going from the cluster inputs through the crossbar, LUT, and output multiplexer.

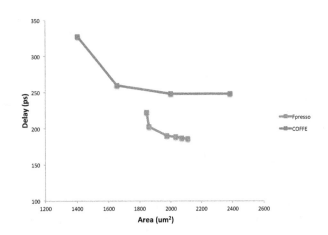

Figure 10: The delay and area Pareto fronts of multiple optimizations performed by FPRESSO and COFFE, for a single architecture ($K = 5$, $N = 6$ and $I = 30$).

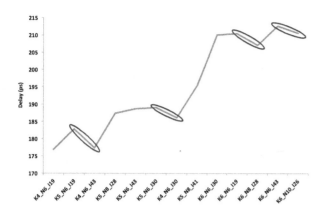

Figure 11: Critical delays reported by FPRESSO for various architectures ordered for growing critical delay as reported by COFFE. Ideally, the graph should be monotonic whereas it is not in a few cases, most pretty marginal. Note that the vertical axis does not start from zero.

elling them. Although this is a tempting claim, we do not think it is a granted one. The reason is that standard cells and a classic semicustom design flow have a number of built-in electrical safeguards to guarantee functionality under any constraint; our flow, purposely, does not. For instance, standard cells never expose pass transistors to the external pins of the cell and this is one of the reasons why standard cell designs cannot match in many practical cases perfectly crafted manual designs. In our case, although on the outputs we always have buffers, we omit input buffers to mimic the way a hand-crafted transistor-level circuit would be built. We have studied some of the circuits resulting from our flow and, within the range of fairly conventional architectures reported here, we have not observed any electrical error; yet, our methodology is such that we do not guarantee functionality for every possible conceivable circuit. At best, we can affirm that our flow helps fast and sound modelling (our prime goal) and actively suggests architectural solutions in the buffering structure which designers may want to study in case they want to produce a production transistor-level implementation. One should note that FPRESSO benefits from the advanced buffer optimization strategies of Design Compiler which largely exceed the resizing capabilities of COFFE, for instance: Design Compiler can not only build multistage optimal buffers when required, but can also add buffers after fanout points when load is divided unevenly across different circuit branches. The frequent Pareto dominance of FPRESSO results over COFFE may be partly due to this effect, but detailed analysis of the results has not been conclusive as yet.

11. STATE OF THE ART

The modelling problem addressed in this paper is very related to the transistor sizing problem of custom circuits. The latter is a well-studied optimization problem that targets the improvement of circuit performance by adequately increasing the size of its transistors. Fishburn et al. [7] show that modelling transistors as linear resistances and capacitances, and calculating the delay of the resulting RC circuits allows the transistor sizing problem to be formulated as a convex optimization problem, which guarantees that any lo-

cal minimum is the global minimum. Accordingly, several algorithms guaranteeing the optimal solution of such formulation have subsequently been proposed [3, 17]. However, all this prior work relies on linear device models that are known to be quite inaccurate, especially in the latest CMOS technology nodes [9].

For the concrete case of FPGAs, Kuon and Rose [11] propose a two-phased approach consisting of an exploratory phase that uses linear device models followed by a SPICE-base fine-tuning phase that adjusts the transistor sizes to account for the inaccuracies of linear models. In contrast, Chiasson and Betz propose COFFE [4], a transistor sizing tool for FPGAs that completely relies on SPICE. FPRESSO differs from both in the fact that it only uses SPICE—a very detailed and slow simulation—in the characterization phase of the components and not in the optimization of every single FPGA architecture. As a result, our tool is capable of modelling new complete architectures significantly faster, provided that there is component reuse, which is typically the case in FPGA architectures (e.g., the same 6-input LUT component can be included in many different architectures). Furthermore, our tool provides full flexibility allowing the user to interconnect the components as desired, as opposed to the reference tools where local interconnects are programmatically encoded. Hence, FPRESSO provides a more versatile solution that enables the exploration of largely different FPGA architectures without requiring any transistor sizing expertise from the users.

12. CONCLUSIONS

Retargetable toolchains are one of the keystones of architectural research, but are somehow more tricky to use than one thinks. In computer architecture, everyone has access to a variety of fairly accurate architectural simulators, customizable in many aspects including, naturally, every aspect of the memory hierarchy. A few years back, someone noticed how difficult it was for most researchers to predict the effect of some architectural changes in the memory hierarchy on its area and latency: understanding most of the implications requires a deep knowledge of the transistor-level implementation options of leading-edge memories, which is clearly outside of the classic skill set of an architect. CACTI [18] was born out of that need: an easy-to-use and sound model for caches and other memory hierarchy elements. Over a couple of decades, six major revisions [14], and continuous new extensions [8], CACTI has helped literally hundreds of research groups in their scientific quest.

We think, as perhaps others in the area, that FPGA architectural research suffers today from the same syndrome that afflicted in the early nineties the computer architectural community: namely, the difficulty of combining in the same researcher or even research group acute architectural intuition and leading-edge transistor-level design skills. Infinitely more modestly compared to the CACTI endeavour, we have shown a new path towards quick and efficient modelling of almost arbitrary FPGA architectures: we can generate within minutes optimized VTR models with reasonably faithful delay and area characteristics. Although we are not there yet, we strive to develop a web interface to our tool that will allow researchers to submit architectural descriptions online and obtain almost immediately reasonable VTR models enabling sound and consistent architectural explorations.

13. REFERENCES

[1] I. Ahmadpour, B. Khaleghi, and H. Asadi. An efficient reconfigurable architecture by characterizing most frequent logic functions. In *Proceedings of the 25th International Conference on Field-Programmable Logic and Applications*, 2015.

[2] E. Ahmed and J. Rose. The effect of LUT and cluster size on deep-submicron FPGA performance and density. *IEEE Transactions on Very Large Scale Integration Systems*, 12(3):288–298, 2004.

[3] C.-P. Chen, C. C. Chu, and D. Wong. Fast and exact simultaneous gate and wire sizing by lagrangian relaxation. *IEEE Transactions on Computer-Aided Design of Integrated Circuits and Systems*, 18(7):1014–1025, 1999.

[4] C. Chiasson and V. Betz. COFFE: Fully-automated transistor sizing for FPGAs. In *Proceedings of the IEEE International Conference on Field Programmable Technology*, pages 34–41, 2013.

[5] D. Chinnery and K. Keutzer. *Closing the Gap Between ASIC & Custom: Tools and Techniques for High-Performance ASIC Design.* Springer US, New York, NY., 2002.

[6] H. Eriksson, P. Larsson-Edefors, T. Henriksson, and C. Svensson. Full-custom vs. standard-cell design flow: an adder case study. In *Proceedings of the Asia and South Pacific Design Automation Conference*, pages 507–510, 2003.

[7] J. P. Fishburn and A. E. Dunlop. TILOS: A posynomial programming approach to transistor sizing. In *The Best of ICCAD*, pages 295–302. Springer, 2003.

[8] N. P. Jouppi, A. B. Kahng, N. Muralimanohar, and V. Srinivas. CACTI-IO: CACTI with OFF-chip power-area-timing models. *IEEE Transactions on Very Large Scale Integration (VLSI) Systems*, VLSI-23(7):1254–67, July 2015.

[9] K. Kasamsetty, M. Ketkar, and S. S. Sapatnekar. A new class of convex functions for delay modeling and its application to the transistor sizing problem [CMOS gates]. *IEEE Transactions on Computer-Aided Design of Integrated Circuits and Systems*, 19(7):779–788, 2000.

[10] J. H. Kim and J. H. Anderson. Synthesizable FPGA fabrics targetable by the Verilog-to-Routing (VTR) CAD flow. In *Proceedings of the 25th International Conference on Field-Programmable Logic and Applications*, 2015.

[11] I. Kuon and J. Rose. Exploring area and delay tradeoffs in FPGAs with architecture and automated transistor design. *IEEE Transactions on Very Large Scale Integration Systems*, 19(1):71–84, 2011.

[12] D. Lewis, E. Ahmed, G. Baeckler, V. Betz, M. Bourgeault, D. Cashman, D. Galloway, M. Hutton, C. Lane, A. Lee, P. Leventis, S. Marquardt, C. McClintock, K. Padalia, B. Pedersen, G. Powell, B. Ratchev, S. Reddy, J. Schleicher, K. Stevens, R. Yuan, R. Cliff, and J. Rose. The Stratix II logic and routing architecture. In *Proceedings of the 13th ACM/SIGDA International Symposium on Field Programmable Gate Arrays*, pages 14–20, Monterey, Calif., Feb. 2005.

[13] D. Lewis, E. Ahmed, D. Cashman, T. Vanderhoek, C. Lane, A. Lee, and P. Pan. Architectural enhancements in Stratix-III^{TM} and Stratix-IV^{TM}. In *Proceedings of the ACM/SIGDA International Symposium on Field Programmable Gate Arrays*, FPGA '09, pages 33–42, New York, NY, USA, 2009. ACM.

[14] N. Muralimanohar, R. Balasubramonian, and N. P. Jouppi. CACTI 6.0: A tool to model large caches. Technical Report HPL-2009-85, Hewlett-Packard Development Company, Palo Alto, Calif., Apr. 2009.

[15] H. Parandeh-Afshar, H. Benbihi, D. Novo, and P. Ienne. Rethinking FPGAs: Elude the flexibility excess of LUTs with And-Inverter Cones. In *Proceedings of the 20th ACM/SIGDA International Symposium on Field Programmable Gate Arrays*, pages 119–28, Monterey, Calif., Feb. 2012.

[16] J. Rose, J. Luu, C. W. Yu, O. Densmore, J. Goeders, A. Somerville, K. B. Kent, P. Jamieson, and J. Anderson. The VTR project: architecture and CAD for FPGAs from Verilog to routing. In *Proceedings of the 20th ACM/SIGDA International Symposium on Field Programmable Gate Arrays*, pages 77–86, 2012.

[17] V. Sundararajan, S. S. Sapatnekar, and K. K. Parhi. Fast and exact transistor sizing based on iterative relaxation. *IEEE Transactions on Computer-Aided Design of Integrated Circuits and Systems*, 21(5):568–581, 2002.

[18] S. J. Wilton and N. P. Jouppi. An enhanced access and cycle time model for on-chip caches. Technical Report WRL-93-5, Digital Equipment Corporation, Palo Alto, Calif., July 1994.

Towards PVT-Tolerant Glitch-Free Operation in FPGAs

Safeen Huda and Jason Anderson
Dept. of Electrical and Computer Engineering,
University of Toronto
Toronto, ON, Canada
Email: {safeen,janders}@ece.toronto.edu

ABSTRACT

Glitches are unnecessary transitions on logic signals that needlessly consume dynamic power. Glitches arise from imbalances in the combinational path delays to a signal, which may cause the signal to toggle multiple times in a given clock cycle before settling to its final value. In this paper, we propose a low-cost circuit structure that is able to eliminate a majority of glitches. The structure, which is incorporated into the output buffers of FPGA logic elements, suppresses pulses on buffer outputs whose duration is shorter than a configurable time window (set at the time of FPGA configuration). Glitches are thereby eliminated "at the source" ensuring they do not propagate into the high-capacitance FPGA interconnect, saving power. An experimental study, using Altera commercial tools for power analysis, demonstrates that the proposed technique reduces 70% of glitches, at a cost of 1% reduction in speed performance.

1. INTRODUCTION

In recent years, field-programmable gate arrays (FPGAs) have become increasingly popular platforms for the implementation of digital systems, as reflected in the increased market share FPGA vendors have enjoyed in the semiconductor industry. However, it has previously been shown that there is a large gap between FPGAs and the alternative medium for the implementation of digital systems, ASICs [1]. While FPGAs (vs. ASICs) suffer from deficiencies in area efficiency and performance, it is the large power consumption – 7-14× as claimed in a recent study [1] – that has particularly inhibited the adoption of FPGAs in a wide variety of current and emerging applications that require strict power budgets. In this paper, we propose a technique to reduce a component of FPGA dynamic power, namely, power dissipated due to *glitches*.

Underscoring the importance of reducing FPGA power, the vendors have adopted a variety of techniques to tackle power consumption at the device, circuit, and architectural levels, and through CAD techniques as well [2, 3, 4]. One particular power optimization, Altera's *Programmable Power Technology* [5], makes use of the fact that a transistor's threshold voltage, V_T can be altered by application of a bias voltage at the base terminal. An increase in $|V_T|$ (by applying a base-terminal (body) bias) results in reduced static power of a device, at the expense of increased delay. However, since designs implemented on FPGAs typically have a large num-

ber of paths with considerable timing slack [6], this technique can be used to reduce the static power of circuitry on such paths. Unfortunately, with the vendors transitioning to FinFETs [7, 8] which do not permit independent body bias control, the future of this technique appears to be limited. Nevertheless, the notion of using excess timing slack to trade-off overall power with delay appears to be a very effective means of power reduction – and is one which we exploit in this work.

We take aim at glitch power in FPGAs, which has previously been shown to account for a significant portion of the total dynamic power dissipated, with one study finding that glitches account for ~26% of total core dynamic power [9]. We propose novel glitch filtering circuitry which serves to completely eliminate glitches of a given pulse-width. The circuitry is incorporated into the buffers present at logic element outputs. Glitches are eliminated immediately after they are generated, and most importantly, before they can propagate into the high-capacitance programmable interconnection network, where they would otherwise result in significant energy waste. We also propose an optimization algorithm to maximize the glitch power reduction (by applying appropriate settings on each glitch filter), subject to timing constraints. We present a full CAD flow which we use to assess the merits of our power reduction technique. Experiments show that glitch power can be reduced by up to ~70% at an area cost of < 3%, with an average critical-path degradation of ~1%. We provide an overview of glitch power in FPGAs and previous techniques proposed to reduce glitches in Section 2. Section 3 describes our proposed glitch filtering circuit. Section 4 provides an overview of our CAD flow and glitch optimization algorithm. Section 5 describes our experimental study and presents results. Finally, Section 6 concludes the paper.

2. BACKGROUND

2.1 Glitch Power Dissipation in FPGAs

Glitches commonly occur in digital circuits, as a consequence of unequal arrival times at the inputs of combinational logic gates, such as the scenario depicted in Figure 1, where input A transitions after input B. The period of time between the two input transitions shown in the figure can potentially give rise to spurious transitions at the output – i.e. glitches – which have no functional value, and are a waste of energy. Each transition consumes CV_{DD}^2 joules of energy, where C is the capacitance of the net being driven by OUT.

Glitches are especially troublesome in FPGAs. Whereas in ASICs there exists the freedom to minimize the disparity between the delays of different paths (and thereby ensure that the arrival times of the input signals to a combinational circuit are well matched), there is no such freedom with FPGAs. For example, consider the circuit shown in Figure 2, which shows an inherent potential mismatch between the delays of the two paths of combinational logic, named *path 1* and *path 2*, which converge at the XOR gate. The delay mismatch is inherent because of the structure of this circuit: *path 1* has

FPGA'16, February 21-23, 2016, Monterey, CA, USA
© 2016 ACM. ISBN 978-1-4503-3856-1/16/02. . . $15.00
DOI: http://dx.doi.org/10.1145/2847263.2847272

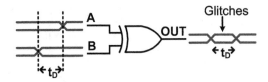

Figure 1: Example showing conditions which result in glitches at the outputs of combinational gates.

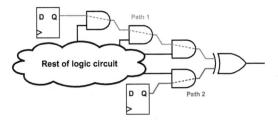

Figure 2: Example showing inherent mismatch in arrival times due to structure of circuit.

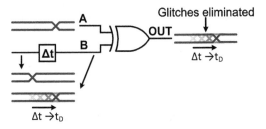

Figure 3: Glitch reduction through input delay balancing.

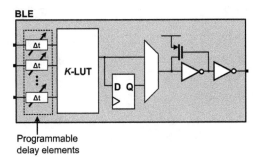

Figure 4: Proposed glitch-free BLE from [12].

more logic gates than *path 2*. If this circuit were implemented in an ASIC, given sufficient freedom in the ability to trade-off power with area or speed, the delay of the single logic gate in *path 2* could be increased (for example, by reducing the sizing of its transistors), or the delays of the gates along *path 1* could be decreased (by increasing the sizing of their transistors), with the objective to equalize and align the arrival times at the inputs to the XOR gate. In contrast, if this circuit were to be implemented in an FPGA, each of the logic gates and inteconnects would be mapped to prefabricated circuits, whose delays cannot be optimized as freely, thus making the problem of equalizing arrival times difficult. Recent work has shown that glitches account for, on average, 26% of total core dynamic power for the MCNC circuits, and up to 50% for specific circuits [9].

2.2 Previous Work on Glitch Power Reduction

Several prior works have addressed glitch power in FPGAs [9, 10, 11, 12]. One recent approach [9] proposed to make use of the prevalent don't-care states in logic circuits to minimize glitches. The authors proposed to set the *don't-care* states to specific values such that when the input vector to a logic circuit momentarily assumes an intermediate (don't-care) state (while it transitions between two states), the output does not make a spurious transition. This technique is a light-weight approach to glitch reduction, as it has zero performance or area overheads, and offers reasonable glitch power reduction: an average of 13.7% over a set of benchmark circuits.

More direct approaches to glitch reduction were proposed in [12] and [13]. While these two works offered different approaches to glitch reduction, the overall strategy was similar to that depicted in Figure 3. The figure shows two signals, *A* and *B*, that are inputs to an XOR gate, and again, *B* arrives earlier than *A*. In theory, glitches can be eliminated if we equalize the delay along the input paths to ensure all signal transitions arrive at the same time at the different inputs to the logic circuit. This is shown in the figure, where a delay, Δt, is added to *B*, and so now the difference in the arrival times of the two signals to the XOR gate is $t_D - \Delta t$, which is also the width of the resulting glitch at *OUT*. Clearly, if the added delay can be calibrated such that it is equal to t_D, then the two signal transitions arrive at exactly the same time to the inputs of the XOR gate, and the glitch is eliminated.

In [13], path delay equalization was proposed by inserting additional routing conductors along paths with early arrival times – the additional delay of each routing conductor slows the path down. While this approach requires no additional changes to the FPGA architecture or circuitry, and does not result in an area penalty (since routing conductors are often underutilized to begin with), the power reductions arising from the elimination of glitches are offset by the increased dynamic power due to the use of additional routing resources. In contrast, [12] proposes a modified logic element (LE) with programmable delay lines at the input pins, shown Figure 4. The programmable delay lines are used to adjust the arrival delays at each input pin so that they may be equalized and glitch power eliminated. While this approach does incur an area overhead associated with programmable delay lines on each input of a LUT (which may not be insignificant for large LUT sizes), the authors claim the ability to completely eliminate glitch power with this approach.

2.3 The Limitations of Path-Delay Balancing

One fundamental problem with the above "path delay equalization" approaches is that in general, circuit delays are a function of temperature and in some process corners, are also a function of logic state, because of unequal rise and fall delays. The reason for these effects is that modern commercial FPGAs are comprised of both CMOS gates and NMOS pass transistors. Multiplexers, which form the core of both programmable logic elements and routing switches, are effectively large trees of NMOS pass-transistors, along with CMOS level-shifters and buffers. These two different styles of circuitry respond differently to changes in operating parameters, such as temperature. Recall that the rise/fall delay of a CMOS circuit is approximately inversely proportional to both μ, the mobility parameter of the gate's transistors, and $(V_{DD} - V_T)$ (this is also true for the *fall* delay of an NMOS pass-gate). While $(V_{DD} - V_T)$ is an increasing function of temperature (by virtue of V_T decreasing with temperature), μ generally decreases with temperature, and so generally, the combined effect results in an overall increased delay with increasing temperature [14]. On the other

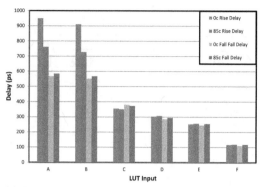

(a) Temperature dependence and rise/fall delay imbalance of LUT delays for each LUT input.

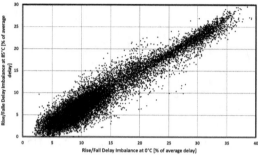

(b) Correlation of routing path rise/fall delay imbalance at 0 °C and 85 °C.

Figure 5: Temperature consequences on FPGA logic and routing delays.

hand, the *rise* delay of an NMOS pass-gate, assuming an ideal transistor model, is approximately:

$$t_{delay} = \frac{C_L V_{DD}}{\mu_N C_{OX}(W/L)(V_{DD}/2 - V_T)(V_{DD} - V_T)} \quad (1)$$

which exhibits an inverse-quadratic relationship between delay and $(V_{DD} - V_T)$. This equation is derived from a differential equation for the voltage at the source terminal of an NMOS transistor when its drain and gate terminals are held at V_{DD}. The increased sensitivity to $(V_{DD} - V_T)$ in this case typically results in an inverse temperature-dependence characteristic – i.e. delay *decreases* with temperature. This characteristic of NMOS pass-gates leads to two observable characteristics: (1) paths which are dominated by pass-transistors have inverse temperature dependence on delay, while paths which are dominated by CMOS gates will more likely experience delay degradation with increased temperature and (2) the inherent asymmetry in rise and fall behaviour of pass-transistors means that the rise and fall delays can only be balanced at a single PVT corner. Under other conditions, the rise and fall delays of pass-transistors are unbalanced. LUT and routing delay data from a design placed and routed in a Stratix III FPGA illustrate these trends, as shown in Figure 5.

Figure 5(a) shows the rise and fall delays for each of the six inputs to a Stratix III LUT at 0 °C and 85 °C. Note that inputs A, B and C, which connect to pass-transistors at deep levels of the LUT's pass-transistor tree, exhibit an inverse temperature dependency (likely owing to the fact that these paths are pass-transistor dominated), while inputs D, E, and F, which connect to pass-transistors closer to the output of the LUT exhibit slight delay degradation with increased temperature. Note also the large rise and fall delay imbalance (~45% of the rise delay) for inputs A and B. Figure 5(b) highlights the unpredictable and temperature-dependent

rise/fall delay imbalance of routing circuitry. The plot shows the relationship between the rise/fall delay imbalance, expressed as a percentage of the average delay, of each routing path in a sample circuit at 0 °C and 85 °C. In the figure, it is apparent that most routing paths exhibit a delay imbalance greater than 5%, with some approaching 40% at 0 °C. Qualitatively, the plot also shows the unpredictability of the delay-imbalance over temperature, since a poor correlation between delay-imbalances at the two temperature points is apparent.

These characteristics of circuit structures in FPGAs means that the relative arrival times of signals at the inputs to a gate is a strong function of both temperature and logic-state (due to rise/fall delay imbalance). This implies that if delay equalization is used to remove glitches at a particular temperature and for a particular state, the glitches may reappear or new glitches may form at a different temperature/logic state. Circuitry to compensate for these variations would be prohibitive from an area point of view, since aside from the required additional circuitry needed to sense different temperature/logic states, these variations are a function of the specific mapping, placement, and routing of a design, thus making the variations highly unpredictable.

As opposed to prior path-delay-balancing techniques, we propose a glitch-reduction technique with low area overhead which has the ability to eliminate all glitches whose pulse-widths are bounded across different process, voltage, and temperature conditions. The following sections detail the proposed circuitry and associated CAD support.

3. PROPOSED GLITCH FILTERING CIRCUITRY

3.1 Circuit Overview

At the core of our proposed glitch power reduction technique is the circuit shown in Figure 6, which we call a *glitch filter*, as it has the ability to suppress glitches. This circuit bears some resemblance to the circuit shown in [15], although there are several subtle differences.

The proposed circuitry is effectively a buffer with a first stage inverter, shown as *B1* in the figure, followed by a second stage inverter, formed by transistors *M5* and *M6*. Transistors *M1* through *M4* form gating circuitry which can disconnect the input stage from the output stage, and this enables the glitch filtering functionality of the proposed circuit, as will be described. The circuit also comprises a programmable *inverting* delay line, shown as *D1* in the figure, whose delay determines the glitch pulse-widths which are filtered out by the circuit. When the glitch-filtering mechanism of this circuit is not needed (i.e. for timing critical paths), the multiplexer shown in the figure allows the input transition to bypass the delay-line and directly drive transistors *M2* and *M3*. The SRAM configuration cells shown connected to the delay line, will be discussed below.

To understand the operation of this circuit, we first begin with a description of the dynamic behaviour of the circuit in response to a single transition at the input, and then describe the response to a glitch (i.e. multiple consecutive transitions). Immediately following a transition at the input to this circuit – say from logic-"0" to logic-"1" – the output of *B1* transitions from logic-"1" to logic-"0", but because of the delay t_D of *D1*, the output of the delay line remains at logic-"0". The combination of signal values (the input to the circuit at logic-"1" while the outputs of *D1* and *B1* at logic-"0") means that *M1* will turn on, thus discharging the gate of *M5* and turning it off. Since *M3* is also off during this time, the gate of *M6* will be briefly floating, but because it was previously driven to V_{DD} (since the input was previously at logic-"0"), *M6* will remain turned off. As such, the output remains at logic-"0" (despite both *M5* and *M6* being momentarily off). After a delay t_D, the transition

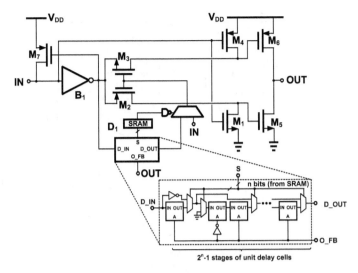

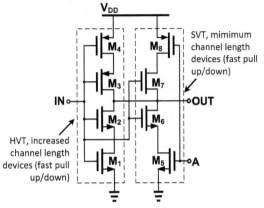

(a) Conventional delay cell.

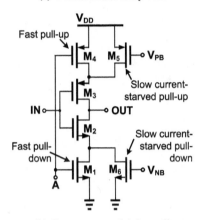

(b) Current-starved delay cell.

Figure 7: Delay-cell implementation options.

Figure 6: Proposed glitch-filter circuit.

at the input of the circuit is seen at the output of $D1$, and this turns $M3$ on. Since the source of $M3$ (which is driven by $B1$) is at this moment logic-"0", the gate of $M6$ is discharged, which turns $M6$ on and results in the output transitioning from logic-"0" to logic-"1".

This analysis of the response of this circuit to a transition at the input highlights an important property: immediately following a transition at the input, the output of the buffer is prevented from following suit and propagating the transition at the input. Instead, the buffer is forced to wait a delay of t_D before the output of $B1$ is connected to the gates of the transistors forming the output stage of the circuit. If however, during this delay t_D, the input transitions back to the previous value (i.e. a glitch has occurred), then the data value during the course of the spurious transition is not "seen" by the output stage when it is reconnected to $B1$. As such, the spurious transition does not propagate to the *output*, and the glitch input to the circuit is prevented from propagating and dissipating power in other areas of the chip. While this discussion highlights how lone pulses may be filtered out, consider what happens when a train of pulses, $x(t)$ appears at the input to the glitch filter: assuming the glitch filter contains an *ideal* delay line, it follows that the delay-line output is equal to $x(t - t_D)$, where t_D is the delay of the delay line. If for example $x(t)$ is a periodic function with a period equal to t_D, then by definition, the output of the delay line will in fact just be $x(t)$, and as such, all glitches will be allowed to pass through from the input to the output. In a more general sense, if the temporal separation, t_S, between glitch i and $i+1$ is less than t_D, glitch $i+1$ will only be partially filtered. If $t_S + t_W = t_D$, where t_W is the pulse-width of a particular glitch, then the glitch will pass from the input to the output of the circuit without any attenuation or pulse-width reduction. Thus, in an analogy to passive electronic filters, while the proposed glitch filter has a low-pass characteristic, in that all glitches with pulse-widths less than t_D may be filtered, it also has a *resonance characteristic*, where the glitches can pass through the filter without any attenuation for certain values of t_S. It can be shown that a mechanism to effectively flush the delay line of its contents following the arrival of a *restoring transition* is required to rectify this problem, and this can be achieved by ensuring that the delay of the delay-line is asymmetric and dependent on the state of its output: if the output of the glitch filter is at logic-"1", then the delay line is to have a slow output-fall delay and fast output-rise delay, while if the output of the glitch filter is at logic-"0", the delay line is to have a slow output-rise delay and fast output-fall delay. This allows a restoring transition to quickly "flush" the delay line, to ensure previous transitions at the input do not continue to stay in flight in the delay line – this helps to significantly mitigate

the resonant effects. It can be shown that a glitch of pulse-width t_W seconds will be filtered without any resonant effects if $t_W < t_D - t_{Df}$ (where t_{Df} is the time required for a restoring transition to propagate through the delay line) with this new topology.

3.2 Delay Line Design

A number of options exist for the implementation of the programmable delay line $D1$. As will be discussed in Section 5, from our experiments we determined that each stage of our delay line had to provide, in the worst case, up to 600 ps of delay (some benchmarks required significantly less delay per stage as will be discussed in Section 5). Given that the FO4 delay in 65nm CMOS (for standard-V_T) is just over 20 ps, achieving such a large delay per stage in an area and power-efficient manner can be challenging. Since the delay of a CMOS gate is approximately a linear function of the product of the gate's drive resistance and its output load capacitance, increasing either of these will result in an increase in delay. However, increasing delay solely through increasing a gate's output capacitance would result in an unacceptably large power overhead, as such we considered two different approaches to effectively increase the drive resistance of the delay cells comprising the delay line, so that our delay targets could be achieved with minimal overhead.

The two alternative delay-cells are depicted in Figure 7. The first delay-cell shown in Figure 7(a), which we call a *conventional delay cell* is effectively a conventional inverter comprising of transistors with increased channel-lengths; a combination of a stack of series transistors (needed when the maximum modeled length by the foundry is less than the length necessary to meet a target delay) and transistors with increased length leads to degraded drive resistance, allowing us to meet target delay. Note that while this technique also increases the input capacitance of the cell (which is the dominant load on the preceding cell in the delay-line), and thus will increase power, the power-overhead is still smaller than a delay-cell which achieves the same delay strictly through increased load capacitance. The second delay-cell shown in Figure 7(b), which is a *current-starved delay cell*, achieves increased delay by restricting the maximum pull-up/down current, by applying a bias voltage which is less (greater) than V_{DD} (GND) on the gates of transistor $M6$ ($M5$). This technique allows us to degrade drive-resistance to meet our delay targets by finding suitable voltages V_{PB} and V_{NB}.

These two techniques have different costs and trade-offs. For the conventional delay cell, an increase to its constituent transistors' channel lengths results in increased area, and as mentioned previously, increased input-capacitance and thus power. In contrast, for the current-starved delay cell, as long as suitable bias voltages V_{BP} and V_{BN} can be generated and distributed throughout the chip in a reliable and cost efficient-manner, the transistors comprising the delay cell can be set to minimum length and width, thus minimizing area and power overheads. However, given than $V_{PB} > GND$ and $V_{NB} < V_{DD}$, transistors $M5$ and $M6$ have degraded overdrive voltage, thereby making them more sensitive to V_T variation, although in this case sensitivity to variation and area overhead can be traded-off since increasing the size of $M5$ and $M6$, will reduce their σ_{VT}. In addition, there may be considerable area/power costs of distributing the voltages V_{PB} and V_{NB}. In this work, however, we assume that both the costs of the bias generation and the current-starved delay-cell's sensitivity to variation are insignificant, as this serves as a *lower-bound estimate* on the area and power overheads of the proposed glitch filtering circuitry. In contrast, the conventional delay cell allows us to form an *upper-bound estimate* on the are and power overheads of the glitch filtering circuit. Rigorous PVT analysis of the current-starved delay cell, as well as design and cost/benefit analysis of the bias generation circuitry is left for future work. Finally, observe that both of the delay cells shown in Figure 7 contain fast pull-up/down paths, which are activated by input A for both cells; these paths enable the cells to have asymmetric, state-dependent delay, which serves to eliminate resonant effects as discussed previously.

3.3 PVT Sensitivity

Given the nature of the way in which glitches are suppressed using this technique, we may draw some conclusions about the ability of this circuit to suppress glitches in the face of variation in PVT. Section 2.3 highlighted the principal shortcoming in preventing glitches using delay balancing: it requires precise knowledge and control of path delays. As discussed previously, varying PVT conditions makes this difficult to guarantee in modern processes, particularly in FPGAs because of the unique combination of various circuit structures which they employ. However, the exact *bounds* of path delays, and thus the bounds on the pulse-widths of resulting glitches, can be determined, and to some degree guaranteed.

The proposed glitch reduction technique in this work relies solely on the expected bounds of the glitches to be suppressed. If it is known in a circuit at a particular node which dissipates a large amount of power, that the vast majority of glitches at that node have pulse widths which are less than some bound W_{max} over all PVT corners, then simply by setting the delay of the delay line of the glitch filter at that node to a value $\geq W_{max}$ ensures that those glitches will be eliminated for all possible operating conditions of the circuit. Moreover, we can always ensure that the delay line delay is greater than W_{max} over all process corners; given that the delay line delay can be expressed as $t_D + \delta_D$, where t_D is the nominal delay of the delay line and δ_D is some random deviation from the nominal delay due to PVT variation, we can guarantee that the de-

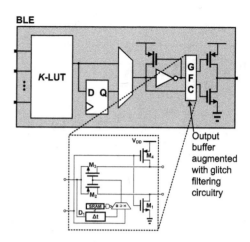

Figure 8: Proposed BLE architecture.

lay line delay is greater than W_{max} by setting $t_D \geq W_{max} + |\delta_D^{(max)}|$, where $\delta_D^{(max)}$ is the worst case variation of the delay line's delay over all PVT corners (which can be modelled and bounded). There may be a resulting timing penalty in this case, but for energy critical applications, this technique provides an ability to guarantee glitch suppression. While the inherent robustness to PVT makes this approach even more appealing, in this paper, we perform glitch suppression using statistics gathered from a single corner. Multi-corner glitch reduction and optimization using this technique is therefore left for future work. In addition to improved robustness compared to delay-balancing glitch reduction approaches, the proposed circuit also offers reduced area overhead, since only a single glitch filter is required at the output of the BLE, whereas a BLE with input delay balancing will need a delay-line and associated circuitry at each input to the BLE, as shown previously in Figure 4.

3.4 Proposed Architecture

Figure 8 shows a proposed Basic Logic Element (BLE) incorporating the proposed glitch filtering circuitry. We assume a conventional BLE will have an output buffer consisting of the inverter and transistors shown in the figure; this buffer exists to restore the voltage at the output of the bypass multiplexer to full CMOS levels, and is necessary to drive the BLE's output load. We propose to augment this buffer with glitch filtering circuitry consisting of transistors M_1-M_4, delay-line D_1, SRAM configuration cells, and additional auxiliary circuits as shown in the figure. The SRAM cells are used to configure the delay of the delay line. Recall that if the delay line is set to a delay t_D, then all glitches input to the glitch filter of a pulse width less than t_D will be filtered out. Thus, given information about the glitch statistics at the input to the glitch filter (which may be profiled through timing simulations of a given design mapped to the FPGA), the delay line can be configured accordingly to maximize glitch suppression and save power. However, the ability to filter glitches comes at a cost, namely an added delay of t_D. The configuration of the glitch filter delays is thus nontrivial. While it is desirable to filter out all possible glitches in the circuit, it may not be desirable from the performance angle. Moreover, the configuration of each glitch filter must take into account effects of an added delay on downstream nodes, since the additional delay introduced by a glitch filter may in fact result in the inception of new glitches downstream. If these downstream glitches propagate through very capacitive interconnect network, there may be a resulting net *increase* in glitch power. The additional delay introduced by a particular glitch filter setting may also leave less room for downstream nodes to filter out glitches due to reduced slack. As such, the optimization of glitch filter settings is a combinatorial optimization problem, wherein *global* glitch power must be reduced

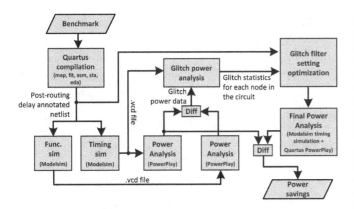

Figure 9: CAD/experimental flow for proposed glitch reduction technique.

under the presence of timing constraints. The CAD flow and glitch optimization approach are described in next section.

The circuits shown above were designed and simulated using commercial 65nm STMicroelectronics models to verify functionality, and extract power and delay overheads. All simulations were conducted using Cadence's Spectre simulator, with typical transistor models, 1V V_{DD}, and at a temperature of 28 °C. We assume a transition time of 150 ps at the input to the buffer, and an output load of 20fF (which is to represent the load of multiplexers and wire capacitance at the output of the BLE, similar to the loading considered in [16]). The delay penalty of the cell when the glitch-filtering mechanism is *not* used (and thus the input signal is allowed to propagate directly through the bypass multiplexer) is approximately 30 ps; this delay represents the signal propagation from the buffer's input through the glitch filter's bypass multiplexor to the gate of transistors M_2 and M_3 in Figure 8, and the signal propagation from the output of the first stage of the buffer through transistor M_3 (M_2) to the gate of transistor M_4 (M_1). These two signal propagations have some overlap, thus the total added delay is not simply their sum. For the baseline output buffer (without glitch filtering circuitry), under the aforementioned PVT conditions, we observed a ∼90 ps delay in our simulations, which grows to ∼120 ps with the addition of the glitch filtering circuitry.

For a glitch filter implemented with current-starved delay cells, the dynamic power overhead is << 1%, while for a conventional delay cell based delay-line, the glitch filter's dynamic power overhead would increase to ∼1.5% (compared to estimated power dissipated in routing, which is typically the dominating component of total dynamic power consumption). The static power overhead is also negligible, since aside from transistors $M1 - M6$, and the transistors comprising the bypass multiplexer and input buffer $B1$, all transistors are HVT (high-threshold voltage transistors).

4. GLITCH FILTER SETTING OPTIMIZATION

4.1 CAD Flow

A proposed CAD flow supporting glitch filter-based power optimization is presented in Figure 9. While packing, placement, and routing remain the same as in a conventional FPGA CAD flow [17], we propose to add the following steps post-routing: glitch power analysis, glitch filter setting optimization, and final power analysis. Other than specific implementation details, overall the additional steps in the CAD flow are agnostic to the original CAD flow being augmented, and as such, we chose to use Altera's Quartus II CAD software as the base CAD flow to extend.

Details for each of the CAD flow steps introduced are as follows: the first step post-routing is glitch power analysis, where

cumulative distribution functions relating glitch pulse-width and glitch power are generated. Total glitch power is calculated on a node-by-node basis by comparing power reports generated from a functional simulation and a timing simulation. Since a functional simulation contains no glitches, differences in power between two different simulations represent glitch power. The exact distribution of pulse-widths are extracted from the timing simulation, and the relative frequency of glitches of a certain pulse width is used to estimate the dissipated power arising from glitches of that pulse width. These statistics, in addition to the netlist and its timing information (i.e. the timing graph), are used by the glitch filter setting optimization step to find the best settings for each glitch filter used in the circuit. The details of this step will be discussed in the following section. Finally, a timing simulation is performed on the model of the circuit augmented with glitch filters (configured to the settings determined in the previous step), and the results of this simulation are used by power analysis to determine the power savings through glitch filtering.

4.2 Glitch Power Optimization

It is worthwhile to consider some of the challenges faced in optimization of glitch filter settings in a circuit. As mentioned above, reduction of all glitches at a node with pulse-width less than t_W results in an increase in delay at that node of t_W. This trade-off must be considered carefully. To begin with, in the optimization of overall power reduction, we ought to allocate more of the timing slack available on a particular path to nodes on that path with the greatest power reduction opportunity (that is, nodes with the highest glitch power). As such, timing data must be used in conjunction with the power reduction opportunities for nodes along a particular path. In addition, we must be careful in considering the consequences a particular glitch filter setting may have on downstream nodes. When a particular node's glitch filter is set to a setting of t_D, all downstream nodes will experience a *delay push-out* of t_D seconds at one (or more, if there are re-convergent paths) of their inputs. This results in the profile of relative arrival times (that is, the difference in time between the signal arrival times at each input) of the inputs to each downstream node being altered, which may result in *new* glitches (and increased power consumption) arising downstream. Even if the power dissipation of downstream nodes does not change, the glitch statistics of downstream nodes will become "stale", and therefore less useful for subsequent decision making.

In the absence of a model that relates changes in glitch-filter settings to altered glitch power characteristics on downstream nodes of the circuit, the glitch power analysis step (outlined above) would have to be executed frequently to ensure: (1) overall glitch power has not increased following changes to the glitch filter settings for a set of nodes and (2) the glitch power and pulse-width statistics for all affected nodes are updated so that they are always relevant and usable for glitch power optimization. This particular approach seemed to be intractable from a run-time point of view, and as such an alternative approach was pursued. Specifically, we opted to ensure that regardless the glitch filter settings applied to the various nodes in the circuit, the relative arrival times at all *consequential* nodes stayed unchanged. By consequential, we mean a node whose worst-case increased glitch power due to an altering of its relative fanin arrival times is significantly large. This means that nodes of relatively low output capacitance, whose worst-case glitch power is small in comparison to the potential glitch power savings elsewhere in the circuit, would be allowed to have altered input arrival times. This approach therefore ensures that the two main concerns previously discussed are avoided. By ensuring the relative arrival times stay unchanged (for consequential nodes), we are assured that no new (consequential) glitches are created at a given node whenever we attempt to filter glitches at other points (specifically, upstream nodes) of the circuit, while this also ensures that the glitch data at each consequential node is never stale. Whenever a consequential node's glitch filter settings are changed to some delay t_D, we ensure that for all nodes downstream, the arrival times at each fanin path is similarly increased by t_D (by applying the necessary delay settings on upstream glitch filters). Admittedly, this is a somewhat conservative approach, and leads to compromised power reduction and development of a strategy to more optimally manage the effects of unequal delay push-out among the fanin paths of consequential nodes is left for future work.

4.2.1 Problem Statement

The optimization of glitch power as described in the preceding sections can in general be formulated as a constrained non-linear optimization problem. We are given as input a timing graph for a circuit, $G(V,E)$ where each vertex, $v \in V$, represents an input or output port of a block in the design (i.e. LUT, DFF, RAM, I/O), while each edge $e = (u,v)$, represents a signal path between ports (i.e. routing or a block's internal timing arc). For each node v in the circuit, we are given a *glitch power density function*, $GP_v(t)$ (this is obtained empirically during the glitch power analysis step in the CAD flow described in Section 4.1), which describes the amount of power dissipated at node v by glitches of width t. The total glitch power at node v is therefore:

$$P_v^{(max)} = \int_0^\infty GP_v(\tau)d\tau. \qquad (2)$$

At each node v, we have a decision variable d_v, which is the specific glitch filter setting at node v. As described previously, the proposed glitch filtering circuitry is able to eliminate all glitches of pulse width less than d_v from appearing at its output when the glitch filter's delay line is set to a delay of d_v. This means that given a glitch filter setting of d_v, the total glitch power at node v would be reduced to:

$$P_v = \int_{d_v}^\infty GP_v(\tau)d\tau. \qquad (3)$$

Therefore, total glitch power in the entire design (which we aim to minimize) is:

$$P_{total} = \sum_{v \in V} \int_{d_v}^\infty GP_v(\tau)d\tau. \qquad (4)$$

At each node v, we wish to keep track of the worst-case arrival time, arr_v, and this expressed as:

$$arr_v = \max_{(u,v) \in E} arr_u + d_u + t_{uv}, \qquad (5)$$

where t_{uv} is the delay from node u to v in the graph, and d_u is the delay push-out caused by the glitch filter setting at u (i.e. it is u's glitch filter delay setting). Let CO be the set of *circuit outputs* – i.e. primary outputs, flip flop inputs, etc. Given a constrained critical path of T, we have the following constraint:

$$\forall v \in CO : arr_v \leq T \qquad (6)$$

As described in the previous section, we also wish to ensure that the delay push-out on each fanin edge of each node v are within some tolerance level of one another. However, this should be a soft constraint, as we only wish to avoid the case of unequal input delay push-out on nodes which are consequential. Similar to arrival time, we can keep track of the minimum and maximum input delay push-out on each node v, $dp_v^{(min)}$ and $dp_v^{(max)}$ respectively, with the following equations:

$$dp_v^{(min)} = \min_{(u,v) \in E} dp_u^{(min)} + d_u \qquad (7)$$

$$dp_v^{(max)} = \max_{(u,v) \in E} dp_u^{(max)} + d_u \qquad (8)$$

We wish to ensure that $dp_v^{(max)}$ and $dp_v^{(min)}$ are within some acceptable threshold of one another, i.e.:

$$dp_v^{(max)} - dp_v^{(min)} \leq K_{tol} \qquad (9)$$

Where K_{tol} is the maximum allowed mismatch between input push-out (which can for example be obtained empirically and set to a constant value). Equation 9 represents a hard constraint, and so we may allow this constraint to be relaxed with the following modification:

$$dp_v^{(max)} - dp_v^{(min)} - K_{eq} \cdot e_v \leq K_{tol} \qquad (10)$$

In contrast to Equation 9, we introduce a large constant K_{eq} (which can be set to some value which provably will always be greater than $dp_v^{(max)} - dp^{(min)}v$, such as the critical path delay), and a *slack variable* e_v, which is binary, and allows the constraint in Equation 9 to be violated for certain nodes. In order to objectively trade-off glitch power reduction opportunities available in the circuit with the requirement that nodes have equal delay push-out on input edges, we introduce a penalty term to Equation 4 to form our objective function:

$$P_{obj} = \sum_{v \in V} \int_{d_v}^\infty GP_v(\tau)d\tau + \sum_{v \in V} P_v \cdot K_p \cdot e_v, \qquad (11)$$

where K_p is an empirically determined penalty factor. The second term in Equation 11 effectively indicates that whenever a node's input fanin delay push-outs are allowed to be unequal to one another, we must pay a penalty in power consumption pessimistically set to $K_p \cdot P_v$ (i.e. all glitch power reduction at node v is now lost, and some additional power penalty may be incurred if $K_p > 1$). This ensures that we are careful in balancing the input delay push-out on consequential nodes, while allowing us to violate this condition on inconsequential nodes if this would allow for greater glitch power reduction in other parts of the circuit. Equations 5 - 8 and Equations 10-11 together define a constrained optimization problem.

4.2.2 MILP Formulation

While the optimization of Equation 11 may at first appear to be intractable given that $GP_v(t)$ are arbitrary non-linear functions, we can simplify the equation by observing that each glitch filter's delay line has finite resolution and a limit on its maximum delay. In other words, $d_v = di_v \cdot res$, where res is the finite resolution of the delay line, and di_v is an integer decision variable (it is effectively the delay line setting for node v's glitch filter) in the range from $0 \leq di_v \leq 2^B - 1$, where B is the number of configuration bits of the delay line. This means that given the finite number of values for d_v, we also have a finite number of possible values for the glitch power dissipated at node v. This observation allows us to recast Equation 11 as a linear equation coupled with linear constraints. First, let $gp_v[k] = \int_{(k-1) \cdot res}^{k \cdot res} GP_v(\tau)d\tau$ where $1 \leq k \leq 2^B - 1$. We can then rewrite Equation 11 as:

$$P_{obj} = \sum_{v \in V} \sum_{k=1}^{2^B - 1} x_v[k] \cdot gp_v[k] + \sum_{v \in V} \int_{t_{DM}}^\infty GP_v(\tau)d\tau + \sum_{v \in V} P_v \cdot K_p \cdot e_v \qquad (12)$$

Where $x_v[k]$ are binary decision variables for node v, and indicate whether or not the glitch power corresponding to $gp_v[k]$ can be eliminated (i.e. if $x_v[k] = 0$, $gp_v[k]$ can be eliminated), and $t_{DM} = (2^B - 1) \cdot res$ corresponds to the maximum delay of the delay line. The second term in this Equation describes glitch power that cannot be reduced due to the finite maximum delay of the glitch filter delay line. As such, this term is a constant, and therefore Equation 12 is a *linear* function of $x_v[k]$ and e_v. We may relate this objective function with the underlying decision variables di_v with the following linear constraints at each node v:

$$\forall_{k \in \{1,\ldots,2^B-1\}} : res \cdot di_v + k \cdot res \cdot x_v[k] \geq k \cdot res \quad (13)$$

This constraint indicates that if $di_v < j$, $x_v[k] = 1$ for $k \geq j$; in other words, the delay line setting is unable to filter glitches of pulse-width greater than or equal to $res \cdot j$, and so the glitch power corresponding to these glitches cannot be eliminated. On the other hand, the constraint is satisfied if $x_v[k] = 0$ for $k \leq di_v$; thus the glitch power corresponding to glitches of width $\leq res \cdot di_v$ can be eliminated.

The *min* and *max* constraints in Equations 5, 7, and 8 also represent non-linearities in our problem formulation, however these too may be recast into a linear form through the following constraints:

$$arr_v \geq \forall_{(u,v) \in E} \; arr_u + d_u + t_{uv} \quad (14)$$

$$dp_v^{(min)} \leq \forall_{(u,v) \in E} \; dp_u^{(min)} + d_u \quad (15)$$

$$dp_v^{(max)} \geq \forall_{(u,v) \in E} \; dp_u^{(max)} + d_u \quad (16)$$

It can be shown that the objective function Equation 12 is minimized whenever arr_v and $dp_v^{(max)}$ are minimized, and whenever $dp_v^{(min)}$ is maximized. Thus, for example, any optimal solution to the objective function will guarantee that arr_v will be suitably minimal, while ensuring that the constraints in Equation 14 are met. As such, for all practical purposes, $arr_v = max_{(u,v) \in E}(arr_u + d_u + t_{uv})$. Similar claims can also be made for $dp_v^{(max)}$ and $dp_v^{(min)}$ to ensure that they are effectively the *max* and *min* of their respective arguments.

Together, the objective function in Equation 12 and the constraints in Equation 6, 10 and Equations 13-16 define a mixed-integer linear program (MILP), with binary variables $x_v[k]$ and e_v, integer variables d_v, and continuous variables arr_v, $dp_v^{(min)}$, and $dp_v^{(max)}$. This MILP can be solved using standard mathematical optimization software. We used the commercial `Gurobi Optimizer` tool, version 6.0.5 [18].

5. EXPERIMENTAL STUDY

To assess the power reductions attainable using our proposed technique, we conducted a set of experiments on the 20 largest MCNC benchmark circuits, as well as the 6 circuits from the UMass RCG HDL Benchmark Collection [19]. Since the glitch analysis step in our CAD flow requires functional and timing simulations, we chose the MCNC benchmark circuits as it is straightforward to generate testbenches for these designs that result in sufficient toggling on their internal nodes without requiring an intimate knowledge and understanding of how each of these benchmarks work. The UMass RCG HDL benchmarks were chosen because ready-made test benches are provided with the benchmark set. We also conducted an architecture study to investigate different trade-offs in area overhead and power reduction corresponding to the parameters of the glitch filter circuit. We considered the impact on power reduction from quantization effects in the reduction in resolution and finite maximum delay of the delay lines. Indeed, a glitch filter whose delay line is infinitely precise and has infinite range would offer the greatest flexibility, and thus the greatest opportunity to reduce power. On the other hand, a delay line with large range and fine granularity would also require many stages and SRAM cells, thus presenting an area overhead. Our experiments shed light on an appropriate choice for these parameters.

Our methodology is summarized in the CAD flow shown in Figure 9. A circuit is first compiled using Altera's Quartus II software,

targetting 65nm Stratix-III devices, to generate a delay-annotated netlist. This delay annotated netlist is then input to ModelSim for timing simulation, and the appropriate input vectors are used for simulation (10000 random vectors are generated for the MCNC circuits, while the UMass RCG HDL benchmark circuits are provided with test benches containing appropriate input vectors). A functional simulation is also performed using the same set of vectors to allow us to characterize the glitch statistics of the circuit. These glitch statistics, along with timing information (also output by Quartus II in Standard Delay Format (SDF)) are then input to the glitch setting optimization framework described in Section 4.

To simulate the glitch statistics after applying our glitch filter settings, we created a behavioural model of our programmable glitch filter circuit – the exact glitch filter settings to be used for this circuit are supplied as parameters. We augment the outputs of combinational logic cells in the original Quartus II-generated netlist with instances of our glitch filter circuit, where each instance would have its glitch filtering parameters set by the previous stage of our CAD flow. This modified netlist is then run with the same set of random vectors used previously, and the output of this timing simulation is used to gauge power using Altera's PowerPlay power estimation tool (via a ModelSim-generated .vcd file for switching activity data).

5.1 Maximum Power Reduction Assuming Ideal Delay Lines

The first set of experiments we conducted were to assess the maximum possible power reductions assuming an ideal delay line (i.e. infinite precision and infinite maximum range). The experiments provide an upper bound on the achievable power reduction, prior to our optimization of the range and precision of the delay-line. Table 1 summarizes the power reduction and critical path degradation results for the case where a glitch-filter uses an *ideal* delay line (which has no limits on range or resolution, and does not have any area/power overhead), and for two specific delay-line implementations which will be discussed in the next section. The table lists glitch power reduction along with the resulting reduction to *logic and routing dynamic power* for each circuit in the benchmark set. It should be noted that the amount of dynamic power dissipated in logic (i.e. BLEs and FFs) and routing versus that dissipated in other parts of an FPGA varies from one design to another. For instance, in the UMass benchmark set, the *turboSram* benchmark's core dynamic power is dominated by the power dissipated in memory blocks, while logic and routing power contributes a small percentage to overall power dissipation. In contrast in other benchmarks, such as the *jpeg*, power dissipated in logic and routing power is dominant. The percentage of total dynamic power resulting from glitches is not shown in the table for the sake of brevity, but is similar to previously obtained statistics on the same benchmark set [9]. Note that the virtually no glitches were observed while simulating the *ava* benchmark from the UMass benchmark set, as such the table entries corresponding to glitch reduction for this benchmark are left empty.

Turning our attention now to the first section of the table, we see that with an ideal delay line, glitch reductions ranging from 45-97%, with an average reduction of 75% may be obtained. Logic and routing dynamic power savings range from -1% (for the *ava* benchmark, the 1% power *increase* corresponds to the glitch filter's power overheads, since no glitch power could be reduced) to 33%. Average logic and routing dynamic power reduction is $\sim 14.7\%$ over the set of benchmark circuits.

For the other two delay-lines shown in the table, we pessimistically assume that these would be composed of the conventional delay cells shown in Figure 7(a). In our results, we include the simulated power overhead of a delay-line which comprises these delay-cells, in addition to the increased routing power resulting from the area-overheads of the glitch filtering circuitry. As will be

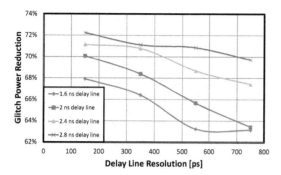

Figure 10: Glitch reductions for delay lines with varying resolution and maximum delay.

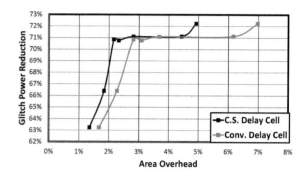

Figure 11: Max glitch reduction vs. area overhead.

described in the subsequent section, for a given delay-line resolution and maximum delay, we may estimate the resulting area overhead. Given an area overhead of x, we estimate that the tile dimensions will increase by a factor of $\sqrt{1+x}$, and thus routing power will (pessimistically) increase by this factor as well. Given the power-breakdown data which can be obtained from PowerPlay's power reports, we are able to estimate the resulting impact to total logic and routing power.

Table 1 also lists the critical path degradation for each circuit. Recall in Section 3 we discussed a delay penalty of 30 ps for the glitch-filter circuit even when the its glitch filtering mechanism is unused (e.g. for timing critical signals). This nominal delay penalty results in a slight impact to the critical path delay for the circuits considered in this work. Observe that the critical path degradation ranges from 0.2% to 2.8%, with an average critical path degradation of 0.9%. Note that the different delay-lines in the table have equal impacts to critical path, since the critical path is unaffected by the range or resolution of the delay-lines.

5.2 Power Reduction with Real Delay Lines

After establishing the maximum possible power savings for each design under ideal circumstances, we experimented with various resolutions and number of bits (i.e. maximum delay line delay) in a bid to identify the delay-line parameters to realize maximum power savings/minimum area overhead. The results of these experiments are shown in Figure 10.

The figure shows 16 different combinations of delay-line parameters, as resolution is varied from 150 ps to 750 ps, while the maximum delay of the delay line is varied from 1.6 ns to 2.8 ns. As expected, the results show monotonic decreases in power consumption as the resolution is increased; reduced resolution is associated with reduced flexibility to eliminate glitches. At the same time, we observe that for the same resolution, the ability to eliminate glitches increases monotonically as the maximum delay of the delay line (and thus, number of configuration bits) increases.

However, the plot reveals an interesting trend: while the delay-line in this study with the finest resolution (150ps) and longest delay (2.8 ns) allowed us to achieve a power reduction of just over 72%, approaching the maximum theoretical glitch reduction of 75%, the other delay lines with coarser resolution and reduced maximum delay were still able to achieve glitch reductions within 5-10% of the theoretical maximum. This compels us to further investigate the area-power trade-offs of these various delay-lines.

We begin by establishing an estimate for the area overhead of the proposed glitch-filter circuit. The number of minimum-width transistors introduced as overhead by this circuit (including configuration memory) for a delay-line constructed with current-starved delay cells is approximately:

$$A_{CS} = 8 + 12n + 6S \qquad (17)$$

Where n is the number of bits, and S is the number of stages in the delay line. For a conventional delay cell based delay-line, the area overhead is approximately:

$$A_{Conv} = 8 + 12n + 10S \qquad (18)$$

We further estimate that a suitably-sized 6-input LUT has an area of 1110 minimum-width transistors, by using transistor sizing data obtained through area-delay optimization of a conventional island-style FPGA architecture [16] (i.e. similar to Stratix III). Also, assuming that the area of an FPGA tile is broken down as follows: 50% routing, 30% LUTs and 20% for miscellaneous circuitry [20], we can form an estimate for the area overhead of the proposed glitch-filters for varying delay-line resolutions and maximum delay-line delays. For the 16 delay-line parameter combinations explored, we may then obtain the greatest power reduction for a given area overhead. The maximum power-reductions, for the two different delay-lines and over the range of area-overheads considered in this work are shown in Figure 11.

Interestingly, the plot shows that for an area overhead of less than 3%, a glitch reduction of ∼ 70% is obtained (which is within 5% of the theoretical maximum), even with the larger conventional delay cell based delay line. This corresponds to a glitch filter with a resolution of 350 ps and maximum delay of 2.4 ns (this requires 3 bits for configuration of the delay-line). The total core dynamic power dissipation in this case is reduced by 12.8%. Another candidate delay-line, with resolution of 550 ps and maximum delay of 1.6 ns (requiring 2 bits for configuration of the delay-line) offers slightly reduced glitch reduction of just over 63%, but this is at an area overhead of under 2%, again for both delay-line types. However, the actual reduction in core dynamic power is 12% in this case, thus making this combination of parameters particularly attractive given its low-cost and a net 2.7% decrease in dynamic power savings compared to the theoretical maximum! The detailed power reductions for these two candidate delay-lines are provided in Table 1.

6. CONCLUSIONS AND FUTURE WORK

This paper presented a glitch reduction circuit and the associated CAD flow/optimization framework needed to maximize glitch power reduction in an FPGA architecture comprising the proposed circuitry. In contrast to prior works, the proposed circuitry offers the ability to reduce glitch power over a wide range of PVT corners because of the nature in which it suppresses glitches, while incurring minimal area/delay overheads. Variations of the proposed circuitry allow glitch power to be reduced from 60-71%, which corresponds to a reduction in core dynamic power of 12-13%, at an area cost of 1.5-3%.

As indicated previously, the fanin delay push-out balancing scheme used in this work is a conservative approach to glitch power optimization, and indeed compromises to some degree our ability to remove glitches. Future work will investigate alternative ap-

Table 1: Detailed glitch and dynamic power reductions for glitch filters with three delay line variants.

Circuit	Critical Path [ns]	Ideal Delay Line			Delay Line Candidate #1: 2.4 ns total delay, 3 bits of resolution			Delay Line Candidate #2: 1.6 ns total delay, 2 bits of resolution		
		Glitch Reduction [%]	Logic and Routing Dynamic Power Savings [%]	Critical Path Degradation [%]	Glitch Reduction [%]	Logic and Routing Dynamic Power Savings [%]	Critical Path Degradation [%]	Glitch Reduction [%]	Logic and Routing Dynamic Power Savings [%]	Critical Path Degradation [%]
alu4	22	70	15	1.3	68	13	1.3	65	12	1.3
apex2	26	81	28	1.1	79	27	1.1	76	25	1.1
apex4	24	73	19	1.3	71	17	1.3	70	17	1.3
bigkey	18	63	18	0.5	56	14	0.5	50	13	0.5
clma	22	65	11	2.2	60	9	2.2	50	7	2.2
des	28	63	19	0.5	59	15	0.5	59	15	0.5
diffeq	18	93	5	0.2	92	4	0.2	92	4	0.2
dsip	17	85	18	0.4	74	15	0.4	53	10	0.4
elliptic	17	74	20	0.2	70	18	0.2	60	15	0.2
ex1010	28	82	33	1	79	30	1	78	29	1
ex5p	26	45	19	1.2	42	17	1.2	42	17	1.2
frisc	17	63	7	0.3	60	6	0.3	55	5	0.3
misex3	24	83	20	1	65	12	1	60	12	1
pdc	31	62	19	1	62	17	1	45	12	1
s298	21	59	5	2.8	57	3	2.8	50	3	2.8
s38417	17	96	25	0.7	96	23	0.7	95	23	0.7
s38584.1	24	84	4	1	80	3	1	58	2	1
seq	23	83	21	1	82	20	1	79	19	1
spla	28	71	24	1.1	70	21	1.1	66	20	1.1
tseng	18	75	7	0.2	55	5	0.2	53	4	0.2
ava	4.3	-	-1	1	-	-1	1	-	-1	1
fdct	7.2	97	17	0.7	94	16	0.7	94	16	0.7
fir_filter	12.6	76	6	0.2	72	5	0.2	72	5	0.2
jpeg	7.8	93	20	0.5	85	18	0.5	85	18	0.5
RS_decoder	7.7	73	3	1.2	71	3	1.2	66	3	1.2
turboSram	4.2	75	3	0.8	65	2	0.8	65	2	0.8
mean		**75**	**14.7**	**0.9**	**70**	**12.8**	**0.9**	**63**	**12**	**0.9**

proaches and/or computationally efficient methods to detect situations in which fanin delay balancing can be neglected, even for consequential nodes. Development of compact and accurate models which allow us to predict glitch statistics given the relative arrival times and switching statistics at input signals would serve this purpose well, and so this would be a promising avenue for future research. Finally, since the proposed circuitry allows for glitches to be suppressed under varying PVT, future work will explore the problem of multi-corner glitch power optimization, thus yielding a truly comprehensive glitch power reduction technique.

7. REFERENCES

[1] I. Kuon and J. Rose, "Measuring the gap between FPGAs and ASICs," *IEEE Trans. On CAD*, vol. 26, no. 2, pp. 203–215, Feb. 2007.

[2] *Virtex-5 FPGA Data Sheet*, Xilinx, Inc., 2012.

[3] S. Gupta *et al.*, "CAD techniques for power optimization in Virtex-5 FPGAs," in *IEEE CICC*, 2007, pp. 85–88.

[4] *Introducing Innovations at 28 nm to Move Beyond Moore's Law*, Altera Corp., 2012.

[5] *Stratix III Programmable Power White Paper*, Altera Corp., 2007.

[6] J. Anderson and F. Najm, "Low-power programmable FPGA routing circuitry," *IEEE Trans. VLSI*, vol. 17, no. 8, pp. 1048–1060, 2009.

[7] *The Breakthrough Advantage for FPGAs with Tri-Gate Technology*, Altera Corp., 2013.

[8] *Xilinx UltraScale: The Next-Generation Architecture for Your Next-Generation Architecture*, Xilinx Corp., 2014.

[9] W. Shum and J. Anderson, "FPGA glitch power analysis and reduction," in *ACM/IEEE ISLPED*, Aug 2011, pp. 27–32.

[10] S. Wilton *et al.*, "The impact of pipelining on energy per operation in field-programmable gate arrays," in *International Conference on Field Programmable Logic and Applications*, Antwerp, Belgium, 2004, pp. 719–728.

[11] T. S. Czajkowski and S. D. Brown, "Using negative edge triggered FFs to reduce glitching power in FPGA circuits," in *ACM/EDAC/IEEE DAC*, 2007, pp. 324–329.

[12] J. Lamoureux *et al.*, "Glitchless: Dynamic power minimization in FPGAs through edge alignment and glitch filtering," *IEEE Trans. VLSI*, vol. 16, no. 11, pp. 1521–1534, Nov 2008.

[13] Q. Dinh *et al.*, "A routing approach to reduce glitches in low power FPGAs," *IEEE TCAD*, vol. 29, no. 2, pp. 235–240, Feb 2010.

[14] W. Lee *et al.*, "Dynamic thermal management for FinFET-based circuits exploiting the temperature effect inversion phenomenon," in *ACM/IEEE ISLPED*, 2014, pp. 105–110.

[15] K. Chakravarthy, "Programmable glitch filter," Dec. 6 2001, US Patent App. 09/864,946. [Online]. Available: http://www.google.ca/patents/US20010048341

[16] C. Chiasson and V. Betz, "COFFE: Fully-automated transistor sizing for FPGAs," in *IEEE FPT*, Dec 2013, pp. 34–41.

[17] J. Rose *et al.*, "The VTR project: Architecture and CAD for FPGAs from verilog to routing," in *ACM/SIGDA FPGA*, 2012, pp. 77–86.

[18] I. Gurobi Optimization, "Gurobi optimizer reference manual," 2015. [Online]. Available: http://www.gurobi.com

[19] "UMass RCG HDL benchmark collection," http://www.ecs.umass.edu/ece/tessier/rcg/benchmarks/.

[20] S. Chin and J. Anderson, "A case for hardened multiplexers in FPGAs," in *IEEE FPT*, Dec 2013, pp. 42–49.

Pitfalls and Tradeoffs in Simultaneous, On-Chip FPGA Delay Measurement

Timothy A. Linscott
Seattle University
901 12th Avenue
Seattle, WA 98122
timothy.a.linscott@gmail.com

Benjamin Gojman[*]
University of Pennsylvania
3330 Walnut St.
Philadelphia, PA 19104
bgojman@acm.org

Raphael Rubin
University of Pennsylvania
3330 Walnut St.
Philadelphia, PA 19104
rafi@seas.upenn.edu

André DeHon
University of Pennsylvania
200 S. 33rd St.
Philadelphia, PA 19104
andre@acm.org

ABSTRACT

Recent work shows how to use on-chip structures to measure the fabricated delays of fine-grained resources on modern FPGAs. We show that simultaneous measurement of multiple, disjoint paths will result in different measured delays from isolated configurations that measure a single path. On the Cyclone III, we show differences as large as ± 33 ps on 2 ns-long paths, even if the simultaneously configured logic is not active. This is over $20\times$ the measurement precision used on these devices and over 50% of the observed delay spread in prior work. We characterize the magnitude of the impact of simultaneous measurements and identify strategies and cases that can reduce the difference. Furthermore, we provide a potential explanation for our observations in terms of self-heating and the configurable clock network architecture. These experiments point to phenomena that must be characterized to better formulate on-chip FPGA delay measurements and to properly interpret their results.

Keywords

FPGA; Timing; Self Measurement; Component-Specific Map

1. ON-CHIP DELAY MEASUREMENT

Recent work [10, 11, 9, 12, 7] shows how to perform on-chip, self measurement of the delay of FPGA resources. In one strategy [10, 7] registers are placed around a path to be measured composed of LUTs and wires (Circuit Under Test, or CUT, Fig. 1). The self test programs the on-chip PLLs to vary the clock period for the registers and identifies

---

[*]Now affiliated with Google, Inc.

FPGA'16 February 21-23, 2016, Monterey, CA, USA

ACM ISBN 978-1-4503-3856-1/16/02.

DOI: http://dx.doi.org/10.1145/2847263.2847334

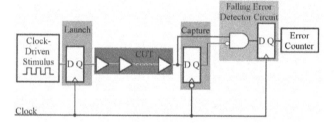

Figure 1: Path-Delay Circuit Under Test (CUT)

when the path fails because the path delay exceeds the clock period.

Gojman showed that a Cyclone III LAB has over 2,400 independently varying delay components [6], meaning even a small FPGA with 963 blocks can have over two million component delays and demand measurement of five to six million paths. Performed serially, each measurement requires both reconfiguration time, T_{reconf}, to define the path and testing time to exercise a configured path.

$$T_{char} \approx N_{path} \times (T_{freq} \times N_{freq} \times N_{samples} + T_{reconf}) \quad (1)$$

T_{reconf} can be 5–200 ms for the Cyclone III [2]. As a result, characterization time, T_{char}, for even a small FPGA could extend to days. Both Wong [10] and Gojman [7] suggest that it might be valuable to perform delay experiments in parallel. Parallel testing could divide the characterization time by the number of simultaneously placed and activated CUTs. Parallelism can scale with the size of the chip such that characterization time need not increase with chip capacity. However, Gojman does not perform measurements in parallel citing the possibility that the experiments could affect each other. Nonetheless, both Wong and Gojman build configurations with multiple CUTs instantiated in each configuration in order to reduce the total number of configurations they must generate and, consequently, the number of times the FPGA must be reconfigured; they do this even when they only enable one CUT at a time.

This prior work left open two important questions:

1. Can we run simultaneous delay measurements without significantly corrupting the measured results? That

is, how much does simultaneous delay measurement impact the measured results?

2. Does placing multiple CUTs onto an FPGA in a single configuration have an impact on the measured results?

This paper provides a direct answer to these questions, quantifying the impact of simultaneous measurement and placement of multiple measurement circuits on an FPGA. We show which effects are present and characterize their magnitude for the 65 nm Cyclone III FPGA used by both Gojman and Wong. The paper also identifies potential sources for the effects and a strategy for minimizing the impact of simultaneous measurements.

2. METHODOLOGY

A simplified version of the measurement circuit is shown in Fig. 1. The measured path—labeled the CUT—contains six LUTs configured as buffers and using only the C and D inputs linked with LAB Local Tracks. Surrounding each CUT are registers that latch on alternate edges of the clock: the launch register at the front latches on the positive edge, and the capture register latches at the falling edge. The input signal is an oscillator running in phase with the clock at half the frequency. If it has had sufficient time to propagate through the CUT after half a clock period, then the two registers will have equal values. If so, we know that the propagation delay over the CUT is equal to or less than half the clock period. However, if the clock period is shorter than the CUT delay, the input will not be able to propagate through the CUT, the outputs of the two registers will differ on the falling edge of the clock, and the AND gate in the Error Detector Circuit will register the error. This will trigger an increment of the Error Counter. For each frequency in our experiments, the input and output of the CUT are compared for $N_{samples} = 2^{15}$ transitions. A failure is reported if at least half of the comparisons are mismatches. We measure timing at this 50% failure point since that is where the results will be most statistically significant. To support this, we use a 14 bit counter. When the count exceeds 2^{14}—half of the number of comparisons we run—it indicates that the CUT has failed at this frequency. In our experiments, we took measurements at both the rising and falling edges of the input clock signal and observed similar effects. For simplicity and brevity, we present only the effects seen at the falling edges of the clock.

Differences in placement and routing of resources could potentially impact delays. Consequently, we took care to control the exact wires and switches used in our experiments following the methodology from [7]. The elements in the measurement circuit, including the CUT, are placed in the same positions, and they use identical switches and wire tracks to connect them. The control structures (shown on the left in Fig. 3) are placed optimally to shorten the connections to the measurement circuits, and the routing from the measurement circuits to the control structures depend on the placement of the CUT; nonetheless, the routes from the control structures are always the same when a CUT is placed in the same position on the array. Boundary registers isolate the routes between the CUTs and the control circuitry and provide fixed locations for these routes. To the right of these registers, the routing is strictly controlled to ensure consistency between measurements and reduce potential crosstalk between wires. We use QUIP to extract and control placement and routing [1].

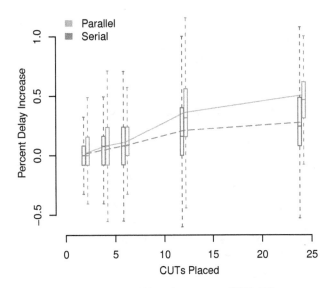

Figure 2: Impact of Simultaneous CUT Placement and Activation on Measured Delay. Lines added to highlight the mean values.

Each tests starts with a binary search to identify the bounds on the circuit operating frequency. Once the binary search has found an approximate frequency, the controller uses a linear search, decreasing the clock period by 1.6 ps until the frequency of failure is found. Five sets of the 2^{15} comparisons are taken from each CUT, and only the result of the last set is used. This allows the circuit to reach a steady-state temperature where the effects of self-heating can be measured uniformly. Previous work established that this methodology gave consistent measurements that were repeatable and independent of the order in which the CUTs were measured [6].

3. SIMULTANEOUS MEASUREMENT

With this setup, we performed an experiment where we first measured a single path in isolation using a single CUT and then measured it with additional CUTs placed at least two LABs away. As noted, the placement and routing for the reference CUT are constrained to be identical across the tests. In the isolation case, aside from control structures (shown on the left of Fig. 3), only a single CUT is placed on the FPGA. For the multiple CUT cases, sets of 2, 4, 6, 12, and 24 CUTs were placed on the FPGA and distributed over at least two rows. Separate measurements were taken for the cases where only one CUT was activated and measured at a time (serial) and cases where all CUTs were simultaneously active and conducting measurements (parallel). An activated CUT will toggle its input to generate a series of transitions that propagate through the path, and, possibly, toggle error counters, while the input to a non-activated CUT does not switch. We collected data across 14 Cyclone III (EP3C16F256C8N) components on Arrow Be-Micro boards. We measured CUT delays between 1.911 ns and 2.110 ns.

Fig. 2 shows the percentage increase of the non-isolated measurement from the isolated measurement. The top (solid blue) line shows the mean percent increase in the parallel case where the other CUTs were simultaneously activated,

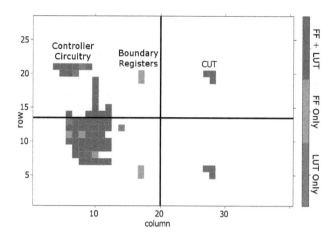

Figure 3: Measurement Test Setup on Cyclone III EP3C16F256C8N

while the bottom (red dashed) line shows the percent increase in the serial case where the added CUTs are not enabled, leaving only the reference CUT active. Both curves include boxplots that show the distribution of the values measured across the various multiple CUT cases; the boxes show the middle two quartiles, while the whiskers show the full range of values measured except for outliers. From these data, we can see that placing additional CUTs increases mean delay. Comparing the serial and parallel trend lines, we can see that more than half of the delay increase comes from the placement of the CUTs, the serial case, rather than their activation. We also see that the effect is not uniform, with some delays decreasing and the largest non-activated delays being as high as the simultaneous activation delays. We saw one, repeatable outlier on one chip whose delay changed by 124 ps.

Depending on the intended use of the measurements, these results may be encouraging or disappointing. The fact that they are within ±1.5%, says that the simultaneous measurements do not change the delays significantly. However, the fact that the delays can change by ±33 ps, even when only one CUT is activated at a time, means the precision of the measurements made is far worse than the precision expected from the clock resolution of 1.3 ps claimed by [10] and 1.6 ps used here and claimed by [7]. Furthermore, the in-LAB LUT chain measurement spreads in [10] are less than 80 ps, and, when measured at the nominal voltage, spreads in [7] are less than 100 ps. This means the delay contribution from simultaneous placement could be 60–80% of these measured delay spreads.

4. WHAT'S HAPPENING?

The CUT used for testing carefully isolates a logic path as a single pipeline stage between registers (Fig. 1). Between the isolated and simultaneous tests, no change is made to the measured CUT logic or physical layout. The only change is that additional, disconnected logic is added elsewhere on the chip. What might cause the measured delay differences?

4.1 Voltage Fluctuation and Self-Heating

Even though the circuit and layout do not change, the delay of the individual circuit elements that make up the CUT may be impacted by environmental changes, including

the local temperature and supply voltage for the circuit as demonstrated in previous work [12]. For MOS gates, the switching time is roughly:

$$\tau \approx \frac{C_{load}V_{dd}}{I_{ds}} \qquad (2)$$

Due to voltage drops on the power distribution lines that supply individual gates on the chip, the local V_{dd} seen by a gate will be smaller than the package V_{dd} and will vary based on the current draw of other gates sharing portions of the power distribution network ($I \times R$ voltage drop). The on-transistor source-drain current, I_{ds}, is impacted by the local supply voltage, V_{dd}, as well as, the threshold voltage and mobility (and hence saturation velocity, v_{sat}) of the MOS-FET, both of which are temperature dependent.

$$I_{ds} = W v_{sat} C_{ox} \left(V_{dd} - V_{th} - \frac{V_{d,sat}}{2} \right)^{\gamma} \qquad (3)$$

As circuitry on the FPGA switches, it dissipates energy (e.g., CV^2 switching energy) as heat. The energy dissipation will heat the die area in the vicinity of the switching, increasing the temperature seen by surrounding circuits and changing their current flow and hence speed. For example, Zick and Hayes show 2.5% change in frequency based on temperature and the ability to control local temperature by controlling switching activity [12]. Consequently, switching activity on the chip can potentially impact the delay of a measured CUT. As expected, the impact increases with the total volume of activity, as Fig. 2 shows. Nonetheless, we might be surprised to see that the magnitude of the effect can be equally large even when circuitry is placed but not activated.

4.2 Configurable Clock Architecture

Modern FPGAs have configurable clock networks that allow portions of the clock distribution tree to be deactivated when not in use in order to save power. Placing a clocked circuit that *could* be activated demands that the clock network be configured to deliver a clock signal to the flip-flops on the circuit. The mere presence of a clocked circuit creates activity in the clock network, even when the circuit is not activated. Furthermore, the buffers in the clock distribution network are typically large in order to drive large clock loads and minimize delay and skew on the clock network, likely much larger than the buffers on logic in a LAB. We believe the activation of different portions of the clock network contributes significant activity that impacts circuit delay in the serial cases where additional CUTs are placed but not simultaneously activated with the measured CUT. Differential loading on clock network in the different clock configurations could also be a contributing factor.

In particular, the Cyclone III clock architecture provides independent control of the clock supplied to each quadrant of the chip, including the ability to disable the clocks to a quadrant [2]. Our measurements suggest that row clock drivers can also be independently disabled on the Cyclone III, similar to more recent Altera architectures [3, 4]. We were able to confirm this conjecture with an Altera architect [5].

5. IMPACT OF SECOND CUT

To better characterize the effects of self-heating on measured CUT delay, we performed a controlled experiment with a single second CUT. A CUT placed in the LAB at

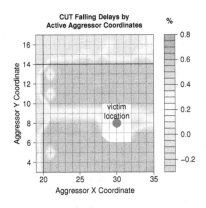 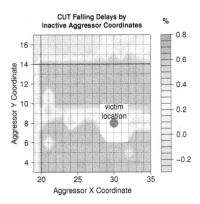

Figure 4: Impact of Relative Position of Two CUTs

(30,8) was used for measurement. It was measured in isolation for a reference point. It was then tested with a second CUT placed at a range of positions around it, both within and outside of its clock quadrant. We call the measurement CUT the *victim* because we are measuring how it is affected by the second CUT, which we call the *aggressor*. The test was conducted once with the aggressor CUT inactive and once with it active (Fig. 4).

Each coordinate in the Fig. 4 map is the location of the aggressor CUT. The value associated with the coordinate is the percent delay increase of the victim CUT with respect to its measurement in isolation. No trials were run where the aggressor was placed in the 3×3 region surrounding the victim. Because the measurement circuits occupy three LABs on the Cyclone III, we left a buffer zone so that the victim and aggressor would never overlap.

The quadrant where the victim CUT is located has its boundaries on x=20 and y=14. When the aggressor CUT is placed outside these boundaries, the victim runs faster—usually close to the delay of the isolated case. When the aggressor is placed in the same quadrant, the victim delays increase by up to 0.74%. Across chips and trials, we see the same pattern—placing the aggressor in the same quadrant increases the victim's delays more significantly than placing it in a different quadrant. This suggests it may be possible to place and measure CUTs simultaneously as long as they reside in separate quadrants.

When the aggressor is placed in the same, or a nearby, row as the victim, the aggressor typically has less impact on the victim. It is possible that the two CUTs share an enabled row clock driver in this configuration, so there is no additional heat or activity generated by activating an *additional* row clock driver within the quadrant. If this effect is robust, it could suggest another option for obtaining low-noise parallel measurements in the same configuration.

6. QUADRANT EXPERIMENT

The previous section suggests there is a strong impact on timing when two CUTs are placed in the same quadrant, but a much smaller effect when they are placed in different quadrants. To further understand this effect, we provide a more directed quadrant experiment. Since the control circuitry lives in the left-hand quadrants (Fig. 3), we limited this experiment to the upper-right and lower-right quadrants. For the same-quadrant experiment, pairs of CUTs were placed in the lower-right quadrant seven rows apart. For the different-

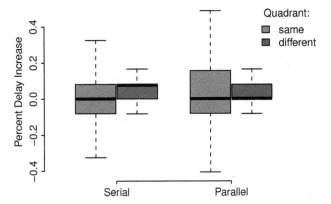

Figure 5: Comparing Impact of Same Quadrant vs. Different Quadrant Aggressors

quadrant experiment, pairs of CUTs were placed with one CUT in the lower-right quadrant of the chip and the second placed in a similar position in the same column in the upper-right quadrant as illustrated in Fig. 3.

When the simultaneously activated CUTs (parallel) are in different quadrants, the difference between simultaneous and isolated measurements is highly concentrated at zero, much more so than when the CUTs are in the same quadrant (Fig. 5). There are still a small percentage of cases where the same-quadrant measurements differ by as much as the different-quadrant measurements as both have occurrences around ±1.5%. Leaving the aggressor CUT inactive (serial) produces similar distributions, also with outliers around ±1.5%.

To determine whether the effect was systematic or unique to particular chips, we differentiated the data based on the measured chip (Fig. 6), using a different symbol for each chip. Some chips are faster than others, as we expect from die-to-die variation. However, no small subset of the chips is uniquely to blame for outliers, nor do they show a tendency to produce results shifted up or down on the graph.

7. DISCUSSION AND FUTURE WORK

The presence of logic, even inactive logic, does impact timing results in on-chip measurements experiments. Vendors know this, and it is one of the timing margins included in their timing analysis [7]. It is necessary to understand how

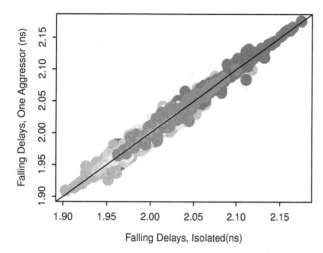

Figure 6: Isolated vs. Simultaneous, Two-CUT, Out-of-Quadrant Measurements by Chip

this simultaneous logic can affect the measurements in order to interpret the results of on-chip timing measurements. The non-isolated measurements are not necessarily wrong—in typical usage scenarios much of the nearby logic will be used, so large portions of the clock network will be enabled as well. When the activity effects are relatively uniform, such that there is a good correlation between component path delay measurements and application-circuit delays, the measurements can still be useful in identifying the relative delay of the resources. *The pitfall comes in comparing the delay of two resources that are differentially impacted by their environment.* As we see in Figs. 2, 5, and 6, while many measured delays change little, some change by much larger amounts, and this differential effect can be misleading. When the magnitude of the difference exceeds the intrinsic delay differences, the measurements can mislead CAD tools (e.g., [8]) and variation characterization.

The primary contribution of this short paper is to identify this issue and provide an initial characterization of the magnitude of the effect. As such, it raises a host of questions that will need to be addressed in future work. For example, how significant are these effects on other FPGA models with different clock architectures? Ideally, we would like to develop a timing model that accounts for thermal and other coupling effects, including modeling the effects of infrastructure logic such as the clock network. E.g.,

$$\tau_{use}(A, B) = \tau_{int}(A, B) + \sum_x \sum_y f(x, y, act(x, y), T_{ext}) \quad (4)$$

This would allow CAD tools to account for coupling delay effects directly. At least, it is necessary to develop a better understanding of the effects upon on-chip delay measurements and develop best practices for collecting delays that are useful and predictive for CAD. It will also be useful to understand how much the coupling effects themselves are subject to variation at various scales and over time.

8. CONCLUSIONS

Even nominally disjoint and quiescent logic placed in proximity to circuitry configured on an FPGA can impact its delay. On a 65 nm Cyclone III we identified effects as high as ±33 ps or about 1.5% of the delay of the paths we were mea-

suring. The effects of the quiescent logic can be explained in terms of circuit activity when we account for the configurable clock network. We show that the average delay effect can be reduced by keeping simultaneous logic in different quadrants or, perhaps, in the same row within a quadrant. Our preliminary experiments suggest there is a rich area to explore to characterize the nature of these coupling effects.

9. ACKNOWLEDGMENTS

Timothy A. Linscott was supported by the National Science Foundation (NSF) Research Experience for Undergraduates (REU) program under contract EEC-1359107. Parts of the research were supported by DARPA/CMO contract HR0011-13-C-0005. Any opinions, findings, and conclusions or recommendations expressed in this material are those of the authors and do not reflect the official policy or position of the National Science Foundation, the Department of Defense, or the U.S. Government.

10. REFERENCES

[1] Altera. QUIP. http://www.altera.com/education/univ/research/quip/unv-quip.html, 2005. 2

[2] Altera. Cyclone III Device Handbook Volume I. http://www.altera.com/literature/hb/cyc3/cyclone3_handbook.pdf, 2011. 1, 4.2

[3] Altera. White paper 01148-2.0: Reducing power consumption and increasing bandwidth on 28-nm FPGAs. https://www.altera.com/en_US/pdfs/literature/wp/wp-01148-stxv-power-consumption.pdf, March 2012. 4.2

[4] Altera. Cyclone V Device Handbook. https://www.altera.com/content/dam/altera-www/global/en_US/pdfs/literature/hb/cyclone-v/cv_5v2.pdf, 2015. 4.2

[5] V. Betz. Cyclone 3 configurable clock architecture. *personal communications*, December 2015. 4.2

[6] B. Gojman. *GROK-FPGA: Generating Real On-chip Knowledge for FPGA Fine-Grain Delays using Timing Extraction.* PhD thesis, University of Pennsylvania, 2014. 1, 2

[7] B. Gojman, S. Nalmela, N. Mehta, N. Howarth, and A. DeHon. GROK-LAB: Generating real on-chip knowledge for intra-cluster delays using timing extraction. *ACM Tr. Reconfig. Tech. and Sys.*, 7(4):5:1–5:23, Dec. 2014. 1, 1, 2, 3, 7

[8] N. Mehta, R. Rubin, and A. DeHon. Limit Study of Energy & Delay Benefits of Component-Specific Routing. In *FPGA*, pages 97–106, 2012. 7

[9] T. Tuan, A. Lesea, C. Kingsley, and S. Trimberger. Analysis of within-die process variation in 65nm FPGAs. In *ISQED*, pages 1–5, March 2011. 1

[10] J. S. Wong, P. Sedcole, and P. Y. K. Cheung. Self-measurement of combinatorial circuit delays in FPGAs. *ACM Tr. Reconfig. Tech. and Sys.*, 2(2):1–22, June 2009. 1, 1, 3

[11] H. Yu, Q. Xu, and P. H. Leong. Fine-grained characterization of process variation in FPGAs. In *ICFPT*, pages 138–145, 2010. 1

[12] K. M. Zick and J. P. Hayes. On-line sensing for healthier FPGA systems. In *FPGA*, pages 239–248, 2010. 1, 4.1, 4.1

FPGP: Graph Processing Framework on FPGA
A Case Study of Breadth-First Search

Guohao Dai, Yuze Chi, Yu Wang, Huazhong Yang
Department of Electronic Engineering, Tsinghua University, Beijing, China
Tsinghua National Laboratory for Information Science and Technology
{dgh14, chiyz12}@mails.tsinghua.edu.cn, {yu-wang, yanghz}@mail.tsinghua.edu.cn

ABSTRACT

Large-scale graph processing is gaining increasing attentions in many domains. Meanwhile, FPGA provides a power-efficient and highly parallel platform for many applications, and has been applied to custom computing in many domains. In this paper, we describe FPGP (**FP**GA **G**raph **P**rocessing), a streamlined vertex-centric graph processing framework on FPGA, based on the interval-shard structure. FPGP is adaptable to different graph algorithms and users do not need to change the whole implementation on the FPGA. In our implementation, an on-chip parallel graph processor is proposed to both maximize the off-chip bandwidth of graph data and fully utilize the parallelism of graph processing. Meanwhile, we analyze the performance of FPGP and show the scalability of FPGP when the bandwidth of data path increases. FPGP is more power-efficient than single machine systems and scalable to larger graphs compared with other FPGA-based graph systems.

Categories and Subject Descriptors

B.4.4 [**Hardware**]: Input/Output and Data Communications—*Performance Analysis and Design Aids*; E.1 [**Data**]: Data Structure

Keywords

Large scale graph processing; FPGA framework

1. INTRODUCTION

We are living in a "big data" era with the great explosion of data volume generated and collected from ubiquitous sensors, portable devices and the Internet. However, large graphs are generally hard to deal with. State-of-the-art graph processing systems are generally limited by IO and computation does not take a large part in the total execution time. FPGA can handle the same computation task while providing much better power-efficiency. Researchers have proposed some dedicated solutions for certain algorithms[2, 3] and some generic solutions[11] on FPGA. The formers are restricted to special applications whereas the latter cannot

scale to the order of millions because all vertices and edges need to be stored on the FPGA board.

In this work, we present FPGP, a scalable graph processing platform on FPGA that can handle billion-scale graphs with a single FPGA board. Our main contributions are as follows:

- **Enable interval-shard based vertex-centric graph processing on FPGA.** Previous work on FPGA either focuses on certain algorithm only, or supports generic algorithms but limited to less than millions of vertices due to the lack of FPGA resources. By cutting vertices into small intervals and fitting them into small on-chip memory while streaming edges from off-board storage, FPGP can scale to graphs with billions of vertices and even more edges.

- **Analyze the performance bottleneck of generic graph systems on FPGA.** Under FPGP framework, we analyze the impact factors of performance and give an optimized strategy to achieve the maximum performance. Given the analysis, we do a case study of breadth-first search to demonstrate the system performance model when the bandwidth varies.

The following of this paper is organized as follows. Section 2 shows some related graph processing systems. Section 3 describes some background ideas about graph computation tasks and introduces the algorithm. We then present the FPGP framework in Section 4. Then, we model the performance of the FPGP framework in Section 5. We demonstrate and discuss some experimental results in Section 6. Section 7 concludes the paper.

2. RELATED WORK

2.1 Single-machine CPU systems

GraphChi[10] is a disk-based single-machine system following the vertex-centric programming model. GraphChi first introduces the concepts of intervals and shards. GraphChi can handle billions of vertices and edges on a single PC.

TurboGraph[8] is another disk-based graph processing system. It presents the *pin-and-slide* model to handle larger graphs. Edges are managed as pages stored on disk and are pinned into memory when necessary. VENUS[5] is more friendly to hard disks. It introduces the Vertex-centric Streamlined Processing (VSP) model such that graph is loaded in serial but updating kernel is executed in parallel. NXgraph[6] divides edges into smaller sub-shards and sorts edges within each sub-shard, achieving a better performance compared with systems above.

All these systems use interval-shard structure to store graphs, providing the locality of data accessing.

2.2 FPGA systems

Bondhugula et al. presents a parallel FPGA-based all-pairs shortest paths solving system in [4]. This system is

This work was supported by 973 project 2013CB329000, National Natural Science Foundation of China (No. 61373026, 61261160501), the Importation and Development of High-Caliber Talents Project of Beijing Municipal Institutions, Xilinx University Program, Huawei Technologies Co., Ltd, and Tsinghua University Initiative Scientific Research Program.

FPGA'16, February 21-23, 2016, Monterey, CA, USA
© 2016 ACM. ISBN 978-1-4503-3856-1/16/02. . . $15.00
DOI: http://dx.doi.org/10.1145/2847263.2847339

Table 1: Notations of a graph

Notation	Meaning
G	the graph $G = (V, E)$
V	vertices in G
E	edges in G
n	number of vertices in G, $n = |V|$
m	number of edges in G, $m = |E|$
v_i	vertex i, or its associated attribute value
$e_{i \to j}$	edge e from v_i to v_j
I_i	interval i
S_i	shard i
$SS_{i.j}$	sub-shard $i.j$
P	number of intervals
B_v	(average) size of a vertex on disk
B_e	(average) size of an edge on disk

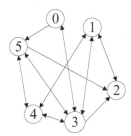

(a) Example graph   (b) Intervals and sub-shards

Figure 1: An example of intervals and sub-shards

dedicated for Floyd-Warshall algorithm and is optimized so that a maximum utilization of on-chip resources is achieved while maximum parallelism is enabled. Betkaoui et al. introduces an FPGA-based BFS solution with high efficiency and scalability with optimization on memory access and coarse-grained parallelism. However, neither of them can address general graph computation problems. GraphGen[11] is an FPGA-based generic graph processing system using the vertex-centric model. However, GraphGen stores the whole graph in the on-board DRAM, which significantly limits the scalability of such a system.

3. PRELIMINARY

In this section, a detailed description of a graph computation task is given first, followed by a brief introduction of graph presentation methodology. The algorithm in FPGP is described in Section 3.3. The notations used in this section is listed in Table 1.

3.1 Problem description

A graph $G = (V, E)$ is composed of its vertices V and edges E. A computation task on G will be updating values on set V according to the adjacency information on set E. By attaching a value to the $<source, destination>$ pair of each edge, FPGP is applicable to both weighted and unweighted graphs. The update function used in graph computation is usually modeled as vertex-centric. In the vertex-centric model, each vertex carries a mutable attribute value, which can be updated by its in-neighbors during the execution stage. Graph algorithms are usually iterative.

3.2 Graph presentation

Many systems use intervals to store vertex attributes and shards to store edges. Moreover, each shard can be divided into sub-shards. All vertices of $G = (V, E)$, or V, should be divided into P disjoint intervals $I_1, I_2, ..., I_P$. All edges of G, or E, should be divided into P disjoint shards $S_1, S_2, ..., S_P$. Each shard S_j is further partitioned into P disjoint sub-shards $SS_{1.j}, SS_{2.j}, ..., SS_{P.j}$. A sub-shard $SS_{i.j}$ consists of all edges in E whose source vertex resides in the interval I_i and destination vertex resides in the interval I_j. This is shown in Figure 1.

3.3 Algorithm description on FPGP

FPGP adopts the updating strategy described in [6] which supports both weighted and unweighted graphs. Updates are performed in unit of intervals. Within each iteration of traversal, FPGP will iterate each interval as the destination interval and perform updates upon it. For example, in the graph presented in Figure 1, FPGP will first choose I_1 as the destination interval. To calculate the updated I_1, FPGP will first use $SS_{1.1}$ and previous values in I_1

to calculate incremental values to I_1. After that, FPGP will use $SS_{2.1}$ and previous I_2 to calculate another incremental values. Then it'll use $SS_{3.1}$ and I_3, ..., etc. When FPGP finishes iteration over source intervals, it will accumulate all the incremental values as well as optional initial values of I_1. In this way, all edges and vertices are effectively traversed and updates are incrementally performed on the destination.

4. FPGP FRAMEWORK

4.1 Framework Overview

The overall framework of FPGP is shown in Figure 2. The Processing Kernels(PKs) provides reconfigurable logic for designers to implement graph updating kernel function on the FPGA chip. On-chip cache stores a portion of graph data using block RAMs(BRAMs) on FPGA, thus PKs can access these data within one or two clock cycles in a random access pattern. Data controller arranges edge or vertex data from either the shared vertex data memory and the local edge data storage. The shared vertex data memory stores the vertex data and can be updated by each PK when executing the graph algorithm. Each local edge data storage stores a portion of edges in the graph and feeds these data for a slice of PKs.

4.2 Reconfigurable Processing Kernel

Designers can implement their own designs for different graph algorithms on PKs. Both the input and output of PKs are from on-chip block RAMs rather than the off-chip memory, thus the long latency caused by the poor locality of graph data is eliminated. Each PK receives an edge e and extracts the value of its source vertex, then performs the $kernel()$ function to update the value for its destination vertex, as shown in Formula (1).

$$e.dst.value = kernel(e.dst.value, e.src.value) \qquad (1)$$

4.3 On-chip Cache and Data Arrangement

FPGP provides a dedicated on-chip cache mechanism for graph data and that ensures the locality when executing the graph algorithm on a subset of a graph. As mentioned in Section 3.2, vertices in the graph are divided into P intervals and edges are divided into P^2 sub-shards. Updating is performed in unit of sub-shards. When executing graph algorithm on a sub-shard $SS_{i.j}$, FPGP stores I_i and I_j in the on-chip vertex read cache and vertex write cache, respectively. The values of vertices in I_j are then updated using the values of vertices in I_i while edges in $SS_{i.j}$ are loaded in a streamlined way from external local edge storage. From the perspective of intervals, Formula (1) can be modified into Formula (2).

$$I_j = update(I_j, I_i, SS_{i.j}) \qquad (2)$$

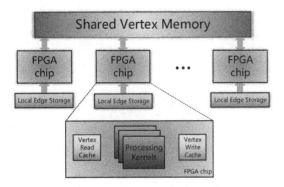

Figure 2: FPGP framework

Algorithm 1 Work flow of FPGP framework[10]

Input: G
Output: updated V in $G = (V, E)$
1: **for** $j = 1$ to P **do**
2:     Load I_j;
3:     Load I_1;
4:     **for** $i = 1$ to P **do**
5:         $I_j = update(I_j, I_i, SS_{i.j})$;
6:         **if** $i \neq P$ **then**
7:             Load I_{i+1};
8:         **end if**
9:     **end for**
10:    Save I_j;
11: **end for**

4.4 Updating Strategy

In the FPGP framework, two kinds of storage are introduced, the shared vertex data memory and the local edge data storage, vertices and edges are stored in them respectively. When performing the vertex-centric updating, edges in the local edge data storage are loaded to FPGA chip sequentially whereas vertices in the shared vertex data memory are manipulated by a controller. Observing that different PKs can update different destination intervals (I_j, I_k, etc.) using the same source interval I_i, I_i can be loaded from the shared vertex data memory and issued to different PKs without increasing the bandwidth requirement of the shared vertex data memory. This storage arrangement and updating strategy makes our FPGP framework scalable as the size of graph increases.

The basic workflow of FPGP is shown in Algorithm 1. FPGP executes the *update* fuction (Line 5 in Algorithm 1) in a streamlined way, as shown in Algorithm 2.

5. PERFORMANCE ANALYSIS OF FPGP

5.1 FPGP Model

Consider the graph $G = (V, E)$ where $|V| = n, |E| = m$. The size of a vertex value is B_v and the size of an edge is B_e. The total space requirement for vertices and edges are nB_v and mB_e, respectively. Assume all intervals have the same size $\frac{nB_v}{P}$ and all sub-shards have the same size $\frac{mB_e}{P^2}$. Here, P represents the number of intervals in the graph.

Two fundamental requirements for FPGP are that all vertices in the graph can be stored in the shared vertex memory and ping-pong operation can be performed, and all local edge storage space is sufficient to store all edges in the graph, which is shown in Formula (3) and Formula (4). For example, in our FPGP implementation, we use on board DRAM ($\sim$GBytes) as shared vertex memory. Assuming $B_v = 4$Bytes, FPGP can support graphs with millions of vertices. Because edge data can be accessed via PCI-e,

Algorithm 2 Streamlined executing of *update* function

Input: $I_i, I_j, SS_{i.j}$
Output: I_j
1: **for** $e \in SS_{i.j}$ **do**
2:     $e.dst.value = kernel(e.dst.value, e.src.value)$
3: **end for**

Table 2: Notations of FPGP

Notation	Meaning
N_{pk}	number of PKs on each FPGA chip
N_{chip}	number of FPGA chips
M_{bram}	size of available Block RAMs on each chip
M_v	size of available shared vertex memory
M_e	size of available local edge storage
f	frequency of FPGA
T_{cal}	time spent on PKs
$T_{load.edge}$	time spent on loading edges
$T_{load.vertex}$	time spent on loading vertices
T_{exe}	time spent on the inner loop of Algorithm 1
$T_{total.exe}$	total executing time of each iteration
BW_{share}	bandwidth of the shared vertex memory
BW_{local}	bandwidth of each local edge storage

the local edge storage can be extended to several TBytes.

$$M_v > 2nB_v \tag{3}$$

$$M_e > mB_e \tag{4}$$

5.2 Memory Size

Assuming the number of FPGA chips is N_{chip} and the block RAM size of each chip is M_{bram}, we implement N_{pk} PKs on each FPGA chip. Each PK executes the *kernel* function to update an I_j using the same I_i. Considering the ping-pong interval (I_i and I_{i+1}) on the FPGA chip, the total on-chip BRAM requirement is $(N_{pk} + 2) \cdot \frac{nB_v}{P}$, thus:

$$M_{bram} > (N_{pk} + 2) \cdot \frac{nB_v}{P} \tag{5}$$

P^2 iterations are required and each FPGA chip executes the *update* function $\frac{P^2}{N_{chip}}$ times (Line 5 in Algorithm 1). Assume each FPGA chip runs at the frequency of f, and the bandwidth of local edge storage is sufficient to provide the input tuple ($e.dst, e.src$), the executing time of calculating the updated value of an interval is $\frac{1}{f} \cdot \frac{m}{P^2}$. Note that the PKs are required to be fully pipelined so that a new edge can be issued every cycle. Thus, the total executing time of calculating the updated value of all vertices V, namely T_{cal}, is shown in Formula (6).

$$T_{cal} = \frac{1}{f} \cdot \frac{m}{P^2} \cdot \frac{P^2}{N_{chip}} \cdot \frac{1}{N_{pk}} = \frac{m}{N_{chip}N_{pk}f} \tag{6}$$

Assuming the total time of loading all edges in a local edge storage is $T_{load.edge}$, Formula (6) is valid when $T_{load.edge} < T_{cal}$. Furthermore, note that calculating the updated value of I_j (Line 5 in Algorithm 1) and loading I_{i+1} are executed concurrently, the total executing time of the inner loop (Line 5 to 8), namely T_{exe}, is

$$T_{exe} = max(T_{cal}, T_{load.edge}, T_{load.vertex}) \tag{7}$$

Formula (7) shows that the total executing time of the inner loop of Algorithm 1 equals to the largest value among T_{cal}, $T_{load.vertex}$ and $T_{load.edge}$. The latter two are closely related to the bandwidth of memory in FPGP, which will be analyzed in Section 5.3.

5.3 Bandwidth

Based on the analysis above, we will show how memory bandwidth affects the performance of FPGP in this section. Assume the bandwidth of the local edge storage is BW_{local}, we can get Formula (8):

$$T_{load.edge} = \frac{mB_e}{N_{chip}BW_{local}} \qquad (8)$$

As illustrated in Figure 2, all FPGA chips can access the shared vertex memory, leading to a decrease on the effective bandwidth when the number of FPGA chip N_{chip} becomes larger. However, noticing that we can update different intervals (I_j, I_k, etc.) with the same interval I_i, we can synchronize all FPGA chips before loading an interval. This is shown in Algorithm 3 (Line 3 and Line 8).

Algorithm 3 Work flow of FPGP framework with synchronization

Input: G
Output: updated V in $G = (V, E)$
1: **for** $j = 1$ to P **do**
2:     Load I_j;
3:     SyncAndIssue();
4:     Load I_1;
5:     **for** $i = 1$ to P **do**
6:         **for** each chip **do** in parallel
7:             $I_j = update(I_j, I_i, SS_{i.j})$;
8:         **end for**
9:         **if** $i \neq P$ **then**
10:           SyncAndIssue();
11:           Load I_{i+1};
12:         **end if**
13:     **end for**
14:     Save I_j;
15: **end for**

We can get $T_{load.vertex}$ according to Formula (9), assuming the bandwidth of the shared vertex memory is BW_{share}.

$$T_{load.vertex} = \frac{P}{N_{chip}} \cdot P \cdot \frac{nB_v}{P} \cdot \frac{1}{BW_{share}} = \frac{PnB_v}{N_{chip}BW_{share}} \qquad (9)$$

Note that according to Formula (5), the lower bound of P is $\frac{(N_{pk}+2)nB_v}{M_{bram}}$. To minimize $T_{load.vertex}$ so that T_{exe} can be minimized, we substitute P with its lower bound. Thus, Formula (7) can be derived into Formula (10):

$$T_{exe} = max\left(\frac{m}{N_{chip}N_{pk}f}, \frac{mB_e}{N_{chip}BW_{local}}, \frac{(N_{pk}+2)(nB_v)^2}{M_{bram}N_{chip}BW_{share}}\right) \qquad (10)$$

Formula (10) shows the executing time of inner loop in Algorithm 3. The total executing time of one iteration, $T_{total.exe}$, is

$$T_{total.exe} = T_{exe} + \frac{2nB_v}{BW_{share}} \qquad (11)$$

The extra item $\frac{2nB_v}{BW_{share}}$ is added because we need to read the new destination interval from the shared vertex memory and write the updated destination interval to the shared vertex memory before changing the subscript j in Algorithm 1 or 3.

5.4 Performance Summary

Implementing more PKs on one FPGA chip may not lead to better performance because larger N_{pk} leads to an increase in the total number of loops, as illustrated in Formula (5). Formula (10) shows that the first item of T_{exe} is inversely proportional to N_{pk}, while the other two is constant

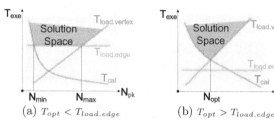

(a) $T_{opt} < T_{load.edge}$ (b) $T_{opt} > T_{load.edge}$

Figure 3: Solution space: when the bandwidth of the local edge storage increases and $T_{load.edge}$ decreases, the bottleneck turns into on-board processing from off-board data accessing

and proportional to N_{pk}, respectively. Assuming (N_{cross}, T_{cross}) is the crossover point of T_{cal} and $T_{load.vertex}$ as N_{pk} varies, we can derive that

$$N_{cross} = \sqrt{1 + \frac{mM_{bram}BW_{share}}{f(nB_v)^2}} - 1 \qquad (12)$$

$$T_{cross} = \frac{(nB_v)^2}{M_{bram}N_{chip}BW_{share}}\left(\sqrt{1 + \frac{mM_{bram}BW_{share}}{f(nB_v)^2}} + 1\right) \qquad (13)$$

We can also get N_{min}, the crossover points of T_{cal} and $T_{load.edge}$, and N_{max}, the crossover points of $T_{load.vertex}$ and $T_{load.edge}$. Note that $N_{min} < N_{max}$ if and only if $T_{cross} < T_{load.edge}$.

$$N_{min} = \frac{BW_{local}}{fB_e} \qquad (14)$$

$$N_{max} = \frac{mB_e BW_{share}M_{bram}}{(nB_v)^2 BW_{local}} - 2 \qquad (15)$$

We can see that T_{cross} reflects the best performance that on-board resources (FPGA chip, DRAM) can provide, while $T_{load.edge}$ only depends on off-board resources (PCI-e bandwidth). Thus, in Figure 3, when $T_{cross} < T_{load.edge}$, the system gets the best performance as $N_{min} < N_{pk} < N_{max}$, and $T_{exe} = T_{load.edge}$. In this situation, the local edge storage becomes the bottleneck, and the bandwidth of the local edge storage is not sufficient to provide data for processing. When $T_{cross} > T_{load.edge}$, the system gets the best performance as $N_{pk} = N_{cross}$, and $T_{exe} = T_{cross}$. In this situation, the bandwidth of the local edge storage is sufficient to provide data for processing, and a larger N_{pk} can lead to a higher degree of parallelism but also increase the times of replacing on-chip intervals, thus the whole system reaches the best performance when N_{pk} gets the optimal point.

6. EXPERIMENTAL RESULTS

In this section, we will introduce a slice of experimental results of our FPGP framework on real-world graphs. We test the system performance and compare the results with the performance analysis in Section 5. We also compare the executing time of FPGP on real-world graphs with state-of-the-art systems.

6.1 Implementation: A case study of BFS

In this section, we implement the BFS under the FPGP framework. Although BFS does not involve much computation, we can extended the results to more complicated algorithms. In FPGP, data are streamlined loaded to FPGA chip so pipeline is applicable for complicated algorithms. We use one Xilinx Virtex-7 FPGA VC707 Evaluation Kit and choose $N_{pk} = 2$ in the implementation (Figure 4). Thus, 4 interval caches are on the chip, including a ping-pong interval cache (I_i and I_{i+1}), and one result interval I_j for each PK.

In our implementation, we use a FIFO between the local edge storage and on-chip logic. By introducing the FIFO, the FPGP is capable of decoding the compressed sparse format used in the sub-shards. The updating results of I_j from two BFS kernels will be merged before written back to the shared vertex memory.

6.2 Experimental Setup

To test the performance of breadth-first search in the FPGP framework, we implement the breadth-first search algorithm according to the detailed implementation in Section 6.1. We choose Xilinx Virtex-7 FPGA VC707 Evaluation Kit as our FPGA prototype, and the FPGA chip is XC7VX485T-2FFG1761. The VC707 Evaluation Kit has an x8 PCI-e Gen2 interface to a host PC and a 1GB on-board DDR3 memory. Our implementation of FPGP on VC707 runs at the frequency of 100MHz. A personal computer is equipped with a hexa-core Intel i7 CPU running at 3.3GHz, eight 8 GB DDR4 memory and a 1 TB HDD. The computer is used to execute GraphChi as a comparison to FPGP, and we choose the Twitter[9] graph (42 millions of vertices and 1.4 billions of edges) and the YahooWeb[7] graph (1.4 billions of vertices and 6.6 billions of edges) as the benchmark.

6.3 System Performance

In this experiment, we compare the FPGP to GraphChi on the Twitter graph when performing the breadth-first search. GraphChi is a disk-based single-machine system following the vertex-centric programming model. It presents the interval-shard based graph computation model for the first time and many other graph processing systems improve the performance based on GraphChi.

There are 37.08 Mbits BRAM resources in total on the XC7VX485T-2FFG1761 chip, we use 90% of these resources. However, only about 1% LUTs are used. Although LUTs can be used as on-chip memory, it can only provide about 20% extra on-chip memory resources compared with BRAMs, which may not provide significant improvement. Meanwhile, LUTs can be used for other logics in our further implementation to improve the performance of FPGP. $N_{pk} = 2$ in our implementation and thus there are 4 interval caches on the FPGA chip, each has the size of 1MBytes, and the resource cost of our FPGP implementation is shown in Table 3.

Table 3: Resource utilization of BFS

Resource	Utilization	Available	Utilization%
FF	610	607200	0.10
LUT	4399	303600	1.45
BRAM	928	1030	90.09
BUFG	1	32	3.13

As shown in Table 3, the bottleneck of our FPGP implementation is the total block RAM resources on one chip. We simulate the performance of FPGP when $BW_{share} = 6.4$ GB/s and $BW_{local} = 0.8$ GB/s. The executing time on Twitter[9] graph of FPGP is 121.992s (13 iterations), while it takes 148.557s on GraphChi and 76.134s on TurboGraph.

Table 4: Executing time of BFS on Twitter

System	GraphChi	Turbograph	FPGP
Time(s)	148.557	76.134	121.992

As we can see, FPGP achieves **1.22x** speedup to GraphChi when $BW_{share} = 6.4$ GB/s and $BW_{local} = 0.8$ GB/s. Note that the VC707 Evaluation Kit can provide up to 12.8 GB/s

of BW_{share} (by using DDR3 on the board) and up to 2 GB/s of BW_{local} (by using PCI-e). Meanwhile, our FPGP system requires less power that the CPU system.

We also test the performance on YahooWeb graph[7], which consists of 1.4 billions of vertices and 6.6 billions of edges. It takes 635.44s on FPGP while takes 2451.62s on GraphChi, thus FPGP achieves **3.86x** speedup to GraphChi. FPGP is scalable to graphs with billions of vertices.

6.4 Bandwidth

As analyzed in Section 5, both bandwidth and memory size have influence on the whole system performance. To get the best performance of FPGP, we almost use all of on-chip BRAM resources and do not change the BRAM size by implementing FPGP on different FPGA chips. The size of DRAM on VC707 board and off-board DRAM via PCI-e is able to meet Formula (3) and Formula (4). Thus in our experiment we just change the bandwidth, BW_{local} and BW_{share}.

Because the data access pattern is organized into a streamlined way in FPGP, we can use the simulated results to demonstrate the actual bandwidth of actual implementation. According to the analysis in Section 5.4, both the bandwidth of the shared vertex memory and local edge memory influence the system performance. Simply improve the bandwidth of either of them will approach a bottleneck when the bandwidth of another is limited. In this section, we simulate the performance of FPGP when the bandwidth of local edge storage and shared vertex memory varies. We choose $N_{pk} = 2$ and the FPGP runs at the frequency of 100 MHz.

BW_{share}. We vary the BW_{share} from 0.4 GB/s to 51.2 GB/s, and $BW_{local} = 0.4$ GB/s and 0.8 GB/s respectively. We test the executing time of FPGP when performing the BFS algorithm per iteration, and the result is shown in Figure 5. As we can see, the performance of FPGP will hardly be improved when BW_{share} is more than 12.8 GB/s, for BW_{local} has become the bottleneck in this situation.

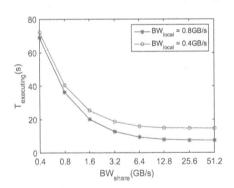

Figure 5: Performance when BW_{share} varies

BW_{local}. The local edge storage typically requires a memory space about 10 to 100 GB to store part of edges in a graph and can be carried out by using disk or via PCI-e. The typical bandwidth of these devices is about 0.5 GB/s. Thus, we simulate the performance of FPGP by varying the BW_{local} from 0.1 GB/s to 0.8 GB/s. The result is shown in Figure 6. When BW_{local} increases, the $T_{load.edge}$ line in Figure 3 continuously decline and the situation changes from Figure 3(a) to Figure 3(b). However, due to the platform limitation, we cannot get a larger bandwidth than ~GBytes via PCI-e, the real situation of our FPGP implementation is more corresponding to Figure 3(a). Thus, improving the bandwidth of local edge storage will enhance the performance of FPGP markedly compared with improving the bandwidth of shared vertex memory, which can be inferred from our experiment results in Figure 6.

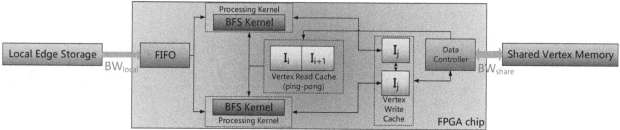

Figure 4: Detailed implementation of Breadth-First Search in FPGP

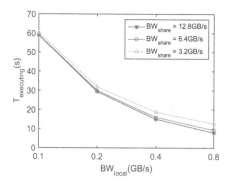

Figure 6: Performance when BW_{local} varies

6.5 Discussion

FPGP provides a framework for implementing different graph algorithms on FPGA. Compared with state-of-the-art CPU-based systems, such as TurboGraph[8] and NX-graph[6], FPGP doesn't achieve better performance on current FPGA chips.

We compare an Intel Haswell architecture CPU (i7-4770) with our Xilinx XC7VX485T-2FFG1761. The i7-4770 has 4 cores and a 256KBytes L2 cache for each core, each core runs at 3.4GHz and the latency of fetch data in the L2 cache is around 10 cycles, thus each core is equivalently running at around 300MHz when fetching data in L2 cache. In our implementation, we have 2 PKs and each PK is attached with a 1MBytes BRAM, running at 100MHz. State-of-the-art systems use more powerful CPUs which have more cores, larger L2 cache size, and run at a higher frequency. Meanwhile, CPU systems store edge data in the main memory and have larger bandwidth compared with the PCI-e implementation in FPGP.

As analyzed above, to improve the performance of FPGP, one way is to improve the bandwidth of both shared vertex memory and local edge storage. However, current implementation uses PCI-e to access edge data and on-board DRAM to access vertex data, FPGP is not as competitive as CPU systems. Thus, using FPGAs with larger on-chip memory becomes a possible way. Larger on-chip memory can provide a higher degree of parallelism. Meanwhile, it can also enlarger the interval size on the FPGA chip, so that the number of intervals can be reduced and the times of replacing intervals can be lowered.

A recent work[1] shows that in-memory-computing is effective to improve the performance of graph processing. "By putting computation units inside main memory, total memory bandwidth for the computation units scales well with the increase in memory capacity."[1] Thus, allocating more memory resources to each graph processing unit is important for improving performance of graph processing, the point of view corresponds to our conclusion that an FPGA chip with lager on-chip memory resources can lead to a better performance in FPGP.

7. CONCLUSION

In this paper, we present an power-efficient large-scale interval-shard based graph processing framework based on FPGA, FPGP, which can handle generic graph algorithms on graphs with billions of edges in several seconds. Meanwhile, we model the performance of FPGP and analyze the bottleneck on a specific hardware platform. In our future work, we will support more graph algorithms under the FPGP framework.

8. REFERENCES

[1] J. Ahn, S. Hong, S. Yoo, O. Mutlu, and K. Choi. A scalable processing-in-memory accelerator for parallel graph processing. In *ISCA*, pages 105–117, 2015.

[2] B. Betkaoui, D. B. Thomas, W. Luk, and N. Przulj. A framework for FPGA acceleration of large graph problems: Graphlet counting case study. In *FPT*, pages 1–8, 2011.

[3] B. Betkaoui, Y. Wang, D. B. Thomas, and W. Luk. A reconfigurable computing approach for efficient and scalable parallel graph exploration. In *ASAP*, pages 8–15, 2012.

[4] U. Bondhugula, A. Devulapalli, J. Fernando, P. Wyckoff, and P. Sadayappan. Parallel fpga-based all-pairs shortest-paths in a directed graph. In *IPDPS*, pages 112–121, 2006.

[5] J. Cheng, Q. Liu, Z. Li, W. Fan, J. C. S. Lui, and C. He. Venus : Vertex-centric streamlined graph computation on a single pc. In *ICDE*, pages 1131–1142, 2015.

[6] Y. Chi, G. Dai, Y. Wang, G. Sun, G. Li, and H. Yang. Nxgraph: An efficient graph processing system on a single machine. *arXiv preprint arXiv:1510.06916*, 2015.

[7] G. Dror, N. Koenigstein, Y. Koren, and M. Weimer. The yahoo! music dataset and kdd-cup'11. In *KDD Cup*, pages 8–18, 2012.

[8] W.-S. Han, S. Lee, K. Park, J.-H. Lee, M.-S. Kim, J. Kim, and H. Yu. Turbograph: A fast parallel graph engine handling billion-scale graphs in a single pc. In *SIGKDD*, page 77, 2013.

[9] H. Kwak, C. Lee, H. Park, and S. Moon. What is twitter, a social network or a news media? In *IW3C2*, pages 1–10, 2010.

[10] A. Kyrola, G. Blelloch, and C. Guestrin. Graphchi: Large-scale graph computation on just a pc disk-based graph computation. In *OSDI*, pages 31–46, 2012.

[11] E. Nurvitadhi, G. Weisz, Y. Wang, S. Hurkat, M. Nguyen, J. C. Hoe, J. F. Martínez, and C. Guestrin. Graphgen: An fpga framework for vertex-centric graph computation. In *FCCM*, pages 25–28, 2014.

GraphOps: A Dataflow Library for Graph Analytics Acceleration

Tayo Oguntebi
Pervasive Parallelism Laboratory
Stanford University
tayo@stanford.edu

Kunle Olukotun
Pervasive Parallelism Laboratory
Stanford University
kunle@stanford.edu

ABSTRACT

Analytics and knowledge extraction on graph data structures have become areas of great interest. For frequently executed algorithms, dedicated hardware accelerators are an energy-efficient avenue to high performance. Unfortunately, they are notoriously labor-intensive to design and verify while meeting stringent time-to-market goals.

In this paper, we present GraphOps, a modular hardware library for quickly and easily constructing energy-efficient accelerators for graph analytics algorithms. GraphOps provide a hardware designer with a set of composable graph-specific building blocks, broad enough to target a wide array of graph analytics algorithms. The system is built upon a dataflow execution platform and targets FPGAs, allowing a vendor to use the same hardware to accelerate different types of analytics computation. Low-level hardware implementation details such as flow control, input buffering, rate throttling, and host/interrupt interaction are automatically handled and built into the design of the GraphOps, greatly reducing design time. As an enabling contribution, we also present a novel locality-optimized graph data structure that improves spatial locality and memory efficiency when accessing the graph in main memory.

Using the GraphOps system, we construct six different hardware accelerators. Results show that the GraphOps-based accelerators are able to operate close to the bandwidth limit of the hardware platform, the limiting constraint in graph analytics computation.

Keywords

FPGA, Graph analysis, Analytics, Dataflow, Accelerator

1. INTRODUCTION

Graph analytics problems have recently attracted significant interest from the research and commercial communities. A large number of important data sets can be usefully expressed as graphs, which efficiently encode connections between data elements. Analytics algorithms executed on

FPGA'16, February 21 - 23, 2016, Monterey, CA, USA

© 2016 Copyright held by the owner/author(s). Publication rights licensed to ACM.
ISBN 978-1-4503-3856-1/16/02. . . $15.00

DOI: http://dx.doi.org/10.1145/2847263.2847337

these data sets can yield valuable insight otherwise difficult to extract from traditional data stores, e.g. relational databases.

The ability of graphs to capture information about relationships makes them easily amenable to a wide variety of data analytics algorithms. The usefulness of these algorithms has been amplified by the prevalence of large data sets, now becoming commonplace in data centers operated by large corporations and research labs. As graphs become a more integral tool in processing unstructured network-based data, the energy efficiency of the operations executed on them begins to assume prime importance.

It is commonly known that the vast majority of large scale efforts in data analytics utilize commodity hardware, for a variety of reasons [6, 9]. Dedicated hardware accelerators usually provide significant performance-per-energy benefits, but are considered unwieldy and difficult to program [10].

In this context, we present *GraphOps*, a hardware library for quickly and easily constructing energy-efficient accelerators for graph analytics algorithms. GraphOps provide a hardware designer with a set of composable graph-specific building blocks necessary to implement a wide array of graph analytics algorithms. The target user is a hardware designer who can design her own logic but would benefit from a library of modular building blocks that are tailored to the domain of graph analytics. The system is built upon a *dataflow* execution platform [17]. GraphOps-based accelerators are defined as sets of *blocks* in which graph data are streamed to/from memory and computation metadata are streamed through the GraphOps blocks as inputs and outputs.

Most graph data structures are inherently sparse – indeed, they are usually represented on disk as sparse matrices. This sparseness manifests itself as a dearth of spatial locality when attempting to traverse a vertex's edges to visit its neighbors. We address this issue by using a modified storage representation to increase spatial locality and enable element-wise parallelism within the GraphOps blocks. GraphOps-based accelerators pre-process the graph on the host machine and store it in the FPGA memory space using our modified storage format. Stubborn hardware implementation details such as flow control, input buffering, rate throttling, and host/interrupt interaction are built into the design of the GraphOps, greatly reducing design time.

The major contributions of this paper are:

- We present a library of flexible, modular hardware modules that can be used to construct accelerators for high-performance streaming graph analytics. We enumerate a subset of the components in Section 5.

- We describe a novel graph representation that is optimized for coalesced access to the properties of the graph elements. This data structure is used in all accelerators and is described in Section 3.

- We illustrate how the GraphOps library can be used to construct new accelerators. As a case study, we construct a PageRank accelerator in Section 4.

- We prototype the hardware library on an FPGA platform by implementing six different hardware accelerators. We present evaluation results of the hardware by comparing against two different types of software systems in Section 6.

2. BACKGROUND

In this section, we provide the terms used in this paper as well as give a short overview of key technologies used in this work.

2.1 Graph Terminology

Research on graphs is extensive, spanning from mathematics to computational science and beyond, and standard terminology is not well established. Our terms are briefly described here.

Graph data structures are built on primitives that naturally mirror the real world: *vertices* (or nodes), *edges* (or relationships) between them, and *properties* (or attributes) associated with each. Properties can be arbitrary data members of any type.

2.2 Dataflow Architectures

Dataflow architectures are a special type of computer architecture in which there is no traditional program counter. Instead, the execution of processing is determined by the flow and availability of data inputs to instructions which are manifested as kernel processors. Data flows from memory to the kernels and also flows between the kernel processors. The computational model is sometimes referred to as a "spatial processing" model. The architecture obviates the need for functionality such as instruction decode, branch prediction, or out-of-order logic. It has been successfully used in applications such as digital signal processing, network routing, and graphics processing.

3. LOCALITY-OPTIMIZED GRAPH REPRESENTATION

It has long been known that computational performance of graph analytics codes is usually bound by memory bandwidth [5]. The memory constraint is compounded by a dearth of spatial locality due to the inherently sparse nature of graph data structures.

Unfortunately, the memory controllers of FPGAs and other accelerator systems are often optimized for throughput – wide memory channels with coarse fetch granularities. Because the GraphOps library relies heavily on data parallelism, naive executions of GraphOps on standard graph data structures suffer heavily from this memory bottleneck. To address this issue when using the FPGA memory system, we propose a novel *locality-optimized graph representation* that uses redundancy to trade off compactness for locality.

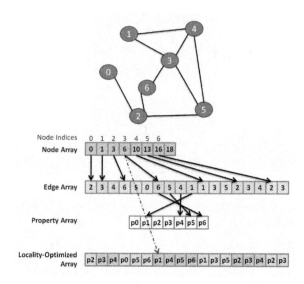

Figure 1: A simple graph and its associated data structures. The locality-optimized array redundantly coalesces properties, making the accessing of a vertex's neighbors' properties be possible with only level of indirection. In particular, the expensive second (random) level of indirection is avoided.

3.1 Traditional Graph Representation

There is abundant prior research on data structures for representing graphs in computer memory [4,5]. Graph formats are designed and optimized based on factors such as the size of the graph, its connectivity, desired compactness, the nature of the computations done on the graph, and the mutability of the data in the graph. Common formats include compressed sparse row (CSR), coordinates list (COO), and ELLPACK (ELL).

The compressed sparse row format is composed of a vertex array (or node array) and an edge array. These arrays are shown, along with their associated graph, in Figure 1. The vertex array is indexed by the vertex ID (an integer). Data elements in the vertex array act as indices into the edge array, which stores the destination vertex of each edge.[1]

3.2 Locality-Optimized Graph Representation

The edge array is an efficient data structure for reading lists of neighbors. However, when accessing associated properties for a neighbor set, the system must perform random access into a property array. This scattering effect is visualized by the accesses to the property array in Figure 1. Unfortunately, accessing neighbor properties is a common paradigm in graph algorithms–many important computations are concerned with the data elements of a vertex's neighbor.

We propose adding a new data structure called the locality-optimized array, also shown in the figure. Instead of an edge list, this array stores the properties associated with those neighbors. Reading neighbor properties now is achieved without random access, significantly increasing spatial locality. Updates are still performed to the original property array.

The new data structure achieves locality by replicating

---

[1]Compressed sparse row (CSR) also features heavily in the domain of sparse matrix computation [1].

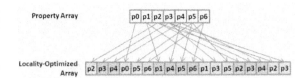

Figure 2: The locality-optimized array is generated and updated offline on the host.

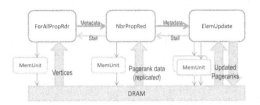

Figure 3: Composition of GraphOps blocks to form the PageRank accelerator.

properties of vertices which serve as neighbors to multiple other vertices. This array needs to be prepared and updated offline. Figure 2 displays the scattering maintenance operation that is performed to prepare the array. This operation is performed on the host machine in-between computation iterations.

4. A MOTIVATING EXAMPLE

Before going into the details of the GraphOps blocks and their architectures, let us first motivate the library and explain how these components are used to compose a practical application. We will focus on a well-known algorithm, *PageRank* [15]. We assume that the accelerator is being run in tandem with the main application on the host system. We present the construction of the application in three categories: block selection, block parameterization, and block composition.

Block Selection

We refer the reader to the reference [15] for a detailed description of the algorithm. Through profiling or code analysis, the designer would determine that the calculation of new pagerank scores for each vertex dominates the runtime of this algorithm. This is the core computation that a GraphOps-based accelerator most naturally accelerates. For every vertex, a reduction is performed using the neighbors of that vertex. Fundamentally, a PageRank accelerator needs to perform three functions:

1. Fetch the necessary sets of data properties (PageRank scores of neighboring vertices, in this case) for each vertex.

2. Perform the arithmetic reduction operation described by the core algorithm.

3. Store the updated values by updating the data structure after each iteration.

The components in the GraphOps library were borne out of necessity, as the authors implemented several prominent graph analytics algorithms within the dataflow model. Patterns emerged across these applications, and we encoded these patterns in the library as GraphOps blocks. The final set of GraphOps blocks result in: (i) natural coverage of a wide, interesting set of graph analytics algorithms and (ii) ease of use when compared with other flows, e.g. HDL and HLS.

For PageRank, the high-level blocks used are *ForAllPropRdr*, *NbrPropRed*, and *ElemUpdate*. The next section goes into more detail about these blocks. The full library has been open-sourced, and further details about the blocks are available online [14].

Block Parameterization

Once a set of blocks has been selected, they must be properly configured to perform the specific computation on the correct graph in memory. Parameters are implemented as static inputs that are driven over the PCIe bus by the host system. We detail the physical implementation of the system in Section 6.

Every block requires a few local parameters, needed for customization. There are also global accelerator-level parameters that can be modified. One common parameter that is used by several different blocks is that of memory addresses for property arrays. Any block that issues a memory request must have this base address from which to determine the memory location of specific graph elements. Further details regarding parameterization are available in the library documentation at the source repository [14].

Block Composition

The final step in constructing the accelerator is to compose all blocks together to form a functioning system. Metadata outputs from each block are routed to the accompanying inputs on downstream blocks. Memory request signals are routed through memory interface units. Figure 3 shows a detailed block diagram of the blocks used in the PageRank algorithm.

5. HARDWARE DESIGN

This section continues the PageRank example of the previous section by presenting the design details of the GraphOps library components used in PageRank. We begin with brief descriptions of each of the library components. Because of space constraints, we will not fully characterize all of the details and parameters involved in all components. We will instead focus on one interesting component in detail, describing its architecture, internal structures, and operation. Using the components presented, we explore other aspects of the hardware design of GraphOps. We finish by providing some of the graph-specific optimizations used to maximize throughput.

We have open-sourced the entire GraphOps dataflow library under the MIT License as a Github repository [14]. The repository documentation contains additional documentation that describes each of the blocks, parameterization suggestions, and composition instructions.

5.1 Enumeration of PageRank GraphOps

The GraphOps library can be broken down into three categories: *data* blocks, *control* blocks, and *utility* blocks. We enumerate blocks of each category used in PageRank.

5.1.1 Data-Handling Blocks

Data blocks are the primary GraphOps components. They handle incoming data streams, perform arithmetic operations, and route outputs to memory or subsequent blocks:

(i) **ForAllPropRdr** issues memory requests for all neighbor property sets in the graph. In order to do this, it first reads all the row pointers in the graph. The incoming row pointer data are used to issue individual memory requests for each set of neighbor properties.

(ii) **NbrPropRed** performs a reduction on a vertex's neighbor set. The unit receives the neighbor property data as a data stream from memory. Each set of neighbor properties is accompanied by a metadata packet as an input to the kernel from a preceding block (e.g. ForAllPropRdr).

(iii) **ElemUpdate** is used to update property values in the graph data structure. The unit receives a vertex reference and an updated value as input. It issues memory read requests for the requisite memory locations and memory update requests for the updated values.

5.1.2 Control Blocks

In GraphOps, the majority of the logic is amenable to dataflow. One key reason for this is that feedback control is rare. There are situations, however, that call for more intricate control difficult to express without state machines. Key control blocks for the PageRank application are:

(i) **QRdrPktCntSM** handles control logic for input buffers in the data blocks. A common use case occurs in the following situation: A metadata input datum dictates how many memory packets belong to a given neighbor set. QRdrPktCntSM handles the counting of packets on the memory data input and instructs the data block when to move on to the next neighbor set.

(ii) **UpdQueueSM** handles control logic for updating a graph property for all nodes. This unit assumes that the properties are being updated sequentially and makes use of heavy coalescing to minimize the number of update requests sent to memory.

5.1.3 Utility Blocks

Additional logic is needed to properly interface with the memory system and the host platform. These are realized via the utility blocks:

(i) **EndSignal** monitors *done* signals for all data blocks and issues a special interrupt request to halt execution when all units are finished.

(ii) **MemUnit** provides a simplified memory interface to the data blocks. It compiles memory profiling information, watches for end-of-execution interrupt requests, and includes control logic for handling very large memory requests.

5.2 NbrPropRed

We now specify the details of one representative block to give the reader an illustration of the type of logic common in data blocks. NbrPropRed is interesting because it interacts with memory streams while performing computation that is fundamental to an algorithm.

Figure 4 shows a detailed diagram of the NbrPropRed block. As described in Section 5.1, this block is used to perform a reduction on the properties of a vertex's neighbor set, a common operation for many analytics algorithms. In the dataflow paradigm, this block would be placed after a

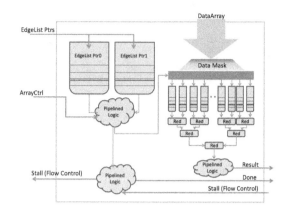

Figure 4: Detailed architecture of the NbrPropRed data block.

block which has already issued memory requests for neighbor properties.

The NbrPropRed has three primary inputs: the property data stream from memory (*DataArray* and *ArrayCtrl*), metadata from the previous requesting block (*EdgeList Ptrs*), and a flow control signal to halt execution when buffers are nearing capacity (*Stall*). There are three primary outputs: the metadata output for this block is the reduction results (*Result*). The other two outputs are common to all data blocks. The *Stall* output is issued when this block has halted, telling upstream blocks to also halt. The *Done* signal is asserted when this block has finished its work.

For each memory request, the corresponding edge list pointers define a data mask that dictates which properties in the data stream are a part of the neighbor set. Simple logic operations are used to generate this mask. The data mask filters the incoming data stream and allows only valid neighbor properties to participate in the reduction tree. For very large neighbor sets, many data packets are required to be reduced. The reduction tree therefore uses accumulation registers to handle these large sets. When the neighbor set is finished processing (as dictated by the edge list pointers), the accumulation registers are cleared and the result is emitted by the block (*Result* output).

6. EVALUATION

We prototyped the GraphOps architecture using a system from Maxeler Technologies. The system FPGA is a Xilinx Virtex-6 (XC6VSX475T). The chip has 475k logic cells and 1,064 36 Kb RAM blocks for a total of 4.67 MB of block memory. For all graph accelerators, we clocked the FPGA at 150 MHz. The FPGA is connected to 24 GB of DRAM via a single 384-bit memory channel with a max frequency of 400 MHz DDR. This means the peak line bandwidth is 38.4 GB/s. Note that the peak bandwidth is achievable largely because of the relatively large width (384 bits) of the memory channel.

The FPGA is connected via PCIe x8 to the host processor system. The host system has two 2.67 GHz Xeon 5650 multi-processors, each having six multi-threaded cores mak-

---

[2]BRAM usage is heavily dependent on the sizing of the numerous FIFO buffers in the design. These FIFOs are often larger than required.

| Algorithm | Resource Usage (%) | | | GraphOps Blocks | |
	FF	LUT	BRAM^2	# MemUnits	Blocks Used
pagerank [15]	33.2	21.3	24.5	5	ForAllPropRed, NbrPropRed, ElemUpdate
bfs	32.1	18.8	36.6	6	NbrPropRdr, NbrPropFilter, ElemUpdate, SetWriter, SetReader
conduct [3]	25.7	16.0	20.6	4	AllNodePropRed, NbrPropRdr, NbrPropRed
spmv	33.0	20.6	24.5	5	ForAllPropRed, NbrPropRed, ElemUpdate
sssp	30.7	18.8	37.0	6	NbrPropRdr, NbrPropFilter, ElemUpdate, SetWriter, SetReader
vcover [16]	23.4	14.7	19.4	3	ForAllPropRed, GlobNbrRed

Table 1: Resource usage and enumeration of GraphOps blocks for each accelerator. The EndSignal block, used in all accelerators, is not included.

ing a total hardware thread count of 24. Each of the two processors has a peak line bandwidth of 32 GB/s and three 64-bit channels to memory.

The GraphOps blocks are implemented on top of a software framework built by Maxeler [17]. The tools provide an HDL and interfaces for accelerating development of dataflow and streaming accelerators. The higher level language is compiled to generate VHDL.

6.1 Applications

We use the GraphOps blocks to implement accelerators for six analytics algorithms. Table 1 breaks down the resource usage of each accelerator and lists the GraphOps components used in their implementations. None of the accelerators are bound by on-chip resources on our Xilinx Virtex-6 FPGA. However, BRAM resources can impose undue pressure on the place-and-route tool if the designer is too liberal with use of FIFO buffers. The throttling and flow control schemes described in Section 5.2 naturally reduce buffer pressure and allow for more conservative sizing. Typical buffer sizes in the GraphOps blocks range from about 2K to 8K elements, with typical element widths being about 32 to 64 bits.

6.2 Software Comparison

We present the performance of the GraphOps-based accelerators by comparing computation done on the accelerators with computation done via an optimized software implementation. The software implementations are C++ multithreaded (OpenMP) versions generated using the Green-Marl graph compilation framework [11]. Software versions are run using the Intel Xeon processors on the host system, described at the beginning of this section. The GraphOps accelerated versions use the run-times of the same applications in a C program with the "inner loop" computation accelerated using the FPGA, as described for PageRank in Section 4. The time to transfer the graph data to/from the host and the FPGA is not included.

Figure 5 compares performance throughput for selected accelerators. The x-axis is the number of vertices in the graph. The degree of the vertices of the graph follows a uniform distribution with the average being eight. This means that the number of edges in each workload is 8*N. The y-axis is millions of edges per second, or MEPS, a measure of the number of edges "processed" per second. Because the notion of processed work for each algorithm is different, MEPS should not be compared across accelerators, but rather used as a relative scale for different systems within one accelerator.

Referring to the legend, SW1 through SW8 are the number of threads used by each software version. GraphOps (150 MHz) is the standard FPGA-accelerated version. HW+Scatter is the accelerated version which also takes into account the time to pre-process the graph data structure on the host system.

All of the graph analytics algorithms displayed are bound by memory bandwidth. This is evident in Figure 5, as all of the lines begin to roughly approach a steady state asymptote with increasing graph size. For smaller graph sizes, we see strong caching effects in the software versions. The data sets fit partially or fully in the CPU cache, greatly improving throughput. Note that both of these effects apply partially to the HW+Scatter version, because the graph pre-processing workload is a normal software function and therefore depends on the cache.

In contrast to the software versions, the GraphOps-based implementations show no caching effects, as there is no significant re-use happening on the FPGA. Therefore, we see that the throughput is roughly constant for all three accelerators. Comparing the performance of the software and hardware versions, we see that the SpMV and Vertex Cover eight-threaded software versions perform better than the FPGA implementation, even for the largest graph size. As stated earlier, the FPGA peak bandwidth is about 38 GB/s while the CPU bandwidth is about 32 GB/s per socket. The eight threads are co-located on the same socket. The reason for the superior software performance is its access to three memory channels as compared with one channel on the FPGA. Using calculations based on the number of data words requested during FPGA execution runs, we determine that the single memory channel causes some memory request queues (and therefore the entire streaming system) to occasionally stall. An ideal prototyping system for GraphOps-based accelerators would have several memory channels, with the most heavily-used memory interfaces having access to a dedicated memory channel.

6.3 Streaming Comparison

We continue the evaluation of the GraphOps library by comparing against a graph processing framework called X-Stream [18]. The X-Stream framework is an apt choice because, similarly to the locality-optimized storage representation used in GraphOps (Section 3), X-Stream is built around maximizing sequential streaming of graph data while minimizing random access. The underlying observation is that sequential memory bandwidth is usually much higher than random access bandwidth, particularly for graphs that do not fit in main memory and require disk access. We refer the reader to the X-Stream reference [18] for a more thorough description of the X-Stream system.

Our locality-optimized storage representation is similar to

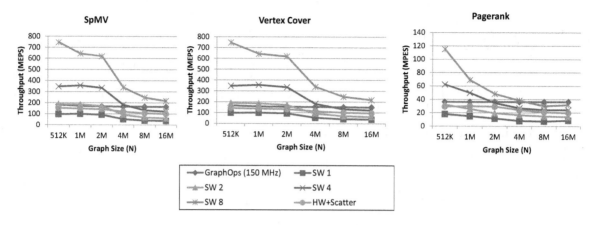

Figure 5: Performance throughput for selected accelerators.

X-Stream primarily because of the shared emphasis on maximizing use of high-bandwidth architectures. LO-arrays generate locality through data replication, similarly avoiding random access into the large edge/property data structure.

We chose a variety of different data sets from the Stanford SNAP project [12] for use in this comparison study. The data sets used are: *amazon0601*, *cit-Patents*, *wiki-Talk*, *web-BerkStan*, and *soc-Pokec*. We refer the reader to the reference for detailed characteristics about the data sets.

Figure 6 compares execution time of the GraphOps and X-Stream frameworks for the workloads discussed. The metric is execution run time, so lower is better. Both frameworks were executed on the same machine, described in the beginning of this section. X-Stream is a software-only framework and used the host system CPU and memory resources, ignoring the FPGA.

The figure provides a breakdown of total execution time for three GraphOps-based accelerators. GraphOps systems compare favorably with the X-Stream applications, despite the slightly inferior total bandwidth available to the GraphOps accelerators. The reader should first note that the preparation and maintenance overhead for the LO-arrays, denoted as *graphops (scatter)*, is a small fraction of the overall runtime for each implementation.

The most problematic data sets for the spmv and pagerank accelerators are wiki-Talk and cit-Patents. Both of these accelerators are dependent upon efficient access to vertex neighbors' properties. Wiki-Talk and cit-Patents are sub-optimal because they have relatively small average degrees, 2.1 and 4.3 for wiki-Talk and cit-Patents respectively. Recall from our discussion of our target hardware system that memory accesses are constrained to rather large data blocks. Indeed, we designed the locality-optimizing storage representation presented in Section 3 with this consideration in mind. Because our system is fundamentally designed around fetching neighbor property sets using large data blocks, small-degree data sets such as wiki-Talk and cit-Patents waste much of the bandwidth designated for that purpose. This observation is also borne out by the superior performance of GraphOps on the soc-pokec-relationships data set, given its average degree of 19.1. The conductance accelerator is built around streaming the entire graph, as opposed to a neighbor traversal, and is thus not subject to this small-degree effect.

6.4 Bandwidth Utilization Calculations

We performed an experiment to determine how well the single memory interface was being utilized by the various memory interfaces. Details are omitted for brevity. The steady state throughput for the PageRank GraphOps accelerator is about 37 MEPS, which corresponds to a throughput of about 220 MB/s. This represents about 1/6 of the available theoretical throughput.

The memory channel must switch among the three other interfaces also issuing requests–this is the primary cause for performance limitation. The secondary cause is that issuing one memory request per neighbor set limits the size of the requests and prevents optimizations at the memory controller level.

7. RELATED WORK

Several approaches have used FPGAs as the vehicle for accelerating graph analytics. Betkaoui et al [2] accelerated the graphlet counting algorithm on an FPGA using an optimized crossbar and custom memory banks. Their work differs from GraphOps, because their framework requires an end user to express his algorithm as a vertex-centric kernel, similar to Pregel [9]. They do the work of mapping it to a Convey hardware system. Nurvitadhi, Weisz, et al [13] created an FPGA backend for a graph algorithm compiler called GraphGen. They also focus only on vertex-centric graph descriptions, an important difference from GraphOps, which is designed to be more general. DeLorimier et al [7] presented Graph-Step, a system architecture for sparse graphs that fit in the block memory of the FPGA. While general, their architecture is severely constrained in the size of dataset possible, particularly in an era of rapidly expanding dataset sizes and DRAM banks.

There has also been some work in the area of using a streaming paradigm to process graphs. Ediger et al [8] used a dynamic graph representation called STINGER to extract parallelism and enable streaming processing. Roy et al [18] proposed X-stream, which we presented in Section 6. GraphOps differs from these approaches, as they are both software-focused efforts. Another key difference is that these approaches attempt to better utilize the memory hierarchy, whereas GraphOps relies on main memory bandwidth.

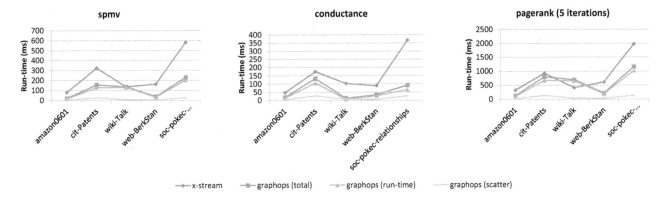

Figure 6: Run-time comparison of GraphOps and X-Stream.

8. CONCLUSION

In this paper, we present the GraphOps hardware library, a composable set of hardware blocks that allow a designer to quickly create an energy-efficient graph analytics accelerator. Using the well-known computation PageRank as a driving example, we explain how GraphOps addresses issues that a designer would otherwise spend valuable time solving and verifying. We evaluate the GraphOps library by composing six different accelerators and using them to process a variety of workloads. We compare with pure software implementations as well as with a software streaming framework. Results show that the GraphOps-based accelerators are able to operate close to the bandwidth limit of the FPGA system. Overall, this paper demonstrates that graph-specific FPGA acceleration can be achieved with a significant reduction in design time if a hardware designer is given a useful set of building blocks.

Acknowledgments

We would like to thank the Maxeler engineering team and the Maxeler University Program for their diligent help and support. We would also like to thank reviewers and the programming chair for their reviews and attention.

This work is supported by DARPA Contract- Air Force, Xgraphs; Language and Algorithms for Heterogeneous Graph Streams, FA8750-12-2-0335; Army Contract AHPCRC W911NF-07-2-0027-1; NSF Grant, BIGDATA: Mid-Scale: DA: Collaborative Research: Genomes Galore - Core Techniques, Libraries, and Domain Specific Languages for High-Throughput DNA Sequencing, IIS-1247701; NSF Grant, SHF: Large: Domain Specific Language Infrastructure for Biological Simulation Software, CCF-1111943; NSF Grant- EAGER- XPS: DSD: Synthesizing Domain Specific Systems-CCF-1337375; and the Stanford PPL affiliates program.

9. REFERENCES

[1] N. Bell and M. Garland. Efficient sparse matrix-vector multiplication on cuda. Technical report, Nvidia Tech Report NVR-2008-004, Nvidia Corporation, 2008.

[2] B. Betkaoui, D. B. Thomas, W. Luk, and N. Przulj. A framework for fpga acceleration of large graph problems. In *FPT 2011*, pages 1–8. IEEE, 2011.

[3] N. Biggs. *Algebraic graph theory*. Cambridge university press, 1993.

[4] R. Che, Beckmann. Belred: Constructing gpgpu graph applications with software building blocks.

[5] J. Chhugani, N. Satish, et al. Fast and efficient graph traversal algorithm for cpus. In *IPDPS 2012, IEEE 26th International*, pages 378–389. IEEE, 2012.

[6] J. Dean and S. Ghemawat. Mapreduce: simplified data processing on large clusters. *Communications of the ACM*, 51(1):107–113, 2008.

[7] M. DeLorimier, N. Kapre, N. Mehta, et al. Graphstep: A system architecture for sparse-graph algorithms. In *FCCM'06.*, pages 143–151. IEEE, 2006.

[8] D. Ediger, K. Jiang, et al. Massive streaming data analytics: A case study with clustering coefficients. In *IPDPSW 2010*, pages 1–8. IEEE, 2010.

[9] M. A. e. a. G. Malewicz. Pregel: a system for large-scale graph processing. In *ACM SIGMOD 2010*, pages 135–146. ACM, 2010.

[10] G. Govindu, L. Zhuo, S. Choi, and V. Prasanna. Analysis of high-performance floating-point arithmetic on fpgas. In *IPDPS 2004*, page 149. IEEE, 2004.

[11] S. Hong, H. Chafi, E. Sedlar, and K. Olukotun. Green-marl: a dsl for easy and efficient graph analysis. In *ACM SIGARCH Computer Architecture News*, volume 40, pages 349–362. ACM, 2012.

[12] J. Leskovec and A. Krevl. Snap datasets:stanford large network dataset collection. 2014.

[13] E. Nurvitadhi, G. Weisz, et al. Graphgen: An fpga framework for vertex-centric graph computation. In *FCCM 2014*, pages 25–28. IEEE, 2014.

[14] T. Oguntebi. Graphops source repository. https://github.com/tayo/GraphOps.

[15] L. Page, S. Brin, R. Motwani, and T. Winograd. The pagerank citation ranking. 1999.

[16] C. H. Papadimitriou and K. Steiglitz. *Combinatorial optimization: algorithms and complexity*. Courier Dover Publications, 1998.

[17] O. Pell, O. Mencer, K. H. Tsoi, and W. Luk. Maximum performance computing with dataflow engines. In *High-Performance Computing Using FPGAs*, pages 747–774. Springer, 2013.

[18] A. Roy, I. Mihailovic, and W. Zwaenepoel. X-stream: edge-centric graph processing using streaming partitions. In *SOSP 2013*, pages 472–488. ACM, 2013.

High Performance Linkage Disequilibrium: FPGAs Hold the Key

Nikolaos Alachiotis
Carnegie Mellon University
nalachio@cmu.edu

Gabriel Weisz
Carnegie Mellon University
gweisz@cmu.edu

ABSTRACT

DNA sequencing technologies allow the rapid sequencing of full genomes in a cost-effective way, leading to ever-growing genomic datasets that comprise thousands of genomes and millions of genetic variants. In population genomics and genome-wide association studies, widely used statistics such as linkage disequilibrium become computationally demanding when thousands of whole genomes are investigated. Long analysis times and excessive memory requirements usually prevent researchers from conducting exhaustive analyses, sacrificing the ability to detect distant genetic associations. In this work, we describe a generic algorithmic approach for organizing arbitrarily distant computations on full genomes, and to offload operations from the host processor to accelerators. We explore FPGAs as accelerators for linkage disequilibrium because the bulk of required operations are discrete, making them a good fit for reconfigurable fabric. We describe a versatile and trivially expandable architecture, and develop an automatic RTL generation software to search the design space. We find that, when thousands of genomes from complex species such as humans, are analyzed, current FPGAs can achieve up to 50X faster processing than state-of-the-art software running on multi-core workstations.

Keywords

population genomics; linkage disequilibrium; accelerator

1. INTRODUCTION

Linkage disequilibrium (LD) is a fundamental technique that is widely used in population genomics and genome-wide association studies (GWAS) in order to understand how mutations interact with each other within a population. The term, coined in 1960 by Lewontin and Kojima [13], refers to the non-random association between alleles (variants of a gene) at different loci. Traditionally, LD-based analyses are conducted on human genomes to gain insight into the genetic composition of populations, as well as changes in this genetic composition that are driven by evolutionary forces

FPGA'16, February 21 - 23, 2016, Monterey, CA, USA

© 2016 Copyright held by the owner/author(s). Publication rights licensed to ACM.
ISBN 978-1-4503-3856-1/16/02. . . $15.00

DOI: http://dx.doi.org/10.1145/2847263.2847271

such as natural selection and genetic drift [8]. Other applications of LD that are of significant importance include disease-gene mapping to understand genetic factors for inherited diseases [20], detecting drug-resistant mutations in pathogens such as HIV [9, 16], or revealing reasons for drug treatment failures [5]. With improvements to DNA sampling techniques and the continuous sequencing of genetic material from more species of flora and fauna, LD-based analyses are now even more pervasively used in the study of population genetics beyond that of humans [21]. The importance of LD-based analyses can be observed from titles of population genetics papers declaring "Population genomics: Linkage disequilibrium holds the key" [10].

Genomic datasets that are suitable for population genetic analyses comprise thousands of genomes from different individuals (also referred to as samples), and millions of genetic variants (e.g., the 1000 Genomes project, *http://www. 1000genomes.org*). Genetic variation is observed in the form of so-called single-nucleotide polymorphisms (SNPs), a term that is used to describe single base-pair changes in a DNA sequence. The amount of genetic variation (discovered polymorphisms) increases with the number of sequenced genomes, leading to escalating dataset sizes. Roughly speaking, doubling the sample size leads to doubling the number of associated variants discovered [24]. Computing LD on this abundance of data can become prohibitively expensive, both in terms of long execution times as well as excessive memory requirements. Typically, researchers opt to narrow the extent of LD computations, using subsets of the available SNPs, in favor of significantly reduced analysis time and memory footprint, sacrificing the ability to detect highly correlated but potentially distant SNPs. Therefore, it is essential to devise high performance implementations that enable rapid and wider LD evaluations on complex populations such as humans ($\approx$ 10 million SNPs in the human genome).

Modern microprocessors are not adequately equipped to deliver high performance for LD computations. While the increase in transistors keeps pace with the rate at which molecular data become available (Fig. 1), the current trend to increase core performance by increasing the SIMD width does not yield a significant performance boost in LD calculations. The performance bottleneck for LD is the calculation of allele and haplotype (pairs of alleles on the same chromosome that tend to be inherited together) frequencies in a population. Since alleles are typically encoded as one- or two-bit entities (depending on certain biological assumptions such as the infinite sites model [12]), the allele and haplotype frequency calculation relies mainly on the enumeration of set bits in registers, an operation widely known as population count. While current microprocessor architectures provide hardware support for population count, in the form of an intrinsic instruction (since Intel Nehalem and AMD K10), the specific intrinsic command operates strictly on regular registers and does not support wider SIMD registers. Therefore, potential performance benefits from the use of SIMD instructions are diminished due to the required employment of a scalar instruction for the population counter at the microkernel level. To avoid reader confusion, we henceforth refer to the bit-enumeration operation as "popcount".

This study explores the potential of FPGAs to accelerate LD computations as required by large-scale population genomic and GWAS analyses. In addition to the apparent need for reducing execution time, a challenge lies in enabling arbitrarily wide LD evaluation on full genomes, a computation exhibiting memory requirements that typically exceed the amount of available memory on present-day accelerator platforms. The contribution of this work is two-fold:

- We implement a versatile accelerator architecture for faster analyses under the widely adopted infinite sites model [12]. In the interest of conducting a rapid design space exploration, as well as reducing development time and debugging effort, the architecture is described in the C language, through a series of custom RTL-specific library calls. Each of the custom library calls augments various instances of a unified data structure, where each instance represents a building component. A Verilog backend is deployed to generate the Verilog RTL description for the accelerator architecture. We find that performance gains become more prevalent (up to 2X higher throughput) when a moderate number of sufficiently wide, pipelined popcount operators are employed in contrast to an excessive number of narrow popcount operators.

- We present a generic algorithm to execute on the host processor in order to schedule and offload computations to the accelerator platform. The host implements an iterative procedure that splits large genomes into variable-size subgenomic regions depending on the distribution of SNPs along the genome, while ensuring that each subgenomic region is of the same size in terms of number of SNPs. The regions are paired on the host in order to cover all required LD computations and the pairs are offloaded to the accelerator. On the FPGA, dedicated circuitry organizes the SNPs into groups and carries out the LD computations for every pair of regions by pairwise combining all the SNP-groups in both regions. This approach facilitates the expansion of the hardware design to comprise more processing cores while not requiring changes on the software side. Furthermore, it permits LD evaluation between arbitrarily wide and potentially distant subgenomic regions without conducting redundant operations or requiring excessive memory space.

The remainder of this paper is organized as follows: In Section 2, we describe the mathematical operations and concepts required to compute LD. Thereafter, we discuss related work on software implementations in Section 3. Section 4 presents the proposed accelerator system, while Section 5 provides implementation details and a design space analysis. In the following Section 6 we present a performance evaluation, and conclude in Section 7.

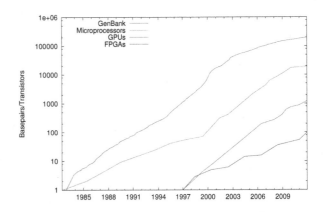

Figure 1: Growth of molecular data available in GenBank as well as of number of transistors in microprocessors, GPUs, and FPGAs (source: [1]).

2. LINKAGE DISEQUILIBRIUM (LD)

The primary source of genetic variation is the mutation. Population genetics investigate mutations by analyzing lists of individuals and their associated DNA sequences. Prior to the analysis, a so-called multiple sequence alignment (MSA) is computed, i.e., a $n \times m$ matrix that comprises n rows (one row per individual) of m columns each (also referred to as alignment sites). If a mutation has occurred at an alignment site, this site becomes a SNP, to differentiate from monomorphic alignment sites which are non-informative for evolutionary purposes. Therefore, a SNP is by definition polymorphic as it represents a single-nucleotide substitution of one DNA base (A, C, G, and T) for another. An example of an MSA of 4 individuals that comprises 30 alignment sites of which 5 are SNPs (highlighted in blue and italics) is shown below.

```
sample_0    ATGGCATACCCCT-CCAACTAGGATTCCAA
sample_1    ATGGCCTACCACTCCCAACTAGGCTTCC-A
sample_2    ATGGCATAC-C-TCCCAAGTAGGTTTTC-A
sample_3    ATGG----CCCCTCCCAACTTGGTTTCCAA
```

2.1 Representation of Genomic Data

Real-world analyses and *in silico* simulations (analyses on synthetic datasets) often adopt the infinite sites model [12] (henceforth denoted ISM). Under this model, it is assumed that there is an infinite number of sites, and consequently each new mutation appears on a site where previously no mutation has occurred. Due to the ISM assumption, SNPs can be represented by binary vectors, where each unset bit ('0') represents the initial–before mutation–state (usually referred to as the ancestral state), while each set bit ('1') indicates a new–after mutation–state (usually referred to as the derived state)[1]. For the rest of this paper, we assume that each SNP is represented by a group of N_{word} w-bit-long words with N_{word} defined as follows:

$$N_{word} = \left\lceil \frac{N_{seq}}{w} \right\rceil,$$

with zero padding if $N_{seq} \bmod w \neq 0$, N_{seq} is the number of samples, and $w = 2^p$ with $p \in \mathbb{N}$. This also implies

---

[1]It should be noted that the assignment of '0' to the ancestral state is arbitrary. One could easily have used '1' to represent the ancestral and '0' for the derived state.

```
0  1  0  1 │0│ 0  0  0  ...  0  1  0  1
⋮          │ │                        ⋮
0  0  0  1 │1│ 1  1  0  ...  1  1  0  0
0  1  0  0 │1│ 0  1  0  ...  1  1  0  1   Sample
⋮          │ │                        ⋮
1  0  1  0 │0│ 1  1  0  ...  1  0  1  0
1  0  0  1 │0│ 1  1  1  ...  1  0  1  0
0  0  0  0 │0│ 0  0  0  0  0  0  0  0   ⇑
0  0  0  0 │0│ 0  0  0  0  0  0  0  0   padding
0  0  0  0 │0│ 0  0  0  0  0  0  0  0   ⇓
              SNP
```

Figure 2: Pictorial representation of samples in the $(k \times w) \times n$ genomic matrix, G. Each row in G represents the genome of an individual (sample). Columns represent SNPs at different locations within the genome.

that the entire genomic dataset can be represented by a $(k \times w) \times n$ matrix, G, where $k = N_{word}$. Each row in G represents a particular sample while each column represents a SNP. We call this the genomic matrix, which is illustrated in Figure 2. We assume here that all monomorphic sites have been discarded through an initial prefiltering stage, and consequently the genomic matrix G is dense and consists solely of SNPs. For clarity reasons, we omit the SNP locations in Figure 2 but keep in mind that neighboring SNPs in the genomic matrix representation can be thousands of sites apart in the genome. In future discussions we represent a SNP as a column vector s.

2.2 Computing LD

The fundamental concept behind the computation of LD deals with the probability of independent events. If the probability of two mutations occurring at two sites in the same sequence is not the same as the product of the probabilities of the two mutations occurring independently, then the event that two mutations appear in the same sequence is said to be not independent, or the two SNPs are in linkage disequilibrium. Mathematically, we want to compute

$$D_{i,j} = P_{i,j} - P_i P_j, \tag{1}$$

for every pair of SNPs, s_i and s_j, where $P_{i,j}$ represents the probability that a sample has mutations in both SNPs, s_i and s_j, and P_i and P_j are the probabilities for the independent events that a mutation has occurred in s_i and s_j, respectively. When $D = 0$, s_i and s_j are in linkage equilibrium, i.e., mutations in s_i and s_j occur independently of each other. More interestingly, $D \neq 0$ if the two SNPs are in linkage disequilibrium.

Given SNPs of length N_{seq}, and ignoring (for the moment) that each SNP is stored as N_{word} words, the probability that a mutation occurs in a SNP s_x, denoted as P_x, can be obtained with the following equation:

$$P_x = \frac{POPCNT(s_x)}{N_{seq}}, \tag{2}$$

which counts the number of '1's in s_x and then divides it with the total number of bits in the s_x.

$P_{i,j}$ can be similarly computed by first counting the number of samples that have mutations in both SNPs, s_i and s_j, and then dividing that number by N_{seq}. Mathematically, $P_{i,j}$ can be computed as follows:

$$P_{i,j} = \frac{POPCNT(s_i \& s_j)}{N_{seq}} \tag{3}$$

Using Equations 2 and 3, we can then compute $D_{i,j}$ for all possible pairs of SNPs, s_i and s_j, using Equation 1.

The formulation of LD in Equation 1 can become problematic since the sign and range of $D_{i,j}$ vary with the choice of representation and the frequency at which different mutations occur. This makes it difficult to compare $D_{i,j}$ across different genomic regions. As such, several standardization methods have been proposed for D, with a commonly used one being the squared Pearson coefficient r_{ij}^2:

$$r_{ij}^2 = \frac{(P_{i,j} - P_i P_j)^2}{P_i P_j (1 - P_i)(1 - P_j)}$$
$$= \frac{D_{i,j}^2}{P_i P_j (1 - P_i)(1 - P_j)} \tag{4}$$

This measure of LD has the advantage that all r_{ij}^2 values remain between 0 and 1, with higher numbers representing stronger association. More importantly, even with this representation of LD computation, notice that the cost of computing the r_{ij}^2 values for all pairs of SNPs is dominated by the cost of D.

3. RELATED WORK

Advances in modeling and statistical analysis for population genetics in the past decade [14, 17, 15] were not accompanied by high performance computing approaches due to the limited amount of available molecular data. More recently, driven by sequencing cost reductions that have generated a plethora of molecular data suitable for population genetics analyses, several software tools capable of analyzing genome-scale datasets have been released.

Pfeifer et al. [18] released PopGenome, an R package for population genetics analyses that can compute a wide range of statistics, including LD, on whole-genome SNP data. Although PopGenome can exploit multiple cores for faster execution, the computational kernel for pairwise LD assessment is not optimized to exploit intrinsics and the cache hierarchy.

Chang et al. [6] released a comprehensive update to the widely used PLINK software [19] for whole-genome association and population-based linkage analyses (over 9,000 citations according to Google scholar). The updated implementation (PLINK 1.9) exhibits significant performance and scalability improvements in comparison with the initial software. It heavily relies on bitwise operations, multithreading, and high-level algorithmic improvements for the most compute-demanding functions, such as distance-based clustering and LD-based pruning. PLINK 1.9 implements the squared Pearson coefficient as a measure of LD and deploys the SSE2-based Lauradoux/Walish popcount algorithm to achieve high performance [6].

Alachiotis et al. [4, 3] released the population genomics software OmegaPlus. Similarly to PLINK 1.9, OmegaPlus computes the squared Pearson coefficient as a measure of LD. The implementation differs at the microkernel level since the performance-critical popcount operation is computed via the intrinsic popcount instruction supported in hardware.

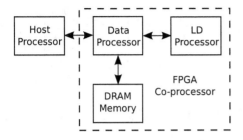

Figure 3: Accelerator system design overview.

FPGA researchers have successfully accelerated compute-intensive bioinformatics kernels in the past, such as sequence alignment [22] and phylogeny reconstruction [25]. However, to the best of the author's knowledge, the work presented here is the first to demonstrate the efficiency of FPGA technology for the acceleration of large-scale LD computations.

4. SYSTEM DESIGN

Our proposed accelerator system consists of four main components (Fig. 3). The host processor parses an input dataset in any of the widely used formats for genomic data (FASTA or VCF for real data, ms [11] or MaCS [7] for simulated data), and constructs the genomic matrix by filtering out the monomorphic–non-informative–sites. Thereafter, it executes the generic algorithm for scheduling and offloading computations to the FPGA co-processor. On the FPGA, the data processor handles the communication/synchronization with the host, as well as the data accesses to/from the on-board DRAM, whereas the LD processor is the computational kernel that carries out the population genomics calculations. Decoupling the data handling (data processor) and the execution (LD processor) parts on the co-processor permits the deployment of LD processors of any size (varying number of LD cores and/or popcount width) without requiring any changes to the data processor, which facilitates the exploration of the design space.

4.1 Host Processor

As already mentioned, a key challenge in conducting wide LD analyses efficiently is to avoid redundant computations. Our solution requires a pair of genomic regions of arbitrary size (number of SNPs), A and B, as input for any LD computation. While current software implementations compute all LD scores between SNPs in the same genomic region, allowing to provide a pair of regions as input attacks the problem of computing long-range LD efficiently. Association studies that investigate long-range LD in genomes might not require the computation of LD scores between SNPs located inbetween the distant regions of interest. For instance, if a study investigates association between two distant genes, computing the association between all intermediate genes as well is only going to result in many unnecessary calculations and excessive memory requirements. Thus, unlike existing software implementations, the generic algorithm on the host can consider only the SNPs in the distant genes to reduce execution time and memory footprint, while the single-region case can be trivially facilitated by setting $A = B$.

To enable the computation of arbitrarily large genomic datasets, the genomic matrix is organized by the host processor into large chunks, depending on the size of available

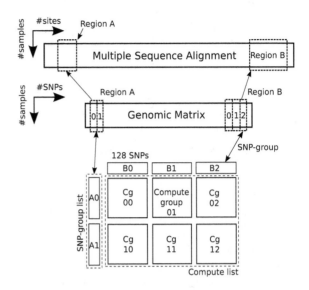

Figure 4: Illustration of the compute-list for arbitrarily distant LD computations.

main memory on the co-processor. Thereafter, each chunk is organized into a number of non-overlapping SNP-groups of fixed size S SNPs (e.g., $S = 128$). A subset of the SNP-groups in the same chunk (if $A = B$) or in two different chunks (if $A \neq B$) are used to construct two SNP-group lists, A_{list} and B_{list}, achieving full coverage of the regions of interest in A and B, respectively. Each pair of SNP-groups is a compute-group that entails all pairwise LD computations between the SNPs in the two SNP-groups. Consequently, each pair of SNP-group lists defines a compute-list that implicitly describes all required LD computations between the two regions of interest in A and B. Once the compute-list is constructed, it is offloaded to the co-processor for execution. Upon completion and return of the results, the steps of compute-list construction and offloading are repeated for the next chunk or pair of chunks until the entire genomic matrix is completed. Figure 4 illustrates the compute-list, where each tile represents the output of a compute-group, essentially a $S \times S$ matrix of LD values.

4.2 Data Processor

The data processor architecture is depicted in Figure 5. To facilitate the trivial instantiation of variously sized design points (varying LD processor size), the data processor is implemented as a series of parameterized FSMs that are configured and controlled by a non-parameterized top-level FSM following a master-worker scheme. The top-level FSM, denoted DTOP in Figure 5, parses a set of configuration instructions that are used by the host processor to offload computations to the LD processor. These instructions are classified as follows: a) load instructions, b) dataset instructions, and c) store instructions. The DTOP FSM decodes the incoming instructions and configures the associated FSM of each class. Once all three worker FSMs are configured, DTOP initiates the LD computations by enabling the three FSMs. Thereafter, the LD processor is controlled by the worker FSMs which cooperate to load the genomic data from main memory, schedule operations on the LD processor, and store the results back in memory. To avoid increased row buffer misses and achieve high memory bandwidth, the SNP-

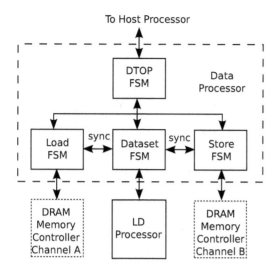

Figure 5: The data processor architecture.

group size S is appropriately set by the host processor to ensure that the SNP-groups, which are retrieved by the data processor during computations, do not exceed the DRAM row buffer size.

4.3 LD Processor

The LD processor architecture is depicted in Figure 6. The processing scheme is similar to searching a database for given queries. The SNPs in one of the two input regions are the queries while the SNPs in the other region are the database objects. A fraction of the query SNPs are initially loaded into a dual-port multi-bank memory subsystem (Data Mem A in Fig. 6). Thereafter, the database SNPs are passed through the two compute grids of LD cores (LD Core Grids A and B in Fig. 6) which calculate the LD scores between the database SNPs and all the query SNPs in Data Mem A. Query SNPs are provided to the two grids of LD cores through the two available ports on every DM Bank. Only a small fraction of the query SNPs are expected to fit in the Data Mem A on-chip memory, thus several iterations are needed to complete the required all-to-all LD calculations. To improve performance, double buffering is employed for loading the database SNPs from memory and streaming them through the LD Core Grids. For this reason, it is of vital importance for performance that the DM Bank size is chosen carefully so that it can store a sufficiently large number of query SNPs to allow enough time to refill the second database input buffer. This is because, each SNP in the database input buffer (not shown in the figure, it is part of the data processor) is parsed as many times as half the number of SNPs in a DM Bank before all query SNPs in Data Mem A are pairwise combined with the database SNPs in any of the two input buffers.

An LD Core Grid consists of $x \times y$ cores, organized into y rows of x cores each. The LD processor instance in Figure 6 contains 8 cores per grid ($x = 4$, $y = 2$). Every LD core matches a query SNP to a database SNP. Every SNP is simultaneously streamed through an LD core and an AFC block (Allele Frequency Calculator, not part of the LD core), which computes the frequency of the allele represented by the set bits. Note that, it is possible to avoid instantiating AFC blocks when genomic sequences without missing data

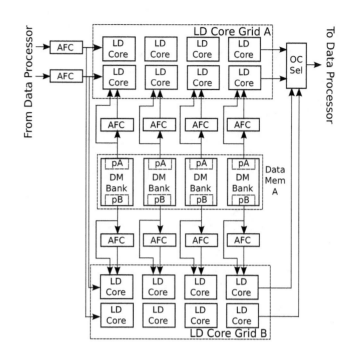

Figure 6: The LD processor architecture for a design point that exhibits 16 LD cores.

are analyzed, since the per-SNP allele frequencies can be computed during the prefiltering stage and added to the genomic matrix as metadata.

Figure 7 shows the pipelines of the AFC block and the LD core to demonstrate how the AFC block operations overlap with the HFC block operations (Haplotype Frequency Calculator), which is part of the LD core. Both AFC and HFC blocks contain a pipelined popcount implementation (POPCNT), which exhibits an array of ROM blocks at the lowest level and an adder reduction tree afterwards, to count the existing alleles and haplotypes, respectively. The SNPs are loaded in segments of size equal to the POPCNT input width. Therefore, the final count of alleles and haplotypes is only available at the output of the accumulator (ACCUM) after all the samples per SNP have been loaded. The frequencies are computed through a floating-point division (DIV) with the total sample size. Note the additional component in the HFC block, denoted HAPCONST, which constructs a bit vector where every set bit represents a valid haplotype. Currently, this is implemented as a logical *and* operation, which covers the cases of high-quality real-world datasets as well as simulated datasets. Additional logic is required in HAPCONST to account for alignment gaps or missing data in the dataset.

When the allele and haplotype frequencies are computed (output of AFC and HFC blocks in Figure 7), the LD Pipe implements Equations 1 and 4 to compute D and r^2, respectively. Changing the LD metric would only require changing the floating-point LD Pipe, and would not affect the rest of the LD processor. The results are temporarily stored in a FIFO buffer. The OC Sel module of the LD processor (see Fig. 6) retrieves LD scores from the FIFOs in a Round-Robin fashion, and transfers them to the data processor. Scores from several FIFOs may be retrieved simultaneously to consume all the available memory bandwidth.

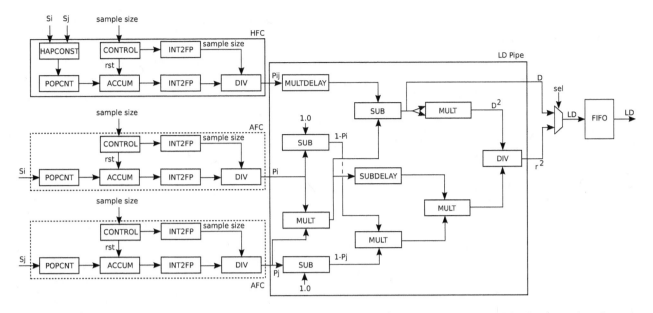

Figure 7: Pipelined datapath of the LD core (HFC and LD Pipe) and the two AFC blocks (one for the query SNP and one for the database SNP) that provide the allele frequencies.

5. IMPLEMENTATION

The generic algorithm executed on the host processor is implemented in C and the parallel processing mechanism of the compute list was modeled using the OpenMP API for parallel programming. The RTL description of the data processor is directly implemented in Verilog HDL, while the LD processor is automatically generated by an appropriately adapted RTL generation software implemented in C, which was initially designed for chemical similarity assessment [2]. Note that, the LD Pipe is also directly implemented in Verilog HDL, and employs single-precision floating-point cores. In the following, we present the input parameters for the RTL generation software, describe the verification process, and analyze the design space of the LD processor.

5.1 Automatic RTL Generation

A single software invocation generates a multi-module Verilog file that contains an LD processor configuration. Two types of tunable parameters are exposed to the user: Type S and Type R. Type S parameters are used to specify the size of the LD processor, such as the LD Core Grid size (number of LD cores vertically and horizontally), the size of the popcount units (input width and latency), the width of the accumulator units (to support arbitrarily large sample sizes), the size of the Data Mem A memory subsystem (number of SNP segments per DM Bank), the size of the FIFO buffer in every LD core (number of floating-point results), and the FIFO-group size (number of FIFOs grouped together to saturate the available memory bandwidth). The optional Type R parameters can be employed to achieve a more balanced distribution of the FPGA resources to the building blocks. The use of Type R parameters deploys synthesis attributes individually for each one of the Core Grids, the Data Mem A memory, and the LD core FIFOs. The popcount units and the accumulators in the LD cores can be implemented on DSP blocks or FPGA LUTs, while the DM Banks and the FIFOs can be mapped on block or distributed RAM. A summary of the parameters is presented

in Table 1, while the RTL generation software is available for download at *https://github.com/alachins/fpga-ld*.

Table 1: RTL generation parameters

	Parameter	Description
	m	popcount width (bits)
	t	popcount latency (cycles)
	n	accumulator width (bits)
Type S	x	LD cores horizontally
	y	LD cores vertically
	z	words in DM Bank
	r	words in FIFO
	o	number of FIFOs grouped together
	gba	AFC synthesis code[2]
	gbb	HFC Core Grid A synthesis code[2]
Type R	$gbbs$	HFC Core Grid B synthesis code[2]
	$qmem$	DM Bank memory type[3]
	$rmem$	FIFO memory type[3]

5.2 Verification

To verify correctness of the accelerator architecture, we generated several LD processor instances and initially conducted extensive post-place and route simulations using Modelsim 6.3f. Additionally, we verified correctness in hardware, deploying a Xilinx ZC706 board with a Zynq Z-7045 FPGA. We configured a Verilog testbench to run a limited-performance design point (8 LD cores, 32-bit popcount operators) at 200 MHz, and used ChipScope to monitor the output of the LD processor.

5.3 Design Space Analysis

Given a sample size l, the popcount width and latency are set according to the following formulas in order to avoid

---

[2]Synthesis codes: 0 for BRAMs and DSPs, 1 for BRAMs and LUTs, 2 for Distributed memory and DSPs, 3 for Distributed memory and LUTs
[3]Memory type: 0 for BRAM, 1 for Distributed memory

excessive allocation of resources (Eq. 5) and to ensure that the bit-enumeration logic does not become the critical path in the design (Eq. 6).

$$m \leq l \tag{5}$$

$$t \geq log2(m) \tag{6}$$

The above formulas ensure that we do not instantiate unnecessarily wide popcount units, i.e., popcount units with input width larger than our target dataset's sample size, as well as restrict the computational path between registers in the adder reduction tree structure to one addition at most, in order to maximize the popcount operating clock frequency.

The LD processor size (total number of LD cores) is given by Eq. 7. Each of the two LD Core Grids contains $x \times y$ cores.

$$Cores_{total} = 2 \times (x \times y) \tag{7}$$

Assume a DRAM bandwidth B, a floating-point precision $prec$ (bit width), and a function $f(B, prec)$ which calculates the number of results that can be offloaded to DRAM per clock cycle. The minimum number of LD cores that need to be instantiated to ensure that performance is not bounded by computation is provided by Eq. 8, while Eq. 9 sets the size of the FIFO groups, i.e., a parameter that configures the OC Sel module to fully utilize the available bandwidth B.

$$Cores_{min} = \left\lceil \frac{l}{m} \right\rceil \times f(B, prec) \tag{8}$$

$$o = f(B, prec) \tag{9}$$

As already mentioned, the data processor employs double buffering to stream one of the two genomic regions, the one considered the database. Each database buffer can store a fixed number of d SNPs, which is set to 64 SNPs in our system. A prerequisite for performance is to overlap the database buffer loading time with computations, which can be achieved by tuning the z parameter according to d. Consider a function $c(d \times y, l, B)$ which calculates the number of clock cycles required to retrieve $d \times y$ SNPs of length l from DRAM at an available bandwidth B. The DM Bank depth z must satisfy the following:

$$d \times \left\lceil \frac{z}{2 \times \lceil \frac{l}{m} \rceil} \right\rceil \times \left\lceil \frac{l}{m} \right\rceil \geq c(d \times y, l, B), \tag{10}$$

where the left-hand side is the number of clock cycles required by an LD core to compute the scores (e.g., D or r^2) between d database SNPs in one of the two database buffers and half of the query SNPs in a DM Bank. Assuming that l is the smallest multiple of m (with zero padding) and z is restricted to be a multiple of $2 \times \lceil \frac{l}{m} \rceil$, then the above formula can be simplified as follows:

$$z \geq \frac{2 \times c(d \times y, l, B)}{d}. \tag{11}$$

6. PERFORMANCE EVALUATION

To assess performance of the FPGA-accelerated system, we used a workstation with an Intel Xeon E5-2630 6-core Sandy Bridge processor running at 2.60 GHz and 32GB of main memory, as a test platform for the software benchmark. For the hardware evaluation, a series of design points were generated and mapped on a Virtex 7 VX980T-2 FPGA. We

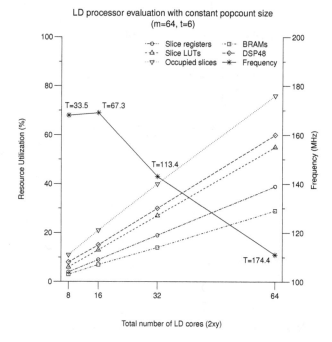

Figure 8: Post-PAR resource utilization, maximum operating clock frequency, and throughput performance T (mLD/sec, based on 2,504 samples) when the total number of LD cores increases.

assess throughput performance in terms of million LD scores per second (mLD/sec). Note that this metric is tightly dependent on the sample size. In our comparisons, we use a subset of 10,000 SNPs from the first chromosome of the human genome (available from the 1000 Genomes project, *http://www.1000genomes.org*), with a sample size of 2,504 genomes (phase 3).

6.1 Tuning Type S Parameters

Initially, we explored the design space of the LD processor by tuning only Type S parameters while maintaining the default Type R values, which map all memory components to BRAMs and attempt to maximize the utilization of DSP slices. Figure 8 illustrates post-place and route (PAR) resource utilization, maximum operating clock frequency, and estimated throughput performance for an increasing number of LD cores. When the number of cores increases, by tuning the x and y parameters, the popcount width and latency are constant and set to $m = 64$ bits and $t = 6$ cycles, respectively. The figure reveals that the highest throughput performance (based on a sample size of 2,504 genomes) which can be achieved with the current configuration is 174.4 mLD/sec. Furthermore, it is observed that DSPs and FPGA slices rapidly become the limiting factors and prevent the instantiation of additional LD cores on the target device. This is not surprising, particularly because the LD pipe heavily relies on floating-point operators.

Thereafter, we explore performance for increasing popcount width and latency. For this configuration, the total number of LD cores is fixed to 16, i.e., 8 LD cores per grid, by setting $x = 8$ and $y = 1$. Figure 9 demonstrates that the highest throughput performance now is 349.4 mLD/sec. This performance improvement over the largest previous

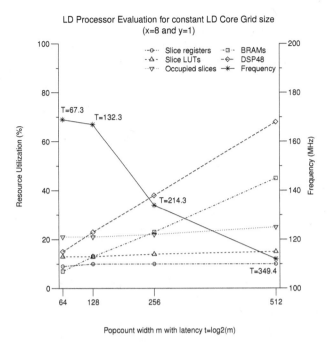

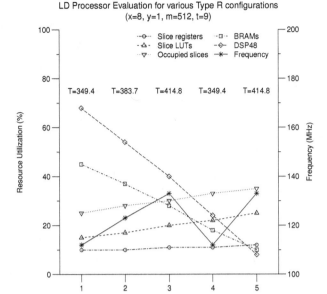

Figure 9: Post-PAR resource utilization, maximum operating clock frequency, and throughput performance T (mLD/sec, based on 2,504 samples) when the popcount width increases.

Figure 10: Post-PAR resource utilization, maximum operating clock frequency, and throughput performance T (mLD/sec, based on 2,504 samples) for various R Type configurations.

configuration (Figure 8) comes from the wider popcount operators which significantly reduce the latency for computing the allele and haplotype frequencies. Reducing the latency for computing or estimating allele and haplotype frequencies has great significance for the population genomics community. The computational demands for computing allele/haplotype frequencies grow with an increasing sample size, and the sample sizes of present-day datasets are only expected to increase (due to the continuous advances in DNA sequencing technologies), whereas the number of SNPs is bounded by the chromosomal length. Furthermore, in addition to association studies that rely on LD, rapid allele and haplotype counts are also required for the evaluation of mutation rates in a population [23], or to investigate the genetic differentiation between populations.

6.2 Tuning Type R Parameters

Driven by the observation that wider popcount operators yield better performance than larger LD Core Grids, we now employ Type R parameters to redistribute the resources of the LD processor configuration that exhibits the largest bit-enumeration-per-cycle capacity, i.e., $x = 8$, $y = 1$, $m = 512$, and $t = 9$. There are five Type R parameters that can be tuned (see Table 1), however only the first three have an effect on the utilization of DSP slices, which is currently the resource with the highest percentage of occupancy. Figure 10 shows resource utilization and performance as more LD processor components are mapped to FPGA LUTs and distributed memory instead of DSP slices and block RAMs. The default LD processor configuration (#1) fully utilizes DSPs and block RAMs. The next two configurations map the HFC blocks of one (#2) and both (#3) LD Core Grids to LUTs and distributed memory. In addition to all HFC

blocks, the final two configurations also map one (#4) and both (#5) arrays of AFC blocks to LUTs and distributed memory.

As can be observed, configuration #4 exhibits the lowest resource utilization over all resources, which is achieved at the price of a longer clock cycle and consequently poorer throughput performance. From the figure, we conclude that it is beneficial to accept a slight increase in occupied slices (configuration #5 versus #4) in order to boost throughput performance by nearly 19%.

6.3 Refining the LD Processor Size

Configuration #5 exhibits the highest throughput performance without excessively occupying the available resources on the target device. This permits to increase the LD processor size to boost performance further. At this point, we opt to continue exploring the design space by increasing the x parameter only, which will add more LD cores to the LD Core Grids horizontally. Increasing the LD Core Grid size by adding more cores vertically (y parameter), or widening the popcount operators (m parameter), requires additional memory bandwidth to sustain performance. On the other hand, placing more LD cores horizontally allows to increase parallelism by matching more query SNPs to the same number of incoming database SNPs.

Figure 11 reveals that increasing the size of the LD processor from 32 to 40 LD cores leads to a significantly longer clock cycle (maximum operating clock frequency drops from 137 MHz to 104 MHz) due to increased routing effort, which diminishes potential throughput performance improvements from the placement of more LD cores in parallel in each LD Core Grid. As can be observed, a 40-core LD processor exhibits poorer performance than a 32-core instance.

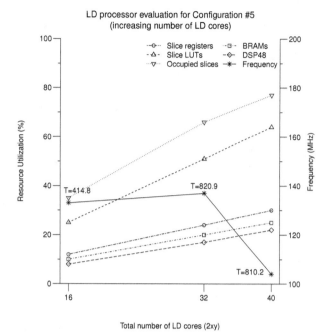

Figure 11: Post-PAR resource utilization, maximum operating clock frequency, and throughput performance T (mLD/sec, based on 2,504 samples) for Type R configuration #5 (all HFC and AFC blocks occupy distributed memory and FPGA LUTs) and increasing LD processor size (number of LD cores).

6.4 Comparison with Reference Software

The open-source tool PLINK 1.9 [6] was selected as the reference software due to superior parallel efficiency in comparison to OmegaPlus [4]. We conducted a preliminary performance comparison (results not shown) between PLINK 1.9 and the multi-grained parallel version of OmegaPlus [3], which was proposed by the authors to improve scalability of the tool. We measured throughput performance when both tools compute $10^4(10^4 + 1)/2$ LD scores. We observed that, for small numbers of threads (up to 4), both tools exhibit comparable throughput performance (OmegaPlus was up to 15% faster), whereas when the number of threads increases, PLINK 1.9 is up to 2X faster. Therefore, we opted to compare the FPGA-accelerated system against PLINK 1.9 to ensure an accurate performance evaluation based on the current state-of-the-art software.

Table 2 shows execution times and throughput performance for the analysis of the test dataset that comprises 10,000 SNPs from the genomes of 2,504 humans. The FPGA performance refers to the fastest LD processor configuration detected through the design space exploration, which comprises 32 LD cores and exhibits 512-bit-wide popcount units with 9 clock cycles latency, while all HFC and AFC blocks are mapped to FPGA LUTs and distributed memory. The comparisons include the memory access time, and exclude the amount of time required for prefiltering.

It could be argued that the execution times in Table 2 are too short to justify the need for acceleration. One should consider however that the 10,000 SNPs in the test dataset account for roughly 0.1% of the total amount of variants

in the human genome. Typically, whole-genome analyses implement a sliding-window approach, where each window covers a narrow subgenomic region that comprises a limited number of SNPs (10,000 SNPs is a reasonable size for such a window). To cover the entire genome of complex species for instance, tens of thousands of sliding-window iterations may be needed, requiring several hours or days to complete an analysis on current workstations. Furthermore, PLINK 1.9 allows only a single region as input, which would require prohibitively large memory footprint on the test platform in order to cover larger genomic space in our tests, whereas our proposed generic algorithm accepts two subgenomic regions as input, which permits the sequential scheduling and calculation of arbitrarily distant LD associations.

Table 3 provides execution times and throughput performance when two simulated datasets with larger sample sizes are analyzed. Both datasets, D.1 and D.2, comprise 10,000 SNPs, while exhibiting sample sizes of 10,000 and 100,000 sequences, respectively. The 32-core LD processor achieves throughput performance of 205.7 mLD/sec for dataset D.1, and 20.4 mLD/sec for dataset D.2.

Table 2: Performance comparison between PLINK 1.9 software (6-core Xeon CPU) and a 32-core LD processor instance (Virtex 7 FPGA).

Threads	PLINK 1.9 Exec. time (sec)	mLD/sec	FPGA LD Proc. Speedup (X)
1	12.3	4.1	200.2
2	9.6	5.2	157.8
4	5.9	8.4	97.7
8	3.8	13.0	63.1
12	3.0	16.4	50.1

Table 3: Performance comparison based on simulated datasets D.1 and D.2 with sample sizes of 10,000 and 100,000 sequences, respectively.

Threads	PLINK 1.9 Exec. time (sec)		mLD/sec		FPGA LD Proc. Speedup (X)	
	D.1	D.2	D.1	D.2	D.1	D.2
1	41.1	389.1	1.2	0.128	171.4	159.3
2	31.4	297.6	1.6	0.168	128.5	121.4
4	19.2	180.2	2.6	0.277	79.1	73.6
8	11.3	109.4	4.4	0.456	46.8	44.7
12	9.9	88.3	5.0	0.566	41.1	36.0

7. CONCLUSIONS

In this study, we explored the potential of FPGAs to be employed as accelerators that boost performance of linkage disequilibrium computations in population genomics and genome-wide association studies. We developed a hardware generation software that allowed rapid design space exploration that reached several high performance design points. Generating custom accelerator instances enables the deployment of the largest/fastest design point for the analysis of the genomic dataset at hand. This has great significance in real-world analyses that typically need to conduct thousands of simulations on synthetic datasets with similar characteristics (e.g., demographic model) and size as the real dataset under investigation to determine whether the results are statistically significant. We find that FPGAs can achieve up to 50X faster analysis than current software implementations executed on multi-core workstations. Finally, we described a generic algorithm that is executed on the host and enables the offloading of long-range association statistics without conducting redundant operations or requiring excessive memory resources.

As future work, we intend to port the generic algorithm on GPUs to explore the potential performance gains, as well as on systems that comprise different types of accelerator devices such as GPUs and FPGAs to exploit the aggregate computational capacity of such heterogeneous systems. Additionally, we intend to further develop the automatic generation software to accommodate other computationally intensive statistics that can benefit from rapid allele and haplotype frequency computations.

Acknowledgments

The authors thank Tze Meng Low (CMU) for constructive discussions, valuable insights on LD, and comments on the manuscript. Furthermore, the authors thank Xilinx for tools and hardware donated to CMU. This work is supported in part by NSF CCF-1320725 and by Intel.

8. REFERENCES

[1] N. Alachiotis. *Algorithms and Computer Architectures for Evolutionary Bioinformatics*. PhD thesis, München, Technische Universität München, 2012.

[2] N. Alachiotis. Generating FPGA accelerators for chemical similarity assessment. In *Field Programmable Logic and Applications (FPL), 2015 25th International Conference on*, pages 1–4. IEEE, 2015.

[3] N. Alachiotis, P. Pavlidis, and A. Stamatakis. Exploiting multi-grain parallelism for efficient selective sweep detection. In *Algorithms and Architectures for Parallel Processing*, pages 56–68. Springer, 2012.

[4] N. Alachiotis, A. Stamatakis, and P. Pavlidis. OmegaPlus: a scalable tool for rapid detection of selective sweeps in whole-genome datasets. *Bioinformatics*, 28(17):2274–2275, 2012.

[5] M. T. Alam, D. K. de Souza, S. Vinayak, S. M. Griffing, A. C. Poe, N. O. Duah, A. Ghansah, K. Asamoa, L. Slutsker, M. D. Wilson, J. W. Barnwell, V. Udhayakumar, and K. A. Koram. Selective sweeps and genetic lineages of Plasmodium falciparum drug -resistant alleles in Ghana. *The Journal of infectious diseases*, 203(2):220–7, Jan. 2011.

[6] C. C. Chang, C. C. Chow, L. C. Tellier, S. Vattikuti, S. M. Purcell, and J. J. Lee. Second-generation PLINK: rising to the challenge of larger and richer datasets. *Gigascience*, (4), 2015.

[7] G. K. Chen, P. Marjoram, and J. D. Wall. Fast and flexible simulation of DNA sequence data. *Genome research*, 19(1):136–42, Jan. 2009.

[8] J. F. Crow, M. Kimura, et al. An introduction to population genetics theory. *An introduction to population genetics theory.*, 1970.

[9] N. G. de Groot and R. E. Bontrop. The HIV-1 pandemic: does the selective sweep in chimpanzees mirror humankind's future? *Retrovirology*, 10(1):53, Jan. 2013.

[10] D. B. Goldstein and M. E. Weale. Population genomics: linkage disequilibrium holds the key. *Current Biology*, 11(14):R576–R579, 2001.

[11] R. R. Hudson. Generating samples under a Wright-Fisher neutral model of genetic variation. *Bioinformatics (Oxford, England)*, 18(2):337–8, 2002.

[12] M. Kimura. The number of heterozygous nucleotide sites maintained in a finite population due to steady flux of mutations. *Genetics*, 61(4):893, 1969.

[13] R. Lewontin and K. Kojima. The evolutionary dynamics of complex polymorphisms. *Evolution*, pages 458–472, 1960.

[14] H. Li. A new test for detecting recent positive selection that is free from the confounding impacts of demography. *Molecular biology and evolution*, 28(1):365–75, Jan. 2011.

[15] R. Nielsen, S. Williamson, Y. Kim, M. J. Hubisz, A. G. Clark, and C. Bustamante. Genomic scans for selective sweeps using SNP data. *Genome research*, 15(11):1566–75, Nov. 2005.

[16] P. S. Pennings, S. Kryazhimskiy, and J. Wakeley. Loss and recovery of genetic diversity in adapting populations of HIV. *PLoS genetics*, 10(1), 2014.

[17] P. Pfaffelhuber, A. Lehnert, and W. Stephan. Linkage disequilibrium under genetic hitchhiking in finite populations. *Genetics*, 179(1):527–537, May 2008.

[18] B. Pfeifer, U. Wittelsbürger, S. E. Ramos-Onsins, and M. J. Lercher. PopGenome: An Efficient Swiss Army Knife for Population Genomic Analyses in R. *Molecular biology and evolution*, 31(7):1929–36, 2014.

[19] S. Purcell, B. Neale, K. Todd-Brown, L. Thomas, M. A. Ferreira, D. Bender, J. Maller, P. Sklar, P. I. De Bakker, M. J. Daly, et al. PLINK: a tool set for whole-genome association and population-based linkage analyses. *The American Journal of Human Genetics*, 81(3):559–575, 2007.

[20] D. E. Reich, M. Cargill, S. Bolk, J. Ireland, P. C. Sabeti, D. J. Richter, T. Lavery, R. Kouyoumjian, S. F. Farhadian, R. Ward, et al. Linkage disequilibrium in the human genome. *Nature*, 411(6834):199–204, 2001.

[21] M. Slatkin. Linkage disequilibrium-understanding the evolutionary past and mapping the medical future. *Nature Reviews Genetics*, 9(6):477–485, 2008.

[22] E. Sotiriades and A. Dollas. A general reconfigurable architecture for the BLAST algorithm. *The Journal of VLSI Signal Processing Systems for Signal, Image, and Video Technology*, 48(3):189–208, 2007.

[23] F. Tajima. Statistical method for testing the neutral mutation hypothesis by dna polymorphism. *Genetics*, 123(3):585–595, 1989.

[24] P. M. Visscher, M. A. Brown, M. I. McCarthy, and J. Yang. Five years of GWAS discovery. *The American Journal of Human Genetics*, 90(1):7–24, 2012.

[25] S. Zierke and J. D. Bakos. FPGA acceleration of the phylogenetic likelihood function for Bayesian MCMC inference methods. *BMC bioinformatics*, 11(1):184, 2010.

LMC: Automatic Resource-Aware Program-Optimized Memory Partitioning

Hsin-Jung Yang
Massachusetts Institute of
Technology, CSAIL
hjyang@mit.edu

Kermin Fleming
Intel Corporation
SSG Group
kermin.fleming@intel.com

Michael Adler
Intel Corporation
SSG Group
michael.adler@intel.com

Felix Winterstein
Imperial College London
CAS Group
f.winterstein12@imperial.ac.uk

Joel Emer
Massachusetts Institute of
Technology, CSAIL
emer@csail.mit.edu

ABSTRACT

As FPGAs have grown in size and capacity, FPGA memory systems have become both richer and more diverse in order to support the increased computational capacity of FPGA fabrics. Using these resources, and using them *well*, has become commensurately more difficult, especially in the context of legacy designs ported from smaller, simpler FPGA systems. This growing complexity necessitates resource-aware compilers that can make good use of memory resources on behalf of the programmer. In this work, we introduce the LEAP Memory Compiler (LMC), which can synthesize application-optimized cache networks for systems with multiple memory resources, enabling user programs to automatically take advantage of the expanded memory capabilities of modern FPGA systems. In our experiments, the optimized cache network achieves up to 49% performance gains for throughput-oriented applications and 15% performance gains for latency-oriented applications, while increasing design area by less than 6% of the total chip area.

1. INTRODUCTION

FPGAs have become increasingly popular as accelerators because of their energy-efficiency and performance characteristics. To maximize efficiency and performance, FPGA programmers have traditionally utilized low-level primitives and programming models, explicitly customizing their implementation both to the target application and *to the target platform*. This approach, while effective, has made FPGA programs difficult to write, limiting both developer productivity and portability across FPGA platforms. As a result, recent research in both FPGA-oriented programming languages [26] [8] [5] [3] and architecture [20] [7] [13] has focused on raising the level of abstraction available to FPGA programmers, with the goal of reducing programmer design efforts.

High-level abstractions provide clearly-defined, generic interfaces that separate user programs from underlying infrastructure implementations. These fixed interface layers allow users to write portable programs, which can run on different FPGA platforms without re-

designing the application code. Low-level platform implementation details are handled by a combination of compilers and system developers. Such abstractions present a significant opportunity for compilers since the extra resources available on modern FPGAs can be used to improve program performance without perturbing the original user program. This is especially the case for coarse-grained resources like board-level memories, the integration of which have traditionally required significant architectural consideration at design time.

To produce efficient, performant, portable FPGA designs, we argue that automated, resource-aware optimization of abstract interfaces is essential for modern FPGAs. In this work, we focus on one aspect of resource-aware optimization: FPGA memory systems. As the availability of more transistors makes it feasible to build both larger, bandwidth-hungry designs and the memory controllers necessary to feed them, modern FPGA boards have begun to include multiple DDR and HBM memories [2]. Moreover, the number of memory controllers appears to be increasing rapidly as vendors move to harden memory interfaces [1] [2]. To improve FPGA system performance, it is critical to enable integration of these increasingly rich and varied memory systems into user programs without drastically increasing design burden.

To allow programs to automatically make use of available memory resources, we propose the LEAP Memory Compiler (LMC), an augmentation to the LEAP compilation flow [13]. Unlike general-purpose processors where the memory hierarchy is fixed at design time based on a set of expected workloads, LMC tailors FPGA memory systems to different applications at compilation time based on the properties of those specific applications. LMC presupposes user programs described in terms of high-level memory interfaces [4] [29], which hide memory implementation details from application designers. In order to improve the performance of user programs, LMC incorporates several optimizations that take advantage of both interface abstraction and the availability of extra memory resources.

LMC operates in three phases: instrumentation, analysis, and synthesis. In the first phase, LMC injects instrumentation infrastructure into the baseline memory system. This instrumentation is used to collect runtime information about the way the program uses memory. Subsequently, LMC analyzes these metrics and applies various optimization techniques to improve the performance of the memory subsystem specific to the application and the target platform. Finally, LMC emits an optimized memory system implementation which passes through a standard tool flow to produce an FPGA image.

The main contribution of our work is in the automated optimization of memory systems. LMC produces as output an optimized

FPGA'16, February 21-23, 2016, Monterey, CA, USA

© 2016 ACM. ISBN 978-1-4503-3856-1/16/02. . . $15.00

DOI: http://dx.doi.org/10.1145/2847263.2847283

cache network, connecting single or multiple user-level caches to the available on-board memory resources. We introduce optimizations for both private and shared memories based on the available on-board memory resources in the system, the number of FPGAs, as well as the user program's bandwidth, which we derive from runtime instrumentation. In support of and in conjunction with our optimizing compiler, we introduce several new memory microarchitectures that enable existing client memory primitives to target multiple board-level memories.

For private memories, we partition the user-level private caches into disjoint groups and connect each group to a shared cache implemented on top of each on-board memory bank. Each partition is connected using a separate, dedicated network, which serves to increase memory throughput while simultaneously reducing memory latency. To improve memory bandwidth, LMC implements an intelligent memory interleaving mechanism, which enables individual private memories to utilize multiple board-level memories. In interleaved memory systems, portions of the memory address space are routed to different memory resources at a relatively fine grain.

For applications using shared memory, we apply memory interleaving techniques to partition the shared memory address space into multiple disjoint regions. We adopt a hierarchical-ring topology in the partitioned coherent cache network. This hierarchical topology reduces the latency of coherence messages, which is essential if designs are spread across several networked FPGAs. Since the coherent memory hierarchy is integrated with the private memory hierarchy, our private memory optimizations can be directly composed with our coherent memory optimizations to further improve overall system performance.

We evaluate LMC using both hand-assembled and HLS-compiled applications by targeting several single-board and networked multiboard FPGA deployments. Our optimizations cost less than 6% of the total chip area. For hand-assembled, throughput-oriented applications, the partitioned network achieves up to 49% performance improvement because of the increased memory bandwidth. For the HLS-compiled application, which involves pointer-chasing and is latency-oriented, the partitioned network provides about 15% performance improvement because of the reduced network latency.

2. BACKGROUND

LMC produces program-optimized memory hierarchies. To produce these hierarchies, LMC requires a collection of primitive elements from which a memory system can be constructed. As a base for LMC, we adopt the primitives and compiler of the LEAP [13] memory hierarchy. In particular, we leverage two prior memory primitives: LEAP private memories [4] and coherent memories [29]. Both of these memory primitives are built on top of LEAP's latency-insensitive channels [11], named communications primitives that are instantiated within user programs and implemented by the compiler at compilation time.

LEAP latency-insensitive channels provide named point-to-point communications for hardware programs. At compilation time, send and receive endpoints in the user program are matched, and a flow-controlled channel implementation is instantiated between them. Additionally, LEAP supplies a ring primitive, in which the compiler assembles all similarly named ringstops into a network. Unlike traditional hardware programming, LEAP named channels enable communication between any two points in a design without explicitly connecting wires through the module hierarchy. This channel construction primitive greatly simplifies tasks such as restructuring memory topologies and instantiating counters for feedback directed compilation. LMC makes use of channel and ring renaming as a mechanism for constructing application-specific memories.

```
interface MEM_IFC#(type t_ADDR, type t_DATA);
    method void readRequest(t_ADDR addr);
    method t_DATA readResponse();
    method void write(t_ADDR addr, t_DATA data);
endinterface
```

Figure 1: A general memory interface for hardware designs.

LEAP private memories provide a general, in-fabric memory abstraction for FPGA programs. Programmers instantiate private memories with a simple read-request, read-response, write interface, shown in Figure 1. Each memory represents a logically private address space, and a program may instantiate as many memories as needed. Memories may store arbitrary data types and support arbitrary address space sizes, even if the target FPGA does not have sufficient physical memory to cover the entire requested memory space. To provide the illusion of large address spaces, LEAP backs the FPGA memory with host virtual memory, while FPGA physical memories, including on-chip and on-board memories, are used as caches to maintain high performance.

LEAP coherent memories [29] extend the baseline LEAP memory interface to support shared memory. Similar to LEAP private memories, LEAP coherent memories provide a simple memory interface and the illusion of unlimited virtual storage. In addition, LEAP coherent memories permit applications to declare multiple, independent coherent address spaces using a compile-time specified name. Cache coherency and weak consistency are maintained among coherent memories that share the same address space.

LEAP's memory system resembles that of general-purpose machines, both in terms of its abstract interface and its hierarchical construction. Like the load-store interface of general-purpose machines, LEAP's abstract memory interfaces do not specify or imply any details of the underlying memory system implementation, such as how many operations can be in flight and the topology of the memory. This ambiguity provides significant freedom of implementation to the compiler. For example, a small memory could be implemented as a local SRAM, while a larger memory could be backed by a cache hierarchy and host virtual memory. LEAP exploits abstraction to build complex, optimized memory architectures on behalf of the user, bridging the simple user interface and complex physical hardware. In this work, we leverage the freedom of abstraction to target systems with multiple on-board memory banks.

LEAP organizes the various memory primitives in the user program into a memory hierarchy with multiple levels of cache. Like memory hierarchies in general-purpose computers, the LEAP memory organization provides the appearance of fast memory to programs with good locality. Figure 2 shows an example of a typical LEAP memory hierarchy which integrates one private memory and three coherent memories instantiated in the user program. LEAP coherent memories are built on top of LEAP private memories both literally and figuratively: each LEAP shared address space is backed by two LEAP private memories as data and coherence ownership stores. As a result of this layering, both types of memories share large portions of the memory hierarchy. LEAP memory clients optionally receive a local cache, which is implemented using on-chip SRAMs. A snoopy-based coherence protocol is implemented to maintain cache coherency among LEAP coherent memory clients' local caches.

The board-level memory, which is typically an off-chip SRAM or DRAM, is used as a shared cache or central cache. The central cache controller manages access to a multi-word, set-associative board-level cache with a configurable replacement policy. Within the cache, each private memory space and shared memory domain is uniquely tagged, enforcing a physical separation. Previously, LEAP

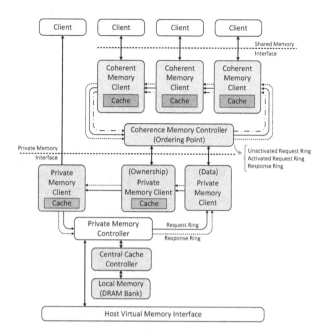

Figure 2: An example of LEAP memory hierarchy

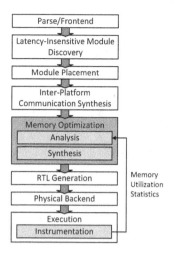

Figure 3: The LEAP compilation flow [14], with our augmentations highlighted. We add a memory optimization phase that performs memory network analysis and synthesis. Memory network analysis is optionally feedback driven.

aggregated all board-level memory resources into a single larger-capacity cache handled by a single central cache controller. In this work, we introduce the capability to treat each board-level memory resource as an independent cache, thereby creating the opportunity for program-specific memory hierarchy organization and partitioning, which we examine in detail in Section 5.

LEAP's compilation flow is shown in Figure 3. The compiler gathers the various LEAP memories in the user program and assembles them into a memory hierarchy, as in Figure 2. By default, the compiler assembles the various memory interfaces into ring networks. For example, coherent memories in each coherence domain are connected via three rings: the unactivated request ring, the activated request ring, and the response ring. These rings are used to implement the channels required by the snoopy coherence protocol. Lower levels of the memory hierarchy are self-assembled in a similar manner, integrating successive backing stores into the hierarchy. In this work, we augment LEAP's name-based network assembly mechanism with a compiler-generated indirection layer which influences the construction of the memory network based on memory system properties and program characteristics.

3. RELATED WORK

Our work presumes the existence of a basic memory abstraction for FPGAs, which we then back with a custom memory network. In this work, we build on the LEAP memory framework, but other frameworks are compatible with our approach. CoRAM [7] advocates memory interaction using control threads programmed with a C-like language. CoRAM does not define the memory hierarchy or network backing its interface, and therefore could use our optimization approach, a work that is ongoing. FPGA-based processor infrastructures [23] [21] [24], especially multicore systems, could also make use of our networks, though the benefit of optimizing such symmetric systems is less obvious.

Much recent work has gone into the microarchitecture of memory systems on FPGAs [9] [6] and the construction of multiple-level memory hierarchies [4] [6] [16] [22], all of which build user-level memory interfaces backed by some off-chip storage. Generally, the memory networks used by these systems are symmetrical and do not explicitly take into account program behavior.

Our technique of memory address interleaving across multiple memory controllers has been used extensively in general-purpose computer architecture to maximize available memory bandwidth and to simplify the microarchitecture of elements of the memory system, like coherency. Memory interleaving dates to early IBM mainframes. An example of memory interleaving is the SGI Challenge [15] line of supercomputers. Challenge's memory subsystem is comprised of multiple *leaf* memory controllers which were aggregated and interleaved in large systems using direct address partitioning. As transistor density has improved, most modern systems have opted to include multiple memory channels and controllers, most of which use various interleaving techniques to improve workload memory bandwidth and latency.

Hierarchical, ring-based coherence protocols also have a long history in computer architecture. Our work resembles some of the coherence architectures developed as part of the Hector project [10]. In this work, sets of processors are connected on coherent buses forming a collection called a *station*. The station controller serves to interface the processor collection to other stations on a local ring and filters messages not needed by the station. Local rings are aggregated to form a global ring. This arrangement of hierarchical rings helps reduce latency and overall network traffic by eliminating irrelevant messages on the local and station networks.

Since the memory networks of traditional computer architectures must be fixed or largely fixed at manufacture, previous work in the area of memory networks has largely focused on symmetric architectures, which are likely to handle a broad class of workloads reasonably well. Our per-program analysis permits us to leverage memory partitioning asymmetrically, if such asymmetry benefits a particular program.

4. LEAP MEMORY COMPILER

To automate the construction of optimized memory systems tailored for different applications, we extend the LEAP compilation flow [14] by adding a series of compilation phases, which we refer to as the LEAP Memory Compiler (LMC). Figure 3 shows the extended compilation flow incorporating LMC. LMC operates in three

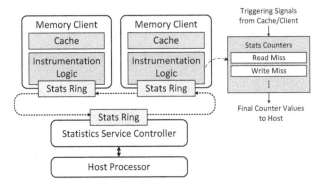

Figure 4: Program instrumentation built with the LEAP statistics collection service

phases: instrumentation, analysis, and synthesis. The combination results in an application-specific memory hierarchy.

The first phase of LMC is program instrumentation. For many FPGA applications, there are multiple memory clients in the system and the memory clients may have highly asymmetric behaviors and implementation needs. For example, a memory client producing a large number of cache misses within a short period of time may require more memory bandwidth from the next-level memory, while a memory client with high cache hit rate may be able to tolerate a larger miss penalty. Evenly distributing memory resources among asymmetric clients without knowing their memory utilization properties may cause bandwidth waste. To understand program behavior, static program analysis may be tractable, especially for HLS-compiled applications [28]. However, in order to target more general and more complicated programs including hand-assembled applications, we resort to FPGA-based runtime instrumentation.

Figure 4 describes our program instrumentation mechanism, which is built on top of the LEAP statistics collection service. Program instrumentation logic is inserted at each memory client to monitor various runtime memory utilization properties, such as the number of cache misses, the number of outstanding requests, and the request queueing delay. These instrumentation results are recorded in local counters at each memory client during program execution. We utilize the LEAP statistics service to collect instrumentation results at the end of the execution. LEAP statistics counters communicate using the standard LEAP named channels and rings. The LEAP compiler automatically connects the instrumentation logic to a centralized statistics controller via a LEAP latency-insensitive ring. When the controller receives a statistics-collection command from the host processor, it forwards the command to the clients and asks them to send back the instrumentation results. The host processor then records the collected results in a statistics file, which can be used in LMC's analysis phase in subsequent compilations.

During the analysis phase LMC analyzes program information, such as the number of memory clients, as well as platform information, including the number of FPGAs and the number of board-level memories. LMC then optimizes the memory hierarchy by assigning memory clients to available memory controllers associated with board-level memories. This phase is optionally feedback-driven: the instrumentation results obtained from previous program execution can be utilized for further optimizations, such as bandwidth-aware partitioning, which we will discuss in Section 5. The output of the analysis phase is an abstract representation of the memory hierarchy, which is passed to the synthesis phase.

The final phase of LMC is the synthesis phase, which produces an implementation of the application-specific memory hierarchy. To construct the synthesized memory hierarchy we leverage the

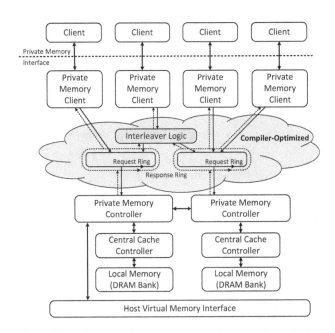

Figure 5: LEAP private memory system with a compiler-optimized cache network

name-based channel assembly mechanism provided by the baseline LEAP compiler, as mentioned in Section 2. Based on the abstract representation of the memory hierarchy obtained from the analysis phase, LMC generates a renaming function as the final output, which maps each client's memory connection to its automatically chosen memory controller. If no optimizations are applied in the analysis phase, we supply identity as the renaming function. After LMC is complete, we leverage the existing network synthesis capabilities of the RTL-generation phase in the baseline LEAP compiler to generate physical networks by matching the newly assigned channel names.

5. CACHE NETWORK OPTIMIZATION

This section introduces the analysis and mechanisms by which we synthesize platform-optimized and program-optimized cache networks for both private and shared memory services. In this work, we target the cases when there is more than one board-level memory controller. Operating from a high-level specification of a memory system, our optimizations produce cache networks that utilize increased memory bandwidth as well as reduce cache network latency.

5.1 Private Cache Network Optimization

To utilize the bandwidth of multiple on-board memories efficiently, we begin by constructing a central cache controller for each memory bank, as shown in Figure 5. The result is a set of distributed caches. Each central cache uses an on-board memory bank to store cache data and tags. The private memory controller, which offers a read/write interface to address spaces, is also duplicated per central cache. The memory controllers are responsible for accessing central cache banks for the associated private memory clients as well as communicating with the host memory backing store.

Since LEAP private memories have disjoint address spaces, they can be freely separated and mapped to different controllers and central caches without any changes in the private memory design. There are many possible mechanisms for assigning clients to memory controllers. A simple solution is random partitioning: we randomly separate private memory clients into (roughly) equal-sized groups, assign a memory controller to each group, and synthesize separate rings to connect all the nodes within the same group. For

1: **procedure** PARTITION(*clientList*, *controllerList*, *statsFile*)
2:      Initialize controller bandwidth to be zero
3:      **if** *statsFile* exists **then**   ▷ Load-balanced partitioning
4:          *clientBandwidth* ← Parse *statsFile*
5:          **while** *clientList* not empty **do**
6:              *s* ← Memory client with maximum *clientBandwidth*
7:              *c* ← Controller with minimum bandwidth
8:              Connect *s* to *c*
9:              Add *s*'s bandwith to *c*'s bandwidth
10:             Remove *s* from *clientList*
11:     **else**   ▷ Random partitioning
12:         *n* ← Length of *controllerList*
13:         *sLists* ← Randomly separate *clientList* into *n* lists
14:         **for** *i* in 1 to *n* **do**
15:             Connect *sLists[i]* to *controllerList[i]*

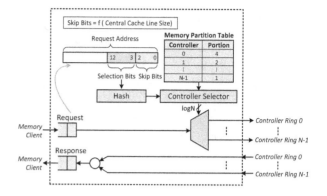

Figure 6: LEAP private memory interleaver logic microarchitecture

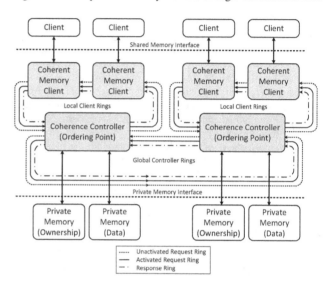

Figure 7: LEAP coherent memories with dual coherence controllers

applications with largely homogeneous memory clients, random partitioning effectively reduces network latency and balances the traffic among multiple controller networks. However, if the behavior of private memories is heterogeneous, i.e., the memory clients have different cache properties and different bandwidth demands, random partitioning may not achieve the best performance.

To improve performance of applications with heterogeneous clients we adopt feedback-driven load-balanced partitioning to separate memory clients into groups. Load-balancing is especially important for throughput-oriented applications, whose memory clients issue multiple outstanding requests to hide long-latency misses and therefore are more sensitive to the available bandwidth in the associated controller network. We utilize LMC's instrumentation mechanism to track the total number of messages sent from each memory client and use this metric as the first-order approximation of the client's bandwidth requirement. We then partition the memory clients based on their bandwidth estimation.

Algorithm 1 describes how we partition the private cache network on a single FPGA. We adapt the classical longest-processing-time (LPT) algorithm [17] to memory bandwidth partitioning. This algorithm approximates optimal load balancing by assigning new memory traffic to the least-loaded memory controller. To partition the cache network across multiple FPGAs, private memories are routed to one of the controllers on the same FPGA using our load balancing algorithm, avoiding long inter-FPGA communication latency.

A weakness of the load-balanced partitioning approach is that a single bandwidth-intensive memory client cannot utilize the full bandwidth of the memory system. To remedy this, LMC implements a memory interleaving mechanism that enables a single memory client to connect to multiple memory controllers. Memory interleaver logic is instantiated to partition a single private memory's address space into multiple, variable-sized interleaved regions. Requests targeting different regions are forwarded to different controller networks, allowing more physical bandwidth and more independent, parallel requests.

When memory clients consume a large amount of bandwidth or when it is difficult to perform load-balanced partitioning, for example, when there is only one private memory in the system, LMC constructs interleaved memories. Individual clients accessing interleaved memories are mapped to multiple controllers by injecting memory interleaver logic. Private memory interleaving is combined with the partitioning method described in Algorithm 1: LMC first deals with the memory clients whose memory needs to be interleaved, connecting them with multiple controllers, and then apportions the remaining non-interleaved memory clients.

Figure 5 shows an example of a compiler-optimized cache network with two on-board DRAM banks in the system. In this example, there is one private memory that connects to two controller networks via the memory interleaver logic. Figure 6 shows the microarchitecture of the private memory interleaver logic. When the memory interleaver receives a request from the associated private memory, it forwards the request to one of the controller rings based on the target request's word-level address. We route consecutive addresses to the same controller to take advantage of spatial locality available at the central cache: each central cache line is comprised of multiple private memory's cache words. We use the mid-order bits in the address field and the memory partition table to select the destination controller. The memory partition table records the portion of the address space assigned to each controller. The address space can be split into non-equal-sized banks, enabling fine-grained load-balanced partitioning. Since some strided access patterns may introduce controller selection conflicts and cause serialization at the memory controllers, we introduce a hashing function to apportion requests in a static but random fashion in order to balance requests between controllers.

5.2 Coherent Cache Network Optimization

Since LEAP coherent memories are built on top of LEAP private memories, applications that use LEAP coherent memories can benefit from previously described private cache partitioning optimizations. However, the optimization space is limited, since each

132

coherence domain only uses two private memories as data and ownership stores (see Figure 2).

To efficiently utilize the underlying memory resources in the case of coherent memories, we introduce a memory interleaving technique for a coherence domain. Coherent memory interleaving is conceptually similar to the private memory interleaving technique described above. The coherent memory address space is partitioned into disjoint regions and assigned to a distributed set of coherence controllers, each handling coherence for a separate region. Figure 7 shows an example of the partitioned coherent cache network that connects four coherent memory clients in a single coherence domain to dual interleaved coherence controllers. Coherent caches and interleaved controllers are connected via a hierarchy of ring networks, which reduces network latency and improves scalability. Although similar to the private memory optimization, the separation of the address spaces for coherent memories is complicated by the need to maintain coherency guarantees.

Within an interleaved coherence domain, each coherence controller is responsible for a portion of the domain address space. The controller connects to the next-level memory by instantiating two LEAP private memories, one to store data and the other to track coherence ownership information for the associated address region. The controller snoops every local request, whose target block address belongs to the controller's associated memory region, and responds to the requester if none of the coherent cache clients owns the data block.

Each controller has an address mapping function that determines whether an incoming request is local or not. The address mapping function is also responsible for converting the address of an incoming request from the global address space to the controller's local address space before the controller accesses the next-level memory. For coarse-grained memory interleaving, the address mapping function can be as simple as an address range filter. For fine-grained memory interleaving, the mapping function can be implemented as a look-up table.

Each coherence controller also serves as a distributed ordering point. In the original ring-based snoopy protocol [29], there is a single, global ordering point on the memory network (see Figure 2). To ensure all coherent memories see coherence requests in the same order, all requests must first go to the global ordering point before being broadcast in a global order, creating congestion at the single ordering point. To improve network performance for an interleaved shared memory system, each coherence controller gathers requests that are local to its memory bank and broadcasts them on the ring separately. Requests targeting different memory banks may be seen in a different order by different coherent memory clients. Coherency is maintained under this optimization because all clients agree with the ordering of operations on a single memory location. As for memory consistency, which specifies the memory ordering behavior for operations on multiple memory locations, coherent memory clients in the original protocol [29] perform out-of-order execution to achieve higher parallelism and thus only provide weak consistency guarantees. Introducing multiple ordering points does not weaken memory consistency. The LEAP coherent memory interface supports fences which can be invoked by clients that require stronger memory consistency to ensure the ordering of operations.

To improve network bandwidth, we partition the original ring network into hierarchical rings as shown in Figure 7. As a baseline, coherent memory clients are partitioned into equal-sized groups in lexical order, but other feedback driven partitioning algorithms can also be applied. Coherent memory clients in the same partition are connected to one of the coherence controllers via local client rings, and the controllers are connected together with global controller rings. As in the original protocol, three LEAP latency-insensitive rings are constructed for three types of coherence messages in each local and global ring network to prevent deadlocks: the unactivated request ring, the activated request ring, and the response ring. The global request and response rings can be viewed as express links that shorten the longest distance between the responder and requester. When memory clients are spread across multiple FPGAs, the hierarchical ring structure further improves network latency since the frequency of long-latency inter-FPGA communication is reduced.

6. EVALUATION

The majority of our evaluation targets the Xilinx VC709 platform. The Virtex-7 FPGA on the VC709 includes two physical memory controllers, each connected to 4GB DDR3 memories. We use these to implement two board-level caches per VC709. We also test two networked FPGA deployments: a dual VC707 and a dual VC709 configuration, to demonstrate how our techniques can be applied to cloud-based networks of FPGAs. We network our FPGAs using two bidirectional 10Gbps SERDES channels. Frequencies are normalized to 100MHz on all platforms to ensure performance results are comparable. For the HLS benchmark [27], we utilize Vivado HLS. We make use of Xilinx Vivado 2015.1 for all synthesis and physical implementation.

We examine a set of benchmarks with different memory access patterns in order to evaluate the benefit of LMC:

Memperf: A kernel that measures the performance of the LEAP memory hierarchy by testing various data strides and working set sizes on a single private memory. *Memperf* is throughput-oriented and can issue as many outstanding requests as the memory system permits.

Heat: A two-dimensional stencil code that models heat transfer across a surface. *Heat* is embarrassingly parallel and can be divided among as many worker engines as can fit on the FPGA. From an algorithmic perspective, *heat* is also very regular: workers march over the shared two-dimensional space in fixed rectangular patterns. As such, *heat* is largely throughput-oriented with a strided access pattern, but with a high degree of locality. Each *heat* worker accesses a LEAP coherent memory, and these coherent memories are largely symmetric in their runtime behavior. However, *heat*'s coherence controllers include private memory clients for data and ownership, and these are asymmetric: the data client uses ten times the bandwidth of the ownership client.

Heat operates on a parametric data size. In this work, we examine two data size parameterizations: 8-bit, which gives a degree of spatial locality in the coherent cache, and 64-bit, which has less locality.

Cryptosorter: *Cryptosorter* [12] sorts a set of encrypted memory arrays using highly parallel merge sort engines. *Cryptosorter* loads a large number of partially ordered lists in a streaming fashion and then merges these lists within the fabric using a high-radix sort tree. *Cryptosorter* is throughput-oriented and can be scaled to consume almost any amount of bandwidth. Since the lists to be sorted are random, the access pattern of *cryptosorter* is also somewhat random. The merge operation and, therefore, the memory access behavior of *cryptosorter* is related to sparse matrix algebra [18], making this workload broadly representative of that class of algorithms.

Cryptosorter itself has a parametric memory system and can instantiate several parallel, banked memory interfaces to improve memory bandwidth. This approach works well for small numbers of sorting engines and banks, but if scaled to an extreme, results in large memory network queuing delays and degraded overall system

Table 1: FPGA resource utilization for memory system components.

Primitive	Slice Registers	Slice LUTS	18K-bit BRAM
Memory Ringstop	876	945	0
Memory Interleaver	1575	1766	0
Unified Central Cache	14499	16513	18
Single Central Cache	13195	15376	18
DRAM Controller	8525	13661	0
Private Memory Client	1660	2010	4
Coherent Memory Client	2985	5721	7
Coherence Controller	6795	7658	19

Table 2: FPGA resource utilization for baseline and best performing memory configurations. In general, our optimizations increase utilization by about 20,000 slices and registers over the baseline. This represents 5.27% of LUTs and 2.44% of registers on the VC709.

Benchmark		Slice Registers	Slice LUTS	18K-bit BRAM
Memperf	Baseline	62317	80722	162
	Optimized	84166	105308	184
Cryptosorter (4 sorters)	Baseline	99284	137314	304
	Optimized	110116	146592	326
Heat (8-bit Data)	Baseline	157361	229276	243
	Optimized	189684	264881	284
Filter	Baseline	158774	185742	457
	Optimized	178039	207333	475
Average Utilization Increase		21067	22765	25.75
VC709 Area (%)		2.44%	5.27%	0.88%

performance. We examine two configurations: a baseline configuration with a single private memory and a configuration with two memory interfaces, which we refer to as *banked*.

Filter: An HLS kernel that implements a filtering algorithm for K-means clustering [19]. K-means clustering partitions a data set of points into K clusters, such that each point belongs to the cluster with the nearest mean. *Filter* first builds a binary tree structure from the input data set and then traverses the tree in several iterations. Our implementation splits the tree into eight independently-processed sub-trees. Each partition tracks its tree traversal using a stack and maintains several sets of candidates for the best cluster centers. *Filter* uses 24 private memories: eight each for the sub-trees, stacks, and candidate center sets. Unlike the other applications, *Filter's* performance is sensitive to the latency of memory read responses. The workload chases data-dependent pointers and thus has limited ability to produce multiple, parallel memory requests.

6.1 Basic Memory Behavior

To build intuition about the behavior of our optimized memory systems, we benchmark three memory system implementations – a baseline implementation and two different interleaved implementations – using a memory performance kernel that varies both the working set size and reference locality (see Figure 8). In regions of high locality, when the working set is small, all three implementations have similar performance, since there are few misses to the backing memory system. As locality decreases and the number of accesses to the backing memory increases, our memory-interleaved implementations begin to outperform the baseline implementation. When all accesses are serviced in the central caches, our interleaved memory subsystems outperform the baseline throughput by 40% due to the availability of bandwidth from both DRAM controllers.

Our direct address interleaving mechanism routes requests based on a granularity related to the central cache line size. For *memperf* strides that are multiples of this granularity, our direct scheme will route all requests to a single memory controller, reverting to baseline performance. To combat this case, we introduce address hashing which recovers most of the DRAM bandwidth by evenly balancing the interleaving.

6.2 Area Consumption

Table 1 describes the area requirements of various components of the LEAP memory hierarchy. We consider two central cache controller implementations: the unified cache controller, which services two DRAM banks, and the single cache controller, which services a single DRAM. Managing a second DRAM bank marginally increases the area utilization of the cache controller, due to the increasing width of buses within the controller.

Within the memory system, the chief consumers of area are

DRAM controllers and central cache controllers. Private and coherent memory clients require much fewer resources than the lower levels of the memory hierarchy. For most applications, the chief cost of implementing our bandwidth partitioning scheme is the introduction of a second central cache controller. Considered at the chip level, this area represents only 3.6% of the overall area of the VC709, which we believe is a small price to pay for the performance gains we will describe in subsequent sections.

The chief overhead of our intelligent network synthesis is the introduction into the memory network of new ringstops. In the case where we simply assign memory clients to different memory networks without interleaving, no new hardware is introduced. Memory network ringstops that are capable of address interleaving, shown in Figure 6, are more than twice the cost of baseline ringstops, since interleaved ringstops must communicate with two or more controller networks. However, the cost of ringstops, and of the network in general, is dwarfed by the cost of implementing the other elements of the memory system: memory controllers and caches.

Table 2 shows the area utilization of baseline and best-performing implementations of each of our benchmarks. As expected, LMC optimization increases the area of each benchmark by approximately the area of a single cache controller. The largest increase occurs in the *heat* benchmark. In addition to a second central cache controller, the optimal instance of *heat* also includes a second coherence controller. However, the average increase in utilization is small relative to the size of the VC709: LUT utilization increases by 5.3% of the full VC709 while register utilization increases by 2.4%.

6.3 Randomized Partitioning

As a baseline for LMC optimization, we examine a random partitioning algorithm, in which memory clients are allocated to memory controllers in a randomized fashion. This balances the number of clients accessing each board-level memory, but is otherwise suboptimal. Figures 9, 10, and 11 show the relative performance of three benchmarks under randomized allocation. In general, random allocation is successful in improving program performance, especially for symmetric applications like *cryptosorter*. However, for throughput-oriented applications with asymmetric memory clients like *heat*, random partitioning gives only limited performance gains.

Like *heat*, *filter* also features asymmetric memory clients. However, random allocation actually performs slightly *better* than more sophisticated allocation schemes. This is because *filter* can sustain only a few outstanding requests per memory client, and is therefore less sensitive to bandwidth balancing. *Filter* is, however, extremely sensitive to latency. Random allocation both halves and balances

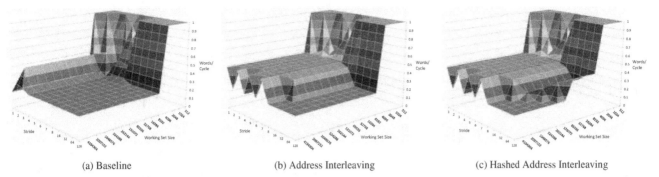

(a) Baseline   (b) Address Interleaving   (c) Hashed Address Interleaving

Figure 8: Performance of various LEAP memory systems. Performance is divided into two regions for each configuration. In the high-locality region, throughput is one word per cycle. In the low-locality region, performance is constrained to the bandwidth of the backing memory system. Our interleaving techniques nearly double the bandwidth over the baseline. Of note is the small region of increased bandwidth in the baseline memory system, which is due to the FPGA-side on-chip caching of DRAM lines.

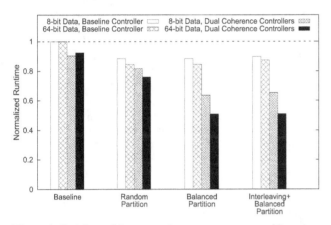

Figure 9: Runtime of *heat* on a 1-mega-entry array with various memory network configurations, normalized to the baseline implementations. *Heat* achieves the highest performance level when coherent and private cache network optimizations are composed.

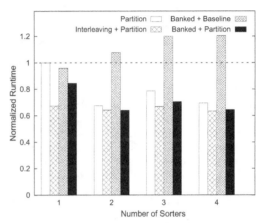

Figure 10: Runtime of *cryptosorter* on 256 kilo-entry lists with various memory network configurations, normalized to the baseline implementations. Generally, *cryptosorter* benefits from additional memory bandwidth. Banked versions of *cryptosorter* add latency and promulgate queuing delay in the memory network, lowering performance for large numbers of sorters.

memory network latency relative to the baseline, and, as a result, improves the performance of *filter* by about 15%.

6.4 Load-balanced Partitioning

The chief weakness of random partitioning is that it can sometimes oversubscribe the bandwidth of a single memory interface, especially when the memory clients are asymmetric in their memory bandwidth utilization. To further improve the system performance, we introduce load balancing. Load-balanced partitioning solves the problems of bandwidth imbalance by spreading memory accesses evenly across all board-level caches. *Heat*, which obtained some performance gains with random partitioning, obtains another 20% performance gain with load balancing, since heavily-loaded clients are evenly spread across the two board-level memories of the VC709. Load balancing naturally preserves the performance of symmetric applications like *cryptosorter*.

Load balancing evens out bandwidth, but ignores latency: low-bandwidth memory clients may all be assigned to the same network. In the case of *filter*, the memory network latencies are slightly imbalanced due to bandwidth balancing, which results in a small performance degradation compared to random partitioning.

6.5 Private Memory Address Interleaving

Load-balanced partitioning provides large performance gains for most of our benchmark cases. However, load balancing can result in

small bandwidth imbalances if the bandwidth characteristics of a particular workload are uneven, or if the number of memory clients is relatively prime to the number of board-level memories. This bandwidth imbalance can lead to suboptimal performance. For example, in Figure 10, a three-sorter instantiation of *cryptosorter* experiences some benefit under load-balancing, but achieves less of a performance gain than either the two or four sorter case. Two of the sorters in the three sorter case must share a single controller. If we introduce memory interleaving, the odd controller's accesses can be spread across both controllers equally, leading to further performance gains. Similarly, applications like *memperf* or a single-sorter *cryptosorter*, which have only one client, can benefit from multiple controllers when using our interleaving approach.

Throughput-oriented applications generally benefit, or at least maintain load-balanced performance, with address interleaving. However, for latency-oriented applications, like *filter*, the extra cycles of latency added to route requests between memory networks result in a performance degradation, even as compared to our baseline implementation. This is the only case which we found in one of our optimizations failed to outperform the baseline, and suggests that care must be taken by the compiler when applying network optimizations to latency-oriented applications.

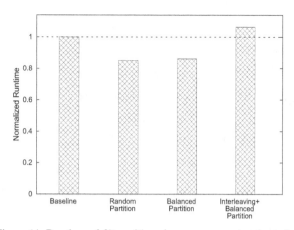

Figure 11: Runtime of *filter* with various memory network configurations, normalized to the baseline. *Filter* is sensitive to latency and thus benefits from random and load-balanced partitioning both of which reduce memory latency.

6.6 Coherent Cache Network Partitioning

Since LEAP coherent memories make use of private memories for intermediate data storage, they can take advantage of our bandwidth allocation and interleaving techniques in addition to our shared-memory-specific optimization. Figure 9 examines the *heat* benchmark under a variety of optimization scenarios.

Because most memory clients in *heat* are LEAP coherent memories, only the coherence controller in *heat* can utilize our private memory network optimizations. As a result, the performance gains for *heat* under our private memory optimizations are limited to about 12% in the best, load-balanced configuration.

Memory interleaving of the coherence domain at the coherence controller level provides a similar performance gain to load balancing, around 10%. However, because coherence controllers use private memory clients, we can compose the coherent memory interleaving technique with private memory optimizations. This composition of optimizations yields a performance gain of 49% for the 64-bit version of the *heat* benchmark and a 36% gain for the 8-bit version. The composed performance gain is actually better than the sum of the individual optimizations. This occurs because coherent memory interleaving introduces new coherence controllers and, thereby, increases the number of private memory clients, improving the effectiveness of our private memory optimizations.

6.7 Multiple FPGAs

Looking forward to cloud deployments [25] comprised of networks of FPGAs, we examine what happens when we stretch our synthesized memory networks between FPGAs. LEAP's named channel semantic permits their implementation as either inter-FPGA or intra-FPGA channels, differing only in latency. The LEAP compiler thus enables programs located on one FPGA to take advantage of potentially unused resources located on a nearby FPGA by automatically constructing a network between the FPGAs. The results of this experiment are shown in Figure 12.

Since inter-FPGA networks add latency, we examine only the throughput-oriented benchmarks: *heat* and *cryptosorter*. On the VC707, which has one DRAM per FPGA, the performance when scaling to two VC707s approaches that of the dual-DRAM VC709 for *heat*. *Cryptosorter* enjoys even larger performance gains when deployed to dual VC707s, and even obtains slightly better performance than a single VC709, indicating that the bandwidth offered by the remote memory outweighs the latency cost of accessing the

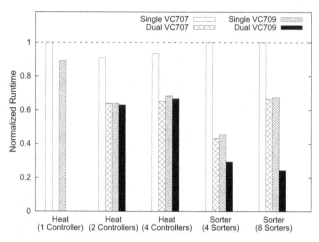

Figure 12: Normalized runtime of best-achieved performance solutions for 8-bit *heat* and *cryptosorter* with various platform configurations. *Heat* results are normalized to the runtime of the solution with a single coherence controller on a single VC707. The results of single-controller dual-FPGA solutions are not included because they simply add latency. *Cryptosorter* results are normalized to the runtime of the optimized single-VC707 solution.

remote memory. We note that it is unrealistic to expect designers to consider such complex systems without the assistance of a compiler to manage communication and resource allocation.

Scaling *cryptosorter* across two VC709s and to four memory banks yields another significant performance improvement. This is particularly pronounced for the eight sorter case, which shows superlinear performance gains: the baseline, single private memory controller case has a large memory network and suffers queuing delay. *Heat* also shows performance improvement when scaled to two FPGAs, but only about 2% over an optimized single VC709 implementation. Although incorporating multiple FPGAs exposes more memory resources, in the case of *heat*, increased bandwidth is counter-balanced by communication latency in the coherency networks. The effect of latency is also visible, to a lesser degree, in the slight performance degradation that occurs when we increase the number of interleaved coherence controllers. Our experience with the memory system of *heat* points to the need for better program analysis when scaling application-specific memory systems, especially if large performance cliffs, like inter-chip latency, are present in the scaled system.

Our results show, particularly for throughput-oriented applications, that bandwidth borrowing or sharing among adjacent, networked FPGAs can be a significant source of performance gains.

7. CONCLUSION

Modern FPGA boards include multiple memory resources to support the increased bandwidth demand of large numbers of computational resources. To alleviate the complexity of designing programs for such systems, we have demonstrated a resource- and application-aware compiler, the LEAP Memory Compiler, that can transparently optimize the memory system of a given application. Using runtime statistics, LMC automatically partitions the network that connects user-specified memory interfaces to board-level memory resources, simultaneously increasing the memory bandwidth and reducing memory latency. We target several platforms wherein multiple on-board memory resources are available, and demonstrate that LMC produces significant performance gains.

To optimize private memory interfaces, we balance the total traffic on each of several partitioned memory networks so that asymmetric memory clients can efficiently share the memory bandwidth. For memory clients that consume large amounts of bandwidth, a compiler-synthesized memory interleaver may be added to partition a single client's address space into multiple disjoint regions. A similar memory interleaving technique is also applied to shared memory interfaces. We also construct distributed coherence controllers to relieve network contention and introduce hierarchical coherence rings to improve the latency of coherent cache networks. Our evaluation shows that the compiler-synthesized cache network provides up to 49% performance gains to throughput-oriented workloads we studied and a 15% performance gain to the latency-oriented workload we studied, while increasing design area utilization by less than 6%. We also demonstrate that FPGA applications can make use of and benefit from remote memory resources accessible by an inter-FPGA network, and that throughput-oriented applications can derive significant performance gains as a result.

In this work, we show that different optimizations are helpful for different applications. One direction for future work is to explore more non-uniform workloads and conduct a more detailed run-time analysis on clients' bandwidth and latency demands to better direct compiler optimizations. For example, such analysis can be used to classify different memory clients within a single application as throughput-sensitive or latency-sensitive, enabling the compiler to synthesize a more complicated network topology. A latency-oriented client would be given a more direct connection to a memory controller, while a throughput-oriented client could be given some quality-of-service guarantees ensuring higher aggregate bandwidth. In addition, we also plan to explore dynamic partitioning for memory clients whose memory demands change over time or between executions.

8. REFERENCES

[1] Achronix semiconductor corp. *http://www.achronix.com/*.

[2] Nallatech 510t FPGA accelerator. *http://www.nallatech.com/nallatech-510t-fpga-datacenter-acceleration/*.

[3] Vivado high-level synthesis. *http://www.xilinx.com/products/design-tools/vivado/integration/esl-design.html*.

[4] M. Adler, K. Fleming, A. Parashar, M. Pellauer, and J. Emer. LEAP Scratchpads: Automatic memory and cache management for reconfigurable logic. In *FPGA*, 2011.

[5] A. Canis, J. Choi, M. Aldham, V. Zhang, A. Kammoona, T. Czajkowski, S. D. Brown, and J. H. Anderson. LegUp: An open-source high-level synthesis tool for FPGA-based processor/accelerator systems. *ACM Transactions on Embedded Computing Systems (TECS)*, 13(2):24, 2013.

[6] J. Choi, K. Nam, A. Canis, J. Anderson, S. Brown, and T. Czajkowski. Impact of cache architecture and interface on performance and area of FPGA-based processor/parallel-accelerator systems. In *FCCM*, 2012.

[7] E. S. Chung, J. C. Hoe, and K. Mai. CoRAM: An in-fabric memory abstraction for FPGA-based computing. In *FPGA*, 2011.

[8] J. Cong, B. Liu, S. Neuendorffer, J. Noguera, K. Vissers, and Z. Zhang. High-level synthesis for FPGAs: From prototyping to deployment. *IEEE Transactions on Computer-Aided Design of Integrated Circuits and Systems*, 30(4):473–491, 2011.

[9] G. Dessouky, M. Klaiber, D. Bailey, and S. Simon. Adaptive dynamic on-chip memory management for FPGA-based reconfigurable architectures. In *FPL*, 2014.

[10] K. Farkas, Z. Vranesic, and M. Stumm. Cache consistency in hierarchical-ring-based multiprocessors. In *IEEE Conference on Supercomputing*, 1992.

[11] K. Fleming, M. Adler, M. Pellauer, A. Parashar, Arvind, and J. S. Emer. Leveraging latency-insensitivity to ease multiple FPGA design. In *FPGA*, 2012.

[12] K. Fleming, M. King, M. C. Ng, A. Khan, and M. Vijayaraghavan. High-throughput pipelined mergesort. In *MEMOCODE*, 2008.

[13] K. Fleming, H. Yang, M. Adler, and J. Emer. The LEAP FPGA operating system. In *FPL*, 2014.

[14] K. E. Fleming. *Scalable Reconfigurable Computation Leveraging Latency Insensitive Channels*. PhD thesis, MIT, Cambridge, MA, 2012.

[15] M. Galles and E. Williams. Performance optimizations, implementation, and verification of the SGI Challenge multiprocessor. In *Hawaii International Conference on System Sciences*, 1994.

[16] D. Göhringer, L. Meder, M. Hübner, and J. Becker. Adaptive multi-client network-on-chip memory. In *ReConFig*, 2011.

[17] R. L. Graham. Bounds on multiprocessing timing anomalies. *SIAM Journal on Applied Mathematics*, 17(2):416–429, 1969.

[18] F. G. Gustavson. Two fast algorithms for sparse matrices: Multiplication and permuted transposition. *ACM Transactions on Mathematical Software (TOMS)*, 4(3):250–269, 1978.

[19] T. Kanungo, D. M. Mount, N. S. Netanyahu, C. D. Piatko, R. Silverman, and A. Y. Wu. An efficient k-means clustering algorithm: Analysis and implementation. *IEEE Transactions on Pattern Analysis and Machine Intelligence*, 24(7):881–892, 2002.

[20] R. Kirchgessner, G. Stitt, A. George, and H. Lam. VirtualRC: a virtual FPGA platform for applications and tools portability. In *FPGA*, 2012.

[21] H. Lange, T. Wink, and A. Koch. MARC II: A parametrized speculative multi-ported memory subsystem for reconfigurable computers. In *DATE*, 2011.

[22] E. Matthews, N. C. Doyle, and L. Shannon. Design space exploration of L1 data caches for FPGA-based multiprocessor systems. In *FPGA*, 2015.

[23] E. Matthews, L. Shannon, and A. Fedorova. Polyblaze: From one to many bringing the Microblaze into the multicore era with Linux SMP support. In *FPL*, 2012.

[24] V. Mirian and P. Chow. FCache: A system for cache coherent processing on FPGAs. In *FPGA*, 2012.

[25] A. Putnam, A. M. Caulfield, E. S. Chung, D. Chiou, K. Constantinides, J. Demme, H. Esmaeilzadeh, J. Fowers, G. P. Gopal, J. Gray, et al. A reconfigurable fabric for accelerating large-scale datacenter services. In *International Symposium on Computer Architecture (ISCA)*, 2014.

[26] J. Villarreal, A. Park, W. Najjar, and R. Halstead. Designing modular hardware accelerators in C with ROCCC 2.0. In *FCCM*, 2010.

[27] F. Winterstein, S. Bayliss, and G. A. Constantinides. Separation logic-assisted code transformations for efficient high-level synthesis. In *FCCM*, 2014.

[28] F. Winterstein, K. Fleming, H. Yang, S. Bayliss, and G. A. Constantinides. MATCHUP: memory abstractions for heap manipulating programs. In *FPGA*, 2015.

[29] H. Yang, K. Fleming, M. Adler, and J. Emer. LEAP shared memories: Automating the construction of FPGA coherent memories. In *FCCM*, 2014.

Efficient Memory Partitioning for Parallel Data Access via Data Reuse

Jincheng Su[1], Fan Yang[1*], Xuan Zeng[1] and Dian Zhou[1,2*]
[1]State Key Lab of ASIC & System, Microelectronics Dept., Fudan University, China
[2]Department of Electrical Engineering, University of Texas at Dallas, TX

ABSTRACT

In this paper, we propose an efficient memory partitioning algorithm for parallel data access via data reuse. We found that for most of the applications in image and video processing, a large amount of data can be reused among different iterations in a loop nest. Motivated by this observation, we propose to cache these reusable data by on-chip registers. The on-chip registers used to cache the re-fetched data can be organized as chains of registers. The non-reusable data are then partitioned into several memory banks by a memory partition algorithm. We revise the existing padding method to cover cases occurring frequently in our method that some components of partition vector are zeros. Experimental results have demonstrated that compared with the state-of-the-art algorithms the proposed method can reduce the required number of memory banks by 59.8% on average. The corresponding resources for bank mapping is also significantly reduced. The number of LUTs is reduced by 78.6%. The number of Flip-Flops is reduced by 66.8%. The number of DSP48Es is reduced by 41.7%. Moreover, the storage overheads of the proposed method are zeros for most of the widely used access patterns in image filtering.

Keywords

high-level synthesis; memory partition; data reuse

1. INTRODUCTION

High-level Synthesis (HLS) becomes more and more popular for complex digital system design. By raising the design abstraction level from RTL to a higher level, HLS is promising to reduce the design and verification efforts and the opportunities of error. It also provides high-quality results close to manual RTL design [1]. The ever-increasing gap between computation system and memory system is one of the most important issues in the area of digital design [2]. This problem tends to be even worse for high-level synthesis,

*Corresponding authors: {yangfan, zhoud}@fudan.edu.cn.

FPGA'16,February 21–23, 2016, Monterey, CA, USA.
© 2016 ACM. ISBN 978-1-4503-3856-1/16/02 ...$15.00.
DOI: http://dx.doi.org/10.1145/2847263.2847264

since it is hard to control the hierarchy and architecture of the circuit when we switch to a higher abstraction level.

In the areas of image/video processing and scientific computing, the parallel computation and pipeline technologies are extensively used. How to meet the requirement of large amount of parallel data accesses with limited number of on-chip memory ports is a major challenge [3]. Duplicating the data to be accessed to multiple copies is a straightforward way to meet the throughput requirements [4]. However, it may result in a significant storage and power overhead as well as the notorious memory coherency problem.

Memory partitioning is an effective way to support parallel data access. It partitions the original memory array into multiple banks. Each bank holds a portion of the original data and supply limited memory ports for data access. As a result, it is possible to access the multiple data elements in parallel by memory partition. Compared with the duplicating method, the overhead of memory partitioning is significantly reduced. In [5], an automatic memory partitioning flow via data structure partitioning is proposed to support parallel access to memory. The flow first detects Linear Memory access Patterns (LMP) by memory profiling and data structure decomposition. The LMP allocation problem is then formulated as a graph-coloring problem. In [6], an automatic partition strategy based on scheduling information is proposed to improve the throughput and reduce the energy consumption. This strategy is extended in [7] as the Automated Memory Optimization (AMO) flow to support memory references with modulo operations. It caches the reusable off-chip data between consecutive iterations of a loop by on-chip SRAM. The memory partition scheme is designed to partition the on-chip SRAM into multiple banks to support parallel access. In [8], a mixed memory partitioning and scheduling algorithm is proposed. It can generate a valid partition scheme for arbitrary affine memory inputs.

The aforementioned partitioning strategies [6–8] are mainly designed for one-dimensional arrays or flattened multidimensional arrays. In [9], a Linear Transformation-Based (LTB) method is proposed to support multidimensional array partitioning. However, it is limited to cyclic partitioning. A Generalized Memory Partitioning (GMP) algorithm is proposed in [10] to support both cyclic and block-cyclic partitioning using the polyhedral model. A constructive algorithm is proposed in [11]. It is very fast but fails to find the optimal bank-mapping scheme in some cases.

Data reuse technique is widely used to improve data access throughput and reduce storage overhead by caching the off-chip data in on-chip SRAMs [12–14]. In [12], a data reuse analysis technique for scratch-pad memory management is proposed to reduce energy consumption while improve system performance. A data reuse approach based on loop transformation is proposed in [14] to reduce the on-chip buffer size where a Data Reuse Graph (DRG) is used to represent the data reuse candidates. The work in [13] formulates a data reuse computation problem to promote all the off-chip data referenced in a loop level to on-chip SRAMs. Nevertheless, all of the existing data reuse techniques focus on caching the off-chip data by on-chip SRAMs.

In this paper, we propose to employ the on-chip registers to cache the SRAM data. In most of the applications such as image and video processing, a large amount of data can be reused among different iterations. We propose a memory partitioning algorithm based on data reuse to support simultaneous affine memory references to multidimensional array. The re-fetched data among iterations are cached by on-chip registers. The non-reusable data referenced in each iteration are then partitioned into several banks by a memory partitioning algorithm. The on-chip registers used to cache the re-fetched data can be organized as chains of registers. With the proposed method, the number of banks and the required hardware resources are significantly reduced while the performance is slightly improved.

The main contributions of our works are:

1. We propose to use the on-chip registers to cache the SRAM data so that the data access throughput can be improved and the storage overhead can be reduced. Previous work only consider to cache the reusable off-chip data by SRAMs.

2. We propose to organize the on-chip registers as register chains to cache the reusable data without extra control logic.

3. We revise the padding method proposed in [10] to cover cases occurring frequently in our method that some components of partition vector are zeros. With the revised padding method, the storage overheads can be reduced to zeros for most of the widely used access patterns in image filtering.

The rest of this paper is organized as follows. We provide a motivational example in Section 2. The memory partitioning problem is formulated in Section 3. In Section 4, we discuss the data reuse strategy following by the memory partitioning strategy discussed in Section 5. Experimental setup and results comparison are given in Section 6. Finally, we give the conclusions in Section 7.

2. MOTIVATIONAL EXAMPLE

We take the 3×3 image convolution kernel, PREWITT, which is an operator widely used for edge detection [15], as our motivational example. Its edge detection code for a 1920×1080 gray-scale image is shown in Fig. 1. The data access pattern is shown in Fig. 2(a). The access pattern can be described by a set of offsets to the top left corner of the access pattern. For the access pattern shown in Fig. 2(a), it can be described as

$$\{(0,0)^T, \quad (0,1)^T, \quad (0,2)^T,$$
$$(1,0)^T, \qquad\qquad (1,2)^T,$$
$$(2,0)^T, \quad (2,1)^T, \quad (2,2)^T\}.$$

```
1:   define A[1920][1080], Z[1920][1080]
2:   for (i₀ = 0; i₀ < 1918; i₀++)
     {
3:       for(i₁ = 0; i₁ < 1078; i₁++)
         {
4:           Z[i₀+1][i₁+1] = foo( A[i₀][i₁], A[i₀][i₁+1], A[i₀][i₁+2], A[i₀+1][i₁],
                 A[i₀+1][i₁+2], A[i₀+2][i₁], A[i₀+2][i₁+1], A[i₀+2][i₁+2])
         }
     }
```

Figure 1: Pseudo-code for edge detection with PREWITT.

As the iteration continues, references to the memory array can be described by a vector $\vec{s} = \lambda(0,1)^T$ plus the offsets, where λ represents the number of iterations.

It is natural to store all the data in memory and then fetch the necessary data elements one by one, which would take 8 clock cycles for one iteration. However, we can use the technique of pipelining to parallelize the execution of successive inner loop iterations to efficiently accelerate the computation. For simplicity, we assume that the loop initiation interval (II) is targeted to be 1, which means we have to access all the 8 data elements in one cycle. The common way to solve this problem is to partition the original memory array into multiple banks.

Memory partitioning methods in previous works typically assign each data element referenced in a pattern to a distinctive memory bank to allow simultaneous accesses and therefore take the number of memory references in a pattern as the optimal bank number for partitioning. For the access pattern of 3×3 PREWITT kernel shown in Fig. 2(a), solutions of works in [9–11] all partition the memory array into 9 banks. However, when it comes to kernels with larger size such as 7×7, 9×9 or larger, partitioning each memory reference in a same pattern to a distinctive memory bank becomes unrealistic because it would take too many banks and thus a large resource overhead. Moreover, more memory banks means larger multiplexers and longer critical path, which would severely degrade the performance.

We notice that for most of the kernels in image filtering, there are plenty of opportunities for data reuse among iterations. In our motivational example, there are 4 re-fetched data elements between the first and the second iterations as the gray dots inside the dashed boxes shown in Fig. 2(b). If we hold these 4 elements with registers, only 4 data elements are needed to be accessed at each cycle. Fig. 2(c) shows that there are 3 re-fetched elements between the first and the third iterations. If we hold these elements with registers as well, we could further reduce the elements needed to be accessed at each cycle to 3.

Our work exploits all the reuse in a given access pattern by reorganizing all the references as a set of data reuse chains. The last reference of every reuse chain is combined together as a new access pattern. Memory partitioning is then applied to this new pattern. Take the pattern in Fig. 2(a) as an example. Three reuse chains are constructed as shown in Fig. 2(d): $(0,0)^T \leftarrow (0,1)^T \leftarrow (0,2)^T$, $(1,0)^T \leftarrow (1,2)^T$ and $(2,0)^T \leftarrow (2,1)^T \leftarrow (2,2)^T$. The arrow pointing from $(0,1)^T$ to $(0,0)^T$ means that the data referenced as $(0,1)^T + \lambda(0,1)^T$ in the λ-th iteration will be reused as the reference $(0,0)^T + (\lambda+1)(0,1)^T$ in the $(\lambda+1)$-th

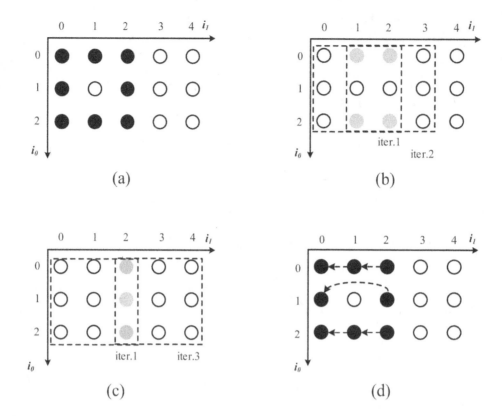

Figure 2: (a) Access pattern of PREWITT kernel, (b) Data reuse between consecutive iterations, (c) Data reuse between the first and the third iterations, (d) Data reuse chains.

iteration. The arrow pointing from $(1,2)^T$ to $(1,0)^T$ means that the data referenced as $(1,0)^T + \lambda(0,1)^T$ in the λ-th iteration will be reused as $(1,2)^T + (\lambda + 2)(0,1)^T$ in the $(\lambda + 2)$-th iteration. As FPGA devices usually own a large amount of Flip-Flops, we use FIFOs consisting of chains of registers to hold the reusable data. Two stage of registers are required for each of the three reuse chains. The last references $(0,2)^T$, $(1,2)^T$ and $(2,2)^T$ of the three chains constitute a new pattern to be partitioned. Since the size of the bank mapping problem now is quite small after caching the reusable data, we use an exhaustive enumeration algorithm similar to [9] to find the optimal bank mapping strategy.

For this motivational example, experimental results show that compared to the GMP method [10], our method reduces the bank number from 9 to 3, and saves up to 83.5% LUTs, 70.5% Flip-Flops, 0% DSP48Es while the performance is improved by 26.7%.

3. PROBLEM FORMULATION

In this section we will formulate the problem for memory partitioning. For simplicity, we assume the bandwidth of the memory is 1 and the initiation interval (II) is target to be 1. It is easy to extend our algorithm to the case where the bandwidth of the memory is B by combining B banks together.

In order to formulate the memory partition problem, we introduce the following definitions.

Definition 1. (**Iteration Space**) Given an l-deep loop nest with l index variables $i_0, i_1, ..., i_{l-1}$, the iteration space D is a l-dimension space bounded by lower and upper bounds of the loop indexes. The column vector $\vec{i} = (i_0, i_1, ..., i_{l-1})^T$ is called **iteration vector**.

Definition 2. (**Data Space**) The data space M is the data set accessed in all iterations in a loop nest. We use $w_0, w_1, ..., w_{d-1}$ to denote the sizes of dimensions of a d-dimensional array. The data space M also denotes the set of all references in a loop nest.

Definition 3. (**Affine Memory Reference** [16]) We say that a memory access in a loop is affine if the following conditions are satisfied.

1. The bounds of the loop are expressed as affine expressions of the surrounding loop variables and symbolic constants;

2. The index for each dimension of the array is also an affine expression of surrounding loop variables and symbolic constants.

Given a d-dimensional array referenced by a l-dimensional iteration vector $\vec{i}$, we describe each affine memory access $\vec{x}$ by a *coefficient matrix* A and a column vector $\vec{c}$:

$$\vec{x} = A \cdot \vec{i} + \vec{c},$$

where $A \in Z^{d \times l} = (\vec{a}_1, \vec{a}_2, ..., \vec{a}_{l-1})$, and $\vec{c} \in Z^l$.

Definition 4. (**Access Pattern**) An access pattern $P = \{\vec{p}_0, \vec{p}_1, \cdots, \vec{p}_{m-1}\}$ is used to describe simultaneous accesses to memory array in an iteration, where $\vec{p}_i = A_i\vec{i} + \vec{c}_i, i = 0, 1, ...m - 1$.

Definition 5. (**Affine Memory Partition** [9]) An affine memory partition of a memory array is to find a pair of functions $(B(\vec{x}), F(\vec{x}))$ where the function $B(\vec{x})$ is index of the bank the reference $\vec{x}$ is mapped to and $F(\vec{x})$ is its intra-bank offset.

A valid memory partition must guarantee that each distinctive reference $\vec{x}$ is mapped to a distinct bank or a unique offset inside a same bank, which formulates the following constraint

$$\forall \vec{x}_j, \vec{x}_k \in M, \vec{x}_j \neq \vec{x}_k, B(\vec{x}_j) \neq B(\vec{x}_k)||F(\vec{x}_j) \neq F(\vec{x}_k).$$

For an access pattern P, we must also ensure that more than one reference to the same bank is not allowed, which formulates another constraint

$$\forall \vec{i} \in D, \forall \vec{p}_j, \vec{p}_k \in P, \vec{p}_j \neq \vec{p}_k, B(\vec{p}_j) \neq B(\vec{p}_k).$$

Problem 1. (**Bank Mapping Problem** [9]) Given a l-deep loop nest with access pattern $P = \{\vec{p}_0, \vec{p}_1, \cdots, \vec{p}_m\}$ on a d-dimensional memory, find the minimum bank amount N which is called **partition factor**, such that:

Minimize N

Subject To

$$\forall \vec{x}_j, \vec{x}_k \in M, \vec{x}_j \neq \vec{x}_k, B(\vec{x}_j) \neq B(\vec{x}_k)||F(\vec{x}_j) \neq F(\vec{x}_k),$$
$$\forall \vec{i} \in D, \forall \vec{p}_j, \vec{p}_k \in P, \vec{p}_j \neq \vec{p}_k, B(\vec{p}_j) \neq B(\vec{p}_k).$$

4. DATA REUSE

In this paper, we focus on the access patterns where the references share the same *coefficient matrix* A [16]. It is based on the following considerations. Firstly, the access patterns sharing the same coefficient matrix can cover most of the patterns in the applications such as image/video processing. Secondly, if the references in the access pattern do not share the same coefficient matrix, the probability of data reuse is low. In such cases, we can use the traditional memory partition strategy such as [9] to handle these cases. We notice that in [11] they also assume that the references of the access patterns share the same coefficient matrix.

4.1 Preliminaries

We introduce the following definition for access patterns with the same coefficient matrix.

Definition 6. (**Access Pattern with the Same Coefficient Matrix**) An access pattern P_A with a coefficient matrix A can be described by a set of constant offset vectors $P_A = \left\{\vec{\delta}^{(0)}, \vec{\delta}^{(1)}, ..., \vec{\delta}^{(m-1)}\right\}$ where $\vec{\delta}^{(j)} = (\delta_0^{(j)}, \delta_1^{(j)}, ..., \delta_{l-1}^{(j)})^T$. $\delta_i^{(j)}$ is a non-negative integer for $\forall 0 \leq i \leq l - 1, 0 \leq j \leq m - 1$.

For example, the references of the access pattern of the 3×3 image convolution kernel PREWITT shown in Fig.

2(a) share the same coefficient matrix

$$A = \begin{bmatrix} 1 & 0 \\ 0 & 1 \end{bmatrix}.$$

As the iteration continues, the accesses to the memory array are defined by the vector $\vec{s} = A\vec{i}$ plus the constant offsets.

We introduce the concept of *Move* to define the advances of iteration vector $\vec{i}$ as iteration continues.

Definition 7. (**Move**) We use a column vector $\vec{e} \in \{0, 1\}^l$ called *increment direction* and a diagonal matrix $\Lambda \in Z^{l \times l}$ called *increment matrix* to denote the direction and increment of iterations in a loop. We call their product $\Lambda\vec{e}$ a move.

Given a move $\Lambda\vec{e}$, the iteration vector $\vec{i}$ will increase by $\Lambda\vec{e}$ each iteration.

4.2 Data Reuse Among References

We first introduce the following theorem for two references sharing the same coefficient matrix A in an iteration.

Theorem 1. *Denote $\Lambda\vec{e}$ a move for iteration vector $\vec{i}$ of a loop nest. Given two different offsets $\vec{c}_j$ and $\vec{c}_k$, $\vec{c}_j \neq \vec{c}_k$ in an access pattern sharing the same coefficient matrix A, if $\vec{c}_j - \vec{c}_k = \lambda A\Lambda\vec{e}$ where λ is a non-negative integer, then the data element referenced by $\vec{c}_j$ can be reused as the data referenced by $\vec{c}_k$ after λ iterations.*

PROOF. Since

$$\vec{c}_j - \vec{c}_k = \lambda A\Lambda\vec{e},$$

we have

$$A\vec{i} + \vec{c}_j - (A\vec{i} + \vec{c}_k) = \lambda A\Lambda\vec{e}.$$

It is equivalent to

$$A\vec{i} + \vec{c}_j = A(\vec{i} + \lambda\Lambda\vec{e}) + \vec{c}_k.$$

$\square$

The element referenced by $\vec{c}_j$ is supposed to be reused as reference $\vec{c}_k$ after λ iterations. If all the iterations can finish in one clock cycle, then a FIFO consisting of λ-stage registers can be used to hold the data without any extra control logic. We define λ as *Reuse Distance* between the references c_j and c_k.

Example 1. A pattern with 5 references denoted by dark dots is shown in Fig. 4. The memory array is one-dimensional for simplicity. The coefficient matrix A and the increment matrix Λ reduce to constants which are both 1 in this example. The increment direction $\vec{e} = (1)^T$ which means the iteration variable i increase by 1 each iteration. For references $c_4 = 4$ and $c_7 = 7$, we have $c_7 - c_4 = 3$. Therefore, they can reuse the same data between the i-th and $(i + 3)$-th iterations and a 3-stage FIFO can be used to hold the reusable data.

We consider the more general cases. As shown in Fig. 3(a), we use a directed acyclic graph(DAG) similar to that in [17] to represent the data reuse in a specified access pattern. Each node c_i in the graph represents a reference to the array. The directed edge CC_{ij} weighted by the reuse distance RD_{ij} denotes the reuse relationship between the nodes c_i and c_j. Note that the reuse relationship is transitive. The DAG can

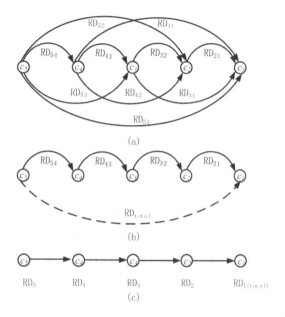

(a)

(b)

(c)

Figure 3: (a) Directed acyclic graph representing data reuse, (b) Simplified DAG, (c) Data reuse chain.

be simplified as the directed graph shown in Fig. 3(b) by pruning the redundant transitive edges and further simplified as the *data reuse chain* shown in Fig. 3(c) by storing the reuse distances in nodes. We give the definition of a data reuse chain as following.

Definition 8. (**Data Reuse Chain**) A data reuse chain is a set of references $\vec{c}_0, \vec{c}_1, ..., \vec{c}_{k-1}$ where the data referenced by $\vec{c}_j$ can be reused by reference $\vec{c}_{j-1}$ for $j = 1, 2, ..., k-1$ after λ_j iterations, where λ_j represents the reuse distance between $\vec{c}_{j-1}$ and $\vec{c}_j$.

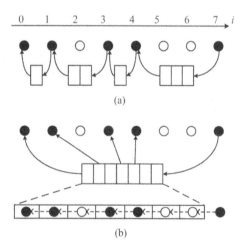

(a)

(b)

Figure 4: (a) Reuse between two references, (b) Data reuse chain.

An example of data reuse chain is shown in Fig. 4(b). Given a data reuse chain, we can always use a chain of FIFOs consisting of different stages of registers to hold the reused data as shown in Fig. 4(b) where the output of a FIFO is

connected to the input of another FIFO. We also call a chain of FIFOs a *register chain*.

One should note that the FIFOs which hold the reusable data should be initialized at the beginning of the loop. The initialization would take a few extra clock cycles. However, the initialization overhead is negligible compared with the large numbers of clock cycles required to process an image/video.

4.3 Constructing Reuse Chains

In this subsection, we propose a heuristic algorithm as shown in *Algorithm 1* to construct the reuse chains for a given pattern. The inputs to the algorithm is a pattern P, a move $\Lambda\vec{e}$ and a coefficient matrix A. For each reference $\vec{c}_i$ in P, if it cannot be inserted to any of the reuse chains in *ReuseChains* or the *ReuseChains* is empty, a new chain containing this reference will be created and inserted to *ReuseChains*. If reference $\vec{c}_i$ can be inserted to a certain reuse chain in *ReuseChains*, the function $insert(\vec{c}_i)$ will be used to insert it to an appropriate position in the reuse chain. We also store its corresponding reuse distance λ in the node. The total reuse distance is stored in the first node of each chain. The last elements of the reuse chains are inserted into the non-reusable pattern NRP for memory partitioning.

For each reference in a pattern, the algorithm traverses all the m references, and finds a proper position of a reuse chain for the reference to insert in. Therefore the complexity of this algorithm for a pattern with m references is $O(m^2)$.

Algorithm 1 Algorithm for Constructing Reuse Chains

Input: Pattern $P = \{\vec{c}_0, \vec{c}_1, \cdots, \vec{c}_{m-1}\}$, move $\Lambda\vec{e}$ and coefficient matrix A
Output: A list of reuse chains *ReuseChains*, and the non-reusable pattern NRP

1: **for** $\vec{c}_i$ in P **do**
2:     flag = false
3:     **for** each element *chain* in *ReuseChains* **do**
4:         $\vec{c}_t$ = last element of *chain*
5:         **if** $\vec{c}_i - \vec{c}_t = k\lambda\Lambda\vec{e}$ **then**
6:             *chain*.insert($\vec{c}_i$)
7:             flag = true
8:             break
9:         **end if**
10:     **end for**
11:     **if** !flag **then**
12:         Create a new reuse chain *chain*
13:         *chain*.push_back($\vec{c}_i$)
14:         Insert *chain* to the list of reuse chains *ReuseChains*
15:     **end if**
16: **end for**
17: **for** each element *chain* in *ReuseChains* **do**
18:     Insert the last element of *chain* to the non-reusable pattern NRP
19: **end for**

---

5. MEMORY PARTITIONING

By caching the reusable data by on-chip registers, we only need to apply memory partitioning to the non-reusable data elements referenced in an access pattern, of which the number is quite small. We can use exhaustive enumeration to find the optimal solution. Our bank mapping strategy is similar to the LTB based memory partition algorithm [9]. We revised the padding method in [10] to cover the case that some components of partition vector $\vec{\alpha}$ are zeros.

5.1 Bank Mapping

For a reference $\vec{x} = A\vec{i} + \vec{c}$ to a d-dimensional array in a l-deep loop nest, we first transform it with a row vector $\vec{\alpha} \in Z^d$ called *partition vector* : $x \to \vec{\alpha} \cdot \vec{x}$. The bank mapping function $B(\vec{x})$ can be expressed as

$$B(\vec{x}) = (\vec{\alpha} \cdot \vec{x})\%N,$$

where N is the number of banks.

Given an access pattern P consisting of m affine memory references, a valid bank mapping function should satisfy

$$\forall \vec{i} \in D, \forall \vec{p}_j, \vec{p}_k \in P, \vec{p}_j \neq \vec{p}_k, B(\vec{p}_j) \neq B(\vec{p}_k) \quad (1)$$

which is equivalent to

$$\nexists k \in Z, \quad s.t. \quad \vec{\alpha} \cdot (\vec{p}_j - \vec{p}_k) = kN. \quad (2)$$

By substituting $\vec{p}_j = A_j\vec{i} + \vec{c}_j$ and $\vec{p}_k = A_k\vec{i} + \vec{c}_k$ into the (2), we have

$$\nexists k \in Z, \quad s.t. \quad \vec{\alpha}(A_j - A_k)\vec{i} + \vec{\alpha} \cdot (\vec{c}_j - \vec{c}_k) = kN. \quad (3)$$

Equation (3) is a typical linear Diophantine equation. We can then apply the GCD (Greatest Common Divisor) testing to check if there is an integer solution to the equation.

Lemma 1. *The linear Diophantine equation [16] $q_0\beta_0 + q_1\beta_1 + ... + q_n\beta_n = r$ has an integer solution for $\beta_0, \beta_1, ..., \beta_n$, if and only if r is exactly divisible by $gcd(\beta_0, \beta_1, ...\beta_n)$.*

With this lemma, the following corollary holds.

Corollary 1. *Two references $\vec{x}_j = A_j \cdot \vec{i} + \vec{c}_j, \vec{x}_k = A_k \cdot \vec{i} + \vec{c}_k$, where $A_j = (\vec{a}_0, ..., \vec{a}_{l-1}), A_k = (\vec{b}_0, ..., \vec{b}_{l-1})$ are mapped to the same bank by a mapping function $B(\vec{x}) = (\vec{\alpha} \cdot \vec{x})\%N$, if and only if $\vec{\alpha} \cdot (\vec{c}_j - \vec{c}_k)$ is exactly divisible by $gcd(\vec{\alpha} \cdot (\vec{a}_0 - \vec{b}_0), ..., \vec{\alpha} \cdot (\vec{a}_{l-1} - \vec{b}_{l-1}), N)$.*

PROOF. Proof omitted as it is straightforward applying the lemma of linear Diophantine equation. □

Because we assume that the references in the access patterns share the same coefficient matrix A, Corollary 1 can be simplified. Two references $\vec{x}_j = A \cdot \vec{j} + \vec{c}_j$ and $\vec{x}_k = A \cdot \vec{k} + \vec{c}_k$ are mapped to the same bank by the mapping function $B(\vec{x}) = (\vec{\alpha} \cdot \vec{x})\%N$, if and only if $\vec{\alpha} \cdot (\vec{c}_j - \vec{c}_k)$ is exactly divisible by N.

The procedure to find the optimal $\vec{\alpha}$ is exhaustive enumeration in the space $\{\vec{\alpha} | 0 \leq \alpha_j \leq N, \text{ for } j = 0, \cdots, d-1\}$, where $\vec{\alpha} = (\alpha_0, \cdots, \alpha_{d-1})$. The enumeration of partition factor N begins from the number of non-reusable references of the access pattern. Note that the partition factor N and components of the partition vector $\vec{\alpha}$ are preferred to be a power of 2, because we can use a bit-shifting operation to implement the multiplications or divisions, and a bit-and operation to implement the modulo operation.

5.2 Intra-bank Offset Mapping

To simplify the procedure of calculating intra-bank offset and thus reduce the resource usage, proper number of data elements is padded on the highest dimension, i.e., the $(d-1)$-th dimension, such that the number of data elements in the

$(d-1)$-dimensional subspaces divides the bank number N exactly. With this method, each of the subspaces contains the same number of data elements for each bank and the intra-bank offset can be calculate as [10]

$$\left(\sum_{t=0}^{d-3} \prod_{j=t+1}^{d-2} w_j \times \lceil \frac{w_{d-1}}{N} \rceil \times x_t \right) + \lceil \frac{w_{d-1}}{N} \rceil \times x_{d-2} + \lfloor \frac{x_{d-1}}{N} \rfloor.$$

For a 3-dimensional array, it is calculated as

$$w_1 \times \lceil \frac{w_2}{N} \rceil \times x_0 + \lceil \frac{w_2}{N} \rceil \times x_1 + \lfloor \frac{x_2}{N} \rfloor.$$

With this mapping strategy, the storage overhead for padding is

$$(N \times \lceil w_{d-1}/N \rceil - w_{d-1}) \times \prod_{j=0}^{d-2} w_j,$$

where $d > 1$ since padding is not needed for one-dimensional array.

5.3 Revised Padding Method

However, the above padding method can be further improved if some components of partition vector $\vec{\alpha}$ are zeros. For the access patterns shown in Fig. 2(a), the optimal partition vector by our method is $\vec{\alpha} = (1, 0)$. The data elements in each row of the original array will be mapped to a single bank, respectively, as shown in Fig. 5. The gray dots represent the reused elements.

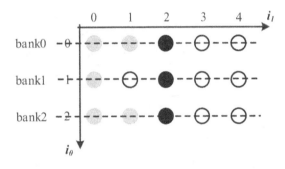

Figure 5: Mapping result for the case that $\vec{\alpha} = (1, 0)$.

We revised the padding method to improve the padding efficiency of the cases of this kind. For $\vec{\alpha} = (\alpha_0, \alpha_1, ..., \alpha_{d-1})$, we assume that $\alpha_0, \alpha_1, ..., \alpha_{k-1} \neq 0, \alpha_k = \alpha_{k+1} = ... = \alpha_{d-1} = 0$. This assumption is based on the technique of *loop permutation [16]*, which permutes the index variables in an iteration vector $\vec{i}$ to transform it to another form. No padding is needed for the dimensions from k to $d-1$, because the k-th to $(d-1)$-th components of the partition vector $\vec{\alpha}$ are zeros. Only the $(k-1)$-th dimension should be padded. Therefore, the intra-bank offset is calculated as

$$\left\{ \left(\sum_{t=0}^{k-3} \prod_{j=t+1}^{k-2} w_j \times \lceil \frac{w_{k-1}}{N} \rceil \times x_t \right) + \lceil \frac{w_{k-1}}{N} \rceil \times x_{k-2} + \lfloor \frac{x_{k-1}}{N} \rfloor \right\}$$

$$\times \prod_{j=k}^{d-1} w_j + \left\{ \left(\sum_{t=k}^{d-2} \prod_{j=t+1}^{d-1} w_j \times x_t \right) + x_{d-1} \right\}.$$

We call the first part enclosed by braces the *Padding Part*, and the second part the *Non-padding Part*. With this revised

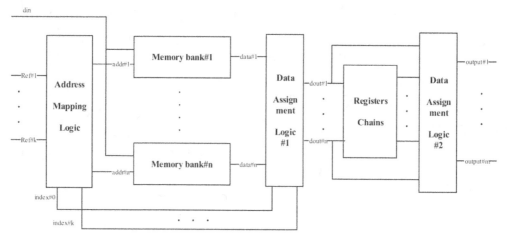

Note: k is the number of references to be mapped to banks, n is the number of banks, m is the number of all references in a pattern.

Figure 6: Top-level schematic of the memory system.

padding method, the storage overhead for padding is

$$(\lceil \frac{w_{k-1}}{N} \rceil \times N - w_{k-1}) \times \prod_{j=0}^{k-2} \prod_{j=k}^{d-1} w_j.$$

Note that if $k = 1$, the padding part reduces to $\lfloor \frac{x_0}{N} \rfloor$, which means that no padding is needed. Take the case in Fig. 2(a) as an example. In this example, $\vec{\alpha} = (1, 0)$. The intra-bank offset for reference $\vec{x} = (x_0, x_1)^T$ is calculated as $addr = \lfloor x0/N \rfloor * w_1 + x_1$ without padding. In fact, padding is not needed for most of the 2-dimensional access patterns commonly used by image filtering, especially for all the benchmarks used in previous works [9–11], since the partition vector $\vec{\alpha}$ is usually $(1, 0)$ applying our data reuse strategy.

6. EXPERIMENTAL RESULTS

6.1 Experimental Setup

The top-level schematic of the memory system supporting simultaneous accesses for experimental comparison is shown in Fig. 6, which is implemented in C++ code generated by our automatic memory partitioning algorithm. The set of non-reusable references to be mapped to banks is transformed by the Address Mapping Logic to a set of addresses to N banks. The data elements from those banks are then assigned to their corresponding references by the Data Assignment Logic 1. We examine each of the outputs of the Data Assignment Logic 1, and shift the data into a register chain if it can be reused. The outputs of the Data Assignment Logic 1 and the outputs of all the register chains are reorganized by Data Assignment Logic 2 to generate outputs corresponding to their references. For patterns with no reusable data, the parts of Register Chains and Data Assignment Logic 2 will not be generated and the schematic would be the same as that in [9, 11].

The generated code is then delivered to the Xillinx Vivado Design Suite 2014.4 [18] targeting the Virtex-7 VC707 Evaluation Platform [19] for high-level synthesis. The RTL output is then synthesised into gate-level netlists for resource

usage, storage overhead and performance analysis. We also implement the memory partitioning algorithms in [10,11] for comparison.

We select eight access patterns as shown in Fig. 7 from [10, 11] for resource (LUT, Flip-Flop and DSP48E) usage comparison. One should note that all the references of these access patterns share the same coefficient matrix. For storage overhead comparison, we choose five different image resolutions: SD (640× 480), HD (1280×720), FullHD (1920×1080), WQXGA (2560×1600) and 4K (3840×2160).

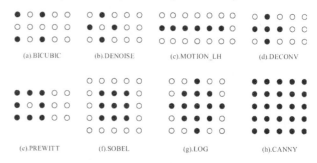

Figure 7: Eight access patterns for comparison.

6.2 Experimental Results and Comparison

For these access patterns, although the number of references can be up to 25, there are many reusable data elements among different iterations and the maximum number of references needed to be partitioned is only 5. Thus our automatic memory partitioning flow runs quite fast. For the largest test case CANNY, the GMP algorithm takes several seconds, our algorithm takes less than one second while the EMP [11] algorithm takes a constant time.

The experimental results of resource, including LUT, Flip-Flop and DSP usage, are presented in Table 1. In Table 1, FF_{total} is the total amount of Flip-Flops used by the memory system, FF_{addr} is the amount of Flip-Flops used by address mapping logic and data assignment logic. We observe that for all the test patterns, the resource usage of EMP is no less than that of GMP. The reason is that the EMP

Table 1: Experimental results and comparisons for overall resources

Benchmark	Access#	Method	Bank#	alpha	LUT	FF_{total}	FF_{addr}	DSP48E	CP
BICUBIC	4	GMP	5	(1,2)	1640	1217	1217	1	2.405
		EMP	5	(1,3)	1937	1387	1387	1	2.405
		ours	3	(1,0)	545	567	439	0	2.299
		Improvement	40%	-	66.8%	53.4%	63.9%	100%	4.4%
DENOISE	4	GMP	5	(1,2)	1667	1265	1265	2	2.401
		EMP	5	(1,3)	1964	1417	1417	2	2.401
		ours	3	(1,0)	826	783	719	2	2.306
		Improvement	40%	-	50.4%	38.1%	43.2%	0%	4.0%
DECONV	5	GMP	5	(1,2)	2143	1482	1482	2	2.441
		EMP	5	(1,3)	2507	1674	1674	2	2.441
		ours	3	(1,0)	628	488	424	2	2.299
		Improvement	40%	-	70.7%	67.1%	71.4%	0%	5.8%
MOTION_LH	6	GMP	6	(1,1)	1753	1397	1397	6	2.604
		EMP	6	(1,6)	1826	1477	1477	6	2.604
		ours	1	(1,0)	47	230	160	0	2.327
		Improvement	83.3%	-	97.4%	84.4%	95.3%	100%	10.6%
PREWITT	8	GMP	9	(1,3)	2966	2496	2496	2	3.138
		EMP	9	(1,3)	2966	2496	2496	2	3.138
		ours	3	(1,0)	490	736	544	2	2.299
		Improvement	66.7%	-	83.5%	70.5%	78.2%	0%	26.7%
SOBEL	9	GMP	9	(1,3)	3561	2723	2723	3	2.917
		EMP	9	(1,3)	3561	2723	2723	3	2.917
		ours	3	(1,0)	614	747	544	2	2.419
		Improvement	66.7%	-	86.2%	73.0%	80.0%	33.3%	21.2%
LOG	13	GMP	13	(1,8)	5550	4319	4319	8	2.438
		EMP	13	(1,5)	5606	4311	4311	8	2.438
		ours	5	(1,0)	1167	1502	1246	4	2.291
		Improvement	61.5%	-	79.0%	65.2%	71.2%	50%	6.0%
CANNY	25	GMP	25	(1,5)	20679	10427	10427	8	3.44
		EMP	25	(1,5)	20679	10427	10427	8	3.44
		ours	5	(1,0)	1160	1832	1192	4	2.291
		Improvement	80%	-	94.4%	82.4%	88.6%	50%	33.4%
Average Improvement			59.8%	-	78.6%	66.8%	74.0%	41.7%	14.0%

[1]FF_{total} is the total usage of Flip-Flops by the memory system
[2]FF_{addr} is the usage of Flip-Flops by the address mapping logic and data assignment logic
[3]Improvement is calculated over GMP

method takes a constructive solution to solve the memory partitioning problem and thus cannot always find the optimal solution. Therefore, we calculate our improvement over the GMP method.

Although we use registers to cache the reused data elements, it does not increase the usage of Flip-Flops. Instead, by using registers to hold the reused data elements, we can substantially reduce the usage of Flip-Flops. This is mainly due to the decrease in the number of memory banks. The address mapping logic is thus greatly simplified. Taking CANNY as an example, 640 Flip-Flops are required to hold the 20 reusable elements. However, with the number of memory banks reducing from 25 to 5, the total usage of Flip-Flops is reduced from 10427 to 1832. Experimental results with FF_{addr} show that we can reduce the amount of Flop-Flops used by address mapping logic and data assignment by 74.0%. Experimental results of FF_{total} show that we can reduce the total amount of Flip-Flops by 66.8%.

Improvement of DENOISE is the least one since only one data element can be reused. However, we can still achieve an improvement of 50.4% in LUTs, 38.1% in Flip-Flops, 4.0% in clock period while use no more DSP48Es. It is because we save 2 memory banks and find a better partitioning solution. The best improvement is with MOTION_LH where we save up to 97.3% in LUTs, 83.5% in Flip-Flops and 10.6% in clock period while reduce the usage of DSP48Es from 6 to 0. This is because we have saved 5 out of 6 banks and use no address mapping logic. The average improvement over GMP shows that for the 8 selected patterns, we can reduce the amount of banks by 59.8%, the amount of LUTs by 75.6%, the amount of Flip-Flops by 64.5%, the amount of DSP48Es by 29.2% and the clock period by 13.1%. The average decrease in number of banks reflects that compared with previous works, there are more than half of the banks that can be reduced for most of the commonly used patterns.

Table 2 is the experimental results of storage overhead. It is calculated as the percentage of padding size compared

Table 2: Storage Overhead Comparisons.

benchmark	method	bank#	storage overhead				
			SD	HD	FullHD	WQXGA	4K
BICUBIC	GMP/EMP	5	0	0	0	0	0
	ours	3	0	0	0	0	0
	improvement		0	0	0	0	0
DENOISE	GMP/EMP	5	0	0	0	0	0
	ours	3	0	0	0	0	0
	improvement		0	0	0	0	0
DECONV	GMP/EMP	5	0	0	0	0	0
	ours	3	0	0	0	0	0
	improvement		0	0	0	0	0
MOTION_LH	GMP/EMP	6	0	0	0	0.125%	0
	ours	1	0	0	0	0	0
	improvement		0	0	0	100%	0
PREWTITT	GMP/EMP	8	1.25%	0	0	0.125%	0
	ours	3	0	0	0	0	0
	improvement		100%	0	0	100%	0
SOBEL	GMP/EMP	9	1.25%	0	0	0.125%	0
	ours	3	0	0	0	0	0
	improvement		100%	0	0	100%	0
LOG	GMP/EMP	13	0.208%	1.111%	1.111%	0.75%	0.423%
	ours	5	0	0	0	0	0
	improvement		100%	100%	100%	100%	100%
CANNY	GMP/EMP	13	4.167%	0.694%	1.852%	0	0.7%
	ours	5	0	0	0	0	0
	improvement		100%	100%	100%	0	100%
Average improvement			35%				

to the original array size. The storage overhead of GMP is the same as EMP. For benchmarks BICUBIC, DENOISE and DECONV, the storage overheads of GMP/EMP for the 5 different image resolutions are zero because w_{d-1} divides the partition factor $N = 5$ exactly. For other test cases, it seems that compared with the original array size, the storage overhead is very tiny. However, because the original array sizes are extremely large, the absolute storage overhead are remarkably large. Taking access pattern LOG as an example, 0.208% storage overhead of image size 640×480 means two 9kb memory blocks.

For the eight selected patterns, our average improvement of storage overhead on the 8 selected patterns over GMP/EMP is 35%. In fact, our algorithm takes no storage overhead for these patterns, because our work can find the optimal intra-bank offset for most of patterns and the padding is not required. Even for patterns where padding is needed, our solution can usually save up the storage overhead by

$$\frac{N_{GMP}\lceil w_{d-1}/N_{GMP}\rceil - N_{ours}\lceil w_{k-1}/N_{ours}\rceil \times \frac{w_{d-1}}{w_{k-1}}}{N_{GMP}\lceil w_{d-1}/N_{GMP}\rceil - w_{d-1}} \times 100\%$$

where N_{GMP} is the partition factor of the GMP method, N_{ours} is the partition factor of our method. $d-1, k-1$ are the corresponding padding dimensions.

7. CONCLUSIONS

In this paper, we developed an efficient algorithm for memory partition by caching the reusable data by on-chip registers. The non-reusable data are then partitioned into several banks by a memory partition algorithm. The on-chip regis-

ters used to cache the re-fetched data are organized as chains of registers. We also proposed a new padding method for the partition vectors with zero components. Experimental results demonstrated that compared to the GMP method our method can reduce the resource usage by 59.8% in the amount of banks, 75.6% in the amount of LUTs, 64.5% in the amount of Flip-Flops, 29.2% in the amount of DSP48Es with 13.1% performance improvement. Furthermore, with our proposed method, the storage overheads for all the 2-dimensional patterns employed in previous works are zero.

8. ACKNOWLEDGEMENT

This research work is supported partly by National Natural Science Foundation of China (NSFC) research project 61474026, 61274032, 61125401, 61376040, 91330201, 61574046 and 61574044, partly by the National Basic Research Program of China under the grant 2011CB309701, partly by the Recruitment Program of Global Experts (the Thousand Talents Plan), partly supported by Chen Guang project supported by Shanghai Municipal Education Commission and Shanghai Education Development Foundation, partly supported by Lam Research Inc. This work is also partially supported by NSF grant 1115556.

9. REFERENCES

[1] M. Fingeroff, *High-level synthesis blue book.* Xlibris, 2010.

[2] D. T. W. Bruce Jacob, Spencer W. Ng, *Memory Systems – Cache, DRAM, Disk.* Denise E.M. Penrose, 2008.

146

[3] Y. Tatsumi and H. Mattausch, "Fast quadratic increase of multiport-storage-cell area with port number," *Electronics Letters*, vol. 35, no. 25, pp. 2185–2187, 1999.

[4] Q. Liu, T. Todman, and W. Luk, "Combining optimizations in automated low power design," in *Proceedings of the Conference on Design, Automation and Test in Europe (DATE)*, 2010, pp. 1791–1796.

[5] Y. B. Asher and N. Rotem, "Automatic memory partitioning: increasing memory parallelism via data structure partitioning," in *Proceedings of the eighth IEEE/ACM/IFIP international conference on Hardware/software codesign and system synthesis*, 2010, pp. 155–162.

[6] J. Cong, W. Jiang, B. Liu, and Y. Zou, "Automatic memory partitioning and scheduling for throughput and power optimization," *ACM Transaction on Design Automation of Electronic Systems (TODAES)*, no. 16, 2011.

[7] Y. Wang, P. Zhang, X. Cheng, and J. Cong, "An integrated and automated memory optimization flow for FPGA behavioral synthesis," in *Asia and South Pacific Design Automation Conf.(ASP–DAC)*, 2012, pp. 257–262.

[8] P. Li, Y. Wang, P. Zhang, G. Luo, T.Wang, and J.Cong, "Memory paritioning and scheduling co-optimization in behavioral synthesis," in *IEEE/ACM International Conference on Computer-Aided Design(ICCAD)*, 2012, pp. 488–495.

[9] Y. Wang, P. Li, P. Zhang, C. Zhang, and J. Cong, "Memory partitioning for multidimensional arrays in high-level synthesis," in *Proceedings of the 50th Annual Design Automation Conference (DAC)*, 2013.

[10] Y. Wang, P. Li, and J. Cong, "Theory and algorithm for generalized memory partitioning in high-level synthesis," in *Proceedings of the 2014 ACM/SIGDA International Symposium on Field-Programmable Gate Arrays (FPGA)*, 2014.

[11] C. Meng, S. Yin, P. Ouyang, L. Liu, and S. Wei, "Efficient memory partitioning for parallel data access in multidimensional arrays," in *Proceedings of the 52th Annual Design Automation Conference (DAC)*, 2015.

[12] I. Issenin, E. Brockmeyer, M. Miranda, and N. Dutt, "A data reuse analysis technique for efficient scratch-pad memory management," in *ACM Trans. Des. Autom. Electron. Syst.*, 2007.

[13] L.-N. Pouchet, P. Zhang, P.Sadayappan, and J. Cong, "Polyhedral-based data reuse optimization for configurable computing," in *Proceedings of the 2013 ACM/SIGDA International Symposium on Field-Programmable Gate Arrays (FPGA)*, 2013.

[14] J. Cong, P. Zhang, and Y. Zou, "Optimizing memory hierarchy allocation with loop transformations for high-level synthesis," in *Proceedings of the 49th Annual Design Automation Conference (DAC)*, 2012.

[15] J. M. S. Prewitt, *Picture processing and psychopictorics*. Academic Press, 1970, ch. Object enhancement and extraction.

[16] M. S. Alfred V.Aho and J. D. Ravi Sethi, *Compilers: Principles, Techniques and Tools*. Pearson Education, 2007.

[17] J. Cong, H. Huang, C. Liu, and Y. Zou, "A reuse-aware prefetching scheme for scratchpad memory," in *Proceedings of the 48th Annual Design Automation Conference (DAC)*, 2011, pp. 960–965.

[18] [Online]. Available: http://www.xilinx.com/support/download/index.html/content/xilinx/en/downloadNav/vivado-design-tools/2014-4.html

[19] [Online]. Available: http://www.xilinx.com/products/boards-and-kits/ek-v7-vc707-g.html

Intel Acquires Altera:
How Will the World of FPGAs be Affected?

Derek Chiou (organizer)
Microsoft and The University of Texas
at Austin
derek@ece.utexas.edu

ABSTRACT

Intel's purchase of Altera is very likely to be the biggest single event in FPGA history and, therefore, have a profound impact on the FPGA world. This panel intends to explore the business and research opportunities that are potentially enabled and potentially squashed by the acquisition.

Questions that will be explored by the panel include:

- What will be the impact on FPGA applications? Clearly, there is the potential of much tighter integration of CPU and FPGA, but what applications and usage models does that really enable?

- What will be the impact on FPGA business?

- What will be the impact on the FPGA research community?

CCS Concepts

• **Hardware~Reconfigurable logic and FPGAs**

Keywords

FPGAs

FPGA'16, February 21-23, 2016, Monterey, CA, USA

ACM 978-1-4503-3856-1/16/02.

DOI: http://dx.doi.org/10.1145/2847263.2857658

PRFloor: An Automatic Floorplanner for Partially Reconfigurable FPGA Systems

Tuan D. A. Nguyen
National University of Singapore
Department of Electrical & Computer
Engineering, Faculty of Engineering
4 Engineering Drive 3, Singapore 117583
tuann@u.nus.edu

Akash Kumar
Technische Universität Dresden
Center for Advancing Electronics Dresden
(cfaed) Chair of Processor Design
Würzburger Str. 46, Dresden, Germany 01187
Akash.kumar@tu-dresden.de

ABSTRACT

Partial reconfiguration (PR) is gaining more attention from the research community because of its flexibility in dynamically changing some parts of the system at runtime. However, the current PR tools need the designer's involvement in manually specifying the shapes and locations for the PR regions (PRRs). It requires not only deep knowledge of the FPGA device, the system architecture, but also many trial-and-error attempts to find the best-possible floorplan. Therefore, many research works have been conducted to propose automatic floorplanners for PR systems. However, one of the most significant limitations of those works is that they only consider the PRRs and ignore all other static modules. In this paper, we propose a novel PR floorplanner called PRFloor. It takes into account all components in the system. The main ideas behind PRFloor are the unique *recursive pseudo-bipartitioning* heuristic using a new, simple, yet effective Nonlinear Integer Programming-based bipartitioner. The PRFloor performs very well in the experiments with various synthetic PR system setups with up to *130* modules, *24* PRRs and *85%* of the FPGA resource. The average maximum clock frequency obtained for the actual PR systems implemented using PRFloor is even *3%* higher than the similar systems without PR capability.

Keywords

partial reconfiguration; FPGA floorplan; bipartition; NLP

1. INTRODUCTION

Nowadays, the number of applications that must be incorporated into a single FPGA-based system is increasing rapidly which requires more hardware resources. One of the solutions is to increase the size of the chips. This is not an efficient or scalable solution because of the size and power consumption constraints. Consequently, dynamic partial reconfiguration [25] is gaining special interests from the research community. Nevertheless, it is not trivial to successfully im-

FPGA'16, February 21-23, 2016, Monterey, CA, USA

© 2016 ACM. ISBN 978-1-4503-3856-1/16/02. . . $15.00

DOI: http://dx.doi.org/10.1145/2847263.2847270

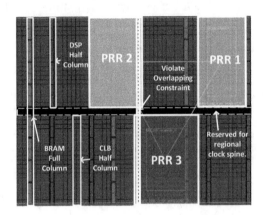

Figure 1: The resources in one clock region of Xilinx Virtex-6 XC6VLX240T. These are BRAM, DSP and CLB, distributed in a columnar fashion. There are 3 rectangular PRRs placed at different locations in the same clock region. The placement of PRR 2 and PRR 3 violates the PR constraint.

plement these kinds of system. One of the reasons is the limitation of the current PR-supported EDA tools, such as Xilinx PlanAhead and Vivado. The designers have to specify the shapes and locations (hereafter called *placements* for simplicity) for all PR regions (PRRs) manually. Moreover, to make a good floorplan, it is essential to plan the layouts of **all** modules in the system with respect to the connections between them and the resource requirements. This process requires expertise in FPGA architecture, the knowledge of the connections between components and many trial-and-error attempts to find the best possible floorplan. Additionally, since the PR systems are getting more complicated with hundreds of components [8,19], it is almost impossible to do the work by hand. Hence, having an automatic floorplanner for PR FPGA-based design is imperative.

Research on floorplanning for VLSI design has been underway since long time ago with many sophisticated advancements [13]. Some well-known methods introduced in [13] are Stockmeyer, Normalized Polish expression, sequence pair, recursive partitioning, etc. However, floorplanning in FPGA design has different challenges and restrictions, especially in state-of-the-art FPGAs. These devices have a variety of resources: Configuration Logic Block (CLB), Block RAM (BRAM), Digital Signal Processing (DSP), PCIe, GTX and so on. All of these resources are predefined, already placed and non-uniformly distributed on the FPGA fabric. They

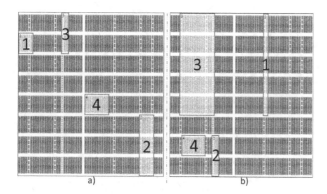

Figure 2: The floorplans given by the tool [20] at *floorplacer.necst.it*. The columns in blue, red and green are CLBs, BRAMs and DSPs, respectively. The weight costs for CLB, BRAM and DSP are 1, 12 and 60. The red boxes represent PRRs.

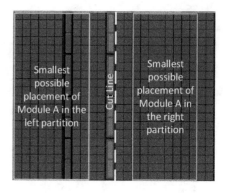

Figure 3: The two possible placements of Module A in two partitions. A requires 4 CLB columns which can be fully satisfied in the right partition. But in the left partition, the placement occupies an extra BRAM column. The bipartitioner may end up assigning A to the left partition because it does not consider the actual resources occupation.

are also arranged in a columnar-fashion as can be seen in Fig. 1. Thus, the aforementioned techniques cannot be applied directly to FPGA. Moreover, in FPGA-based PR systems, the following constraints must be satisfied. **(1)** There is at *most* one PRR in any column in one clock region [25] as shown in Fig. 1. **(2)** In Xilinx PlanAhead, the proxy logics [25] are used for the input/output signals to/from PRRs. Therefore, the number of CLBs along the edges of the PRRs should be large enough to avoid routing congestion and to enhance the timing of the design.

In fact, many research works have been conducted to propose such floorplanners [3, 6, 14, 15, 17, 20, 24]. But none of those considers the possible placements for all components in the system with different constraints for static modules and PRRs. They only analyze the connections between PRRs which, in some cases, may not have any direct link in the systems with Network-on-Chip (NoC) [8, 19]. Even worse, they overlook the resource requirements of the static modules in the system. It leads to the situation where there are not sufficient resources for static modules. These problems are illustrated in Fig. 2. In Fig. 2a, Region 1 and 2 are communicating indirectly via NoC. Therefore, it would be better if they are placed close to each other to facilitate the place and route (PnR) process in placing the NoC. In Fig. 2b, Region 3 requires only 50 CLBs, 40 BRAMs and 20 DSPs. However, the placement for that region occupies 40 DSPs. Consequently, it is not possible to implement static modules if they require 10 DSPs since there are only 8 blocks left. The authors in [3] were aware of this problem but they suggested treating static modules similar to PRRs which puts unnecessary PR constraints on them. Alternatively, the work described in [2] does floorplan both static modules and PRR but they only support one PRR. As a result, these floorplanners are only suitable to the systems with no or small number of static modules and PRRs.

Besides, one of the most widely used methods in VLSI floorplanning is recursive cut-size driven multilevel netlist bipartitioning [5, 13, 26]. It reduces the problem size through bipartitioning and finds the appropriate relative locations of the modules in the system. These methods are only applicable for *homogeneous* FPGA as contended in [16, 21]. Although [16, 21] and even [11] support multi-resource aware bipartitioning, they do not anticipate an important issue: the resources occupied by the placements of module in two

partitions may not be the same. It is because of the non-uniform distribution of FPGA resources as illustrated via an example in Fig. 3. Thus, estimating module resources based solely on the synthesized netlist is not accurate.

Contribution: In this work, all of the above issues are addressed by our novel floorplanner for PR systems, PRFloor. Our contribution is twofold.

- We propose a unique *recursive pseudo-bipartitioning* heuristics using a new, simple, yet effective Nonlinear Integer Programming (NLP) [12] bipartitioner. The NLP bipartitioner supports heterogeneous FPGA. Besides, the resources occupied by the modules in different partitions can be different.

- PRFloor finds the placements for PRRs in the system considering not only the connections between them but also between the static modules and the resources requirements of all modules.

The experiments are carried out using the set of PR systems proposed by [19] with up to *24* PRRs. The largest FPGA utilization is *85%*. The numbers of modules (including PRRs) in the experimental systems are from *99* to *130*. These systems are significantly larger than the experiments reported in most of the PR floorplanners in literature. The longest time taken by the PRFloor is less than *9* minutes for the systems with 24 PRRs. Interestingly, by using the PRFloor, the average maximum clock frequency obtained for the synthesizable PR systems is even *3%* higher than the comparable systems without PR capability. Given the fact that the PR systems usually have lower clock frequency than the similar static ones; this result clearly shows how effective our PRFloor is in producing high quality floorplans. The NLP-based bipartitioner also produces good results. It reduces the average cut-size by *15%* as compared to the state-of-the-art bipartitioner [11] in a set of random systems with up to *300* modules.

The remaining paper is organized as follows. The recent PR floorplanners are discussed in Section 2. The proposed algorithm is presented in Section 3, followed by experimental results in Section 4. Finally, the conclusions and future works are presented in Section 5.

2. RELATED WORK

The general floorplanners for FPGAs have been addressed extensively in classical works such as [1, 4, 7, 22]. Nonetheless, we only consider the ones that support the recent heterogeneous FPGA and are compliant with PR constraints [2, 3, 6, 14, 15, 20, 24]. The application-specific PR-supported floorplanner proposed in [17] is not covered here because it is only applicable to their pipeline architecture.

The Floorplacer in [14] is based on Simulated Annealing (SA). The SA places the PRRs from the bottom-left of FPGA towards the upper-right and tries to minimize the resource wastage of these PRRs. The Floorplacer expects that the remaining area would be feasible for static modules. The communication aspects of the system are ignored. The authors further improved the method in [15]. They added the *distance to corresponding Input/Output Blocks* minimization objective to the SA algorithm. However, the problem of static modules is still not addressed properly.

Another SA method proposed by Bolchini et al. [3] is based on the sequence pair representation. The method has some improvements in local search and violation constraints to speed up the process. The approach does take the connections between PRRs and static modules into account if needed. However, the method handles PRRs and static modules in the same manner which imposes unnecessary strict PR constraints to the regions dedicated to static modules. For instance, in their approach, the PRRs have to span the whole clock regions. However, this condition is not necessary for static modules. As a result, the floorplanner will be more likely to fail to place the PRRs when the resource utilization is high.

The floorplanner suggested in [24] uses a greedy approach called Columnar Kernel Tessellation. For each PRR, all the kernels are generated from the available resources of the FPGA. The kernels are then replicated in the columnar fashion to satisfy the requirements of the PRR. The smallest kernel is chosen for that PRR and the next PRR is processed. The procedure is repeated several times with different initial kernels to find the best floorplan. The post process procedure is executed after the above operation to further optimize the wirelength by moving or swapping the PRRs vertically. Similarly, Duhem et al. [6] suggest an exhaustive method to find all possible placements for each PRR. The resulting regions are then sorted with respect to the cost of the shapes and resource wastages. After that, the regions are greedily selected for each PRR considering non-overlapping constraint and the threshold for the physical distances between *only* PRRs. Again, these approaches do not consider the static modules at all.

The only approach that takes into account both static and PR modules (PRMs) is proposed in [2]. They suggested a three-stage process. First, it creates a dummy module which is the union of all PRMs that are mapped to one PRR. Then, the PnR is run for the new non-PR design consisting of this dummy module and the other static modules. The center of mass of this dummy module is identified. Finally, a placement which is closest to that center is selected among all possible placements of the PRR. For more than one PRR, the authors suggest executing the above process iteratively for each PRR but it is left for future work.

The most recent floorplanner is proposed in [20]. It is based on Mixed-Integer Linear Programming (MILP). The analytical model formulated only for the set of PRRs with respect to their resource requirements and connectivities.

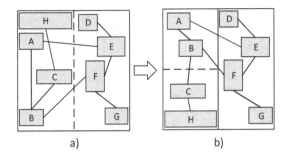

Figure 4: The cut-size driven recursive bipartitioning. The connections between modules are illustrated by the solid lines. In *a)*, **the** *vertical cut* **(dashed line) is done to vertically separate the region into two halves. Similarly, in** *b)*, **the next** *horizontal cut* **(dashed line) is performed for the newly created partition on the left.**

Since the MILP takes into account the global search space, it is proven to provide better floorplans compared with the previous works [3, 24]. Nevertheless, this method overlooks the static modules as illustrated in Fig. 2.

As can be seen from the above literature review, except the work [2], there is no floorplanner that considers all modules in the PR system therefore they all suffer from the problems discussed in Section 1.

3. PROPOSED APPROACH

3.1 NLP-based Bipartitioner

3.1.1 Recursive bipartitioning

Recursive cut-size driven multilevel netlist bipartitioning is used widely in VLSI floorplanning [5, 13, 26]. The basic idea of the cut-size driven recursive bipartitioning is shown in Fig. 4. In general, the cuts are recursively performed to divide the circuit into two partitions such that the cut line crosses the least amount of wires while balancing the weights of modules in two new partitions. The order of the cuts, i.e *vertical* and *horizontal cuts*, is not known a priori and it must be decided by the algorithm based on the analysis of the circuit. Nonetheless, further details of this problem are beyond the scope of this paper; the reader can refer to [5, 13, 26] for more information.

3.1.2 The proposed bipartitioner

As discussed in Section 1, the prior approaches cannot be applied directly to FPGA because the FPGA resources are predefined and placed in specific locations. Additionally, none of the current multi-resource aware partitioners [11, 16, 21] can provide a solution for the resource occupation issue. That is the resources taken by the possible placements of one module in two partitions can be different. Therefore, we propose a novel bipartitioner that is capable of **(1)** minimizing the number of nets crossing two partitions and **(2)** supporting multi-resource bipartitioning in which:

- The available resources, type and quantity, in two partitions can be different.

- The resources occupied by the possible placements of **one** module in **two** partitions can be different.

- The resources occupied by the modules in two partitions can be balanced individually with respect to each type of resource.

The partitioning algorithms presented in [16, 21] support the hypergraph representation of the connections between modules. Our bipartitioner and [11] work on the graph representation instead. Our method transforms a group of nodes connected by one particular hyperedge to a *fully connected* graph. Even though using hypergraph is more straight forward to represent the connections between modules in a circuit, in practice, converting them to graph has minor effect on the quality of the bipartitioning solutions. The correctness of the bipartitioning solutions is not affected. The only concern is the extra memory used to store the graph. However, using graph makes it easier to construct the NLP model for our bipartitioner.

In our bipartitioner, the partitioning problem is modeled as an NLP optimization problem [12]. The binary variable m_i, of which value is either 0 or 1, represents the partition assignment for module i. The objective function is the total number of nets between modules that cross two partitions (this number is *cut-size*). Equations 1 and 2 show how to calculate the cut-size $nets_{ij}$ between two modules i and j which are connected by n_{ij} wires. Intuitively, $nets_{ij} = n_{ij}$ when $m_i \neq m_j$.

$$nets_{ij} = n_{ij} * (1 - m_i) * m_j + n_{ij} * m_i * (1 - m_j) \quad (1)$$
$$= n_{ij} * (m_i + m_j - 2 * m_i * m_j) \quad (2)$$

The objective function of the NLP program is the summation of all $nets_{ij}$. This function (derived from Equation 2) is presented in Equation 3 followed by the constraints on the resources occupation in Equations 4, 5, 6 and 7.

Objective:

$$\sum_i m_i * \sum_{j \neq i} n_{ij} - 2 * \sum_i m_i * \sum_{j \neq i} (n_{ij} * m_j) \quad (3)$$

Subject to:

$$Total0_{CLB} = \sum_i ((1 - m_i) * CLB0_i) <= MAX0_{CLB} \quad (4)$$

$$Total1_{CLB} = \sum_i (m_i * CLB1_i) <= MAX1_{CLB} \quad (5)$$

$$ub_{lower} * Total0_{CLB} <= ub_{upper} * Total1_{CLB} \quad (6)$$
$$ub_{lower} * Total1_{CLB} <= ub_{upper} * Total0_{CLB} \quad (7)$$

The objective is to minimize Equation 3 while satisfying the maximum resource constraints. That is the total resources of the modules assigned to one partition should not exceed the available resources of that partition. The constraints on the total number of CLBs occupied by the modules assigned to partition 0, $Total0_{CLB}$, and partition 1, $Total1_{CLB}$, are shown in Equations 4 and 5. In the equations, $MAX0_{CLB}$ and $MAX1_{CLB}$ represent the numbers of CLBs available in partition 0 and 1 respectively. The possible numbers of CLBs occupied by a module i in either partition are $CLB0_i$ and $CLB1_i$.

Another constraint is to balance the resources in two partitions by the unbalance factor, ub, similar to [11]. This factor controls the ratio of the resources occupied by the modules in two partitions. This ratio must be within the range $(0.5 - ub, 0.5 + ub)$. Let $ub_{lower} = 0.5 - ub$ and $ub_{upper} = 0.5 + ub$. The unbalance constraints for the CLB resource are illustrated in Equations 6 and 7.

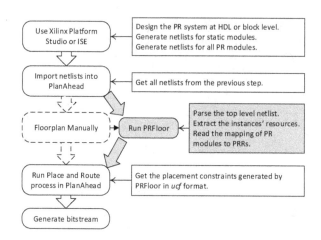

Figure 5: The new design flow with PRFloor.

Similar constructs of the above constraints are done for the remaining resources such as DSP and BRAM. The NLP program is then solved by the Gurobi Optimization tool [9]. The experiment results of the proposed bipartitioner is provided in Section 4.1.

3.2 The PRFloor

3.2.1 The Design Flow

Fig. 5 shows the flow of designing a PR system as suggested by [25]. However, the manual floorplanning step is replaced by the separate execution of the PRFloor outside of PlanAhead. The PRFloor reads the top level netlist of the design to get the information of all modules in the system and the connections between them. Thereafter, the resources of each module are parsed from its netlist. The *total resources required for one PRR* is the **union** of the resources of the PRMs that are mapped to that PRR. In this work, it is assumed that the mappings of PRMs to PRRs are already carried out. In addition, the PRMs which are mapped to one particular PRR are also implemented with a common interface wrapper [25]. Finally, PRFloor executes the *recursive pseudo-bipartitioning heuristic* to floorplan all modules in the design. The placement constraints for PRRs is written in the *ucf* format. Hereafter, the PRR is considered as generic module with implied PR constraints.

3.2.2 Overview of the PRFloor

All the steps executed inside the *PRFloor* are summarized in Algorithm 1. It starts by building the model of the FPGA device used in the design. The empty ROOT partition which is an entire FPGA is created. A list of static and PR modules is parsed from the netlist. All possible placements for each module are computed. After that, the recursive pseudo-bipartitioning process is executed to determine the preferred position for each module. The placements are then heuristically filtered and sorted. Finally, the feasible combination of them is found using the recursive trial-and-error algorithm. The details of the aforementioned major steps are discussed in the subsequent sections.

3.2.3 The FPGA Model

In this section, the architecture of the FPGA is analyzed and the representations of the FPGA resources are simplified to ease the search process in the algorithm. The FPGA

Algorithm 1 PRFloor
```
 1: Build the FPGA model {Section 3.2.3}
 2: Create ROOT partition containing all the modules and the
    current bounding box is the entire FPGA
 3: Find all possible placements {Section 3.2.4}
 4: while NOT SUCCESS do
 5:    Do recursive vertical cut for ROOT {Section 3.2.5}
 6:    Do recursive horizontal cut for ROOT {Section 3.2.5}
 7:    Calculate the normalized wastage and distances to anchor
       points for all placements
 8:    Select the placement candidates {Section 3.2.6}
 9:    Sort the placements of each module in the increasing order
       of their OBJ_placement values {Section 3.2.6}
10:    Sort the modules in the decreasing order of the resource
11:    Find the feasible floorplan {Section 3.2.7}
12:    if NOT SUCCESS then
13:       Shift the first vertical cut line to the right
14:    end if
15: end while
16: return final placements
```

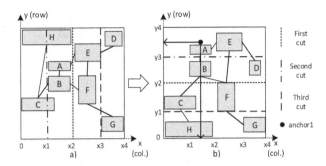

Figure 6: The pseudo vertical cuts (*a*) and horizontal cuts (*b*) used to estimate the preferred anchor points of the modules. The vertical cuts are performed first to scatter the modules horizontally across the FPGA. In *a*, the first cut separates the entire FPGA into two halves, the second cut is applied to the partition on the left (from 0 to $x2$), and so on. Likewise, in *b*, the horizontal cuts are done to spread the modules vertically.

considered in this paper is Xilinx Virtex-6 XC6VLX240T (hereafter, called Virtex-6). However, the method is general enough that it can be extended to support other devices such as Virtex-4, Virtex-5 and Virtex-7.

The Virtex-6 is divided into 6-by-2 clock regions. The clock region is further divided into roughly 50 columns (depending on the region on the left or the right side of the FPGA), each of them can be CLB, BRAM, DSP or special resources such as IOB, PCIe, GTX or even empty. The resources in each clock region do not need to be the same across the entire FPGA. Also noted that there is a blank space in the middle of the clock region, as can be seen in Fig. 1. It is reserved for the regional clock spine, separating the columns into two halves. Each half of CLB, BRAM and DSP column consists of 20 CLBs, 4 BRAMs (if configured as 18-bit-width RAM, there are 8 blocks) and 8 DSP blocks respectively. The smallest addressable *configuration frame* spans the entire column, which is equivalent to the 40-CLB height. This is the reason why PRR-2 and PRR-3 violate the overlapping constraint since one frame cannot contain configuration bits for more than one PRR.

In our approach, instead of looking at the fine-grain granularity of resources, the *half-column* resource is preferred. This half-column granularity balances the trade-off between the number of configuration frames and the occupied resources. For instance, the PRR-1 in Fig. 1 requires 8 DSP blocks. If the full-column granularity is used as suggested by [20, 24], we have to assign the entire DSP column containing 16 DSP blocks to it. The costs saved and the configuration time overhead by using half-column granularity are discussed in Section 4.2. Our method uses an accurate half-column model of the Virtex-6, including the PCIe, GTX and other resources. The wastage cost of each placement is also calculated similar to the related works [20, 24]. Each resource is given a weight based on its scarcity in the FPGA and the cost is the *weighted sum* of those resources. The connections of the modules to the external IO pins are not considered in this paper. However, it does not affect the general idea of the algorithm because the IO pins can be handled as generic fixed-location modules.

3.2.4 Find the possible placements

Since the actual occupied resources as well as the position of the placements of the module cannot be predicted as discussed in Fig. 3, all possible rectangle-shape placements

of each module (subjected to PR constraints described in Section 1 if it is PRR) across the aforementioned simplified FPGA model are generated. It is possible to generate L-shape placements. However, these shapes may hinder the place and route process from satisfying the timing constraints of the whole system. Therefore, rectangle-shape is preferred. All placements that overlap with user-defined or hard-macro regions are not entertained.

3.2.5 The Recursive Pseudo-bipartitioning Heuristic

The difficulty in using the cut-size driven recursive bipartitioning for FPGA is that the resources are limited and their locations are predefined. It is not possible to strictly determine a region for a module before having knowledge of the resources under that region. Therefore, we propose the *recursive pseudo-bipartitioning heuristic* as the solution for this problem. That is, except the *first vertical cut* which is actually used to partition the circuit, the *subsequent cuts* are *pseudo*. These vertical and horizontal pseudo cuts are done independently without back-tracing. The objective is to **(1)** scatter the modules across the FPGA device as evenly as possible. **(2)** The cut-size at every cut is minimized. **(3)** The newly created partitions must have sufficient resources to accommodate the modules. These cuts are performed to have the global view of the preferred positions, or *anchors*, of all modules with respect to the FPGA fabric. The cuts are illustrated in Fig. 6. The anchor point is represented by the (x, y) pair corresponding to $(column, row)$ axes of the FPGA. It is calculated based on the final partition where the corresponding module is assigned to as shown in Fig. 6. Equations 8 is used to compute the (x, y) coordinate of the anchor *anchor*1 of Module A. The *recursive pseudo-bipartitioning heuristic* is presented in the Algorithm 2.

$$anchor A_x = (x1 + x2)/2; \; anchor A_y = (y3 + y4)/2 \quad (8)$$

The modules may not fit entirely in the assigned partition (Module C in Fig. 6a). In FPGA floorplanning, the shape of a placement cannot be freely adjusted by changing the ratio of its edges to fit in the partition because it depends on the locations of the FPGA resources. Therefore, the pseudo cuts are relaxed in such a way that a placement only belongs to one partition if *at least* 90% of its area is inside that

Algorithm 2 Recursive Pseudo-bipartitioning Heuristic

Require: $parent\_partition \neq \emptyset$ **and** valid cut_line **and** cut_type

1: create $partition0 \leftarrow \emptyset$ from cut_line and $parent\_partition$
2: create $partition1 \leftarrow \emptyset$ from cut_line and $parent\_partition$
3: $list\_mod \leftarrow \emptyset$ {list of modules used for bipartition process}
4: $area\_constraint \leftarrow 90\%$
5: **if** cut_type = vertical cut **and** first cut **then**
6: $\quad area\_constraint \leftarrow 100\%$
7: **end if**
8: **for all** module $\in$ parent_partition **do**
9: $\quad list\_placement0 \leftarrow \emptyset; \ list\_placement1 \leftarrow \emptyset$
10: $\quad$ **for all** placement of module $\in$ parent_partition **do**
11: $\qquad area\_ratio0 \leftarrow area\_of\_placement \cap partition0$
12: $\qquad area\_ratio1 \leftarrow area\_of\_placement \cap partition1$
13: $\qquad$ **if** $area\_ratio0 \geq area\_constraint$ **then**
14: $\qquad\quad$ add placement to $list\_placement0$
15: $\qquad$ **else if** $area\_ratio1 \geq area\_constraint$ **then**
16: $\qquad\quad$ add placement to $list\_placement1$
17: $\qquad$ **end if**
18: $\quad$ **end for**
19: $\quad$ **if** $list\_placement0 = \emptyset$ **and** $list\_placement1 = \emptyset$ **then**
20: $\qquad$ deduct the resource of $module$ from the total resource of $partition0$ and $partition1$
21: $\quad$ **else**
22: $\qquad resource0 \leftarrow estimate\_resources(list\_placement0)$
23: $\qquad resource1 \leftarrow estimate\_resources(list\_placement1)$
24: $\qquad$ add $module \rightarrow list\_mod$
25: $\quad$ **end if**
26: **end for**
27: run $NLP\_Bipartitioner(list\_mod, partition0, partition1)$
28: **if** SUCCESS **then**
29: $\quad$ update anchor points of modules
30: $\quad$ execute Recursive Pseudo-bipartitioning for partition0
31: $\quad$ execute Recursive Pseudo-bipartitioning for partition1
32: **end if**

Algorithm 3 Estimate Occupied Resources

1: $a = \bar{x}$
2: **if** $a > \tilde{x}$ **then**
3: $\quad a = \tilde{x}$
4: **end if**
5: $result = a - 1.5 * \sigma_x$
6: **if** $result < minimum\_occupied$ **then**
7: $\quad result = minimum\_occupied$
8: **end if**
9: **return** $result$

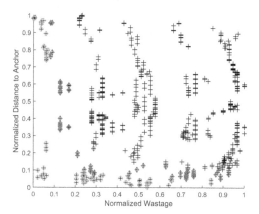

Figure 7: The Pareto-ranking selection technique for the placement candidates of one module. This is the real data obtained from the experiments. The ones in green circle are the first-rank points. The other points in red diamond are the second-rank.

partition (this requirement is drawn empirically from our experiments). If all possible placements of a module do not belong to any partition due to that area constraint, that module will not be considered for the subsequent cuts as the case of Module H in Fig. 6a. Its resources will be deducted from the corresponding partitions. This process is described between lines 8 and 20 in Algorithm 2. The anchor point is still determined based on the partition that it is previously assigned to as shown in Equation 9.

$$anchor H_x = (0 + x2)/2; \ anchor H_y = (0 + y1)/2 \quad (9)$$

During the recursive bipartitioning process, all possible placements of each module in each interim partition are filtered based on the 90%-area constraint. The resources occupied by each module in two partitions are then estimated (lines $22 - 23$ in Algorithm 2). For each of two sets of these placements, the *arithmetic mean* $\bar{x}$, median $\tilde{x}$ and *standard deviation* σ_x of each type of the occupied resources (CLB, DSP, BRAM) are calculated. Algorithm 3 shows how the resource is estimated. The *minimum_occupied* is the smallest possible number of resources occupied by the module. This calculation makes sure that the estimated resources will not be skewed by the unusually large placements.

However, this 90% area constraint is not applicable for the *first vertical cut* as mentioned before (lines $4 - 7$ in Algorithm 2). The placements must be completely inside either of the partitions. This is to reduce the problem size without compromising the quality of the floorplan. The reason is that the initial *ROOT* partition, which is the entire FPGA, is bigger than most modules; dividing it by half should not cause any difficulty in finding good placements for modules.

Besides, our algorithm will shift the first vertical cut line along the x-axis to enlarge one of the partitions if some of the modules are too big to fit in neither half of the FPGA.

3.2.6 Select the placement candidates

At this stage, the *anchor points* of all modules are identified. The *geometric* distances from them to the center points of the placements of the corresponding modules are calculated. These distances are then normalized to the largest distance from the placements of the module. Similarly, the wastage cost of these placements are normalized. Then for each module, the Pareto-ranking selection technique [18] is performed for all placements. Only the first and second-rank points are selected for the next steps as presented in Fig. 7.

In PRFloor, the objective of the recursive bipartitioning process is to minimize the cut-size and the connected modules tend to stay closer to each other. The wirelength between connected modules is optimized indirectly via the distance to the anchor point metric. Therefore, when the designer specifies the preferences between the *total wirelength* and the *resource wastage* using the 2-tuple weight (α, β), it can be applied directly to the distance to the anchor point and the resource wastage. Then, the selected placements of each module are sorted in the increasing order of the objective values calculated using the Equation 10.

$$OBJ_{placement} = \alpha * wastage + \beta * dist\_to\_anchor \quad (10)$$

3.2.7 Find the feasible floorplan

At this step, the number of possible placements for each module is reduced significantly thanks to the selections done in Section 3.2.6. The modules are then sorted in the de-

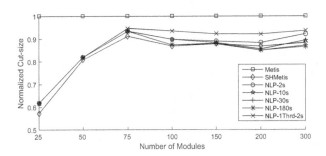

Figure 8: Comparison between the proposed NLP bipartitioner, Metis [11] and SHMetis [10]. The Gurobi solver [9] used for the NLP bipartitioner is configured to stop after 2, 10, 30 and 180 seconds to compare how good the result is for a certain time constraint. The line NLP-1Thrd-2s represents the results obtained from Gurobi solver when it is executed with one thread. All the results are normalized to the ones provided by Metis.

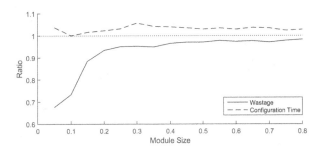

Figure 9: The ratio of the wastage and configuration time between the FPGA modeled in half-column and full-column granularity. The x-axis represents the maximum sizes of the randomly generated modules compared to the size of Virtex-6.

creasing order of the resources requirement and the number of wires in its input/output interface. The recursive trial-and-error algorithm is executed to obtain the final floorplan. The possible combinations of the placement candidates (with separate constraints for PRRs) are considered. Nevertheless, the algorithm is optimized such that it does not back-trace all the possible combinations of small modules. These modules usually have large number of possible placements to choose from. Therefore it is easier to find suitable placements for them. The algorithm stops immediately when the first feasible floorplan is found. If the algorithm cannot find any, it shifts the first vertical cut gradually closer to the right edge to enlarge one of two partitions to facilitate the placement of big modules (lines 12 − 14 in Algorithm 1). The heuristic is restarted with the new cut line.

At first sight, our algorithm (generating all placements then finding the feasible combination of them) may look similar to [6,24]. However, the PRFloor is better than those because it has the sophisticated bipartitioning process to estimate the possible locations of modules and the selection of the placement candidates to filter out bad placements. These processes play an important role in making the recursive algorithm finish very fast as reported in Section 4.3.

4. EXPERIMENTS

4.1 The NLP-based Bipartitioner

Fig. 8 shows the quality of the results obtained from the proposed NLP bipartitioner in comparison with Metis [11] and SHMetis [10]. SHMetis is the single-resource hypergraph partitioning tool created by the same group which develops Metis. In the experiments, the resources requirement for each module in two partitions are set to be the same; the available resources in two partitions are also equal. We only perform *one cut* to separate the modules into two halves. Since SHMetis does not support multi-resource bipartitioning, the multiple resources are converted into one weighted sum function. We use SHMetis in the experiments for reference purposes only because it cannot be directly compared with the multi-resource bipartitioners. The NLP program is solved by the Gurobi Optimization tool [9] with default configurations and various run time constraints.

As can be seen in Fig. 8, the NLP bipartitioner provides better cut-size than Metis in all configurations of number of modules. The cut-size given by our method is up to 38% smaller than Metis [11]. The average cut-size is *15%* smaller. The results are becoming better when the run time constraint for the solver is increased. This is the advantage of using NLP bipartitioner compared to the heuristic one. We can increase the run time constraint to cope with the situations in which it is difficult to solve the NLP program. These situations happen when the number of modules is high or the sizes of the modules are too large.

Given that the number of modules is not expected to be very large because we only floorplan the top-level modules in the system, the features supported by the NLP bipartitioner and the quality of the results, our method is the viable solution for the problem mentioned in Section 1.

4.2 The costs saved by using the half-column model compared to the full-column model

In this section, the resource cost saved by using the half-column granularity model compared to the full-column model is examined. The half-column model is used in our proposed approach, while the full-column model is used by [20, 24].

In the experiments, the resource requirements of the modules are randomly generated. They do not exceed a predefined maximum proportion of the total resources of the Virtex-6. The modules can have any of the CLB, BRAM and DSP resources. For each range up to the maximum proportion, 500 modules are uniformly randomly generated. The smallest possible placements for each module in half-column and full-column model are recorded. The final results are the average of those placements of 500 modules. The average configuration times of the modules are also reported.

The experiments are carried out with various maximum size proportions. The resource wastage and configuration time ratios between the half-column and full-column models are reported in Fig. 9. As shown, the resource wastages of the placements of modules found by using half-column model are always smaller than the ones found in full-column model. The saving ranges from 2% to 32%.

The average configuration time of the modules in half-column model is 6% higher than the full-column model. In half-column model, the placements for modules tend to be wider to cover the required resources. They require more configuration frames because the minimum addressable Xilinx configuration frame spans the entire column [25]. Nevertheless, the controller for the Internal Configuration Access

Table 1: The set of experimental systems with the actual utilization values. For each resource type, the first number is the utilization of PRRs, the second one is of the whole system.

No. PRRs	No. Mod.	%CLB		%BRAM		%DSP	
		PRR	All	PRR	All	PRR	All
3 (65%)	99	40.8	66.2	8.9	42.3	3.8	6.4
3 (70%)	99	45.8	71.2	27.2	60.6	13.5	16.1
3 (75%)	99	50.1	75.5	21.9	55.3	10.0	12.6
3 (80%)	99	55.5	80.9	24.5	57.9	10.7	13.3
3 (85%)	99	60.1	85.5	26.2	59.6	10.7	13.3
8 (65%)	116	35.6	65.3	16.1	27.9	11.1	14.5
8 (70%)	116	40.7	70.4	17.3	29.1	11.2	14.6
8 (75%)	116	45.8	75.6	18.3	30.0	11.7	15.1
8 (80%)	116	50.7	80.5	15.9	27.6	11.2	14.5
8 (85%)	116	56.3	86.1	19.2	31.0	11.7	15.1
15 (65%)	130	34.4	65.1	28.1	46.6	22.1	25.5
15 (70%)	130	39.8	70.5	29.6	48.1	23.2	26.6
15 (75%)	130	44.9	75.6	34.6	53.1	23.4	26.8
15 (80%)	130	49.8	80.5	31.3	49.8	24.7	28.1
15 (85%)	130	57.1	87.8	27.4	45.9	25.1	28.5
24 (65%)	126	33.0	66.0	31.7	55.5	31.3	31.9
24 (70%)	126	37.5	70.5	33.2	57.0	26.6	27.2
24 (75%)	126	42.3	75.3	21.6	45.4	23.4	24.1
24 (80%)	126	47.1	80.1	31.7	55.5	28.1	28.8
24 (85%)	126	52.3	85.3	36.1	59.9	22.7	23.3

Port proposed in [23] can reach the maximum theoretical speed of *3.2 Gbps* which is fast enough to handle the increased configuration time. Besides, our approach can easily discard the placements for modules with high reconfiguration time overhead if the designer wants to do so with the expense of possible higher wastage.

4.3 The PRFloor

4.3.1 Experiment with synthetic systems

To evaluate the PRFloor, the PR heterogeneous multiprocessor system-on-chip (PR-HMPSoC) [19] is used with different number of PRRs (or Tiles as described in that work). In the original systems, there is no direct connection between PRRs because they are connected indirectly by the Network-on-Chip (NoC). In this experiment, the systems are modified such that the PRRs are also connected with each other via PLB buses to observe the wirelength between them in the final floorplan. For each system configuration, the different sets of PRMs mapped to PRRs are semi-randomly chosen such that the overall CLB utilization ranges from 65% to 85%. Additionally, each PRRs are required to have at least 1 BRAM block and 1 DSP block to make it harder for the floorplanner to find a feasible floorplan. The details of the experimental systems are shown in Table 1. The data in the rows is used to show how big the PRRs are compared to the whole system, the average size of each PRR and the heterogeneity of the PRRs (CLB, BRAM, DSP). For example, the first row indicates that there are 99 modules in the system including 3 PRRs. The whole system utilizes 66.2% CLB of the FPGA while three PRRs utilize 40.8% CLB of the FPGA. The similar interpretation can be drawn for the BRAM and DSP columns.

The average execution times of the PRFloor for each system configuration in Table 1 are presented in Fig. 10. As seen, the largest runtime of PRFloor is about 530 seconds for the system with 24 PRRs and the CLB utilization is 70%. The execution time is increasing almost linearly with the number of modules in the system and the number of PRRs. It can also be noticed that for the same system architecture,

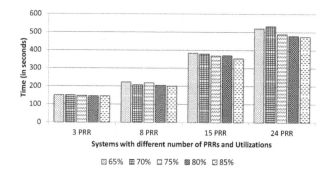

Figure 10: The execution time of PRFloor in different system configurations presented in Table 1.

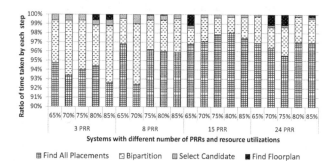

Figure 11: The ratios of time taken by the major steps in PRFloor. They are: finding all placements for modules, recursive bipartitioning, selecting placement candidates and finding final floorplan.

the execution time slightly decreases as the utilization increases. The reason is that when the resources requirement of the PRRs are larger, the number of placement candidates becomes smaller because there is lesser freedom to move the PRRs around. Thus, the trial-and-error process described in Section 3.2.7 takes lesser time to complete.

Fig. 11 provides the ratio of time taken by the major steps in PRFloor which are: finding all placements for modules, recursive bipartitioning, selecting placement candidates and finding final floorplan. As stated earlier, the recursive process used to find the final floorplan finishes very fast. It takes only at most 1.2% of the total runtime and in most cases, the percentage is almost 0. The most time-consuming process is finding all placements for modules. It constitutes more than 92% of the total runtime. This process can be further optimized in future work by having a smarter way to restrict the search space for each module instead of the whole FPGA as implemented in this work.

The experiment on the effect of varying the 2-tuple weight (α, β) in Equation 10 is also carried out. Fig. 12 plots the wirelength (the Manhattan distance) between the centroids of the PRRs and the total wastage of the PRRs. The α runs from 0 to 1 and $\alpha + \beta = 1$. The data is normalized to the results when $\alpha = \beta = 0.5$. As shown, the resource wastage decreases gradually with the increment of α. However, the wirelength does not react the same to the changes of β. In most cases, the differences are very small. It may be the cause of the Manhattan distance metric used in our current measurement. The larger the α, the smaller the placements, therefore the shorter the distance between the centroids of the placements. Another possible explanation

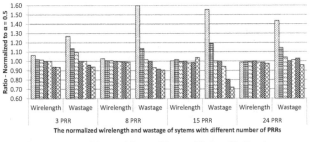

Figure 12: The effect of varying weight of the wastage in different system configurations.

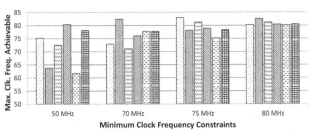

Figure 13: The maximum clock frequency achievable with different minimum clock constraints.

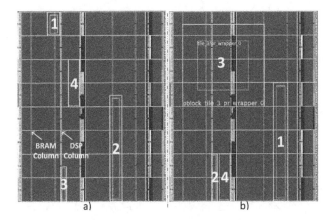

Figure 14: The floorplans provided by PRFloor for the same systems used in the examples in Fig. 2. The floorplans in *a)* and *b)* correspond to Fig. 2a and Fig. 2b respectively.

Table 2: The resource requirements of the PRRs used in the experiments in Section 4.3.3.

PR Regions	Fig. 14a			Fig. 14b		
	CLB	*BRAM*	*DSP*	*CLB*	*BRAM*	*DSP*
PRR 1	100	4	0	100	20	0
PRR 2	50	18	0	50	0	14
PRR 3	50	0	10	50	40	20
PRR 4	200	0	0	200	0	0

is the computation of the anchor points. They are simply the center points of the partitions in which they reside. In future works, we would use another metric such as the half perimeter wirelength to have a more accurate observation on the distances between PRRs. The calculation of the anchor points can also be improved by shifting the anchor point of a module toward the other modules connected to it.

4.3.2 Experiment with actual systems

The quality of the floorplans produced by PRFloor is further verified with the actual synthesizable systems. The maximum clock frequency achievable for PR systems is compared against the ones without PR capability. In this experiment, the original PR-HMPSoCs described in [19] are used in which there is no direct connection between Tiles. All Tiles are Xilinx Microblaze processor configured with default settings. In the static systems, these Tiles are static. In PR systems, they are partially reconfigurable. We use the Xilinx XPS 14.4 with default settings to implement the static systems. The PR systems are implemented by the Xilinx PlanAhead 14.4 with similar settings. The placement constrains for PRRs are generated by the PRFloor. The minimum clock constraint is varied from 50 MHz up to 80 MHz. The achievable clock frequencies for these systems are shown in Fig. 13. As can be seen from the chart, in all cases, the minimum clock frequency constraints are satisfied. Moreover, in most cases, the PR systems even have higher maximum clock frequency than the static systems. On average, it is 3% higher.

4.3.3 Comparison with the previous work

For comparison with the related work, it is not possible to compare our work directly with them. The problem that our method is dealing with is different from all the existing works discussed in Section 2. Moreover, there is no standard benchmark for FPGA floorplanning. Intuitively, in terms of the complexity of the experimental systems, we have much larger number of modules (including PRRs). The communication architecture between static modules and PRRs is also more complicated. However, we do have two use-cases to compare the PRFloor with [20]. The same systems given in Fig. 2 are fed into PRFloor with the identical FPGA, Xilinx Virtex-5 XC5VLX110T. The final floorplans are illustrated in Fig. 14. In these systems, the PRRs are connected indirectly by NoC and the PRFloor is run with $\alpha = \beta = 0.5$. The weight costs for CLB, BRAM and DSP are 1, 12 and 60 respectively. The resource requirements of the PRRs used in the experiments are provided in detail in Table 2.

Regarding the system in Fig. 14a, the total wastage cost given by [20] is 652 while ours is 19% lower, 530, thanks to the half-column granularity described in Section 3.2.3. The PRRs in our floorplan are also placed closer to each other. The total Manhattan distances (with weight 1) between four PRRs in our floorplan is 35% lower than [20].

For the system in Fig. 14b, one of the static modules requires 10 DSP blocks; therefore the PRFloor reserves that resource for it between PRRs 2 and 3. On the other hand, in Fig. 2b, the floorplanner [20] does not take into account the static modules. Hence, the remaining number of DSP blocks after floorplanning is just 8 which is not sufficient to implement the static module.

5. CONCLUSIONS AND FUTURE WORKS

This paper presents an automatic floorplanner for PR systems using the proposed NLP-bipartitioner to address the differences between the FPGA and VLSI floorplanning problem. Unlike other previous works, PRFloor takes into account the complex connections between both static modules and PRRs rather than just between PRRs. The experiments with various system setups show that PRFloor can provide results in a couple of minutes. The quality of the floorplan is demonstrated via the higher maximum clock frequency achievable than the comparable static systems.

The forthcoming works are to improve the performance and the quality of the algorithm. It would be extended to support bitstream relocation at runtime with tighter constraints for the placements of the PRRs.

6. ACKNOWLEDGMENTS

This work is supported in part by the German Research Foundation (DFG) within the Cluster of Excellence "Center for Advancing Electronics Dresden" (cfaed) at the Technische Universität Dresden.

7. REFERENCES

[1] P. Banerjee, M. Sangtani, and S. Sur-Kolay. Floorplanning for partially reconfigurable FPGAs. *Computer-Aided Design of Integrated Circuits and Systems, IEEE Transactions on*, pages 8–17, 2011.

[2] C. Beckhoff, D. Koch, and J. Torreson. Automatic floorplanning and interface synthesis of island style reconfigurable systems with GOAHEAD. In *Architecture of Computing Systems–ARCS 2013*, pages 303–316. Springer, 2013.

[3] C. Bolchini, A. Miele, and C. Sandionigi. Automated resource-aware floorplanning of reconfigurable areas in partially-reconfigurable FPGA systems. In *Field Programmable Logic and Applications International Conference on*, pages 532–538. IEEE, 2011.

[4] L. Cheng and M. D. Wong. Floorplan design for multimillion gate FPGAs. *Computer-Aided Design of Integrated Circuits and Systems, IEEE Transactions on*, 25(12):2795–2805, 2006.

[5] J. Cong, M. Romesis, and J. R. Shinnerl. Fast floorplanning by look-ahead enabled recursive bipartitioning. *Computer-Aided Design of Integrated Circuits and Systems, IEEE Transactions on*, 25(9):1719–1732, 2006.

[6] F. Duhem, F. Muller, W. Aubry, B. Le Gal, D. Négru, and P. Lorenzini. Design space exploration for partially reconfigurable architectures in real-time systems. *Journal of Systems Architecture*, 59(8):571–581, 2013.

[7] Y. Feng and D. P. Mehta. Heterogeneous floorplanning for FPGAs. In *VLSI Design, 2006. Held jointly with 5th International Conference on Embedded Systems and Design., 19th International Conference on*, pages 6–pp. IEEE, 2006.

[8] D. Göhringer, M. Hübner, E. N. Zeutebouo, and J. Becker. Operating system for runtime reconfigurable multiprocessor systems. *International Journal of Reconfigurable Computing*, 2011.

[9] Gurobi. Gurobi Optimization version 6.0.2. http://www.gurobi.com, April, 2015.

[10] G. Karypis and V. Kumar. hMETIS 1.5: A hypergraph partitioning package, 1998.

[11] G. Karypis and V. Kumar. Metis - A Software Package for Partitioning Unstructured Graphs, Partitioning Meshes, and Computing Fill-Reducing Orderings of Sparse Matrices Version 5.1.0. *Technical report*, 2013.

[12] D. Li and X. Sun. *Nonlinear integer programming*, volume 84. Springer Science & Business Media, 2006.

[13] S. K. Lim. *Practical problems in VLSI physical design automation*. Springer, 2008.

[14] A. Montone, F. Redaelli, M. D. Santambrogio, and S. O. Memik. A reconfiguration-aware floorplacer for FPGAs. In *Reconfigurable Computing and FPGAs, 2008. ReConFig'08. International Conference on*, pages 109–114. IEEE, 2008.

[15] A. Montone, M. D. Santambrogio, F. Redaelli, and D. Sciuto. Floorplacement for partial reconfigurable FPGA-based systems. *International Journal of Reconfigurable Computing*, 2011.

[16] S. Mukhopadhyay, P. Banerjee, and S. Sur-Kolay. Balanced bipartitioning of a multi-weighted hypergraph for heterogeneous FPGAS. In *Programmable Logic (SPL), 2011 VII Southern Conference on*, pages 91–96. IEEE, 2011.

[17] C. E. Neely, G. Brebner, and W. Shang. ReShape: Towards a High-Level Approach to Design and Operation of Modular Reconfigurable Systems. *ACM Transactions on Reconfigurable Technology and Systems (TRETS)*, 6(1):5, 2013.

[18] P. Ngatchou, A. Zarei, and M. El-Sharkawi. Pareto multi objective optimization. In *Intelligent Systems Application to Power Systems. Proceedings of the International Conference on*, pages 84–91. IEEE, 2005.

[19] T. D. Nguyen and A. Kumar. PR-HMPSoC: A versatile partially reconfigurable heterogeneous Multiprocessor System-on-Chip for dynamic FPGA-based embedded systems. In *Field Programmable Logic and Applications (FPL), 24th International Conference on*, pages 1–6. IEEE, 2014.

[20] M. Rabozzi, J. Lillis, and M. D. Santambrogio. Floorplanning for Partially-Reconfigurable FPGA Systems via Mixed-Integer Linear Programming. In *Field-Programmable Custom Computing Machines (FCCM), Annual International Symposium on*, pages 186–193. IEEE, 2014.

[21] N. Selvakkumaran, A. Ranjan, S. Raje, and G. Karypis. Multi-resource aware partitioning algorithms for FPGAs with heterogeneous resources. In *Proceedings of the 41st annual Design Automation Conference (DAC)*, pages 741–746. ACM, 2004.

[22] L. Singhal and E. Bozorgzadeh. Multi-layer floorplanning on a sequence of reconfigurable designs. In *Field Programmable Logic and Applications (FPL). International Conference on*, pages 1–8. IEEE, 2006.

[23] K. Vipin and S. Fahmy. A high speed open source controller for fpga partial reconfiguration. In *Field-Programmable Technology (FPT), 2012 International Conference on*, pages 61–66, Dec 2012.

[24] K. Vipin and S. A. Fahmy. Architecture-aware reconfiguration-centric floorplanning for partial reconfiguration. In *Reconfigurable Computing: Architectures, Tools and Applications*, pages 13–25. Springer, 2012.

[25] Xilinx. *Xilinx Partial Reconfiguration User Guide UG702 (v14.5)*, 2013.

[26] J. Z. Yan and C. Chu. DeFer: deferred decision making enabled fixed-outline floorplanning algorithm. *Computer-Aided Design of Integrated Circuits and Systems, IEEE Transactions on*, 29(3):367–381, 2010.

The Stratix™ 10 Highly Pipelined FPGA Architecture

David Lewis, Gordon Chiu, Jeffrey Chromczak, David Galloway, Ben Gamsa,

Valavan Manohararajah, Ian Milton, Tim Vanderhoek, John Van Dyken

Altera Corporation, 150 Bloor St. W., Suite 400, Toronto, Ont., Canada M5S 2X9

dlewis@altera.com

Abstract

This paper describes architectural enhancements in the Altera Stratix™ 10 HyperFlex™ FPGA architecture, fabricated in the Intel 14nm FinFET process. Stratix 10 includes ubiquitous flip-flops in the routing to enable a high degree of pipelining. In contrast to the earlier architectural exploration of pipelining in pass-transistor based architectures, the direct drive routing fabric in Stratix-style FPGAs enables an extremely low-cost pipeline register. The presence of ubiquitous flip-flops simplifies circuit retiming and improves performance. The availability of predictable retiming affects all stages of the cluster, place and route flow. Ubiquitous flip-flops require a low-cost clock network with sufficient flexibility to enable pipelining of dozens of clock domains. Different cost/performance tradeoffs in a pipelined fabric and use of a 14nm process, lead to other modifications to the routing fabric and the logic element. User modification of the design enables even higher performance, averaging 2.3X faster in a small set of designs.

Keywords

FPGA, logic module, routing

1. INTRODUCTION

This paper describes core logic architecture enhancements in the Stratix™ 10 HyperFlex™ FPGA architecture. This device is manufactured in a 14nm FinFET CMOS process [16], and offers logic capacity of up to 5M equivalent 4 LUTs. While Moore's law continues to offer density increases of approximately 2X per generation, it also introduces new challenges for FPGA architecture. Although RC delay per logical distance changes slowly with process, the RC delay per physical distance increases with process shrink, making it necessary for users to pipeline designs that span increasing logical area. This increases the demand for registers, as well as the importance of providing high speed long distance routing.

Stratix 10 introduces a highly pipelined logic and routing fabric to address these problems. The key innovation compared to previous work on pipelined FPGAs is the introduction of a pulse latch based register in every routing multiplexer. The shift from pass gate to direct drive based routing enables a low-cost flip-

FPGA'16, February 21-23, 2016, Monterey, CA, USA. Copyright is held by the owner/author(s). Publication rights licensed to ACM.
ACM 978-1-4503-3856-1/16/02…$15.00
DOI: http://dx.doi.org/10.1145/2847263.2847267

flop embedded in the routing fabric, while introducing minimal delay when it is not used. While the cost of providing a flip-flop in every routing multiplexer is minor, other support not considered in previous papers increases the cost and has consequences on the rest of the fabric. Further extending on previous pipelined fabrics, the Stratix 10 architecture development included the exploration of clocking structures to handle the dozens of clocks present in real customer designs.

The highly pipelined routing fabric also motivates changes to the logic element structure. Flip-flop control signals such as clear and clock enable affect retiming, and must be optimized differently. The routing fabric is also affected by the different properties of the 14nm process and the needs of a pipelined architecture, and is modified for better performance.

The remainder of the paper is organized as follows. First, in Section 2, we give a brief overview of Stratix-style architectures. Section 3 provides an overview of some previous work in pipelined architectures, while Section 4 describes the Stratix 10 pipelined fabric. Section 5 details the CAD flow used for architecture exploration and in production tools. Section 6 describes pipelining experiments and Section 7 modifications to the logic element and routing. Section 8 provides a few examples of designs modified to target Stratix 10 and discusses the production tools that provides design modification advice. Section 9 concludes the paper.

2. STRATIX™ ARCHITECTURE

To help understand the remainder of the paper, we provide a background on Altera architectures. Stratix architectures use logic elements (LEs) of different types arranged into logic array blocks (LABs). Each LAB contains some number of LEs, which in the case of Stratix II and later are adaptive logic modules (ALMs). The term LAB in this paper also refers to the programmable routing fabric associated with each group of LEs, so throughout this paper, a Stratix LAB means 10 ALMs and associated inter-LAB and intra-LAB routing.

Figure 1 shows LABs and other embedded blocks such as memories and DSP blocks arranged in a row-column fashion, conceptually between the horizontal and vertical routing wires; in reality the wires pass over the LABs. Each block in the array can communicate with the inter-LAB routing on three of the four logical sides of the block. Each block output can drive onto either of the adjacent vertical routing channels and one horizontal routing channel, and the block inputs can receive signals from any of those three channels [11]. Figure 2 illustrates that routing wires are driven by multiplexers called driver input muxes (DIMs). DIMs select signals from other routing wires, to implement stitching and corner turning, as well as from the outputs of the LAB. Inputs to the LAB are provided by LAB input muxes (LIMs), which select from the nearby routing wires and LAB outputs, and drive the LAB lines. Inputs to the LEs are driven by LE input muxes (LEIMs), which select from the LAB lines. In common nomenclature the DIMs correspond to the S-box, the LIMs to C-box inputs, and the LEIMs to local interconnect muxes.

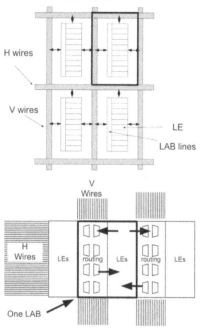

Figure 1: LAB inputs and outputs connect to 3 routing channels; logical view on top, physically oriented view on bottom. A LAB consists of both logic and routing.

It is important to understand the detailed implementation of the routing muxes, as the efficient implementation of the Stratix 10 pipelined routing fabric is highly dependent on this. Figure 2 shows a typical routing mux constructed as a two stage cascade of NMOS pass transistors followed by two inverters. For example, a 16:1 mux can be constructed as a set of four 4:1 muxes with common control signals, followed by a 4:1 mux. We refer to the two stages of inverters as buffer and driver respectively. The buffer has a PMOS feedback to ensure that the input rises to Vdd. The configuration RAM cells (CRAMs) are supplied with a higher Vdd (Vddh) to give greater drive strength to the NMOS pass gates. This improves speed at minimal power cost from increased gate and CRAM leakage.

The logic element is an adaptive logic module (ALM) that contains a 6-LUT that can be fractured into two 5-LUTs [12]. In the case of two 5-LUTs in a single ALM, there must be no more than eight unique inputs, so that a pair of 5-LUTs must share at least two inputs.

In arithmetic modes, the 6-LUT can be used as four 4-LUTs, where two pairs of 4-LUTs provide inputs to a two-bit adder. Each pair of 4-LUTs has common inputs. Control signal conditioning selects and conditions wide fanout signals such as clears and clock enables. Figure 3 shows a simplified overview of a LAB, using a 4-LUT LE for simplicity. Note that global signals such as clocks and clears are distributed on separate high speed networks, and brought into the LAB either using separate global network routing muxes or using conventional routing, and distributed to the LEs in that LAB.

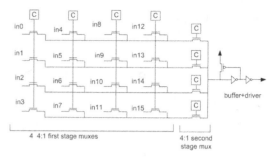

Figure 2: Example 16:1 Routing Mux and Driver

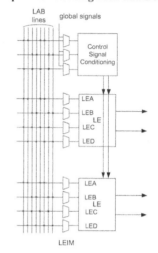

Intra-LAB Routing

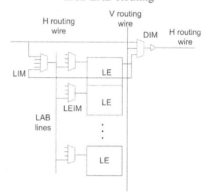

Figure 3: LEs with local routing on LAB lines. Connectivity of LEs and LEIM to DIM and LIM, with local connectivity from LE outputs to LIM inputs (no direct feedback.)

3. PREVIOUS PIPELINED FABRICS

Several researchers have previously explored the inclusion of pipeline registers in a FPGA routing fabric, together with a CAD flow to automatically retime the user design. Tsu et al [7] described a hierarchical array with pipelined fabric to achieve a fixed clock cycle. However this had approximately a 100% area overhead due to the large number of full edge-triggered flip-flops. Singh [2] described the key concepts of a registered fabric and a retiming flow to exploit it. They included some fraction of pipelined routing tracks and measured the area and performance increase of a set of designs. They varied the fraction of pipelined routing tracks and measured the performance improvement, achieving, for example, about 19% performance improvement at 18% area increase for 50% registered tracks. Weaver [17] described the HSRA which includes capacity-depopulated S-boxes and fully populated C-boxes, as well as pipeline registers in the routing and LE inputs, but at an area cost nearly 4X that of a comparable commercial FPGA.

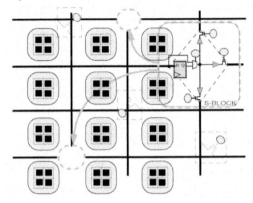

Figure 4: Pipelined routing from Singh [2] using pass transistor architecture

Singh concludes that registered routing fabrics are not generally useful, but suited to high speed pipelined designs. Over the subsequent 14 years, we suggest that this style of design has become more common as long range routing delays increase relative to clock cycles.

Eguro [10] performed an extensive study into pipelined fabrics and CAD. He explored both pipeline-aware routing in conventional fabrics and the addition of pipeline registers to the routing fabric. He concluded that pipelined interconnect was capable of only a modest speed improvement. However the reported delay of a single wire is 8 times more than a LUT delay, [10, p. 120] unlike modern direct drive architectures, where a LUT delay is comparable to a single routing wire. Consequently his conclusion is not applicable to modern architectures, and the change to direct drive architectures may in part be responsible for the performance achieved here. Eguro concludes that pipelined routing fabrics are not desirable [10, p. 147].

Sharma et al [5] describe a pipelining-aware router that was implemented for the RaPiD architecture [8], which is a coarse-grained architecture. Goldstein et al [9] describe PipeRench which is another coarse-grained fabric with pipelining. These papers address some of the issues in pipelined designs, but the coarse-grained single clock domain area is not directly applicable to the general purpose FPGA applications that we address here.

4. STRATIX 10 PIPELINED ARCHITECTURE

A primary goal of our work is to enable pipelining at a sufficiently low area cost that designs that do not use this feature do not incur a significant cost penalty. Further, rather than take the design unmodified, we assume that the user will perform some work to make it amenable to pipelining. Previous work in pipelined routing fabrics has focused on complete edge-triggered flip-flops, as well as using pass transistor based architectures, with large area cost. Subsequent to these papers, FPGA architectures adopted direct drive multiplexer based routing [11,14], which this paper will show allows ubiquitous pipeline registers at a minimal cost.

A common feature of previous work is that clocking of the pipelined fabrics is largely ignored. Modern FPGAs offer complex clock networks to support commercial designs that typically have dozens of clocks, and designs in our benchmark set can contain over 50 clocks. While clustering may naturally find collections of related flip-flops to place in each LAB, the routing used in a LAB may contain signals from several clock domains, and it is unclear how many clocks will be required to effectively pipeline designs. Since a clock mux can have significant cost, a low cost clocking structure is important. The global clock networks provide sufficient clocks to the fabric, so our focus is on the distribution of this to the pipeline registers.

The key concept that enables a low-cost pipelined fabric is shown in Figure 5. The routing mux is modified by converting the buffer into a tristate, and adding a feedback latch to the internal node. Note that this is a single stage latch, and it is used as a pulse latch to emulate an edge triggered flip-flop. The feedback latch may be close to minimum size since it is not critical. The PMOS feedback also needs to be split off from the feed forward using a new independent inverter, since the feedforward is not necessarily enabled. A total of 10 transistors, of which 8 can be minimum size, are added to a conventional routing mux to implement this latch, compared to the total of 73 transistors, of which 4 are large, in a basic 16:1 mux, CRAM, and driver. In isolation, the cost of adding a pulse latch to every routing mux and to select internal paths in the ALM is approximately 5% of LAB area, considerably less than previously reported pipelined architectures. This 5% does not include the cost of clock selection and other control-related circuits, which dominate the total increase in area.

Fig. 5 also shows a CRAM and clock enable circuit for the flip-flop. When the flip-flop is not needed, the circuit is enabled in combinational mode, with a small increase in delay due to the series transistors in the buffer and added parasitic loading of the latch. The CRAM **rcomb** controls whether the routing mux is pipeline or transparent, while **cp** is a clock pulse generated by a pulse generator much as in Stratix V [13]. In practice a more complex clock selection circuit is needed, but is deferred until our consideration of clocks.

The low cost of this circuit and the need for a regular layout drove us towards effectively using an architecture where every routing mux is pipelined, rather than depopulation of the routing flip-flops.

Our early architectural experiments considered a set of k flip-flops contained in each routing multiplexer. Only for the case that $k=1$ is it possible to use a pulse latch. When $k>1$ the second and all subsequent flip-flops must be edge-triggered in order to avoid race through. Consequently the cost increases dramatically for $k>1$, and the delay when not used also increases as a separate multiplexer to select from or bypass the flip-flops is required.

The most natural place to expect $k>1$ to be beneficial is in the inputs to the LEs. Due to the ubiquitous flip-flops we can selectively enable them in routing paths. However we anticipate that due to reconvergent fanout of routing signals, there will potentially be an imbalance in the desired number of flip-flops at the LEs.

Control signals are also problematic for a pipelined architecture. Although most published work assumes a simple LUT + flip-flop, Altera architectures have evolved to contain a rich set of control signals that are shared among all flip-flops in a LAB. These include ACLR (asynchronous clear), SCLR (synchronous clear), CE (clock enable), and SLD (synchronous load). Fig 6 shows a logical view of the relevant circuits. The gating logic and multiplexers that select and enable the clock and the control signals are not shown.

In previous architectures, CE functionality was implemented by gating LAB-wide clocks. In a pipelined architecture where flip-flops are mobile and may migrate into the routing fabric as part of a retiming step, CE functionality is realized with a feedback as illustrated in Figure 6. Another modification that facilitates retiming flip-flops with CEs is the ability to select the output of the LE from either the input or the output of the FF. This allows a "copy" of the flip-flop to migrate to another location while the original remains fixed.

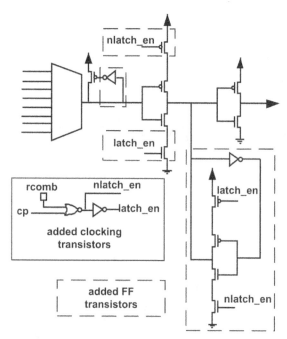

Figure 5: Pulse latch included in Stratix 10 routing multiplexers

Control signals such as CE, SCLR, and SLD are potentially shared by a large number of flip-flops in a LAB, and retiming any one of those flip-flops may create a situation where a flip-flop imbalance is created on a subset of the control signals in the LAB. We address this in the architecture by allowing for *k* optional flip-flops on the control signals as we did for other LE inputs. The addition of these flip-flops creates a different cost/benefit tradeoff for the number of each of these control signals compared to previous architectures.

Figure 7 gives a simplified view of the relevant parts of the clock network. Various clock trees distribute a large number of global or regional clocks to vertical spines. Row clock muxes select six of these which are driven across a 1 row high region typically 1/4 to 1/8 of the width of the die. Each LAB selects two of these that are again selected at the ALM level. In Stratix 10, the global/regional clock trees are replaced by a routable clock network, but the details of this are not relevant to this paper, as the clocking available to the LAB remains the same.

5. CAD FOR PIPELINED ARCHITECTURES

Two different CAD flows were used in our experiments. All architectural experiments in this paper were performed using

Altera's FPGA Modeling Toolkit (FMT) which is an extended version of the VPR placement and routing software [1], and the design modification experiments in section 8 were done using an early version of Quartus™ II (QII) with added CAD support for Stratix 10.

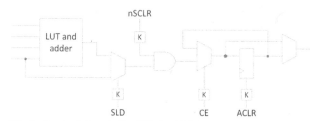

Fig 6: Control signals for FFs in ALM

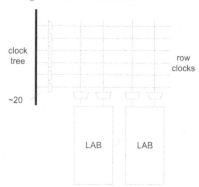

Fig. 7: Row level clock network and LAB level clock selection

The FMT uses QII logic synthesis software to map designs to the ALMs, memories, and DSP blocks present in the target architecture, and then carries out placement and routing using a set of flexible algorithms which allow a range of architectural parameters to be evaluated. For a given architectural configuration, the area and speed of each circuit is calculated and an overall area/performance tradeoff is determined.

Production QII software lacks the generality of FMT, but it is highly optimized to take advantage of the particular architectures it supports. A number of changes were required to both QII and FMT to take advantage of the ubiquitous flip-flops present in the architecture. Specifically, the flip-flops allow the implementation of a retiming step much later than is possible in conventional architectures.

5.1 Post-Route Register Retiming

Register retiming is a well-known sequential optimization technique historically used to increase the maximum frequency of operation of circuits in both FPGA and ASIC design [20]. In conventional FPGA CAD, register retiming optimizations are usually performed either during synthesis, or as a post-placement fixup step [19]. When performed early in the flow, conventional timing-driven register retiming is often limited by the poor timing predictions available (as placement and routing are not yet known). When performed late in the flow, the optimization is often limited by the need to re-legalize the placement and routing after a register retiming optimization, to accommodate the addition or removal of registers in the design.

The flexibility offered by the Stratix 10 architecture enables a new variant of register retiming that can occur much later than conventional register retiming. This allows for better timing prediction, while the architecture allows us to not incur the traditional legalization cost of retiming. By operating post-route, where both placement and routing are fixed, the retimer has perfect knowledge of the delays in the circuit, bypassing the challenges normally associated with delay prediction [18]. The design of the ubiquitous flip-flops allows the registers to be configured post-routing (either "enabled" to expose a registered path, or "disabled" to expose a combinational bypass path). This enables the post-routing retiming flow to perform a register retiming by simply enabling (adding) and disabling (removing) registers throughout the design, without the costly legalization of the placement or routing that is conventionally required.

Fig. 8: Conventional retiming vs Stratix 10 retiming

Register retiming in QII is implemented with a variant of the architecturally constrained retiming technique introduced by Singh [3]. First, we create a retiming graph which models all potential locations for flip-flops in the circuit. Second, we derive a set of constraints to ensure the legality of the retiming solution: constraints that ensure architectural restrictions are not violated (ensuring zero or one flip-flops are placed at every flip-flop location), and constraints that ensure both setup and hold timing constraints are met. Next, this set of constraints can be expressed as a set of difference inequalities that are solved via a constraint satisfaction algorithm for an optimal period or frequency of the circuit. Finally, registers are configured as per the solution to the constraint set.

FMT implements the same architecturally constrained retiming step, but uses a slightly simpler algorithm to solve the retiming problem than the production version found in QII.

5.2 Retiming-Aware Place & Route

The post-route retiming step can make dramatic changes to a circuit's critical path and the CAD steps that precede the final retiming may target their optimizations on the wrong set of paths without any awareness of the final retiming solution. Specifically, synthesis, placement, and routing steps must be modified to focus on paths that cannot be timing optimized by retiming. Timing driven optimizations in QII and FMT are guided by slacks and slack ratios [1] computed by a timing analysis engine. A simple approach to making these optimizations aware of the late pipelining and retiming is to use *post-retiming slacks* to guide the timing-driven optimizations.

We modify the conventional CAD flow so that at each point in the flow where a traditional timing analysis is requested, we perform a fast estimation of the retiming solution.

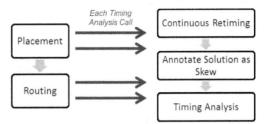

Fig 9: Retiming aware place and route

First, we use continuous retiming techniques [23] to estimate the maximum frequency of operation of the circuit, and we compute the amount of delay retimed across each flip-flop location in the continuous retiming solution. We apply this delay as a skew to the flip-flop's clock path. Applying the equivalence between retiming and skew optimization [4], the resulting timing analysis of the circuit with skewed clocks closely resembles the expected timing after a full retiming step. By using continuous retiming in this manner, the retiming estimation step is approximately 50 times faster on average than the full discrete retiming that is performed at the end of the flow. It should be noted that our approach of using a continuous retiming solution to guide CAD is less powerful than the approach of using cycle slack as in [3], but is much faster to compute.

6. ARCHITECTURE EXPERIMENTS

The architectural experiments in this section were performed over a range of time from 2011 onwards using customer designs as well as Altera-generated designs. One circuit set used in many of the experiments contains 82 circuits with sizes up to 728K equivalent 4-LUTs. These designs contain from 1 to 67 clocks in the core logic and routing, with 14 clocks on average.

One of the challenges in evaluating a highly pipelined architecture is the lack of designs targeted for the architecture. We addressed this problem by making minor modifications to the existing suite of designs, and by considering three different experimental flows to model the expected use of Stratix 10.

Asynchronous clears limit the movement of registers in a pipelined architecture. We believe most designs will clear in a well-disciplined manner, and therefore we convert the ACLR signals in the design netlists to SCLR.

We use three experimental flows to evaluate designs on the pipelined architecture. In the strictest flow, retiming, we assume that the cycle by cycle behavior of each design must be exactly preserved, and the circuit may only be retimed by moving existing flip-flops. The *retiming flow* does not change the functionality of the design in any way, but allows retiming on each clock domain. In the *pipelining flow*, we assume that the user is willing to tolerate added latency in each clock domain but otherwise requires the same functional behavior. The pipelining flow is allowed to add any number of flip-flops to all of the inputs of each clock domain and to retime them into the circuit. In the *user modification flow*, we take a small number of actual designs and explore the limiting factors for pipelining, and manually restructure the design to preserve functionality but add latency. This corresponds to the expected use of Stratix 10 by customers willing to perform redesign to exploit the maximum potential of the architecture. The retiming and pipelining flows can be evaluated on all designs purely with

CAD modifications while the user modification flow requires designer interaction, so has only been done on a handful of designs.

6.1 Limits of Pipelining and Retiming

Early in the development of the highly pipelined architecture, a study of the potential benefits of pipelining and retiming were done on an existing architecture. An Arria™ 10 fabric model was modified to allow registers to be placed at every routing mux, and up to 4 registers were allowed at LE inputs and control signals (Arria 10 is a 20nm implementation of the Stratix V architecture). A post-route retiming step was introduced to pipeline and reposition the existing flip-flops in the design (pipelining flow) to achieve the optimal retimed frequency (fmax).

Figure 10 summarizes the improvement in fmax observed when the largest clock domain in each circuit is pipelined and retimed.

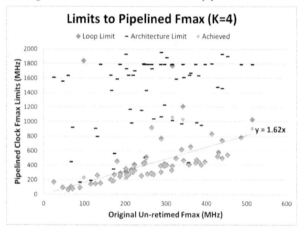

Fig. 10: The limits of pipelining and retiming

There are two limits that prevent this flow from achieving a higher fmax. First, there is an *architectural limit* created by slow internal paths which have no pipeline registers, or have other competing demands on a resource. This limit is illustrated in the figure by the dashes. Second, there is a *loop limit* which is created by sequential feedback loops in the circuit which cannot be pipelined without breaking design functionality. This limit is illustrated in the figure by the diamonds.

We address the architectural limit by ensuring that slow internal paths have optional pipelining registers and adequate clocking flexibility is present in the pipelined routing. A discussion of the clocking flexibility is provided in Section 6.4.

There are two ways to address the loop limit. The first is via the retiming-aware CAD changes described in Section 5.2 which make the optimization steps preceding the final retiming step aware of the paths that become critical when pipelining and/or retiming is employed. This awareness helps the CAD tools focus on minimizing the delay of circuit loops while placing a lower priority on acyclic paths. The impact of retiming-aware CAD is illustrated in Figure 11. The normalized geomean fmax for a suite of designs using the pipelining flow in FMT is shown as the clustering, placement, and routing steps are made retiming aware. Further gains are possible by making the synthesis step retiming-aware, but due to time constraints we were not able to carry out those modifications.

A second approach to the loop limit problem is to make design modifications that minimize the size of circuit loops, and we discuss this approach in Section 8.

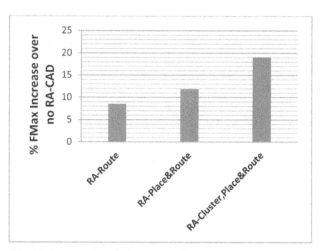

Fig. 11: Impact of retiming aware CAD

6.2 Impact of K

Figure 12 illustrates the impact of changing k, the number of optional flip-flops at LE data and control inputs. This sweep was done using the pipelining flow and each point represents the normalized geomean fmax for a suite of designs. A modest gain is possible by going to $k=2$, but this comes at a significant area cost as this requires edge-triggered flip-flops and bypass circuitry for $k>1$. Further software improvements that do a better job of predicting the demand for pipeline registers while physically constructing k=1 may improve performance beyond the present value, with an upper bound of the k=∞ performance. For example, if the routing step is aware of the flip-flop requirements that may exist at LE inputs, it can use longer routes to fulfill the requirement. While the first FF costs us about 5% area, the subsequent ones cost more area (~10%) as well as a significant delay penalty due to the need for full edge triggered FF and mux. Therefore the cost of k>1 is not justified by the performance gain, so we build k=1. Future performance gains may be possible purely through software improvements.

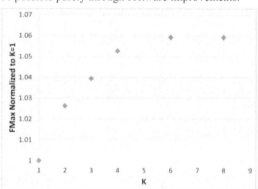

Fig. 12: Impact of K on Fmax

6.3 Impact of Hold Time

Clock skew, as well as the transparency window of pulse latches, causes significant hold time requirements, which have been ignored in preceding experiments. Although the basic FMT does not model hold time, in this work it has been enhanced to model hold time requirements in the routing FFs. Figure 13 shows the performance impact of a hold value on the fmax achieved in the pipelining flow. Larger values of hold render many routing flip-flops unusable during retiming and lead to performance degradation. Roughly 200ps of hold time is tolerable before performance begins to decline. This data is used to guide design of the clock network to achieve acceptable cost and performance degradation due to skew.

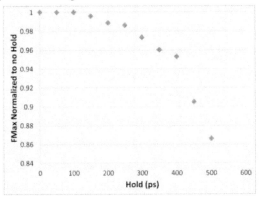

Fig. 13: Impact of hold on Fmax

6.4 Clocking

A low-cost clocking architecture is as important as the cost of the pipeline FFs. The global clocking structure provides six row clocks and, although it is implemented differently [6], has no functional changes relevant to the pipelined fabric, so is not discussed here. Our focus is the distribution of clocking to the pipeline FFs. As the pipeline FFs in the routing add only 10 small transistors per mux, the cost of a single CRAM and a 2-input gate to merely tie off the clock exceeds the cost of the FF. Additional clock muxing increases the cost further, so it is desirable to minimize clocking flexibility.

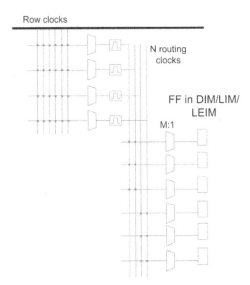

Fig 14: Pipeline FF clock architecture

We tried several different structures for clocking the routing FFs. A simple, regular structure that minimizes the cost of the clock selection at each FF is desirable since there are >200 routing FFs per LAB. Fig 13 shows a general overview of a clocking structure for a single LAB. The row clock structure is unchanged, but N clock muxes and pulse generators are added to select N routing clocks from the six row clocks. Each of the FFs can select from a subset M of the N routing clocks. There may be more than one group of FFs selecting from the N clocks, so N >= M. In the discussion below, the M-sized subsets are disjoint,

so N is the sum of all their sizes. The per-FF clock mux can also tie the routing FF in transparent mode. The cost per additional fanin M is very high since it affects all, or some large subset, of the >200 muxes per LAB, but N is very inexpensive since each such mux occurs once per LAB. Consequently we focus on finding a reasonable number of N clocks, and minimizing the value of M by partitioning the routing muxes into distinct subsets. In particular, we expect all of the logic in a LAB to be closely related in terms of the clocks but the inter-LAB routing to carry a wide variety of clocked signals. Therefore we anticipate separate clock sets for various groups of DIMs vs. LIM and LEIM, as well as simpler clocking for the LIM/LEIM.

It is also possible to consider heterogeneous values of M for routing muxes in the various sets. This leads to highly irregular layouts that are undesirable as well as complicated CAD, and was not pursued after the simpler structures proved feasible.

Table 1 summarizes a set of DIM and LIM clocking experiments. The geomean fmax achieved by the pipelining flow is reported for each choice in DIM and LIM clocking flexibility. The DIMs in this experiment are the short wire DIMs (length 10 and under). All fmax values have been normalized to the case where every DIM and LIM has access to the full set of row clocks. In the first three cases, every DIM and LIM selects from a subset of M=4,3,2 or 1 clocks selected from the row clocks. In the remaining cases where the value of N exceeds the total of MLIM + MDIM, the DIMs are split into multiple groups, each of which has access to MDIM unique clocks of the N available; similarly each LIM can select from MLIM clocks. Therefore N = DIM groups * MDIM + MLIM. Performance is largely unaffected by restricting the clocking flexibility at LIMs, but there is some performance degradation by restricting flexibility at DIMs. By carefully grouping the DIMs by direction and by type of wire driven, this degradation can be avoided. In the architecture we implemented a modified version of clocking flexibility indicated by the last row using four groups of DIMs with 2 clocks each. In addition to this clocking, we allow the DIMs driving long vertical or horizontal wires full access to the available row clocks. There are four such DIMs at each LAB location and this increase in clock flexibility can be achieved with a negligible increase in area.

Table 1: Impact of clocking flexibility on Fmax

N	DIM Groups	MDIM	MLIM	Fmax
8	1	4	4	1.00
6	1	3	3	0.99
4	1	2	2	0.99
5	2	2	1	0.99
3	2	1	1	0.98
5	4	1	1	0.98
9	4	2	1	1.00

Although this paper will not give detailed results of the impact of LEIM clocking flexibility on performance, it is similar to LIM clocking flexibility. Performance is largely unaffected by a limited LEIM clocking flexibility, since the logic in a LAB most commonly uses one clock. In the architecture we allow the LEIMs a choice of one clock selected from the row clocks.

6.5 Impact of Pipelined Architecture

Figure 15 summarizes the performance impact of the pipelined architecture and CAD flow on a suite of test circuits. Each point is a geomean fmax value computed for a design by weighting the fmax obtained for each clock domain by its size. Retiming provides a geomean performance increase of 10% and when pipelining is used in conjunction with retiming, performance increases by 53%. The improvement from Fig 10 due to CAD (Fig 11) has been essentially negated by the change to k=1, introduction of hold time, and generalizing the metric for multiple clock domains. However, higher performance levels are possible if the users restructure their circuits as we demonstrate in Section 8.

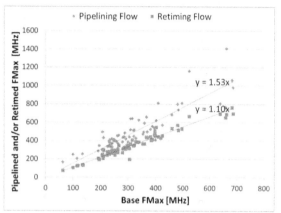

Fig 15: Impact of the pipelined architecture on performance

7. ROUTING AND LOGIC ELEMENT ARCHITECTURE CHANGES

The 14nm finFET process we used offers a wider variation of metal thicknesses and pitches compared to our previous products. Previous Stratix architectures used a mix of one or two lengths in each direction (horizontal and vertical) of mid length wires (such as 3, 4, or 6). They also supplied one length in each direction of long wires (16, 24, 27, 32) on a very thick and wide pitch metal layer, largely optimized towards optimal delay for long distance connections. In contrast, the finer gradations of metal in the 14nm process result in a corresponding increase in the heterogeneity of the wire lengths. Fig. 16 summarizes experiments exploring the mix of different wire lengths and their allocation to various metal layers. The first phase explored wire lengths using the existing allocation of wires to layers, while the second pass varied the allocation of wires to layers to obtain a small incremental improvement in performance.

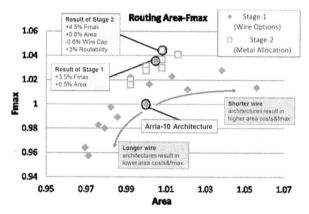

Fig 16: Routing optimization

Table 2: Stratix 10 Routing Fabric

H wire	H wire fraction	V wire	V wire fraction
H2	10%	V2	12%
H4	28%	V3	38%
H10	50%	V4	33%
H24	12%	V16	17%

The combination of wire length and layer optimization produced a 4.5% improvement in fmax compared to simply porting the Arria 10 architecture. Although a longer H10 wire is introduced, no such wire is added in the vertical direction because the Altera LAB is considerably taller than it is wide, so the physical length of an H10 and V4 are in fact comparable. Related to this, a shorter V2 wire is introduced for faster vertical connections. The longest wires (H24 and V16) are still shorter than electrically optimal in the thickest metal, and designed according to routability and metal constraints. The Stratix 10 routing fabric contains 8 distinct wire types as shown in Table 2.

7.1 ALM Simplification

The Stratix ALM was introduced in Stratix II [12] and contains a 6-LUT that can be configured as two 5-LUTs with two shared inputs. It can also be configured as two 6-LUTs with identical functions and four shared inputs (shared LUT mask, or SLM mode [15]). The ALM also contains an adder, FFs, and control signals. It has survived relatively unchanged since Stratix II, except for the addition of two FFs and various power/area/performance tradeoffs. The introduction of pipelined routing changes the cost/benefit of some of these features.

SLM mode allows two 6-LUTs with four shared inputs to be implemented, with the addition of a few extra multiplexers for the later stages of the LUT. In a pipelined fabric SLM introduces a coupling in the pipeline structure of the first four stages of the LUTs, which use one physical multiplexer to implement two independent LUTs with shared inputs. This makes it impossible to independently retime the four inputs of the two logical LUTs. Consequently SLM is removed in Stratix 10. The two 5-LUT mode uses independent hardware for each of the 5-LUTs, which can be retimed independently by providing separate pipeline registers for the two 5-LUTs. Although the two 5-LUTs share two inputs, these may be retimed independently by using two independent registers for each input.

As mentioned earlier, it is expected that the designer will restructure his design to use synchronous, rather than asynchronous clears. This potentially increases the number of SCLR signals needed. However the ACLR must be preserved for backwards compatibility. To enable this without excessive cost for retiming registers, we merge the ACLR and SCLR into a set of two ASCLR signals that are each capable of being used for either purpose.

Previous generations of the ALM also contained a synchronous load, which has been removed in Stratix 10 due to the increased cost of the function when support for retiming the control signals is included.

The adder was also simplified based on observations that it is rarely used in its most powerful modes, which allow the use of all 8 inputs to provide the operands for a two bit addition.

Further the 3 input mode straddles 2 ALMs and was difficult to use in a pipelined fashion. In Stratix 10 the operands enter through only the 6 inputs shared across four 4-LUTs, allowing some of the addition logic to be implemented in the LUT, thus saving area.

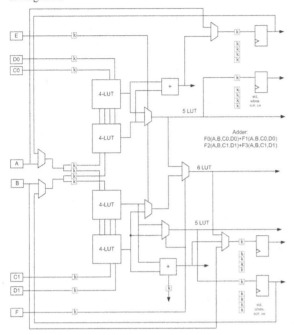

Fig 17: ALM with simpler arithmetic, removal of SLM and inclusion of pipeline registers

Further area savings are realized by removing the dedicated intra-LAB routing (compare Fig 2 with local lines [13] Fig 2) and replacing them with inputs into the LIMs, similar to [25]. The number of LIMs and LAB lines is increased from 52 to 60 to compensate for the larger average number of used signals now on the LAB lines, while 20 local lines are eliminated. LEIM fanin is reduced from 36 to 32 and large local line drivers are eliminated. There is a small delay increase due to the fact that a local routing now goes through a mux instead of a driver. This change was introduced in Arria 10.

8. DESIGN MODIFICATIONS

We have used an early version of QII with support for Stratix 10 to identify limiting factors in several customer designs and to modify them to improve performance. We modified several modules in these customer designs, in the context of the entire design when available, to ensure that the results reflect actual design performance improvement. We compared the fmax of Stratix 10 under the various flows to a Stratix V baseline.

As noted in Section 6.1, when a design can be pipelined it is common for it to be limited by loops. Although our CAD flow can partly address this, it may only identify but not remove, some bottlenecks. Manually restructuring the design is used in these cases to dramatically improve performance. Simple Shannon factoring of the loop is a common technique that can provide significant speedup when a few signals are the limiting factor [21]. This section presents results on several actual customer engagement designs. Naturally, the ability to achieve increased performance depends on the exact functionality of the design and improvement can vary dramatically. We did not necessarily pursue maximum optimization of each design due to time limits, but enough to demonstrate optimization potential to

the customer. Nevertheless the results shown below clearly demonstrate the benefits of design optimization. To show the purely architectural benefits of Stratix 10, we then back-port the redesign to Stratix V and measure the performance improvement. Table 3 shows the results for the 4 designs.

Design 1 refactored a critical loop in module A. Modules B and C have not been modified to date.

Table 3: Performance Fmax (MHz) and Improvement

Des	S V	Retime S10	Pipe S10	Redesign S10	Redesign SV
1A	320	380 (+19%)	460 (+44%)	489 (+53%)	329 (+3%)
1B	327	482 (+47%)	626 (+91%)		
1C	319	432 (+35%)	457 (+43%)		
2A	250	429 (+72%)	454 (+82%)	942 (+277%)	347 (+39%)
3A	191	290 (+52%)	291 (+52%)	748 (+292%)	359 (+88%)
4A	403	599 (+49%)	638 (+58%)	725 (+80%)	411 (+2%)
4B	384	555 (+45%)	570 (+48%)	695 (+81%)	391 (+2%)
Geo %		45%	48%	136%	23%

Design 2 restructured critical loops to have a single FF in the loop and simplify the logic, and achieved one of the highest gains in performance.

Design 3 represented a case where performance improvement was a priority and area increase could be tolerated to achieve this. Design 3 has a large and logically deep loop, so we employed loop unrolling [22] to increase performance with some area cost. The selected area/performance tradeoff is a not particularly favorable one but improves performance from 191MHz to 748MHz, a factor of 3.9X.

In Design 4 the loop was modified to reduce the logic depth, and some complex calculations were moved into a feedforward stage. This achieves 80% improvement in performance.

The geomean performance of modified clock domains across all 4 designs is a factor of 2.36X faster, 1.49X faster than the unmodified pipelined designs. Since it is possible that the design modifications can benefit the older architectures, we also evaluated the performance of the redesign in Stratix V. Two modules that use loop unrolling benefit reasonably (geomean 62%) but others benefit minimally. On average the design improvements have a 23% fmax benefit, which compared to the 136% fmax benefit of design modifications and architecture, means that the redesigns in Stratix 10 are on average 92% faster due to architecture and process technology.

8.1 Design Optimization Advisor

A key assumption in the design of the Stratix 10 architecture is that designers are willing to make changes to their circuits in order to achieve higher levels of performance. The architecture was evaluated with three experimental flows, the *retiming flow*, the *pipelining flow*, and the *modification flow*, as per Section 6. To enable the performance of the retiming flow, a designer must convert asynchronous reset elements in their design to synchronous resets. To enable the performance of the pipelining flow, a designer must add additional latency at the inputs or outputs of each clock domain (or primary inputs/outputs) of the circuit.

We enhance the post-route register retiming algorithm to provide two key pieces of information to designers. Where in the design must asynchronous elements be converted to synchronous, and where in the design should additional pipeline latency be added? At the conclusion of the post-route retiming step, the performance limit of the circuit can be analyzed. In our constraint-driven retimer, this performance limit manifests as an infeasible set of constraints in our retiming graph, for which provably no solution exists. This set of constraints can be analyzed to suggest a specific modification to the circuit, be it the conversion of an asynchronous clear to synchronous, or the addition of a register at an appropriate boundary point. We can then modify the retiming graph to implement this suggestion, which enables the retiming optimization to continue exploring circuit performance that was previously blocked by this limit. In the end, we can report both an attainable performance of the circuit as well as an actionable set of steps for the designer to take to achieve that performance.

9. CONCLUSIONS

The Stratix 10 architecture introduces a highly pipelined logic and routing fabric to improve performance at a relatively modest cost. The use of direct drive routing enables low-cost ubiquitous pipeline registers in the routing fabric, implemented with a simple pulse latch. The global clock network is logically unchanged, but the LAB level clock network is designed to minimize cost at no performance loss, using a modest number of clocks for routing multiplexers, and only a single clock within a LAB. The relatively simple concept of a pulse latch in the routing multiplexers has ramifications on the overall architecture once the cost of the clocking structure and its effects on control signals is included, leading towards simplification of the logic element to avoid an excessive number of pipeline registers in the LE.

Stratix 10 enables moderate performance gains with fully automated retiming flows, but pipelining can boost performance significantly. A skilled designer can often restructure logic to achieve more than 2X performance, although this is highly dependent on the fundamental logical structure of the design.

10. REFERENCES

[1] V. Betz, J. Rose, and A. Marquardt, "Architecture and CAD for Deep-Submicron FPGAs", Kluwer Academic Publishers, 1999

[2] D. Singh and S. Brown, "The Case for Registered Routing Switches in Field Programmable Gate Arrays", *Proc. FPGA 2001*, pp. 161-169

[3] D. Singh and S. Brown, "Integrated Retiming and Placement for Field Programmable Gate Arrays", *Proc. FPGA 2002*, pp. 67-76

[4] R. Deokar and S. Sapatnekar, "A Fresh Look at Retiming via Clock Skew Optimization", *Proc. DAC 1995*, pp. 304-309.

[5] A. Sharma, C. Ebeling, and S. Hauck, "PipeRoute: A Pipelining-Aware Router for Reconfigurable Architectures", *IEEE TCAD*, Mar. 2006, pp. 518-532

[6] C. Ebeling, D. How, D. Lewis and H. Schmit, "Stratix™ 10 High Performance Routable Clock Networks", *Proc. FPGA 2016*

[7] W. Tsu *et al*, "HSRA: High-Speed, Hierarchical Synchronous Reconfigurable Array", *Proc. FPGA 1999*, pp. 125-134

[8] D. Cronquist, C. Fisher, M. Figueroa, P. Franklin, and C. Ebeling, "Architecture Design Of Reconfigurable Pipelined Datapaths", *Conf. Advanced Research in VLSI*, 1999, pp. 23-40

[9] S. Goldstein, H. Schmit, M. Budiu, S. Cadambi, M. Moe R. Taylor, "PipeRench: A Reconfigurable Architecture and Compiler", *Computer*, April 2000, pp. 70-77

[10] K. Eguro, "Supporting High-Performance Pipelined Computation in Commodity-Style FPGAs", PhD thesis, University of Washington, 2008

[11] D. Lewis et al, "The Stratix™ Routing and Logic Architecture", *Proc. FPGA 2003*, pp. 12-20

[12] D. Lewis et al, "The Stratix-II™ Logic and Routing Architecture", *Proc. FPGA 2005*, pp. 14-20

[13] D. Lewis et al, "Architectural Enhancements in Stratix-V™", *Proc. FPGA 2013*, pp. 147-156

[14] G. Lemieux and D. Lewis, "Circuit Design of FPGA Routing Switches", *Proc. FPGA 2002*, pp. 19-28

[15] B. Pedersen, "Logic Circuitry with Shared Lookup Table", US Patent 7317330

[16] C.-H. Jan et al, "A 14nm SoC Platform Technology Featuring 2nd Generation Tri-Gate Transistors, 70nm Gate Pitch, 52nm Metal Pitch, and 0.0499um2 SRAM Cells, Optimized for Low Power, High Performance and High Density SoC Products", *Symp. VLSI*, 2015, pp. T12-T13

[17] N. Weaver, J. Hauser, J. Wawrzynek, "The SFRA: A Corner-Turn FPGA Architecture", *Proc. FPGA 2004*, pp. 3-12

[18] V. Manohararajah, G. Chiu, D. Singh, and S. Brown, "Predicting Interconnect Delay for Physical Synthesis in a FPGA CAD Flow", *IEEE TVLSI*, Aug 2007, pp. 895-903

[19] D. Singh, V. Manohararajah, and S. Brown, "Two-stage Physical Synthesis for FPGAs", *CICC 2005*, pp. 171-178

[20] C. Leiserson and J. Saxe, "Optimizing Synchronous Systems", *Symp. Foundations of Computer Science*, 1981, pp 23-36

[21] C. Soviani, O. Tardieu, and S. Edwards, "Optimizing Sequential Cycles Through Shannon Decomposition and Retiming", *IEEE TCAD*, Mar 2007 pp. 456-467

[22] D. Lewis, B. Thomson, P. Boulton, and E. S. Lee, "Transforming Bit Serial Communication Circuits into Fast, Parallel VLSI Implementations", *IEEE JSSC*, April 1988, pp. 549-557

[23] P. Pan, "Continuous Retiming: Algorithms and Applications", *Proc. ICCD 1997*, pp. 116-121

[24] W. Feng and S. Kaptanoglu, Designing Efficient Input Interconnect Blocks for LUT Clusters Using Counting and Entropy, *Proc. FPGA 2007*, pp. 23-30

Case for Design-Specific Machine Learning in Timing Closure of FPGA Designs

Que Yanghua
quey0001@e.ntu.edu.sg

Chinnakkannu Adaikkala Raj
adaikkal001@e.ntu.edu.sg

Harnhua Ng[1]
harnhua@plunify.com

Kirvy Teo[1]
kirvy@plunify.com

Nachiket Kapre
nachiket@ieee.org

School of Computer Engineering, Nanyang Technological University, Singapore 639798
[1]Plunify Inc., 67 Ayer Rajah Crescent, Singapore 139950

ABSTRACT

We can achieve reliable timing closure of FPGA designs using machine learning heuristics to generate input parameter settings for FPGA CAD tools. This is enabled by running multiple instances of CAD tool with different sets of these input parameters and logging of resulting timing slack values into a database. We incrementally build this database and run learning routines to develop suitable classifier models that correlate input parameter combinations to resulting slack. As each CAD run in independent, we can trivially parallelize our exploration. The classifier model developed using this approach can help predict whether a given combination of tool parameters will improve the timing score of that particular FPGA design. Through repeated trials and use of cheap cloud computing resources, we are able to reliably improve timing scores for a variety of industrial and academic FPGA designs. We show how to build design-specific classifier models that easily outperform generic models that are trained by combining results across all circuits in a benchmark.

1. INTRODUCTION

With FPGA capacities rising to millions of LUTs per chip, the ambition and complexity of modern FPGA designs is growing proportionally larger. FPGAs today can fit designs requiring millions of LUTs, thousands of hard DSP-blocks, thousands of on-chip Block RAMs, hundreds of IO ports supporting a rich set of IO protocols, and complex wiring requirements. Modern CAD tools have struggled to keep up with this increase in design size and heterogeneity of the underlying FPGA fabric resulting in long compilation cycles for these designs. A typical single run of the CAD tool can take hours to days of compilation time under user-supplied constraints. Developers often iterate through this painful compilation process multiple times hoping to improve timing scores by modifying their RTL through pipelining, logic

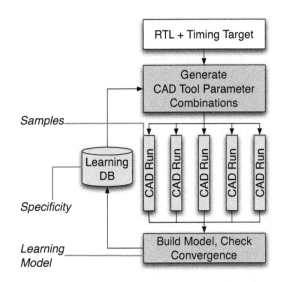

Figure 1: Organization of InTime Flow. Overall goal is to achieve timing closure for a given RTL design. In-Time runs the RTL through multiple rounds of parallel CAD runs with different CAD parameter configurations. Based on history of what improved timing, we modify the configurations for subsequent rounds of execution.

restructuring and providing suitable constraints to the CAD tool. They can fail and in many cases are prevented from modifying verified RTL source (*e.g.* black-box IP) thereby restricting their freedom.

When RTL modifications are not possible, we can still rely on the tuneability and configurability choices available in the CAD algorithms itself. However, modern CAD tools are a complex series of NP-complete heuristics that are hard to understand and configure properly for a given design. A typical FPGA developer may require years of experience before mastering the art of guiding the CAD tool to produce desired results. These tools are organized as a series of passes such as synthesis, technology mapping, placement, and routing before the bitstream is produced. These key stages are NP-complete problems that are driven by tuneable heuristics. Consequently, they significantly affect solution quality. The exact selection of CAD tool parameters (command-line options, GUI switches, and drop-down boxes) depends heavily on the specifics of the user design and user constraints, and its interaction with the exact device family selected for mapping.

In this study, we use InTime [2, 3], a plugin for CAD tools, that can efficiently select these parameters for each combination of RTL design, FPGA device, and timing constraint combination. InTime helps designs achieve timing closure by running multiple CAD runs in parallel with different parameter selections and refines these selections per design through machine learning. This addresses the long runtimes of the CAD tools inherent in the edit-compile-debug loop of a typical FPGA design, as well as select input CAD parameters for the CAD tool in an automated fashion. In this paper, we focus on the selection of appropriate machine learning algorithms and techniques to identify and tune the most promising solution. The goal is to deliver timing closure with high classifier accuracy and consequently fewer iterations to timing closure. The principle of operation of InTime has already been established in prior work [2, 3].

The key contributions of this report include:

- Development of plugins for InTime to evaluate the impact of design specificity on the overall solution of our learning algorithms.

- Quantification and characterization of design-specific learning routines across various real-world open-source benchmarks.

2. INTIME

2.1 Execution Flow

As described in [2, 3], InTime is a plugin for FPGA CAD tools from Altera and Xilinx that helps the developer select a suitable combination of CAD tool parameters to achieve timing closure. Modern FPGA CAD tools employ tuneable heuristics that export hundreds of parameters. Some of these are boolean (on/off) parameters, some offer discrete choices, while others are continuous. In all these cases, selecting the combination of assignments to these parameters to guide timing closure is hard and usually handled through experience or trial-and-error. For Altera Quartus 14.1 CAD tool with 80 selected boolean parameters, a trivial brute-force exploration of all possible combinations will take 2^{80} runs of the CAD tool which is clearly infeasible using contemporary computing technology. Instead, InTime *learns* these insights through automated parallel trials of far fewer combinations and accumulating wisdom through machine learning. As shown in Fig. 1, InTime is organized as an iterative computation broken down into a series of parallel CAD *runs*. Each *iteration* (or *round*) is an opportunity to acquire data for the learning database. Typically, we need 30 runs in each *round* to acquire sufficient data points to drive the learning algorithms. In [3, 2], InTime used a Naive Bayesian learning framework to classify the timing results and drive the learning process (maximum observed accuracy of $\approx 70\%$). While these results were promising, our work differs from InTime by clearly exploring design specificity.

We evaluate the classifier accuracy gap between general models that are trained in a single-shot with all design data vs. a design-specific learning flow where each circuit trains its own classifier. FPGA vendor DSE (design space exploration) tools typically use the generic approach to greatly save on the compute time and compute costs required by running a pre-calibrated set of CAD parameter combinations. More importantly, we also consider the scenario where different machine learning routines may be suitable for different kinds of benchmarks. This requires a further meta analysis of how to select the most appropriate learning approach for a given circuit benchmark.

2.2 Formal Model

The key idea in InTime is to track which CAD parameter combinations improve timing slack and which combinations make timing worse over a reference baseline. Thus, we can formulate a supervised learning approach to develop a classifier model that can determine if a given combination of CAD parameter assignments will help the design converge towards timing closure. The combinations themselves can be generated statistically. We represent this formally in Figure 2 where x_{ij} are the boolean parameters for each CAD parameter i and y_j is a timing slack result for a given CAD execution j.

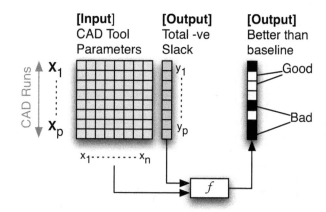

Figure 2: Data Structures used to build classifier model. We tabulate all combinations of CAD parameters tested in various runs, and record the resulting TNS (Total Negative Slack). This is used to drive a supervised learning routine that classifies timing scores better than a reference baseline as GOOD or BAD. This then trains a model which is used to generate better candidates for subsequent CAD runs.

3. METHODOLOGY

In this section, we introduce our set of benchmark circuits used to evaluate the various learning algorithms, and the system setup required to run these experiments.

3.1 R Packages

We wrote machine learning routines as plugins for InTime using R [5] and appropriate R libraries and packages. The interface supplies a CSV-formatted dataset with input columns containing the boolean values of the various input CAD parameters and an output column containing the resulting timing score. We make extensive use of *caret* [1] to train our models. It provides a unified interface to use multiple machine learning algorithms. The runtime of running these algorithms on the data are minuscule (few seconds) compared to the much longer runtimes of the CAD algorithms.

3.2 Benchmarks

In Table 1, we list the key characteristics of the FPGA benchmarks used in this study that are taken from Open-Cores as well as industrial designs. These benchmarks were compiled using Quartus 14.1 and mapped to the Cyclone devices using the free Web Edition licenses. Certain industrial designs also targeted other Altera devices and tool versions. These benchmarks occupy a range of sizes and the operating frequencies also cover a spectrum of values thereby stress-testing our toolflow with design-specific requirements and constraints. In particular, the `viterbi` benchmark has a high TNS score and highest number of failing paths and is painful for timing closure. Our framework also works with Xilinx ISE and Vivado flows and the resulting mapping costs are listed in Table 2.

Table 1: Opencore Benchmarks (Altera)

Bench.	FFs	LUTs	P&R mins.	Freq. MHz	TNS	Fail/Tot. Paths
Open-Cores Examples						
aes	6K	11K	22	500	0.2	5/5.7K
switch	0.5K	2.6K	15	250	0.7	14/2.3K
vga	0.7K	1K	12	400	1.7	17/262
viterbi	1.6K	4K	20	285	22.8	300/6.6K
xge	1672	2.5K	17	333	10.8	79/1.7K
bitcoin	14K	22.3K	28	78	2.8	10/96K
Industrial Examples						
SOC	4.9K	3.5K	5	150	0.6	10/42K
flow	20.7K	21.8K	12	320	5.9	47/87K
vip	62.3K	80.1K	58	150	0.6	15/435K
eight	3.3K	3.5K	2	174	1.02	10/16K

Table 2: Opencore Benchmarks (Xilinx)

Bench.	FFs	LUTs	P&R mins.	Freq. MHz	TNS	Fail/Tot. Paths
aes	6K	11K	0	500	1219	4630 / 5775
switch	800	2.4K	0	200	42.3	57 / 2190
vga	966	106	0	400	108	128 / 290
viterbi	3.5K	4K	0	333	5081	4399 / 7299
xge	1.6K	1.6K	0	250	50	229 / 1778

3.3 Compute Resources

We ran all our experiments on the Google Compute Engine [4]. We configured an *instance group* template using `n1-standard-2` CPU configuration with 2 virtual CPUs (Intel Xeon E5s) and 7.5G RAM each. We chose this configuration over the dense 32-CPU configurations to make optimum use of the free web-edition licenses and to ensure sufficient RAM state is available for the CAD tool executions. We also enabled the Google `auto-scaling` feature to trigger the launch of parallel VM instances (up to 10 machines launched in parallel) when the CPU utilization threshold got over 65%. This allowed us to keep costs low and only spawn machines are needed during the benchmarking process. The cumulative costs of using the Google machines for our entire experiment set for over a fortnight was under ≈500$ USD[1]. This means

[1]summer 2015 prices, not considering InTime licensing costs.

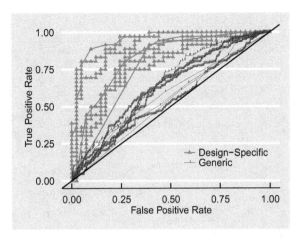

Figure 3: Comparing ROC [6] characteristics of various Machine Learning routines for the `aes` benchmark. Each curve is a particular Machine Learning algorithm. Even the worst-performing Design-Specific model does better than the best-performing Generic model.

for a single design we roughly needed a couple of days of cloud compute time which compares favorably against an RTL engineer struggling to manually deliver timing closure.

4. RESULTS

To evaluate the effectiveness of the various machine learning algorithms, we measure several metrics: (1) Prediction Accuracy, (2) F1 score or FMeasure, and (3) ROC [6] (Receiver Operating Characteristics) plots. To understand these metrics mathematically, we define TP as True Positives, TN as True Negatives, FP as False Positives and FN as False Negatives in our prediction set. Ideally, we want high TP and TN and low values for FP and FN. These are defined based on a classification threshold and can be thought of as a tag or attribute assigned to each row in Figure 2 of the testing set. High prediction accuracy $A = \frac{TP+TN}{TP+TN+FP+FN}$ is useful as it helps us correctly determine how a given combination of FPGA CAD parameters affects timing slack. However, this is not sufficient as we are ultimately interested in generating good candidates that are positively correlated with reducing timing slack. Additionally, false positive rate (FPR) helps us determine if we are making judicious use of our parallel compute resources during the exploration phase by avoiding wasted compute on false positives. It should be noted that we do want certain bad combinations (FP combinations) to teach us what kinds of combinations to avoid in the future. Even a failed CAD run is a teachable moment for InTime flow. We also calculate the FMeasure that is a harmonic mean of precision and recall metrics $F = \frac{2 \cdot P \cdot R}{P+R}$ that provides a unified view of the classifier effectiveness. Precision is the fraction of positive predictions that are relevant $P = \frac{TP}{TP+FP}$ while Recall is the fraction of relevant predictions that are positive $R = \frac{TP}{TP+FN}$. A great visual tool for evaluating the effectiveness of the machine learning algorithm is the ROC (Receiver Operating Characteristics) curve. This provides a complete picture of the tradeoffs between accuracy of the prediction and wasted time on fruitless CAD runs.

Table 3: Features Ranked by Chi-Squared (χ^2) for *aes*.

Rank	Design-Specific	Generic Model
1	Optimize_Ioc_Register_ Placement_For_Timing	Remove_Redundant_ Logic_Cells
2	Physical_Synthesis_ Register_Retiming	Remove_Duplicate_ Registers
3	State_Machine_Proces.	Auto_Ram_Recog.
4	Physical_Synthesis_ Map_Logic_To_ Memory_For_Area	Not_Gate_Push_Back
5	Auto_Rom_Recognition	Physical_Synthesis_ Register_Duplication
6	Synth_Timing_ Driven_Synthesis	Allow_Synch_Ctrl_Usg.
7	Extract_Vhdl_ State_Machines	Auto_Resource_Shar.
8	Dsp_Block_Balancing	Physical_Synthesis_Eff.
9	Fitter_Aggressive_ Routability_Optimiz.	Allow_Any_Ram_Size_ For_Recognition
10	Cycloneii_Optimiz._ Technique	Optimize_Timing

One may be tempted to consider building a generic global model for timing score in a manner that is not specific to a particular design. FPGA vendors are likely to prefer a single design-agnostic model that they can train using their customer benchmarks in-house and ship a single model with their CAD tools to all customers. A key benefit of such an approach is the ability to construct such a model off-line across a wide range of benchmarks without resorting to an online learning-based incremental approach advocated in this paper. Additionally, the model can operate in feed-forward manner and execute a set of canned strategies (CAD parameter mixes) based on some design criteria. In contrast, a design-specific model is tailored to each individual design and involves an online learning phase with feedback as described earlier in Section 2.

4.1 ROC for Design-Specific Models

In Fig. 3, we show the ROC plot for the various machine learning routines applied to the **aes** benchmark. Here, we observe that the cluster of design-specific models offer higher accuracy at the expense of higher false positives. Across other benchmarks as well, the prediction accuracy of the general model hovers around 50–55% which is no worse than a random coin toss. It is interesting to note that even the worst-fitted model built from the design-specific scenario is still better than the best-case generic model. There is a clear case for constructing and developing the correct model tailored for each individual design.

4.2 CAD Parameter Ranking

Next, we rank the most important CAD tool parameters with the χ^2 metric in Table 3. This ranking is computed by identifying the CAD tool parameters when modified cause the most impact on the final TNS result. Here, again, we see that the top-10 features for the **aes** benchmark have nothing in common with the top ranked features when considering the generic model that ignores the effect of design-specific preferences. While this is admittedly an extreme case scenario, it highlights the need for a design-specific model yet again. The kind of CAD parameter that matters for a given design is also related to the underlying architecture when we see the Cyclone-II specific optimizations becoming prominent. In general, we expect the combination of design, FPGA architecture and possibly even the CAD tool version having a joint influence on these rankings. This implies we need our models to be built in a manner that is specific to the FPGA architecture and CAD tools version in addition to design alone.

5. CONCLUSIONS

Machine learning algorithms can be configured to deliver timing closure for digital designs in the presence of rising complexity and noise in modern FPGA CAD toolflows. To achieve these goals, we use cheap, parallel cloud computing resources to run multiple instances of the CAD tools guided by these machine learning routines. Across a range of benchmarks, we show that design-specific learning routines outperform generic models. Overall, we observe that InTime works well when the timing constraints are realistic and we observed a few cases where none of the machine learning algorithms delivered useful performance.

6. REFERENCES

[1] M. K. C. from Jed Wing, S. Weston, A. Williams, C. Keefer, A. Engelhardt, T. Cooper, Z. Mayer, B. Kenkel, the R Core Team, M. Benesty, R. Lescarbeau, A. Ziem, and L. Scrucca. *caret: Classification and Regression Training*, 2015. R package version 6.0-52.

[2] N. Kapre, B. Chandrashekaran, H. Ng, and K. Teo. Driving timing convergence of fpga designs through machine learning and cloud computing. In *Field-Programmable Custom Computing Machines (FCCM), 2015 IEEE 23rd Annual International Symposium on*, pages 119–126, May 2015.

[3] N. Kapre, H. Ng, K. Teo, and J. Naude. Intime: A machine learning approach for efficient selection of fpga cad tool parameters. In *Proceedings of the 2015 ACM/SIGDA International Symposium on Field-Programmable Gate Arrays*, FPGA '15, pages 23–26, New York, NY, USA, 2015. ACM.

[4] S. Krishnan and J. L. U. Gonzalez. Google compute engine. In *Building Your Next Big Thing with Google Cloud Platform*, pages 53–81. Springer, 2015.

[5] R Core Team. *R: A Language and Environment for Statistical Computing*. R Foundation for Statistical Computing, Vienna, Austria, 2015.

[6] T. Sing, O. Sander, N. Beerenwinkel, and T. Lengauer. Rocr: visualizing classifier performance in r. *Bioinformatics*, 21(20):7881, 2005.

Just In Time Assembly of Accelerators

Sen Ma
Department of CSCE
University of Arkansas
Fayetteville, AR 72701, USA
senma@uark.edu

Zeyad Aklah
Department of CSCE
University of Arkansas
Fayetteville, AR 72701, USA
zaklah@uark.edu

David Andrews
Department of CSCE
University of Arkansas
Fayetteville, AR 72701, USA
dandrews@uark.edu

ABSTRACT

Despite the significant advancements that have been made in High Level Synthesis, the reconfigurable computing community has failed at getting programmers to use Field Programmable Gate Arrays (FPGAs). Existing barriers that prevent programmers from using FPGAs include the need to work within vendor specific CAD tools, knowledge of hardware programming models, and the requirement to pass each design through synthesis, place and route. In this paper we present a new approach that takes these barriers out of the design flows for programmers. Synthesis is eliminated from the application programmers path by becoming part of the initial coding process when creating the programming patterns that define a Domain Specific Language. Programmers see no difference between creating software or hardware functionality when using the DSL. A run time interpreter is introduced that assembles hardware accelerators within a configurable tile array of partially reconfigurable slots at run time. Initial results show the approach allows hardware accelerators to be compiled $100\times$ faster compared to the time required to synthesize the same functionality. Initial performance results further show a compilation/interpretation approach can achieve approximately equivalent performance for matrix operations and filtering compared to synthesizing a custom accelerator.

Keywords

FPGA;Overlay;Just-In-Time Hardware Compilation.

1. INTRODUCTION

Just In Time (JIT) compilation and run time interpretation has been effective at delivering portability within the software world. In this work we investigate if the same JIT run time interpretation philosophy can be used to enable programmers, not hardware designers, to assemble hardware accelerators at run time on todays FPGAs.

This is no small challenge. Creating such a capability requires rethinking what is synthesized, when synthesis should

FPGA'16 February 21-23, 2016, Monterey, CA, USA
© 2015 ACM. ISBN 123-4567-24-567/08/06...$15.00
DOI: http://dx.doi.org/10.1145/2847263.2847341

occur, and how certain steps within the place and route sequence can be moved into the run time system.

Synthesis cannot be totally eliminated, but can be moved out of a programmer's compilation path. Domain Specific Languages (DSLs) provide a path forward [1, 6, 8]. Our assertion is that synthesis can be taken out of the application developers path if it is made part of the standard coding process when the Domain Specific Language (DSL) is created. This is before an application programmer attempts to combine and compile individual programming patterns into an application.

Individual programming pattern bitstreams can be made available as executable library routines. These library routines can be symbolically referred to during compilation as yet another form of a dynamically linked run time executable. Thus the bitstreams are treated no differently during compilation as traditional libraries of binary executables. The place and route steps that traditionally occur when bitstreams are combined together before synthesis can be moved into the run time system.

Java compilers produce platform independent Java bytecodes that are translated into native machine code during run time by the Java Virtual Machine (JVM). The symbolic links to the individual bitstreams can be output from a compiler as pointers to the hardware module equivalents of the native methods. They are just spatial instead of temporal representations.

The hardware native methods (bitstreams) then need to be substituted in place of the symbolic links at run time. We define a new run time interpreter to perform the equivalent function of the JVM. Instead of substituting byte codes with native machine code, the run time interpreter will substitute the symbolic links with the relocatable hardware modules.

The interpreter needs spaces within the FPGA to place the hardware modules and a programmable interconnect that can route data between the modules. FPGAs already provide the structure to support this through partial reconfiguration [9]. We create a network overlay with programmable interconnects. Partial reconfiguration regions are provided into which the interpreter can place the modules and route them together at run time.

Figure 1 shows our end to end design flow. The left side shows what occurs by a system programmer when creating a Domain Specific Language (DSL) for the application programmers. During the normal coding process that occurs when programming patterns are created, we add the additional step of synthesizing each individual pattern into a bitstream. This is discussed in section 3. The bottom left

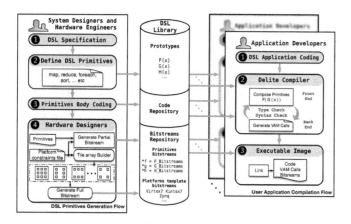

Figure 1: Design Flow.

of Figure 1 shows the introduction of a new type of overlay network. This overlay is created once when the programming patterns are coded and synthesized. The new overlay is discussed in section 2. The programming patterns, bitstreams, and overlay are placed into libraries shown in the middle of Figure 1 and can be accessed by all application programmers.

The application programmers use the flow on the right in Figure 1 to create their applications. They work with standard software DSL primitives just as if they are coding their application for a traditional software implementation. However when the programmer composes DSL primitives that have bitstream representations, the compiler inserts symbolic links to the bitstreams and builds a data flow graph representation of how the programming patterns are composed to represent the accelerator.

The compiler outputs a series of interpreter instructions that are used by an interpreter to assemble the bitstreams within the overlay and set the data connections. This is discuss in section 4.

1.1 Contributions

The main contributions of this work are:

- *PR Tile Overlay* A new overlay that uses partial reconfiguration tiles within a 2D Array and flexible word width switch boxes. The overlay represents the framework within which the run time system assembles accelerators. We provide a scripting tool to automatically create different configurations of the overlay for a DSL and FPGA.

- *Platform Independent Interpreter Language* A set of platform independent interpreter calls used by an interpreter to assemble accelerators on different configurations of the PR tile overlay at run time.

- *Run Time Interpreter* We created a C implementation of the interpreter. The interpreter dynamically places and routes the programming patterns within different configurations of the overlay. The interpreter calls are compiled and linked as sys_calls within a pthreads compliant multithreaded programming model middleware library.

- *Case Studies and Evaluation* Case studies showing a complete end to end capability. Case studies show

how accelerators are formed from the programming patterns of a DSL, compiled, JIT assembled and run within different overlays. We show the portability of the approach by running the same compiled accelerator in different overlays, including single and multiprocessor systems on chip architectures on Virtex7 and Kintex7 FPGAs. Run time performance and area overhead comparison studies are provided that compare the approach to traditional synthesis flows.

2. INTERMEDIATE FABRIC

Commercial off-the-shelf FPGAs have served and will continue to serve as the defacto component for reconfigurable computing research. This is not because they are ideal, in fact they are far from it. Course Grained Reconfigurable Arrays (CGRAs) have been proposed as alternatives to FPGA fabrics for reconfigurable computing [4]. CGRAs replace Lookup tables (LUTs) and Flop Flops with programmable Arithmetic Logic Units (ALUs) and word width interconnects as compilation targets. CGRA structures promise to close the semantic gap between high level languages and hardware and change design flows from synthesis to compilation [3]. Even though interest in CGRAs remains high no devices are available.

Intermediate Fabrics, or overlays have been proposed that allow CGRA type structures [5] as well as more higher level computational components such as vector processors [10] to be embedded within FPGAs. The potential advantage of such overlays is that circuits and hardware acceleration can be achieved through compilation instead of synthesis on existing FPGAs. Common approaches for enabling CGRAs on an FPGA are to replace LUTs and Flip Flops with small programmable computational units such as ALUs as the compilation target. The ALUs are embedded within a network of switch boxes and channels.

The interconnect structures are defined to support wider word widths instead of bit level interconnections. The general approach introduces some overhead inefficiencies associated with need to provide additional resources to form the overlay, routing delays between the computational units, and limitations on the granularity of parallelism that can be exploited. New approaches to addressing overhead and latency issues continue to be investigated [2].

We defined a hybrid type of overlay to support JITing bitstreams.

Our overlay includes a nearest neighbor programmable word width interconnect similar to traditional CGRA type overlays. Different from traditional CGRA overlays, we expose the lookup tables and flip flops of the FPGA as partially reconfigurable tiles instead of abstracting them into programmable computational units. This combination of pre-formed interconnects and partial reconfiguration regions allows the bitstreams for the programming patterns to be downloaded at run time into the intermediate fabric. Figure 2 shows the structure of the hybrid overlay. The basic structure is a 2D array of partial reconfiguration tiles and programmable switches that are connected as a nearest neighbor interconnect network.

2.1 PR Tiles

The specific 3×3 array configuration shown in Figure 2 was constructed of partial reconfiguration tiles sized at 9,600 LUTS, 360KB BRAM, and 80 DSPs. This particular con-

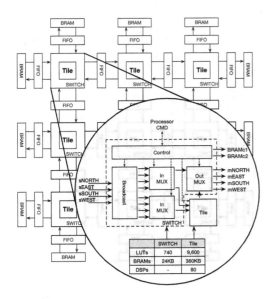

Figure 2: 3×3 **Tile Array and Interconnect Network.**

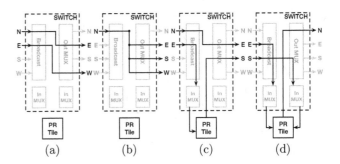

Figure 3: Switch Routing.

figuration was sized to hold the largest bitstream generated from our test DSL. The exact size of the tiles is variable and can be set when the DSL is first created.

The number of the tiles is derived based on the size of the tiles and the number of resources available on a target FPGA logic family.

2.2 Programmable Switch

Figure 3 provides an exploded view of a switch. Figure 3 shows the types of routing patterns that can be programmed into switch. The routing patterns were defined to enable each switch to direct inputs and outputs through the tile, as well as serving as a pass through for routes between distant tiles.

Routes can be set statically or dynamically. Dynamic settings can be used for allowing the switch to support different time varying routing needs such as when multiple accelerators are resident within the overlay. Each switch may serve as a pass through for one accelerator, and then source and synch data for a tile that is part of a different accelerator.

2.3 Local Memory

The boundary cells in the overlay include connections to blocks of local memories (BRAMs). These BRAMS can be used as addressable local memories or as FIFO data buffers for streaming data.

Block data transfers use DMA (not shown) between the BRAMs and Global DRAM memory. The BRAMs are placed within the global address map of the system, allowing any processor or bus master device to transfer data into and out of a local memory. The BRAMS have buffer full/empty handshaking signals that are connected through the switches to enable processing to be dynamically triggered.

3. THE PROGRAMMERS PERSPECTIVE

Domain Specific Languages (DSLs) are common within software development flows and offer a reduced set of programming patterns tailored for a particular application domain.

An advantage of a DSL approach is that domain s pecific

optimizations can be applied to the programming patterns before they are translated into lower level intermediate representations.

The programming patterns themselves hide complexity and allow the compiler and run time system to better decompose and map the computations across different configurations of architectures and computational resources. For these reasons, DSLs are gaining interest within the general purpose computing domain as a approach to increase performance and productivity for heterogeneous multiprocessors [8].

Our approach deviates from the current approaches that combine programming patterns prior to synthesis. When the programming patterns that define a DSL are first created, there is no reason why they cannot be synthesized before they are combined. The individual bitstream versions of the programming patterns can be placed within a corresponding library of linkable executables. The compiler can then refer to executables using symbolic links just like dynamically linked software routines.

This view presents a subtle but important difference from today's current approaches. Consider the differences in flows, design skills and development time needed to create the two separate hardware accelerators acc_1 and acc_2 using the following three generic functions $f(x), g(y), h(z)$. $acc_1 := f(g(h(z)))$; $acc_2 := g(g(h(z)))$;

Creating the first accelerator (acc_1) under current hardware design flows would require a programmer to work within a CAD tool to first combine and then synthesize the composed functionality within an HLS tool (such as Vivado). Coding each function would require the programmer to know HLS tool specific coding styles as well as board requirements. This effort typically includes inserting platform specific control, command/control and data interfaces, all requiring knowledge of low level signaling protocols. Creating the second accelerator (acc_2) would require a repeat of these steps. Under the proposed approach shown in Figure 1 the bitstreams for each function are created once by a hardware designer as part of the coding process for each individual function. Software prototypes can be provided for the programmers to represent the function calls. Application programmers can now compose and compile the function prototypes to create an accelerator as if they were working within a traditional software DSL framework. Assembling the individual bitstreams for $f(x), g(y), h(z)$ into a complete accelerator is moved from design time to run time.

4. INTERPRETER

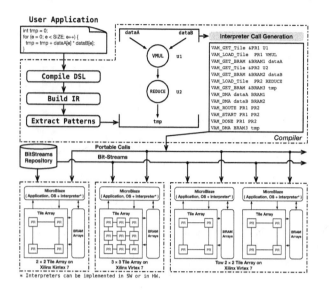

Figure 4: Design Portability with JIT.

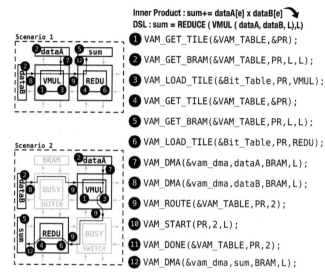

Figure 5: Interpreter Calls For Inner Product.

In this section we show how the interpreter executes the calls of the running example of Figure 4 on the two overlay configurations shown in Figure 5.

Function Placement and Loading: We chose to manage the free PR tiles in a simple queue (the VAM_TABLE). For each ***VAM_GET_TILE*** (steps 1, 4) the interpreter pops a free tile from the queue. The tiles returned for two consecutive ***VAM_GET_TILE*** calls may not be adjacent within the overlay array. This is shown in Figure 5. On the left the interpreter selected two adjacent tiles while on the right, the top right and bottom left tiles were selected. Function bitstreams are then loaded into free tiles using ***VAM_LOAD_TILE*** (steps 3, 6).

The run time interpreter manages input and output buffers for the accelerator in a similar fashion to tiles. For each input variable the ***VAM_GET_BRAM*** (steps 2, 5) returns a list of available local BRAMs to be selected as an input buffer.

Function Routing: After the interpreter transfers the bitstreams into the tiles, and BRAMs are selected, data paths are formed from the ***VAM_ROUTE*** (step 9) calls. For our prototype systems we implement a simplified version of the standard maze-routing algorithm [7]. The right side of Figure 5 shows the route formed from the top right tile (VMUL) to the bottom left tile (REDU). This route first traverses down to the bottom right tile, and then left to the bottom left tile.

Data Transfer: After the accelerator has been configured, the interpreter transfers input data from DRAM into the local input buffer BRAMS using ***VAM_DMA*** (steps 7, 8). The outputs of the accelerator are transferred from the output BRAM buffer back into DRAM using ***VAM_DMA*** (step 12).

Control Operations: The ***VAM_START*** (step 10) initiates the execution of the array. The ***VAM_DONE*** (step 11) returns status from the accelerator.

5. EXPERIMENTATION AND ANALYSIS

Figure 4 shows the three base platform systems created to evaluate our approach. The first system contains a 2×2

array built on a Kintex7. The second contained a 3×3 overlay on a Virtex7. The third system was built on a Virtex7 and contained two 2×2 overlays. In all cases the overlays were interfaced to a MicroBlaze processor as tightly coupled accelerators.

All systems were built and synthesized using Vivado 14.2 tools.

The interpreter was written in C and cross compiled with the operating system. As all systems used a MicroBlaze we were able to compile the interpreter once and reuse it on all systems. Interpreter calls invoked through sys_calls. Sequential portions of the test programs were cross compiled and run as a thread, or in the case of mulitprocessor system, as concurrent threads on the two MicroBlazes.

5.1 Creating the Accelerators

The first column in Table 1 list the functions we selected as our benchmarks. These functions are representative of computations that a programmer might wish to accelerate from high performance computing and signal processing codes. The second column lists the lines of code that were run through our Vivado HLS tool to create custom accelerator versions of each function for comparisons.

We defined the programming patterns shown in Table 2 as our test DSL. Prototypes (function definitions) were created for each programming pattern, and the body of each programming pattern was coded in C as part of the DSL creation process. The C bodies were passed through Vivado HLS to generate bitstreams. We added an additional flag to the standard compilation flow to allow the C versions of the DSL to be compiled for test and evaluation, or cross compiled to run on the MicroBlaze processors for comparison. Switching the compiler flag was all that was needed to generate interpreter calls with symbolic links to the bitstreams.

The right hand column of Table 1 shows how we composed the programming patterns to implement the test functions. Inner product was computed using the REDUCE and VMUL programming patterns. Matrix × Vector used the matrix multiply pattern with the number of columns set to 1. Matrix × Matrix × Matrix was computed by composing

176

Table 1: Code Complexity

Benchmarks	Lines of Code (HLS)*	Composed Expression
Inner Product	35	dataC=**REDUCE**(**VMUL**(dataA, dataB, Size), Size);
$M_1 \times V_1$	60	MatrixC=**MM**(MatrixA, VectorB, rowA, colA, 1);
$M_1 \times M_2 \times M_3$	65	MatrixD=**MM**(**MM**(MatrixA, MatrixB, rowA, colA, colB), MatrixC, rowA, colB, colC);
Correlation	90	diff1=**SVSUB**(dataA, **AVG**(dataA, Size), Size); diff2=**SVSUB**(dataB, **AVG**(dataB, Size), Size); VAR1=**REDUCE**(**VSQR**(diff1, Size), SIZE); VAR2=**REDUCE**(**VSQR**(diff2, Size), SIZE); Cov=**IPR**(diff1, diff2, Size);

*Lines of HLS code includes data interface and accelerator control protocol.

Table 2: Prototype Programming Patterns

Patterns	Semantics	Description
REDUCE	$S = REDUCE(dataA, SizeA)$;	$sum = \sum_{i=0}^{n} a_i$
VMUL	$dataC = VMUL(dataA, dataB, Size)$;	$\vec{v_c} = \vec{v_a} \cdot \vec{v_b}$
MM	$MatrixC=MM(MatrixA,MatrixB,rowA,colA,colB)$;	$M_c = M_a M_b$
AVG	$S = AVG(dataA, SizeA)$;	$avg = (\sum_{i=0}^{n} a_i)/n$
SVSUB	$dataB = SVSUB(dataA, S, SizeA)$;	$\vec{v_c} = \vec{v_a} - S$
VSQR	$dataB = VSQR(dataA, SizeA)$;	$\vec{v_c} = \vec{v_a} \cdot \vec{v_a}$
IPR	$dataC = IPR(dataA, dataB, Size)$;	$ipr = \sum_{i=0}^{n} a_i \times b_i$

Table 3: productivity

Benchmarks	Compile time* (s)	HLS Synthesis & PAR (s)†	Improvement
Inner Product	≤5	865	173×
$M_1 \times V_1$	≤5	889	178×
$M_1 \times M_2 \times M_3$	≤5	1034	207×
Correlation	≤5	1068	214×

*JIT (This Approach).
†Vivado Synthesis & PAR for accelerator.

Table 4: Resource utilization on Virtex7

Benchmark	Approach	Patterns	BRAM	DSP	FF	LUTs
Inner Product	JIT	VMUL	0	4	232	320
		REDUCE	0	0	167	318
		Total	0	4	399	638
	HLS		0	4	232	320
$M_1 \times V_1$	JIT	mm	24	5	848	2,254
		Total	24	5	848	2,254
	HLS		10	5	813	2,118
$M_1 \times M_2 \times M_3$	JIT	mm×2	24	5	848	2,254
		Total	48	10	1,696	4,508
	HLS		32	5	848	2,298
Correlation	JIT	AVG×2	0	2	984	2,214
		IPR	0	5	588	1,024
		SVSUB×2	0	2	427	658
		VSQR×2	0	5	588	1,024
		REDUCE×2	0	0	167	318
		Total	0	28	5,508	10,476
	HLS		32	5	2,009	3,865

two matrix multiply patterns. Correlation was computed using the five programming patterns SVSUB, AVG, REDUCE, VSQR, and IPR.

The composed expressions were compiled and our VAM call generator backend to produce the interpreter instructions. The run time interpreter executed the interpreter calls on each system. Qualitatively this verifies the portability of the interpreter calls over different versions of our overlay.

5.2 Discussion: Programmer Accessibility

Compiling is a fundamental step in getting application developers to use FPGAs; CAD tools and synthesize need to be removed from their development paths. Table 3 shows accelerators could be compiled and run time assembled in our overlay in less than five seconds. The reported times to compile is independent of the target overlay (2×2, 3×3) or platform (Virtex7, Kintex7). Synthesis times reported in Table 3 are averages. The variance in synthesis, P&R times for our test system on the Virtex7 and Kintex7 were not sufficiently different to report.

The actual time to compile just the programming patterns was more realistically under a second. The reported times include the time to compile and link the application program, middleware and operating system within our automated system build toolchain. Still the results show that compilation occurred between 170× to 214× faster than synthesis.

Table 4 shows the area cost of achieving this productivity in terms of LUTs, flop flops, and DSP blocks just for the accelerators excluding the overlay. The correlation benchmark showed the greatest increase in resources. The number of LUTS and flip flops increased 2.7× compared to synthesizing a custom version. The size of the individual programming patterns were fairly small, averaging 550 LUTS. But creating the equivalent functionality required using four of the programming patterns twice. The inner product (IPR) used two patterns, VMUL and REDUCE. Each individual pattern was smaller than the custom synthesized version, but combined resulted in a 1.9× increase in resources. This basic pattern is also present for the Matrix × Matrix × Matrix, which used the same programming pattern twice and resulted in 1.9× increase in resources. The Matrix × Vector benchmark showed approximately the same resource utilization (1.06×).

Two factors contribute to the size of the patterns. The first is the choice of programming pattern functionaltiy. These patterns were created to be general and not derived to support any one particular application. A more careful definition of pattern functionality based on application needs could eliminate using certain patterns twice. Second, no effort was put forth to optimize any of the programming patterns to reduce their footprint. The size of the programming patterns would be reduced by a skillful and careful designer. How much the sizes could be realistically reduced is unknown at this time and needs further study.

Additional resource overhead is incurred by the overlay architecture itself. Each switch required 740 LUTs. The 2×2 and 3×3 overlays required 2960, and 6660 LUTs respectively. This is a characteristic of using an overlay. A redesign and optimization of the overlay can reduce it's resource requirements.

5.3 Discussion: Performance Analysis

It was anticipated that run time assembling accelerators would suffer some measure of degraded performance compared to a single custom synthesized version. We further anticipated that our initial prototypes would suffer additional performance degradations compared to later optimized revisions. Clearly the performance of any accelerator is dependent on many different factors, including how the code is structured, the time taken to optimize the code, and the designers hardware design skills. We made every attempt to

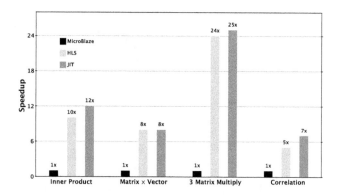

Figure 6: Speedup of Benchmarks.

apply the same types of coding style to the creation of both custom accelerators and programming patterns to eliminate any bias in comparing performance. To set a base case for comparison we also ran a software version of each benchmark on the MicroBlaze. We used the execution time of the software to compute speedups for the synthesized version and the accelerator running using our functor based approach. Figure 6 shows results generated on the Virtex7 on the 3×3 overlay. The results on the 2×2 array on both the Virtex7 and Kintex7 for the inner product, Matrix × Matrix × Matrix, and Matrix × Vector showed no significant differences. The Correlation benchmark required 9 programming patterns and hence 9 PR slots, so was only run on the Virtex7 3×3 overlay.

We were intrigued to observe the speedups in Figure 6 which showed the approach was as good or better than an equivalent synthesized custom accelerator. While the results are promising we are reluctant to draw any conclusions on performance based on these relatively few and simple benchmarks.

From a conservative perspective what we conclude is that the results simply do not negate the validity of the approach. Clearly, more DSLs and more applications need to be evaluated before any meaningful performance trends can be reported. What can be inferred is that the approach does allow a programmer to rapidly create and evaluate the execution times of accelerators. At a minimum the approach represents a powerful capability for rapidly prototyping and evaluating the performance of accelerators.

The interpreter was implemented in software as part of the operating system running on a MicroBlaze. This overhead would be seen at startup when the accelerator is assembled and does not enter into the execution time of the accelerator. In our preliminary work did run test applications to verify the ability to run time assemble different accelerators within the body of two threads running on the multiprocessor system using two MicroBlazes and two 2×2 arrays. Specifically in one thread we run time assembled the inner product benchmark and in the other a matrix multiply. The performance relationship between run time assembling and a custom accelerator is identical to the results shown in Figure 6 and is therefore not reported separately.

6. CONCLUSION

A new approach was presented to enable programmers to use standard software development flows to create hard-

ware accelerators and bypass CAD tools and synthesis. The approach introduced a new PR tile overlay and set of interpreter calls that brings portability into the process. This will greatly facilitate the use of FPGAs within our software dominated information technology sector. Results were presented showing a complete end to end capability; from working within a DSL to assembling the accelerator at run time. Results also show the costs in terms of additional resource overheads for the accelerator functionality as well as the overlay.

7. REFERENCES

[1] J. Bachrach, H. Vo, B. Richards, Y. Lee, A. Waterman, R. Avizienis, J. Wawrzynek, and K. Asanovic. Chisel: Constructing hardware in a scala embedded language. In *Design Automation Conference (DAC), 2012 49th ACM/EDAC/IEEE*, pages 1212–1221, June 2012.

[2] D. Capalija and T. Abdelrahman. A high-performance overlay architecture for pipelined execution of data flow graphs. In *Field Programmable Logic and Applications (FPL), 2013 23rd International Conference on*, pages 1–8, Sept 2013.

[3] J. a. M. P. Cardoso, P. C. Diniz, and M. Weinhardt. Compiling for reconfigurable computing: A survey. *ACM Comput. Surv.*, 42(4):1–65, June 2010.

[4] J. Cong, H. Huang, C. Ma, B. Xiao, and P. Zhou. A fully pipelined and dynamically composable architecture of cgra. In *Field-Programmable Custom Computing Machines (FCCM), 2014 IEEE 22nd Annual International Symposium on*, pages 9–16, May 2014.

[5] J. Coole and G. Stitt. Adjustable-cost overlays for runtime compilation. In *Field-Programmable Custom Computing Machines (FCCM), 2015 IEEE 23rd Annual International Symposium on*, pages 21–24, May 2015.

[6] N. George, H. Lee, D. Novo, T. Rompf, K. Brown, A. Sujeeth, M. Odersky, K. Olukotun, and P. Ienne. Hardware system synthesis from domain-specific languages. In *Field Programmable Logic and Applications (FPL), 2014 24th International Conference on*, pages 1–8, Sept 2014.

[7] C. Lee. An algorithm for path connections and its applications. *Electronic Computers, IRE Transactions on*, EC-10(3):346–365, Sept 1961.

[8] H. J. Lee, K. Brown, A. Sujeeth, H. Chafi, K. Olukotun, T. Rompf, and M. Odersky. Implementing domain-specific languages for heterogeneous parallel computing. *Micro, IEEE*, 31(5):42–53, Sept 2011.

[9] S. Ma, Z. Aklah, and D. Andrews. A run time interpretation approach for creating custom accelerators. In *Field Programmable Logic and Applications (FPL), 2015 25th International Conference on*, pages 1–4, Sept 2015.

[10] P. Yiannacouras, J. G. Steffan, and J. Rose. VESPA: Portable, Scalable, and Flexible FPGA-Based Vector Processors. In *CASES '08: Proceedings of the 2008 International Conference on Compilers, Architectures and Synthesis for Embedded Systems*, pages 61–70, New York, NY, USA, 2008. ACM.

CASK - Open-Source Custom Architectures for Sparse Kernels

Paul Grigoras
Department of Computing
Imperial College London
paul.grigoras09@imperial.ac.uk

Pavel Burovskiy
Department of Computing
Imperial College London
p.burovskiy@imperial.ac.uk

Wayne Luk
Department of Computing
Imperial College London
w.luk@imperial.ac.uk

ABSTRACT

Sparse matrix vector multiplication (SpMV) is an important kernel in many scientific applications. To improve the performance and applicability of FPGA based SpMV, we propose an approach for exploiting properties of the input matrix to generate optimised custom architectures. The architectures generated by our approach are between 3.8 to 48 times faster than the worst case architectures for each matrix, showing the benefits of instance specific design for SpMV.

1. INTRODUCTION

Sparse matrix vector multiplication (SpMV) is an important kernel in many large scale scientific applications where it is a typical component of linear solver algorithms for large sparse systems of equations [1]. For the HPC community to use FPGAs effectively, SpMV kernels need to have good performance. However, the dynamic nature of the data flow in SpMV [2, 3] requires expensive and complex circuitry and it becomes a challenge to achieve effective use of arithmetic and logic resources and on-chip and off-chip memory bandwidth. Furthermore, performance varies greatly based on the matrix instance [4–6].

While many general purpose solutions have been proposed for reconfigurable architectures, they do not provide a viable alternative to CPU or GPU based computing [4,5,7,8]. We believe that an instance specific approach, in which properties of the sparse matrix such as its sparsity pattern and numerical value range are adequately exploited, is the key to generating high performance sparse matrix kernels on FPGAs. This work takes the first step towards instance specific design methods for SpMV kernels. Our contributions are: *1)* a framework for generating customised *iterative double precision floating point sparse matrix vector multiplication* designs based on sparse matrix instances, taking into account the matrix order and sparsity pattern, *2)* an open-source implementation of the proposed framework for the

FPGA'16, February 21-23, 2016, Monterey, CA, USA
© 2016 ACM. ISBN 978-1-4503-3856-1/16/02...$15.00
DOI: http://dx.doi.org/10.1145/2847263.2847338

Maxeler Vectis (Virtex 6) and Maia (Stratix V) platforms[1] and *3)* evaluation on a set of matrices from the University of Florida sparse matrix collection [9] to demonstrate the scope for instance specific design on SpMV.

2. BACKGROUND

SpMV refers to the multiplication of a *sparse* matrix A by a vector x to produce a result vector b. A matrix is considered *sparse* if sufficient entries are zero to allow adequate representation and algorithms to reduce the storage size or execution time of various operations [1]. In this work, sparse matrices are represented using the Compressed Sparse Row (CSR) format [1]. CSR encodes a sparse matrix of dimension n with N_{nnz} nonzero elements using three arrays: the `values` and `col_ind` arrays have one element for each nonzero value representing its value and column index. The `row_ptr` array encodes the start and end of each row as indices in the `values` and `col_ind` arrays. The notation introduced in this paragraph will be used throughout this work.

Early papers on reconfigurable architectures cover optimisations to reduce resource usage [6,8], but have not studied instance specific optimisations. [7] proposes a method to process multiple CSR rows in parallel by using independent channels. A methodology for improving memory bandwidth utilisation is described in [4]. However, the proposed format (equivalent to a block CSR of width 16) is not parametric so it is not possible to optimise it based on the matrix sparsity pattern. In addition [4] also studies the use of compression to reduce memory traffic. This has also been proposed in other work [10,11] to improve performance when memory bound matrices are involved and remains an important point for future development in this work. However, for matrices on which SpMV is not memory bound, careful architectural tuning is more effective than compression.

The cost of pre-processing is acceptable for iterative SpMV implementations. Although early implementations introduced too much overhead [12], recent preprocessing, scheduling and partitioning techniques have been employed successfully [2,7]. Pre-processing has become essential for modern SpMV based applications and it is also used in our approach to enable partitioning and blocking.

To quantify, understand and correctly apply the numerous optimisation opportunities for SpMV, a systematic method is required to explore the various implementation trade-offs on particular sparse matrices. We present such a method in this work and start by providing an overview in the next section.

---

[1]caskorg.github.io/cask

3. OVERVIEW

To support instance specific design for SpMV problems we introduce **CASK**, an open-source framework for exploring custom architectures for sparse kernels. The key novelty of **CASK** is the capability of adapting parts of the flow to better suit the problem instance which may lead to more efficient architectures.

At the application level, **CASK** is designed for *iterative double precision floating point SpMV*. We assume the input is a CSR encoded sparse matrix, with double precision floating point values and 32 bit index pointers (`col_ind` and `row_ptr`). SpMV kernels are most commonly part of iterative algorithms, such as linear or non-linear solvers where the structure and possibly values of the sparse matrices will not change for the duration of the algorithm. We assume the resulting optimised SpMV architecture is to be used as part of an iterative algorithm. In such applications the pre-processing time (up to a linear bound) is regularly ignored [2, 4, 7, 10].

At the system level, we assume an accelerator model: an FPGA co-processor is used in conjunction with a multi-CPU host system. Therefore data are initially stored in the CPU DRAM where they are generated as part of a wider application (e.g. Finite Element Method [13]). Data are transferred from CPU DRAM to accelerator DRAM via an interconnect such as PCIe or Infiniband. An iterative computation is implemented on-chip: matrix and vector data are transferred once over the slow interconnect, many iterations are performed on-chip and the output is transferred to the CPU. A large on-board memory is assumed (24 – 48 GB) and the bandwidth between on-board DRAM and the FPGA is assumed to be significantly larger than over the interconnect and significantly smaller than from the on-chip storage.

The three main steps of the **CASK** workflow are *analysis*, *generation* and *execution*.

The *analysis* step identifies the best architecture based on the input sparse matrix by using a performance model which is a function of the architectural parameters shown in Section 4. The performance model provides an accurate estimation of the execution time and resource usage of an SpMV operation on a particular architecture for a specific matrix instance. To support customisation during this step, **CASK** exposes important aspects of the optimisation process ranging from data layout strategies (partitioning and blocking) to architectural characteristics (such as datapath replication and cache structure). In addition, the framework can be extended with new architectures and execution models entirely.

The *generation* step compiles the optimised architecture identified previously. It then generates an x86 executable that configures the FPGA with this architecture and performs the SpMV.

The *execution* step uses the resulting implementation to perform the SpMV as shown in Figure 1 and consists of three main phases: *1) pre-processing, 2) accelerator execution, 3) post-processing*.

First, *pre-processing* is performed on the CPU. The input matrix is *partitioned* in work items which can be parallelised and operated on independently. Since the CSR format is used, partitioning can be achieved by row slicing: splitting the matrix into disjoint sets of adjacent rows. In accelerator DRAM, partitions are stored at different addresses and a number of independent memory streams are used for

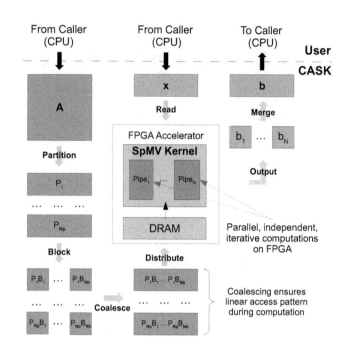

Figure 1: Overview of SpMV steps in CASK

each partition. While this allows better workload distribution, the number of streams is constrained which means that only a small number of partitions can be processed simultaneously. Each partition is then *blocked*. Blocking splits a partition in independent sets of adjacent columns, each set smaller than the size of the on-chip cache, to allow fully storing the required elements of x in the limited on-chip memory. Blocks are *coalesced* to merge the CSR representation of each block into a single input stream. This is required to ensure a linear access pattern of maximal length for accelerator DRAM which is an important factor in achieving good performance. As an optimisation, this process also merges the `values` and `col_ind` arrays, to reduce the number of required memory streams and therefore increasing the maximum number of partitions supported.

Second, during the *accelerator execution* phase, partitions are distributed to accelerator DRAM. The distribution strategy is exposed, so users can experiment with various schemes to improve effective bandwidth, for example by using a better distribution of data across DRAM banks. Then partitions are processed independently in parallel processing units which we refer to as *pipes*; each *pipe* can process multiple matrix nonzero entries from the same row per cycle. This step is described in more detail in Section 4.

Finally, *post-processing* is performed on the CPU to merge the resulting outputs. We note that in many iterative algorithms the order of partitions is irrelevant (due to commutativity of operations) and an iterative algorithm could operate on the current data distribution without additional merging steps.

4. ARCHITECTURE

A flexible, parametric architecture is a prerequisite of the analysis and generation steps. Therefore, the architecture introduced in this section exposes a number of parameters, resulting in more effective customisation. Our architecture is also generic, since it supports any problem up to the size of the on-board memory of the accelerator. Supporting large problems through blocking has long been a subject for future work [6, 7] since it introduces significant optimisation challenges. For example, the inter-block reduction strategy and efficient handling of empty rows (inevitably introduced by blocking) can have significant impact on performance as shown in Section 5. In [4] a model which effectively constrains the block size to 16 is introduced, but as we find in Section 5, the optimal block size may be as large as 15K on some of the matrices in our benchmark, for our architecture. This is why in our architecture, the blocking strategy is flexible.

An overview of the proposed architecture is shown in Figure 2. It can evaluate k nonzero values per clock cycle of one row and N_p rows in parallel (from different partitions). Intuitively larger values of k improve performance on denser matrices, while larger values of N_p improve performance on sparser matrices. To achieve this design the components shown in Figure 2 are required. Depending on the properties of the input matrix, the generated design may be composed of multiple replicated processing pipelines as described above. As shown in Figure 2, these pipelines are fully replicated, without sharing resources.

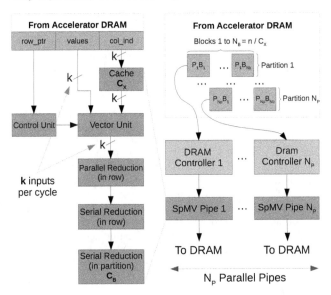

Figure 2: Parameterised SpMV architecture with number of pipes (N_p), reduction cache size (C_b), multiplicand cache size (C_x), vector input width (k)

The control unit implements the sequence of operations in the proposed architecture. Following the steps described in the previous Section, the matrix partitions have been loaded in the accelerator DRAM. From there the execution continues as outlined in Algorithm 1 for each iteration and for each partition. This logic is implemented in a state machine which can decode one CSR entry per clock cycle. Since each parallel pipeline has one such control unit, a total of N_p CSR entries (from different rows) can be decoded per cycle.

The on-chip cache is used to store elements of the multiplicand x. Since the arithmetic unit in each pipe may work on k nonzero entries of a row, the vector element cache should be able to produce k elements per cycle at peak. This is achieved by replicating the vector storage for each arith-

---

Algorithm 1 Architecture operation on a single iteration.

> **for all** p in partitions **do**
>   **for all** b in p.blocks **do**
>   **for** i in 1, size(b) **do**   ▷ Load vector block on chip
> $v[i] \leftarrow vectorValue[blockNumber * size(b) + i]$
>   **end for**
> $part_p \leftarrow SpMV(b, v, part_{p-1})$
>   **end for**
> $output(part_p)$
> **end for**

---

metic unit, in total of k times per pipe. During the load stage, all copies can be updated in parallel; during the SpMV arithmetic stage all copies can produce data in parallel.

To ensure efficient retrieval of elements from the cache (at the rate of exactly k elements per clock cycle) we introduce the Arbitrary Length Burst Proxy (ALBP). The ALBP consists of k FIFOs to store the bursts retrieved from DRAM. When a burst is retrieved (we request a multiple of k elements in each burst from DRAM to improve transfer efficiency), data are pushed in the FIFOs in a circular pattern such that element i of a burst is assigned to the FIFO $o + i$ mod k, where o is the position after processing the previous burst. $m_t \leq k$ data items may be pulled from the FIFOs, in parallel, by the compute kernel. m_t is determined at runtime, and if fewer than k items are requested, $k - m_t$ zeros are padded to match with the regular k width architecture of the SpMV pipe. Since the FIFOs are implemented in BRAMs, both push and pull can be processed in a single cycle. The ALBP also maintains the count of nonzero elements in a row left to process in order to deliver less than k matrix elements to the arithmetic pipe at the end of matrix row at one cycle, and continues processing k matrix entries of a new matrix row at the next cycle (provided the matrix row has more than k nonzeros to process).

The SpMV arithmetic pipeline processes the current block once the vector elements have been loaded in the on-chip cache. It operates on k elements of the current block as shown in Algorithm 2. Once a block is computed, its results are accumulated with previous results from the current partition. This is done, in parallel, for each partition in the design.

Algorithm 2 Operation of arithmetic pipeline

> **for all** r in b.rows **do**   ▷ Compute new block
> $t_r \leftarrow 0$
>   **for all** (value, idx) in r.subrows **do**   ▷ Compute new row
> $t_r \leftarrow t_r + value \times v[idx]$
>   **end for**
> **end for**
> $output(part_{p-1} + t_r)$ ▷ Inter-partition accumulation

At the first stage of the arithmetic pipeline a vectorized multiplication is performed on up to k elements of the current row with corresponding vector elements. The outputs are sum-reduced using a balanced adder tree composed of deeply pipelined floating point units, so at every cycle, k values are reduced to a single output. For rows of more than k elements, additional reduction stages are required. Therefore the outputs of the adder tree, one per clock cycle, are reduced using a feedback adder. Due to the latency of double precision floating point addition, a sequence of at least $F_{AddLatency}$ partial sums will be generated in this stage, one per clock cycle. These sums are reduced using a variation of a partially compacted binary reduction tree (PCBT) [14]. Our modification to the standard PCBT supports reducing an arbitrary number of inputs (up to a design parameter maximum) without stall before processing the next reduction set. It is also capable of skipping *inactive* cycles: data does not shift through the tree levels, thus not modifying its internal data storage, in the case where no input is available. This modification is motivated by the fact that sparse matrix rows may also be shorter than $F_{AddLatency}$. In this case the third stage reduction circuit reduces a number of terms equal to the row length, and the PCBT should produce a correct result for the whole matrix row. This case is even more likely in the presence of blocking, which may reduce the row length per block even further.

Finally, the results from each block must be accumulated with previous results within the same partition. This is done in the *inter-block reduction unit*. For large matrices, this accumulation is performed using DRAM. For small matrices, the number of cycles between writing the result of row i in block b and requiring this value to compute the new value of row i in block $b+1$ may not be high enough to cover the large latency of the write and read to DRAM. Therefore, for small matrices an on-chip buffer (C_b) is employed to perform the accumulation. Of course, it may be preferable to use this on-chip buffer to perform the accumulation for large memory bound matrices to reduce memory traffic.

The proposed architecture also supports empty rows efficiently. Although empty rows are not common in initial sparse matrices since they would correspond to ill-formed systems of equations, they can appear frequently as a result of the blocking strategy required to deal with larger matrices. For example, in banded matrices which are common in practice, a large number of cycles will be wasted on handling empty rows. In fact we observe that for banded matrices, for every C_x columns there will be only at most $2 \times C_x$ rows containing nonzeros on those columns as long as the matrix band is smaller than C_x. Since we should maximise the size of C_x to reduce DRAM transfer overhead due to inter-block accumulation, in practice the matrix band is very likely to be smaller than C_x. Therefore, the rest of $n - 2 \times C_x$ rows on every group of C_x columns are empty. Assuming one cycle of processing for each empty row (as in the current architecture, with one partition) gives a total quadratic workload overhead of $(n - 2 \times C_x) \times n/C_x = O(n^2)$. We propose a simple approach to reduce the number of clock cycles for processing a sequence of empty rows to 1, provided that the inter-block accumulation results can be buffered on chip, that is $n < C_b$ for some architectures.[2] First, we modify the current CSR format to support a run length encoding of empty rows; we note that without this modification it would not be possible to deal with sequences of empty rows, since the decoding process is serial, requiring at least on cycle per row; every sequence of empty rows will be encoded as an unsigned 32 bit integer for which the most significant bit is the encoding bit[3] and the least significant 31 bits are the length of the empty sequence. Second, we modify the inter-block reduction circuit to allow skipping over empty rows, by providing arbitrary increments to the address counter

which controls the write address for the accumulated sum; the address skip is passed from the control unit based on the length of the decoded sequence. In practice the ability to deal with empty rows efficiently can result in substantial speedup.

In summary, the proposed architecture can be used to perform a blocked sparse matrix vector multiplication up to the limit of the on-board DRAM. The architecture is parametric and its most important parameters are k the width of vector pipelines; C_x the multiplicand cache size; C_b the partial result cache size; and N_p the number of parallel pipelines. Tuning the values of these parameters for a specific input matrix can have a strong impact on performance.

5. EVALUATION

The evaluation is performed on a set of matrices from the University of Florida sparse matrix collection [9]. This set is chosen to match the matrices that were used as benchmarks in some of the previous SpMV work on FPGAs [4,5,7]. There is no inherent restriction on the properties of the sparse matrices which are supported, other than they must fit into accelerator DRAM. The benchmark is summarised in Table 1. We note that matrices mc2depi and conf5_4-8x8-05 are not real-valued matrices, so are omitted from our analysis.

We compare our model and implementation on the Maxeler Vectis and Maia platforms with recent implementations targeting the Convey HC-1 platform [4,5] and a Stratix V development board [7]. The main parameters of these systems are summarised in Table 2. It is difficult to perform an accurate comparison since the DRAM bandwidth, number of FPGAs, type of FPGAs and arithmetic precision differ. To aggregate these results we report a double precision GFLOPs value per FPGA. This is computed for our design as $2 \times N_{nnz}/T$, where the execution time T is measured as explained below. For [7] we optimistically halve the performance of the design, although the resource cost of floating point units increases quadratically with word length and using double precision storage for x reduces the applicability of the design from supporting $16K$ order matrices to $8K$ order matrices. This is considerably smaller than those supported in all other works (including our own, which supports up to main DRAM limit).

Table 2: System properties for previous implementations and this work (Maia and Vectis)

Implementation	[4,5]	[7]	Maia	Vectis
FPGA	4 x LX330	SV D5	SV D8	V6
Freq. (MHz)	150	150	120	100
Bwidth. (GB/s)	80	21.3	58	38.4
Precision	Double	Single	Double	Double

Figure 3 shows a comparison of the *best* architecture proposed by our framework as shown in Table 1 with implementations of previous work. The execution time on the Maxeler systems is measured using a high resolution clock in the chrono library of C++11. It includes the time to load scalar values, to send the compute request from the CPU to the FPGA, to queue initial memory commands and to perform the entire SpMV (including memory transfers on the FPGA). It does not include the time to pre-process and transfer the matrix, the input vector x and the output vector y from CPU to FPGA (and back).

---

[2] a memory controller extension could be provided to support this optimisation for larger problem sizes but is beyond the scope of this work

[3] when the *encoding bit* is high the number represents an encoded sequence of empty rows

Table 1: Required architectures for each matrix, produced in our approach (for Maxeler Vectis)

Name	Order	Nonzeros	Nnz/row	Cx	k	N_p	Cb	Logic/DSP/BRAM %	GB/s	GFLOPs
	Matrix			**Architecture**				**Place & Route**	**Peak Performance**	
dense	2048	4194304	2048.00	2048	16	2	2048	42.63 / 23.41 / 43.14	38.4	6.30
psmigr_2	3140	540022	171.98	4096	16	2	3584	42.02 / 23.41 / 54.23	38.4	4.76
raefsky1	3242	294276	90.77	4096	16	2	3584	42.02 / 23.41 / 54.23	38.4	3.99
rma10	46835	2374001	50.69	7168	16	2	47104	42.91 / 23.41 / 84.87	38.4	1.63
consph	83334	3046907	36.56	9216	8	2	83456	37.46 / 12.30 / 82.61	19.2	1.37
cant	62451	2034917	32.58	11264	8	2	62464	37.15 / 12.30 / 80.92	19.2	1.60
shipsec1	140874	3977139	28.23	14336	16	1	141312	30.24 / 11.71 / 79.65	19.2	0.78
torso2	115967	1033473	8.91	15360	16	1	116224	30.97 / 11.71 / 78.62	19.2	0.19
t2d_q9_A_01	9801	87025	8.88	10240	8	2	10240	36.24 / 12.30 / 60.81	19.2	0.87
epb1	14734	95053	6.45	15360	8	2	14848	37.06 / 12.30 / 75.94	19.2	0.69
mac_econ	206500	1273389	6.17	15360	8	1	206848	27.31 / 6.10 / 73.07	9.6	0.08
scircuit	170998	958936	5.61	14336	16	1	171008	30.39 / 11.71 / 84.54	19.2	0.08
dw8192	8192	41746	5.10	8192	8	3	8192	45.59 / 18.45 / 78.57	28.8	0.68

First, we observe that on the denser matrices (`dense`, `psmigr_2`, `consph`, `cant`) we outperform other implementations. This is due to the ability to select the correct values of k, N_p, C_x and C_b to maximise the achieved bandwidth while allowing sufficient spare resources to place and route the design. We note that when increasing the memory controller frequency to maximise bandwidth, the additional buffering and pipelining logic for the memory streams occupies as many resources as the SpMV kernel itself. So finding the configuration that enables the design to place and route and run correctly is an achievement in itself.

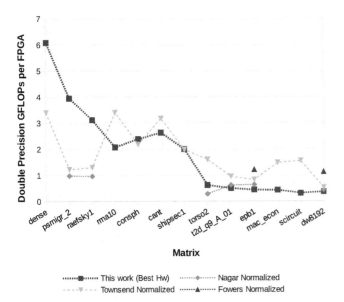

Figure 3: Comparison of the best Maia or Vectis design with prior work for matrices in our benchmark

For sparse matrices (`torso2` to `dw8192`), the platform used in [4] is better suited: with a monolithic memory controller and a large burst size, the Maxeler platforms (both Maia and Vectis) are better suited to linear access patterns with a large number of consecutive bursts; with multiple controllers, and high effective bandwidth for random access, the Convey platform is a better fit to the sparser matrices.

On matrices with few unique values, which therefore compress well (`rma10`, `cant`) our implementation is outperformed

by [4] which uses compression techniques to improve effective memory bandwidth while we do not. On `epb1` and `dw8192` the flexible cache structure results in better utilisation of available memory bandwidth, but the approach is not directly applicable to large matrices in our benchmark.

Table 1 shows that on many matrices the proposed architectures are not bound by memory throughput on the Maxeler Vectis (and similarly Maia) platforms. Figure 4 shows projected results for the proposed architecture on the Vectis platform assuming increased memory bandwidth (100GB/s) and increased logic resources and hard blocks such as BRAM. Architectures for denser matrices such as `dense`, `psmigr_2`, `raefsky1` benefit substantially from larger memory bandwidth and are hence memory bound. Architectures for sparser matrices could benefit from more resources, by deploying more independent processing pipes to achieve a better utilisation of on-board DRAM bandwidth.

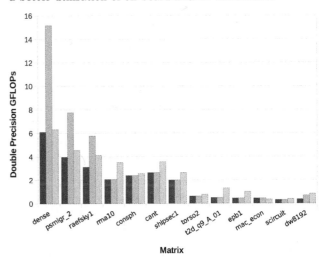

Figure 4: Projections for increased bandwidth or resources

We note that all implementations on FPGA so far are outperformed by CPU and GPU implementations. For example scaling the results of [15] for a modern dual CPU Xeon server would indicate performance on the order of 4.4 – 12 GFLOPs and [4] observes performance in the range of 12

– 30 GFLOPs for an Intel MKL implementation running on a dual Intel Xeon E5-2690 server. Furthermore NVIDIA cuSPARSE [16] claims speedup in the range of 2 - 5x using a modern Tesla K40 GPU over Intel MKL running on one E5-2649. A more conservative estimate based on scaling the results in [17] for the bandwidth of a K40 GPU suggests performance in the range of $9 - 24$ GFLOPs could be achieved.

Nevertheless, we believe that through the use of systematic instance specific optimisations, FPGAs would be able to compare favourably with these platforms in the near future. Table 1 also shows the need for an automated, instance specific design method: to maximise performance on the 13 matrices in our benchmark, no fewer than 12 distinct configurations for the Vectis platform have been identified, with various sizes of C_x, k and N_p found to be most effective based on the problem size (the number of rows, which also constrains C_b) and matrix sparsity pattern. A similar set of configurations has been built for the Maia platform, but has been omitted for brevity.

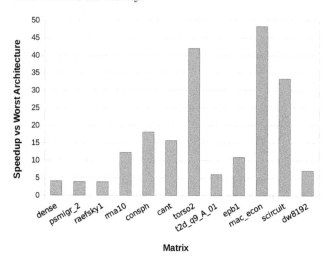

Figure 5: Speedup of best architecture versus worst architecture configuration

Finally, we note that not only do we require a large number of distinct configurations to achieve maximal performance, but also selecting the wrong configuration can reduce performance significantly, by a factor of almost 50 in the worst case, as shown in Figure 5.

6. CONCLUSION

We have introduced **CASK**, an open source tool for exploring custom architectures for sparse kernels. We have shown that **CASK** can use properties of the input sparse matrix such as the sparity pattern to generate customised, instance specific architectures for SpMV. This approach can lead to improved performance and applicability of FPGA based SpMV implementations.

Opportunities for future work include the use of compression techniques [10, 11], instance specific word-length optimisation and support for additional parameters such as clock frequency, memory controller frequency and various low level, FPGA specific optimisations. These improvemets can bring the performance of SpMV kernels on FPGAs closer to that on optimised CPU and GPUs systems, paving the way for wide adoption of FPGAs in HPC.

Acknowledgments

This work is supported in part by the EPSRC under grant agreements EP/L016796/1, EP/L00058X/1 and EP/I012036/1, by the Maxeler University Programme, by the HiPEAC NoE, by Altera, and by Xilinx.

7. REFERENCES

[1] Y. Saad, *Iterative Methods for Sparse Linear Systems.* Society for Applied and Industrial Mathematics, 2003.

[2] G. Chow, P. Grigoras, P. Burovskiy, and W. Luk, "An Efficient Sparse Conjugate Gradient Solver Using a Benes Permutation Network," in *Proc. FPL*, 2014.

[3] X. Niu, W. Luk, and Y. Wang, "EURECA: On-Chip Configuration Generation for Effective Dynamic Data Access," in *Proc. FPGA*, 2015.

[4] K. Townsend and J. Zambreno, "Reduce, Reuse, Recycle (R 3): A design methodology for Sparse Matrix Vector Multiplication on reconfigurable platforms," in *Proc. ASAP*, 2013.

[5] K. K. Nagar and J. D. Bakos, "A Sparse Matrix Personality for the Convey HC-1," in *Proc. FCCM*, 2011.

[6] L. Zhuo and V. K. Prasanna, "Sparse Matrix-Vector Multiplication on FPGAs," in *Proc. FPGA*, 2005.

[7] J. Fowers, K. Ovtcharov, K. Strauss, E. S. Chung, and G. Stitt, "A High Memory Bandwidth FPGA Accelerator for Sparse Matrix-Vector Multiplication," in *Proc. FPGA*, 2014.

[8] L. Zhuo, G. R. Morris, and V. K. Prasanna, "Designing Scalable FPGA-based Reduction Circuits Using Pipelined Floating-point Cores," in *Proc. ISPDP*, 2005.

[9] T. A. Davis and Y. Hu, "The University of Florida Sparse Matrix Collection," *ACM Transactions on Mathematical Software*, vol. 38, no. 1, p. 1, 2011.

[10] S. Kestur, J. D. Davis, and E. S. Chung, "Towards a Universal FPGA Matrix-Vector Multiplication Architecture," in *Proc. FCCM*, 2012.

[11] P. Grigoras, P. Burovskiy, E. Hung, and W. Luk, "Accelerating SpMV on FPGAs by Compressing Nonzero Values," in *Proc. FCCM*, 2015.

[12] M. DeLorimier and A. DeHon, "Floating-point Sparse Matrix-Vector Multiply for FPGAs," in *Proc. FPGA*, 2005.

[13] P. Burovskiy, P. Grigoras, S. J. Sherwin, and W. Luk, "Efficient Assembly for High Order Unstructured FEM Meshes," in *Proc. FPL*, 2015.

[14] L. Zhuo, G. R. Morris, and V. K. Prasanna, "High-performance reduction circuits using deeply pipelined operators on FPGAs," *IEEE Trans. PDS*, vol. 18, no. 10, pp. 1377–1392, 2007.

[15] S. Williams, L. Oliker, R. Vuduc, J. Shalf, K. Yelick, and J. Demmel, "Optimization of Sparse Matrix–vector Multiplication on Emerging Multicore Platforms," *Parallel Computing*, vol. 35, no. 3, pp. 178–194, 2009.

[16] NVIDIA, "Nvidia cuSPARSE Framework." [Online]. Available: https://developer.nvidia.com/cuSPARSE

[17] N. Bell and M. Garland, "Implementing Sparse Matrix-vector Multiplication on Throughput-oriented Processors," in *Proc. SC*, 2009.

GPU-Accelerated High-Level Synthesis for Bitwidth Optimization of FPGA Datapaths

Nachiket Kapre
School of Computer Engineering
Nanyang Technological University
Singapore 639798
nachiket@ieee.org

Deheng Ye
School of Computer Engineering
Nanyang Technological University
Singapore 639798
ye0014ng@e.ntu.edu.sg

ABSTRACT

Bitwidth optimization of FPGA datapaths can save hardware resources by choosing the fewest number of bits required for each datapath variable to achieve a desired quality of result. However, it is an NP-hard problem that requires unacceptably long runtimes when using sequential CPU-based heuristics. We show how to parallelize the key steps of bitwidth optimization on the GPU by performing a fast brute-force search over a carefully constrained search space. We develop a high-level synthesis methodology suitable for rapid prototyping of bitwidth-annotated RTL code generation using gcc's GIMPLE backend. For range analysis, we perform parallel evaluation of sub-intervals to provide tighter bounds compared to ordinary interval arithmetic. For bitwidth allocation, we enumerate the different bitwidth combinations in parallel by assigning each combination to a GPU thread. We demonstrate up to 10–1000× speedups for range analysis and 50–200× speedups for bitwidth allocation when comparing NVIDIA K20 GPU implementation to an Intel Core i5-4570 CPU while maintaining identical solution quality across various benchmarks. This allows us to generate tailor-made RTL with minimum bitwidths in hundreds of milliseconds instead of hundreds of minutes when starting from high-level C descriptions of dataflow computations.

1. INTRODUCTION

FPGAs have long empowered the circuit designer to build hardware tailored completely to the particular performance, cost and accuracy requirements of the application. A key aspect of this flexibility is the ability to select the data representation for signals in the circuit. As different applications have varying accuracy requirements, the exact number of bits necessary may change. This is in stark contrast to ISA-based processors where a small set of types are supported (char, short, int, long, float, double). While the low-level tuning of bits may seem time-consuming and excessive, it is a well-known approach [8, 15, 22, 23, 2, 1, 24] for saving resource costs by as much as 2–4× while improving cir-

cuit performance by as much as 20–30% without compromising quality of the output signals. In particular, with the promise of approximate computing, we must ask how many bits are actually needed to represent data (or signals) to deliver an acceptable computational outcome for our designs. The objective of the bitwidth optimization problem is to determine the cheapest data representation (fewest bits) for all variables in the computation subject to a user-supplied accuracy constraint. This can be achieved through static compile-time analysis of variable bounds and error.

While the benefits are clear, unfortunately, bitwidth allocation is an NP-hard problem [8]. Broadly speaking, we can classify existing approaches for solving this problem based on the focus of their optimization – (1) **tighter analysis of error** [2, 1, 16, 17] that focuses on fast arithmetic techniques for producing tight error bounds, and (2) **intelligent search algorithms** [15, 22, 23, 12] that use specially-formulated automated heuristics. To perform bitwidth allocation on CPUs, all heuristics typically examine a limited set of bitwidth combinations during the search process to keep runtimes low. More importantly, these approaches solve the problem in a sequential manner by refining the bitwidth combination in each sequential iteration while learning from the previous trials.

Commercial tools such as Matlab HDL Coder[1] provide a floating-point to fixed-point conversion toolflow but exposes the accuracy analysis to a simulation-driven workflow that requires developer involvement. LegUp [7] provides no precision analysis engine while Vivado HLS merely allows expression of templated types for fixed-point arithmetic without providing the necessary automation to analyze error and select bitwidths. A key limitation that prevents integration of automated analysis engines in these tools is the large computational cost of the automation which translates into minutes to hours of runtime for even simple dataflow blocks of code. In fact, pure CPU-based fixed-point simulations to determine bitwidths of a simple FIR filter with 10^5-element-long input test vector can take 40 days [4] of runtime. In this paper, we provide an automated precision analysis engine for gcc based on GIMPLE backend. We also show how to speedup the optimization problem using GPUs with a carefully constrained brute-force approach backed by an intelligent pruning of the search space. The use of GPUs in the FPGA CAD process needs to expand and grow to help tackle the series of slow, NP-hard heuristics that have traditionally constrained the design development process. The bitwidth optimization problem is one such slow heuristic that needs

FPGA'16, February 21–23, 2016, Monterey, CA, USA.
Copyright is held by the owner/author(s). Publication rights licensed to ACM.
ACM 978-1-4503-3856-1/16/02 ... $15.00.
DOI:http://dx.doi.org/10.1145/2847263.2847266.

---

[1] http://www.mathworks.com/products/hdl-coder/

Table 1: Different Phases of the Precision Analysis Flow for $y = a*x^2 + b*x + c$.
Assume a, b, c are integer constants, W_i represents the number of bits required to represent variable i

Dataflow Graph (DFG)	DFG Node	Range Analysis	Error Propagation	Resource Modeling
	x	$[0,1]$	$2^{(-W_x-1)}$	W_x
	a	$[a,a]$	0	W_a
	b	$[b,b]$	0	W_b
	c	$[c,c]$	0	W_c
	$a*x$	$[0,a]$	$\max(a*2^{(-W_x-1)}, 2^{-W_{m1}}))$	$W_a * W_x$
	$b*x$	$[0,b]$	$\max(b*2^{(-W_x-1)}, 2^{-W_{m2}}))$	$W_b * W_x$
	$a*x^2$	$[0,a]$	$\max(a*2^{-W_x}, 2^{-W_{m3}}))$	$W_a * W_x^2$
	$a*x^2+b*x$	$[0,a+b]$	$\max((a+b/2)*2^{-W_x}, 2^{-W_{a1}}))$	$\max(W_a*W_x^2, W_b*W_x)$
	$a*x^2+b*x+c$	$[c,a+b+c]$	$\max((a+b/2)*2^{-W_x}, 2^{-W_{a2}}))$	$\max(W_a*W_x^2, W_b*W_x, W_c)$

faster evaluation for broader adoption and seamless integration with high-level synthesis (HLS). The key enabling idea here is rapid evaluation of dynamic range, error and resource costs estimates for multiple bitwidth combinations in data-parallel fashion. By choosing *where* to explore and by evaluating multiple candidate solutions in parallel, we can accelerate the time to optimized solution. Unlike multi-core CPUs, GPUs are well-suited for this kind of brute-force exploration as they support hundreds of thousands of concurrent threads. We formulate our search space in a manner that fits entirely within the GPU memory capacity while maximizing the likelihood of finding the optimal solution fast. We develop heuristics that prune the search space to bound variable bit width ranges based on error propagation. For large problem sizes, we use simulated annealing-based heuristics running on the CPU to constrain the search space before transferring the computation to the GPU for acceleration. This proposal is in the same spirit as end-case optimal layout algorithms for ASICs [5], where the final branch of the design space is solved optimally while the parent heuristic is still retained.

In this paper, we make the following key contributions:

- Development of a high-level synthesis flow suitable for rapid prototyping of bitwidth optimization transforms that compile C descriptions of dataflow computations into RTL by exploiting gcc's GIMPLE backend.

- Development of optimized GPU-based kernels for (1) accelerated sub-interval analysis to derive higher dynamic range bounds, and (2) parallel error analysis and FPGA resource model kernels for bitwidth optimization.

- Engineering of CPU-based pruning heuristics that intelligently constrain the search to make it feasible to perform brute-force exploration on the GPU.

- Quantification of speed and quality of bitwidth optimization when comparing the NVIDIA K20 GPU to state-of-the-art simulated annealing-based heuristics on an Intel Core i5-4570 CPU across a variety of benchmarks.

2. BACKGROUND

Precision analysis is typically performed before detailed RTL design and pipelining. We must determine the exact number of bits required for various datapath variables and encode these into the RTL descriptions of our computation. This static analysis procedure can be automated and potentially integrated with high-level synthesis to generate tailor-made RTL for a given accuracy constraint. We now describe the basic concepts underlying precision analysis that are important to explain our parallelization approach. The precision analysis flow for bitwidth optimization can be broken down into a sequence of three steps (1) range analysis, (2) error propagation, and (3) resource modeling. We will use the example expression $a \cdot x^2 + b \cdot x + c$ to illustrate this flow as shown in Table 1.

Range Analysis: We need to first identify the dynamic range of all variables in our computation which requires calculating the smallest and the largest values they may attain. This is essential as the implemented circuit only needs to be correct over this range which is typically much smaller than the range of real numbers (or floating-point for canonical implementations). The underlying algorithm to achieve this simply propagates the interval of the input iteratively through the feed-forward dataflow computation while evaluating the range at the output of each arithmetic operator. For example, in the polynomial expression of Table 1 (column Range Analysis), if $x \in [0,1]$, then $y \in [c, a+b+c]$ can be computed through a top-down range propagation using Interval Arithmetic (IA). However, purely relying on IA often produces bounds that are over-estimated (loose), because they ignore input correlations. Loose bounds affect our final solution quality by requiring more bits than strictly necessary to meet the error constraints. One option is to use Affine Arithmetic (AA) [9] which allows us to produce accurate estimates of intervals by identifying correlations in the inputs at the expense of tracking correlation terms that are proportional to the number of inputs to the expression (thereby trickier for parallelism). However, Affine Arithmetic (AA) formulations are trickier to parallelize on GPUs due to the growth in correlation terms. In this paper, we choose to use the well-known sub-interval analysis approach to addresses this limitation of traditional IA. This is achieved by splitting each input interval into multiple sub-intervals, performing range analysis on all input sub-interval combinations, and composing the final range by merging the results of each sub-interval evaluation. This allows us to trivially exploit parallel processing capacity on the GPU across sub-intervals even while an individual sub-interval is sequentially evaluated. Our formulation using sub-interval arithmetic helps us generate tight bounds while exposing GPU-friendly parallel behavior.

Error Propagation: Once we know the range of each variable, we can estimate rounding and truncation errors due to each arithmetic operation. These errors depend on the number of fraction bits used in the variable representation. We assume sufficient number of integer bits are allocated for the largest fixed-point number to eliminate overflow errors. While many error models are available such as mean squared error (MSE) in signal processing systems, we use the worst-case quantization error models [21] for fixed-point implementations that are evaluated over operating intervals of the variable. For our implementation, we exact and verify the error model equations as expressed in the error analysis tool Gappa [3]. The errors are propagated from the input to output of the arithmetic expression based on the number of bits for each arithmetic operation as shown in Table 1 (column Error Propagation). Here, we observe that each arithmetic operation introduces an error term that is then carried forward downstream in the expression tree. Structurally this is similar to range propagation, but here we need to repeat this analysis for each proposed bitwidth combination. For a given combination, this is a sequential operation that processes error values from the inputs and calculates output error of that operation. CPU-based analysis tools are typically driven by heuristics such as simulated annealing that iteratively generate bitwidth combinations for evaluation and terminate once a sufficiently low-cost solution is found. Our insight here is that we can generate and evaluate multiple precision combination proposals for the variables in the arithmetic expression and process them in parallel. Again, this form of large-scale exploration is inappropriate on multi-core platforms due to the limited number of threads that are possible and the large scope of the combinations that must be considered. However, GPU-based systems with thousands of lightweight data-parallel threads are ideally suited to exploit this parallel pattern.

Resource Modeling: In this paper, our optimization problem is geared towards minimization of resource utilization of the implemented circuit. The goal is flexible, and we can substitute resource minimization for speed, latency or power if required (or some combined figure of merit). To support resource minimization, we develop highly-accurate analytical resource models of arithmetic operators by performing a complete FPGA implementation flow (synthesis, place and route). This accounts for internal optimizations and interactions between the various FPGA CAD stages. Based on these compilations, we build analytical resource models using regression-fit for LUT and DSP count usage as a function of the number of bits in the arithmetic operation using Weka [10], a popular data mining toolkit. This approach is in stark contrast to the simplistic models in [8, 15, 22, 23, 2, 1] and helps improve our optimization accuracy. For a given precision combination, this computation is a simple accumulation of cost estimates for each operation as shown in Table 1 (column Resource Modeling). For all precision combinations processed in parallel, we filter those

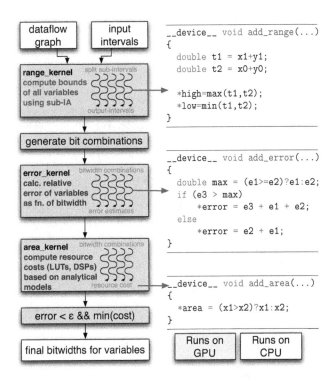

Figure 1: Compute Flow for GPU-Accelerated Precision Analysis (with sample GPU code for **add** operator)

that satisfy a user-supplied error constraint, and calculate the cheapest cost implementation using a GPU-optimized **reduce** operation.

3. GPU ACCELERATION

Bitwidth optimization on sequential CPUs is typically performed using heuristics such as simulated annealing (SA) that help drive the optimization towards a final solution while avoiding getting trapped in local minima through hill climbing. The state-of-the-art precision analysis tools [15, 22, 24] use this approach for formulating and tuning the optimization. They use the Adaptive Simulated Annealing (ASA) [11] package which is an highly-tuned optimization software that uses SA with intelligent selection of solution candidates to approach the optimal solutions. We use this state-of-the-art tool as reference for comparing time and solution quality.

In this section, we discuss the design of the key kernels used in our GPU approach that implements this search in a different manner. Unlike sequential CPU implementations of ASA, where a single combination of bitwidths is considered in a given iteration, on the GPU, we exploit the opportunity to consider multiple combinations in parallel.

3.1 GPU Kernel Design

The parallel bitwidth allocation problem on GPUs is implemented across three kernels (1) sub-interval range analysis, (2) error propagation, and (3) resource modeling calculations. We show a high-level view of the flow in Figure 1 for the **add** operator. Each of these three kernels is data-parallel. In function **add_range**, x0 and y0 are the lower bounds of the two input operands respectively, while x1 and y1 are the upper bounds. In function **add_error**, e1 and e2 are the inherent errors of the two operands respectively, and e3 is the propogation error. In function `add_area`, `x1` and `x2` are the area costs of the two operands respectively, derived from regression-fitted analytical models. Sub-interval Analysis is parallelized by trivially distributing the sub-interval combinations across the GPU threads while the Error propagation and Resource Modeling phases are parallelized across multiple bitwidth combinations that are considered. These approaches are *brute-force* approaches and are ultimately limited by the number of parallel threads that can run on your GPU and the amount of DRAM space available to store all intermediate results. With the availability of GPUs that can process thousands of threads in parallel and store GBs of data in the DRAM (*e.g.* NVIDIA K20 can handle $\approx$26K threads and 5–6 GB of RAM), we can start tackling brute-force approaches to optimization problems with relative ease.

For range analysis, each GPU thread is programmed to evaluate a small sub-interval slice of the complete input range. For multiple inputs, this means we must consider all possible combinations of input sub-intervals across all threads. Each thread uses a unique thread index to automatically identify the sub-interval it is supposed to explore. An individual GPU thread propagates the sub-intervals through the graph to calculate the sub-ranges of the intermediate and output variables. Once this is done, we fuse the results of the multiple sub-intervals to form complete tight bounds on all variables in the program. While this procedure is highly-parallel, we are ultimately limited by the memory capacity required to hold all intermediate sub-ranges. For error analysis, we allocate each GPU thread to evaluate one combination of bitwidths. Each thread locally determines the combination of bitwidths it must explore based on the limit of precision choices possible for all variables and the unique thread index. We discuss how the precision limits for the variables are identified shortly in Section 3.2. Given a bitwidth combination, a thread can process the error equations and resource model expressions to determine the cumulative error of the output variable and resource costs. Finally, across all threads, we filter out those threads that do not satisfy the user-supplied error constraint. From this set of threads (precision combinations), we pick the thread with the cheapest implementation cost as the solution.

When developing our GPU code for arithmetic operators we derive our error models from [21] and [3], except we consider rounding to the nearest while they use truncation directly. Furthermore we adapt the models to better account for constant integer inputs. When using fixed-point to represent integer constants, we can have no rounding or truncation errors by choosing the bitwidth properly. As such, the number of bits required for such integers can be predetermined. For area modeling of the arithmetic operators, instead of using analytical models based on theoretical expectations as used in [15], and [23], we use regression-fitted models derived from the real-world results of a complete FPGA CAD flow to capture the effect of CAD tools on implementation costs (LUTs and DSPs). In this regard, our approach requires a first-pass evaluation and mapping of all basic arithmetic building blocks through the FPGA CAD flow to help expose the DSP-LUT partitioning and allocation of resources that may differ from a simplistic theoretical models used in [15], and [23]. We quantify the impact of this accurate assessment of resource costs in Fig-

ure 4 later to show the resulting benefits. In these experiments, we observed a 30% improvement in prediction accuracy when considering the post-synthesis mapping results to select bitwidths.

In Table 2, we show the preliminary performance results for the range, error and area evaluation kernels on the GPU across various arithmetic operations. We observe 100-400× faster processing on the GPU when compared to OpenMP-optimized, multi-threaded (8-thread) implementation on the CPU. This initial experiment suggests high parallel potential for GPU evaluation of the constituent kernels. As we scale to larger GPUs, we expect this gap over multi-cores to grow as multi-core CPU trends do not align with the sheer degree of data-parallel thread capacity of modern GPU architectures and their rising DRAM capacity and associated bandwidths.

Table 2: NVIDIA K20 GPU Speedups over Intel Core i5-4570 CPU for Kernels used in Precision Analysis

Kernel	Speedup				
	add	mult	div	exp	log
Range analysis	312×	213×	119×	298×	254×
Error propagation	246×	80×	103×	261×	297×
Resource estimation	272×	266×	251×	414×	407×

3.2 Search Space Pruning

Instead of using sequential ASA-like heuristics directly on the GPU, we develop a GPU-optimized solution that uses a brute-force approach to explore multiple combinations in parallel. However, a naive brute force approach will quickly exhaust available GPU memory capacity, limiting the usefulness of this technique to toy problems. To allow the search space to fit within the memory limits of the GPU, we develop a pruning heuristic that restricts the combinations considered during the search. The pruning is also necessary for smooth execution of ASA running on the CPU. For our benchmark set introduced later in Section 5.1, ASA without pruning simply fails to converge and runs for hours before aborting. On the GPU, what pruning allows us to do is to optimally solve the subspace extracted from the pruning, unlike the multi-core CPUs which still explore this space suboptimally based on heuristics. We show a high-level sketch of our pruning heuristic in Algorithm 1. Bitwidth combinations that result in error larger than the user-supplied error constraint are invalid. Our pruning heuristic must maximize the coverage of valid bitwidth combinations in our search. At the start, we choose a uniform fixed point bitwidth (*target_fb* in line 1 in Algorithm 1) for all variables in the code and keep increasing precision until we satisfy the user-supplied error constraint (line 2–4 in Algorithm 1). The uniform bitwidth is designed to satisfy the worst case error and forces all variables to use the corresponding worst case precision. Thus, the uniform bitwidth *uniform_bit* will be over-provisioned for some variables that could be implemented with fewer bits. Hence, we now decrease the bitwidth one variable at a time (line 6–12 in Algorithm 1) while keeping the other bitwidths equal to *uniform_bit*. By doing this across all variables, we get the lowest possible precision (*lowest*) for each variable independently. We now replace each variable's precision with their respective *lowest* but in this configuration we will most likely violate the error constraint. As the last step, we increase the precisions of all variables simultaneously one bit at a time (line 14–15 in Algorithm 1) until it meets the required error criteria once again. In some instances, this pruning is excessively aggressive, and we relax the constraints by adding extra padding bits (*guard_bit* in line 17 in Algorithm 1) to help cover potentially better solutions. Overall, our heuristic is able to compress the number of potential precision choices of each variable into ranges that make them feasible for brute-force exploration within the GPU memory space.

Algorithm 1: Search Space Pruning Heuristic

Data: The number of variables N; Targeted
   Fixed-point Precision
Result: Bounded search space
1 $bit\_width(0{:}N{-}1) \leftarrow target\_fb$;
2 **while** $current\_error > error\_constraint$ **do**
3 | $bit\_width(0{:}N{-}1)$ ++;
4 **end**
5 $uniform\_bit = bit\_width[0]$;
6 **foreach** $n=0{:}N{-}1$ **do**
7 | **while** $current\_error \leq error\_constraint$ **do**
8 | $bit\_width(n)$ −−;
9 | **end**
10 | $lowest(n) \leftarrow bit\_width(n)$;
11 | $bit\_width(n) \leftarrow uniform\_bit$;
12 **end**
13 $bit\_width(0{:}N{-}1) \leftarrow lowest(0{:}N{-}1)$;
14 **while** $current\_error \leq error\_constraint$ **do**
15 | $bit\_width(0{:}N{-}1)$++;
16 **end**
17 $highest(0{:}N{-}1) \leftarrow bit\_width(0{:}N{-}1) + guard\_bit$;

For very large problems, this pruning is still insufficient to make the design feasible for brute-force exploration on the GPU. In these cases, we rely on preliminary cost-reducing moves in sequential ASA to assist in the pruning process. In this arrangement, we split the computation between CPU and GPU by allowing the first 10–100 iterations to run sequentially on the CPU and then switch to the GPU once the search space becomes feasible for GPU exploration. We keep the lower bound of the possible bitwidth identical as before and use the best observed precision combinations as the new upper bound for search. We achieved identical solution quality as the CPU-only solution after ≈ 25 iterations.

3.3 Overcoming GPU Limits

While the GPU is a great platform for rapid parallel evaluation of data-parallel problems, we consider several architectural optimizations that enhance performance of the FPGA CAD computations.

GPU Global Memory Capacity: A key constraint to consider is the size of the search space. For instance, on the NVIDIA K20 GPU with a 5GB DRAM, we are able to explore search spaces with precision combinations as large as 2^{24} with a single GPU call. Similarly we were only able to scale from 1K–8K sub-intervals before we run out of memory resources to store intermediate sub-ranges.

Kernel Fusion: The GPU kernels for error propagation and resource modeling are logically separate and can be invoked independently. However, we achieve significant reductions in kernel invocation and synchronization time if we fuse them together into a single call.

CPU-GPU Offload: While it is tempting (and easy) to offload all data-parallel computations to the GPU, in our

case, we saw significant degradation in performance of the error kernel when evaluating truncation error of the form 2^{-t} using the `pow` CUDA function. Since the possible values of precision we consider are limited ($t < 128$ bits), we precompute these values offline on the CPU only once and simply pass them to the kernels as a lookup table.

Memory Bandwidth: To avoid needless data transfers between the CPU and GPU, we allocate sub-intervals, error and resource arrays directly in the GPU main memory. We only need to access summarized data, such as the unified final interval and the minimum cost implementation result from these large arrays. Furthermore, we identify thread-local state for storing per-variable structures into fast memory (registers and shared memory) instead of allocating them on the GPU global memory space. When we stored intermediate results in GPU shared memory space we were able to minimize needless memory traffic to the off-chip DRAM and obtain additional ≈2× speedup across our kernels.

4. HIGH-LEVEL SYNTHESIS TOOLFLOW

Contemporary attention in FPGA high-level synthesis is focussed on the robust and popular LLVM framework [14] (*e.g.* LegUp, VAST HLS). While LegUp [7] is a popular choice for development of HLS compiler transformations in the academic community, we choose an alternative methodology using `gcc`. We are able to rapidly prototype our optimization algorithms based on the `GIMPLE` backend in the `gcc` compiler, while retaining all the existing optimization benefits of the compiler flow. Transformations described on the three-register `GIMPLE` syntax can be developed independently of the compiler and need not be constrained to the language or development quirks of the compiler framework itself. Ultimately, once the technology is demonstrated and interest generated, the toolflow can and should be integrated with more robust tools such as LegUp, Vivado HLS or OpenCL compilers for broader distribution.

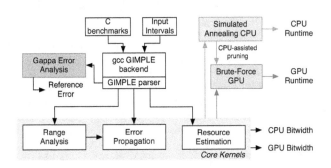

Figure 2: Compilation Flow for Precision Analysis

In Figure 2, we show a high-level block diagram of our compiler flow. We support simple feed-forward computations written in C through the `gcc`'s `GIMPLE` [6] backend. It is an Intermediate Representation (IR) provided to support development of plugins and optimization passes. For precision analysis, we process the C input files along with user-annotated range information to generate intermediate `GIMPLE` IR for post-processing. We then translate the `GIMPLE` IR into a suitable assembly-like, dataflow format for GPU processing that captures the dependencies and range information in a compact data structure. We develop a generic interpreter on the GPU that iterates over this suitably encoded dataflow graph. This not only allows us to avoid needless recompilations on the GPU for each benchmark input, but enables optimized GPU kernel design that works across all benchmarks.

We verify the correctness of our GPU-calculated error bounds by generating Gappa scripts for the given benchmark. Once again, the simplicity of the `GIMPLE` IR makes it feasible to rapidly assemble a translator for Gappa syntax. Gappa [16] is a static analysis tool that proves numerical properties of programs through formal techniques. Our CPU-based ASA annealer also operates on the exact same `GIMPLE` IR and the exact same error and resource models as the GPU implementation for a fair comparison.

Table 3: Auto-generated Assembly and Gappa Code

(a) ASM Code	(b) Gappa Script
LD, 0, 0, 1	x_fx = fx1 (x); a_fx = fx2 (a);
LD, 1, 1, 1;	b_fx = fx3 (b); c_fx = fx4 (c);
LD, 2, 1, 1;	d_fx = fx5 (a_fx * x_fx);
LD, 3, 1, 1;	e_fx = fx6 (b_fx * x_fx);
MUL, 4, 0, 1;	f_fx = fx7 (d_fx * x_fx);
MUL, 5, 0, 2;	g_fx = fx8 (e_fx + f_fx);
MUL, 6, 0, 4;	y_fx = fx9 (g_fx + c_fx);
ADD, 7, 5, 6;	y = a*x*x + b*x + c;
ADD, 8, 3, 7;	{ a in [1, 1] /\ b in [1, 1] /\
ST, 9, 8, -1;	c in [1, 1] /\ x in [0, 1]
	-> y_fx in ? /\ (y_fx - y) in ? }

In Table 3, we show the auto-generated GPU dataflow code and Gappa code for an example circuit $y = a*x^2 + b*x + c$. Here, we assume a, b, c are constants all with numerical value 1, x is an input variable with range $[0, 1]$. Each entry in the GPU dataflow code contains 4 fields for – instruction code, destination register, first source register, and second source register. The opcodes cover common arithmetic operations that we wish to analyze such as addition, multiplication, division, square-root, exponential, logarithm and conditionals. In addition, we support load and store instructions (shown as `LD` and `ST` respectively, in Table 3) that serve as a convenient place to pass in the various input intervals to the GPU threads. For CPU-based Gappa analysis, we generate a script that follows Gappa's custom syntax. Gappa analysis requires custom type specifications for each variable precision as indicated by the `fx` type-casts for each operation. We also generate VHDL (not shown) from the same input C to synthesize pipelined hardware. The full FPGA CAD flow is only invoked once after the optimized bitwidth combination is determined.

4.1 Compatibility with ASICs and need for FPGA-specific Flow

Like many tools developed for FPGAs, such as LegUp [7], our GPU-accelerated tool can also be made to work with ASICs while remaining a valuable and useful tool within the FPGA community. FPGA-based designs are likely to benefit to a greater extent from a complete per-variable customization of computation unlike ASIC-based designs that must factor in safety margins to handle changes to accuracy requirements after fabrication. Rapid prototyping in a high-level synthesis environment may be of stronger ap-

Table 4: Benchmark Problem Characteristics

Benchmark	#Vars	Arithmetic Operations	Inputs	Search Space
Level1$_{linear}$[24]	10	8	3	1K
Poly[15]	12	8	1	2K
Diode[24]	8	4	2	2K
Bellido[19]	13	9	3	24K
Approx1[24]	12	9	3	35K
Poly6[15]	19	12	1	52K
Level1$_{satur}$[24]	14	10	3	2M
Caprasse[19]	16	10	4	8M
Poly8[15]	22	21	1	160M
Approx2[24]	19	17	4	15G

peal to a time-conscious FPGA developer than an ASIC developer who may also be slightly more tolerant of longer development cycles. An unconstrained bitwidth optimization problem already takes minutes to hours for modest-sized problems which is comparable to FPGA CAD times. Our approach reduces this to seconds or minutes to help make this particularly attractive as an optimization for an FPGA developer hunting for resource wins. To adapt our flow for ASICs, we would need to engineer an appropriate ASIC backend toolchain and construct resource and cost models for the particular technology.

5. EXPERIMENT SETUP

5.1 Benchmarks

We evaluate our framework using a variety of typical benchmarks that have been used frequently in previous range and precision analysis work [15], [24], [23]. These are taken from the Alias-COPRIN benchmark set, the Minibit circuits, Mix FX-SCORE examples and others. Our benchmark set contains a mixture of problems with multiple inputs and outputs, complex non-linear operations (e.g. exponential and logarithm) and varying search space sizes. We tabulate their characteristics in Table 4. While the variable count may seem small, these generate enormously large search spaces ($\approx$15G data points) that are tricky to cover effectively. The key to enabling precision analysis as a routine optimization on larger problems (multiple basic blocks) in high-level synthesis flow is to make this exploration tractable – using GPUs as shown in this paper.

5.2 Tools and Hardware

We compare the sequential annealing (ASA) implementation on an Intel Core i5-4570 CPU @ 3.2 GHz against our approach mapped to an NVIDIA K20 GPU. We use CUDA 6.5 along with Thrust library (version 1.7.0) for simplified transfer of data between CPU and GPU and also for efficient GPU reduction routines. For precision analysis on the CPU, we use two tools that we have mentioned previously (1) simulated annealing package ASA v30.15, and (2) numerical analysis package Gappa v1.1.1. ASA uses the same CPU versions of our GPU thread code for range analysis, error propagation and resource estimation. We modify Gappa to add support for `exp` and `log` operations. For FPGA compilations, we use Vivado Design Suite v2013.4 targeting the Kintex-7 XC7KLX160 FPGA to generate regression models for the various fundamental arithmetic operators. We use off-the-shelf `gcc-4.8` compiler that ships with Ubuntu 14.04 but expect our toolflow to be compatible with even older versions of `gcc` (2007 onwards) but we have not tested this.

6. EVALUATION

In this section, we evaluate the experimental results of our GPU-assisted range analysis and bitwidth allocation. We show the results of FPGA resource utilization as a function of desired accuracy as well as the sensitivity of the FPGA mapping to fidelity of the resource models. For speedup calculations we compared optimized CPU and GPU implementations and include the pruning time on the CPU when calculating total GPU time for speedup calculations. Furthermore, our GPU timing calculations also include CPU-GPU memory transfer times.

6.1 Resource Utilization

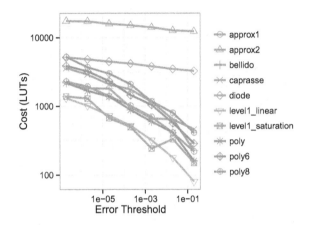

Figure 3: Impact of Error Threshold on FPGA Resource Utilization (LUTs). As we relax the error threshold, we observe that smaller designs are possible

When the resulting computation accuracy is flexible, we can achieve significant reductions in FPGA resource utilization. In our compilation framework, we are able to provide a desired level of accuracy when driving the search for datapath variable precision. We show the sensitivity of the solution quality as a function of the reference error threshold for valid solutions in Figure 3. As is evident, we can generate 2–10× reduction in LUT count when considering various desired error thresholds. We observe that most benchmarks show reduced implementation cost at varying error thresholds indicating significant resource savings are possible for real-world accuracy requirements. Certain benchmarks with `exp` and `log` operators do not show as impressive reductions in cost as seen from the `approx2` and the `diode` benchmark. In these instances, the larger resource utilization of the `exp` and `log` operator dominates the system. Thus, for applications where approximate computations are allowed, our compiler can deliver a suitably optimized solution that aims to deliver exactly the accuracy that is desired and no more. Overall, our bitwidth optimization saves FPGA resource costs by as much as 4× (mean 2.5×) when compared to a baseline double-precision implementation. These qualitative results are better than the ones reported in [15, 22,

24], as we use a superior pruning heuristic and cover every single combination within the pruned search space.

6.2 Resource Model Accuracy

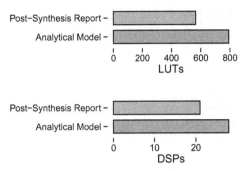

Figure 4: Comparing Quality of Results

As mentioned earlier in Section 3, due to the multi-stage nature of the FPGA CAD compilation flow, we need to build our resource model with particular care. We investigate the efficacy of using different area models on the final observed cost of the mixed precision results for the `level1-saturation` model. We compare: (1) approximate analytical area model, and (2) accurate post logic synthesis report. In each case, we run the full GPU-accelerated optimization to evaluate bitwidths and use the calculated resource numbers to filter out and select the best bitwidth. However, we generate final resource utilization after a complete place-and-route at the optimized bitwidths to compare the predicted model with actual real results. The optimizations considered at the different stages of the FPGA CAD process affect the accuracy of the predictive capabilities of the resource models in each of the CAD process Ideally, we should use post-place-and-route result as the optmization goal of ASA, which requires invoking place-and-route calls inside ASA for every annealing iteration. This would lead to astronomically large runtimes. Therefore, we restrict our experiments until the post-logic synthesis stage. In Figure 4, we observe the reductions in LUTs and DSPs as we improve the fidelity of our resource model for `level1-saturation` by using downstream CAD tool results. If we perform bitwidth optimization solely relying on approximate analytical models, we need to spend 800 LUTs (post place-and-route). We can reduce this to 550 LUTs along with a DSP count reduction by 8 when we re-run the bitwidth optimization using the post-synthesis models. Logic synthesis tools are better at exploiting freedom of choice between LUTs vs. DSPs. Our post-synthesis models are better capable of exploiting this knowledge when driving the optimization.

6.3 Range Analysis

We first perform GPU-accelerated sub-interval analysis to improve the quality of the variable bounds. We obtain tighter interval bounds between 1–4× that of vanilla interval arithmetic across our benchmarks. In Figure 5, we show the performance impact of GPU acceleration on subinterval analysis as we vary the number of sub-intervals. Here, we compare optimized GPU runtime with sequential GPU Gappa runtimes when using Gappa's *dichotomy search* feature when keeping the number of sub-intervals identical in

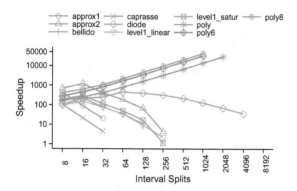

Figure 5: GPU Speedup for Sub-Interval Analysis
(16-thread CPU runtimes can be minutes to hours)

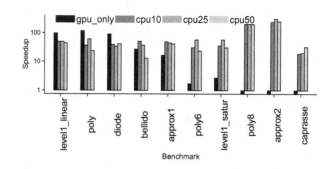

Figure 6: Bitwidth Allocation Speedups. Here cpuX means
X iterations of ASA on CPU run before GPU invoked),
CPU runtimes again run into dozens of minutes and
sometimes ASA must be terminated early as it runs for
hours without termination.

both cases. While we observe peak speedups of 3000×, we achieved best pruning results below 128 sub-intervals with associated speedups of 10–1000×. Fewer sub-intervals generate limited parallelism for GPU acceleration while larger sub-intervals exceed the GPU storage limits and become infeasible. The maximum number of permissible sub-intervals for GPU-compatible acceleration varies with the number of inputs to the benchmark (listed in the **Inputs** column of Table 4). Benchmarks with few inputs 1–2 such as poly8, poly6, and poly deliver continued speedups upto 8192 sub-intervals while the rest saturate between 8–64 sub-intervals.

6.4 Bitwidth Allocation

We now show results for the bitwidth exploration phase of the problem. The CPU-based method typically ran for dozens of minutes on average and was reduced to dozens of seconds when using GPU acceleration. Certain instances of ASA did not terminate even after running for hours, and we inserted an early exit condition to restrict runtimes. These runtimes are for the small dataflow kernels listed in Table 4 which roughly correspond to the size of basic blocks in modern compilers. Larger programs in HLS must handle hundreds of such basic blocks resulting in a large overall runtime for the complete program when using CPUs alone. In Figure 6, we show the overall speedups for GPU accelerated brute-force exploration compared to sequential CPU implementation of ASA. We make the following key observations on analyzing the nature of speedups:

- For smallest benchmarks with very small search space sizes such as the poly, diode, and level1_linear, we observe that the single-shot GPU evaluation delivers a performance improvement greater than 10× without needing pruning assistance from ASA running on the CPU. This is to be expected and is unsurprising.

- For medium-sized benchmarks such as the poly6, approx1, level1_satur, and bellido, the GPU-only approach delivers larger but still modest speedups. We record substantial speedup improvements when using the first 10–25 ASA iterations as pruning assistance. Switching to the GPU after ≈25 iterations generally delivers the best balance between spending sequential pruning time on the CPU and fast evaluation of smaller search space on GPU.

- For the largest benchmarks such as the approx2, poly8 and caprasse, if we purely rely on the pruning heuristic in Algorithm 1, the search space is too large to fit in the GPU memory capacity. In this setting, the GPU-only approach is simply infeasible (shown as 0 speedup in Figure 6). For these cases, we use the ASA-assisted pruning to move the search space into a feasible region. We observe significant speedups due the sheer size of the search space to be explored on the CPU.

6.5 Quality-Time Tradeoffs

Finally, we show the quality-time tradeoff trends in Figure 7. Here, we report the best-observed resource cost (cost = 1/quality) of the sequential ASA search after each trial as a function of CPU runtime across various benchmarks. It is useful to see the convergence towards the final results (normalized costs converge close to 0) often shows significant gains in the first 10% of the overall runtime. This enables us to utilize the fast convergence property of ASA to perform search space pruning, as shown in Section 6.4. While the runtime of ASA runing on the CPU is tunable, the thousands of threads running on the GPU allow highly data-parallel search. For the GPU-accelerated evaluation, our one-shot GPU approach gives us the best answer as a single co-ordinate in this space at the same solution quality.

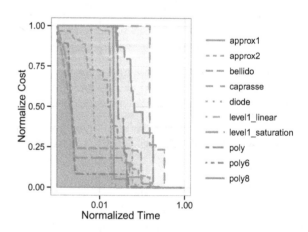

Figure 7: Quality-Time Tradeoffs for ASA (CPU-only)

7. DISCUSSION AND CONTEXT

7.1 Review of Previous Work

Research on range and precision analysis has evolved from simulation-based methods [13] to analytical approaches [15], [23], due to their speed in error modeling and range calculation. Interval Arithmetic (IA) [20] is the most well-known analytical method to calculate true bounds for general numerical algorithms. Some previous studies develop improved arithmetic techniques for producing more accurate error estimations. Lopez et al. [17] present quantized affine arithmetic (AA) [9] which only considers inputs' uncertainty into affine expansions, thereby reducing the complexity of AA representation. Kinsman et al. [12] use SAT-Modulo Theory (SMT) to break input ranges into sub-ranges for allocating optimal bit-width targeting a given precision specification, but is limited to range analysis only. Boland et al. [1] invent a polynomial algebra-based analytical approach to find provable and tight error bounds. This line of work mainly handles the accuracy issue of bit-width error modeling, but does not help with the optimization speed directly. Another set of work focuses on how to speed up the process of bit-width optimization using custom heuristics. In [15] and [24], the authors utilize simulated annealing for picking global optimized bits that minimize area cost. In [22], Osborne et al. perform partitioning followed by simulated annealing to improve runtime of [15]. [18] uses greedy algorithm for a coarse-grained search to find initial solutions, in tandem with Tabu search for refining the results' quality. Vakili et al. [23] propose two semi-analytical heuristics: progressive selection algorithm and tree-based search algorithm, dealing with fastness and optimality of precision analysis respectively. A GPU-based approach in the context of fixed-point analysis of VLSI circuits is presented in [4]. However, the speedups are compared against single-core CPUs on a single toy FIR-filter benchmark and the speedup is lower than the ones reported in this paper. They are only $\approx 58\times$ which is at the low end of our speedups and our speedups are over a faster baseline 16-threaded implementation.

7.2 Case for GPU-based Brute-Force Acceleration

More broadly, the use of GPU-based acceleration provides a model for limited brute-force exploration in FPGA CAD. At multiple heuristics stages of the CAD flow (*i.e.* placement, routing, synthesis), we are often forced to make suboptimal decisions due to our inability to fully explore potential solutions. A GPU-accelerated approach can open the door to using single-shot brute-force techniques at leaf stages of the search tree inherent in the CAD algorithms. In the context of ASIC cell layout, the idea of fast, optimal end-case placement exploration has been explored earlier in [5]. This approach still uses branch-and-bound at the leaf but optimally solves the small end-case solution when the problem size becomes small enough. In our approach, we explore all-possible combinations in the end-case using parallel GPU-based threads. In the long run, exploring the entire search space will stay intractable even with advances in GPU technology (as FPGA problem sizes will keep growing), we expect this technique to be used at stages of the search trees when the search spaces are sufficiently small for brute-force exploration and optimal solutions to the subproblem are desirable.

8. CONCLUSIONS

In this paper, we show how to accelerate precision analysis for bitwidth optimization by 10–1000× for range analysis and 50–200× for bitwidth allocation and when comparing an NVIDIA K20 GPU to an Intel i5-4570 CPU. We demonstrate the design and engineering a high-level synthesis approach suitable for rapid prototyping of bitwidth optimization algorithms. Using our HLS framework with tuneable accuracy targets, we are able to reduce FPGA resource utilization by as much as 10× if suitable approximate results are acceptable to the computation. To exploit GPU potential, we parallelize sub-interval analysis to improve interval analysis bounds and carefully prune the search space to enable single-shot exhaustive exploration of the search space. For range analysis, speedups correlated with the number of inputs and bitwidth allocation speedups tracked the size of the search space. As part of future work, we intend to extend this work to support Monte-Carlo sampling-based methods and integrate Affine Arithmetic models.

Our framework is available for download from `http://yedeheng.github.io/bitgpu`. The LLVM-based [14] LegUp license specifically restricts the use of the open-source compiler to non-commercial, not-for-profit development[2]. In contrast, our own tool is released under the GPLv3 copyleft license[3] and includes customized ASA code as part of the distribution. The ASA package is originally available under a permissive BSD 3-Clause license.

The Tesla K20 used for this research was donated by the NVIDIA Corporation.

9. REFERENCES

[1] D. Boland and G. A. Constantinides. Automated precision analysis: A polynomial algebraic approach. In *FCCM*, pages 157–164, 2010.

[2] D. Boland and G. A. Constantinides. A scalable approach for automated precision analysis. In *FPGA*, pages 185–194, 2012.

[3] S. Boldo, J.-C. Filliâtre, and G. Melquiond. Combining coq and gappa for certifying floating-point programs. *Intelligent Computer Mathematics*, pages 59–74, 2009.

[4] G. Caffarena and D. Menard. Many-core parallelization of fixed-point optimization of vlsi circuits through gpu devices. In *Design and Architectures for Signal and Image Processing (DASIP), 2012 Conference on*, pages 1–8, Oct 2012.

[5] A. E. Caldwell, A. B. Kahng, and I. L. Markov. Optimal partitioners and end-case placers for standard-cell layout. *Computer-Aided Design of Integrated Circuits and Systems, IEEE Transactions on*, 19(11):1304–1313, 2000.

[6] S. Callanan, D. J. Dean, and E. Zadok. Extending gcc with modular gimple optimizations. In *Proceedings of the 2007 GCC DevelopersâĂŹ Summit*, pages 31–37, 2007.

[7] A. Canis, J. Choi, M. Aldham, V. Zhang, A. Kammoona, J. H. Anderson, S. Brown, and T. Czajkowski. Legup: high-level synthesis for fpga-based processor/accelerator systems. In *Proceedings of the 19th ACM/SIGDA international*

---

[2]http://legup.eecg.utoronto.ca/license.php
[3]https://www.gnu.org/licenses/licenses.html

symposium on Field programmable gate arrays, pages 33–36. ACM, 2011.

[8] G. Constantinides and G. Woeginger. The complexity of multiple wordlength assignment. *Applied Mathematics Letters*, 15(2):137 – 140, 2002.

[9] L. H. De Figueiredo and J. Stolfi. Affine arithmetic: concepts and applications. *Numerical Algorithms*, 37(1-4):147–158, 2004.

[10] M. Hall, E. Frank, G. Holmes, B. Pfahringer, P. Reutemann, and I. H. Witten. The weka data mining software: an update. *ACM SIGKDD explorations newsletter*, 11(1):10–18, 2009.

[11] L. Ingber. Very fast simulated re-annealing. *Mathematical and computer modelling*, 12(8):967–973, 1989.

[12] A. Kinsman and N. Nicolici. Finite precision bit-width allocation using sat-modulo theory. In *Design, Automation Test in Europe Conference Exhibition, 2009. DATE '09.*, pages 1106–1111, April 2009.

[13] K.-I. Kum and W. Sung. Combined word-length optimization and high-level synthesis of digital signal processing systems. *Computer-Aided Design of Integrated Circuits and Systems, IEEE Transactions on*, 20(8):921–930, Aug 2001.

[14] C. Lattner and V. Adve. Llvm: A compilation framework for lifelong program analysis & transformation. In *Code Generation and Optimization, 2004. CGO 2004. International Symposium on*, pages 75–86. IEEE, 2004.

[15] D.-U. Lee, A. A. Gaffar, R. C. C. Cheung, O. Mencer, W. Luk, and G. A. Constantinides. Accuracy-guaranteed bit-width optimization. *IEEE Trans. on CAD of Integrated Circuits and Systems*, 25(10):1990–2000, 2006.

[16] M. D. Linderman, M. Ho, D. L. Dill, T. H. Meng, and G. P. Nolan. Towards program optimization through

automated analysis of numerical precision. In *Proc. IEEE/ACM Int. Symp. on Code Generation and Optimization*, CGO '10, pages 230–237, New York, NY, USA, 2010. ACM.

[17] J. Lopez, C. Carreras, and O. Nieto-Taladriz. Improved interval-based characterization of fixed-point lti systems with feedback loops. *Computer-Aided Design of Integrated Circuits and Systems, IEEE Transactions on*, 26(11):1923–1933, Nov 2007.

[18] D. Menard, N. Herve, O. Sentieys, and H.-N. Nguyen. High-level synthesis under fixed-point accuracy constraint. *JECE*, 2012, 2012.

[19] J.-P. Merlet. The COPRIN benchmarks. `http://www-sop.inria.fr/coprin/logiciels/ALIAS/Benches/benches.html`.

[20] R. E. Moore, R. B. Kearfott, and M. J. Cloud. *Introduction to Interval Analysis*. SIAM, 2009.

[21] A. Nayak, M. Haldar, A. Choudhary, and P. Banerjee. Precision and error analysis of MATLAB applications during automated hardware synthesis for FPGAs. In *Proc. of Conf. on Design, Automation and Test in Europe*, DATE '01, pages 722–728, 2001.

[22] W. G. Osborne, R. C. C. Cheung, J. Coutinho, W. Luk, and O. Mencer. Automatic accuracy-guaranteed bit-width optimization for fixed and floating-point systems. In *Int. Conf. on Field Programmable Logic and Applications (FPL)*, 2007.

[23] S. Vakili, J. Langlois, and G. Bois. Enhanced precision analysis for accuracy-aware bit-width optimization using affine arithmetic. *Computer-Aided Design of Integrated Circuits and Systems, IEEE Transactions on*, 32(12):1853–1865, 2013.

[24] D. Ye and N. Kapre. MixFX-SCORE: Heterogeneous fixed-point compilation of dataflow computations. In *Proceedings of the 2014 IEEE 22nd International Symposium on Field-Programmable Custom Computing Machines*, FCCM '14, 2014.

Resolve: Generation of High-Performance Sorting Architectures from High-Level Synthesis

Janarbek Matai*, Dustin Richmond*, Dajung Lee†, Zac Blair*, Qiongzhi Wu*, Amin Abazari*, and Ryan Kastner*

*Computer Science and Engineering, †Electrical and Computer Engineering
University of California, San Diego, La Jolla, CA 92093, United States
{jmatai, drichmond, dal064, zblair, qiw035, maabazari, kastner}@ucsd.edu

ABSTRACT

Field Programmable Gate Array (FPGA) implementations of sorting algorithms have proven to be efficient, but existing implementations lack portability and maintainability because they are written in low-level hardware description languages that require substantial domain expertise to develop and maintain. To address this problem, we develop a framework that generates sorting architectures for different requirements (speed, area, power, etc.). Our framework provides ten highly optimized basic sorting architectures, easily composes basic architectures to generate hybrid sorting architectures, enables non-hardware experts to quickly design efficient hardware sorters, and facilitates the development of customized heterogeneous FPGA/CPU sorting systems. Experimental results show that our framework generates architectures that perform at least as well as existing RTL implementations for arrays smaller than 16K elements, and are comparable to RTL implementations for sorting larger arrays. We demonstrate a prototype of an end-to-end system using our sorting architectures for large arrays (16K-130K) on a heterogeneous FPGA/CPU system.

1. INTRODUCTION

Sorting is an important, widely studied algorithmic problem [13] that is applicable to nearly every field of computation: data processing and databases [6, 11, 20], data compression [5], distributed computing [9], image processing, and computer graphics [4, 15]. Each application domain has unique requirements. For example, text data compression applications requires sorting arrays with few hundred elements. MapReduce sorts millions of elements. Database applications sort both large and small size arrays.

The importance of sorting has led to the development and study of parallel sorting algorithms [1] on CPUs [8], GPUs [22], and FPGAs [14]. Each platform has its advantages. CPUs are relatively easy to program, but often lack performance compared to GPU and FPGA counterparts. GPUs are more difficult to program than CPUs, but they provide high performance. FPGAs typically provide the best performance for per Watt compared to CPUs and GPUs, but they are the most difficult to develop.

Designing efficient sorting applications using FPGAs is difficult because it requires substantial domain specific knowledge about hardware, the underlying FPGA architecture, and the compiler tools. High-level synthesis (HLS) tools aim to improve the accessibility of FPGAs by minimizing required domain specific knowledge by raising the level of programming abstraction, which results in an increase in productivity. Unfortunately, HLS is not a panacea. As reported in previous works, HLS generates efficient hardware when the input code is written in a specific coding style [10, 17], which we call *restructured* code. Therefore, creating optimized hardware using HLS still requires intimate understanding of the underlying hardware architecture and knowledge about how to effectively utilize the HLS tools.

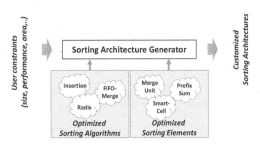

Figure 1: The Resolve sorting framework.

In this paper, we develop a framework that generates high performance sorting architectures by composing basic sorting architectures implemented with optimized HLS primitives. This concept is shown in Figure 1. We note that this is similar to `std::sort` routine found in standard template library (STL), which selects a specific sorting algorithm from a pool of sorting algorithms. For example, STL uses insertion sort for small lists (less than 15 elements), and then switches to merge sort for larger lists. We believe a routine like `std::sort` for HLS is important to facilitate FPGA designs for non-hardware experts. Our framework uses RIFFA [12] to integrate sorting cores into a fully functional heterogeneous CPU/FPGA sorting system. The result is a system that minimizes knowledge required to design high performance sorting architectures for an FPGA.

The specific contributions of this paper are:

1. The design and implementation of highly optimized sorting primitives and basic sorting algorithms.

FPGA '16, February 21–23, 2016, Monterey, CA, USA.

© 2016 ACM. ISBN 978-1-4503-3856-1/16/02. . . $15.00

DOI: http://dx.doi.org/10.1145/2847263.2847268

2. A framework to generate hybrid sorting architectures by composing these basic primitives.

3. A comparison of these generated sorting architectures with other sorting architectures implemented on a FPGA.

4. Integration with RIFFA [12] to demonstrate full end-to-end sorting system.

This paper is organized as follows: Section 2 provides a case study of insertion sort to demonstrate HLS optimizations. Section 3 discusses related work. Section 4 describes the optimization of standard sorting primitives, and how to use them to create efficient architectures for ten basic sorting algorithms. Section 5 presents our Resolve framework. Section 6 provides experimental results. We conclude in Section 7.

2. CASE STUDY: INSERTION SORT

Listing 1 shows a common implementation of an insertion sort algorithm. Implementing this directly using a high-level synthesis (HLS) tool would not provide an efficient architecture. We must optimize it specifically for a hardware implementation.

```
1  void InsertionSort(int array[n])
2  {
3    L1:
4    int i, j, index;
5    for (i=1; i < n; i++)
6    {
7      L2:
8      index = array[i];
9      j = i;
10     while ( (j > 0) && (array[j-1] > index) )
11     {
12       L3:
13       array[j] = array[j-1];
14       j--;
15     }
16     array[j] = index;
17   }
18 }
```

Listing 1: *Typical source code for insertion sort. This does not create an optimized architecture using HLS tools.*

HLS tools typically provide optimization directives that are embedded in input source code as a *pragma*. Throughout this work, we use semantics specific to the Xilinx Vivado HLS tool. However, these ideas are generally applicable to other HLS tools. Some common optimization directives are pipeline, which exploits instruction level parallelism, unroll, which vectorizes loops, and partition, which divides arrays into multiple memories. We denote three potential locations for these directives: L1, L2, and L3. For example, we can direct the HLS tool to exploit instruction level parallelism by applying the `pipeline` pragma to the body of the inner for loop at point L3; similarly, we can apply other HLS optimizations at L1, L2, and L3. Unfortunately, as we will shortly see, designers cannot rely on these directives alone, and must often write special code, which we call restructured code, to generate the best results. This restructured code requires substantial hardware design expertise [10, 17].

Table 1 presents the Initiation Interval (II), achieved clock period, and utilization (slices) results for five different optimizations at the different locations L1, L2, and L3. Design 6 is a restructured implementation, i.e., it completely refactors the code with an eye towards an HLS style of coding. We will discuss Design 6 in more detail in Section 4.

Table 1: *Case study for insertion sort optimization in HLS*

	Optimizations	II	Period	Slices	Category
1	L3: pipeline II=1	661	3.75	29	slow/small
2	L3: unroll factor=2 cyclic partition array by factor=2	730	3.84	112	slow/small
3	L2: pipeline II=1	1194	3.06	47	slow/small
4	L2: unroll factor=2 and cyclic partition array by factor=2	1193	3.50	144	slow/small
5	L1: pipeline II=1 and complete partition array	1	440.85	27291	faster/huge
6	Code restructuring	64	2.90	374	fastest/small

We categorize the performance and area results from Table 1 into three groups: 1) slow/small, 2) faster/huge, and 3) fastest/small. Ideal design from HLS would be fast with small area. The first four designs are very slow and have small area. Design 5 achieves higher performance (II=1 and very large clock period) with unrealistically large area due to aggressive HLS optimizations. Design 6 is hand written by an expert HLS designer to create an optimal architecture; it achieves the highest performance with small area.

This case study demonstrates several concepts: First, writing efficient HLS code requires that the designer must understand hardware concepts like unrolling and partitioning. Second, the HLS designer must be able to diagnose any throughput problems, which requires substantial HLS tool knowledge. Third, and most importantly, in order to achieve the best results – high performance and low-area, it is typically required to re-write the software-centric code to create an efficient hardware architecture.

The aim of this work is to make it easy to design optimized sorting algorithms (like that of Design 6) from higher-level languages by providing a framework of optimized sorting algorithms in HLS. This requires several steps: 1) understand the sorting algorithms, 2) study existing hardware implementations (often written in register transfer level Verilog or VHDL), and 3) modify the sorting algorithms to optimally synthesize to the FPGA. In the remainder of this paper, we address each of these issues.

3. RELATED WORK

There are two main bodies of past work related to this paper; these are hardware sorting architectures and high-level synthesis code generation.

Hardware sorting architectures: The first body of work focuses on implementing hardware sorters (usually a single algorithm) on an FPGA. There are a variety of published works exploring sorting architectures on FPGA platforms. Several works have implemented a single sorting algorithm on a FPGA [3, 7, 16, 18, 21, 23], and some have explored high performance sorting of large size inputs [6, 7, 14].

All the above work focuses on designing a specific hardware architecture for a particular algorithm. Our work enables the user to generate a vast number of different sorting architectures from high-level languages without writing low-level code. Additionally, our work does this automatically from high-level languages, where previous works have used low level hardware description languages. Our framework allows full parameterization, the composition of hybrid architectures from multiple algorithms, and the ability to perform quick design space exploration. Finally, the sorting architectures generated from our work can be integrated with RIFFA to provide an an end-to-end system.

There are also a few works that study sorting in the context of high-level languages. Arcas-Abella et al. [2] looked at the feasibility of implementing bitonic sort and spatial insertion sorting units using existing HLS tools (BlueSpec, Chisel, LegUP, and OpenCL). This work is similar to ours since it studies the implementation of sorting algorithms using HLS tools. Zuluaga et al. [23] presented a method for generating sorting network architectures from a domain-specific language. At a high level, the use of a domain-specific language seems similar to our architecture-generation approach. There are several main differences between aforementioned work and our work. First, we study multiple algorithms instead of focusing on a single algorithm. Second, we generate optimized sorting architectures by composing one or more algorithms. Finally, we can address much larger input sizes and the architectures generated from our work are orders of magnitude better than [23]. Section 6 provides a more detailed comparison of these works and the results generated from our Resolve framework.

HLS code generation: The work by George et al. [10] proposed a domain-specific language based FPGA design using existing high-level synthesis tools. This is similar to our approach by allowing non-hardware designers to write code (in their case using Scala) to generate optimized HLS code. Their work targets specific computational patterns. Our work targets a specific domain (sorting) and creates a framework for the user to explore a vast number of different sorting architectures using sorting primitives and basic sorting algorithms.

4. HARDWARE SORTING

Figure 1 shows the structure of our framework. It has three components: 1) Block 1 is a library of optimized parameterizable sorting primitives. These sorting primitives are the building blocks of our framework. Block 2 represents our basic sorting algorithms. The algorithms use the sorting primitives to implement all the basic sorting algorithms on an FPGA using high-level synthesis. Block 3 is the sorting architecture generator. Here we use the sorting primitives and basic algorithms to generate optimized hybrid sorting architectures to meet different system constraints. The following describes each of these components in more detail.

4.1 Sorting Primitives

This section presents optimized HLS implementations of sorting primitives. Previous works presented a list of several common sorting primitives, e.g., compare-swap, select-value, and a merge unit [14]. After analyzing more common sorting algorithms, we added three more primitives to this list: prefix-sum, histogram, and insertion-cell. Our basic sorting algorithms (presented in Section 4.2) are implemented efficiently in hardware using these six sorting primitives. Figure 2 shows the initial hardware architectures generated from HLS code for our sorting primitives. Section 2 described how *restructured* HLS code is necessary to generate an efficient hardware from HLS. We now present the optimization of prefix sum, merge, and insertion-cell.

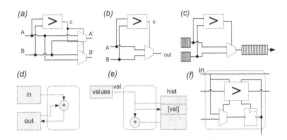

Figure 2: Initial hardware architecture of sorting primitives generated from HLS. a) compare-swap, b) select-value element, c) merge, d) prefix-sum, e) histogram, f) insertion cell

```
1 #pragma PARTITION out
      cyclic factor=4
2 #pragma PARTITION in
      cyclic factor=4
3 for(i=0;i<SIZE;i++){
4   #pragma UNROLL
          factor=4
5   #pragma PIPELINE
6   out[i]=out[i-1]+in[i]
7 }
```

Listing 2: Prefix sum (SW)

```
1 A=in[0];
2 #pragma PARTITION out
      cyclic factor=4
3 #pragma PARTITION in
      cyclic factor=4
4 for(i=0;i<SIZE;i++){
5   #pragma UNROLL
          factor=4
6   #pragma PIPELINE
7   A = A+in[i];
8   out[i] =  A;
9     }
```

Listing 3: Prefix-sum (HW)

Prefix Sum: Listing 2 shows "software-style" C code for prefix sum. Even for this simple prefix sum primitive, we have to restructure the code in non-intuitive ways to produce optimized hardware. First, we apply unroll and pipeline optimizations to expose data and instruction level parallelism. We also perform cyclic partitioning on the arrays *in* and *out* to match the memory access patterns required by unrolling. By pipelining the loop, we expect to get $II = 1$, and by unrolling, we expect to get a speed up by a factor of 4. However, the data dependencies between $out[i-1]$ and $out[i]$ prevent us from achieving the expected results. Figure 2 (d) shows the hardware architectures for the code in Listing 2. Optimized architecture with an $II = 1$ is shown in Figure 3 (a), and Listing 3 shows the HLS code for this optimal hardware architecture.

```
1 #pragma HLS DATAFLOW
2 //omitted partition
3 //pragmas
4 stage1(IN, TEMP);
5 ...
6 stage(TEMP, OUT);
7 }
```

Listing 4: Prefix sum dataflow

```
1 stage1(in, t) {
2   for(i=0; i<SIZE;
          ++i) {
3     #pragma HLS UNROLL
              factor=4
4     #pragma HLS
              PIPELINE
5     t[i] =
            in[i-1]+in[i];
6  }}
```

Listing 5: Prefix sum stages

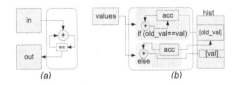

Figure 3: Optimal hardware architectures for prefix sum and histogram that give $II = 1$

As an additional example, we present another optimized HLS block for prefix sum which implements the reduction pattern. The reduction pattern uses $\log(n)$ parallel stages to compute a prefix sum of size n in parallel. The individual stages do not have the data dependency seen in the previous example. Listing 4 shows a high-level prefix sum implementation using a reduction pattern. The **stage** functions are implementations of the parallel stages without the data dependency. Listing 5 shows the code for the first **stage** function. Since there is no data dependency, it is straightforward to get a speed up of $4\times$ or more by unrolling and cyclically partitioning as in Listing 5. Multiple versions of optimized sorting primitives such as in Listing 3 and Listing 4 will facilitate to do easy design space exploration with these primitives. For example, the prefix sum in Listing 3 achieves the desired unrolling factor with reduced frequency, while the prefix sum in Listing 4 with the same unrolling factor achieves higher frequency.

```
1  void MergeUnit(hls::stream<int> &IN1,
       hls::stream<int> &IN2, hls::stream<int> &OUT ,
       int n){
2    int a,b;
3    int subIndex1 = 1, subIndex2 = 1;
4    IN1.read(a); IN2.read(b);
5    for(int i=0; i < n; i++){
6    #pragma HLS PIPELINE
7        if(subIndex1 == n/2+1) {
8            OUT[i] = b;
9            IN2.read(b);
10           subIndex2++;
11       } else if (subIndex2 == n/2+1) {
12           OUT[i] = a;
13           IN1.read(a);
14           subIndex1++;
15       } else if (a < b) {
16           OUT[i] = a;
17           IN1.read(a);
18           subIndex1++;
19       } else {
20           OUT[i] = b;
21           IN2.read(b);
22           subIndex2++;
23       }
24   }
25 }
```

Listing 6: FIFO based streaming merge primitive

Merge: The merge primitive combines two sorted $n/2$ size arrays into a sorted array of size n. Figure 2 (c) shows the hardware architecture. Listing 6 shows the HLS implementation of streaming FIFO-based merge unit. Implementation of merge unit with C arrays is straightforward. Here the IN1 and IN2 are two sorted arrays and OUT is the merged output. The **for** loop in Line 5 runs n times where $n/2$ is the size of IN1 and IN2. It reads one element from either IN1 or IN2 on each iteration and writes it to the output until the end of the FIFO is reached. We pipelined this loop to get an $II = 1$ so it does one read operation every cycle.

Insertion Cell: Insertion cell is a hardware sorting primitive for insertion sort algorithms. The hardware architecture has an input, an output, a comparator, and a register – see Figure 2 (f). The insertion-cell compares the current input with the current value in current register. The smaller (or larger depending sort direction) of current register and the current input is given as an output.

```
1  T InsertionCell(hls::stream<int> &IN,
       hls::stream<int> &OUT){
2    static int CURR_REG=0;
3    int IN_A=IN.read();
4    if(IN_A>CURR_REG) {
5      OUT.write(CURR_REG);
```

```
6      CURR_REG = IN_A;
7    } else
8      OUT.write(IN_A);
9    return CURR_REG;
10 }
```

Listing 7: The code for the sorting primitive insertion-cell.

The code for insertion-cell is shown in Listing 7. The function takes one input argument IN and one output argument OUT. It uses a `hls::stream<>` type to indicate that these input and outputs can use a FIFO interface. The cell holds the previous value in the `CURR_REG` static variable. It must save this value across function calls, and thus declares it as a `static` variable. The architecture compares the input value to the previous value, and outputs the larger of these two values. The next section shows how to use this primitive to create a linear insertion sort algorithm.

4.2 Sorting Algorithms

In this section, we elaborate on the HLS implementations of four kinds of sorting algorithms: nested loop, recursive, non-comparison, and sorting network. Table 2 summarizes the results of our HLS implementations.

4.2.1 Nested Loop Sorting Algorithms

The *selection sort* algorithm iteratively finds the minimum element in an array and swaps it with the first element until the list is sorted . This algorithm runs in $O(n^2)$, where n is the number of array elements. In HLS, we can pipeline the inner loop to get $II = 1$, which still gives us $O(n^2)$ time. We can create a better design by sorting from both "sides", i.e., finding the minimum and maximum elements in parallel, which reduces the number of iterations in the outer loop by $2\times$. This gives us $O(n^2/2)$ time. In general, selection sort does not translate into high performance hardware using HLS. However, selection sort can be used to produce an area-efficient sorting algorithm implementation.

The *rank sort* algorithm sorts by computing the rank of each element in an array, and then inserting them at their rank index. The rank is the total number of elements greater than or less than the element to be sorted. Sequential rank sort has a complexity of $O(n^2)$. The rank sort algorithm can be fully parallelized in HLS: sorting an array of size n has n units operating in parallel computing the rank of each element. However, this process uses $2 \times n^2$ storage to sort the array of size n. Rank sort can be useful when designing sorting hardware in HLS because it is a good algorithm for exploring area and performance trade-offs.

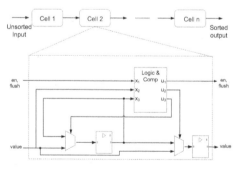

Figure 4: Hardware architecture of linear insertion sort

Insertion sort iterates through an input array maintaining sorted order for every element that it has seen. Insertion

Table 2: Sorting Algorithms evaluations when implementing them using HLS. n=number of elements to sort. *n=number of insertion sort cells, t*= number of compare-swap elements

| Algorithm name | SW Complexity | Parallel HLS Implementation | | | |
		Parallel tasks	Complexity (II)	Storage	Main Sorting Primitives
Selection sort	$O(n^2)$	2	$O(n^2/2)$	$O(2 \times n)$	Compare-swap
Rank sort	$O(n^2)$	n	$O(n)$	$O(n^2)$	Histogram, Compare-swap
Bubble sort	$O(n^2)$	2	$O(2 \times n^2)$	$O(2 \times n)$	Compare-swap
Insertion sort	$O(n^2)$	-	$O(n)$	n*	Compare-swap, insertion-cell
Merge sort	$O(n \log n)$	-	$O(n)$	$O(2 \times \sum \log n)$	Merge Unit
Quick (Sample) sort	$O(n \log n)$ or $O(n^2)$	t	$O(n/t \log n/t)$	$O(n \times t)$	Prefix sum
Counting sort	$O(n \times k)$ (k=3)	3	$O(n)$	$O((k-1)n)$	Prefix sum, Histogram
Radix sort	$O(n \times k)$ (k=4)	4	$O(n)$	$O((k-1)n)$	Prefix sum, Histogram, Counting Sort
Bitonic sort	-	t	$O(\log^2 n)$	$O(n \times t)$	Compare-swap
Odd-even transposition sort	$O(n^2)$	t*	$O(n^2/t^*)$	$O(t*)$	Compare-swap

sort has a complexity of $O(n^2)$. Listing 1 shows a software-centric HLS implementation of insertion sort. We discussed some naive HLS optimizations for insertion sort in Section 2. These used different optimization directives (**pragmas**) in an attempt to create a better hardware implementations. These designs (Designs 1 - 5 in Table 1 did not result in the optimal implementation. Design 6 give the best result. Here we describe code restructuring optimizations of Design 6.

An efficient hardware implementation of insertion sort uses an linear array of insertion-cells [2, 3, 16, 21] or a sorting network [19]. Here we focus on a linear insertion sort implementation; we discuss sorting network implementation later. Figure 4 shows architecture from Arcas-Abella et al. [2]. In this architecture a series of cells (insertion-cell primitives) operate in parallel to sort a given array. It compares the current input (IN) with the current value in current register (CURR_REG). The smaller of current register and the current input is given as an output to *OUT*.

Listing 8 shows the source code that represents the hardware architecture in Figure 4. A cascade of insertion-cells is implemented in a pipelined manner using the **dataflow** pragma, and series of calls to the **InsertionCell** function from Listing 7. Note that we have four different versions of the function – **InsertionCell1**, **InsertionCell2**, etc.. It is necessary to replicate the functions due to the use of the **static** variable. Each of these functions has the same code as in Listing 7. This implementation achieves $O(n)$ time complexity to sort an array of size n.

```
1  void InsertionSort(hls::stream<T> &IN,
       hls::stream<T> &OUT){
2    #pragma HLS DATAFLOW
3    hls::stream<T> out1, out2, out3;
4    // Function calls;
5    InsertionCell1(IN, out1);
6    InsertionCell2(out1, out2);
7    InsertionCell3(out2, out3);
8    InsertionCell4(out3, OUT);
9  }
```

Listing 8: Insertion Sort code for HLS design based on the hardware architecture in Figure 4. The *InsertionCell* functions use the code from Listing 7.

4.2.2 Recursive Algorithms

A pure software implementation of *merge sort* and *quick sort* are not possible in HLS due to the use of recursive functions. HLS tools (including Vivado HLS) typically do not allow recursive function calls. Changing from a recursive

implementation to one that is synthesizable requires a modification of software implementation to remove the recursive function calls in the code.

Merge sort has two primary tasks. The first task partitions the array into individual elements, and the second merges them. The majority of the work is performed in the merging unit, which is implemented with a merge primitive. This was described in Section 4.1.

Merge sort is implemented in hardware using merge sorter tree [14] or using odd-even merge sort. Listing 9 provides an outline of the code for streaming merge sorter tree. In this code, IN1, IN2, IN3 and IN4 are $n/4$ size inputs, and OUT is a size n output. **MergePrimitive1** and **MergePrimitive2** merges two sorted lists of array size $n/4$ and $n/2$, respectively. Using the **dataflow** pragma, we can perform a functional pipeline across these three functions. Merge sort based on odd-even merge also uses merge sorting primitive to sort a given n size array with II of n. Merge sort can be optimized in hardware by running $n \log n$ tasks in parallel.

```
1  void CascadeMergeSort(hls::stream<int> &IN1,
2      hls::stream<int> &IN2, hls::stream<int> &IN3,
3      hls::stream<int> &IN4, hls::stream<int>
         &OUT){
4    #pragma HLS DATAFLOW
5    #pragma HLS stream depth=4 variable=IN1
6    for(int i=0;i<SIZE/4;i++) {
7      //read input data
8    }
9    MergePrimitive1(IN1, IN2, TEMP1);
10   MergePrimitive1(IN3, IN4, TEMP2);
11   MergePrimitive2(TEMP1, TEMP2, OUT);
12 }
```

Listing 9: FIFO based streaming merge sorter tree

Quick sort uses a randomly selected pivot to recursively split an array into elements that are larger and smaller than the pivot. After selecting a pivot, all elements smaller than pivot are moved left of the pivot, i.e., they are in a lower index in the array. This process is repeated for the left and right sides separately. The software complexity of this algorithm is $O(n^2)$ in the worst case and $O(n \log n)$ in the best case. Non-recursive (iterative) version of quick sort can be implemented in HLS with slow performance. Instead, we chose to implement a parallel version of quick sort known as sample sort. In sample sort, we can run t tasks to divide the work of **pivot_function** to sort n size array into n/t. The integration of t results from tasks can be done using the prefix sum primitive. Essentially, this implementation sorts an n size array in $O(n)$ time with higher BRAM usage.

4.2.3 Non-comparison based

Counting sort has three stages. First the counting sort computes the histogram of elements from the unsorted input array. The second stage performs a prefix sum on the histogram from the previous stage. The final stage sorts the array. Final stage first reads the value from the unsorted input array. Then it finds the first index of that element from the prefix sum stage and writes it to the output array. Then it increments the index in the prefix sum by one. Figure 5 (a) shows an example of the counting sort algorithm on an 8 element input array. The first stage performs a histogram on the input data. There are only three values (2, 3, 4), and they occur 3, 2, and 3 times in the unsorted input array, respectively. The second stage does a prefix sum across the histogram frequencies. This tells us the starting index for each of the three values. The value 2 starts at index 0; the value 3 starts at index 3; and the value 4 starts at index 5. The final stage uses these prefix sum indices to fill in the sorted array. Parallel counting sort can be designed using function pipelining of three stages. It runs in $O(n)$ time using $O(n \times k)$ (k is constant) memory storage.

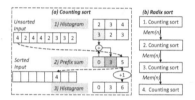

Figure 5: An example hardware architectures for counting sort and radix sort

Radix sort works by applying counting sort for each digit of the input data. For example, to sort 32-bit integers, we can apply counting sort four times to each of the four hexadecimal (radix 8) digits. We can implement a fully parallel radix sort in HLS using functional pipelining of each counting sort. An individual counting sort operation has a throughput of n, thus fully parallel radix sort will also have a throughput of n. To store the outputs of intermediate stages, we need $n \times k$ storage. Here k is usually 4 for 32-bit number or 8 for 64-bit number. Thus to sort 32-bit number in parallel, we use $3 \times n$ storage (3 intermediate memory storage) as shown in Figure 5 (b).

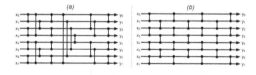

Figure 6: a) Bitonic sort, b) Odd-even transposition sort

4.2.4 Sorting networks

Sorting networks [19] is a set of compare-swap primitives connected by wires. *Bubble sort* is an instance of a sorting network. Two examples of sorting networks (bitonic and odd-even transposition) are shown in Figure 6. For each vertical connection, the minimum of two inputs is assigned to the upper wire and the maximum goes to the lower wire.

Due to parallel nature of sorting networks, they are easier to implement in HLS than other sorting algorithms. However, sorting networks does not scale well in hardware [14]

due to required IO throughput. This requires balancing the parallelism and area in HLS and will be discussed later. For example using parallel n compare-swap elements, odd-even transposition sort can sort an n size array in $O(n)$.

5. SORTING ARCHITECTURE GENERATOR

In this section, we describe our framework for generating sorting architectures. A user can perform design space exploration for a range different application parameters. And once she has decided on a particular architecture, the framework generates a customized sorting architecture that can run on out of the box on a heterogeneous CPU/FPGA system. It creates the RTL code if the user wishes to integrate it into the system in another manner.

The flow for our sorting framework is shown in Figure 8. We define user constraint as a tuple $UC(T, S, B, F, N)$ where T, S, B, F and N are throughput, number of slices, number of block rams, frequency, and the number of elements to sort. We define V as a set of sorting designs that can perform sorting on an input array of size N. The sorting architecture generation is a problem to find a design D of the form $D(T, S, B, F, N)$ that satisfies the UC.

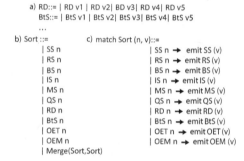

Figure 7: Grammar of domain-specific language. SS=Selection sort, RS=Rank sort, BS=Bubble sort, IS=Insertion sort, MS=Merge sort, QS=Quick sort, RD=Radix sort, BtS=Bitonic sort, OET=Odd-even transposition sort, OEM=Odd even merge sort. a) Sorting architectural variants for particular algorithm, b) Sort function grammar, c) Code generator

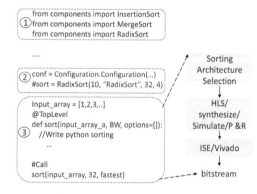

Figure 8: Design flow of Resolve.

Our framework is implemented as a small domain-specific language. Figure 7 shows simplified grammar of the language. The sorting architectures defined in previous sections are defined by types for instance, *RD* and *IS*. Each sorting algorithm has a number of different implementations, called *variants*. For example, radix sort (RD) has five variants: $RD\_v1, RD\_v2, RD\_v3, RD\_v4, RD\_v5,$. The *sort* function can use any sorting algorithm or a composition of one or more algorithms. If we wanted to create an implementation that sorts n elements, we could define it as any of the basic sorting algorithms from Figure 7. For example, SS n creates a selection sort implementation, and BS n uses the bubble sort algorithm for the implementation. If we wish to create a hybrid sorting architecture we could perform Merge(QS n/2, QS n/2), which uses quick sort on the two halves of the input data and merges the results together. The expression: Merge(Merge(RD n/4, RD n/4), Merge(RD n/4, RD n/4)) splits the input data into quarters, and then merges them twice. The elements for the quarter arrays can be sorted using different sorting algorithms in our framework. In this example, radix sort is used to sort the quarter arrays. Based on the Sort function, the emit function generates specific variant of sorting architecture. Thus our framework completely abstracts the underlying architectural details from the user, and allows the user to generate an optimized architecture in a matter of minutes.

To use the framework, the user writes Python code as described in Figure 8. It has three components: Part ① is a library of the template generator classes for existing sorting algorithms (e.g., InsertionSort, MergeSort). There are currently eleven classes, some with multiple architecture variants. All these classes inherit from base class called Sorting. The Sorting class provides common class methods and members (e.g., size, bit width) for all the sorting algorithms. Each class provides parameterizable functions tailored to specific sorting algorithm. For example, $RadixSort.optimized\_II1(size, bit-width)$ generates optimized Radix sort with $II = 1$, while $functional\_pipelining$ $(size, bit\_width)$ generates a dataflow pipelined radix sort for a given parameters. Part ② is HLS project generator and configuration class. The configuration class accepts several parameters. These are the FPGA device, frequency, clock period, simulate_true, implement_true, and name of the module. If simulate_true=1 then the generated design is simulated and verified with a selected simulator inside HLS. If the implement_true=1, then the design is physically evaluated by RTL synthesis.

The users write their top level function in Part ③; this calls the sorting routine. TopLevel is a Python decorator which allows us to add additional information to the existing Python function. Once TopLevel decorator starts executing, it does several things. First, it generates a customized sorting architecture tailored to user provided parameters using Algorithm 1. Here V is a set of all different variants of existing sorting architectures, and D and R are returned sorting design and respective simulation/implementations results. The user provides UC. UC must contain at least one element which is size of array to sort (N). If UC is one, then sorter generates a design from existing designs which has the highest throughput using SorterGenerator function. The emitCode function generates optimized sorting architectures using existing HLS architectures (templates) wrapped in python code. The SorterGenerator includes CalculateThroughput function that calculates throughput TS of current design using initial II of each variant. We assume the II of each variant is known. For

---

Algorithm 1: Customized Sorting Architecture Generation

Data: UC=$\{T, S, B, F, N\}$, V=$\{V_1, V_2, ..V_m\}$,
　　　　P=$\{N/2, N/4..\}$
Result: D=architecture for UC, R=performance area
　　　　results

1 **if** UC *is* 1 **then**
2 　| $[D, R]$=SorterGenerator(V, N)
3 **end**
4 **else**
5 　| **foreach** *(P)* **do**
6 　| 　| $[D, R]$=SorterGenerator(V, P)
7 　| 　| **if** $CheckUserConstraints(UC)$ **then**
8 　| 　| 　| emitMerge(D, P)
9 　| 　| 　| **if** $sim/impl$ *is* 1 **then**
10 　| 　| 　| 　| R = Simulate D
11 　| 　| 　| 　| R =Implement D
12 　| 　| 　| **end**
13 　| 　| **end**
14 　| **end**
15 **end**
16 **Procedure** SorterGenerator(V, N)
　　Data: V, N
　　Result: $D : Design, R : Report$
17 　| $TS(1, 2, .., m)$=CalculateThroughput(V, N)
18 　| $S = min(V_1(t), V_2(t), ..V_m(t))$
19 　| $[D, R]$=emitCode S
20 　| **if** $sim/impl$ *is* 1 **then**
21 　| 　| Simulate D Implement D
22 　| **end**

---

example, we know linear insertion sort (LIS) has $II = 1$, so the $TS(LIS) = 1 \times N$. Then it generates design D and returns report R. In the case of $|UC| > 1$, we must satisfy user constraints; In Algorithm 1, we present a case where there is not a design in the current pool that satisfies UC (other case where there is a D that satisfies UC is straightforward). We use a heuristic approach that continuously divides N into halves until it finds a design that satisfies UC. For a returned design D from SorterGenerator, we call CheckUserConstraints to check these conditions: $UC(T) > D(T), UC(S) < D(S), UC(B) < D(B)$, $UC(F) > D(F)$. If these conditions meet, then emitMerge generates HLS code from pre-wrapped templates in python.

6. EXPERIMENTAL RESULTS

In this section, we present the performance and utilization results for a representative set of architectures generated by our framework, and the end-to-end (CPU/FPGA) implementation of selected sorting architectures. Finally, we compare our designs with existing implementations of sorting hardware architectures.

Basic Sorting Algorithms: We implemented basic sorting algorithms – selection sort, rank sort, linear insertion sort, merge sort (two variants), sample sort, radix sort (two variants), bitonic sort, and transposition sort (two variants) – for three different problem sizes (32, 2014, 16384). The results are shown in Table 3. Results presented in Table 3 are obtained after RTL synthesis targeting the Xilinx xc7vx1140tflg1930-1 chip using Vivado HLS 2014.3. The performance results are presented in terms of megabytes per

Table 3: *Implementation results for different sorting architectures. Tasks=number of parallel sorting processes. Entries with '-' are omitted since the sorting architecture is not good for that particular size (e.g., the utilization is too high to fit on the target device).*

Algorithm name	Tasks	32				1024				16384			
		Slices	BRAM	Freq	MB/s	Slices	BRAM	Freq	MB/s	Slices	BRAM	Freq	MB/s
Selection sort	2	26	0	266	50	410	12	232	3.5	599	192	171	97
Rank sort	2	119	4	389	508	162	16	419	4	504	256	348	< 10
Linear insertion sort	n	374	0	345	1380	12046	0	310	1243	-	-	-	-
Merge sort (P)	log n	1526	18	164	954	2035	40	239	482	484	608	155	1244
Merge sort (UP)	log n	666	18	180	550	1268	40	281	899	2474	832	177	567
MergeStream (P)	log n	529	8	211	794	1425	20	189	756	2487	140	166	666
Sample sort	-	-	-	-	-	2777	218	228	911	5174	2838	127	510
8-bit Radix sort	4	1420	19	227	42	1500	36	230	202	1743	456	222	220
4-bit Radix sort	8	2146	30	353	223	2470	60	362	356	3352	960	289	289
Bitonic sort	-	4391	0	268	1073	3239	56	268	1048	7274	1280	230	922
Odd-even trans	8*2	929	33	342	96	1254	36	301	15	1361	128	225	0.8
Odd-even trans	16*2	1326	0	323	70	2209	68	270	29	2370	128	212	1.64
Merge (Stream)	-	221	0	395	1407	231	0	374	1490	255	0	368	1474
Merge4 + Radix	-	-	-	-	-	-	-	-	-	1010	168	244	411
Merge8 + Radix	-	-	-	-	-	-	-	-	-	2584	240	245	782
Merge16 + Radix	-	-	-	-	-	-	-	-	-	4786	320	148	858

second (MB/s). We show a broad set of implementations to highlight the ability of our framework to create a broad number of Pareto optimal designs rather than simply show the best results.

Selection sort and rank sort both have small utilization with limited throughput especially as the input size increases. Linear insertion sort has very high throughput, but it does not scale well as the number of slices has a linear relationship (to sort n size array, n insertion-cell is required) with the input size since we are directly increasing the number of insertion sort cells. Thus linear insertion sort architecture should only be used to sort arrays with small sizes (e.g, 512).

The designs Merge sort (P) and Merge sort (UP) are pipelined and unpipelined versions of cascade of odd-even merge [13]. Merge Stream (P) is the streaming version of the cascade of odd-even merge sort. Pipelined version of merge sort achieve better II except for size 1024. This is caused because HLS tool is doing loop level transformations when we do not have pipeline for size 1024. Sample sort tends to achieve higher throughput but uses more BRAMs than other sorting architectures.

The 8-bit radix sort has four parallel tasks; the 4-bit radix sort has eight parallel tasks. Radix sort provides a good area-throughput tradeoff. In the 4-bit implementation, doubling the area produces a greater than 4× speedup for 32 inputs. This trend does not continue for larger input sizes though the throughput does increase in all cases. This indicates that radix sort is suitable for medium size arrays. Bitonic sort achieves high throughput for, but it tends to use more BRAMs than merge sort. Thus, bitonic sort is suitable for sorting medium size arrays.

In the second part of Table 3, we present four hybrid sorting architectures. Merge (Stream) is a streaming version of merge sort that operates on pre-sorted inputs. It is designed for heterogeneous CPU/FPGA sorting where the smaller arrays are pre-sorted in CPU. Merge4+Radix is generated with the user constraints $UC(T = H, n = 16384, S < 1500, B < 170)$. This architecture uses merge primitve to combine four 4096-element radix sorts, which gives the highest throughput design with less than 170 Block RAMs ($B < 170$). Merge8+Radix and Merge16+Radix architectures divides the input array (similar to Merge4+Radix except they

use more parallelism 8-way and 16-way) into 8 and 16, respectively. Then uses radix sort to sort the sub arrays.

Table 3 presents some of the basic sorting architectures. Once we have these kinds of sorting architectures, it is straightforward to generate even more sorting architectures for different user constraints. For example, we presented slices, achieved clock period and throughput results for streaming merge sort (pipelined (P) and unpipelined (UP)) in Figure 9. These results are obtained for different sizes and different user specified clock period. We only presented one case study here; we can generate broad number of Pareto optimal designs for aforementioned different sorting algorithms to meet different user constraints.

End-to-end sorting system: To the best of our knowledge, there is no published end-to-end system implementation of large sorting problems using architectures created from HLS. We implemented and tested a number of different sorting algorithms on a hybrid CPU/FPGA system using RIFFA 2.2.1 [12]. The HLS sorting architectures use AXI stream. The corresponding AXI signals are connected to signals of RIFFA. We present the area and performance of the several prototypes (sizes) in Table 4. In the first row of Table 4, we present the area results for RIFFA using only loop-back HLS module (i.e., an empty HLS module). This shows the overhead of RIFFA. The remaining results include RIFFA and the sorting algorithm. Results for 16384 and 65536 are obtained using the xc7vx690tffg1761-2 FPGA running at 125MHz, and PC with Intel Core i7 CPU at 3.6 GHz and 16 GB RAM. The CPU is used only to transmit and receive data. The sorting implemented on the FPGA can sort data at a rate of 0.44 - 0.5 GB/s. Our end-to-end system does not overlap communication and sorting times. Thus, it has an average throughput of 0.23 GB/s. The last line of Table 4 shows hybrid sorter results for 131072 size formed by two 65536 size sorters. CPU merges outputs of sub sorters. These results can be improved linearly by using more channels on RIFFA or increasing the clock frequency.

Comparison to previous work: We compare the results from our framework with the sorting networks from the Spiral project [23], interleaved linear insertion sort (ILS) [21], and merge sort [14]. We selected these because insertion sort is usually best suited for small size arrays, sorting networks are used for both small and medium size arrays, and a

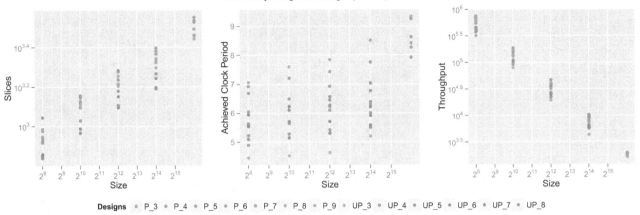

Figure 9: Design space expiration of generated architectures: P_X (X is user specified clock period and X = 3 to 10): piplelined and UP_X (X=3 to 10): unpipelined versions of merge sort.

*Table 4: Area and performance of end-to-end system. *HLS result of 131072 size hybrid sorter. +indicates CPU merging time).*

Design	Size	FF/LUT	BRAM	II
RIFFA	N/A	19472/16395	71	N/A
RIFFA+Sorting IP	16384	25118/20368	141	18434
RIFFA+Sorting IP	65536	26353/21707	333	73730
RIFFA+Sorting IP	131072	38436/31816	609	*73730+

merge sort is best for larger size arrays. Finally, we compare against the sorting architectures implemented in various different high-level languages [2].

First we compare our results (streaming merge sort) to sorting architectures from the Spiral project [23]. We used the same parameters in both cases: 32-bit fixed point type for all architectures, Xilinx xc7vx690tffg1761-2, streaming width of one (one streaming input and one streaming output), and 125 MHz frequency. Spiral generates five different sorting architectures (SN1, SN2, SN3, SN4, and SN5). SN1 and SN3 are high performance fully streaming architectures with large area. SN2 and SN4 balance area and throughput. And SN5 is an architecture optimized for area [23]. We compare against SN1, SN2, and SN5 because they provide a good balance between performance and area. For SN2, we generate fully streaming (SN2_S) and iterative (SN2_I) versions. We only compared our result against to the SN5 fully steaming version because the iterative version of SN5 has a very low performance (e.g., throughput of SN5 iterative version for size 1024 is 102621). We implemented these designs (SN1, SN2_I, SN_S, and SN5) using Vivado 2015.2. All of the results are presented after place-and-route.

Table 5 compares the four architectures from Spiral to our work. The throughput (II) is the number of clock cycles need to sort an array of n elements. We obtained Spiral throughput results from the report generated by online tool (http://www.spiral.net/hardware/sort/sort.html). The throughput of our work is obtained from Vivado HLS co-simulation. In each case, this is the II for sorting one n size array. The best design (fastest, small area) from Spiral project is SN2_S for 1024. SN_S uses 17.9× more BRAMS, 4.6× more FFs, 2.1× more LUTs than our merge sort imple-

mentation for the 1024 element array. The smallest design from Spiral is SN2_I. For example, to sort a 16384 element array, SN2_I uses 13.7× more BRAMs, and its throughput is 14× worse than our merge sort implementation. SN1 and SN5 for 16384 size could not fit on target device (e.g., SN5 requires 8196 BRAMs while target device has only 1470).

We also compared our results to work by Chen et al. [7] which designs an energy efficient bionic sort on the same target device. Their designs uses 19927 LUTs and 2 BRAMS for sorting 1024 elements, and it uses 36656 LUTs and 88 BRAMs for sorting 16384 elements. The LUTs and BRAMs are calculated using the utilization percentage from [7].

Table 6: Streaming insertion sort generated in this paper (Resolve) vs. Interleaved linear insertion sorter (ILS) [21].

	64	128	256
ILS Throughput (MSPS) [21]	4.6	2.33	1.16
Resolve Throughput (MSPS)	5.3	2.54	1.29
Ratio	**1.13X**	**1.08X**	**1.1X**
ILS Slices [21]	1113	2227	4445
Resolve Slices	792	1569	3080
Ratio	**0.7X**	**0.7X**	**0.69X**

Table 6 presents the throughput and utilization results of interleaved linear insertion sorter (ILS) and our streaming insertion sort for different sizes (64, 128, 256). We calculated the slices of ILS by using slices per node × number of elements (size). The slices per node for $w = 1$ is obtained from [21]. The throughput is the number of MSPS for a given size (64, 128, 256). Our insertion sorter has average 1.1X better throughput while using 0.6X fewer slices.

Arcas-Abella et al. [2] develop a spatial insertion sort and bitonic sort using Bluespec, LegUp, Chisel, and Verilog. Table 7 shows comparison of our spatial insertion / bitonic sort designs to implementations of this work. We achieve higher throughput and use less area. Our bitonic sort achieves the same throughput with comparable area results.

Koch et al. [14] use partial reconfiguration to sort large arrays. They achieve a sorting throughput of 667 MB/s to 2 GB/s. We can improve our throughput by increasing the frequency (our HLS cores run at 125 MHz) and using additional RIFFA channels. Our system consumes more BRAMs because they implement a FIFO-based merge sort using a

Table 5: Comparison to Spiral [23]. II is the number of clock cycles to produce one sorted array.

	64			1024			16384		
	FF/LUT	BRAM	II	FF/LUT	BRAM	II	FF/LUT	BRAM	II
Spiral SN1	5866 / 1775	10	64	34191 / 28759	162	1024	-	-	-
Spiral SN2_I	2209 / 880	5	397	4053 / 2002	45	10261	6790/2547	964	229405
Spiral SN2_S	5912 / 1803	10	64	16165 / 5991	125	1024	62875 /2744884	1395 / 16384	16384
Spiral SN5	9386 / 3023	18	64	27130 / 11104	225	1024	-	-	-
Resolve	1560 / 1401	2	68	3486 / 2848	7	1028	6515 / 4901	70	16388

Table 7: Comparison of our work to [2]. * calculated with II=1

	Spatial Insertion		Bitonic	
	FF/ LUT	MB/s	LUT/FF	MB/s
Verilog	2081/ 641	1301	10250/ 2640	38016
BSV	2012/ 1701	1310	10250/ 2640	38326
Chisel	2012/ 720	1317	10272/ 2649	38447
LegUp	1115/ 823	3.13	4210/ 5180	1034
Resolve	605/ 661	1415	6404/ 9827	38016*

shared memory blocks for both input streams. Writing to a FIFO using two different processes during functional pipelining is not supported by HLS tools that we used.

7. CONCLUSION

The Resolve framework generates optimized sorting architectures from pre-optimized HLS blocks. Resolve comes with a number of highly optimized sorting primitives and sorting architectures. Both the primitives and basic sorting algorithms can be combined in countless manners using our domain specific language, which allows for efficient design space exploration to enable a user to meet all of the necessary system design constraints. The user can customize these hardware implementations in terms of sorting element size and data type, throughput, and FPGA device utilization constraints. Resolve integrates these sorting architectures with RIFFA, which enables designers to call these hardware accelerated sorting functions directly from a CPU with a PCIe enabled FPGA card.

References

[1] S. G. Akl. *Parallel sorting algorithms.* AP, Inc, 1985.

[2] O. Arcas-Abella et al. An empirical evaluation of high-level synthesis languages and tools for database acceleration. In *International Conference on Field Programmable Logic and Applications.* IEEE, 2014.

[3] M. Bednara et al. Tradeoff analysis and architecture design of a hybrid hardware/software sorter. In *International Conference on Application-Specific Systems, Architectures, and Processors*, pages 299–308. IEEE, 2000.

[4] V. Brajovic et al. A sorting image sensor: An example of massively parallel intensity-to-time processing for low-latency computational sensors. In *International Conference on Robotics and Automation*, volume 2, pages 1638–1643. IEEE, 1996.

[5] M. Burrows and D. J. Wheeler. A block-sorting lossless data compression algorithm. 1994.

[6] J. Casper et al. Hardware acceleration of database operations. In *International symposium on Field-programmable gate arrays*, pages 151–160. ACM, 2014.

[7] R. Chen et al. Energy and memory efficient mapping of bitonic sorting on fpga. In *International Symposium on Field-Programmable Gate Arrays*, pages 240–249. ACM, 2015.

[8] J. Chhugani et al. Efficient implementation of sorting on multi-core simd cpu architecture. *Proceedings of the VLDB Endowment*, 1(2):1313–1324, 2008.

[9] J. Dean et al. Mapreduce: Simplified data processing on large clusters. *Communications of the ACM*, 51(1):107–113, 2008.

[10] N. George et al. Hardware system synthesis from domain-specific languages. In *Field Programmable Logic and Applications*, pages 1–8. IEEE, 2014.

[11] G. Graefe. Implementing sorting in database systems. *ACM Computing Surveys (CSUR)*, 38(3):10, 2006.

[12] M. Jacobsen et al. Riffa 2.1: A reusable integration framework for fpga accelerators. *ACM Transactions on Reconfigurable Technology and Systems (TRETS)*, 2015.

[13] D. E. Knuth. *The art of computer programming, volume 3: sorting and searching.* Addison-Wesley Professional, 1998.

[14] D. Koch et al. Fpgasort: A high performance sorting architecture exploiting run-time reconfiguration on fpgas for large problem sorting. In *International symposium on Field programmable gate arrays*, pages 45–54. ACM, 2011.

[15] C. Lauterbach et al. Fast bvh construction on gpus. In *Computer Graphics Forum*, volume 28, pages 375–384. Wiley Online Library, 2009.

[16] R. Marcelino et al. Sorting units for fpga-based embedded systems. In *Distributed Embedded Systems: Design, Middleware and Resources*, pages 11–22. Springer, 2008.

[17] J. Matai et al. Enabling fpgas for the masses. In *First International Workshop on FPGAs for Software Programmers*, 2014.

[18] R. Mueller et al. Data processing on fpgas. *Proceedings of the VLDB Endowment*, 2(1):910–921, 2009.

[19] R. Mueller et al. Sorting networks on fpgas. *The VLDB Journalâ ĂŤThe International Journal on Very Large Data Bases*, 21(1):1–23, 2012.

[20] R. Mueller, J. Teubner, and G. Alonso. Data processing on fpgas. *Proceedings of the VLDB Endowment*, 2(1):910–921, 2009.

[21] J. Ortiz et al. A streaming high-throughput linear sorter system with contention buffering. *International Journal of Reconfigurable Computing*, 2011.

[22] N. Satish et al. Designing efficient sorting algorithms for manycore gpus. In *IPDPS*, pages 1–10. IEEE, 2009.

[23] M. Zuluaga et al. Computer generation of streaming sorting networks. In *Design Automation Conference*, pages 1245–1253. ACM, 2012.

SEU Mitigation and Validation of the LEON3 Soft Processor Using Triple Modular Redundancy for Space Processing

Michael Wirthlin, Andrew Keller,
Chase McCloskey and Parker Ridd
NSF Center for High-Performance
Reconfigurable Computing (CHREC)
Deptartment of Electrical and Computer
Engineering
Brigham Young University
Provo, UT 84606, USA

David S. Lee[1] and Jeffrey Draper[2]
[1]Sandia National Laboratories
Albuquerque, NM 87123, USA
Information Sciences Institute
[2]Ming Hsieh Department of Electrical
Engineering
University of Southern California
Marina del Ray, CA, USA

ABSTRACT

Programmable processors are an essential component in most satellite payload electronics and handle a variety of functions including command handling and data processing. There is growing interest in implementing programmable processors within satellites on commercial FPGAs because of their reconfigurability, large logic density, and I/O bandwidth. Commercial FPGAs, however, are sensitive to ionizing radiation and systems developed for space must implement single-event upset mitigation to operate reliably. This paper investigates the improvements in reliability of a LEON3 soft processor operating on a SRAM-based FPGA when using triple-modular redundancy and other processor-specific mitigation techniques. The improvements in reliability provided by these techniques are validated with both fault injection and heavy ion radiation tests. The fault injection experiments indicate an improvement of $51\times$ and the radiation testing results demonstrate an average improvement of $10\times$. Orbit failure rate estimations were computed and suggest that the TMR LEON3 processor has a mean-time to failure of over 70 years in a geosynchronous orbit.

Categories and Subject Descriptors

B.8.1 [**Performance and Reliability**]: Reliability, Testing, and Fault-Tolerance; B.7.2 [**Design Aids**]: Automated TMR, Manual Mitigation

Keywords

FPGA; Soft-core Processor; LEON3; TMR; Fault-Tolerance

1. INTRODUCTION

Modern satellite systems depend on reliable, radiation-hardened (rad-hard) processors to perform various mission-

ACM acknowledges that this contribution was authored or co-authored by an employee, or contractor of the national government. As such, the Government retains a nonexclusive, royalty-free right to publish or reproduce this article, or to allow others to do so, for Government purposes only. Permission to make digital or hard copies for personal or classroom use is granted. Copies must bear this notice and the full citation on the first page. Copyrights for components of this work owned by others than ACM must be honored. To copy otherwise, distribute, republish, or post, requires prior specific permission and/or a fee. Request permissions from permissions@acm.org.

FPGA'16, February 21-23, 2016, Monterey, CA, USA

© 2016 ACM. ISBN 978-1-4503-3856-1/16/02... $15.00

DOI: http://dx.doi.org/10.1145/2847263.2847278

critical operations such as payload processing, command handling, and satellite control. These rad-hard processors, however, are extremely expensive and are often based on architectures that are much older and slower than commercially available processors. A soft processor can be an attractive alternative to a rad-hard processor by providing processor-specific customization, the ability to add custom reliability techniques, and the ability to provide customized FPGA logic [1]. Further, modern FPGAs provide a significant amount of configurable logic and access to a large amount of serial I/O bandwidth.

Any design operating in an SRAM-based FPGA, including soft processors, are susceptible to ionizing radiation [2]. The presence of high energy protons, heavy ions, and galactic cosmic rays in the space orbits cause a number of problems for electronics, including FPGAs. This radiation can induce a number of negative effects including upsets in the internal state of the device. These upsets, known as single-event upsets or SEUs, can cause several problems in FPGA-based systems. First, SEUs can corrupt the configuration memory of the device causing the design configured on the device to operate incorrectly. Second, the internal state of the design's flip-flops or block memories may be corrupted resulting in data corruption. Third, the internal state of custom hardware blocks within the FPGA may be corrupted (PLLs, clock managers, DSPs, etc.).

Fortunately, a number of mitigation techniques have been developed to address these concerns. One of the most common ways of applying structural mitigation is using triple-modular redundancy or TMR [3]. TMR provides masking of single errors by triplicating the circuit and providing majority voters (see Figure 1). As long as two of the three copies of the circuit are operating correctly, the system will tolerate a failure in any of the three copies. Systems that employ TMR must also provide a mechanism for repairing the failures and resynchronizing the state of the three circuit copies. This repair and resynchronization is usually done through a technique called configuration scrubbing [4, 5]. TMR has been shown to provide significant improvements in FPGA reliability in harsh radiation environments [6].

While TMR along with scrubbing have been shown to improve reliability, applying TMR to the entire system may not be the most effective SEU mitigation approach. Complex systems with a variety of resources and different de-

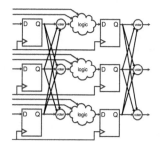

Figure 1: Triple Modular Redundancy (TMR).

sign approaches may respond more reliably to a variety of SEU mitigation approaches. This work investigates hybrid mitigation approaches that are targeted specifically for soft processors operating within an FPGA. In particular, this paper will describe a processor SEU mitigation technique that involves TMR, custom memory mitigation, and custom control structures.

This paper describes a SEU mitigation strategy applied to the LEON3 soft processor core operating on the Xilinx Kintex-7 FPGA. This mitigation strategy is validated using both fault injection and radiation testing with heavy ions. The results of this validation effort demonstrate that the techniques used to improve SEU reliability are improved by a factor of 51× using fault injection and 10× in radiation testing. Estimation of orbit failure rates suggest that at a minimum, these techniques will increase the mean-time to failure of this processor from 1.4 years to 76 years.

This paper will begin by reviewing related efforts in developing reliable soft processors within FPGAs. Next, the LEON3 soft processor core will be described along with the configuration used in this testing and the software used during the validation of the mitigation techniques. Next, the mitigation approaches applied to the LEON3 are described along with the increase in size and reduction in clock speed. The approach for validating the mitigation techniques are presented using fault injection and radiation testing. The impact of these techniques are compared with the non-mitigated processor and suggestions for future work are provided.

2. RELATED WORK

A number of projects have investigated methods for improving the reliability of soft processors operating in commercial SRAM FPGAs. A variety of both structural and temporal redundancy are used to improve soft processor response to single-event upsets. The LEON2 soft processor core was mapped to the Virtex II architecture and tested using fault injection [7]. This work compared three different version of the processor: the standard processor, the processor with TMR, and a "fault tolerant" architectural variation. A custom 16-bit "configurable fault-tolerant processor (CFTP)" was created for an FPGA-based computing satellite and uses TMR and scrubbing to mitigate against configuration upsets [8]. This platform was designed for use in the U.S. Naval Academy's MidSTAR-l satellites and launched in March of 2003.

A NIOS-II soft processor [9] was implemented on an Altera Cyclone-II device and implements time redundancy to address the effects of soft errors and fault injection. Ex-

periments were completed to validate the benefits of this technique. A general approach for lock-step processing with dual soft processors has been proposed [10, 11] which uses traditional software reliability techniques such as lockstep, checkpointing, and rollback. This work was tested using the LEON processor with three variants: the default LEON processor, a TMR LEON processor, and the proposed dual-lockstep core with software fault tolerant techniques.

A triple modular small Xilinx PicoBlaze soft processor was tested on the Xilinx Virtex 5 architecture using a tile-based approach and resynchronization through partial reconfiguration [12]. A duplicated LEON3 was implemented with a special bus monitor to detect processor failures at run time [13]. The reliability of a TMR version of the Microblaze processor was tested with fault injection [14] and a related effort tested the reliability of the microblaze processor operating on the radiation hardened by design (RHBD) Virtex V5QV FPGA [15].

3. LEON3 PROCESSOR ARCHITECTURE

The LEON3 is an open-source soft processor core distributed by Cobham Gaisler AB as part of their GRLIB IP Library. It conforms to the IEEE Standard for a 32-bit Microprocessor Architecture and Version 8 of the Scalable Processor Architecture (SPARC V8) [16, 17]. It features a 7-stage integer pipeline with a Harvard architecture. The LEON3 is a popular option for processing in space environments. First, the LEON3 core utilizes a very small portion of available resources on a commercial FPGA such as the Xilinx Kintex-7 XC7K325T. The remaining resources are available for use in SEU mitigation techniques and for additional IP. Second, additional peripherals may be easily incorporated into a LEON3 system due to its bus centric system-on-chip design. As part of the GRLIB IP Library, the LEON3 connects to additional IP cores via an on-chip bus. The GRLIB IP library supports the AMBA-2.0 AHB/APB bus – a widely used royalty free industry standard. Third, the LEON3 is well documented and supported by a large user group. Fourth, the processor is independent of any FPGA architecture and has been ported to several different FPGA architectures. Fifth, the processor is available as a radiation-hardened custom circuit to facilitate migration from a soft implementation to a higher-performance, more reliable custom implementation [18].

The LEON3 used in this experiment originated from the LEON3/GRLIB Release 1.4.0-b4154. For this test a minimal configuration was given to the "leon3-xilinx-kc705" design – which targets the Xilinx Kintex-7 KC705 development board. A stripped-down configuration of the LEON3 processor was chosen for this experiment to test the sensitivity of the core internal architecture and to simplify the construction of the test. This simplified configuration *excluded* the following default architectural components:

- Instruction and Data Caches
- Interrupt Controller
- Memory Management Unit (MMU)
- Debug Support Unit
- External Memory Controllers

All unnecessary I/O peripherals were excluded and all instruction and data memory was held in internal BRAM resources to avoid the need for an external memory controller. In addition, the PLL clock controllers were removed and a 200 MHz external clock was internally divided by four to create a 50 MHz global clock. Figure 2 reflects the final configuration of both the LEON3 processor core and connected peripherals via the on-chip bus.

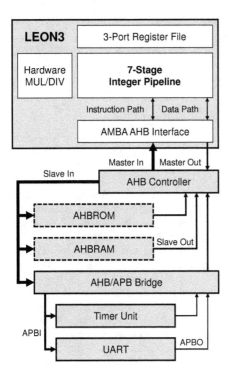

Figure 2: LEON3 System Architecture Under Test

The LEON3 processor is programmed to execute the Dhrystone Version 2.1 benchmark. Dhrystone is designed to test integer performance of a processor like that of the 7-stage integer pipeline found in the LEON3. The benchmark is composed of common instructions surveyed in system-level software such as operating systems and compilers [19]. This program assists in validation of functional correctness under testing when compared against another processor core running the same benchmark program in parallel. Once Dhrystone is loaded into RAM the LEON3 begins execution at the decompressed address. In this experiment Dhrystone is run for 10,000 iterations in a continuous loop.

The LEON3 processor begins the boot process by accessing a read only memory (AHBROM) composed of onboard BRAMs that contains a boot loader and the compressed application program.The boot loader sets the system clock and the baud-rate for UART and then decompresses the benchmark from AHBROM to the AHBRAM peripheral.The Dhrystone C code was cross-compiled for the SPARC V8 architecture and integrated into the LEON3 boot loader using GRTools-20150121 [20].

The Dhrystone output is sent across UART for external monitoring. The benchmark executes continuously to guarantee that the LEON3 processor remains active throughout the test. The caches are disabled to force the processor to communicate more frequently on the bus and facilitate more frequent error checking.

4. LEON3 SEU MITIGATION STRATEGY

The SEU mitigation strategy used in this work involves the combination of several different techniques. The primary mitigation technique used is triple modular redundancy (TMR). Automated tools are used to triplicate the LEON3 netlist and insert voters strategically throughout the design. In addition to TMR, the internal memories of the processor are manually replaced with hand-designed memories that include scrubbing to prevent the accumulation of errors within the memory. These techniques are augmented with configuration scrubbing which occurs in the background to prevent the accumulation of configuration errors. Each of these mitigation techniques used will be described in detail below.

4.1 Automated TMR

Triple Modular Redundancy uses redundant hardware to mask SEUs by triplicating the original module and inserting majority synchronizer voters (see Figure 1). If at least two of the circuit copies are correct, the output of the system will be correct as well. To avoid single point failures, voters themselves are often triplicated as well [21]. The granularity of TMR affects the amount of SEUs a design can tolerate before failure; fine grain TMR (i.e., TMR of the smallest components) is able to withstand more faults at the cost of additional area and delay due to increased voter insertion [22]. There are a number of automated CAD tools that are capable of applying TMR to an FPGA design such as: Xilinx XTMR tool [23], Mentor Graphics Precision Rad-Tolerant Synthesis [24], and an open source tool called BL-TMR [25]. For this test, TMR will be leveraged as much as possible to increase reliability by applying full TMR at a fine granularity to the final LEON3 system configuration of Figure 2.

The BL-TMR open-source tool was used to perform fine granularity TMR of the LEON3 system architecture. It achieved this by manipulating the Xilinx ISE 14.7 generated EDIF netlist of the design allowing for Xilinx 7-series primitives, (e.g., LUT6, FDRE, MUXF8, etc.), to be triplicated with majority voters placed throughout the design. This tool places voters in feedback paths so as to resynchronize the triplicated processor when repaired through configuration scrubbing [21]. The resulting netlist is then instantiated in the test design harness for validation.

All components of the LEON3 system were triplicated except for the AHB memories as indicated by their dashed outline in Figure 2. The global clock was triplicated using three independent clock buffers enabling each LEON3 TMR domain to have its own unique clock. All ports of the LEON3 system module were triplicated and are utilized in the test design harness for validation.

4.2 Internal Memory Mitigation

Internal memories that contain large amounts of state pose a unique challenge when faced with SEUs. Although a number of memory coding techniques can be used, these techniques do not adequately protect the memory from the accumulation of multple upsets in memory words. This problem is especially prevalent on memories whose contents do not change very often (such as read only memories). Affected memories in Xilinx 7-series FPGAs include: BRAMS, LUTRAMs, SRLs, DRP registers, etc. In order to prevent accumulation of upsets that may invalidate TMR and other memory reliability techniques, such as ECC, some form of memory scrubbing is needed [26]. The memories in this processor are manually modified to implement both fault masking and memory scrubbing.

Although the 7 series BRAMs offer ECC support [27], this ECC is not used in this processor for several reasons. First, the ECC is only available when the BRAM is configured in 64-bit mode. The memory used in the LEON3 is configured with a data width that is smaller than 64 bits. Second, the use of a single BRAM with ECC introduces single-point failures in the memory. For example, there are several signals such as the "write enable" that could be corrupted by a single SEU and completely break the operation of the single, ECC-enabled BRAM. While ECC can mask a single bit error when reading from BRAM, it does not actually repair the error within the BRAM. Therefore, ECC is not able to handle the accumulation of SEUs in BRAM unless the corrected data is written back into the memory. To ensure there are no single-point failures in the memory architecture and to prevent accumulation of upsets, triplicated BRAMs with self-scrubbing will be used.

By providing memory scrubbing, memories affected by SEUs will not accumulate upsets and TMR can be used to mask single errors that occur in the memories. The two memories that were protected in this processor are a single-port read only BRAM configuration for the AHBROM peripheral and a single-port BRAM read/write configuration for the AHBRAM peripheral. In each case scrubbing logic is added that takes advantage of the unused second BRAM memory port (see Figure 3). This scrubber "cleans" the memory contents by alternating between a read and write operation through each address of the memory. The complete contents of the BRAM are scrubbed every 400 μs. Data reads from the triplicated memories are voted upon to obtain a corrected value for the current address. This value is then written back to the memory. Scrubbing is disabled in the AHBRAM while it is being written to by the processor to avoid memory conflicts.

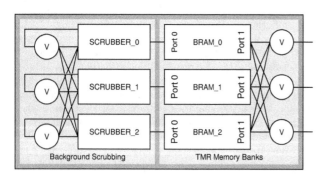

Figure 3: Memory Mitigation with TMR and Memory Scrubbing.

These scrubbing memories were created manually in HDL using inferred BRAMs. The BL-TMR tool merged the netlist of the manually mitigated scrubbing memories with the triplicated netlist of the LEON3 system.

4.3 Configuration Scrubbing

An important component of the mitigation strategy used in this system is configuration scrubbing [4, 5]. Configura-

tion scrubbing involves the rapid and continuous writing of the configuration memory to repair upsets. The reliability of a system can be significantly improved when both configuration scrubbing (repair) and TMR (fault masking) are used together. Without configuration scrubbing, the benefits of TMR are limited (especially for long missions).

Configuration scrubbing is usually performed external to the FPGA and does not impact the design of the mitigated LEON3 processor. A JTAG configuration scrubbing mechanism is used for this experiment and will be described in more detail in Section 6.

4.4 Testing Infrastructure

Two different versions of the LEON3 processor were developed. The first is the unmitigated version which implements the LEON3 processor without any modification. This unmitigated version will serve as a reference to identify baseline reliability. The second is a mitigated version and implements the TMR and memory mitigation described above. The improvements in reliability will be compared against the baseline unmitigated processor.

Both the unmitigated and mitigated LEON3 processors were tested under fault injection and a heavy ion radiation beam. In order to validate the LEON3 processor under these tests a mechanism must be put in place to identify when the LEON3 processor fails. One common approach is to provide a "golden" copy of the design and compare the "golden" copy of the processor with the design under test or "DUT". While this is an effective mechanism, it is difficult to synchronize two separate systems making it a cumbersome strategy to implement.

The strategy used for detecting failures in this experiment is to instance *two* copies of the LEON3 system inside a test design harness and provide an internal cycle-by-cycle comparison of the processors from *within* the FPGA. Fault tolerant detection circuitry is added to detect when the two processors disagree (see Figure 4). When a failure occurs in one of the two processors, the faulty processor will not match the non-faulty processor and the detection circuitry will identify the error. Once an error is identified a triplicated register is set and remains set so external monitoring methods may record the failure.

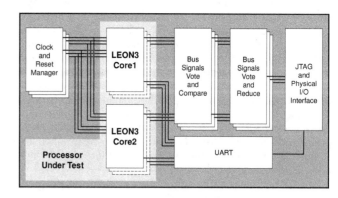

Figure 4: Internal Testing Infrastructure.

The following signals were used to compare the processor execution state and monitor the health of the test design harness:

- Global system clock heartbeat and a heartbeat for each of the triplicated clock domains
- Triplicated disagreement signals set only when processors disagree
- Triplicated failure detection signals asserted if any disagreement occurred
- Triplicated activity signals for each processor core indicating that the bus signals being compared are changing over time (i.e., that the processor is active).
- UART output of the Dhrystone (2.1) benchmark for monitoring correct behavior.

Each bit of the bus signal state was compared between the two processors using triplicated comparison circuitry giving a total of 104 bits of comparison status. Triplicated reduction circuitry reduced these 104 bits to a single triplicated bit. If ever two or more copies of this triplicated bit go high (i.e., the bus signals of the processors do not agree across two or more copies of the comparison logic), an additional register is set and remains set to *catch* the disagreement so that the failure may be recorded externally from the chip.

Two methods of off chip status retrieval were incorporated into this test. First, the status signals were made available via JTAG using an instanced Xilinx Boundary Scan primitive (BSCAN). This allows the status to be queried as part of the configuration scrubbing or fault injection, enabling dynamic control of the test (e.g., automated recording and full device reconfiguration upon failure for fault injection). Second, the triplicated status signals were tied to physical I/O ports and monitored via Xilinx FPGA Mezzanine Card XM105 Debug Cards using an additional Xilinx KC705 Evaluation Board. A Xilinx Virtual I/O Module was instanced on this out-of-beam monitor device and Xilinx ChipScope was used to allow real time monitoring of the DUT during radiation testing. Figure 8 shows the physical configuration of the DUT with the monitoring board. Once off chip the triplicated status signals may be voted upon to determine the correct status of the design under test (i.e., one of the three failures signals may erroneously be set due to an SEU in the comparison logic and should not be considered as a LEON3 system failure).

4.5 Design Implementation Results

Both the unmitigated and mitigated designs were mapped to the Xilinx XC7K325T device on the KC705 evaluation board. The FPGA utilization of both designs is summarized in Table 1. The mitigated version of the LEON3 uses $3.3\times$ more slices than the unmitigated version. The mitigated dual LEON version uses roughly 30% of the FPGA resources suggesting that up to six mitigated LEON3 processors could fit within the XC7K325T device. The internal FPGA layout of both designs is shown in Figure 5.

Although both processors operate at 50 MHz during the tests, the unmitigated processor has a higher maximum clock rate than that of the mitigated processor. The maximum operating frequency of the two designs is shown in Table 2. To understand the effect of the detection logic on maximum operating speed, both designs are implemented in two forms: with and without the detection circuitry. In both cases, the unmitigated circuit operates faster than the mitigated circuit. With detection circuitry added, the mitigated circuit is much slower than that of the unmitigated circuit ($.55\times$) suggesting that the critical path is within the detection circuitry.

Resource Utilization	Testing Overhead	LEON3 Core 1	LEON3 Core 2	Total	Device NonTMR/TMR
Slices	1753	1383	1410	4546	50950
(TMR)	1960	6567	6767	15294	8.9%/30.0%
Slice Reg	2726	1950	1950	6626	407600
(TMR)	2726	6165	6165	15056	1.6%/3.7%
LUTS	3324	4077	4069	11470	203800
(TMR)	3265	18046	18051	39362	5.6%/19.3%
LUTRAM	1	15	15	31	64000
(TMR)	1	45	45	91	.048%/.142%
BRAM	0	50	50	100	445
(TMR)	0	150	150	300	22.5%/67.4%
DSP48E1	0	1	1	2	840
(TMR)	0	3	3	6	.238%/.714%
BUFG	4	0	0	4	32
(TMR)	4	0	0	4	12.5%/12.5%

Table 1: Dual-LEON3 Design Utilization

	NonTMR	TMR
No Detection	164 MHz (6.10 ns)	140 Mhz (7.15 ns)
Detection	132 MHz (7.56 ns)	73.7 MHz (13.56 ns)

Table 2: Post-PAR Timing Summary

5. FAULT INJECTION

A useful way of learning more about the SEU sensitivity of an FPGA design and to understand the benefits of a mitigation technique is to apply artificial fault injection within the configuration memory [29]. Fault injection involves *intentionally* inserting corrupt data into the configuration memory by partially configuring FPGA frames with configuration data in which one or more configuration bits are opposite from their original values (faults are usually injected one at a time). After the faulty configuration data has been applied, the behavior of the circuit is monitored to detect deviations from the expected output. If the circuit deviates from its expected value, then the corresponding upset configuration bit is labeled as *sensitive*. Those configuration bits that do not impact the circuit behavior are labeled *insensitive*. Fault injection can be used to measure the relative sensitivity of various designs to upsets in the configuration memory.

Fault injection has its limitations and does not model all of the negative behavior of FPGAs operating in the presence of ionizing radiation (flip-flops or upsets in the proprietary internal state of an FPGA). As such, a number of failure modes seen in radiation testing will not appear in fault injection. In spite of these limitations, fault injection is a very helpful tool that provides important, preliminary information on the effectiveness of a given mitigation scheme. The goals of fault injection for this work are first, estimate the configuration sensitivity of both the unmitigated LEON3 processor and the mitigated processor. second, validate the ability of the test infrastructure to detect processor errors, and validate the testing infrastructure and software before radiation testing.

5.1 Fault Injection Setup

The fault injection tool used for this project is based on custom tool called the "JTAG Configuration Manager" or JCM. The JCM is a Linux-based embedded system that provides the ability to generate high-speed JTAG sequences

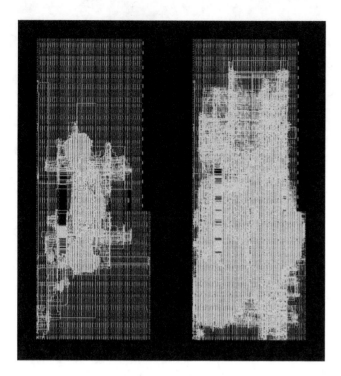

Figure 5: FPGA Layout of Unmitigated Design (left) and the Mitigated design (right)

Figure 6: JTAG Configuration Manager. The board at the bottom is the Xilinx KC705 which contains the Kintex DUT. The small board on the top is the Linux-based JTAG Configuration Manager. A standard 14-wire JTAG cable connects the JCM to the KC705.

for FPGA configuration, readback, and configuration scrubbing. The JCM is capable of configuring an individual frame through JTAG in under 85 μs. The injection of faults can be controlled programmatically by the host Linux system to customize the fault injection campaign to the goals of the experiment. A picture of the JCM fault injection system and the KC705 board is shown in Figure 6.

The fault injection campaign applied to the LEON3 was designed to emulate the random nature of configuration upsets that are expected in a radiation beam. The fault injector is programmed to upset a single configuration bit at a random location and to continue inserting upsets until the processor system fails. The specific steps of this fault injection campaign are as follows:

1. Randomly select a configuration bit and invert the value of the configuration bit through partial configuration.
2. Wait 1 ms to allow the effects of the upset to propagate through the system.
3. Monitor the behavior of the two processor comparator circuit through the JTAG BSCAN interface.

   - If the processor is unaffected by the upset, repair the configuration bit and proceed.
   - If the processor behavior is affected by the upset, reconfigure the FPGA to restore the correct operating state.

The JCM injects faults at an average rate of 120 faults per second.

5.2 Fault Injection Results

The fault injection system was applied to both LEON3 designs: the unmitigated design and the SEU mitigated design.

The results from this fault injection campaign are summarized in Table 3. This table lists the number of faults injected into each design (n) and the number of observed failures on the design (k). From these results the mean-upsets to failure (MUTF) can be estimated as n/k.

	Unmitigated	Mitigated
Faults Injected (n)	1,831,859	29,443,885
Observed Failures (k)	6,501	2,037
MUTF	282	14,455
Sensitivity (95% Conf. Interval)	.355% (.346%,.363%)	.00692% (.00662%,.00722%)
Est. Sensitive Bits	240,539	4,689
Improvement	1.0	51.3

Table 3: Fault Injection Results.

The sensitivity of the design or the estimated percentage of configuration bits with each FPGA design that are sensitive to upsets, is estimated by using the maximum likelihood estimator, $\hat{r}$, of the Binomial distribution:

$$\hat{r} = \frac{k}{n},$$

The standard deviation of the maximum likelihood estimator is:

$$\sigma = \sqrt{\frac{k}{n^2}\left(1 - \frac{k}{n}\right)}.$$

The standard deviation of the estimator can be used to determine the 95% confidence interval bounds of the sensitivity estimate. The number of total sensitive bits in the design can be estimated by multiplying the sensitivity estimate, $\hat{r}$, by the total number of configuration bits (67,779,264) in block 0 of the configuration bitstream (i.e., the configuration bits associated with the logic and routing).

These results suggest that the mitigated LEON3 design is 51.3× *less* sensitive to upsets than the unmitigated design in spite of the fact that the mitigated design is 3.4× larger than the unmitigated design. These results indicate that the mitigation techniques described in Section 4 significantly reduce the sensitivity of the LEON3 processor to upsets in the configuration memory.

In spite of these mitigation techniques, however, there are a number configuration bits in the mitigated design that are still sensitive to single-event upsets. This suggests that the design still contains a number of single points of failure. There are several known single points of failure including the clock network and external I/O. In addition to these known single points of failure, it is possible that some configuration bits in the routing may corrupt more than one net associated with different TMR domains as suggested by [30]. Future work will investigate the cause of these remaining single-points of failure to further improve the reliability.

6. HEAVY ION RADIATION TEST

The results from the fault injection campaign suggest that the mitigation approaches are working and the configuration sensitivity is significantly reduced. The next step in the validation of the mitigated LEON3 processor is to test the processor with a high energy radiation beam. Radiation testing provides a number of advantages over fault injection. First, a radiation beam can upset *any* internal state of the FPGA including that states not tested by fault injection (user flip-flops, block memory, and internal proprietary FPGA state). Second, radiation testing will induce other faults such as single-event transients, multi-cell upsets, and possibly single-event latch-up. Because of these additional failure modes, it is expected that the improvements of the mitigation design will be *lower* with radiation testing than with fault injection.

Figure 7: Delidded and Thinned XC7K325T Die.

6.1 Radiation Test Setup

A radiation test was performed on both the mitigated and non-mitigated LEON3 designs with heavy ions at the Texas A&M K500 Cyclotron in August of 2015. A sample XC7K325T device was prepared for the test by removing the lid and thinning the substrate to allow the ions to penetrate the substrate and reach the active region of silicon (see Figure 7). During radiation testing many configuration bits (and other state) will be upset and configuration scrubbing must be employed to rapidly restore the configuration memory to its proper state. The JTAG Configuration Manager described in Section 5 was used to provide active, high-speed configuration scrubbing during the test. Figure 8 shows the KC705 test board mounted on a base plate along with the configuration scrubber, power monitor, and external I/O connector. Next to the base plate is a second KC705 board that receives the I/O signals for review by the test operator. The base plate mounted in front of the beam cap is shown in Figure 9.

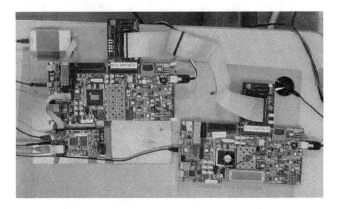

Figure 8: Experiment setup for radiation testing. The radiation test setup is on the left and the remote monitor is on the right.

The organization of the radiation test is very similar to the fault injection testing. The FPGA is configured with either the mitigated or non-mitigated LEON3 design and executes the Dhrystone benchmark. The correctness of the processor execution is monitored through the external I/O signals as well as the standard UART output of the processor. There are a few minor modifications to the radiation test. First, the configuration scrubber is enabled to actively repair configuration upsets when the beam is turned on. Second, a secondary processor correctness interface is added to detect processor failure in the event that the JTAG interface is disabled by radiation. This interface involves several digital I/O signals that are sent to a remote data acquisition board for manually monitoring the processor status.

The procedure for each test is as follows. First, the FPGA is configured and the scrubber initialized to make sure the system is running properly without the radiation beam. Second, the shutter for the radiation beam is removed to enable the radiation beam and induce faults in the circuit. Once the beam is enabled, upsets will occur throughout the FPGA and the configuration scrubber is repairing and logging these upsets. At some point, the radiation will cause the processor to fail. When this failure is detected by the operator, the operator closes the beam shutter and records the beam fluence that accumulated during the beam run. The accumulated fluence is the primary data associated with each run (fluence to failure) and multiple runs are performed to provide an average fluence to failure with greater confidence.

To obtain an accurate estimate of the failure rate of the

Figure 9: Heavy Ion Radiation Test Setup in Beam.

LEON3 processors in a space environment, the heavy ion radiation test must be performed at multiple energies as the space environment is a complex environment with a range of particle flux and energies (see Figure 11). The parameter used in this type of testing is Linear Energy Transfer or LET which describes the amount of energy that an ionizing particle transfers to the material per unit distance ($MeV\ cm^2/mg$). Different values of LET can be obtained by changing the ion used in the beam and inserting degrader material into the beam path.

6.2 Radiation Test Results

Both the unmitigated and mitigated designs were tested at six different LET values as shown in Table 4. As described above, multiple runs were performed at each LET to measure the accumulated beam fluence to failure. The average cross section at each LET was determined by dividing the number of failures observed by the total fluence at the given LET. As shown in the fourth column, the mitigated designs tolerated on average ten times as much fluence as the unmitigated design suggesting that the mitigation techniques provided significant, measurable improvements in radiation tolerance over the unmitigated design.

LET (Ion) (MeV-cm²/mg)		Unmitigated (cm²/proc.)	Mitigated (cm²/proc.)	Improv.
3.4	(Ne)	2.40E-5	3.65E-4	15.2
4.7	(Ne)	2.76E-5	2.58E-4	9.4
6	(Ne)	5.07E-5	5.38E-4	10.6
9	(Ne)	5.75E-5	5.59E-4	9.7
11.9	(Ar)	6.94E-5	5.43E-4	7.8
18.5	(Ar)	3.13E-5	2.69E-4	8.6

Table 4: Measured SEU Sensitive Cross Section.

Unlike fault injection where thousands of runs can be performed automatically in a relatively short amount of time (see k in Table 3), it is very labor intensive to perform a run with radiation testing and only a dozen or so runs can be performed at each LET. The low number of runs produces much larger confidence intervals than the fault injection runs.

6.3 Radiation Test Challenges

Although the radiation test successfully demonstrated an order of magnitude improvement in radiation tolerance for the mitigated design, there were a number of significant problems that occurred at the test. First, the scrubbing hardware was incorrectly configured to the wrong FPGA device and was only scrubbing the first third of the configuration memory. With much of the FPGA not being scrubbed, it is likely that the TMR mitigation scheme failed due to the accumulation of upsets (i.e., more than one TMR domain failing). Second, the scrubbing hardware ran relatively slowly in comparison to the configuration upset rate. In a deployed system, the scrub rate is set to operate at several orders of magnitude greater than the individual configuration upset rate. In radiation testing, however, this is not possible since the upset rate is many orders of magnitude higher than the rate in a space environment. For this experiment, the FPGA experienced an average of 5.11 configuration upsets per second in the first third of configuration memory that was scrubbed. The configuration scrubber operated at 2.88 seconds per scrub allowing about 14.72 configuration upsets to accumulate before completing a scrub cycle. Future radiation tests will be conducted to address these issues and hopefully achieve improved reliability results.

7. ORBIT FAILURE RATE ESTIMATES

The radiation test results were used to estimate the failure rate in a near-earth interplanetary/geosynchronous orbit under "solar minimum" solar conditions (maximum cosmic-ray conditions). This estimate is made by first estimating a cross-section curve (or failure probability curve) as a function of LET. It is customary to use the Weibull distribution to model cross-section curves. The parameters of the Weibull distribution are estimated by using the data samples at each LET from the radiation test. Figure 10 shows a Weibull cross-section curve (in green) based on the size LET test samples. The test samples are shown with blue circles and the corresponding error bars.

Once cross-section curve estimates are created, the orbit error rate is estimated using a tool called CREME-96 [31]. This tool begins by estimating the particle flux of the given orbit based on previous orbit measurements – the GEO orbit particle flux is shown in Figure 11. This tool adjusts the radiation environment seen by the spacecraft due to shielding and then convolves the design cross section (Figure 10) with this modified environment (as a function of LET).

The estimated failure rate and the corresponding mean-time to failure (MTTF) of both designs is shown in Table 5. The estimated failure rate of the mitigated LEON3 processor is roughly 76 years. This estimate suggests that the implemented mitigation methods provide sufficient reliability for many space applications. It is important to emphasize that the estimated orbital failure rates are not exact and that much of the uncertainty is based on the parameters chosen for the Weibull cross section curves More radiation testing

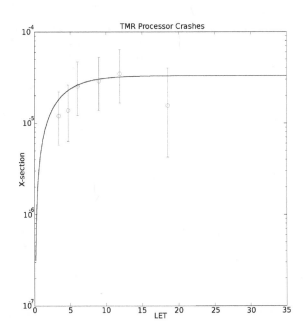

Figure 10: Weibull Cross Section Curve for Mitigated Processor.

is needed at other LET values to increase the accuracy of the Weibull curve fit.

Design	Failure Rate (λ) (failures/processor/s)	MTTF (days/years)
Unmitigated	2.77E-8	501/1.4
Mitigated	4.15E-10	27,889/76

Table 5: Estimated Failure Rate of LEON3 in the GEO Orbit.

8. CONCLUSION

This work investigated the improvements in reliability of the soft core LEON3 processor operating on a commercial Xilinx Kintex 7 FPGA. TMR, internal memory scrubbing, and configuration scrubbing were all used to mitigate against single-event upsets that occur in the configuration memory, user flip-flops, and other FPGA state. Fault injection tests indicated a 51× reduction in SEU cross section, and rough orbit failure rate estimates suggest a MTTF of over 76 years in space. All of these results suggest that the collection of mitigation techniques used to improve the LEON3 reliability were successful and that the mitigated LEON3 processor may be reliable enough to consider for use in space.

Although improvements in reliability were seen in both fault injection and radiation testing, the amount of improvement was not as high as expected. The results suggest that additional SEU mitigation may provide even higher improvements in reliability. A number of single-points of failure still exist in the design (clocking and some I/O) and not all memory structures of the processor were improved with

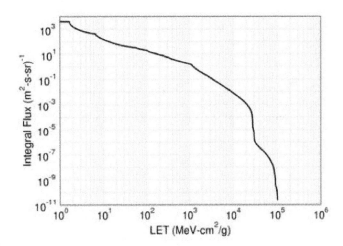

Figure 11: GEO Orbit LET Spectra Expected at Device After Shielding.

scrubbing. In addition, significant improvements in the radiation testing procedure will likely provide additional improvements in the radiation validation. These obvious opportunities for additional improvements in reliability suggest that the reliability estimates in this work can be significantly improved.

To integrate a processor in a complex system, additional features and processor architecture within the LEON3 must be tested. Future work will investigate the reliability of a complex LEON3 system with caches, memory controllers, and other essential I/O peripherals. With this architecture support, complex operating systems like Linux can be used and complex software systems can be deployed. The success of this future work will facilitate the adoption of soft core processors operating in commercial FPGAs in future space systems.

9. ACKNOWLEDGEMENTS

This work was supported by the I/UCRC Program of the National Science Foundation under Grant No. 1265957.

10. REFERENCES

[1] J.G. Tong, ID.L. Anderson, and M.AS. Khalid. Soft-core processors for embedded systems. In *Microelectronics, 2006. ICM '06. International Conference on*, pages 170–173, Dec 2006.

[2] R. Katz, K. LaBel, J.J. Wang, B. Cronquist, R. Koga, S. Penzin, and G. Swift. Radiation effects on current field programmable technologies. *IEEE Transactions on Nuclear Science*, 44(6):1945–1956, December 1997.

[3] F. Lima Kastensmidt, L. Sterpone, L. Carro, and M. Sonza Reorda. On the optimal design of triple modular redundancy logic for SRAM-based FPGAs. In *Proceedings of the Conference on Design, Automation and Test in Europe - Volume 2*, DATE '05, pages 1290–1295, Washington, DC, USA, 2005. IEEE Computer Society.

[4] Carl Carmichael, Michael Caffrey, and Anthony Salazar. Correcting single-event upsets through Virtex

partial configuration. Technical report, Xilinx Corporation, June 1, 2000. XAPP216 (v1.0).

[5] I. Herrera-Alzu and M. Lopez-Vallejo. Design techniques for Xilinx Virtex FPGA configuration memory scrubbers. *Nuclear Science, IEEE Transactions on*, 60(1):376–385, Feb 2013.

[6] L. Sterpone and M. Violante. Analysis of the robustness of the TMR architecture in SRAM-based FPGAs. *Nuclear Science, IEEE Transactions on*, 52(5):1545 – 1549, oct. 2005.

[7] M.A. Aguirre, J.N. Tombs, F. Muoz, V. Baena, H. Guzman, J. Napoles, A. Torralba, A. Fernandez-Leon, F. Tortosa-Lopez, and D. Merodio. Selective protection analysis using a SEU emulator: Testing protocol and case study over the Leon2 processor. *Nuclear Science, IEEE Transactions on*, 54(4):951–956, Aug 2007.

[8] C.A. Hulme, H.H. Loomis, A.A. Ross, and Rong Yuan. Configurable fault-tolerant processor (CFTP) for spacecraft onboard processing. In *Aerospace Conference, 2004. Proceedings. 2004 IEEE*, volume 4, pages 2269–2276 Vol.4, March 2004.

[9] J. Perez Acle, M.S. Reorda, and M. Violante. Implementing a safe embedded computing system in SRAM-based FPGAs using IP cores: A case study based on the Altera NIOS-II soft processor. In *Circuits and Systems (LASCAS), 2011 IEEE Second Latin American Symposium on*, pages 1–5, Feb 2011.

[10] F. Abate, L. Sterpone, C.A. Lisboa, L. Carro, and M. Violante. New techniques for improving the performance of the lockstep architecture for SEEs mitigation in FPGA embedded processors. *Nuclear Science, IEEE Transactions on*, 56(4):1992–2000, Aug 2009.

[11] M. Violante, C. Meinhardt, R. Reis, and M.S. Reorda. A low-cost solution for deploying processor cores in harsh environments. *Industrial Electronics, IEEE Transactions on*, 58(7):2617–2626, July 2011.

[12] C. Gauer, B.J. LaMeres, and D. Racek. Spatial avoidance of hardware faults using FPGA partial reconfiguration of tile-based soft processors. In *Aerospace Conference, 2010 IEEE*, pages 1–11, March 2010.

[13] Frederico Ferlini, Felipe A. da Silva, E.A. Bezerra, and Djones V. Lettnin. Non-intrusive fault tolerance in soft processors through circuit duplication. In *Test Workshop (LATW), 2012 13th Latin American*, pages 1–6, April 2012.

[14] Gregory Miller, Carl Carmichael, and Gary Swift. Mitigation, design flow and troubleshooting a soft processor in a complex FPGA. In *Military and Aerospace Programmable Logic Devices (MAPLD) Workshop*, 2008.

[15] Gregory Miller, Carl Carmichael, Gary Swift, Mike Pratt, and Gregory R. Allen. Preliminary analysis of a soft-core processor in a Rad Hard by Design Field Programmable Gate Array. In *Military and Aerospace Programmable Logic Devices (MAPLD) Workshop*, 2009.

[16] IEEE standard for a 32-bit microprocessor architecture. *IEEE Std 1754-1994*, pages 1–, 1995.

[17] Aeroflex gaisler LEON3 processor. http://www.gaisler.com/index.php/products/processors/leo

[18] Luo Pei and Zhang Jian. A high reliable SOC on-board computer based on Leon3. In *Computer Science and Automation Engineering (CSAE), 2012 IEEE International Conference on*, volume 1, pages 360–363, May 2012.

[19] Michael R. Gardiner. An evaluation of soft processors as a reliable computing platform. Master's thesis, Brigham Young University, 2015.

[20] GRTools. http://www.gaisler.com/index.php/downloads/grtools.

[21] Jonathan M. Johnson and Michael J. Wirthlin. Voter insertion algorithms for FPGA designs using triple modular redundancy. In *Proceedings of the 18th Annual ACM/SIGDA International Symposium on Field Programmable Gate Arrays*, FPGA '10, pages 249–258, New York, NY, USA, 2010. ACM.

[22] M. Niknahad, O. Sander, and J. Becker. A study on fine granular fault tolerance methodologies for FPGAs. In *Reconfigurable Communication-centric Systems-on-Chip (ReCoSoC), 2011 6th International Workshop on*, pages 1–5, June 2011.

[23] Brendan Bridgford, Carl Carmichael, and Chen Wei Tseng. Single-event upset mitigation selection guide. Technical Report 1, Xilinx Corporation, 2008. Xilinx Application Note XAPP987.

[24] R. Do. The details of triple modular redundancy: An automated mitigation method of I/O signals. In *The prooceedings of the Military and Aerospace Programmable Logic Devices*, 2011.

[25] BL-TMR and BYU Edif Tools. http://sourceforge.net/projects/byuediftools/.

[26] N. Rollins, M. Fuller, and M.J. Wirthlin. A comparison of fault-tolerant memories in SRAM-based FPGAs. In *Aerospace Conference, 2010 IEEE*, pages 1–12, March 2010.

[27] Xilinx Coproration. *7 Series FPGAs Memory Resources: User Guide*. UG473 (v1.11), November 12, 2014.

[28] Daniel P. Siewiorek and Robert S. Swarz. *Reliable Computer Systems*. A. K. Peters, 1998.

[29] F. Lima, C. Carmichael, J. Fabula, R. Padovani, and R. Reis. A fault injection analysis of Virtex FPGA TMR design methodology. In *Proceedings of the 6th European Conference on Radiation and its Effects on Components and Sysemts (RADECS 2001)*, 2001.

[30] M.S. Reorda, L. Sterpone, and M. Violante. Multiple errors produced by single upsets in FPGA configuration memory: a possible solution. In *Test Symposium, 2005. European*, pages 136–141, May 2005.

[31] A.J. Tylka, J.H. Adams, P.R. Boberg, B. Brownstein, W.F. Dietrich, E.O. Flueckiger, E.L. Petersen, M.A. Shea, D.F. Smart, and E.C. Smith. Creme96: A revision of the cosmic ray effects on micro-electronics code. *Nuclear Science, IEEE Transactions on*, 44(6):2150–2160, Dec 1997.

Optimal Circuits for Streamed Linear Permutations Using RAM

François Serre, Thomas Holenstein, and Markus Püschel

Department of Computer Science
ETH Zurich
{serref, holthoma,pueschel}@inf.ethz.ch

ABSTRACT

We propose a method to automatically derive hardware structures that perform a fixed linear permutation on streaming data. Linear permutations are permutations that map linearly the bit representation of the elements addresses. This set contains many of the most important permutations in media processing, communication, and other applications and includes perfect shuffles, stride permutations, and the bit reversal. Streaming means that the data to be permuted arrive as a sequence of chunks over several cycles. We solve this problem by mathematically decomposing a given permutation into a sequence of three permutations that are either temporal or spatial. The former are implemented as banks of RAM, the latter as switching networks. We prove optimality of our solution in terms of the number of switches in these networks.

Keywords

Streaming datapath; Data reordering; Connection network; Matrix factorization; Stride permutation; Matrix transposition; Bit-reversal

1. INTRODUCTION

Many algorithms and applications implemented on FPGAs require permutations or data reorderings as intermediate stages. If all data are available in one cycle, a hardware implementation is simply a set or wires as shown in Fig. 1(a)[1]. However, if data arrive streamed in chunks over several cycles as in Fig. 1(b), usually memory is required, as data may be reordered also in time. Accordingly, the efficient implementation becomes non-obvious [1, 2, 3, 4, 5].

In this paper, we present a method to implement streamed linear permutations (SLPs) on 2^n elements with proven minimal logic. Linear permutations are the permutations that

---

[1]Because of the mathematical formalism used later, we view circuits with inputs coming from the right.

FPGA'16, February 21 - 23, 2016, Monterey, CA, USA

© 2016 Copyright held by the owner/author(s). Publication rights licensed to ACM.
ISBN 978-1-4503-3856-1/16/02. . . $15.00

DOI: http://dx.doi.org/10.1145/2847263.2847277

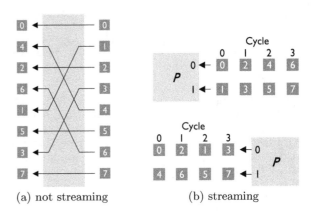

Figure 1: Sketch of two implementations of the bit reversal permutation on 2^3 elements. On the left, the structure has as many ports as the dataset. Thus a simple rewiring is enough. On the right side, data are streamed on two ports. Therefore, the dataset enters within 4 cycles (top), and is retrieved within 4 cycles (bottom).

operate as linear mappings on the bit representation of indices. They include many of the most important occurring permutations including stride permutations and the bit reversal. They are needed in fast Fourier transforms (FFTs; see Fig. 2(a)), fast cosine transforms, sorting networks (see Fig. 3(a)), Viterbi decoders, and many other applications.

Streamed means that the 2^n elements arrive in chunks of size 2^k over 2^t cycles, where $n = k + t$. Therefore, the resulting architecture has 2^k input and output ports. In Fig. 1(b), $2^t = 4$ and $2^k = 2$. Streaming permutations enable the implementation of designs that scale with large datasets (see Fig. 2(b) and 3(b) for instance) while maintaining a high throughput.

Our contribution is a systematic method to construct SLPs with proven minimal logic under the assumption that routing is done only by wires and 2×2-switches. Specifically:

- We prove a lower bound for the switching complexity for an SLP, i.e., for the number of switches needed.

- We provide a method to derive a (switching)-optimal SLP. The method decomposes a given linear permutation into a sequence of spatial and temporal permutations that can be implemented, respectively, as (memoryless) switching networks and banks of RAM.

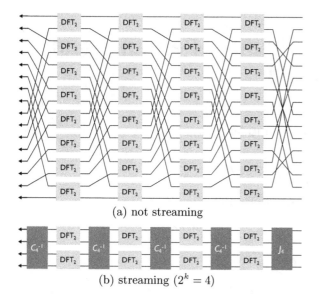

(a) not streaming

(b) streaming ($2^k = 4$)

Figure 2: On the top, dataflow of a Pease FFT on 2^4 elements. After a bit-reversal permutation, a set of 8 parallel DFTs on 2 elements followed by a stride permutation is repeated 4 times. This graph can be directly used for a direct fully-parallel implementation. On the bottom, the same implementation is "folded" with $k = 2$, allowing to reduce the use of DFTs to sets of 2 parallel units.

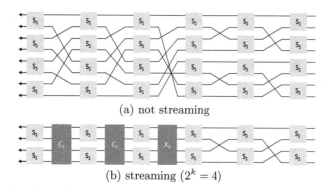

(a) not streaming

(b) streaming ($2^k = 4$)

Figure 3: A sorting network working on 2^3 elements [6]. The "S_2" blocks represent two input sorters. On the top, a fully-parallel implementation. On the bottom, the same implementation "folded" with $k = 2$, allowing to halve the number of sorters [7].

We show that this decomposition is equivalent to a matrix factorization problem in which the minimization of certain ranks of submatrices is equivalent to minimizing the logic of the resulting circuit.

- Finally, we demonstrate our method by generating streamed bit reversal permutations for a Virtex FPGA, and by comparing our optimal solutions to prior art.

2. BACKGROUND AND NOTATION

We provide background on linear permutations, starting with two special cases before we give a general definition.

Bit-reversal permutation. Used in FFTs, the bit-reversal permutation has been studied extensively [8]. It maps each element to the position given by reversing the binary representation of its index. Formally, we denote the binary representation of an index i with a column vector i_b of n bits, such that the most significant bit is at the top. For example, if $n = 3$,

$$6_b = \begin{pmatrix} 1 \\ 1 \\ 0 \end{pmatrix},$$

which the bit reversal maps by flipping upside down to obtain 3_b. Formally, it maps positions as $i_b \mapsto i_b' = J_n \cdot i_b$, where

$$J_n = \begin{pmatrix} & & 1 \\ & .^{.^{.}} & \\ 1 & & \end{pmatrix}. \tag{1}$$

This $n \times n$ bit matrix describes how the bit reversal operates "on the bits," and should not be confused with the $2^n \times 2^n$ permutation matrix that encodes how it maps the data.

Perfect shuffle. The perfect shuffle on 2^n elements interleaves the first and the second half:

$$i \mapsto \begin{cases} 2i, & \text{if } 0 \leq i < 2^{n-1}, \\ 2i - 2^n + 1, & \text{if } 2^{n-1} \leq i < 2^n. \end{cases}$$

On the bit representation it can be represented as cyclic shift: $i_b \mapsto i_b' = C_n \cdot i_b$, where

$$C_n = \begin{pmatrix} & 1 & & \\ & & \ddots & \\ & & & 1 \\ 1 & & & \end{pmatrix} \tag{2}$$

is a bit matrix.

If P is an $n \times n$ matrix that describes the way a permutation works on the binary representation of the elements, we denote this permutation with $\pi(P)$. Formally, $\pi(P)$ is the permutation of $\{0, \ldots, 2^n - 1\}$ such that, for all i in this set,

$$(\pi(P)(i))_b = P \cdot i_b.$$

General linear permutations. Generalizing the previous special cases we consider an arbitrary invertible bit matrix[2] P. Then the mapping $i_b \mapsto P \cdot i_b$ defines a permutation on $\{0, \ldots, 2^n - 1\}$ that we denote with $\pi(P)$. We call such permutations linear [9, 10] and there are $\prod_{i=0}^{n-1} (2^n - 2^i)$ of them. In particular, not every permutation on 2^n elements is linear; for example, linear permutations always leave the first element unchanged (since 0_b is the all-zero vector and thus mapped to $P \cdot 0_b = 0_b$).

For instance, if

$$V_n = \begin{pmatrix} 1 & & & \\ \vdots & \ddots & & \\ 1 & & & \\ 1 & & & 1 \end{pmatrix},$$

then $\pi(V_3)$ is the permutation: $0 \mapsto 0$, $1 \mapsto 1$, $2 \mapsto 2$, $3 \mapsto 3$, $4 \mapsto 7 \mapsto 4$, $5 \mapsto 6 \mapsto 5$. More generally, $\pi(V_n)$ is the permutation of 2^n elements that leaves the first 2^{n-1}

---

[2]Mathematically, $P \in \mathrm{GL}_n(\mathbb{F}_2)$, where $\mathbb{F}_2$ is the Galois field with two elements. Hence, the set of linear permutations is a group, i.e., closed under multiplication and inversion.

elements unchanged, and that reverses the list of the others. It occurs in fast cosine transforms [11].

Composition of linear permutations. Composing two linear permutations corresponds to multiplying the associated matrices:

$$\pi(P) \circ \pi(Q) = \pi(PQ).$$

Additionally, we have $\pi(I_n) = I_{2^n}$ and therefore[3]:

$$\pi(P^{-1}) = \pi(P)^{-1}.$$

As an example, every stride permutation on 2^n elements is a power r of the perfect-shuffle $\pi(C_n)$. Therefore, these are linear permutations as well with the associated matrix C_n^r.

3. STREAMING LINEAR PERMUTATIONS (SLPS): THEORY

Based on the prior formalism, we introduce the problem of streaming linear permutations (as in Fig 1(b)) using bit matrices. Then we discuss two special cases: temporal permutations that do not permute across ports and thus can be implemented using banks of RAM only, and spatial permutations that only permute elements within each cycle and thus can be implemented using switching networks (SNWs). Our approach is then to decompose the general case into these special cases, for which implementations can readily be derived.

Finally, we prove a lower bound on the switching complexity of a given permutation. This bound will later turn out to be sharp and is one main contribution of this paper.

Matrix formalism. As in the introduction, we index each element from 0 to $2^n - 1$ such that for 2^k ports, the element with index $i = c \cdot 2^k + p$ enters during the cth cycle on the pth input port. This means c_b are exactly the upper $t = n - k$ bits of i_b and p_b are the lower k bits. For instance, for $t = 3$ and $k = 2$, the element with the index

$$22_b = \begin{pmatrix} 1 \\ 0 \\ 1 \\ 1 \\ 0 \end{pmatrix} = \begin{pmatrix} 5_b \\ 2_b \end{pmatrix}$$

will arrive during the 5th cycle on port 2.

Therefore, it is natural to block a given bit matrix P as

$$P = \begin{pmatrix} P_4 & P_3 \\ P_2 & P_1 \end{pmatrix}, \quad \text{such that } P_4 \text{ is } t \times t. \quad (3)$$

Hence, the associated streaming permutation maps the input element that arrives on port p during cycle c to the output port $P_1 p_b + P_2 c_b$ at cycle $P_4 c_b + P_3 p_b$.

Next we introduce two special cases of SLPs that will form the building blocks of our general solution.

Spatial permutations. We define (memoryless) spatial permutations as SLPs that permute only within cycles. Therefore, P must leave the upper t bits c_b of each address unchanged, i.e., satisfy $P_4 c_b + P_3 p_b = c_b$, which yields the form

$$P = \begin{pmatrix} I_t \\ P_2 & P_1 \end{pmatrix}. \quad (4)$$

These can be implemented using a switching network that consists of controlled 2×2-switches (see Fig. 4 later). The cycle number controls the setting of the switches. The implementation using a shortened Omega network will be discussed in Section 4.1.

If, in addition, the same reordering is performed in each cycle, we call the spatial permutation steady. This is the case if and only if $P_2 = 0$. Such permutations can be implemented with a simple rewiring without control (similar to Fig. 1(a)), and we consider its cost to be zero.

Temporal permutations. These are the dual of spatial permutations, in the sense that they leave the port number unchanged but permute across cycles. Hence, these permutations are represented by matrices of the form

$$P = \begin{pmatrix} P_4 & P_3 \\ & I_k \end{pmatrix}. \quad (5)$$

They can be implemented using 2^k banks of RAM as explained in Section 4.2.

General linear permutations: Switching complexity. We implement general linear permutations $\pi(P)$ by first decomposing them into temporal and spatial permutations, i.e., by factoring P (blocked as in (3)) into matrices of the form (4) and (5). We will later see that three such matrices always suffice. Interestingly, with this assumption on the building blocks we can already prove a lower bound on the number of switches needed. The reason is that only the switches can map between ports, and their number is thus determined by "how much variety" in mapping between ports is required across the different cycles.

THEOREM 1. *A full-throughput implementation of an SLP for P with 2^k ports that only uses 2×2-switches for routing requires at least $\operatorname{rk} P_2 \cdot 2^{k-1}$ many switches, where $\operatorname{rk} P_2$ denotes the rank of the matrix P_2.*

PROOF. As the implementation has full throughput, each element passes at most one time through a given switch. We denote with $\ell_{p,c}$ the number of switches that the element that arrives on port p at cycle c passes through.

If we accumulate across cycles for all inputs at port p, the bit representations of the corresponding output ports, we get

$$\{P_1 p_b + P_2 c_b \mid 0 \leq c < 2^t\} = P_1 p_b + \operatorname{im} P_2.$$

This set (as a coset of direction $\operatorname{im} P_2$) contains $2^{\operatorname{rk} P_2}$ elements. This means that each input port has to communicate with $2^{\operatorname{rk} P_2}$ different output ports.

Let now p' be one of the $2^{\operatorname{rk} P_2}$ possible output ports for an element from input port p. Further, let $\bar{c}$ be an input cycle of an arbitrary element which transits from p to p'. The set of cycles for which an element transits from p to p' is:

$$\{c_b \mid p_b' = P_1 p_b + P_2 c_b\} = \bar{c}_b + \ker P_2.$$

This set (as a coset of direction $\ker P_2$) contains $2^{t - \operatorname{rk} P_2}$ elements. As this number is independent from p', the distribution over the possible output ports is uniform. Therefore, elements that arrive on port p must at least go through $\operatorname{rk} P_2$ switches in average (since $\log_2(2^{\operatorname{rk} P_2}) = \operatorname{rk} P_2$ bits are needed to describe the output port):

$$\frac{1}{2^t} \sum_{c=0}^{2^t - 1} \ell_{p,c} \geq \operatorname{rk} P_2, \quad \text{for every } p. \quad (6)$$

---
[3]π is a group-homomorphism.

217

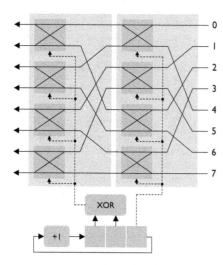

Figure 4: An SNW consisting of two Omega network stages. Each stage contains a perfect shuffle followed by a column of 2^{k-1} switches controlled by a single common bit. Here, the first stage is controlled by a single bit of a counter, while the second one is controlled by the sum of the two other bits of this counter.

We now denote with s the number of switches in an implementation. Since each switch has two inputs, two elements per cycle pass through it. In total, $2 \cdot 2^t$ elements pass through a single switch. Hence

$$\sum_{\substack{0 \leq c < 2^t \\ 0 \leq p < 2^k}} \ell_{p,c} \leq 2 \cdot s \cdot 2^t. \tag{7}$$

Combining (6) and (7), we get:

$$s \geq \frac{1}{2^{t+1}} \sum_{p=0}^{2^k-1} \sum_{c=0}^{2^t-1} \ell_{p,c} \geq \frac{1}{2} \sum_{p=0}^{2^k-1} \mathrm{rk}\, P_2,$$

which yields the desired result. $\square$

As examples, we see that the number of switches for a spatial permutation is at least $\mathrm{rk}\, P_2 \cdot 2^{k-1}$, whereas for a temporal permutation that lower bound is 0, as expected, since no switches are needed.

4. IMPLEMENTATION OF SPATIAL AND TEMPORAL PERMUTATIONS

In this section, we explain how to implement the two special cases of SLPs. In the next section we solve the general case by optimally decomposing it into these.

4.1 Spatial Permutations

We show how to optimally implement a given spatial permutation using a switching network (SNW) with $\mathrm{rk}\, P_2 \cdot 2^{k-1}$ 2×2-switches, thus matching the lower bound of Theorem 1. The network we construct is an Omega network [10] with $k - \mathrm{rk}\, P_2$ stages removed. An optimal solution is already given in [2]; our description here is somewhat simpler and included for completeness.

A stage of an Omega network consists of a perfect shuffle followed by a column of 2^{k-1} 2×2-switches: see Fig. 4, which

shows 2 stages. We first consider one column of switches. If these switches are all controlled by a common bit, then, when this bit is set, pairs of elements are exchanged:

$$\begin{cases} p \mapsto p + 1 & \text{if } p \text{ is even} \\ p \mapsto p - 1 & \text{if } p \text{ is odd,} \end{cases} \tag{8}$$

otherwise the column of switches leaves the data unchanged.

We add a counter c of t bits that is incremented at every cycle. Then, for a fixed vector v of t bits, it is possible to compute $c_b \cdot v$ using xor gates, and we use the result to control the column of switches. This structure performs the permutation (8) when $c_b \cdot v = 1$, and does nothing otherwise. In other words, we have implemented $\pi(K_v)$, where

$$K_v = \begin{pmatrix} I_t & & & \\ & 1 & & \\ & & \ddots & \\ v^T & & & 1 \end{pmatrix}.$$

The perfect shuffle that precedes within the stage is a steady spatial permutation, i.e., a rewiring. Therefore, with our formalism, one stage in Fig. 4 is described by the matrix:

$$S_v = K_v \cdot \begin{pmatrix} I_t & \\ & C_k \end{pmatrix}.$$

We now construct an implementation for a spatial permutation given by (4). First, we find an invertible $k \times k$-matrix L such that LP_2 has $\mathrm{rk}\, P_2$ non-zero lines v_i^T at the top (Gauss elimination):

$$LP_2 = \begin{pmatrix} v_1^T \\ \vdots \\ v_{\mathrm{rk}\, P_2}^T \\ 0 \\ \vdots \\ 0 \end{pmatrix}.$$

Direct computation shows that:

$$P = \begin{pmatrix} I_t & \\ & L^{-1} C_k^{k-\mathrm{rk}\, P_2} \end{pmatrix} S_{v_{\mathrm{rk}\, P_2}} \ldots S_{v_1} \begin{pmatrix} I_t & \\ & LP_1 \end{pmatrix}.$$

This yields an implementation with $\mathrm{rk}\, P_2$ Omega network stages framed by two rewirings. Thus, the number of switches used is $\mathrm{rk}\, P_2 \cdot 2^{k-1}$.

Finally, 2×2-switches can easily be implemented using two 2-to-1 multiplexers. However, some platforms may support larger multiplexers more efficiently. In this case, it is possible to group several switches of different stages as shown in Fig. 5 with an example.

4.2 Temporal Permutations

We consider a temporal permutation associated with a matrix (5), and implement it using 2^k RAM banks, each capable of storing 2^t elements.

Implementation principle. Each port is associated with one bank: the input port p is connected to the write port of the pth bank, and the read port of this bank is connected to the corresponding output port. A possible scheme consists in writing incoming elements linearly in the bank (using a counter c of t bits, as in the spatial permutation case), and to retrieve them in the permuted order, i.e. at

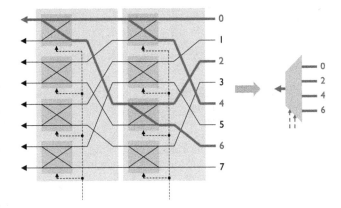

Figure 5: Implementation of the first output port of a switching network using a 4-to-1 multiplexer.

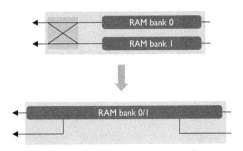

Figure 6: Merging two banks with a 2×2-switch in a large dual-ported bank.

the address $P_4^{-1}c_b + P_4^{-1}P_3p_b$. This address can be computed jointly for every banks using xor gates on the bits of c. Then, inverters specialize these addresses for each bank by adding $P_4^{-1}P_3p_b$.

However, depending on the permutation, this scheme may not be suitable for full-throughput, as some elements of a dataset may be written to a memory address that contains an element of the previous dataset that has not been retrieved yet. Depending on the technology available for the memory, different strategies can be used to overcome these conflicts.

Single-ported RAM. In the case where it is only possible to write or to read an element during a cycle, [4] proposes a double-buffering method. Each port is associated with two RAM banks. One set is written in one of them, while elements of the previous set are retrieved from the second one. This method doubles the memory consumption, and requires an additional multiplexer per port, but has little overhead in control complexity.

If the RAM allows a simultaneous read and write at the same address, [5] proposes a method that uses only one bank per port to perform a temporal permutation σ. Each incoming element is written at the address where the element of the previous set is being read. For example, if the first set is written linearly in the memory, then the second set is written where the first set is read, i.e. at address $\sigma^{-1}(c)$. The ith set is then read at address $\sigma^{-i}(c)$.

In the case of linear permutations, this address becomes:

$$P_4^{-i}c_b + (P_4^{-i} + \cdots + P_4^{-1})P_3p_b. \qquad (9)$$

This method is well suited in the case where P_4 is the identity, equal to its inverse, or more generally, if $(P_4^i)_i$ has a low period. In this case, all possible addresses can be computed using xor gates, and a counter i suffices to control a multiplexer choosing the appropriate address. Otherwise, it becomes interesting to store the different values of P_4^{-i} and of $(P_4^{-i} + \cdots + P_4^{-1})P_3$ in a ROM. In the worst case, this ROM would contain $(k+n) \cdot t \cdot 2^t$ bits[4]. The address (9) can then be computed using and and xor gates.

Dual-ported RAM. If the RAM used allows two simultaneous read and write at two different addresses, it is possible to absorb a potential array of 2×2-switches that would

follow the temporal permutation. Two banks connected to the same switch are fused into one large bank (see Fig. 6), and the read/write addresses corresponding to the two ports are swapped according to the control bit of the switch.

Reuse. If $0 < r \le t$, and P has the form:

$$\begin{pmatrix} I_r & & \\ & * & * \\ & & I_k \end{pmatrix},$$

it means that the associated temporal permutation is periodic with a period of 2^{t-r} cycles[5]. Therefore, it is possible to divide the memory consumption by 2^r by implementing only the permutation represented by the lower principal submatrix, and reuse it 2^r times[6].

5. GENERAL LINEAR PERMUTATIONS

In this section, we discuss the implementation of a general SLP $\pi(P)$ using the previous structures. This is equivalent to decomposing P into spatial and temporal permutations, i.e., permutations of the form (4) and (5).

A first idea is to use one spatial and one temporal permutation. Indeed, if the block P_4 is invertible, Gauss elimination yields

$$P = \begin{pmatrix} I_t & \\ P_2P_4^{-1} & P_1 + P_2P_4^{-1}P_3 \end{pmatrix} \begin{pmatrix} P_4 & P_3 \\ & I_k \end{pmatrix}.$$

This means that $\pi(P)$ can be implemented using a memory block followed by an SNW. For the spatial part, $\text{rk } P_2P_4^{-1} = \text{rk } P_2$, i.e., our implementation will have $\text{rk } P_2 \cdot 2^{k-1}$ switches, which matches the lower bound of Theorem 1.

Conversely, it is possible to decompose an SLP using an SNW followed by a memory block, if P_1 is invertible. Again, the construction will be optimal.

However, if neither P_1 nor P_4 are invertible, none of the solutions above exist. Hence, three blocks are needed and two possibilities exist, depicted in Fig. 7: the SNW-RAM-SNW structure (Section 5.1), and the RAM-SNW-RAM structure (Section 5.2).

---

[4]The period of $(P_4^{-i}+\cdots+P_4^{-1})_i$ is at most twice the period of $(P_4^i)_i$, which is itself at most 2^t [12].

[5]This is a consequence of $\pi(I_r \oplus A) = I_{2^r} \otimes \pi(A)$ in the notation of [2].

[6]This optimization has the theoretical advantage of yielding an empty implementation for the trivial temporal permutation $\pi(I_n)$.

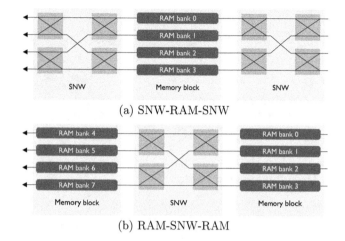

(a) SNW-RAM-SNW

(b) RAM-SNW-RAM

Figure 7: Two possible architectures for a streaming permutation.

5.1 SNW-RAM-SNW

An SNW-RAM-SNW implementation (Fig. 7(a)) corresponds to the factorization

$$P = \begin{pmatrix} I_t & \\ L_2 & L_1 \end{pmatrix} \begin{pmatrix} M_4 & M_3 \\ & I_k \end{pmatrix} \begin{pmatrix} I_t & \\ R_2 & R_1 \end{pmatrix}. \qquad (10)$$

Using our method of implementation, the number of switches involved equals $(\mathrm{rk}\, L_2 + \mathrm{rk}\, R_2)2^{k-1}$. Thus we want to minimize $\mathrm{rk}\, L_2 + \mathrm{rk}\, R_2$ for an optimal implementation. This decomposition has been studied in [13], summarized in the following theorem:

THEOREM 2. *If P is an invertible $n \times n$ matrix, then* (10) *verifies:*

$$\mathrm{rk}\, L_2 + \mathrm{rk}\, R_2 \geq \max(\mathrm{rk}\, P_2, n - \mathrm{rk}\, P_4 - \mathrm{rk}\, P_1).$$

Further, there exists a decomposition (10) *reaching this bound.*

This theorem provides the minimal number of switches possible for the assumed architecture SNW-RAM-SNW, along with the existence of a solution reaching this bound. An algorithm to compute this solution in cubic arithmetic time in n is provided in [13][7].

However, if $\mathrm{rk}\, P_4 + \mathrm{rk}\, P_2 + \mathrm{rk}\, P_1 < n$, the solution has more switches than suggested by Theorem 1 (which does not fix the architecture). It turns out that in this case the next architecture is optimal in terms of the number of switches, at the price of twice the RAM.

5.2 RAM-SNW-RAM

A RAM-SNW-RAM implementation (Fig. 7(b)) corresponds to the factorization

$$P = \begin{pmatrix} L_4 & L_3 \\ & I_k \end{pmatrix} \begin{pmatrix} I_t & \\ M_2 & M_1 \end{pmatrix} \begin{pmatrix} R_4 & R_3 \\ & I_k \end{pmatrix}. \qquad (11)$$

---

[7]The "rank exchange" section in [13] can be used in some cases to balance the ranks of L_2 and R_2. For instance, if $\mathrm{rk}\, L_2$ and $\mathrm{rk}\, R_2$ are both odd, it is interesting to reduce the rank of L_2 by one and increase the rank of R_2 by one, thus making them both even, and therefore easier to implement using 4-input multiplexers.

A switching-optimal solution is guaranteed by the following theorem:

THEOREM 3. *If P is an invertible $n \times n$ matrix, there exists a decomposition* (11) *that verifies $\mathrm{rk}\, M_2 = \mathrm{rk}\, P_2$.*

The existence of such a decomposition is again shown in [13], with an algorithm that computes such a decomposition in cubic arithmetic time in n.

In summary, the RAM-SNW-RAM solution is always optimal in terms of the number of switches. However, if $\mathrm{rk}\, P_4 + \mathrm{rk}\, P_2 + \mathrm{rk}\, P_1 \geq n$, SNW-RAM-SNW offers a better solution with half the RAM.

6. RESULTS

We evaluate our method in two ways. First, we consider one particular, but important example: the streamed bit reversal. We compare our two proposed architectures (one of which is optimal) against a prior solution. Second, we compare our streamed permutations against all four prior solutions that we found in the literature. We show a table summarizing the similarities and differences and illustrate these with three example settings.

Example: Bit-reversal. We consider for $k = t = n/2$ the bit-reversal permutation $\pi(J_n)$. Since $P_2 = J_k$, Theorem 1 states that at least $k \cdot 2^{k-1}$ switches are needed. However, Theorem 2 shows that an SNW-RAM-SNW structure requires twice this amount: $k \cdot 2^k$ switches, based on, for example,

$$P = J_n = \begin{pmatrix} I_k & \\ J_k & I_k \end{pmatrix} \begin{pmatrix} I_k & J_k \\ & I_k \end{pmatrix} \begin{pmatrix} I_k & \\ J_k & I_k \end{pmatrix}.$$

If, on the other hand, we choose a RAM-SNW-RAM structure, we can reach the minimal number of switches with, for example,

$$P = J_n = \begin{pmatrix} I_k & J_k \\ & I_k \end{pmatrix} \begin{pmatrix} I_k & \\ J_k & I_k \end{pmatrix} \begin{pmatrix} I_k & J_k \\ & I_k \end{pmatrix}.$$

The price is twice the RAM capacity. Note in both cases the simplicity of the control logic: only a k-bit counter and k inverters are needed.

Fig. 8 shows throughput versus area for a bit reversal on 2^{11} 16-bit elements for the two different architectures implemented with $k \in \{1, \ldots, 5\}$, i.e., 2 to 32 ports, and $t = 11-k$. In this case, our SNW-RAM-SNW solution is equal to the one proposed by [2]. For each of the two solutions we also implemented the FPGA-specific optimization that uses 4-input multiplexers as sketched in Fig. 5, which yields significant area gains.

We compare against the RAM-SNW-RAM solution in [14], which is more general in that it can handle (fixed) arbitrary, also non-linear permutations. The target is a Virtex-7 xc7vx1140tflgl1930 FPGA, using Xilinx Vivado 2014.4.

Comparison against prior work. Table 1[8] summarizes the similarities and differences between our solutions (SNW-RAM-SNW and RAM-SNW-RAM) and four prior works. As the table shows, only ours provide guaranteed optimal switching complexity at similar RAM cost.

To show the difference with an example, Fig. 9 compares, for different streaming scenarios, the number of switches

---

[8]We suppose here that [5] uses a switch based Beneš permutation network to implement their crossbars.

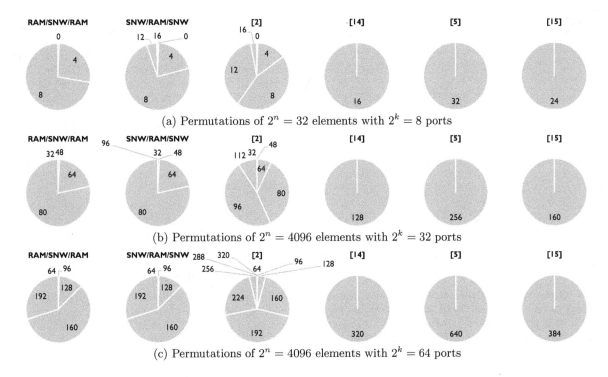

(a) Permutations of $2^n = 32$ elements with $2^k = 8$ ports

(b) Permutations of $2^n = 4096$ elements with $2^k = 32$ ports

(c) Permutations of $2^n = 4096$ elements with $2^k = 64$ ports

Figure 9: Number of switches needed for 10^7 random SLPs with different architectures.

Architecture	Permutations	Memory	Number of switches	Optimal routing?
RAM/SNW/RAM	Linear only	2^{k+1} banks of 2^t words	$\mathrm{rk}\, P_2 \cdot 2^{k-1}$	Always
SNW/RAM/SNW	Linear only	2^k banks of 2^t words	$\max(\mathrm{rk}\, P_2, n - \mathrm{rk}\, P_4 - \mathrm{rk}\, P_1) \cdot 2^{k-1}$	Iff $\mathrm{rk}\, P_4 + \mathrm{rk}\, P_2 + \mathrm{rk}\, P_1 \geq n$
[2]	Linear only	2^k banks of 2^{t+1} words	$\geq \max(\mathrm{rk}\, P_2, n - \mathrm{rk}\, P_4 - \mathrm{rk}\, P_1) \cdot 2^{k-1}$	Generally not
[14]	All	2^{k+1} banks of 2^{t+1} words	$(k - 1/2) \cdot 2^k$	Never for SLPs with $k \geq 2$
[5]	All	2^k banks of 2^t words	$(k - 1/2) \cdot 2^{k+1}$	Never for SLPs
[15]	All	2^k banks of 2^t words	$k \cdot 2^k$	Never for SLPs

Table 1: Comparison of different architectures using RAMs, in the case of a full-throughput SLP.

used by the different architectures. In (a) all specified SLPs are considered, in (b) and (c), the full number is too large and we chose 10^7 random samples instead. The pie charts show the distribution of the number of switches needed for these SLPs. As shown in the paper, one of our solutions (the two leftmost in the table) always minimizes the number of switches needed. We observe the improvement over prior work and also that for larger scenarios, most of the permutations can be implemented optimally using SNW-RAM-SNW. As we have seen, this is not true for the bit-reversal.

7. RELATED WORK

Switching networks for sets of permutations. Switching networks that can execute all permutations (in a non-streamed way) are a classic topic in computer science [16, 17]. A variant of this problem occurred in Section 4.1 where we implemented streamed spatial permutations. Namely, we had to build a minimal switching network capable of passing a subset of permutations.[9] Our solution was based on a reduced Omega network and we

---

[9]Specifically a coset Hg, where g is a linear permutation, and H a subgroup of bit complement permutations, i.e., permutations that map an index i to $i_b + v$, where v is a given bit vector.

proved optimality. The complete Omega network has been heavily studied in [9, 10, 18, 19]. Beyond that, the problem of finding a minimal switching network to perform a given set of permutations appears to have not received much attention in the literature. An exception is the last section in [18], which, however, produces only upper bounds for few cases.

SNW-RAM-SNW structure. We now restrict ourselves to the structure proposed in Section 5.1. This architecture has already been proposed for streamed linear permutations in [2], which also proves optimality for the special case of permutations that permute the bits of the indexes (a group called PIPID in [10] or BP class in [19]), i.e., where P has only one 1 in each row and column. In particular, this includes stride permutations (2) and bit-reversal (1). For these permutations, our solution is equal (Fig. 8 shows one example).

However, [2] has two shortcomings that we resolve in this paper. First, the method to derive an SNW-RAM-SNW implementation is in general not optimal (see Fig. 9). Second, [2] does not consider the alternative architecture RAM-SNW-RAM, which, in some cases provides solutions with fewer switches at the cost of twice the RAM. In this paper we resolve both problems completely by establishing an

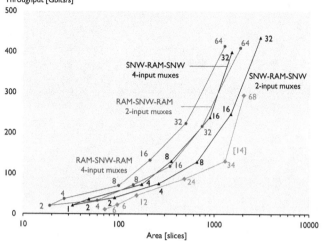

Bit-reversal, 2^n = 2048 on Xilinx Virtex-7 FPGA

Figure 8: Comparison of our two structures for a bit-reversal permutation on 2048 16-bit elements for different multiplexer sizes vs. [14]. Labels: number of BRAM tiles. In this example, the SNW-RAM-SNW structure that uses 2-input muxes is equivalent to [2].

architecture-oblivious sharp lower bound for the number of switches needed and a technique for obtaining that optimal solution using the SNW-RAM-SNW or RAM-SNW-RAM architecture. We precisely characterize the cases where the latter wins.

As a minor point, the solution in [2] uses a double-buffering method to achieve full-throughput (as they mention a memory requirement of 2^{n+1} words in the last section). We propose an alternative method in Section 4.2 that does not require additional RAM capacity.

This SNW-RAM-SNW architecture has also been used in [5] to implement the streaming permutations needed in a bitonic sorting network (which are all linear). They achieve an efficient memory usage, but the method used (folding a Clos permutation network) doesn't harness the specificity of the particular permutations they consider, and the resulting design requires two complete switching networks (that allow any permutation), which also makes the control logic much more complex.

Similarly, [15] offers a solution based on a Beneš network to build a streamed solution for any, also non-linear, given permutation on 2^n elements. Because it is more general, it is not optimal for the linear case. Additionally, the generated datapath is independent of the desired permutation. The control logic is also more complex, as it uses ROM look-up tables to store memory addresses and the control bit of every switches for every cycles. This allows flexibility in the sense that different permutations can be implemented simply by modifying these tables, but is clearly suboptimal for a single fixed permutation. In Fig. 9, we showed how our solutions outperform this method.

RAM-SNW-RAM structure. The RAM-SNW-RAM structure was considered in [14] to implement any (including non-linear) streaming permutation of any size. A shortcoming is that the central SNW has to be able to pass any spatial permutation. Further, it considers only double-buffering for

its temporal permutations. We compared our different architectures in Fig. 8 and 9.

Other architectures for streamed permutations. Other approaches for building a fixed permutation technique include [1], which proposes a register based implementation, and [20], which is specific to implementing stride permutations. These two methods have in common that they use registers to delay elements. In this paper we choose a more regular architecture using RAM banks instead, which are available on FPGAs, to spare logic.

Acknowledgement

We thank Peter A. Milder for his help with implementing [14], and the anonymous reviewer who suggested to use 4-input multiplexers on FPGAs, which we incorporated in our results (Fig. 8).

8. CONCLUSIONS

The main theoretical result of this paper is the exact switching complexity of streamed linear permutations. We established this result by first proving a lower bound, and then providing a constructive method that achieves this lower bound. Our method implements optimal SLPs using switches and RAMs using two different architectures. One always has optimal switching complexity, but requires a RAM capacity of twice the size of the dataset. The other proposed architecture is switching-optimal for some permutations (that we precisely characterized) and requires only half the RAM capacity. We have implemented the technique to test on given permutations; but the main contribution of the paper is the theory and the underlying key idea: to phrase the problem as a specific matrix factorization and apply techniques from linear algebra to construct solutions and prove their optimality.

9. REFERENCES

[1] K. K. Parhi, "Systematic synthesis of DSP data format converters using life-time analysis and forward-backward register allocation," *IEEE Transactions on Circuits and Systems II: Analog and Digital Signal Processing*, vol. 39, no. 7, pp. 423–440, 1992.

[2] M. Püschel, P. A. Milder, and J. C. Hoe, "Permuting streaming data using RAMs," *Journal of the ACM*, vol. 56, no. 2, pp. 10:1–10:34, 2009.

[3] M. Püschel, P. A. Milder, and J. C. Hoe, "System and method for designing architecture for specified permutation and datapath circuits for permutation," 2008. US Patent 8,321,823.

[4] P. A. Milder, F. Franchetti, J. C. Hoe, and M. Püschel, "Computer generation of hardware for linear digital signal processing transforms," *ACM Transactions on Design Automation of Electronic Systems (TODAES)*, vol. 17, no. 2, 2012.

[5] R. Chen, S. Siriyal, and V. Prasanna, "Energy and memory efficient mapping of bitonic sorting on FPGA," in *International Symposium on Field-Programmable Gate Arrays (FPGA)*, pp. 240–249, 2015.

[6] D. E. Knuth, *The Art of Computer Programming, 2Nd Ed. (Addison-Wesley Series in Computer Science and*

Information. Boston, MA, USA: Addison-Wesley Longman Publishing Co., Inc., 2nd ed., 1978.

[7] M. Zuluaga, P. A. Milder, and M. Püschel, "Streaming sorting networks," *ACM Transactions on Design Automation of Electronic Systems (TODAES)*, 2016. Accepted for publication.

[8] A. H. Karp, "Bit reversal on uniprocessors," *SIAM Review*, vol. 38, pp. 1–26, Mar. 1996.

[9] M. C. Pease, "The indirect binary n-cube microprocessor array," *IEEE Transactions on Computers*, vol. 26, no. 5, pp. 458–473, 1977.

[10] J. Lenfant and S. Tahé, "Permuting data with the Omega network," *Acta Informatica*, vol. 21, no. 6, pp. 629–641, 1985.

[11] G. Steidl and M. Tasche, "A polynomial approach to fast algorithms for discrete Fourier-cosine and Fourier-sine transforms," *Mathematics of Computation*, vol. 56, no. 193, pp. 281–296, 1991.

[12] M. Darafsheh, "The maximum element order in the groups related to the linear groups which is a multiple of the defining characteristic," *Finite Fields and Their Applications*, vol. 14, no. 4, pp. 992 – 1001, 2008.

[13] F. Serre and M. Püschel, "A lower-upper-lower block triangular decomposition with minimal off-diagonal ranks," *ArXiv e-prints*, 2014. arXiv:1408.0994.

[14] P. A. Milder, J. C. Hoe, and M. Püschel, "Automatic generation of streaming datapaths for arbitrary fixed permutations," in *Design, Automation and Test in Europe (DATE)*, pp. 1118–1123, 2009.

[15] R. Chen and V. Prasanna, "Automatic generation of high throughput energy efficient streaming architectures for arbitrary fixed permutations," in *Field Programmable Logic and Applications (FPL)*, pp. 1–8, 2015.

[16] V. E. Beneš, *Mathematical Theory of Connecting Networks and Telephone Traffic.* Academic Press, 1965.

[17] A. Waksman, "A permutation network," *Journal of the ACM*, vol. 15, no. 1, pp. 159–163, 1968.

[18] D. Steinberg, "Invariant properties of the shuffle-exchange and a simplified cost-effective version of the Omega network," *IEEE Transactions on Computers*, vol. 32, no. 5, pp. 444–450, 1983.

[19] D. Nassimi and S. Sahni, "A self-routing Benes network and parallel permutation algorithms," *IEEE Transactions on Computers*, vol. 30, no. 5, pp. 332–340, 1981.

[20] T. Järvinen, P. Salmela, H. Sorokin, and J. Takala, "Stride permutation networks for array processors," in *International Conference on Application-Specific Systems, Architectures and Processors Proceedings (ASAP)*, pp. 376–386, 2004.

High Level Synthesis of Complex Applications: An H.264 Video Decoder

Xinheng Liu[1], Yao Chen[2,3], Tan Nguyen[3], Swathi Gurumani[3], Kyle Rupnow[3], Deming Chen[1]

[1] Electrical and Computer Engineering, University of Illinois at Urbana-Champaign, USA
{xliu79, dchen}@illinois.edu

[2] College of Electronic Information and Optical Engineering, Nankai University, China
yaochen@mail.nankai.edu.cn

[3] Advanced Digital Sciences Center, Singapore
{tan.nguyen, swathi.g, k.rupnow}@adsc.com.sg

ABSTRACT

High level synthesis (HLS) is gaining wider acceptance for hardware design due to its higher productivity and better design space exploration features. In recent years, HLS techniques and design flows have also advanced significantly, and as a result, many new FPGA designs are developed with HLS. However, despite many studies using HLS, the size and complexity of such applications remain generally small, and it is not well understood how to design and optimize for HLS with large, complex reference code. Typical HLS benchmark applications contain somewhere between 100 to 1400 lines of code and about 20 sub-functions, but typical input applications may contain many times more code and functions. To study such complex applications, we present a case study using HLS for a full H.264 decoder: an application with over 6000 lines of code and over 100 functions. We share our experience on code conversion for synthesizability, various HLS optimizations, HLS limitations while dealing with complex input code, and general design insights. Through our optimization process, we achieve 34 frames/s at 640x480 resolution (480p). To enable future study and benefit the research community, we open-source our synthesizable H.264 implementation.

1. INTRODUCTION

Advances in high level synthesis (HLS) in recent years have led to increasing adoption of HLS as a primary design methodology. HLS promises advantages in design effort, design space exploration, debugging of high level specifications, and automation of test generation infrastructure. There are many active academic and commercial HLS projects continually improving design quality [4, 5, 23, 36–38].

Due to this rapid rise in adoption there has also been a proliferation of HLS design studies; both studies that happen to use HLS as a design method, but do not comment on HLS efficiency in particular [6, 7, 21, 22] and studies that attempt to analyze the efficiency of HLS features and draw conclusions about HLS-based design methodologies [11, 26]. However, although there are increasing HLS-based studies, there are several limitations of existing studies: Whether the input code was written from scratch or converted from a C/C++ reference software, benchmarks tend to be small and simple. Even for benchmarks that consume large total area, the input source tends to be limited in lines of code, complexity of data-structures, and function hierarchy.

In addition, design studies do not differentiate between alternate design methodologies using HLS. Although all methods translate high level language (HLL) inputs to register transfer level (RTL) hardware implementations, there are substantial differences between writing HLL code from scratch for an HLS design and converting existing HLL code for HLS suitability. There are also differences between targeting a HW/SW platform with HLS-generated hardware used as an accelerator compared to stand-alone hardware. Furthermore, there are substantial differences between a bottom-up methodology that performs block-level design followed by system-level integration compared to a top-down method that synthesizes the entire function as a single core.

This variety demonstrates the many different HLS-based design methodologies. However, not all approaches are equally effective, and the best method depends both on design goals and the application. The differences between design methodologies are emphasized by application complexity; whereas a simple application may be efficiently designed and optimized with many methods, a complex application may be more efficient with approaches that break the application into pieces for efficient piecewise optimization. However, this is not necessarily desirable; partitioning and block-level integration may require substantial design effort that negates the design effort benefits of HLS.

As we demonstrate in this paper, real applications such as H.264 video coding include the types of complexities that make a top-down approach challenging, particularly when starting from C-reference software not originally intended for HLS. Video encoding and decoding accelerator cores are widely used to perform fast and power/energy efficient encoding and/or decoding of videos, particularly in mobile

FPGA'16, February 21-23, 2016, Monterey, CA, USA

© 2016 ACM. ISBN 978-1-4503-3856-1/16/02. . . $15.00

DOI: http://dx.doi.org/10.1145/2847263.2847274

platforms. H.264[1] is a highly used video coding standard [1], with many major platforms such as YouTube using H.264 encoded videos, and accelerators built into many common embedded SoCs such as Apple's A5 through A9x processors, and the popular Qualcomm Snapdragon processors.

Video encoding is representative of the application complexity that is increasingly demanded of HLS-based designs. Complex applications from other domains such as computational genomics, computational physics, computer vision, and deep learning also have complex input source codes that make synthesis of the entire input source challenging. Although H.264 and other applications remain computationally intensive and excellent candidates for acceleration, code complexity creates new challenges for effective use of HLS-based design methodologies.

In this paper, we perform HLS of a complete H.264 decoder starting from a C reference [13]. We convert for synthesizability, and optimize to achieve throughput of 542 frames per second (fps) at 176x144 (QCIF[2]) resolution and 34 fps at 640x480 (480p) resolution. This paper contributes to the study of HLS with:

- A study of top-down HLS of applications with significantly more complex input code, data-structures, and optimization strategies
- Analysis and observations of both best-practices for complex application optimization and future challenges for supporting such applications
- An open-source implementation of synthesizable H.264 that achieves real-time 34 fps decoding at 640x480 (480p) resolution

The rest of this paper is organized as follows: Section 2 presents the related works in HLS and H.264 implementations. Section 3 discusses the H.264 algorithm. Section 4 presents the HLS related optimizations. The experiments and results of the optimized design are presented in Section 5. We conclude with our observations in Section 6.

2. RELATED WORK

In recent years there have been many design studies that use HLS and studies that have created RTL implementations of H.264 or block-level implementation using HLS. We will first discuss HLS case studies in general, then concentrate specifically on design studies of H.264.

2.1 HLS Case Studies

There have been many prior studies focussed on generating hardware modules using HLS tools. Case studies using HLS tools have been primarily used to (i) present tool- or input-language-specific design methodology [3,10,16,21,25], (ii) study the suitability of HLS for specific domains [14,15], or (iii) evaluate quality of results, coding guidelines and performance optimizations for HLS [6,20,26,28–30,35]. Together, these studies present promising results for continuing to expand adoption of HLS tools in digital design flows.

Commercial and academic HLS tool providers have developed case studies to demonstrate unique features of their design methodology and efficiency of their tool. These tool-specific design studies include C2R [3] for AES cryptography,

FOSSY [10] for SystemC TLM translation of JPEG, the No-instruction set compiler toolkit (NISCT) [25] for an architecture specific C-to-RTL of audio codecs, Labview HLS [21] for object detection, and the CAL actor language [16] for video codecs. All of these tool-specific studies demonstrate their respective tools, but do not generalize design methodologies, optimization strategies or tool use observations that can be applied to other flows.

Some case studies do use complex applications such as Monte Carlo-based pricing for finance applications [15], and compare multiple HLS design tools such as Vivado, Altera OpenCL, and Maxeler MaxCompiler. However, the study was a usability study from a software engineering perspective rather than a study of how to effectively use those tools. Similarly, a case study of AES [14] studied suitability of Vivado HLS for cryptography, and demonstrated that Vivado can compete with hand-written RTL, but AES is a comparatively simple benchmark.

Many prior works have also presented evaluations of state of the art HLS tools, but all of these works use simple algorithms from filtering [35], matrix multiplication [29], DSP algorithms (e.g. DCT, FIR and FFT) [6], or edge detection [20]. Although some used and evaluated HLS tools [20, 31], detailed analysis and performance optimizations were not presented. Others perform block-level designs, but do not perform complete system-level design [5, 17]. Benchmark suites for HLS are small and simple; CHStone benchmarks [12] have between 200 and 1400 lines of code (LoC) and less than 20 functions, and MachSuite [24] has between 100 and 500 LoC with 10-18 functions. Although widely used to study HLS, these benchmarks are small and simple block designs that are not representative of the large, complex applications used with modern tools. Some works do present coding guidelines and code transformations to improve quality of results [26,35], but again the applications are small and comparatively simple.

In this work, we select H.264: a complex, widely popular real-world application to study HLS. The Main Profile of H.264 alone has 6000 lines of code and more than 100 functions. H.264 contains complex data structures and control flow, which tests the capabilities of HLS beyond conventional strengths in block-level design.

2.2 H.264 Hardware Implementations

There have been several prior works [2,18,19,27,34] using RTL for H.264 implementation. Due to the complexity of H.264, many [18,19,27,34] only implement parts of H.264. However, rapid development requires a fast design method to implement efficient, optimized hardware for the codecs. The code complexity in applications such as H.264 creates new challenges for effective use of HLS-based design flows.

Previous HLS studies [8,32,33] have mapped H.264 algorithms to hardware. Cadence's C-to-Silicon [33] was used to design individual functional blocks based on a SystemC model but the individual blocks were later integrated using RTL into a system-level decoder. The integration and verification at the system-level is performed manually. The study presented in [32] also used a similar methodology albeit different block-level partitioning of the H.264 decoder. Bluespec SystemVerilog (BSV) was used to synthesize a complete H.264 decoder in [8]. Though BSV provides a comparatively higher level of abstraction than traditional RTL, the

---

[1]Also known as MPEG-4 Part 10, Advanced Video Coding or MPEG-4 AVC

[2]Quarter Common Intermediate Format

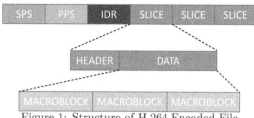

Figure 1: Structure of H.264 Encoded File

designer still focusses on hardware specific details such as data buffering and internal module connection.

In this work, we use an open-source C reference model along with Vivado HLS to explore the design methodology for developing a complete H.264 decoder in HLS. We present the design considerations, challenges and advantages in the HLS design of an H.264 decoder. Our top-down HLS-based implementation of H.264 performs code restructuring and performance optimizations that can be generalized for similar applications with significantly complex input code and data-structures.

3. BACKGROUND

Before we describe our design and optimization process, we first introduce the H.264 video format and decoding process, as well as high level synthesis, common design methodologies, and key challenges in HLS-based design from a reference software platform.

3.1 H.264 Video Decoding

The H.264 standard is a family of specifications covering a variety of encoding features, resolutions, and frame rates. Thus, when designing a decoder, the developer must define which H.264 profile they will support, which covers encoding features such as bit-depth per sample, chroma sampling, and supported frame types (among others). Depending on the performance, an implementation has achieved a *level* from 1 (30 fps at 128x96) to 5.2 (60 fps at 4K (4096x2160)). In this paper, we implement a decoder for the Main Profile, normally used with standard definition video broadcasting.

An encoded H.264 video file is based on a stream of YUV colorspace pixels, where Y corresponds to luminance and the U and V components correspond to two chrominance components. The YUV format is designed to encode colors considering that humans are more sensitive to brightness (luminance) than color (chrominance), and thus chrominance data is often sub-sampled to improve encoding efficiency.

An H.264 file is encoded frame by frame, where I-frames are stand-alone frames encoded independently, P-frames use data from previously encoded frames, and B-frames use data from both past- and future-frames in the video stream. An encoded file is stored as a bit-stream, where a frame may be a non-byte multiple series of bits. The file format specifies each frame's type. In addition, an encoded file specifies some global parameter sets at the beginning of the file. An overview of the H.264 input file format is shown in Figure 1.

The SPS and PPS units contain basic decoding parameters including frame size. IDR is the first slice in a sequence of pictures, where each picture is further divided into macroblocks. Each slice's header contains basic slice information including slice identifier, the number of macroblocks, reference frame settings and quantification parameters.

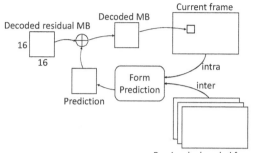

Figure 2: Prediction process in H.264.

Table 1: Pragma Classes Suported by Vivado HLS

Pragma Class	Operation
Interface	Define function interface
Function Call	Function inlining/off
	Flow optimization
	Seperate instantiation of functions
Loop Optimization	Loop pipelining
	Loop unrolling
	Loop merge operations
Memory Control	Array partition, etc.

The decoder receives a compressed bit-stream from the file and entropy decodes the data elements to produce a set of quantized coefficients, as shown in Figure 2. These quantized coefficients are passed to an inverse DCT and dequantized to form a residual image. The residual information is combined with previously decoded data and prediction information to reconstruct a final decoded image.

In this paper, we target the Main Profile[3] with as high of resolution and frame rate as possible. Importantly, we wish to design the core independently of the target resolution(s) that are supported. Therefore, we must consider a design process where we use parameterized internal buffers for temporary storage, but references to large, full-frame buffers are left as external references. Thus, we can resynthesize the same code with modified parameters for any input resolution, and framerate will scale with total workload.

3.2 High Level Synthesis

High level synthesis performs automated translation of high level language inputs to register transfer level (RTL) implementations. HLS flows perform allocation of registers and functional units, scheduling of operations to state machine states, and binding of operations to functional units. HLS tools also generate I/O interfaces to connect the HLS-produced modules with memories or other communication interfaces [9, 20].

Many HLS tools include pragmas to guide optimization of area and performance. Efficient use of pragmas, together with code reorganizations to make pragmas effective is the key design and optimization technique for HLS. In this paper, we use Vivado HLS; Vivado supports several classes of pragmas (Table 1). Unrolling, pipelining, and memory partitioning pragmas are critical performance optimizations, but although it is well known that these optimizations are important, we will demonstrate the complexities of applying these optimizations to H.264, and effective transformations

---

[3]6000 LoC is for Main Profile only

to use these pragmas in Section 4. As discussed earlier, HLS can be used with multiple design flows including:

Design from Scratch.

Experienced hardware designers increasingly use HLS with C/C++ as a primary design entry language due to advantages in C-level verification of an executable specification, and design space exploration among others. These designs may be used as stand-alone hardware or accelerators in a CPU-based system. Furthermore, the design flow may use bottom-up generation of hardware implementations for small pieces and successive expansion of the accelerator, or by top-down specification of the desired hardware module.

Translate from Reference.

Either due to lack of domain expertise or hardware design expertise, some users of HLS choose to start from reference software, translate the C-code to achieve synthesizability, and then optimize the C-code to meet area and performance goals. Although the input source is not specifically organized and designed for HLS, this is a common development case; a designer is commonly lacking either domain expertise or sufficient hardware expertise to define a block-level hardware implementation from scratch before beginning.

As in design from scratch, translation from reference may be used with both stand-alone hardware and accelerators. The design may be performed bottom up by generating hardware units for multiple functions connected at the system level, or top-down synthesis of a single function to accelerate the entire application. Due to code organization and communications interfaces, bottom-up synthesis may be complex or infeasible – especially due to code reuse with overlapping dependencies. If two communicating functions reuse sub-functions, then all of sub-functions must be duplicated, and access to shared data structures may make system level integration complex or entirely infeasible.

Although translating from reference software is common and a desirable use case for HLS, there are particular challenges of starting from reference software. In particular, reference software:

- May have significant command-line interpretation, GUI and user interface code that needs to be partitioned from the code to be synthesized
- May describe a variety of features and use cases, of which only a subset are desired for implementation (e.g. in H.264, reference software describes many profiles, but we only implement a single profile)
- May have function hierarchy that is efficient and elegant for software reuse, but introduces variable bounds computational loops for hardware
- May include substantial hierarchy that is efficient in software, but incurs call/return overheads in HLS-based hardware
- Software code organization may not correspond to a desired hardware block diagram, with computation blocks and communications merged and partitioned among the many functions.

4. METHODOLOGY

We will now discuss the design methodology to generate an optimized, synthesizable implementation of the H.264 decoder. We particularly study the complexities in handling a full, complex system-level design by performing HLS to create a single top-level module to decode a frame of video.

The overall design process includes consideration of the desired use-case for the hardware module, verification requirements, selection of reference software, and subsequent conversion for synthesizability and iterative optimization of the source considering single-function, multiple-function call stack, and system level optimizations.

4.1 Reference Code Selection

The H.264 standard is a family of standards including multiple profiles for 2D and 3D videos. Each profile requires a different subset of coding features, subsampling, and bit-depth. Thus, in the selection of reference code, even though we are targeting a decoder for a single profile, it is critical that we also have access to a conformant video *encoder* so that we can generate input files that properly conform to our selected profile.

In addition, we consider that the desired use case for the generated hardware is a decoder hardware block that directly decodes input H.264 files to an OS-controlled memory buffer or display. However, for the purposes of verification the software reference should create golden output reference files. Finally, due to our requirement to partition the reference code for decoding from software that, in addition to other H.264 profiles, may include graphical interfaces, command line processing or user interaction code, we also look for reference software that can be simply partitioned. Furthermore, the reference software should not include platform-specific performance optimizations such as embedded assembly, which are not supported and would require translation to a C-level implementation.

Thus, in our selection of reference software, we look for software with the following characteristics:

- Both encoder and decoder implementations available
- Ability to generate golden outputs for verification
- Ability to partition decoder from other application code
- No patent or software licensing restrictions
- No embedded assembly or platform-specific performance optimizations

Based on these evaluation criteria there are several source distributions that provide both encoder and decoder reference software, but several of the distributions include significant user interface code, integration with other codecs (e.g. libavcodec implements over 100 codecs), or is restricted by licensing (e.g. OpenH264 is free as a library, but if the source is used and modified, it is restricted). Thus, we select an open encoder decoder reference from Fraunhofer HHI [13].

4.2 Algorithmic Code Conversion

Starting from our selected reference software platform, we partition the decoder logic from the rest of the reference source, eliminate non-synthesizable constructs, and prepare the code for iterative optimization.

4.2.1 Reference Software Partitioning

Based on our selection of the H.264 Main Profile (MP) as the target decoder implementation, we traverse the entire decoder software and determine which portions of software to eliminate. The eliminated code consisted of both (i) entire functions that are unused by the main profile and (ii) conditions within functions that will never occur in the main profile (e.g. if-else conditions based on data-structure identifiers, where the specified frame type never occurs in a MP-encoded video file).

To ensure correctness of the result, we first insert software assertions in all functions or conditional blocks that are candidates for removal, and decode several large reference video files to ensure that none of the candidate blocks are actually used. Then, we remove the code blocks and again verify that decoded videos remain functionally identical. Finally, we also insert test statements into all remaining functions and conditional blocks to ensure that every remaining block is used by main profile videos. It is important that we must manually eliminate these code blocks – the unused code blocks are only dead-code based on data-dependence with the input encoded video file, so static analysis by a compiler cannot determine which functions and/or blocks are unused.

4.2.2 Non-synthesizable Constructs

It is well known that HLS tools do not support dynamic memory allocation, recursive functions or general use of linked list type data structures. Although some tools handle special cases of these issues when static analysis can be used (e.g. static worst-case call depth for recursive functions, or static analysis that a pointer actually refers to a fixed memory buffer), it is generally better to eliminate use of these code constructs before further optimization.

Dynamic Memory Allocation.

First, the H.264 reference software makes heavy use of dynamic memory allocation in order to minimize the memory footprint of the software. However, we also consider the use case for this hardware: some dynamic memory allocation is used for internal buffers that we convert to parameterized static allocations of the largest potential buffer size. However, other dynamic memory allocation is used for large buffers based on the input video file resolution. Although we could also convert that to a static allocation, it is not desirable to design hardware that only supports a single maximum resolution. This would require re-design and optimization for each target resolution, and increases optimization challenges if a significant amount of internal memory is used for large buffers.

We convert large input frame buffers (both encoded frame data and decoded reference frames) into top-level memory interfaces. The memory interfaces will not create or use memory banks but merely create the required address and data ports to transfer data. Thus, we optimize the kernel computation independent of video resolution, and a system level design can choose to instantiate either on-chip frame buffers, or create frame buffers in off-chip memory.

File I/O.

As discussed in section 3.1, the video file format is a structured data stream with sets of parameters, decoding settings and compressed data. The reference software used file I/O in appropriate locations to read relevant variables instead of creating a single data structure to hold the data. Based on the Network Abstraction Layer (NAL) data structure for H.264 data over communications channels, we create a local structure to store one frame of encoded data and associated parameters. The variables and their usage of the NAL_t data structure are shown in Table 2. To maintain consistency with the software reference for verification, we

also create a *StorablePicture* data structure for the decoded output frames. During system deployment, we eliminate StorablePicture parameters not required for streaming video output, and retain only pixel data output buffers.

Pointer-based Data Structures.

The H.264 reference software also uses several linked lists to support reordering of picture display order with respect to the decode order. In the decode process, we may need to decode a later video frame first so that the proper pre-decoded reference images are available. In particular, when decoding a B-frame, we use both past- and future-decoded frames as references, so B-frames are always decoded out-of-order with respect to display order. Rather than supporting pointer manipulation, we instead statically allocate a fixed number of buffers, and maintain index variables to track which buffer is used. In addition, each buffer has an associated reference flag so that we can track which buffers are in use, and manage buffer reuse.

Recursive Functions.

Several of the original function implementations used recursions. We replace all recursive functions with appropriate non-recursive algorithms (e.g. we manually replaced a recursive quick-sort with non-recursive bubble-sort).

4.2.3 Preparation for Optimization

At this point, we have properly partitioned the H.264 decoder from System Calls, File I/O, graphical and non-graphical user interfaces. Furthermore, we have removed all unused functions and code-blocks, and eliminated non-synthesizable constructs. During this process, we considered the target hardware kernel use case to ensure that our source code can be designed and optimized independent of the target resolution. Now, to prepare for optimization, we generate several standardized input files, create appropriate scripts to compile and execute in both CPU-only and synthesized SystemC simulation, and perform profiling of both CPU and synthesized hardware outputs.

4.3 HLS Based Application Optimization

Starting from the synthesizable source reference, we can now begin iteratively optimizing the application. In small and simple applications, we would first perform customizations to minimize area and then simply maximally parallelize and pipeline the minimal area implementation. However, in a complex application, we cannot simply apply global parallelization; the area cost is too high, so we must be more selective about which portions of the application to optimize for area vs. portions to optimize for performance.

Thus, as a first step, we perform profiling of the synthesizable source both at the C-level and based on HLS results. Importantly, Vivado HLS provides area estimates and per-functional-call latency estimates, but it does not gather call stack information or count the number of function calls. Thus, we combine C-level profiling information on number of function calls and critical function call stack with information on the per-function call area and latency to determine optimization priorities.

The H.264 application contains 6000 lines of code and over 100 functions; through our optimization process, most of these functions are modified, rewritten, or entirely eliminated. However, we classify our optimization process into

Table 2: Data structure of NAL_t

Data	Description
unsigned len	The length of byte information in the array buffer
unsigned max_size	Constantly equal to MAXNALBUFFERSIZE
int nal_unit_type	The type of NAL, specify whether an SPS, a PPS or a slice is contained
int nal_reference_idc	Specify the reference functionality
int forbidden_bit	Error check bit, should be 0
unsigned long int bit_offset	Bit indicator of next bit to be read in
unsigned long int bit_length	Constantly equal to bit_offset/8
unsigned char buf[MAXNALBUFFERSIZE]	Buffer to store the data part of on NAL unit

```
//Original Clip3() function
int Clip3(int y, int z, int x) {
  return (x<y) ? y : ((x>z) ? z : x); }

//Clip a number within range (0, 255)
//Clip3(0, 255, x)
int Clip1_1(int x) {
  return (x & 0x80000000) ?
    0 : ((x & 0x7FFFFF00) ? 0xFF : x); }

// Use case of Clip1_1()
Sluma[startx+i][starty+j] =
    Clip1_1(predL4x4[i][j]+rMbL4x4[i][j]);
```

Figure 3: Multifunctional Function rewrite.

three general steps: (1) single function optimization, (2) function call stack optimization, and (3) system-level (cross call stack) optimization. We will now discuss these general steps and the types of optimizations we apply in more detail.

4.3.1 Single Function Optimization

Based on the profiling information, we first identify the set of leaf functions that account for the greatest percentage of time. When optimizing single functions, at this stage, we do not want to apply optimizations that consume significant extra area; instead, we concentrate on analyzing the efficiency of functions in terms of work performed per function call.

We classify single function optimizations into several groups of optimizations; however, in practice, we must apply several conceptual optimizations in order to optimize each function.

Function Specialization.

In reference C code, it is good for small utility functions to be re-usable by multiple callers through proper use of input parameters. However, for HLS, instead of implementing a single function with complex control flow, we specialize the function implementation considering call-site-specific optimizations. For example, in the reference code, a function that limits one input variable to be between a minimum and maximum value is sometimes used with constant limits; as shown in Figure 3, we create several versions to optimize for those constant inputs.

Function Call Efficiency.

In HLS, each call/return incurs overhead beyond the function computation latency due to extra state machine states for transitions. Thus, it is important that each function call accomplishes as much work as possible. In the reference code, several functions were written to read one bit at a time for reusability in multiple location, but this syntax incurred substantial overhead. Thus, after specialization, we also de-

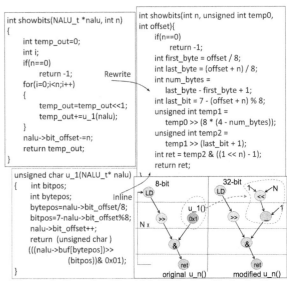

Figure 4: Function Bitwidth Widening Optimization

termine that instead of reading one-bit per call we modify the code to read up to 32-bit at a time with a small increase of the number of memory operations.

As shown in Figure 4, the u_1() function originally performed a single-bit read on the external memory buffer per function call. However, in its call site u_n(), u_1() is called N times in a for loop to construct an n-bit number. That would require N memory load operations. We modified the function by loading 32-bit data buffer into a local variable, then performed appropriate bit shifting and masking to read appropriate bits. Therefore, we reduce the memory overhead and also eliminate the variable-bound for loop which benefits functional-level pipelining.

After specialization and call efficiency optimizations, we also see that in many cases, the specialized implementation(s) are only used in one call site, so we also inline the implementations directly in order to eliminate that call overhead and further optimize the function implementation at the call site. In the general case, function inlining can be expensive due to hardware duplication; however, with simple functions that are further specialized for each call-site, the overhead of inlining can be mitigated by the specializations.

Memory Access Reuse.

CPU implementations of reference software implicitly depend on caching to make temporal locality of memory references efficient. However, in a hardware implementation, each use of a shared memory resource may be expensive; even if the shared memory is a local BRAM block, the port

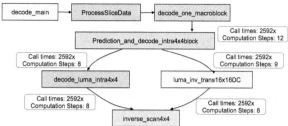

Figure 5: Cross function call analysis.

limitations may be a performance bottleneck in the system. Thus, splitting of local data arrays into individual registers, or creation of locally reused buffer copies of BRAM data can be important to performance.

Small data arrays can be partitioned to use registers; thus to determine whether we should partition a local array, we determine (1) if the function(s) using the array are in the set of important single functions, and (2) if those functions have data-parallelism that can be leveraged if the memory ports are not a limitation or (3) if reducing BRAM use is more important than preventing register use.

We apply this strategy to existing buffers from the reference source. However, if the size of a local buffer makes complete partitioning inefficient or infeasible (e.g. complete partitioning of a large macroblock buffer is expensive), we can create additional local buffers for locally-reused data and fully partition that new local buffer. For example, in each iteration of a loop, 6 data items are read, but between successive iterations 5 of 6 data items overlap, and only one new item is read. Therefore, we create a local buffer and read one new item every iteration.

Pipelining and Unrolling.

Now that each low level function call is optimized for efficiency and memory reuse, we can also consider further optimizations that generally incur area overhead. Pipelining and unrolling pragmas are powerful directives that can significantly improve performance, but can also use significant additional area. Depending on the number of loop iterations, we explore using both pipelining and loop unrolling in order to further improve the performance of important leaf-function implementations.

4.3.2 Cross-Function Analysis and Optimization

After optimizing important function calls, we turn to optimization of important sequences of function calls. Although we could continue to optimize leaf functions in descending order of importance, it is more effective to optimize important call sequences. We update the profiling data and then determine several sequences of function calls that include the (already optimized) important leaf-functions, but also include several other functions along the call stack.

We analyze both the latency of each function and the number of calls on the call stack. Based on this data, we determine the critcal path(s) in the call stack. For example, in the call graph shown in Figure 5, there are two important paths from decode to the function *inverse_scan4x4()*. Thus, direct improvements to both *inverse_scan4x4()* and the buffering steps in the sequence are necessary.

Loop Reordering.

Control flow inside a loop can prevent pipelining entirely or degrade performance due to a conditional check per loop iteration. Therefore, we reorder loops and conditional checking to optimize both the latency per loop iteration as well as the loop's suitability for pipelining.

Function Inlining.

In the single function optimization, we found several cases where function inlining is superior in both latency and area due to specialization during inlining. Here, the function inlining may not necessarily have significant opportunity or benefit of specialization. Nonetheless, there is a tradeoff between lowered function call overheads and increased area due to resource duplication. Through inlining pragmas or compiler directives, we could universally inline (or prevent inlining of) a function. However, for HLS, we should carefully analyze each call-site – if all call sites benefit from inlining (or all but one), we can inline at all sites. However, there may also be cases where it is superior to inline for only a subset of frequently used call sites and retain a shared implementation for less important call sites.

We explore function inlining by first identifying important locations for potential savings. Then, for candidate functions, we determine all call sites and use profile data to determine whether all call sites are equally important, and if the function is used identically from all call sites. Then, we explore multiple alternative inlining options and evaluate for area cost and latency savings; rather than using inlining directives, we finalize all inlining choices by manually inlining the function implementation.

Buffer Optimization.

As discussed in single function optimization, local buffers can play an important role in extracting the parallelism in the algorithm. In the first stage, we performed local buffer insertion to optimize individual leaf-functions, but did not consider where to define those buffers in order to maximize parallelization benefit throughout the call stack. Here, we analyze each buffer and determine where in the call stack to define it. At higher levels in the call stack, the buffer can impact parallelism of more sub-functions, but also introduces complexity in inter-block interfaces, incurs overhead to copy from global interfaces, and potential data sharing conflicts when multiple subfunctions reuse the same buffer. For each local buffer, we analyze the call stack and define it at the earliest point where sub-functions obtain benefit through parallelism, and buffering overheads are minimized.

4.3.3 System Parallelism

After call stack optimizations, we have optimized individual functions as well as the most important sequences of functions in the call stack. As before, we could continue optimizing successively less important functions or sequences of instructions, but we instead shift focus to optimize data buffering and communications across portions of the decoder that do not directly communicate through the function call stack. We again return to the profiling data to find top-level function dependencies and then determine how dependency in the top function corresponds to data dependency between buffers in our call stack.

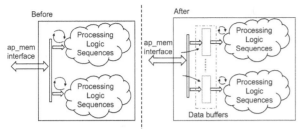

Figure 6: Critical path buffer related hardware.

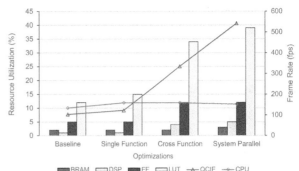

Figure 7: QCIF Resolution for each Optimization step

Buffer Insertion.

Due to the complex input data stream, external data reading remains the critical limiting factor in performance after local and call-stack buffer insertion. Because we wish to design the core independent of target resolution, some of the memory references access the external memory bus for data rather than local memories. Furthermore, although our locally inserted buffers are defined and well-optimized for the local function parallelism, they do not necessarily facilitate reuse across call state regions.

Using the profiling information, we determine the critical functions and then cluster the function call graph. With this clustering, we analyze the functions to find groups of functions that access the same portion of the external memory. Then, we create additional system-level local data arrays for larger subsets of data that can be either directly used (in cases that do not need substantial parallelism) or copied into another level of local buffers that is fully partitioned. This extra copying incurs overhead, but saves latency due to localization and data reuse (Figure 6). We again determine which subfunctions can use the local buffer based on analysis of their buffering requirements and importance in terms of processing time.

Task Parallelism.

Originally, there were more than 100 functions in the H.264 decoder. After specialization and inlining, there are still over 60 functions. To this point we have primarily optimized individual functions or call sequences, but disregarded task-level parallelism. We additionally consider task-level parallelism through two methods (1) buffer duplication if multiple functions access the same input data, but produce independent outputs, and (2) interface duplication to partition data inputs into two or more independent parts that can be accessed and processed independently.

5. RESULTS

For the original synthesizable software (Baseline) and each intermediate optimization stage we use a Xilinx VC709 evaluation board as our synthesis target. We also perform on-board verification using an Omnitek Zynq 7045 board both using the ARM CPU for data movement as well as using the Zynq as a standalone FPGA. We use Vivado HLS 2014.4 for C-to-RTL translation then perform logic synthesis, place and route (P & R) with Vivado 2014.4 to determine the area and achievable frequency of each design. To measure performance, we perform simulation of input video files as well as board level implementation; in an H.264 video file, there is a repeating pattern of frames: one I-frame, one P-frame and two B-frames in a I-B-P-B pattern. Because frame decode latency is data-dependent for all frame-types, we determine

the worst case latency (in cycles) for each frame type, then perform a weighted average (with B-frames twice as important as I or P frames). Then, that average latency in cycles is multiplied by achievable frequency to determine the latency (in seconds) per frame on average. In addition, we measure the frame rate of the reference software on an Intel Xeon CPU E5-2630 v3 (2.4 GHz) to evaluate the CPU performance effects of our modifications.

Although our core design is resolution independent, we verify that the design operates efficiently at multiple input resolutions by using QCIF(176x144) and 480p (640x480) input files. In addition, we analytically estimate our performance at different resolutions; we compute the average latency per macro-block by dividing the average latency above by the number of macroblocks per frame, and then scale performance estimates by the number of macroblocks in other resolutions. We use this analytical estimate to compare our performance results to prior H.264 implementations.

5.1 Performance and Implementation Results

We first compare performance and synthesis results when processing QCIF input video. In Figure 7, we show the area and performance of synthesized implementations at each stage of our optimization, as well as the CPU performance of the reference software at each stage. Single function optimizations improved performance of the implementation at little cost to implementation area, but these optimizations also improved CPU performance, indicating that the reference software may have been well organized for function reuse, but not necessarily for performance. However, as we perform cross-function optimizations that include local buffering (and buffer partitioning) to make unrolling and pipelining optimizations effective, the performance rises substantially. The area scales primarily in DSP, FF and LUT resources, as the BRAMs are used primarily for system-level frame-buffers and only a few small local buffers. With system-level parallelization, our implementation achieves 542 fps in QCIF video, and 34 fps in 480p video, as we show next. These system-level optimizations also show a decrease in CPU performance, demonstrating divergence in goals (and characteristics of *good* software) between CPU and HLS.

Comparing the QCIF results to the 480p results in Figure 8, we see similar trends, but further emphasized. The area of the two implementations is similar, with higher BRAM usage for local buffering of macroblocks. Although the design does not use full frame buffers, and thus remains resolution independent, we do increase local buffering at higher resolution to even better maintain data access locality of pre-decoded reference images (for P- and B-frames). In this

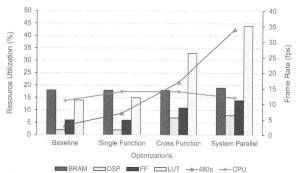

Figure 8: 480p Resolution for each Optimization step

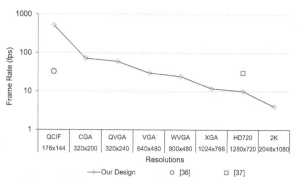

Figure 9: Comparison with Prior H.264 Designs

higher resolution version, we achieve 34 fps in the final system parallelization step, and the reduction in performance for the CPU version is emphasized.

Although our simulations do not model system-level memory bandwidth, H.264 is a compute intensive application that processes compressed input data, and thus not a memory bound application. Xilinx Virtex-7 FPGAs have been demonstrated to achieve as much as 1.8 Gb/s, whereas an H.264 480p video file at 30 fps only demands 14 Mb/s. Even a 4K video stream at 60 fps only requires 240 Mb/s, which is still substantially less than platform abilities. For this reason, we also simply model expected framerate of our implementation at other input resolutions by scaling the computation time per macroblock while ignoring any possible effects of average memory latency. In Figure 9, we show the analytical results of our own performance, and the performance with prior H.264 designs.

A Bluespec implementation [8] for ASIC achieved 30 fps for 720p resolution, but required substantial manual redesign using the Bluespec programming model. Another HLS-based design that quotes performance of full H.264 decoding is a block based design in SystemC [32], but only achieves 33 fps rate in QCIF resolution on a Virtex 4 platform. Three other recent papers discuss block-level designs of portions of H.264[18, 27, 34], but do not present performance results of full H.264 decoding.

5.2 Best-practices and Future Directions

H.264 is a representative complex application for evaluating HLS-based design and optimization. Through single-function, cross-function and system-level optimizations, we are able to demonstrate substantial optimization: achieving 34 frames per second with 480p video decoding. From this case study, we draw several conclusions for design and optimization of such complex applications.

First, we emphasize that our optimization process is using the same mechanisms as HLS-based design in general. In Vivado HLS, the set of pragmas and optimizations are fixed, and the design and optimization process revolves around transforming code to be suitable for pragma-based optimizations, and choosing which portions of the source code are critical for optimization. To that end, instead of concentrating on the usage and efficiency of typical Vivado pragmas, we discuss optimization phases covering function-level, function-callstack-level, and system-level optimizations.

Local optimizations of single, critically important functions remain important to expose further parallelism opportunity, but benefits of these optimizations are not necessarily immediately apparent. Thus, it is important to select a set of critical functions to optimize first and integrate those optimizations with higher-level buffering and parallelization. Although these optimizations are required to achieve gains, iteratively optimizing leaf-functions one by one until we reach targets is less likely to be an effective optimization technique.

In contrast, the majority of gains comes from cross-function optimizations. In complex applications, optimizations of buffering, call stack depth, and loop iteration bounds can account for the majority of opportunity. Function call overhead and loop iteration overheads can be substantial, and even further emphasized with data-dependent loop iterations that prevent optimizations through pipelining or loop unrolling. Although single function optimizations remain important, optimization of the call stack has a multiplicative effect on the importance of leaf-functions.

In particular, buffer insertion for localization of temporal and spatially local memory accesses, as well as partitioning for parallel data access is critically important. In Vivado HLS, it is important to select where to apply unrolling and pipelining pragmas in order to tradeoff between area cost and performance benefit. However, a naive exploration technique can simply apply pragmas everywhere, and Vivado will simply do nothing if data-dependence limits unrolling or pipelining. However, buffer insertion and memory partitioning are often required to enable unrolling or pipelining optimizations, and yet they are not as easily explored: existing buffers may not support partitioning, and users must manually insert local buffers and appropriate data copying in order to create optimizable local data structures.

Based on these observations, we propose several comparatively simple extensions to Vivado HLS (or HLS tools in general) to better support such complex applications:

1. Integrated Call-graph and function call frequency profiling, to better guide optimization priority
2. OpenMP-style pragmas to define creation and partitioning of local structures, including appropriate options for no-copy, copy-first, or copy-last options to support handling of global vs. local data buffer copies
3. Improved optimization of looping and function-call overheads, particularly in relation to ability to pipeline a loop of function calls

6. CONCLUSIONS

We studied and performed a top-down HLS of a complex application using H.264 decoder as a case study. Starting from a reference C software, we converted the code for synthesizability and performed several optimizations to achieve throughput of 34 fps at 480p resolution. We presented our observations of both best practices for HLS optimizations of complex applications and future tool improvements for supporting such applications. The synthesizable and optimized pragma-inserted C code of the H.264 decoder as a complex HLS benchmark is available for use under the MIT license at http://dchen.ece.illinois.edu/tools.html.

7. ACKNOWLEDGEMENT

This study is supported in part by the research grant for the Human-Centered Cyber-physical Systems Programme at the Advanced Digital Sciences Center from Singapore's Agency for Science, Technology and Research (A*STAR).

8. REFERENCES

[1] H.264: Advanced video coding for generic audiovisual services.

[2] L. V. Agostini, A. P. Azevedo Filho, W. T. Staehler, V. S. Rosa, B. Zatt, A. C. M. Pinto, R. E. Porto, S. Bampi, and A. A. Susin. Design and FPGA prototyping of a H.264/AVC main profile decoder for HDTV. *Journal of the Brazilian Computer Society*, 12(4):25–36, 2007.

[3] S. Ahuja, S. Gurumani, C. Spackman, and S. Shukla. Hardware Coprocessor Synthesis from an ANSI C Specification. *Design Test of Computers, IEEE*, 26(4):58–67, 2009.

[4] CALYPTO. Catapult C Synthesis. http://www.calypto.com/catapult-c-synthesis.php.

[5] A. Canis, J. Choi, M. Aldham, V. Zhang, A. Kammoona, J. H. Anderson, S. Brown, and T. Czajkowski. LegUp: high-level synthesis for FPGA-based processor/accelerator systems. In *FPGA*, pages 33–36, 2011.

[6] E. Casseau and B. Le Gal. High-level synthesis for the design of FPGA-based signal processing systems. In *SAMOS*, pages 25–32, 2009.

[7] Z.-H. Chen, A. Su, M.-T. Sun, and S. Hauck. Accelerating Statistical LOR Estimation for a High-Resolution PET Scanner Using FPGA Devices and a High Level Synthesis Tool. In *FCCM*, pages 105–108, 2011.

[8] K. Fleming, C. C. Lin, N. Dave, G. Raghavan, J. Hicks, et al. H. 264 decoder: A case study in multiple design points. In *MEMOCODE*, pages 165–174. IEEE, 2008.

[9] S. Georgakakis and J. Evans. Overview of high level synthesis tools. *Journal of Instrumentation*, 6(02):C02005, 2011.

[10] K. Gruttner, F. Oppenheimer, W. Nebel, F. Colas-Bigey, and A.-M. Fouilliart. SystemC-based Modelling, Seamless Refinement, and Synthesis of a JPEG 2000 Decoder. In *DATE*, pages 128–133, 2008.

[11] S. Gurumani, H. Cholakkal, Y. Liang, K. Rupnow, and D. Chen. High-level synthesis of multiple dependent CUDA kernels on FPGA. In *ASP-DAC*, pages 305–312, 2013.

[12] Y. Hara, H. Tomiyama, S. Honda, and H. Takada. Proposal and quantitative analysis of the CHStone benchmark program suite for practical C-based high-level synthesis. *Journal of Information Processing*, 17:242–254, 2009.

[13] F. HHI. JM H.264 Reference Software. http://iphome.hhi.de/suehring/tml/.

[14] E. Homsirikamol and K. Gaj. Can high-level synthesis compete against a hand-written code in the cryptographic domain? A case study. In *ReConFig*, pages 1–8, 2014.

[15] G. Inggs, S. Fleming, D. Thomas, and W. Luk. Is high level synthesis ready for business? A computational finance case study. In *FPT*, pages 12–19, 2014.

[16] J. Janneck, I. Miller, D. Parlour, G. Roquier, M. Wipliez, and M. Raulet. Synthesizing hardware from dataflow programs: An MPEG-4 simple profile decoder case study. In *SiPS*, pages 287–292, 2008.

[17] K. Karras, M. Blott, and K. Vissers. High-Level Synthesis Case Study: Implementation of a Memcached Server. *arXiv preprint arXiv:1408.5387*, 2014.

[18] G. Khurana, A. Kassim, T. P. Chua, and M. Mi. A pipelined hardware implementation of in-loop deblocking filter in H.264/AVC. *Consumer Electronics, IEEE Transactions on*, 52(2):536–540, 2006.

[19] R. Kordasiewicz and S. Shirani. Hardware implementation of the optimized transform and quantization blocks of H. 264. In *Canadian Conference on ECE*, volume 2, pages 943–946, 2004.

[20] W. Meeus, K. Van Beeck, T. Goedemé, J. Meel, and D. Stroobandt. An overview of today's high-level synthesis tools. *Design Automation for Embedded Systems*, 16(3):31–51, 2012.

[21] E. Ortiz-Lopez, M.-A. Ibarra-Manzano, J. Andrade-Lucio, J. Cervantes, and O. Ibarra-Manzano. Implementation and Test of Appearance-Based Vision Algorithms Using High-Level Synthesis in FPGA. In *CERMA*, pages 143–148, 2011.

[22] E. Oruklu, R. Hanley, S. Aslan, C. Desmouliers, F. M. Vallina, and J. Saniie. System-on-chip design using high-level synthesis tools. *Circuits and Systems*, 3(01):1, 2012.

[23] A. Papakonstantinou, K. Gururaj, J. Stratton, D. Chen, J. Cong, and W.-M. Hwu. FCUDA: Enabling efficient compilation of CUDA kernels onto FPGAs. In *SASP*, pages 35–42, 2009.

[24] B. Reagen, R. Adolf, Y. S. Shao, G.-Y. Wei, and D. Brooks. MachSuite: Benchmarks for accelerator design and customized architectures. In *IISWC*, pages 110–119, 2014.

[25] M. Reshadi, B. Gorjara, and D. Gajski. C-based design flow: A case study on G.729A for Voice over internet protocol (VoIP). In *DAC*, pages 72–75, 2008.

[26] K. Rupnow, Y. Liang, Y. Li, D. Min, M. Do, and D. Chen. High level synthesis of stereo matching: Productivity, performance, and software constraints. In *FPT*, pages 1–8, 2011.

[27] E. Sahin and I. Hamzaoglu. An efficient intra prediction hardware architecture for H. 264 video decoding. In *DSD*, pages 448–454. IEEE, 2007.

[28] S. Sarkar, S. Dabral, P. Tiwari, and R. Mitra. Lessons and Experiences with High-Level Synthesis. *Design Test of Computers, IEEE*, 26(4):34–45, 2009.

[29] S. Skalicky, C. Wood, M. Lukowiak, and M. Ryan. High level synthesis: Where are we? A case study on matrix multiplication. In *ReConFig*, pages 1–7, 2013.

[30] G. Stitt, F. Vahid, and W. Najjar. A Code Refinement Methodology for Performance-improved Synthesis from C. In *ICCAD*, pages 716–723, 2006.

[31] B. D. Technology. An independent Evaluation of High-Level Synthesis Tools for Xilinx FPGAs. http://www.bdti.com.

[32] M. Thadani, P. Carballo, P. Hernández, G. Marrero, and A. Núñez. ESL flow for a hardware H.264/AVC decoder using TLM-2.0 and high level synthesis: a quantitative study. In *Proc. SPIE*, pages 1–12, 2009.

[33] R. N. Tomé, A. N. Ordóñez, and P. P. Carballo. High level synthesis of a H. 264/AVC decoder on FPGA platform.

[34] T.-C. Wang, Y.-W. Huang, H.-C. Fang, and L.-G. Chen. Parallel 4× 4 2D transform and inverse transform architecture for MPEG-4 AVC/H. 264. In *ISCAS*, volume 2, pages II–800. IEEE, 2003.

[35] F. Winterstein, S. Bayliss, and G. Constantinides. High-level synthesis of dynamic data structures: A case study using Vivado HLS. In *FPT*, pages 362–365, 2013.

[36] Xilinx. Vivado High-Level Synthesis. http://www.xilinx.com/products/design-tools/vivado/integration/esl-design.html.

[37] H. Zheng, S. Gurumani, L. Yang, D. Chen, and K. Rupnow. High-level synthesis with behavioral level multi-cycle path analysis. In *FPL*, pages 1–8, 2013.

[38] H. Zheng, S. T. Gurumani, K. Rupnow, and D. Chen. Fast and Effective Placement and Routing Directed High-level Synthesis for FPGAs. In *FPGA*, pages 1–10, 2014.

Automatically Optimizing the Latency, Area, and Accuracy of C Programs for High-Level Synthesis

Xitong Gao, John Wickerson, and George A. Constantinides
Circuits and Systems Research Group, Department of Electrical and Electronic Engineering
Imperial College London, United Kingdom
{xi.gao08, j.wickerson, g.constantinides}@imperial.ac.uk

ABSTRACT

Loops are pervasive in numerical programs, so high-level synthesis (HLS) tools use state-of-the-art scheduling techniques to pipeline them efficiently. Still, the run time performance of the resultant FPGA implementation is limited by data dependences between loop iterations. Some of these dependence constraints can be alleviated by rewriting the program according to arithmetic identities (*e.g.* associativity and distributivity), memory access reductions, and control flow optimizations (*e.g.* partial loop unrolling). HLS tools cannot safely enable such rewrites by default because they may impact the accuracy of floating-point computations and increase area usage. In this paper, we introduce the first open-source program optimizer for automatically rewriting a given program to optimize latency while controlling for accuracy and area. Our tool, SOAP3, reports a multi-dimensional Pareto frontier that the programmer can use to resolve the trade-off according to their needs. When applied to a suite of PolyBench and Livermore Loops benchmarks, our tool has generated programs that enjoy up to a $12\times$ speedup, with a simultaneous $7\times$ increase in accuracy, at a cost of up to $4\times$ more LUTs.

1. INTRODUCTION

There are many reasons why FPGA implementations of numerical algorithms are best obtained via high-level synthesis (HLS) from C: less development effort, the abundance of software engineers compared to hardware designers, the relative ease of testing C code on an ordinary microprocessor, the opportunities for rapid design space exploration, and so on [1]. Great advances have been made in this area recently, and the output from HLS tools is nowadays competitive with hand-crafted designs [2].

Numerical C programs typically spend most of their time in loops. For this reason, HLS tools adopt state-of-the-art scheduling algorithms to synthesize loops to run as fast as possible [3]. This is achieved by pipelining them to maximally exploit parallelism across loop iterations. However,

their ability to perform pipelining is fundamentally constrained by data dependences that are carried across iterations, *i.e. inter-iteration dependences*. To relax these constraints, we must use equivalence rules in real arithmetic (*e.g.* associativity and distributivity), in tandem with conventional rules (*e.g.* partial loop unrolling and array access pattern changes) to enable much more efficiently pipelined RTL designs. A simple example of this is the summation of all elements in an array:

```
float sum = 0;
for (int i = 0; i < N; i++)
    sum += a[i];
```

This code can be partially unrolled and the sequence of additions can be rewritten using tree adders to reduce its latency, and we will see in Sec. 8 that more efficient implementations are possible.

Unfortunately, in the presence of floating-point arithmetic, these program transformations could affect numerical accuracy. For instance, under single-precision floating-point arithmetic with rounding to the nearest, the result of $(2^{-24} + 2^{-24}) + 1 = 1.00000012\ldots$ is exact, but $(1 + 2^{-24}) + 2^{-24}$ is rounded to 1. The difference between the actual result in real arithmetic and the rounded result is known as the *round-off error*. Round-off errors, when accumulated, can have a devastating effect on numerical accuracy [4]. Round-off errors in a numerical program are dependent on every arithmetic operation and every input value, and with the impact on floating-point accuracy being so esoteric, it is challenging for engineers to understand the repercussions of switching between "(a + b) * c" and "a * c + b * c" in their programs.

Experienced engineers apply expression rewriting intuitions in numerical programs. For instance, when summing a sequence of floating-point values, one can sometimes reduce round-off error in the result by summing the inputs in ascending order. On the other hand, one can often reduce latency by applying *expression balancing, i.e.* rearranging operators in an expression to construct a balanced tree, so that more operators can work in parallel. These heuristics cover a very limited number of possible transformations and may not always improve the original code. A straightforward process therefore does not exist to apply steps of transformations using equivalence rules to *optimally* trade off latency, resources and numerical accuracy.

Existing HLS tools consider these rewrites to be unsafe, and thus make little of them when restructuring floating-point data-paths. For instance, *Vivado HLS* (VHLS) [5] has only a simple *expression balancing* feature that uses associativity to improve latency, and only expressions with either additions or multiplications are optimized. Moreover, it does not produce optimal loop pipelining, because it does not take into account the implications of these transformations on inter-iteration dependences and does not explore partial loop unrolling. In addition, VHLS cannot reason about how this feature affects numerical accuracy; there is no guarantee that this transformation will not result in a catastrophically inaccurate implementation.

In response, we have developed a tool, SOAP3—a fully automatic source-to-source optimizer—that augments VHLS by optimizing a given program using these transformations. Our optimizer discovers not only one, but a wide spectrum of program candidates. When synthesized in VHLS, these candidates trade off three performance metrics of great importance to engineers: run time, resource usage and round-off error. Here, run time refers to the latency in clock cycles, resource usage refers to the number of look-up tables (LUTs) and digital signal processing (DSP) elements. Some of these performance metrics could be in conflict. For example, higher performance tends to require more circuitry, and how to resolve this trade-off depends on the user's requirements. As a result, SOAP3 produces a *set* of optimized programs, known as the *Pareto frontier*: those programs P for which the tool has found no P' that improves on P in all three metrics.

In contrast to the expression balancing optimization pass in VHLS, SOAP3 *automatically* produces results that are significantly better than *manually* tuning partial unrolling factors and expression balancing #pragmas in VHLS, because it is fully aware of how data dependences are carried across iterations, and uses this to steer the optimization process. SOAP3 also considers the impact these transformations could have on round-off errors, and minimizes them in the optimization process, as we treat numerical accuracy as one of the three simultaneous objectives. Furthermore, VHLS only generates one result which does not necessarily improve over the original code.

Generating candidate optimizations naïvely would produce a combinatorial explosion, even for small input programs. For instance, a simple summation of n variables could have $(2n-1)!!^1$ equivalent expressions [6, 7]. We therefore base our optimizer on the open-source SOAP2 framework [6, 8], which specifically tackles the efficient discovery of equivalent structures in numerical programs, by intelligently pruning the set of candidates as it progresses up the input program's abstract syntax tree. We also exploit SOAP2's ability to analyze the numerical accuracy of a given program. To analyze the run time and resource utilization of a given program, we use a variant of the *iterative modulo scheduling* algorithm [9] that computes fundamental lower bounds of these metrics.

We evaluated SOAP3 on a suite of 11 programs from the Livermore Loops [10] and PolyBench [11] benchmark suites. Our tool obtained a wide selection of Pareto-optimized programs. Programs with the best latency obtained speedups of up to $12\times$ ($7\times$ on average across the suite), and increases in accuracy of up to $7\times$ ($2.7\times$ on average), while using up to $4\times$ ($2.5\times$ on average) more LUTs. We were unable to decrease the resource utilization in any of the benchmarks, as they have no redundant computations.

$^1(2n-1)!! = 1 \times 3 \times 5 \times \cdots \times (2n-1).$

Our contributions

- We described how standard program equivalences that do not affect program behavior (*e.g.* partial loop unrolling, and rules that remove extraneous array accesses) can enable non-standard transformation rules (*e.g.* arithmetic rules) to significantly impact latency, resource usage and accuracy in a loop (Sec. 5.2).
- We significantly improved the performance of the algorithm for discovering equivalent programs through improved accuracy analysis (Sec. 6.3), graph partitioning, and intelligent pruning of optimization candidates (Sec. 5.1).
- We designed a new scheduling analysis that estimates the latency and resource usage of a given optimization candidate (Sec. 6).
- Incorporating the above-mentioned techniques, we developed the first optimizer to *automatically* and *safely* produce optimized programs (and subsequent RTL implementations with Vivado HLS) on the four-dimensional Pareto frontier of options that trade off run time, accuracy, and area (LUTs and DSP elements). Our improvements in latency are significantly better than the only ones produced by Vivado HLS's *unsafe* optimizations. We have evaluated SOAP3 on a suite of Livermore Loops and PolyBench benchmarks (Sec. 8).

2. MOTIVATION

Figure 1 gives an implementation of the 5-point Seidel stencil computation, modified from PolyBench's 9-point version [11], where initially all values in the array A are single-precision floating-point values between 0 and 1. It resembles the code frequently used in fluid dynamic simulations for solving partial differential equations and systems of linear equations.

```
for (int t = 0; t < 20; t++)
    for (int i = 1; i < 1023; i++)
        for (int j = 1; j < 1023; j++)
            A[i][j] = 0.2 * (A[i-1][j] +
                A[i][j-1] + A[i][j] +
                A[i][j+1] + A[i+1][j]);
```

Figure 1: An excerpt from the Seidel stencil [11]. The inter-iteration data dependence of the innermost loop is underlined.

We start by synthesizing this program in VHLS. We enable *loop pipelining* in VHLS, which asks it to optimize the loop by overlapping its iterations. However, we can observe that this program has very limited opportunity for pipelining, because each iteration j of the innermost loop ends by writing to A[i][j], and the next iteration j+1 begins by reading from A[i][j]; this inter-iteration dependence is highlighted in Figure 1. Hence, it serves as our example to demonstrate the power of SOAP3.

VHLS generates a schedule where each iteration requires 49 cycles (the *depth*, D, of the loop), and there are 46 cycles between the starts of consecutive loop iterations (the *initiation interval*, II), as enforced by the data dependences above. The innermost loop runs for 1022 iterations (the *trip count*, N), so the overall latency of the innermost loop is $((N-1) \times II) + D = 47015$ cycles.

We then enable VHLS's *expression balancing* (EB) optimization. When synthesized, this optimization pass tries to reorder the sequence of additions in the loop body into a tree structure, thus reducing the II to 28 cycles, and D to 42 cycles, while $N = 1022$ remains the same, thus $L = 28630$ cycles. The overall resource usage remains roughly the same. However, as we mentioned in Sec. 1, VHLS is not aware of the inter-iteration data dependence. Although enabling EB did produce a faster implementation, there is still room for improvement. We further discovered that if we partially unroll the loop, VHLS's EB did not improve the total run time, despite using a lot more resources. As we have explained in Sec. 1, EB only makes use of associativity, and does not make use of other equivalence rules. These limitations pose great restrictions on VHLS's ability to produce a significantly faster implementation. Most importantly, VHLS does not guarantee that this optimization will not result in catastrophic numerical inaccuracies.

We then use SOAP3 to automatically discover equivalent programs from the program in Figure 1. Because SOAP3 explores a large number of paths that lead to a Pareto frontier of implementations, here we illustrate one of the many paths that could be taken by minimizing latency, while trying to optimize accuracy and resource usage. By using just arithmetic equivalences, SOAP3 specifically applies transformations to alleviate the constraints on the inter-iteration dependence, and discovers that the innermost loop can be rewritten to minimize latency in the following form:

```
for (int j = 1; j < 1023; j++)
  A[i][j] = 0.2 * (A[i][j-1] +
    ((A[i][j] + A[i][j+1]) +
    (A[i+1][j] + A[i-1][j])));
```

Although this loop still has a data dependence between consecutive iterations, this transformation greatly reduces latency because most of the loop iterations can now be overlapped. We find that this simple transformation can reduce II to 19, which speeds up the original program by $2.3\times$, using almost the same number of LUTs and DSP elements as the original program. At the same time, the sequence of additions are now reordered to minimize round-off errors, improving the accuracy by 18%.

SOAP3 also supports more complex control flow restructuring transformations, such as partial loop unrolling, in tandem with rules that optimize memory accesses and arithmetic calculations. This can further reduce the loop's latency. In this example, unrolling the loop by a factor of two (*i.e.* updating two matrix elements on every iteration and halving the trip count) and applying other rules, results in a program with $II = 19, D = 152, N = 511$. When implemented on a device it is $4.8\times$ faster than the original, and almost twice as accurate, at a cost of 17% more LUTs:

```
for (int j = 1; j < 1023; j += 2) {
  float t0 = A[i][j-1], t1 = A[i][j+1];
  float t2 = (A[i][j] + t1) +
    (A[i+1][j] + A[i-1][j]);
  float t3 = 0.04f * t2 + 0.2f *
    ((t1 + A[i][j+2]) +
    (A[i+1][j+1] + A[i-1][j+1]));
  A[i][j] = 0.2f * (t0 + t2);
  A[i][j+1] = 0.04f * t0 + t3;
}
```

Further increasing the optimization effort, which enables the loop to be further unrolled, leads to a program that is $7\times$ as fast as the original, but uses $2.8\times$ as many LUTs. To summarize, in Table 1, we compare VHLS with EB, against one of the many implementations that we have explored using SOAP3 with the increased optimization effort. For each implementation, the round-off errors are computed using static analysis, a part of our optimization procedure. Our tool estimates latency in clock cycles and the total counts of LUTs and DSP elements, but we performed place-and-route manually for exact statistics.

	VHLS	VHLS with SOAP3	VHLS with EB
Clock Period (ns)	2.60	2.66	2.65
Latency (cycles)	961 k	135 k	585 k
Program Run Time (ms)	2.50	0.358	1.56
LUTs / DSP Elements	620/5	1778/8	623/5
Round-off Error	10.68 μ	4.31 μ	unknown

Table 1: Comparison between the fastest implementations. The three columns respectively shows the original program with loop pipelining enabled, what VHLS can achieve alone, and the capability of SOAP3. It is important to note that the round-off error is unknown for VHLS with EB, because it cannot predict the impact of its unsafe optimizations on accuracy.

3. HIGH-LEVEL OVERVIEW

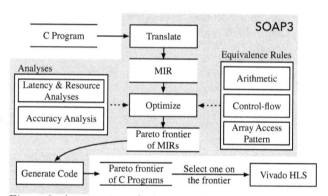

Figure 2: An overview of our automatic program optimization process. The shaded region shows our internal tool flow.

We start by introducing a high-level overview of our program optimization process (Figure 2). Our automatic optimization process starts by taking as an input, the original numerical program written in C, and translates it into a MIR (metasemantic intermediate representation graph). A MIR is a directed acyclic graph (DAG), and it serves as an abstract representation of the original program. It discards information about *how* a program is executed, which is dependent on how the program is structured in C, but retains the *effect* of program execution, keeping only the structure that leads to the final result. This procedure, explained in detail in Sec. 4, greatly reduces the number of program transformations we need to explore. We then discover equivalent MIRs using our efficient optimization procedure discussed in detail in Sec. 5. The optimized C programs can then be generated from the MIRs, using the SOAP2 framework's code generation routines, to be synthesized in Vivado HLS to obtain RTL implementations.

Our optimization flow can be applied to nested **for** loops with constant loop bounds and step counts. It can be relatively easily extended to lift this restriction with polyhedral methods [12].

As we apply transformation rules to discover equivalent MIRs, we estimate latency, resource usage and analyze round-off errors for each MIR we have discovered. Non-Pareto-optimal MIRs—the ones with all three performance metrics (latency, resource usage and accuracy) worse than another MIR—are pruned immediately to keep the size of total MIRs discovered tractable. Sec. 6 explains in depth how we analyze latency, resource usage and accuracy.

4. INTERMEDIATE REPRESENTATION

There are infinitely many ways to rewrite numerical C programs, and many of these rewrites produce programs that have the same resource usage, accuracy and latency characteristics. For instance, the following two programs are equivalent, but syntactically different, as they carry out the same computations.

$$P_1 : \texttt{x = x+1; y = 2*x; x = 3+x;}$$
$$P_2 : \texttt{y = x+1; x = y; y = y*2; x = x+3;} \quad (1)$$

In practice, it is desirable to eliminate as much as possible the need for these syntactic rewrites that do not affect our performance metrics. Following Gao *et al.*, we therefore perform transformations not on the program text directly, but on a DAG representation of the program called a MIR [8]. It expresses how each program variable is updated, but abstracts away the order in which the updates occur, and ignores any temporary variables that are not marked as program outputs. As an example, P_1 and P_2 can be automatically translated into an identical MIR:

$$\begin{bmatrix} \texttt{x} \mapsto + & \texttt{y} \mapsto \times \\ 3 \nearrow \nwarrow & + \nearrow \nwarrow 2 \\ & \texttt{x} \nearrow \nwarrow 1 \end{bmatrix} \quad (2)$$

This representation is useful to us, because a single MIR is able to capture a class of syntactically-distinct programs, all of which have the same resource usage, accuracy, and latency characteristics. By searching for transformations on MIRs, we drastically reduce the size of our search space. Note that expressions in the MIR can share common structures; this is useful for modeling the sharing of common subexpressions and makes the search for optimizations much more efficient.

MIRs also abstract the control structure of a program, preserving only the computations that lead to the outputs. For instance, by using the ternary conditional operator "?" from C, programs with conditionals such as:

    x = x + 1; if (b) x = 2 * x;

can be represented in MIR form as follows:

$$\begin{bmatrix} \texttt{x} \longmapsto ? \\ \texttt{b} \nearrow \times \\ 2 \nearrow \texttt{x} \nearrow + \nwarrow 1 \end{bmatrix} \quad (3)$$

MIRs are also capable of representing loops [8], but we do not exploit that in this paper, despite the centrality of loops to our work. When we optimize loop nests, we are

specifically applying transformations to the kernels of the flattened loop nests. Therefore, we find that when analyzing the latency and resource usage of a loop, we need only have the *body* of the loop as a MIR.

4.1 Representing arrays

Gao *et al.* [8] did not include support for arrays in their original description of the MIR format. However, the examples that motivate our work all include arrays, so in this paper, we extend MIRs to be able to represent programs that use single- or multi-dimensional arrays.

In many imperative languages such as C, arrays are stateful objects, *i.e.* they are used to store information, and changes to them are reflected to concurrent parts of the program that may be oblivious to the changes. This characteristic is known as the lack of *referential transparency*. Such behavior is not present in arithmetic expressions, many functional programming languages, SSA, as well as MIRs. This proves to be a challenge to us, because our efficient program optimization relies on recursively dividing the program into smaller subprograms that can be optimized independently, without affecting other subprograms.

To remedy this, we treat arrays as immutable. We use a function $update(A, \bar{x}, e)$ to return a new array that is the same as A but with (multi-dimensional) index $\bar{x}$ now containing e. Similarly, the function $access(A, \bar{x})$ returns the element of A at index $\bar{x}$. As a simple example, a loop body:

    A[i + 1] = 2 * A[i];

can be translated into the following MIR:

$$\begin{bmatrix} \texttt{A} \mapsto update & \times \\ \texttt{A} \nearrow & + \uparrow & access \\ & \texttt{i} \nearrow 1 & 2 \nearrow \texttt{A} \nearrow \nwarrow \texttt{i} \end{bmatrix} \quad (4)$$

The consequences of making arrays immutable are twofold. Firstly, we disallow pointer aliasing to keep the translation simple, *i.e.* "**float** *b = a;**" is not allowed in the C code. However this is not a problem for us because the programs that can benefit from our optimizations usually do not manipulate pointers. This issue can also be addressed in the future by performing pointer analysis. Secondly, diverged paths in array updates could occur if we naïvely optimize MIRs. For instance, if A is an input array, consider the two expressions in a MIR, $update(A, \bar{x}, e)$ and $update(A, \bar{x}, e')$, where e, e' are equivalent. They respectively update the x-th element of the *same* immutable A with e and e' and return *different* arrays. A C program cannot be generated from this MIR without duplicating A. We solve this problem by partitioning the MIR at "*update*" nodes using the method described in Sec. 5.

5. STRUCTURAL OPTIMIZATION

From a numerical program, we can generate a MIR using the translation in Sec. 4. The next step is to transform the MIR, and discover MIRs that are equivalent to the original MIR in real arithmetic, but may execute differently in finite-precision arithmetic because of round-off errors.

5.1 Algorithm

As discussed in Sec. 1, even a small expression could have a huge number of equivalent ones. Exhaustively discovering all equivalent MIRs would result in combinatorial explosion of

```
function OPTIMIZE(op(e_1, e_2))
    s_1 ← OPTIMIZE(e_1),  s_2 ← OPTIMIZE(e_2)
    s' ← ∅,  s ← {op(e'_1, e'_2) | e'_1 ∈ s_1 ∧ e'_2 ∈ s_2}
    while s ≠ s' do
        s' ← s,  s'' ← ∅
        for r ∈ transformation_rules, e ∈ s do
            for e' where e ↝ʳ e' do
                s'' ← s'' ∪ {e'}
            end for
        end for
        s ← PRUNE(s'')
    end while
    return s
end function
```

Figure 3: The algorithm we used for the efficient discovery of equivalent structures in MIRs.

the number of equivalent MIRs in the search space. For this reason, we base ourselves on an algorithm from SOAP2 that searches efficiently, by discovering equivalences in a bottom-up hierarchy. In this section we discuss the improvements we have made to the algorithm which further increases the performance of this algorithm.

Our first contribution is that instead of optimizing the MIR immediately, we start by partitioning the MIR into multiple smaller sub-MIRs. In turn, each is optimized separately and generate a set of equivalent sub-MIRs. We then select combinations from these sub-MIRs to be merged. This generates a set of MIRs that are equivalent to the original. Finally, we preserve those MIRs merged on the Pareto frontier.

Figure 3 shows the pseudocode of the optimization algorithm. It takes as an input a MIR graph, and produces a set of equivalent graphs that are estimated to be Pareto-optimal when converted into C programs and synthesized into circuits. Although this algorithm deals with a special case, *i.e.* a root node *op* with two child subtrees e_1, e_2, it can easily be generalized to an arbitrary number of child subtrees. Here, $e \overset{r}{\leadsto} e'$ means e' can be obtained by transforming part of the graph e in accordance with the transformation rule r. The next section discusses the transformation rules we used.

The algorithm starts by discovering equivalences in the leaves of a MIR, and progresses upwards for equivalent structures of the individual components that make up the graph, until the roots of the graph, where we have a set of MIRs equivalent to the original MIR. As it traverses through the MIR, the algorithm calculates the performance metrics at each node, using the analyses presented in the next section. Transformations that are not Pareto-optimal are immediately pruned from the search space, thus reducing the average complexity of the algorithm.

Our second contribution is the PRUNE function. We rely on this function to efficiently steer the direction of our Pareto frontier as we discover new candidates. It takes as an input the set of equivalent MIRs that we have discovered, and prunes MIRs in this set to reduce its size, keeping the number of MIRs discovered tractable. The SOAP2 framework prunes the MIRs that are Pareto-suboptimal, leaving only those that are on the Pareto frontier. However, because our Pareto frontier is 4D, there is a large increase in the number of Pareto-optimal MIRs. This Pareto pruning approach is no longer feasible for our benchmark examples. To tackle

Arithmetic Rules	
Associativity	`(a + b) + c` ↝ `a + (b + c)`
Commutativity	`a + b` ↝ `b + a`
Distributivity	`(a + b) * c` ↝ `a*c + b*c`
Negation	`a - b` ↝ `a + (-b)`
Subtraction	`(a + b) - (a + b)` ↝ `0`
Const. prop.	`(a * b + c / d) * 0` ↝ `0`
Division	`a / (5 / b)` ↝ `a * b * 0.2`

Control Flow Restructuring Rules	
Partial loop unrolling	`for(i=0;i<1000;i++){C_i;}` ↝ `for(i=0;i<1000;i+=2){C_i; C_{i+1};}`

Access Reduction Rules	
Multiple reads	`x=A[i--]; y=A[i+1];` ↝ `x=A[i--]; y=x;`
Multiple writes	`A[i++]=x; A[i-1]=y;` ↝ `A[i++]=y;`
Read after write	`A[i++]=x; y=A[i-1];` ↝ `A[i++]=x; y=x;`
Indep. accesses (where $i \not\equiv j$)	`A[i]=x; y=A[j];` ↝ `y=A[j]; A[i]=x;`

Table 2: Before-and-after examples to demonstrate the transformation rules we used. The arithmetic and control flow rules are inherited from Gao *et al.* [8]; the access reduction rules are introduced in this work.

this, we introduce another step in PRUNE to further decrease the number of MIRs in the set by sampling. We developed a new sampling algorithm, inspired by Poisson-disk sampling algorithm [13], which samples the Pareto frontier by first randomly selecting one point, then iteratively growing the set of points by adding the neighbours from the point that are separated by at least a certain distance. We search by bisection for the distance that keeps 20% of all points in the Pareto frontier. This method is superior to random sampling, because random sampling often samples points that are close together, which usually are very similar implementations.

We found that with our improvements, the algorithm is significantly faster than the original optimization algorithm in SOAP2, with a 5-fold increase in speed, at a cost of fewer points on the Pareto frontier.

5.2 Transformation Rules

This section details the transformation rules used in our structural optimization algorithm in Figure 3. Each transformation rule on its own is not revolutionary, but for the first time, we bring them together to show a much better automatic structural optimization on the latency, resource usage and accuracy of numerical programs, than is possible using only a subset of them.

SOAP2 provides a range of equivalence rules that are used in the optimization, such as associativity, distributivity, commutativity, constant propagation, and partial loop unrolling. In Table 2, we list those rules that proved effective when minimizing loop latencies. Although these rules are used to transform MIRs, we present before-and-after examples written in C to allow the effect of each rule to be readily understood.

Our new rules, the access reduction rules, with formal definitions below and examples in Table 2, remove extraneous data dependences that arise after partial unrolling.

238

These rules, along with partial loop unrolling, mostly do not impact latency, because they are well studied in polyhedral loop dependence analysis, and tools such as LegUp can make use of them automatically. However, they give the necessary freedom to arithmetic rules to affect latency. The rules are as follows, where A is an array, $\bar{i}, \bar{j}$ are subscripts, and e, e' are expressions:

- *Multiple reads*, eliminates the second of two reads of the same location. This arises naturally from the MIR, as common subexpressions are shared.
- *Multiple writes*, eliminates a write that is overwritten: $update\,(update\,(A, \bar{i}, e), \bar{i}, e') \rightsquigarrow update\,(A, \bar{i}, e')$.
- *Read after write*, eliminates a read from a location that has just been written: $access\,(update\,(A, \bar{i}, e), \bar{i}) \rightsquigarrow e$.
- *Independent accesses*, allows two array operations to be reordered if it can be proved that they never access the same location: $access\,(update\,(A, \bar{i}, e), \bar{j}) \rightsquigarrow access\,(A, \bar{j})$, if $\bar{i} \not\equiv \bar{j}$. We visualize this rule also in the following sample MIR transformation:

$$
\begin{bmatrix} & \text{y} \mapsto access & \\ \text{A} \mapsto update & & \text{j} \\ \text{A} & \text{i} & \text{x} \end{bmatrix} \rightsquigarrow \begin{bmatrix} & \text{y} \mapsto access & \\ \text{A} \mapsto update & & \text{j} \\ \text{A} & \text{i} & \text{x} \end{bmatrix} \quad (5)
$$

These access reduction rules may not seem powerful on their own, but when combined with other structural rules, they enable SOAP3 to detect dependences that can be removed in the MIR. This in turn allows more opportunities for the rules to further reduce loop latency. Conversely, it is not possible to relax scheduling constraints due to inter-iteration dependences without arithmetic equivalence rules, as these reduction rules are there to assist transformation rules that could really make a difference in latency. Therefore all the rules in Table 2 are essential to the optimization of latency in numerical programs.

6. PERFORMANCE ANALYSIS

This section explains how we analyze MIRs for our three performance metrics: latency, resource usage, and accuracy.

6.1 Latency Analysis

We measure the latency of a numerical program by estimating the total number of cycles required to execute it to completion. The most accurate estimate can be calculated with a complete scheduling of a numerical program. However, this would be computationally expensive, and would need to be repeated for tens of thousands of equivalent programs. Instead, our latency analysis computes the minimum initiation interval ($II_{\min}$) that must not be violated by any scheduling algorithm. (Recall from Sec. 1 that the initiation interval is the number of clock cycles that must elapse between the starts of two consecutive loop iterations, and is determined by data dependences and resource constraints.) We then compute the overall latency of the loop, and subsequently, the total latency of the program.

Following LegUp [14], we compute $II_{\min}$ values using *iterative modulo scheduling* [9]. For our work, we have adapted this analysis to apply directly to MIRs. The structure of MIRs already captures intra-iteration data dependences; to this, we add extra latency information as attributes on the edges of MIRs, plus new edges to form cycles that capture inter-iteration data dependences. The analysis is carried out in three stages.

The analysis starts with the MIR of the loop under analysis. Each edge in the MIR, say $s \to t$, represents a data dependence: the operation at node s must be evaluated fully before the operation at t can begin. The first step is to add a pair $\langle l, d \rangle$ for each edge of the MIR. Here, l is the *latency* of the edge (the number of *clock cycles* that must elapse between the start of s and the start of t) and d is the *dependence distance* (the number of *loop iterations* that must elapse between the start of s and the start of t). Because all operations in the MIR are performed in a single iteration, all edges have $d = 0$. The value of l is given by the latency of the operation at node s; if s corresponds to an input variable or a numerical constant, then $l = 0$.

The second stage is to add edges to form a cyclic dependence graph that captures *read after write* (RAW) dependences across loop iterations. This step involves checking whether each pair of "access" and "update" nodes has a dependence, and if so, adding a new edge between them with latency and dependence distance attributes. As an example, consider the MIR in (4) and assume each iteration increments i by 1. Because in the original program, A[i] and A[i+1] are respectively reading from and writing to the same array A, we need to check if these accesses could touch the same memory location in different iterations. For this, our analysis formulates an integer linear programming problem for the dependence distance, and solves it using the Integer Set Library [12]. In this example, the dependence distance is 1 because the value written to A[i+1] in the current iteration i is immediately used in the next iteration i+1. Similarly, we also add new edges for reads and writes to the same variable, which can be treated as a special array with only one element. Our analysis yields the following graph, and we call it a MIR with dependences (MIR^{dep}):

$$
\begin{bmatrix} \text{A} \longmapsto update & & & \\ 0,0 & 10,0 & 7,0 & -2,1 \\ \text{A} & & 0,0 \times 2,0 & \\ 0,0 + 0,0 & 2 & 0,0\ access\ 0,0 \\ \text{i} & 1 & \text{A} & \text{i} \end{bmatrix} \quad (6)
$$

Note the new dashed edge from the *update* node to the *access* node, which is labeled $\langle -2, 1 \rangle$. The first value, -2, signifies that the latency of the edge between $\times$ and *access*, which is 2 cycles, is canceled out because the multiplier can reuse its output from the previous iteration as the input for the current iteration. The second value, 1, indicates that there is a data flow dependence from iteration i to iteration $i + 1$.

We assume no limit on the number of operators we can allocate, so operators do not constraint II. However, in Vivado HLS, each array is usually translated into a dual-port RAM, which allows only two accesses per clock cycle [5], and thus constrains $II_{\min}$. For instance, for a loop to perform 3 accesses to a single array in each iteration, II must be greater than 1. This lower bound on II is known as *resource-based minimum initiation interval*, $II_{\min}^{\text{res}}$ [9]. It is defined as $\max_A \lceil n_A / r_A \rceil$, where A ranges over all arrays in the loop body, n_A is the number of accesses to the array A, and r_A is the maximum number of accesses allowed per cycle, which is 2 in our case.

The final step is to calculate an integer $II_{\min}^{\text{rec}}$ which is defined as $\max_c \lceil l(c) / d(c) \rceil$, where c ranges over all cycles in the MIR^{dep} graph, and we use $l(c)$ and $d(c)$ to respectively denote the sums of all latencies and dependence distances of the edges in the path c. This value is known as the *recurrence-based minimum initiation interval* [9]. Because a typical MIR with array accesses could have a very large number of cycles, we efficiently search for an $II_{\min}$ using a modified Floyd–Warshall algorithm [9]. Finally, we estimate the total latency L_{est}, an approximation of the actual L, of the loop with:

$$L_{\text{est}} = (N-1)II_{\min} + D, \text{ where } II_{\min} = \max\left(II_{\min}^{\text{rec}}, II_{\min}^{\text{res}}\right)$$

where, recalling from Sec. 1, N is the maximum *trip count*, *i.e.* the loop's total number of iterations, and D is the loop's depth, *i.e.* the total number of cycles per iteration.

Because we optimize programs in a bottom-up hierarchy, as described in Sec. 5, when an expression in a loop is optimized, its latency is estimated by scheduling its operations by using an As-Late-As-Possible (ALAP) [15] scheduling algorithm, where each operation is scheduled to the latest opportunity, while respecting the order of data dependences. Because the expression is eventually used in a loop, and the II of the loop is critical to how fast the loop can execute, it is necessary to start optimizing for II as soon as possible. Therefore, in our latency analysis of a MIR that is a fragment of a loop, our algorithm automatically shortens any paths between any pair of dependent accesses in the MIR, as we use the latency analysis as a component to manoeuvre our optimization on the Pareto frontier. Moreover, we place greater weights on dependent accesses with smaller dependence distances, because these impact the resulting loop II more than larger distances. We use the following formula as the analyzed latency value to guide the optimization for II for subexpressions in a loop, where Deps is a set of paths in the MIR, where each path is a sub-path of a cycle in the loop's MIR^{dep}:

$$L_{\text{est}} = \max_{p \in \text{Deps}} \frac{l(p)}{d(p)} \quad (7)$$

6.2 Resource Utilization Analysis

The hardware resource usage analysis of Gao *et al.* [8] captures the sharing of common subexpressions, but cannot analyze resource binding, which allows common operations to be shared across clock cycles. For instance, in the floating-point expression $a + (b + c)$, the two additions can be computed using one addition operator only. In this paper, we develop a new resource usage analysis that fully understands how resources are shared in an FPGA implementation of numerical programs.

We rely on the foundation of SOAP2, which counts the number $n_\otimes$ of each type of operation $\otimes$, while maximally sharing common subexpressions. In a pipelined loop, we compute a lower bound $a_\otimes$ on the number of instances of $\otimes$ that must be allocated, using the equation $a_\otimes = \lceil n_\otimes / II_{\min} \rceil$. For instance, if we know that a pipelined loop has $II_{\min} = 3$, and each iteration uses 6 multiplications, then we can compute that we need to synthesize at least 2 multipliers. Integer operators are typically not shared [16], so the number of operations is the number of allocated instances.

For straight-line code, non-pipelined loops, and consecutive loops, we use a simple ALAP scheduling [15] to estimate resource utilization.

Finally, we accumulate the number of LUTs and DSP elements for all allocated operators, which is the estimated resource utilization for the full program.

6.3 Accuracy Analysis

We build on the accuracy analysis of Gao *et al.* [8], which analyzes an upper bound of the absolute difference between the actual output of a numerical program and the expected output as if it is executed in real arithmetic. Because our benchmark suite consists of programs with large arrays, we further extend their work to support arrays, and keep the analysis efficient by treating an *entire* array as a pair of a floating-point interval and an interval of accumulated round-off errors. These intervals accumulate all values that are assigned to the array, and never shrink the range bounded by these intervals when we assign new values to an array location. Additionally, because most of the loops in our benchmark programs consist of nested loops and have large iterations, we modified the analysis routine in SOAP2 to analyze only a small fraction of loop execution, and use our dependence analysis to detect whether errors are accumulated across iterations, in order to extrapolate the total round-off errors from the results.

7. TOOL USAGE

SOAP3 is a source-to-source optimizer that specifically targets numerical program statements written in a subset of standard C99. It introduces the "**#pragma** soap begin" and "**#pragma** soap end" directives to delimit the code fragment to be optimized. We can also use "**#pragma** soap in" and "**#pragma** soap out" to provide input ranges and to declare output variables, respectively. SOAP3 supports arithmetic and Boolean expressions, assignment statements, **if** statements, **while** loops and **for** loops. The numerical data types we allow are **int** and **float**, as well as single- and multi-dimensional array types.

Figure 4 shows an example usage of SOAP3 in a C program. Note that it specifies the input values are respectively a two-dimensional array A, where its elements are single-precision floating point values between 0 and 1, and an integer T equal to 20. It also indicates the only output that we care about from this code is the resultant A.

```
#define N 1024
#pragma soap begin
#pragma soap in \
    float A[N][N] = [0, 1], int T = 20
#pragma soap out A
for (int t = 0; t < T; t++)
  for (int i = 1; i < N-1; i++)
    for (int j = 1; j < N-1; j++)
      A[i][j] = 0.2 * (A[i-1][j] +
        A[i][j-1] + A[i][j] +
        A[i][j+1] + A[i+1][j]);
#pragma soap end
```

Figure 4: An example C program that can be optimized with SOAP3.

Our tool is an open-source command-line utility, which only requires the user to provide a program written in C extended with the above **#pragma** statements. The Pareto optimal programs are all automatically generated by our tool, each is accompanied with our estimations of its latency and resource usage, and an analyzed bound on round-off errors. These programs can then be given to Vivado HLS to be synthesized into circuits.

Name	DSPs	LUTs	ratio	Error	ratio	Clock (ns)	Latency (cycles)	(s)	ratio
sum	2	303	0.257	914μ	7.93	2.54	41.0k	104μ	12.8
	4	1181		1.15μ		2.54	3.21k	8.17μ	
dotprod	5	411	0.231	926μ	7.29	2.54	41.0k	104μ	12.4
	10	1781		127μ		2.62	3.23k	8.44μ	
tridiag	5	470	0.288	63.1μ	1.06	2.54	17.8M	45.3m	3.41
	8	1631		59.4μ		2.69	4.93M	13.3m	
2mm	5	781	0.385	209	3.40	2.79	20.4G	57.0	7.46
	8	2029		61.4		2.92	2.62G	7.64	
3mm	5	760	0.207	114	6.76	2.55	32.3G	82.3	9.13
	10	3677		16.9		2.82	3.19G	9.01	
atax	5	627	0.507	353m	1.54	2.60	176M	457m	5.42
	5	1237		230m		2.61	32.4M	84.3m	
bicg	5	427	0.304	887μ	6.72	2.54	160M	407m	8.98
	5	1406		132μ		2.78	16.3M	45.3m	
gemm	5	524	0.234	1.99	2.97	2.54	10.8G	27.4	9.13
	10	2240		0.67		2.69	1.12G	3.00	
seidel	5	620	0.349	10.7μ	2.46	2.60	960M	2.50	7.16
	8	1778		4.31μ		2.66	131M	0.349	
gemver	5	809	0.382	7.28M	4.46	2.87	23.1M	66.2m	3.15
	5	2120		1.63M		2.77	7.60M	2.10m	(8.29)
mvt	5	701	0.251	91.0μ	3.32	2.56	23.1M	59.1m	7.49
	10	2793		27.4μ		2.80	2.82M	7.89m	(9.30)
syr2k	5	709	0.259	250μ	4.07	2.89	14.0G	40.3	6.95
	10	2740		61.4μ		2.71	2.14G	5.80	(7.62)
	Geomean		0.289		3.69				7.19 (8.01)

Table 3: Comparisons of the original (non-shaded rows) and the optimized program with lowest latency (shaded rows), for each benchmark. Values in parentheses are obtained after slightly tweaking our experimental set-up; see Sec. 8.3. We performed place-and-route for exact statistics.

8. EVALUATION

8.1 Method

We have evaluated SOAP3 on a suite of benchmark examples which consists of several applications that have recurring inter-iteration dependences:

- A simple loop, sum, that sums all elements in an array;
- Two kernels from Livermore Loops [10]: dotprod, which calculates the dot product of two vectors, and tridiag, which solves a tridiagonal system of linear equations; and
- Nine kernels from PolyBench [11], which calculate matrix/vector transpositions, additions and multiplications (2mm, 3mm, atax, gemm, gemver, mvt), the biconjugate gradient stabilized method (bicg), the Seidel stencil computation (seidel), and symmetric rank-2k operations (syr2k).

All elements of input arrays and matrices are set to be single-precision floating-point values between 0 and 1. We optimized all of these benchmark examples using SOAP3, specifically targeting the Xilinx Virtex7 device running at 333 MHz, for the three objectives of accuracy, resource utilization and latency simultaneously. We then used Vivado HLS 2015.2 [5] to synthesize the resulting optimized programs into RTL implementations for exact latency information, and performed place-and-route using Vivado Design Suite 2015.2 [17], to obtain exact resource utilization statistics. Our tool produces a 4D Pareto frontier for each program; to better present our results, in the following section we only consider three dimensions, namely, accuracy, latency and LUTs.

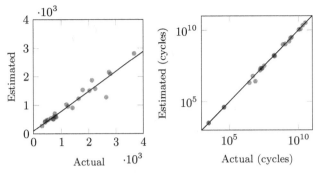

(a) LUT count estimates   (b) Latency estimates (log-log)
Figure 5: Comparisons of our estimated resource and latency statistics against Vivado HLS.

8.2 Results

Table 3 compares, for each benchmark in our evaluation set, the performance metrics of the original program against those of the program with the smallest latency discovered by SOAP3. We synthesized each program to a circuit to obtain exact statistics, which are shown in Table 3.

Figure 5a compares our estimated LUT counts (vertical axis) against the exact LUT counts (horizontal axis) obtained by synthesizing RTL implementations of each program in Table 3. Although our estimates deviate from the exact values, because we compute lower bounds on resource utilizations, and finite state machines synthesized and address calculation are not taken into account, our estimate can still accurately predict the general trend—a linear regression of all scatter points finds $R^2 = 0.9344$.

Figure 5b compares our estimated latency (vertical axis) against the actual latency values (horizontal axis). The solid line represents the linear regression of data points that we have gathered in Table 3. This line is a tight fit with our data, with $R^2 = 0.9959$, which indicates that our latency estimation can accurately predict the exact latency of synthesized implementations.

Returning to our motivating example from Sec. 2, Figure 6 demonstrates the range of optimized programs discovered by SOAP3 when applied to the Seidel stencil loop kernel. All optimized programs are discovered in 876 seconds with SOAP3. In the figure, ×-points indicate the original program. By using only the rules of real arithmetic, our tool finds a more efficient program that can improve run time by 2.5×, as shown by the ○-points. However, by enabling partial loop unrolling and our dependence elimination rules, the performance is further improved, resulting in a 6.7× reduction of total run time. Furthermore, we have found that numerical accuracy can often be optimized at the same time as we optimize the initiation intervals of loops. Because by partially unrolling loops, the sizes of the expressions in loop grow, which provides SOAP3 a greater freedom in terms of discovering more accurate expressions. In this example, the most efficient program is also the most accurate one: it minimizes round-off errors by approximately 2.5×. It is worth noting that our tool can detect that as it explores deep levels of partial loop unrolling, we start to see a diminishing return in performance as it hits a bottleneck in memory bandwidth. This is due to the fact that Vivado HLS synthesizes dual port RAMs for arrays, and in one clock cycle we can only read from the memory allocating array twice.

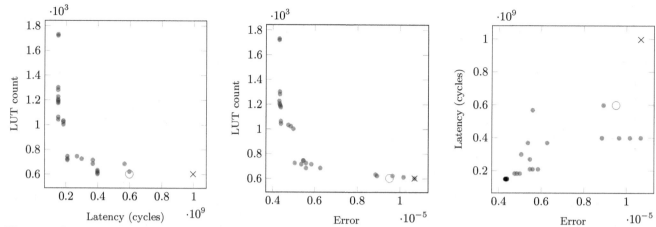

Figure 6: Pareto-optimal variants of the Seidel stencil program from Figure 1. Each graph shows a 2D projection of the Pareto frontier. In each graph, the original program is marked ×, and the lowest-latency variant obtained by arithmetic transformations alone is marked ○.

Our optimization flow discovers this bottleneck and stops exploring further loop unrolling.

Similar graphs for the other benchmarks can be viewed online,[2] each showing three projections from different axes of the Pareto frontier. Our web page can be used to interactively explore the positions of each data point on the three projections simultaneously, and view the corresponding generated C programs.

8.3 Discussion

As demonstrated by Figure 5b, SOAP3 generally produces accurate latency estimates. However, we have discovered a few notable discrepancies. For instance, gemver, mvt and syr2k all have significant differences between our estimated latency and the actual latency from synthesized RTL implementations. An inspection of these programs reveals that they all share a common programming idiom:

```
for (int i=0; i<N; i++)
  for (int j=0; j<N; j++)
    x[i] += ...;
```

We found that Vivado HLS occasionally fails to find the optimal schedule, predicted by SOAP3, that could pipeline this loop as tightly as possible. We fix this problem by rewriting the above code into:

```
for (int i=0; i<N; i++) {
  float sum = x[i];
  for (int j=0; j<N; j++)
    sum += ...;
  x[i] = sum;
}
```

This enables Vivado HLS to generate a hardware implementation with the expected II. The ratios in parentheses in Table 3 reflect the speedup by performing this simple fix.

9. RELATED WORK

Our work conducts program transformations on the MIR intermediate representation of Gao *et al.* [8]. Alternative program representations include *static* and *dynamic single*

assignment forms (SSA, DSA) [18, 19], and *control and data flow graphs* (CDFG) [20]. These representations are less suitable for our work because they are all statement-based and do not identify as many equivalent programs as MIRs do. Dependence graphs [9], on the other hand, are designed for the purpose of capturing data flow dependences in scheduling techniques, but they generally do not preserve enough information for us to reconstruct a program from the graph itself.

Several HLS tools exploit dependence graph restructuring to improve loop parallelism, which allows for a smaller initiation interval, and in turn faster programs. Tree height reduction [21] aims to balance an arithmetic expression tree using associativity and distributivity. Xilinx's Vivado HLS has a similar feature called *expression balancing* [5]. Neither of these methods produce optimal loop pipelining, as they do not examine the implications of loop-carried dependences. Canis *et al.* [3] propose a similar approach called *recurrence minimization*. They specifically tackle loop pipelining by incrementally restructuring dependence graphs to minimize longest paths of recurrences. Their method is subsequently incorporated in LegUp [14], an open-source academic HLS tool. However, both LegUp and Vivado HLS only apply associativity in their restructuring.

Most importantly, none of the above mentioned techniques and tools aim to minimize, or even analyze, the impact of their transformations on resource usage and accuracy. In many numerically sensitive programs, small round-off errors would result in catastrophic inaccurate results. Therefore, HLS tools generally disable this feature by default for floating-point computations. For this reason, we have developed SOAP3 to optimize not only program latencies, but also resource usage and accuracy.

Several authors have considered program transformations that improve accuracy or resource usage. Damouche *et al.* [22] and Panchekha *et al.* [23] propose methods for optimizing numerical accuracy in software using equivalences from real arithmetic, but they consider individual expressions only, and have no control structure manipulation, such as optimizing across basic blocks or partial loop unrolling. Hosangadi *et al.* [24] minimize resource usage by employing symbolic algebra to reduce the number of operations, and Peyman-

---

[2]https://admk.github.io/soap/plot.html

242

doust *et al.* [25] factorize polynomials using Gröbner bases; both only deal with polynomial arithmetic expressions. The SOAP2 tool of Gao *et al.* [8] simultaneously optimizes numerical programs for resource usage and accuracy, but is unable to analyze latency.

10. CONCLUSION

Minimizing the latency of loops is a central task for HLS tools that obtain FPGA implementations from numerical C programs. Loop latency can often be reduced by performing simple rewrites to minimize inter-iteration data dependences, but HLS tools cannot enable such rewrites by default because they may impact the accuracy of floating-point computations. This paper has presented the first tool that is able to automatically rewrite a given program to optimize latency, while controlling for accuracy and resource usage. Our experimental results suggest that, in fact, latency and accuracy are often *not* in conflict: that programs aggressively optimized for latency can also have minimal round-off errors, albeit with greater resource usage. We have demonstrated that SOAP3 can optimize commonly used code fragments from PolyBench [11] and Livermore Loops [10] to have up to a $12\times$ increase in performance, and up to $7\times$ reduction of round-off errors, at the cost of up to $4\times$ more resource utilization. Our tool is open-source and can be downloaded here: `https://github.com/admk/soap`.

Currently, SOAP3 supports only single-precision floating-point data types; we intend to extend this to multiple-precision floating-point and fixed-point types, and explore the impact on latency, resource utilization and numerical accuracy. This could, for instance, allow us to automate the manual design space exploration of matrix/vector multiplication architectures in [26].

11. ACKNOWLEDGMENTS

This work is supported by EPSRC (Grants EP/I020357/1, EP/K015168/1, and EP/I01236/1), Royal Academy of Engineering, and Imagination Technologies.

12. REFERENCES

[1] W. Meeus, K. Van Beeck, T. Goedemé, J. Meel, and D. Stroobandt, "An Overview of Today's High-Level Synthesis Tools," *Design Automation for Embedded Systems*, vol. 16, no. 3, pp. 31–51, 2012.

[2] Berkeley Design Technology, Inc., "An Independent Evaluation of: High-Level Synthesis Tools for Xilinx FPGAs," 2010. [Online]. Available: http://www.xilinx.com/technology/dsp/BDTI_techpaper.pdf

[3] A. Canis, S. D. Brown, and J. H. Anderson, "Modulo SDC scheduling with recurrence minimization in high-level synthesis," in *FPL*, 2014.

[4] N. J. Higham, *Accuracy and Stability of Numerical Algorithms*, 2nd ed. Philadelphia, PA, USA: Society for Industrial and Applied Mathematics, 2002.

[5] Xilinx, Inc., "Vivado Design Suite User Guide—High-Level Synthesis," 2015.

[6] X. Gao, S. Bayliss, and G. A. Constantinides, "SOAP: Structural optimization of arithmetic expressions for high-level synthesis," in *FPT, 2013*.

[7] C. Mouilleron, "Efficient computation with structured matrices and arithmetic expressions," Ph.D. dissertation, ENS LYON, 2011.

[8] X. Gao and G. A. Constantinides, "Numerical program optimization for high-level synthesis," in *FPGA*, 2015.

[9] B. R. Rau, "Iterative Modulo Scheduling: An Algorithm for Software Pipelining Loops," in *MICRO*, 1994.

[10] J. Dongarra and P. Luszczek, "Livermore Loops," in *Encyclopedia of Parallel Computing*. Springer US, 2011, pp. 1041–1043.

[11] L.-N. Pouchet, "PolyBench/C—the Polyhedral Benchmark suite," http://web.cse.ohio-state.edu/~pouchet/software/polybench/.

[12] S. Verdoolaege, "isl: An Integer Set Library for the Polyhedral Model," in *ICMS*, 2010.

[13] R. Bridson, "Fast poisson disk sampling in arbitrary dimensions," in *SIGGRAPH Sketches*, 2007.

[14] A. Canis, J. Choi, M. Aldham, V. Zhang, A. Kammoona, J. H. Anderson, S. Brown, and T. Czajkowski, "LegUp: High-level Synthesis for FPGA-based Processor/Accelerator Systems," in *FPGA*, 2011.

[15] G. Wang, W. Gong, and R. Kastner, "Operation Scheduling: Algorithms and Applications," in *High-Level Synthesis*. Springer, 2008.

[16] P. Li, P. Zhang, L.-N. Pouchet, and J. Cong, "Resource-aware throughput optimization for high-level synthesis," in *FPGA*, 2015.

[17] Xilinx, Inc., "Vivado Design Suite User Guide—Synthesis," 2015.

[18] B. Rau, "Data Flow and Dependence Analysis for Instruction Level Parallelism," in *Languages and Compilers for Parallel Computing*, ser. LNCS. Springer, 1992, vol. 589, pp. 236–250.

[19] R. Cytron, J. Ferrante, B. K. Rosen, M. N. Wegman, and F. K. Zadeck, "Efficiently computing static single assignment form and the control dependence graph," *ACM TOPLAS*, vol. 13, no. 4, pp. 451–490, Oct. 1991.

[20] D. D. Gajski and L. Ramachandran, "Introduction to high-level synthesis," *IEEE Design and Test of Computers*, vol. 11, no. 4, pp. 44–54, Oct. 1994.

[21] A. Nicolau and R. Potasmann, "Incremental tree height reduction for high level synthesis," in *DAC*, 1991.

[22] N. Damouche, M. Martel, and A. Chapoutot, "Intra-procedural optimization of the numerical accuracy of programs," in *Formal Methods for Industrial Critical Systems*, ser. LNCS. Springer, 2015, vol. 9128, pp. 31–46.

[23] P. Panchekha, A. Sanchez-Stern, J. R. Wilcox, and Z. Tatlock, "Automatically improving accuracy for floating point expressions," in *PLDI*, 2015.

[24] A. Hosangadi, F. Fallah, and R. Kastner, "Factoring and eliminating common subexpressions in polynomial expressions," in *ICCAD*, 2004.

[25] A. Peymandoust and G. De Micheli, "Using symbolic algebra in algorithmic level DSP synthesis," in *DAC*, 2001.

[26] D. Boland and G. Constantinides, "Revisiting the reduction circuit: A case study for simultaneous architecture and precision optimisation," in *FPT*, 2013.

Reducing Memory Requirements for High-Performance and Numerically Stable Gaussian Elimination

David Boland

Department of Electrical and Computer Systems Engineering
Monash University, Clayton, VIC 3800, Australia
david.boland@monash.edu

ABSTRACT

Gaussian elimination is a well-known technique to compute the solution to a system of linear equations and boosting its performance is highly desirable. While straightforward parallel techniques are limited either by I/O or on-chip memory bandwidth, block-based algorithms offer the potential to bridge this gap by interleaving I/O with computation. However, these algorithms require the amount of on-chip memory to be at least the square of the number of processing elements available. Using the latest generation Altera FPGAs with hardened floating-point units, this is no longer the case. It follows that the amount of on-chip memory limits performance, a problem that is only likely to increase unless on-chip memory dominates FPGA architecture. In addition to this limitation, existing FPGA implementations of block-based Gaussian elimination either sacrifice numerical stability or efficiency. The former limits the usefulness of these implementations to a small class of matrices, the latter limits its performance.

This paper presents a high-performance and numerically stable method to perform Gaussian elimination on an FPGA. This modified algorithm makes use of a deep pipeline to store the matrix and ensures that the peak performance is once again limited by the number of floating-point units that can fit on the FPGA. When applied to large matrices, this technique can obtain a sustained performance of up to 256 GFLOPs on an Arria 10, beginning to tap into the full potential of these devices. This performance is comparable to the peak that could be achieved using a simple block-based algorithm, with the performance on a Stratix 10 predicted to be superior. This is in spite of the fact that the underlying algorithm for the implementation in this paper, Gaussian elimination with pairwise pivoting, is more complex and applicable to a wider range of practical problems.

Keywords

Gaussian Elimination; Pairwise Pivoting; FPGA; Linear Algebra

1. INTRODUCTION

Computing the solution to a system of linear equations of the form $Ax = b$ (where A is a square matrix of order N, b and x

FPGA'16, February 21-23, 2016, Monterey, CA, USA

© 2016 ACM. ISBN 978-1-4503-3856-1/16/02. . . $15.00

DOI: http://dx.doi.org/10.1145/2847263.2847281

are vectors of length N) forms the basis of many problems in engineering and science. Gaussian elimination is perhaps the most well-known method to solve this type of problem, particularly for dense linear systems. As a result, methods to accelerate Gaussian elimination have been studied extensively. This paper revisits some of these ideas and shows how to apply them to modern FPGAs.

Gaussian elimination involves using a sequence of elementary row operations to transform a matrix into an upper triangular matrix. These operations include swapping two rows, multiplying a row by a non-zero value and adding a multiple of one row to another. A simple algorithm to create an upper triangular matrix involves first selecting a pivot element before subtracting multiples of the row containing the pivot element from the remaining rows. All remaining rows will then have a zero in the column of the pivot element. This process, known as forward elimination, can be repeated until an upper triangular matrix is formed. After applying the same transformations to the vector b, the solution to the system of linear equations can then be quickly computed using back substitution.

The primary method to speed up Gaussian elimination using hardware is through the use of parallelism. For the simple method discussed earlier, this could be achieved by subtracting multiple rows from the pivot row at once. However, the amount of parallelism obtainable is limited either by the amount of on-chip memory, if the matrix is pre-loaded onto the FPGA, or the I/O bandwidth if the matrix is loaded from off-chip RAM.

An alternative is to use a block-based matrix decomposition algorithm. Under such an approaches, the matrix is first broken into blocks, these blocks are then loaded into the on-chip memory, processed, and the resultant matrix is then passed back to global memory. Through double-buffering the matrix, it is possible interleave I/O with computation. However, as we will see in Section 2.1, on modern Altera FPGAs with hardened floating-point units [1], the amount of on-chip memory will limit the performance achievable of such approaches.

This paper demonstrates that through constructing a feed-forward datapath to perform Gaussian elimination, it is possible to take advantage of the matrix being held within the pipeline to mitigate this problem. Furthermore, because this datapath is simple and requires limited memory, it is possible to utilize many more of the available floating-point units in order to obtain a high performance. Furthermore, the design presented in this paper makes use of pairwise pivoting. This ensures that the algorithm is numerically stable, meaning it will be able to solve many more practical problems than basic block-based approaches.

The key contributions of this paper are:

- A scalable feed-forward numerically stable datapath to perform Gaussian elimination and solve practical problems for large matrices.

- A discussion how to pipeline inputs into this datapath to obtain a high sustained performance and some simple optimizations to boost efficiency.

- Highlighting the potential limitations of block-based algorithms on future generation FPGA architectures and emphasizing the importance of creating specialized designs to efficiently use the available hardware.

2. BACKGROUND

This section first discusses literature on simple block-based LU decomposition algorithms, which exhibit high performance. These designs are then compared with more numerically stable FPGA-based implementations of Gaussian elimination, highlighting the performance gap associated with these more complex algorithms.

2.1 Block-based LU decomposition

The FPGA designs exhibiting the best performance for Gaussian elimination or LU decomposition are implementations of block-based LU decomposition, pivoting along the main diagonal. There are many contributions in this area, some of the most recent include that by Zhang et al. [2], Wu et al. [3] and Jaiswal et al. [4]. These approaches divide a matrix into blocks, load blocks into memory and perform parallel computation on these blocks. Suppose an $M \times M$ block of memory is loaded into on-chip memory. The idea is that since the number of computations performed on this block is $O(M^3)$, but the number of cycles to load this block into on-chip memory is $O(M^2)$, if $O(M)$ operations are performed in parallel, it is possible to overlap computation with I/O and achieve high-performance. The work by Zhang et al. achieved 47 GFLOPs in single-precision arithmetic on a Stratix III, Wu et al. achieved 8.5 GFLOPs in double-precision on a Virtex 5 and Jaiswal achieved 15 GFLOPs in double-precision arithmetic on a Virtex 5, with all designs operating at near 100% efficiency (the design by Wu et al. at a lower clock frequency).

In all of these implementations it was stated that the maximum performance was limited by the number of DSPs. However, this is dependent on the target architecture. For example, on a Stratix V, the limitation is likely to move to the number of ALMs. This is because soft floating-point units are made up of a combination of ALMs and DSPs and comparing the top of the range Stratix III and Stratix V, the number of DSPs has increased by approximately a factor of 8, while the number of ALMs increased by approximately a factor of 2. However, more interestingly, on the new Altera FPGAs with hardened floating-point units, for the implementations by Jaiswal et al. and Zhang et al., the limitation of is likely to move to the amount of on-chip memory (the approach by Wu et al. is more scalable, but obtains a lower performance).

To illustrate why on-chip memory will become a bottleneck, we will analyse the approach by Zhang et al. Let us assume that the matrix must be stored in on-chip RAM. Using single precision data (32-bit) we can store up to 512 32-bit words using an Altera M20K. Using the buffering approach as described by Zhang et al. [2,4], we must store five matrices in on-chip RAM. Currently, in the Arria series, the largest number of available M20Ks is 2713 on the Altera Arria GT 1150. Five 512×512 matrices require $512 \times 5 = 2560$ M20Ks, which is the largest matrix that can be stored using these embedded RAMs. This is because storing a matrix of order greater than 512 would require an extra M20K per column. As a result, increasing the matrix order further would rely on the use of MLABs, at the cost of using valuable logic resources and increasing routing congestion. This memory limitation affects the performance because according to the approach by Zhang et al., the maximum

number of processing elements (PEs), each consisting of a floating-point multiply and subtract, is equal to the block size. The number of DSPs on the same chip is 1518, with each DSP able to perform a single precision floating-point multiply and subtract. This means that approximately only one third of the DSPs will be used. Applying the same analysis on a Stratix 10 GX2800 with 11721 M20Ks and 5760 DSPs, the maximum block size that could be stored on chip is 1024 (using 10240 M20Ks), meaning approximately one fifth of the available DSPs would be used.

The problem of on-chip memory limiting performance is likely to increase with future generation FPGAs, unless FPGA architectures move towards memory occupying an increasing portion of the chip, a decision that would negatively impact processing performance. This is because a block size of M will require M processing elements, but at least M^2 words to be stored in memory.

A second, but perhaps more important limitation of all of the block-based LU factorization schemes described earlier is that they are not numerically stable. Since none of the approaches perform any search for a pivot element, instead choosing the diagonal as a pivot row, it follows that these implementations are block-based implementation of a Gaussian elimination without partial pivoting. Unless the input matrix is diagonally dominant, this algorithm is unlikely to return a valid solution [5]. As such, in cases where the performance is limited by the number of floating-point operators that can fit on a chip, these simplified algorithms should be seen as an upper-bound on performance obtainable for any implementation of Gaussian elimination with partial pivoting, or its associated derivatives that are discussed in the following subsection.

2.2 Numerically stable Gaussian Elimination

Gaussian elimination with partial pivoting is the most well-known variant of Gaussian elimination. While not as numerically stable as full pivoting, it still exhibits strong numerical performance and requires far fewer operations to choose the pivot than full pivoting [5]. The algorithm is described in Figure 1. In this figure, $A_{i,j}$ represents the element of matrix A in the ith row and j^{th} column, $A_{i,:}$ represents the vector for the ith row of A and $A_{:,j}$ represents the vector for the jth column of A.

```
for i = 1; i ≤ N; i + + do
    pivot = max(abs(A_{:,i})) // Select pivot row
    temp = A_{pivot,:}
    A_{pivot,:} = A_{i,:}
    A_{i,:} = temp
    for j = i + 1; j ≤ N; j + + do // Forward Substitution
        for k = j; j ≤ N; j + + do
            A_{j,k} = A_{j,k} - (A_{j,i}/A_{i,i}) × A_{i,k}
        end for
        b_j = b_j - (A_{j,i}/A_{i,i}) × b_j
    end for
end for
for i = N; i > 0; i − − do // Back substitution
    temp2 = 0;
    for j = i + 1; j ≤ N; j + + do
        temp2 = temp2 + A_{i,j} × x_j
    end for
    x_i = (b_i − temp2)/A_{i,i}
end for
```

Figure 1: Gaussian elimination with partial pivoting.

The work by Matos et al [6] analyses this algorithm. This work assumes dedicated datapaths are used for the main operations (partial pivoting, forward elimination and back substitution), and some controller that manages dataflow and memory use. To boost performance, the pivot row is stored in on-chip RAM, but this limits the maximum matrix order. However, the greater limitation is that, as stated by the authors, "the inversion performance is directly proportional to the number of banks", or the I/O bandwidth. While FLOPs have not been quoted in this work, because this module essentially consists of loading an element onto the chip, performing a multiplication and subtraction, then passing the result back to external memory, one can estimate an upper bound on performance. If we assume pins are required for input and output we can give the following estimate: $\frac{\#\text{pins}/2 \times \text{max frequency} \times 2}{precision}$. For 512 pins and 32 bits (single precision) and a clock frequency of 400 MHz, this translates to about 6 GFLOPs.

Various authors have created similar approaches, each presenting different innovations. These include merging forward and backward elimination for improved memory storage [7], or computing the pivot at the same time as performing row reductions in double-precision [8]. However, all these approaches are limited by I/O bandwidth. For example, the architecture from [8] could only process four matrix elements in parallel per clock cycle. An alternative which stores the matrix in on-chip RAM achieved much higher performance, but was limited to matrix orders of less than 40, using a Virtex 5 [9, 10]. A related design consisting of a pipeline of processing elements, each buffering columns of the matrix achieved 6 GFLOPs (single) on a Stratix II [11]. However this implementation was designed to solve matrix orders of up to 1000, and even with this restriction, the amount of parallelism was limited by the on-chip RAM, a restriction we seek to eliminate in this paper.

The need for fast and numerically stable Gaussian elimination has led to the development number of alternative algorithms. These have been studied experimentally by the scientific computing community and been shown to exhibit similar numerical stability to Gaussian elimination with partial pivoting in practice [12]. However, to the best knowledge of the author, there is only one FPGA implementation: Tai et al. [13] developed an FPGA design for Tiled LU factorisation [14].

The algorithm for Tiled LU factorisation is given in Figure 2 and shown diagramatically in Figure 3. This consists of 4 kernels: DGETRF, which performs LU decomposition with partial pivoting for a tile; DGESSM, which applies the transformations returned from the LU decomposition to all tiles to the right; DTSTRF, which performs an LU decomposition on the block below the previous LU decomposition, compares this with the previous LU decomposition and performs partial pivoting between these decompositions to update the corresponding transformation matrices; DSSSSM, which applies the new transformation matrices to all tiles to the right.

```
for p = 0; p ≤ N/M; p + + do
    L_pp, U_pp, P_pp = DGETRF (A_pp);
    for q = p + 1; q ≤ N/M; q + + do
        U_pq = DGESSM (A_pq, L_pp, P_pp);
    end for
    for r = p + 1; r ≤ N/M; r + + do
        U_pp, L_rp, P_rp = DTSTRF (U_pp, A_rp);
        for q = p + 1; q ≤ N/M; q + + do
            U_pq, A_rq = DSSSSM (L_rp, P_rp, U_pq, A_rq);
        end for
    end for
end for
```

Figure 2: Tiled LU Decomposition algorithm [14] of a matrix A, where A is divided into $M \times M$ tiles.

Clearly this algorithm is much more complex than the block-based LU decomposition methods described in the previous subsection. As a result, the approach by Tai et al. only obtained a sustained performance of up to 9.8 GFLOPs in double precision on the same chip as the work by Jaiswal et al. This peak performance came at an efficiency of approximately 65%, using 37 processing

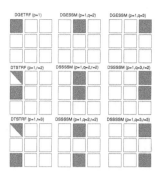

Figure 3: Tiled LU Decomposition [14].

elements on a tile size of 194, but peak efficiency of 83% was obtained with 20 processing elements and a block size of 247. Moreover, the author predicted that on future generation FPGAs, while the performance will increase with greater numbers of processing elements, its efficiency will decrease further, restricting its usefulness on more modern FPGAs that can hold many more processing elements. Once again, in contrast, the simpler solvers by Zhang et al., Wu et al. and Jaiswal et al., achieve close to 100% efficiency.

Tai et al. had suggested various methods to boost the efficiency, such as double-buffering the matrix blocks, but it is unclear precisely how much this could boost efficiency. In particular, the DGETRF and DTSTRF kernels are unlikely to reach maximum efficiency because of the required divisions, comparisons and row swaps. Note that because each M20k could be configured as 512×40, it is easy to share RAMs for the lower triangular matrices L_{rp} and binary permutation matrices P_{rp}. This implies that the performance limitation due to available memory is not increased in comparison to the method by Zhang et al.

Creating rectangular blocking methods to use more PEs: The block based methods discussed thus far have chosen the number of PEs to be less than or equal to the block size. This is suitable provided the block size is less than or equal to 512, because assuming each M20k is configured as 512×32 (or 512×33 to pack the L_{rp} and P_{rp} matrices), all of the internal memory bandwidth is being used. To demonstrate this, consider a parallel implementation of DSSSSM. If every PE requires input values from four matrices $L_{rp}, P_{rp}, U_{pq}, A_{rq}$ per clock cycle, 512 PEs will require input from 512×3 RAMs. For sustained performance, an additional 2×512 RAMs are required for double buffering of data. It makes sense to ensure each of these RAMs contain 512 elements.

However, for a Stratix 10, a näive choice of block size of 1024 by 1024, which uses 1024 processing elements would not make use of all the internal memory bandwidth. Instead, it may be preferable to adopt a rectangular block-based method. For example, once the leftmost matrices have been computed according to DGETRF and DTSTRF, then it is possible to perform DSSSSM for blocks to the right in parallel. Since the leftmost matrices could be re-used, each parallel implementation of DSSSSM would require 2 matrices (U_{pq} and A_{rq}) to be held in RAM and 2 further matrices for double buffering. Given 11721 M20Ks on a Stratix 10, using a block size of 512, one could store up to 22 blocks, allowing up to 5 parallel instances of DSSSSM to run. Since each instance could use 512 processing elements, this would use approximately $2.5\times$ the number of processing elements of the näive blocking approach using a block size of 1024 discussed earlier. However, 5 parallel instances of DSSSSM would require $5\times$ the I/O bandwidth for a single instance of block size 1024. Therefore, unless I/O bandwidth scales with the number of processing elements on future generation FPGAs, this limits the effectiveness of developing rectangular block-based algorithms.

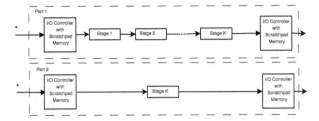

Figure 4: High-level view of datapath.

3. A NEW APPROACH

Throughout this paper, we assume that we are aiming to solve a large matrix that is held in off-chip memory and loaded into the FPGA. The high-level view of the circuit is summarized in Figure 4. This circuit consists of two parts, with the order in which these two parts update a matrix shown in Figure 5. Compared to the Tiled LU approach, Part 1 implements the equivalent of DGETRF, DGESSM, DTSTRF and DSSSSM for 2^K rows and Part 2 implements the equivalent of DTSTRF and DSSSSM for 2^K rows. However, we do not actually implement these kernels, instead, the work in this paper is based on the idea of pairwise pivoting [15].

Gaussian Elimination with pairwise pivoting performs row eliminations between pairs of rows of the matrix, returning one unchanged row and one row with a leading zero. This is done in parallel for several rows of the matrix. It then performs row elimination between pairs of unchanged rows and pairs of rows that now have a leading zero. This is repeated until an upper triangular matrix is formed, back substitution is then performed to return the final result. This article focuses only on forming the upper triangular matrix. It is assumed that back-substitution could be quickly performed on a CPU, given that it requires far fewer operations. In contrast to Gaussian elimination with partial pivoting, pairwise pivoting avoids the search to find the best pivot element for each column. This has a minor detrimental impact on the numerical stability, but has been found to still work on many practical problems [12] and allows the algorithm to be easily parallelised.

To maximise performance, the two parts of Figure 4 are made up of stages, each consisting of a parallel array of processing elements. This forms a deeply-pipelined feed-forward datapath that utilises most of the available resources on an FPGA. Through careful ordering of the input matrix into this pipeline, we are able store the matrix in this pipeline, limiting the memory requirements whilst still being able to obtain a high-performance by effectively utilizing the processing elements. The basic processing elements are first introduced in Section 3.1, before discussing work based on 2D systolic arrays [16] that has inspired the architecture for this paper in Section 3.2. A pipelining approach to improve performance is then discussed in Section 3.3, a method to make use of a shared divider in Section 3.4, an approach to scale this method to larger matrices in Section 3.5 and various optimizations in Section 3.6.

3.1 Processing elements

The basic processing element (PE) consists of a RAM, multiplexers, a multiplier, subtractor, various pipeline registers and some minimal control, as shown in Figure 6. This element takes in two rows of the matrix and produces two rows. As required for pairwise pivoting, one of the rows is unchanged, the other subtracts a multiple of the unchanged row from itself. For numerical stability, we want the row with the larger absolute value to remain unchanged. Therefore, before any processing, we perform a comparison of the leading elements of these two rows and swap the two rows accordingly.

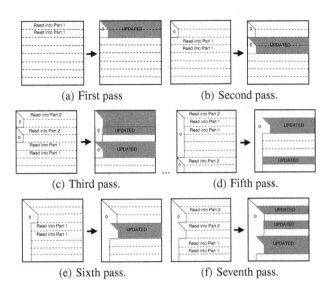

(a) First pass (b) Second pass.

(c) Third pass. (d) Fifth pass.

(e) Sixth pass. (f) Seventh pass.

Figure 5: Overview of how this approach updates a large matrix.

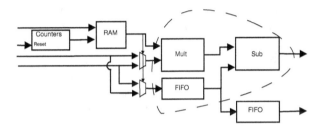

Figure 6: Basic Processing Element.

In this figure, the dotted line highlights three components that are all incorporated within a single DSP on an Arria 10 or Stratix 10 (assuming single precision). The control for a PE is very simple, consisting of counters and some hard-coded enable signals for the RAM. This helps to ensure that the overall design can run at a high clock frequency. Also note that in this diagram, there is no divider or comparator. The reason for this is that the divider and comparator are only used once for every row entering the PE. In contrast, the multiplier and subtractor are used for every element in the row. Instead, the divider and comparator are considered to be external shared resources, discussed in Section 3.4. At the beginning of a row, each processing element receives the appropriate multiplicand and stores this in the RAM. The importance of using RAMs instead of registers will become clear when discussing how the input to the matrix is pipelined in Section 3.3.

3.2 Ahmed-Delosme-Morf array

The design in this paper to perform pairwise pivoting is inspired by the Ahmed-Delosme-Morf 2-D systolic array [16]. In addition to parallelism, the major advantage of this systolic array over a software design is that the row swaps are performed without any writing back to memory. If desired, the lower triangular and permutation matrices can be recovered from this array [16]. However, to simplify the analysis in this paper, it is assumed that this is not required and we are only attempting to perform Gaussian elimination for an augmented matrix.

A slightly modified representation of the Ahmed-Delosme-Morf array is provided in Figure 7 to show its equivalence to the chosen representation used for this paper in Figure 8 (consider if the for-

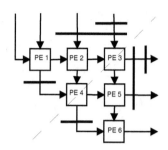

Figure 7: Ahmed-Delosme-Morf systolic array.

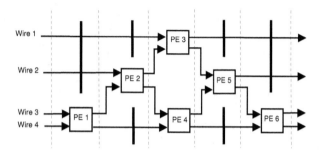

Figure 8: Alternative representation of Ahmed-Delosme-Morf systolic array. This performs the equivalent operations of Stages 1 and 2 of the new design.

mer circuit is rotated around the dotted line). In theses figures, and all subsequent figures in this paper, solid lines over wires are used to represent pipeline registers in the form of first-in-first-out (FIFO) buffers. The depth of these buffers is equivalent to the latency of an individual PE and allows the pipeline to be correctly synchronised. Since all the data moves in a single direction in this alternative representation, it is easier to understand and allows us to describe how the final design is developed in Section 3.3.

To get an intuitive understanding of how the circuit in Figure 8 works, we run through a simple example. In this example, we perform traditional Gaussian elimination with partial pivoting, as described in Figure 1, and also using the circuit described in Figure 8. For the traditional method the output is shown after each column has been eliminated. For the Ahmed-Delosme-Morf array, we see how the matrix flows through the circuit. To illustrate this flow, in Figure 9(c), the values corresponding to where a wire intersects a vertical dotted line on the circuit of Figure 8 are shown for several time steps, where a time step is equal to the delay of a PE. The stars (*) in this figure highlight the elements that are passed into the shared divider, discussed later in Section 3.4.

From this figure, it should be clear that each processing element reduces one of the two rows by a multiple of the other and that the upper output path holds the un-modified row. In particular, observe how after 5 PE delays, the second and third rows have been swapped. Finally, note that although the final matrices in Figure 9 are different for each method, after back substitution they will return the same solution.

In comparison to the Ahmed-Delosme-Morf array, the final design presented in this paper uses many fewer processing elements and less I/O bandwidth. In addition, whereas the Ahmed-Delosme-Morf array assumes that each PE contains its own divider, this approach makes use of a single divider through the use of pipeline stalls. Most importantly, whereas the Ahmed-Delosme-Morf array is designed to compute an upper-triangular matrix in a single pass, this design uses multiple passes. This allows us to perform Gaussian elimination for large matrices.

3.3 Increasing Parallelism

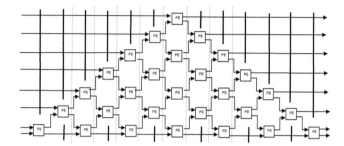

Figure 10: Ahmed-Delosme-Morf array with input bandwidth of 8 values.

Parallelism is increased in the Ahmed-Delosme-Morf array simply by expanding the array. This is demonstrated in Figure 10. This circuit assumes an input bandwidth of 8 elements.

Unfortunately, using this method to boost parallelism increases the I/O bandwidth requirements; this will restrict the maximum amount of parallelism. In contrast, in this paper we use pipelining and subsequent stages to boost the amount of parallelism.

The suggested pipelining structure involves changing the order in which elements are accessed from off-chip memory. In the example given in Figure 9, for the Ahmed-Delosme-Morf array, the first four values fed into the circuit are $A_{1,1}, A_{2,1}, A_{3,1}$ and $A_{4,1}$, which we denote as $A_{1:4;1}$. Using a similar notation, the next four values fed into the circuit are $A_{1:4;2}$, then $A_{1:4;3}$. The pipelining approach proposed in this paper only uses half the input bandwidth. We first feed the two values $A_{1:2;1}$ into the circuit, next we feed the values $A_{3:4;2}$ into the circuit. The subsequent pairs are $A_{1:2;2}$, then $A_{3:4;2}$.

In Figure 13, we analyse the output from the circuit given in Figure 11 for the same problem as in Figure 9. We assume this circuit is fed with this alternative input strategy. Note that for this analysis, we make use of the RAMs seen in Figure 6 to store the relevant multipliers and inputs to the multiplexers to switch the rows if necessary (i.e on even cycles the multiplier is $\frac{A_{2,1}}{A_{1,1}} = \frac{1}{2}$, on odd cycles it is $\frac{A_{4,1}}{A_{3,1}} = -\frac{1}{2}$).

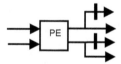

Figure 11: Stage 1. The output FIFOs are for one clock cycle.

Now compare Figure 9(c) with Figure 13(a). Notice that after 1 PE delay + 1 cycle, the output of Figure 11 is of a similar format to the inputs to PE 3 and PE 4 of Figure 8 after 2 PE delays. Similarly, after 1 PE delay + 3 cycles, the output of Figure 11 is of a similar format to the input to PE 3 and PE 4 of Figure 8 after 3 PE delays. It follows that using the structure of PE 3, PE 4, PE 5 and PE 6 from Figure 8, we could create an upper triangular matrix. The resulting circuit is given in Figure 12.

To illustrate how this circuit works, Figure 13(b) shows how the data has flows through the circuit of Figure 12 for the same problem from Figure 9. In this analysis, we assume that the outputs from Stage 1 are sampled every other clock cycle. Note that once again this creates a different final matrix, but after back substitution, the final result is still the same.

$$A = \begin{bmatrix} 16 & 4 & 8 & -12 & 4 \\ 8 & 10 & 12 & -10 & 4 \\ 4 & -7 & -3 & 7 & 11 \\ -2 & -4.5 & -3.5 & 10.5 & 3.5 \end{bmatrix} \text{ and } b = \begin{bmatrix} 4 \\ 4 \\ 11 \\ 3.5 \end{bmatrix} \qquad \text{Augmented matrix: } \begin{bmatrix} 16 & 4 & 8 & -12 & 4 \\ 8 & 10 & 12 & -10 & 4 \\ 4 & -7 & -3 & 7 & 11 \\ -2 & -4.5 & -3.5 & 10.5 & 3.5 \end{bmatrix}$$

(a) Compute the solution to $Ax = b$

Row operations for 1st column:
$$\begin{bmatrix} 16 & 4 & 8 & -12 & 4 \\ 0 & 8 & 8 & -4 & 2 \\ 0 & -8 & -5 & 10 & 10 \\ 0 & -4 & -2.5 & 9 & 4 \end{bmatrix}$$

Row operations for 2nd column:
$$\begin{bmatrix} 16 & 4 & 8 & -12 & 4 \\ 0 & 8 & 8 & -4 & 2 \\ 0 & 0 & 3 & 6 & 12 \\ 0 & 0 & -1.5 & 7 & 5 \end{bmatrix}$$

Row operations for 3rd column:
$$\begin{bmatrix} 16 & 4 & 8 & -12 & 4 \\ 0 & 8 & 8 & -4 & 2 \\ 0 & 0 & 3 & 6 & 12 \\ 0 & 0 & 0 & 4 & -1 \end{bmatrix}$$

(b) Method 1: Traditional Gaussian elimination

Initial Inputs:
```
16  0  0  0  0  0
 8  0  0  0  0  0
 4* 0  0  0  0  0
-2* 0  0  0  0  0
```

After 1 PE delay:
```
  4   16  0  0  0  0
 10    8* 0  0  0  0
 -7    4* 0  0  0  0
-4.5   0  0  0  0  0
```

After 2 PE delays:
```
  8    4  16*  0  0  0
 12   10   8*  0  0  0
 -3   -7   0   0  0  0
-3.5  -8   0   0  0  0
```

After 3 PE delays:
```
-12    8   4   16  0  0
-10   12  10    0  0  0
  7   -3 -12*   0  0  0
10.5  -5  -8*   0  0  0
```

After 4 PE delays:
```
 4  -12   8    4   16  0
 4  -10  12    8*   0  0
11    7  -9  -12*   0  0
3.5  14  -5    0    0  0
```

After 5 PE delays:
```
0   4  -12   8    4  16
0   4  -10   8  -12   0
0  11   12  -9    0   0
0   9   14   1    0   0
```

After 6 PE delays:
```
0  0  4  -12   8    4
0  0  4   -4  -9  -12
0  0  9   12   2*   0
0  0  9    6   1*   0
```

After 7 PE delays:
```
0  0  0  4  -12   8
0  0  0  2   12  -9
0  0  0  9    4   2
0  0  0  3    6   0
```

After 8 PE delays:
```
0  0  0  0  4   12
0  0  0  0  9  -12
0  0  0  0  8    4
0  0  0  0  3    4
```

After 9 PE delays:
```
0  0  0  0  0   4
0  0  0  0  0   9
0  0  0  0  0   8
0  0  0  0  0  -1
```

Final matrix output:
$$\begin{bmatrix} 16 & 4 & 8 & -12 & 4 \\ 0 & -12 & -9 & 12 & 9 \\ 0 & 0 & 2 & 4 & 8 \\ 0 & 0 & 0 & 4 & -1 \end{bmatrix}$$

(c) Method 2: Ahmed-Delosme-Morf. Output shown for locations where wires cross dotted lines in Figure 8 after different numbers of delays for each processing element.

Figure 9: Example comparing traditional Gaussian Elimination with Gaussian elimination with pairwise pivoting using the Ahmed-Delosme-Morf array. We assume back substitution is subsequently performed on a CPU.

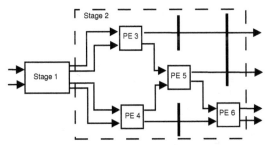

Figure 12: Stages 1 and 2.

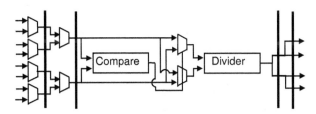

Figure 14: Pipelined Divider.

3.4 Shared divider

The use of a shared divider can save substantial area. For simplicity, one divider per stage is implemented. The implementation is simple: the input to every PE is also given to a multiplexer that feeds the common divider, the output from the divider fans out to every processing element. This divider includes a comparator to determine whether to swap rows; this output is also fanned out to the various PEs. This is possible because at no time is the divider required by more than one processing element. This can be seen from the flow in Figure 9(c), where the two values that are passed into the divider are highlighted using a '*'.

The control to the multiplexer is therefore straightforward, consisting of a counter and comparator. A minor problem is that the number of inputs to the multiplexer and fanout to the various processing elements can create long delays. In order to overcome this issue, we implement a pipelined multiplexer and pipelined fanout. Figure 14 illustrates this for a divider circuit choosing between four different pairs of inputs. In this diagram, the solid vertical lines represent pipeline registers. Note that the amount of pipelining could be reduced to save resources (for example, using four-to-one multiplexers instead of two-to-one multiplexers).

3.4.1 Pipeline Stalls

One complexity of using this shared divider is that it requires pipeline stalls. During a pipeline stall, we must pause the input to the circuit and store the outputs from each processing element for the duration of a stall. However, pipeline stalls introduce very little additional hardware. This is because we know the order of operations a priori, meaning we can work out when to stall inputs to the circuits, and when to store outputs. The control for each processing element can be implemented using counters and hard-coded enable signals. A similar controller is required for the input scratchpad memory buffer.

Table 1 illustrates a simplified schedule for this circuit consisting of two stages. This schedule assumes that each processing element requires a single cycle to process data and the divider requires two cycles. During each cycle, the element of the matrix that is inputted to each PE is shown (the numbers for each PE correspond to the numbers in Figures 11 and Figures 12), assuming that no swapping has been performed (note swapping will not affect the schedule, only the output from a PE). This table also show which inputs are passed to the divider.

Looking from cycle 19 onwards in this table, the processing elements from Stage 1 are fully utilised, whilst the processing ele-

Initial inputs:		After 1 PE delay:		After 1 PE delay+1 cycle:		After 1 PE delay+2 cycles:		After 1 PE delay+3 cycle:	
	0		0		16		4		4
16*	0	4*	16	4	4	-7	4	8	-7
8*	0	$-2*$	0	10	0	-4.5	8	12	8
	0		0		0		0		-8

(a) Simplified stage 1. Output on each wire corresponding to Figure 11

Initial Inputs:				After 1 PE delay:				After 2 PE delays:				After 3 PE delays:				After 4 PE delays:			
16*	0	0	0	4	16	0	0	8	4	16	0	-12	8	4	16	4	-12	8	4
4*	0	0	0	-7	0	0	0	-3	$-8*$	0	0	7	-5	-8	0	11	10	-5	-8
0	0	0	0	8*	0	0	0	8	8*	0	0	-4	8	0	0	2	-4	3*	0
0	0	0	0	$-8*$	0	0	0	-5	0	0	0	14	3	0	0	9	10	3*	0

After 5 PE delays:				After 6 PE delays:				After 7 PE delays:				Final matrix output:				
0	4	-12	8	0	0	4	-12	0	0	0	4	16	4	8	-12	4
0	10	10	-5	0	0	10	10	0	0	0	10	0	-8	-5	10	10
0	2	6	3	0	0	12	6	0	0	0	12	0	0	3	6	12
0	11	10	0	0	0	11	4	0	0	0	-1	0	0	0	4	-1

(b) Stage 2. Output on each wire corresponding to Figure 12

Figure 13: Example performing Gaussian Elimination using the pipelining approach described in Section 3.3, using the circuits from Figure 11 for Stage 1 from Figure 12 for Stage 2. We assume back substitution is subsequently performed on a CPU.

Table 1: Example schedule and pipeline stalls for inputs to various PEs and Divider for Stage 1 and Stage 2 with interleaved rows. $A_{1,2;1}$ represents $A_{1,1}$ and $A_{2,1}$ entering the associated PE. S represents a pipeline stall for the associated PE.

Cycle	Stage 1	Stage 2				Divider
	PE	PE 3	PE 4	PE 5	PE 6	
1	S					$A_{1,2;1}$
2	S					
3	$A_{1,2;1}$					
4	S					$A_{3,4;1}$
5	S					
6	$A_{3,4;1}$					
7	S	S				$A_{1,3;1}$
8	$A_{1,2;2}$	S				
9	$A_{3,4;2}$	$A_{1,3;1}$	$A_{2,4;1}$			
10	S	S	S	S	S	$A_{2,4;2}$
11	S	S	S	S	S	
12	S	$A_{1,3;2}$	$A_{2,4;2}$	$A_{2,3;1}$		
13	$A_{1,2;3}$	S	S	S	S	$A_{2,3;2}$
14	$A_{3,4;3}$	S	S	S	S	
15	$A_{1,2;4}$	$A_{1,3;3}$	$A_{2,4;3}$	$A_{2,3;2}$	$A_{3,4;1}$	
16	$A_{3,4;4}$			$A_{2,3;3}$	$A_{3,4;2}$	
17	S	S	S	S	S	$A_{3,4;3}$
18	S	S	S	S	S	
19	$A_{1,2;5}$	$A_{1,3;4}$	$A_{2,4;4}$		$A_{3,4;3}$	
20	$A_{3,4;5}$			$A_{2,3;4}$		
21	$A_{1,2;6}$	$A_{1,3;5}$	$A_{2,4;5}$		$A_{3,4;4}$	
22	$A_{3,4;6}$			$A_{2,3;5}$		

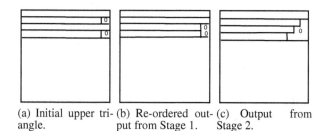

(a) Initial upper triangle. (b) Re-ordered output from Stage 1. (c) Output from Stage 2.

Figure 15: Summary of operations in Stage 1 and Stage 2.

that its output is similar to the input to the second half of the circuit shown in Figure 8. Therefore, using an appropriate circuit, described in Figure 12, we can eliminate further rows, forming a larger initial upper triangular matrix, as shown in Figure 15(c).

To form an even larger initial upper triangular matrix, we perform a similar process. The corresponding circuit is shown in Figure 17. First, we interleave the input rows slightly differently: we first read $A_{1,2;1}$, then $A_{3,4;1}$, then $A_{5,6;1}$ and finally $A_{7,8;1}$; we then read $A_{1,2;2}$, then $A_{3,4;2}$, then $A_{5,6;2}$ and finally $A_{7,8;2}$. In Stage 1, which consists of a single processing element, we perform four row eliminations producing an output as shown in Figure 16(a). In Stage 2, we then take these outputs and form two initial upper triangles of double the height, as shown in Figure 16(c). If we then re-order the outputs from Stage 2 to be of the form of Figure 16(d), we can use a circuit similar to the second half of the circuit for Figure 8 with twice the input bandwidth (this corresponds to the second half of the circuit shown in Figure 10) to form a final upper triangular matrix, as shown in Figure 16(e).

With infinite hardware, we could repeat this process until we form an upper triangular matrix. However, for very large matrices this is not possible in practice. Instead, as shown in the high-level view of this approach in Figure 5, to ensure sustained performance we wish to create a different output format. To achieve this, suppose we replaced PEs 8, 11, 13, 14, 15 and 16 from Figure 17 with FIFO buffers (or equivalently, replaced PEs 8 and 11 with FIFO buffers and remove PEs 13, 14, 15 and 16 and all FIFO buffers above these elements). If you consider that the lower path for each PE introduces a zero, one could imagine that the output of the circuit would appear as shown in Figure 16(f). The final stage (Stage K) will take this form.

ments from Stage 2 are utilised every other cycle. Importantly, this means that the pipeline stalls have little impact on the sustained performance (Section 3.5 discuss how to use fewer PEs and spread the computation over two cycles to boost the efficiency), and this is true in the general case with careful scheduling.

3.5 Pipelining for Stages 2 to K

This section first provides a high-level summary of the pipelining approach described in Section 3.3 before illustrating how it could be extended to larger matrices.

We first form an augmented matrix of A and b, and read the first four rows of the input matrix into a single processing element in an interleaved fashion. This processing element performs two row eliminations producing an output as shown in Figure 15(a). The output rows are then re-ordered, as shown in Figure 15(b), such

250

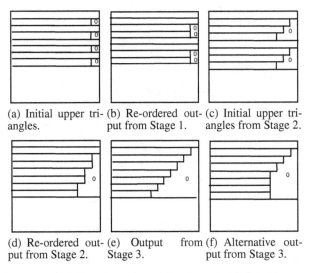

(a) Initial upper triangles. (b) Re-ordered output from Stage 1. (c) Initial upper triangles from Stage 2.

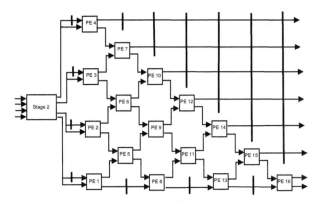

(d) Re-ordered output from Stage 2. (e) Output from Stage 3. (f) Alternative output from Stage 3.

Figure 16: Summary of operations in Stages 1, 2 and 3.

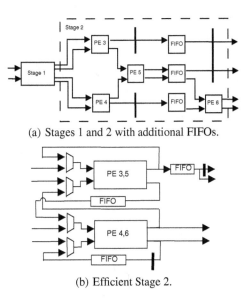

(a) Stages 1 and 2 with additional FIFOs.

(b) Efficient Stage 2.

Figure 18: Optimizing Stage 2 using FIFOs.

Unfortunately, for subsequent stages the number of FIFOs required, as well as the delay of the FIFOs would increase exponentially. This would eventually consume most of the memory of the FPGA, which this approach attempts to avoid. An alternative circuit with substantially reduced memory requirements is suggested in Figure 19(a). This uses a separate PE to process the work that would be performed by PE 6. Note that this circuit has an additional output FIFO because a single PE performs the work that would be performed by PE 3 and PE 5, producing an output every cycle. The size of this FIFO is the delay of one PE.

This alternative scales much better with increasing number of stages. The associated circuit for Stage 3, which receives valid data every four cycles, is given in Figure 19(b). Using this circuit, during one cycle, we perform the operation that would be performed by PEs 1, 2, 3 and 4 from Figure 17, the next cycle the work by PEs 5, 6 and 7, then the work by PEs 8, 9 and 10 and finally the work by PEs 11 and 12. To avoid introducing any additional delay, using a second circuit consisting of two PEs, in the next cycle we perform the operation that would be performed by PEs 13 and 14, the next cycle the work by PE 15, and finally the work by PE 16. Since this second circuit also only receives valid data every four cycles, this sharing will not cause any problems. For this circuit the size of the FIFO is equal to the delay of the second circuit (3 times the delay of one PE).

In general, for stage M, 2^{M-1} words are received every 2^{M-1} clock cycles. Using M PEs in the first half of the circuit and $M/2$ PEs in the second half of the circuit and a FIFO of depth $M/2 - 1$ times the delay of a PE, we can implement the desired behavior without introducing any additional delay. Note that using the alternative approach of FIFOs, such as that shown for Stage 2 in Figure 18(b), we would not require the $M/2$ PEs for the second half of the circuit. It follows that this alternative approach is only 66% efficient. Furthermore, for Stage-K, where fewer PEs are required, as discussed in Section 3.5, this efficiency decreases to 50%. However, unlike the work by Tai et al, this efficiency will not decrease further with greater numbers of PEs.

3.7 I/O requirements

Stage 1, as described in Figure 11, assumes an input bandwidth of two words per cycle. Once the pipeline is full, it will output 2

Figure 17: Stages 2 and 3.

3.6 Optimizing Stages 2-K

The problem with the initial design described in Figures 12 and 17 is that because Stage 2 only receives valid data every other clock cycle, its PEs will only perform useful computation half of the time. Similarly, Stage 3 will only receive valid data every four clock cycles, meaning its PEs will only perform useful computation one quarter of the time, and Stage K will only receive valid data every 2^{K-1} clock cycles. This section provides some suggestions regarding how to re-use hardware.

For Stage 2, since we only receive valid data every other cycle, ideally we would share the work from 4 PEs using 2 PEs. During one cycle, we perform the operation that would be performed by PEs 3 and 4 from Figure 12, in the other cycle we perform the operation that would be performed by PEs 5 and 6. Unfortunately, PE 6 needs the lower output from PE 5 before it can run, making this more difficult to achieve.

One method to achieve this, is based on an alternative design, shown in Figure 18(a), where FIFOs are added to all wires between PE 5 and PE 6. Clearly the addition of FIFOs will not affect the output of the circuit, only delay it. Provided the depth of these FIFOs is greater than two times the delay of a PE, then because we only received valid input every other cycle, we could create a simple architecture that would only require 2 PEs for this circuit. This is given in Figure 18(b). Once the pipeline is full, this circuit would be 100% efficient.

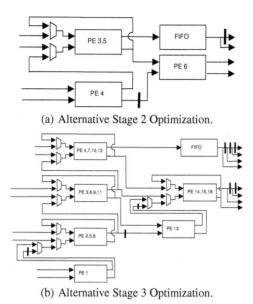

(a) Alternative Stage 2 Optimization.

(b) Alternative Stage 3 Optimization.

Figure 19: Optimizing Stages 2 and 3 without introducing any additional delay.

words per cycle. Stage 2 receives these 2 words every cycle and produces 4 words every 2 cycles. Stage 3 receives these 4 words every 4 cycles and produces 8 words every 4 cycles. It follows that Stage K will produce 2^K values every 2^{K-1} cycles. Provided the output from Stage K to external memory is spread over these 2^{K-1} cycles, altogether, the circuit must on average read two values and write two values every clock cycle. Since the additional Stage K in Part 2 of Figure 4 will have the same I/O behavior, a total of four values are read and written every cycle. The external I/O bandwidth requirements are therefore the word size (32 bits for IEEE single precision) $\times 8 \times$ the operating frequency. Assuming a frequency of 250MHz, this is $32 \times 8 \times 0.25 = 64$ Gbps.

Let us assume the matrix is held in off-chip DRAM. An Altera Arria 10 supports DDR4 up to 2666Mbps. The memory access pattern for this technique is regular — columns of 2^K elements are read to and written back to memory — so assuming the matrix is transposed, the DRAM should perform quite efficiently. Therefore, through using a memory controller with a scratchpad memory to buffer the data from DRAM before it is passed into the circuit, the I/O requirements should be well within the capability of a single $\times 72$ DDR4 SDRAM interface.

If necessary, there are simple methods to reduce the I/O requirements for this circuit. These include performing more sharing between the processing elements (for example, if we halved the input data rate to Stages 2 to K, we would only require half the processing elements per stage, we could then add more stages to use all the available processing elements on an FPGA), or removing the separate Stage K in part 2 of Figure 4. Instead the single Stage K could be re-used, with only a slight modification of the method to update a large matrix described in Figure 5. Alternatively, one could employ coding schemes to improve external memory bandwidth [17], or make use of additional DDR interfaces.

Of greater importance is that the external I/O bandwidth requirement is independent of the number of stages K. Thus assuming future devices could support greater numbers of processing elements, memory bandwidth is not likely to become an issue, unlike using a rectangular blocking approach, as discussed in Section 2.

4. RESULTS

The circuit described in Section 3 was simulated using Modelsim to verify the functionality, then synthesized, targeting an Arria 10 GT 1150. All of the floating-point units were generated using Altera Megafunctions. As stated previously, it is assumed that the FPGA is attached to off-chip DDR4 SDRAM to store the entire large matrix. For the simulation, a testbench was used to delay the input as required for the pipeline stalls, simulating the behavior of the memory controller mentioned in Section 3.4.1. Therefore this part of the circuit is not taken into account in the synthesis results, neither are any external memory controllers. However, this should require relatively little additional hardware and have minimal impact on the results.

Table 2 states the post place and route resource use for various entities and the overall design with $K = 9$ (where K corresponds to the number of stages, as shown in Figure 4). This table highlights that the individual processing elements require little hardware: a DSP implementing the multiplication and subtraction, an MLAB to create the FIFO, a M20K to store the multipliers and switch signals and some extra control logic. It should be noted that since the maximum number of multipliers stored for any PE is is given by 2^{K-1}, each PE may require additional M20Ks for larger designs, but this will still be less than that required by block based methods. The additional 3 M20Ks and 4 DSPs for Stage 1 are for the divider. Stages 1 and 9 use one divider, Stages 2 to 8 use two. Ignoring the divider, the ALMs and DSPs for each stage increase exponentially. This is expected because the number of PEs doubles for each stage, as well as the hardware required for the pipelined multiplexer and pipelined fanout for each shared divider and any other pipeline registers. The additional M20Ks between Stages 2 and 8 are because Quartus has implemented some of the output pipelined stage delays using M20Ks instead of MLABs. This corresponds to up to two additional M20Ks per PE, but once again, this is still less than that required by the block-based algorithms and could be reduced with some optimization.

In Figure 20, the GFLOPs for these implementations is plotted. This is calculated as the total number of operations required to perform forward substitution for Gaussian elimination, divided by the total runtime (number of cycles times the operating frequency). The operating frequency was found to be 250MHz.

Table 2: Resource use for various entities for design of $K = 9$

	Resource Use		
Entity	ALMs (1000s)	DSPs	M20Ks
Individual PE	0.15	1	1
Stage 1	0.9	5	4
Stage 2	2.6	11	18
Stage 3	3.6	14	27
Stage 4	5.7	20	45
Stage 5	10	32	80
Stage 6	19	56	146
Stage 7	35	104	280
Stage 8	70	200	542
Stage 9	95	260	395
Full design	338	962	1932

This graph highlights that high performance has been attained on an Arria 10. For comparison purposes, we briefly estimate the performance of block-based LU decomposition algorithms on these devices. On an Arria 10, as stated in Section 2, using the method by Zhang et al., the maximum block size would be 512. Assuming a similar clock frequency to the design of this paper, this translates to up to $512 \times 2 \times 0.25 = 256$ GFLOPs (assuming 100% efficiency). While this is comparable to the design of this paper, the method by Zhang et al. will only work on diagonally dominant matrices. A comparison to the approach by Tai et al. applying Tiled LU,

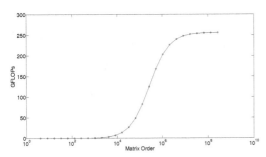

Figure 20: Performance vs matrix size.

which would be comparable in terms of numerical performance, is difficult due to the predicted decreasing efficiency with increasing number of PEs, however, it is will almost certainly be less than that achievable using the simpler block-based methods.

4.1 Predicted performance on next-generation FPGAs

While the results from the previous section demonstrate high-performance on the Altera Arria 10, it is possible that it may have an even greater impact on the next-generation FPGAs. Since Altera is yet to provide the device support files for this architecture to compile this design, the performance on a Stratix 10 GX2800 (933K ALMs, 5760 DSPs, 11520 M20Ks) is estimated by extrapolating the synthesis results in Table 2. A design containing two instances of this circuit, one for $K = 9$ and one for $K = 10$ should fit on the device. This is a conservative estimate and ignores any architecture optimizations in Stratix 10 which may reduce logic use further. The I/O constraints for two circuits should be easy to satisfy assuming multiple DDR interfaces, given the analysis in Section 3.7. Assuming a similar clock frequency, the performance of such a design would be approximately 765 GFLOPs.

Comparing once again against a basic block-based algorithm, assuming a maximum block size of 1024 on a Stratix 10 and a similar clock frequency, this translates to up to $1024 \times 2 \times 0.25 = 512$ GFLOPs (assuming 100% efficiency), which is significantly lower. If it were possible to create a rectangular block-based method, as proposed in Section 2, this may translate to up to $2560 \times 2 \times 0.25 = 1280$ GFLOPs. However, the latter design will require significantly greater I/O bandwidth. One should also note that CPU designs have also achieved high performance; for example in [12], it is claimed up to 225 GFLOPs (double) using 2 8-core Sandy-Bridge CPUs clocked at 2.6 GHz. However, as stated in previous literature on FPGA-based Gaussian elimination, one can expect a considerable performance-per-watt improvement using the FPGA design [2–4]. Such analysis is reserved for future work.

5. CONCLUSION

This paper presents a novel approach to perform Gaussian elimination with pairwise pivoting. Through carefully ordering the inputs, it is possible to store the matrix within a deeply-pipelined feed-forward datapath in order to extract parallelism. This ensures that the maximum performance is limited by the number of floating-point units that can be placed on the FPGA. This paper also highlighted that the performance of block-based methods on latest generation FPGA architectures will by limited by on-chip memory, and argues that this limitation will become increasingly important unless FPGA manufacturers choose to use a significantly larger proportion of the chip as on-chip memory. Finally, since this design is based on pairwise pivoting, it is more numerically stable than the existing high-performance basic block-based implementa-

tions on an FPGA. This means that it is applicable to many more practical problems. At the same time, this design can still achieve comparable or potentially superior performance to these simpler block-based methods and outperform all existing numerically stable implementations of Gaussian elimination on on FPGA. In the future, methods could be investigated to improve this architecture by boosting its efficiency further. This will involve more careful re-use of processing elements. It would also be interesting to analyze the numerical behavior of this circuit as a function of precision in order to understand any benefits an FPGA may have over a processor due to the freedom to implement variable precision arithmetic.

6. REFERENCES

[1] M. Parker, "Technical White Paper: Understanding Peak Floating-Point Performance Claims," Altera, Tech. Rep., 06 2014.

[2] W. Zhang, V. Betz, and J. Rose, "Portable and Scalable FPGA-based Acceleration of a Direct Linear System Solver," *ACM Trans. Reconfigurable Technol. Syst.*, vol. 5, no. 1, pp. 6:1–6:26, 2012.

[3] G. Wu, Y. Dou, J. Sun, and G. Peterson, "A High Performance and Memory Efficient LU Decomposer on FPGAs," *IEEE Transactions on Computers*, vol. 61, no. 3, pp. 366–378, 2012.

[4] M. Kumar Jaiswal and N. Chandrachoodan, "FPGA-Based High-Performance and Scalable Block LU Decomposition Architecture," *IEEE Transactions on Computers*, vol. 61, no. 1, pp. 60–72, 2012.

[5] N. Higham, "Gaussian elimination," *Computational Statistics*, vol. 3, pp. 230–238, 2011.

[6] G. de Matos and H. Neto, "On Reconfigurable Architectures for Efficient Matrix Inversion," in *Int. Conf. on Field Programmable Logic and Applications*, 2006, pp. 1–6.

[7] ——, "Memory Optimized Architecture for Efficient Gauss-Jordan Matrix Inversion," in *Southern Conference on Programmable Logic*, 2007, pp. 33–38.

[8] R. Duarte, H. Neto, and M. Vestias, "Double-precision Gauss-Jordan Algorithm with Partial Pivoting on FPGAs," in *Euromicro Conference on Digital System Design, Architectures, Methods and Tools*, 2009, pp. 273–280.

[9] J. Arias-Garcia, R. Jacobi, C. Llanos, and M. Ayala-Rincon, "A suitable FPGA implementation of floating-point matrix inversion based on Gauss-Jordan elimination," in *Southern Conference on Programmable Logic*, 2011, pp. 263–268.

[10] J. Arias-Garcia, C. Llanos, M. Ayala-Rincon, and R. Jacobi, "A fast and low cost architecture developed in FPGAs for solving systems of linear equations," in *IEEE Third Latin American Symposium on Circuits and Systems*, 2012, pp. 1–4.

[11] G. Wu, Y. Dou, Y. Lei, J. Zhou, M. Wang, and J. Jiang, "A Fine-grained Pipelined Implementation of the LINPACK Benchmark on FPGAs," in *Int. Symp. on Field Programmable Custom Computing Machines*, 2009, pp. 183–190.

[12] S. Donfack, J. Dongarra, M. Faverge, M. Gates, J. Kurzak, P. Luszczek, and I. Yamazaki, "On Algorithmic Variants of Parallel Gaussian Elimination: Comparison of Implementations in Terms of Performance and Numerical Properties," LAPACK Working Note, Tech. Rep. 280, 2013.

[13] Y.-G. Tai, C.-T. Dan Lo, and K. Psarris, "Scalable Matrix Decompositions with Multiple Cores on FPGAs," *Microprocess. Microsyst.*, vol. 37, no. 8, pp. 887–898, 2013.

[14] A. Buttari, J. Langou, J. Kurzak, and J. Dongarra, "A Class of Parallel Tiled Linear Algebra Algorithms for Multicore Architectures," *Parallel Computing*, vol. 35, no. 1, pp. 38–53, 2009.

[15] J. H. Wilkinson, *The Algebraic Eigenvalue Problem*. Oxford University Press, 1965.

[16] Y. Robert, *The Impact of Vector and Parallel Architectures on the Gaussian Elimination Algorithm*. New York, NY, USA: Halsted Press, 1990.

[17] P. Grigoras, P. Burovskiy, E. Hung, and W. Luk, "Accelerating SpMV on FPGAs by Compressing Nonzero Values," in *Int. Symp. on Field-Programmable Custom Computing Machines*, 2015, pp. 64–67.

FGPU: An SIMT-Architecture for FPGAs

Muhammed Al Kadi, Benedikt Janssen, Michael Huebner
Chair for Embedded Systems for Information Technology
Ruhr University of Bochum
{muhammed.alkadi, benedikt.janssen, michael.huebner}@rub.de

ABSTRACT

Driven by its high flexibility, good performance and energy efficiency, GPGPU has taken on an increasingly important role in embedded systems. In this paper, we present the basic core of FGPU: a GPU-like, scalable and portable integer soft SIMT-processor implemented in RTL and optimized for FPGA synthesis with a single-level cache system. Compared to a performance-optimized MicroBlaze implementation on the same FPGA, the biggest implemented core of FGPU achieves average wall clock speedups of 49x and a measured power saving of 3.7x with an area overhead of 17.7x. Compared to an ARM CPU with a NEON vector processor, we measured an average speedup of 3.5x over the used benchmark. FGPU is highly parametrizable and it does not contain any manufacturer-specific IP-cores or primitives.

Keywords

GPGPU; SIMT; soft GPU; FPGA

1. INTRODUCTION

The official birth of General Purpose computing on Graphical Processing Units (GPGPU) was announced by Nvidia in 2007 as CUDA was introduced [14]. One year later, the Khronos group published the OpenCL specifications [10] as the manufacturer-independent programming language in this domain. Since that time, the application areas of GPUs expanded remarkably: not only on top of graphic cards in personal computers, but also in high performance computing platforms and embedded systems. GPUs have been used as accelerators in many supercomputers all over the world [1]. Nowadays, they can be programmed efficiently using high level languages, such as MATLAB [13].

Industry quickly recognized the advantages of GPGPU in embedded applications. Embedded GPUs, programmable with CUDA [15] or OpenCL [6], have been available since 2008. Current embedded Systems-On-Chips (SoCs) tend to integrate a hard GPU-core next to an ARM-CPU [6] or the

FPGA Programmable Logic (PL) [23]. Researchers in contrast, have put less focus on developing GPU architectures. Instead, many projects have focused on synthesizing tasks for FPGAs from high level GPU languages [16][17][22]. Others have tried to schedule kernels on a pre-synthesized overlay on the FPGA fabric [18][8]. Multi-processor platforms, programmable with GPU languages, have been realized by replicating modified soft microprocessors (like MIPS [11], LEON3 [2] or MicroBlaze [12]) and balancing the workload over them at runtime.

The main advantages of soft- over hard-GPUs do not differ from those in the microprocessors domain. Soft solutions enable application-specific adaptations and accelerate design space exploration [25]. They are easier to realize, multiply or integrate with other system parts. Because the physical characteristics of FPGAs have been steadily improving, system architects are now more willing to trade extra area for more integration flexibility and a shorter development cycle. Hence, as long as the design goals are met, portable software implementations on soft GPUs are more attractive than programming HDL in many applications.

Directly synthesizing kernels from GPU languages to FPGA logic with High Level Synthesis (HLS) tools may be more efficient than using soft GPUs [3]. But when multiple tasks have to be performed or the task size changes, the HLS-approach does not scale well: adding new tasks implies more occupied area and extra consumed power. Even when combined with partial reconfiguration, the time and the power needed to reconfigure the FPGA may be significant. On the other hand, performing software tasks on soft GPUs is a much more flexible solution.

FGPU (**F**PGA general purpose **G**raphical **P**rocessing **U**nit) it is a portable, scalable and flexible soft Single-Instruction Multiple-Thread (SIMT) processor developed in VHDL-2002. Although it has been optimized and tested for the 7series FPGA architecture from Xilinx, it does not include any IP-cores or FPGA-primitives. It depends on the capabilities of the synthesis tool to infer the right FPGA logic like DSP or BRAM blocks from the VHDL code. It does not replicate, even partially, any other GPU architecture. The platform and execution models of FGPU follows those of the OpenCL standard [10]. FGPU has its own ISA, which is a extended subset of the MIPS assembly. The extra instructions are inspired from the execution model of OpenCL. The timing characteristics degrade very little as the size of the implemented core increases. FGPU has its own configurable 1-Level cache system, which can be connected to one or more 32- or 64bit AXI4 interfaces.

FPGA'16, February 21-23, 2016, Monterey, CA, USA

© 2016 ACM. ISBN 978-1-4503-3856-1/16/02...$15.00

DOI: http://dx.doi.org/10.1145/2847263.2847273

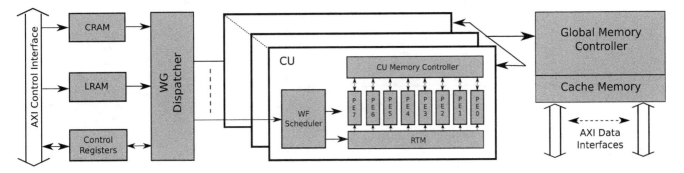

Figure 1: FGPU architecture

This paper is organized as follows: Section 2 presents the FGPU architecture, along with its execution model. The details about optimizing and synthesizing FGPU for FPGAs are discussed in Section 3. Testing and evaluating the proposed architecture and comparing it to other solutions is described in Section 4. Section 5 gives an overview of related work and a comparison to similar projects. Section 6 concludes the paper and future work is briefly described in Section 7.

2. FGPU ARCHITECTURE

2.1 Execution Model

The FGPU execution model can be considered as a simplified version of the one described in the OpenCL standard [10]. For each task to be executed, an *index space* has to be defined: its size and the number of dimensions are determined at runtime. For each point in this space, a work-item will be launched[1]. The programmer may parallelize the execution by linking the coordinates of each work-item to a part of the data to be processed. For example, in order to perform a vector addition, the programmer may define a 1-dimensional index space of the size L, where L is the length of any of the input vectors. The work-item launched for index $0 \leq i < L$ may add the elements located at the ith entries in each input vector and write the result into the ith location in the result vector.

The index space has up to 3 dimensions and it is decomposed in equally-sized work-groups. The depth of the index space along any dimension may be up to 2^{32} and must be a multiple of the work-group size along the same dimension. A work-group can include up to 512 work-items. A work-item is uniquely identified by its 3D-coordinates tuple in the index space, named *global ID*. The *Global Offset* of a work-group is the smallest global ID of any included work-item. The *local ID* of a work-item reveals its relative coordinates inside the work-group and it is calculated by subtracting its work-group global offset from its own global ID.

2.2 Memory Model

In the current version of FGPU, each work-item can use two types of memories to perform its computations:

- *Private Memory*: Each work-item has 32 registers of 32bits. The registers are not accessible from other work-items. The first register (R0) is read-only and contain the value 0. Private memory is the closest memory to the ALUs as well as the fastest one.

- *Global Memory*: It is external to FGPU and can be read or written from any work-item. Its address is limited to 32bit and hence its size to 4GB.

2.3 Platform Model

FGPU accommodates several *Compute Units (CUs)*, each holds a single array of *Processing Elements (PEs)* (see Figure 1). All member PEs in an array share the same program counter. The whole platform is controlled over a single 32bit AXI4 *Control Interface* while data can be transferred through multiple other AXI4 *Data Interfaces*.

To run a task on FGPU, its binary code has to be stored in the *Code RAM (CRAM)*. Other information that can not be determined at compile time, e.g. the number of work-items to be launched, linkage information to assign the parameter values, the address of the first instruction of the task in CRAM, all have to be stored in the *Link RAM (LRAM)*.

When the execution is started, the *Work-Group (WG) Dispatcher* begins to assign groups of up to 512 work-items to free CUs. A *Wavefront (WF) Scheduler* divides a WG further into multiple wavefronts, each of 64 work-items, and schedule them on the PE array. The *RunTime Memory (RTM)* is written whenever a WG or a WF is scheduled with all runtime-relevant information that may be accessed by the work-items during execution, e.g. the coordinates of each scheduled work-item in the index space and the parameter values. Reads and writes to global memory are handled by a local memory controller. CUs have no local memories or caches.

Memory operations issued by CUs are forwarded to a central memory controller (see Section 2.5). It includes an internal multi-bank direct-mapped cache. Accesses to the global memory are shaped in bursts and sent over a configurable number of AXI4 interfaces.

2.4 Compute Unit Architecture

2.4.1 Compute Vector

The 8 processing elements within a compute unit are placed into a compute vector module (see Figure 2). They are designed with a very deep pipeline of 18 stages for better timing performance. To overcome the high pipeline latency, a 2x faster clock is used for the compute vector with respect to the clock of other CU components. Each PE has 2048 registers to be used by 64 work-items, where each work-item

---

[1]The term *work-item* is defined in the OpenCL execution model and it is equivalent to *thread* in CUDA terminology.

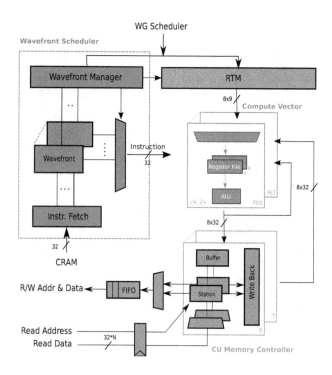

Figure 2: Compute unit overview

can access exclusively 32 registers. Physically, two dual-ported BRAMs are multiplexed in time to hold the register files. Any ALU operation may have up to three operands, which enables performing a multiply-and-accumulate (macc) within a single instruction. Executing any instruction is repeated over 8 clock cycles on all PEs, which corresponds to executing the same instruction from 64 work-items. Selecting the corresponding register file for the work-item under execution is achieved without extra latency through setting the address inputs of the BRAMs accordingly. Despite of the deep pipeline and even if an instruction depends on the results computed in a previous one, it is possible to execute the instructions within a wavefront after each other without inserting delays in between as long as no memory access is required.

2.4.2 Wavefront Scheduler

When a CU gets a work-group assigned by the WG dispatcher, the corresponding number of wavefronts have to be consequently scheduled and managed internally in the CU. On a single CU, it is possible to concurrently execute up to 8 WFs from different work-groups.

A WF has a single program counter and its instructions are executed in-order. After requesting a memory operation, the WF is placed on standby until its requests have been served. The WF scheduler is responsible of updating the program counters, fetching next instructions and waking up a WF when its memory requests have been served. It is also responsible of initializing the RTM before the execution begins. In order not to overrun the CU memory controller with 64 memory requests at once, a WF gets broken into quarter WFs when the execution reaches a memory operation. A quarter WF gets scheduled only when the CU memory controller is capable of handling new requests.

2.4.3 Runtime Memory

The RTM is a 2 ported-RAM with one write and one read 72bits ports. It is written either by the WG dispatcher when a WG gets assigned on the CU or by the WF scheduler when a wavefront is scheduled internally in the CU. It holds miscellaneous data which can only be determined at runtime, e.g. the global offset of scheduled work-groups or the local indices of work-items in their corresponding WGs. RTM can be read by work-items during execution by calling special assembly instructions. RTM enables realising the *Work-Item Built-In Function* defined in the OpenCL standard [10]. These functions can be linked to macros of assembly instructions that copy the corresponding content from RTM into the register files.

2.4.4 CU Memory Controller

Whenever a memory operation is executed on the compute vector, its outcomes get latched in a buffer. Then, the individual memory requests are handled by a vector of controllers or *stations*.

a) In case of a *write* operation: the requested address and the written data are forwarded into a FIFO (see Figure 2). The station can handle new requests directly after writing the FIFO.

b) In case of a *read* operation: after pushing the request into the FIFO, stations listen to the data read out from the cache. The cache has multiple banks and it serves several data words at once. If the address of the served data matches, the corresponding word is selected and latched. The *Write Back* module collects the read data from stations and writes them back into the register files.

Before pushing a new read request into the FIFO, a check is done whether the last waiting read request will serve the new one. In this case, the new request gets ignored. It is very probable that the work-items will access sequential addresses when reading or writing the global memory. Because the register files consists physically of two ram blocks and runs at double the frequency of the memory controller, the read data can be written back while the register files are being updated by other instructions without causing any congestion.

2.5 Memory Controller

FGPU has a central memory controller that can be connected to a single or multiple memory blocks over a configurable number of 32- or 64bit AXI4 interfaces (see Figure 3). To overcome the latency when reading the global memory, multiple read transactions with different IDs can be initiated and managed on the same AXI4 read channel. The controller can serve multiple CUs and it includes a direct-mapped data cache with one read and one write ports. Both ports spans over N data words. All read and write transaction to global memory are performed as bursts, where the burst size is the same of a cache block. To minimize data traffic to global memory, a write-back strategy is used. The controller includes a *Byte Dirty* memory to mark dirty bytes within a cache block.

A incoming memory request from a CU is caught by a free *Station*. Then, the station checks if the corresponding cache block has been already mapped to a physical location in the global memory (*Tag Valid Bit*), to which location it has been mapped (*Tag Address*) and if the cache block has been populated by data from global memory (*Block Valid Bit*):

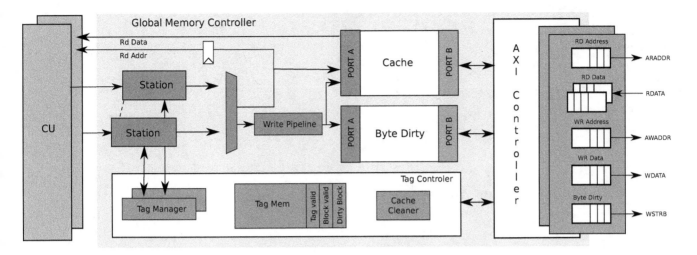

Figure 3: Global Memory Controller

- In case of a *Cache Hit*:

  - For Write Operations: the write command enters the *Write Pipeline* and the dirty bit gets set for the updated block as well as the corresponding bits in the *Byte Dirty* memory.

  - For Read Operations: If the *Block Valid* bit is set, the cache can be read safely. Otherwise, a *Tag Manager* gets signalized to populate the cache block with the corresponding content from global memory.

- In case of a *Cache Miss*: the station asks a tag manager to allocate the corresponding tag.

  - For Write Operations: As soon as the tag memory is updated accordingly, the write command enters the *Write Pipeline*. The tag manager does not read the global memory to fill the cache block. This is done only for read operations.

  - For Read Operations: the tag manager checks if the cache block is dirty. Only in this case, cache content will be written back into the global memory and the corresponding *Dirty Bit* gets cleared. The content of the *Byte Dirty* memory enables to selectively write the dirty parts of the cache block. After that, the global memory is read and the cache block gets populated with the requested data.

Then, reads and writes can be executed on cache. Each outstanding request is assigned an increased priority as more time is spent on waiting. Reading stations compare the read address port of the cache with their own ones and retire when a match is detected. Since the cache read port spans over multiple data words, many stations can be served at once. Write requests have to go through the *Write Pipeline* before they get marked as served. The pipeline gives the necessary time to announce the address that is going to be written to other stations, check if any one is waiting to write the same cache entry, gather data and perform the write for as many stations as possible at once. When the tag value of a cache block is changed, all outstanding stations that

are waiting to read from the block will restart the whole procedure and go to the first step in serving their requests. To avoid race conditions when modifying tag values, every new tag is protected for a minimum time from being deallocated. The protection time should enable the corresponding outstanding stations to finish before they get restarted. After all work-items finish, the *Cache Cleaner* module checks the whole cache and writes back any dirty data it finds into global memory.

When a cache location is read and written by multiple CUs, the requests may be served in any order. Overwriting data that has been already written by some CUs when validating the content of a cache block is even possible. Anyway, the OpenCL standard does not enforce constraints on synchronising the memory accesses outside the borders of a CU[2]. Serving a read request may take at least 8 clock cycles. When a cache block has to be cleaned and new data has to be read from global memory, a latency of over 50 clock cycles is typical in realistic situations[3].

2.6 Instruction Set Architecture

FGPU has its own ISA. It can be divided into two parts: i) *a CPU-like* part whose instructions can be considered as a subset of MIPS ISA, and ii) *an OpenCL-relevant* part whose instructions are built to support the execution of unmodified OpenCL-kernels in future. These instruction are designed to replace OpenCL built-in functions. Figure 4 shows a simple FIR filter implemented in FGPU ISA next to an equivalent OpenCL implementation. In this example, the *get_global_id(0)* OpenCL function is replaced by the first three assembly instructions. To run the benchmarks presented in Section 4, it was enough to implement a total of 18 assembly instructions. All instructions have the same 32bit format.

---

[2]Global atomics enable avoiding race conditions when multiple CUs read and modify the same memory location. They will be supported and implemented as an extension to the current architecture in future work.

[3]This number does not take into account the response latency of the global memory slave AXI4 interface.

```
__kernel void fir(                        # FIR filter using 1D index space. It has 4 Paramaters:
    *input_array,                         #  0 : address of the first element in input array
    *filter,                              #  1 : address of the first element in coefficients array
    int *res_array,                       #  2 : address of the first element in results array
    int filter_len)                       #  3 : filter length (L)
{                                         LID  r1, d0 # local ID: load the local work-item index in its work-group into r1
                                          WGOFF r2, d0# Work-Group Offset: load the work-group global offset into r2
    int index = get_global_id(0);         ADD  r1, r1, r2 # ADD integers: r1 has now the global id of the work-item
                                          LP   r2, 3 # Load Parameter: r2 has filter length
    int i = 0;                            LP   r3, 0 # Load Parameter: r3 is a pointer to the input array
                                          LP   r4,   # Load Parameter: r4 is a pointer to the coefficients array
    int acc = 0;                          ADDI r5, r0, 0 # ADD Immediate: r5 will be the loop index (initialized with 0)
                                          ADDI r6, r0, 0 # ADD Immediate: r6 will contain the result (initialized with 0)

    do                                    begin: LW r10, r4[r5] # Load Word: load a coefficient  into r10
    {                                     ADD  r11, r5, r1 # ADD integers: calculate the index of an element in input array
                                          LW   r11, r3[r11] # Load Word: load the input element into r11
        acc += input_array[indx+i] * filter[i];  MACC r6, r10, r11 # Multiply and ACComulate: update the result
        i++;                              ADDI r5, r5, 1 # ADD Immediate: update loop index
    } while(i < filter_len);              BNE  r5, r2, begin # Branch if Not Equal: repeat the iteration if necessary

                                          LP   r20, 2 # Load Parameter: r20 is a pointer to the result array
    res[index] = acc;                     SW   r6, r20[r1] # Store Word: store the result r6 into the index r1 in result array
}                                         RET  #RETurn: end of task
```

| (a) FIR filter as OpenCL kernel | (b) Equivalent implementation in FGPU ISA |

Figure 4: FIR filter in OpenCL and FGPU assembly

3. FGPU IMPLEMENTATION

3.1 Scalability

To synthesize a scalable GPU-like architecture on FPGAs, the following issues must be considered:

3.1.1 Implementing Register Files

Running more work-items simultaneously on the FPGA requires more register files to be synthesized. For example, 4K work-items with 32 registers of 32bits require 4M bits of RAM, or equivalently 64K 6-input LUTs. This corresponds to about a third of the available LUTs on the Xilinx z7045 FPGA, which has been used during development. It is possible to realize the same storage just with 64 modules or about 12% of the available BRAMs on the same FPGA. The main challenge when using BRAMs is getting the instruction operands out of a smaller number of access ports. Three read- and one write-operations must be performed per clock cycle on any register file. Therefore, we have doubled the clock frequency of the BRAMs that hold the register files and used two BRAMs in every PE. Hence, a single BRAM has to deliver three operands for the next ALU instruction every four "fast" clock cycles. Considering the two BRAMs, the needed number of operands for a single instruction can be read out per single "slow" clock cycle with a latency of another "slow" clock cycle.

3.1.2 Using DSP Blocks

Using DSP blocks that are available on most modern FP-GAs would spare a significant amount of LUTs and improve the operating frequency as well. These blocks are capable of performing integer multiplication, addition or even logical shift. To extend these operations on 32bit words, multiple DSP blocks have to be chained and signals that go through the DSPs will form the most critical paths. This problem is avoided in FGPU by using the additional pipeline registers inside and at the borders of the DSP blocks. Five pipeline stages are used when performing 32bit multiplication. To

reduce the additional pipeline latency, DSP blocks operate in the same double-frequency domain as the register files.

3.1.3 Preserving the Operating Frequency

To mitigate the degradation in the operating frequency as the design gets bigger, many FPGA-specific techniques have been applied, e.g. minimizing the use of reset signals and activating the optional output registers of BRAM blocks. Since two different clocks have been used, the most critical paths after place and route were the ones that cross over the borders of any clock domain. Therefore, additional pipeline stages have been added to remove any logic located on the crossing paths. Sometimes empty pipeline stages have been inserted in the same clock domain just before crossing to the other one. High-fanout signals have been determined and limited through multiple manual place and route iterations. Slice registers have been placed on some signals, e.g. the read data bus driven by the central memory controller which has to reach all CUs that are expected to be placed apart from each other over the whole FPGA chip.

3.2 Portability

Although FGPU architecture targets specific FPGA resources like DSP or byte-enabled true dual-port BRAM blocks, no IP-cores or primitives have been used. But a successful and efficient implementation on any FPGA depends primarily on the ability of the manufacturer's synthesis tools to infer the targeted blocks from the VHDL code. Although FGPU has been synthesized and tested only for the 7series from Xilinx, it is absolutely possible to implement it on other FPGA families without modifying the RTL Code. But a closer look to the synthesis outcomes is recommended when porting the design to other types of FPGAs for the first time. Fanout limitations are included in the RTL code as signal attributes and they are manufacturer-dependent[4]. They may need to to be adjusted when targeting other FPGA chips

---

[4]Synthesis tools ignore VHDL attributes that could not be interpreted. This enables having multiple manufacturer-dependent ones in the same design.

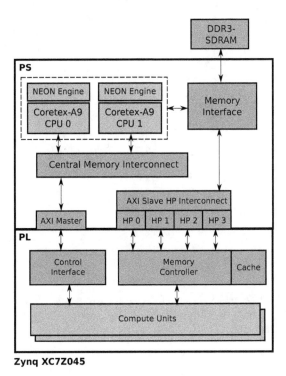

Figure 5: Development Platform

Zynq XC7Z045

Table 1: Area requirements for different configurations

	LUTs	FFs	BRAM	DSPs
Available	219K	437K	545	900
8 CUs	124K (57%)	159K (36%)	167 (31%)	192 (21%)
4 CUs	76K (35%)	88K (20%)	99 (18%)	96 (11%)
2 CUs	57K (26%)	60K (14%)	65 (12%)	48 (5.3%)
2 CUs (min)	21K (9.6%)	35K (8.1%)	47 (8.5%)	48 (5.3%)
MicroBlaze	7K (3.2%)	5.6K (1.3%)	27 (5.0%)	6 (0.7%)

Table 2: Adjustable parameters with direct influence on design scalability

Module	Parameter	Range
CU	# CUs	2, 4, 8
	# Outstanding mem. requests	16, 24, 32
Memory Controller	Cache Size	1 to 8KB
	# Cache Read Banks	2, 4, 8
	# Outstanding mem. requests	32, 64
	# AXI4 interfaces	1, 2, 4
	# Tag Managers	2, 4, 8, 16

from the same manufacturer to achieve better performance. Anyway, they are optional and they do not affect the portability at all.

3.3 Flexibility

FGPU is a highly customizable architecture and offers a large space for design exploration. The user can customize the design to fit to the available FPGA resources. All parameters have to be determined before synthesis in a VHDL-package file. To generate the results presented in this paper, we focused on studying the parameters of direct influence on scalability. Other non scalability-critical ones have been fixed on realistic and near-optimal values found during behavioral simulations, e.g. the size of a cache blocks or the number of tag managers in the central memory controller.

4. RESULTS

4.1 Development Platform

The ZC706 FPGA board with z7045 Zynq has been used for development (see Figure 5). The on-chip ARM Cortex-A9 processor includes two cores: one is used to control FGPU and the other for power measurements. The on-board 1G DDR3-SDRAM PS memory is considered as a global memory. FGPU accesses the DDR through the four AXI HP (High Performance) ports of the ARM.

All applications are programmed in FGPU ISA and the binaries are automatically generated with a special tool developed in C++. To optimize FGPU architecture and discover bottlenecks and bugs, we depended on cycle accurate simulations using Questa Sim v10.4. A realistic and highly customizable model for the global memory with a adjustable number of AXI4 interfaces is developed and integrated. The simulation platform offers many statistical measurements

that we have used to make architectural decisions. In addition, it enables testing any application intensively with different settings and offers automated check for the correctness and the completeness of the data that must be written back in the global memory. This check is also done after a task is executed on the hardware platform.

The CRAM has 16KB of storage and its content is included in the bitstream. The LRAM size is set at 4KB which is enough to hold the settings of 16 kernels. Its content has been defined in an XML file and integrated in the bitstream but it was modified at runtime to change the task size. The conversion from the XML representation to binary has been automated with awk script. FGPU has two 16bit control registers, namely *Start* and *Finish*. By setting the ith bit in the start register, the kernel at index i in LRAM will be launched. When it finishes, the corresponding bit in the finish register gets set. The execution time on FGPU is measured between setting the start register and reading the corresponding value from the finish register.

4.2 Area Requirements

Table 1 gives an overview of the needed resources when FGPU is synthesized with 8, 4 and 2 CUs. All other parameters listed in Table 2 are configured for maximum performance. The entry "2 CUs (Min)" indicates the case where all parameters are configured form minimum resource usage. All implementations could be successfully placed and routed without frequency degradation at 200 and 400MHz for the normal and double clock domains, respectively. This

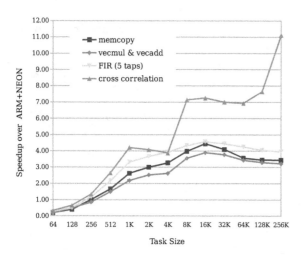

Figure 6: Wall clock time speedup for 8 CUs over ARM+NEON implementation for variable task size

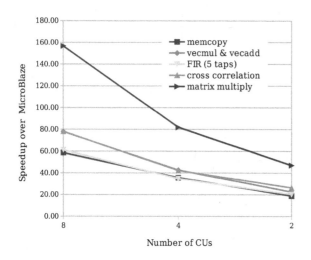

Figure 7: Wall clock time speedup for FGPU with different number of CUs over MicroBlaze implementation for a task size of 16K

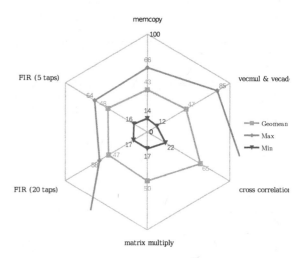

Figure 8: Wall clock time speedup for 8 CUs over MicroBlaze implementation for task size between 256 and 256K

is very close to the practical maximum operating frequency of BRAMs on the used FPGA which is 454MHz [24]. The most critical resources when implementing FGPU are the LUTs. Anyway, this applies only to the 7series FPGAs from Xilinx, which have 2 FFs per LUT. When implementing FGPU on older FPGA families where this ratio becomes 1 FF per LUT, the most critical resources will be the FFs.

4.3 Speedup

The benchmark used in this work includes 7 typical application for GPGPU computing that have been considered in related work. To measure the efficiency of the designed memory controller, the *memcopy* task has been added. An equivalent software implementation of the benchmark in C++ is compiled and executed as bare-metal application on two architectures: a single hard ARM core with the NEON vector engine and a soft MicroBlaze processor. The ARM CPU is clocked at 667MHz and its cache system is enabled. The

NEON SIMD has been always used, where auto vectorization is performed by the compiler. The reference MicroBlaze is configured by the default settings for maximum performance and it runs at 185MHz. The ARM as well as the MicroBlaze compilers are configured for maximum optimization -O3 and no debug symbols are generated. The FGPU and the reference MicroBlaze are synthesized using Vivado 2015.2 with a performance-oriented strategy for synthesis, placement and routing. We varied the problem size from 64 to 256K integers. The size of work-groups was set on 64 work-items. Similar to any other GPU architecture, the work-group size should be a multiple of the wavefront size to get optimal performance on FGPU. All time measurements are repeated and averaged over 10 runs and they include flushing the content of the written cache region after the execution ends. FGPU performs cache flushing automatically when all work-items retire.

Figure 6 illustrates the relationship between the speedup and the task size for some considered applications. To execute a task on FGPU, a minimum execution time of 4 us is needed for the initialization of RTM memories at the beginning and flushing the dirty cache content at the end. When taking the ARM with the NEON engine as a reference, a minimum task size of 256 is needed to achieve any speedup with FGPU. The effect of the number of CUs on speedup is depicted in Figure 7. Even for applications that are less computationally intensive, remarkable improvements can be achieved by using more CUs. This is because of the improved throughput to the global memory. The memory operations generated by a single CU usually target memory addresses with minimum stride. As more CUs are involved, much more cache blocks have to be updated and hence the central memory controller has more requests to serve. The latency for populating a cache block or cleaning it will have less effect on the overall performance.

Figure 8 shows the wall clock time speedup of FGPU with 8 CUs over MicroBlaze on the whole benchmark. After averaging all speedups for task sizes from 256 to 256K and then taking the average over the whole benchmark, a speedup of

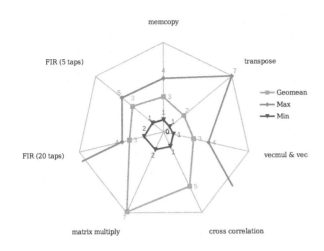

Figure 9: Wall clock time speedup for 8 CUs over ARM+NEON implementation for task size between 256 and 256K

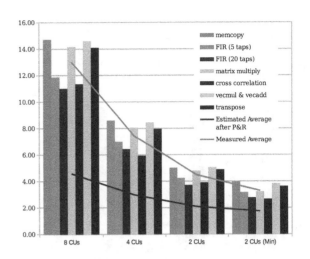

Figure 10: Measured and estimated ratios of the power consumption of different FGPUs to the one consumed by MicroBlaze over the benchmark

49x could be achieved with FGPU. The minimum accelerations are measured for applications like vector additions or FIR filtering. For the most computational intensive tasks, speedups up to 105x for cross correlation and 166x for matrix multiplication have been measured. The achieved speedup improves as the ratio of the number of performed arithmetic operations to the required number of memory accesses increases. Even when FGPU is used like a DMA, a bandwidth up to 7.7Gbps could be achieved, which is 66x faster than the MicroBlaze implementation. When compared to the ARM+NEON implementation, FGPU managed to provide remarkable improvements with similar relative changes over the different applications of the benchmark (see Figure 9). FGPU could provide an average speedup of 3.5x over the whole benchmark with a maximum of 35x when multiplying matrices of 512x512 integers.

4.4 Power Consumption

The power measurements have been done via the Texas Instruments UCD90120A power-supply sequencer and monitor on the Xilinx ZC706. The measurements were done on the second core of the ARM processor using the PMBus protocol, while the first core controlled task execution on FGPU. The voltage and current values of all supply rails have been periodically sampled. Because measuring one value pair takes about 1.7ms, we set the task size at maximum during power measurements and repeated the task execution many times when necessary to make at least 500 samples. The two ARM cores synchronized the measurement procedure with task execution over a flag located in the DDR memory. All reported power measurements are averaged over the whole amount of taken samples. Because the power consumed by the PL represents only a part of the measured one, the following trick was used: we measured the power consumed when PL is not programmed, the first ARM core is idle, and only the power measurement runs on the second core. Then, we subtracted the value we got from all future measurements. Figure 10 shows the ratio of the power consumed by different FGPU implementations to the

one consumed by MicroBlaze over the whole benchmark. In average, the biggest and smallest FGPUs consumed 13.0x and 3.3x more power than MicroBlaze, respectively. If the estimated power consumptions for the different designs after place & route with Vivado are considered, the previous ratios should have been be at 4.6x and 1.7x, respectively (see Figure 10). Absolute values for the measured consumed power through the UCD90120A chip were 5.19W for the biggest FGPU, 1.94W for the smallest one and 1.18W for the MicroBlaze. Despite of the high power consumption of FGPU, taking the speedups into account leads to the fact that FGPU is capable of providing a minimum power saving of 3.2x over MicroBlaze. The power measurements of the ARM+NEON implementation could not be made because the PS power supply is not included completely in the UCD90120A chip.

Figure 11 illustrates a comparison of many FGPU implementations and MicroBlaze in different aspects. Since LUTs are the most critical resource for all architectures when implemented on the z7045 FPGA, their usage is considered as a metric to compare area requirements of all designs. Even in the worst cases, FGPU was in average at least as fast as the ARM+NEON solution.

5. RELATED WORK

5.1 Soft GPGPUs

Because of their complexity and in contrast to soft CPUs, there have been quite few attempts to implement GPUs as configurable or application-specific soft cores on FPGAs for general purpose computing. In [2], a soft GPU based on the LEON3 processor was presented and tested only for matrix multiplication. Speedups up to 3x were achieved over the original LEON3 implementation. Andryc, et al. [5] tried to replicate the Nvidia G80 architecture[5] on a Virtex6 FPGA in the FlexGrip project. The reported implementation is capable of executing 27 integer CUDA instructions of compute

---

[5]G80 is the first generation architecture of CUDA-programmable GPUs released in 2006 [14].

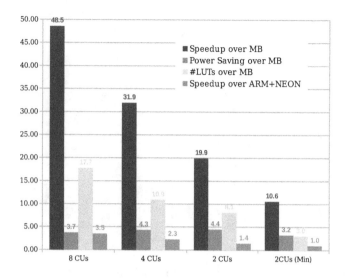

Figure 11: Average wall clock time speedup, power saving and area overhead for different FGPUs over MicroBlaze and ARM+NEON implementations

capability 1.0 and supports thread-level branching in hardware. On the VLX240T FPGA, it was possible to synthesize 8, 16, or 32 scalar processors (SPs) at 100 MHz organized in a single compute unit where all SPs execute the same instruction at once. Instructions and data were accessed by FlexGrip through a single 32bit AXI4-interface connected to a MicroBlaze processor. Taking the performance of the MicroBlaze processor as a reference, FlexGrip was capable of achieving an average speedup of 22x in simulation for 32 SPs over a benchmark of 5 applications. The best simulated speedup was 29x for matrix multiplication and the worst one was about 11x for autocorrelation. The best average power saving was %66 for the 32 SP implementation.

MIAOW is an open source GPGPU [7] which introduces a similar architecture to the southern Islands from AMD and uses its ISA [4]. It targets a hybrid implementation: register files, on-chip networks and memory controllers are provided as behavioral C/C++ modules while the rest is implemented in RTL. MIAOW is capable of running many unmodified OpenCL benchmarks. The developed compute unit has been synthesized with 32nm technology[6]. It occupies 15mm^2 and can run at 222MHz. The developers reported an FPGA-implementation of MIAOW, named *Neko*: It consists of a single compute unit next to a MicroBlaze on a Virtex7 FPGA. Neko's CU has 16 floating-point ALUs with no memory controller. The MicroBlaze has to schedule wavefronts on the CU and perform memory accesses. Neko needs 195285 LUTs and 137 BRAMs for the whole CU. No timing informations or test results have been reported. To the best of our knowledge, there has been no successful attempt to synthesize a soft GPU with multiple compute units on a single FPGA.

---

[6] A compute unit in MIAOW accommodates 4 vectors of 16 floating-point ALUs with 1024 vector- and 512 scalar-registers.

5.2 Soft Vector Processors

In contrast to soft GPGPUs, soft vector processor architectures have been extensively studied in many projects. The VENICE architecture [20] implements up to 4 ALUs next to a NIOS soft processor. An average speedup of 21x and up to 72x have been reported @190MHz on a Stratix IV device for the biggest design. In VESPA [26], a MIPS with a soft vector processor has been implemented. An average speedup of 11.3x was achieved with 32 ALUs @ 96MHz on Stratix III. MXP [21] has a similar architecture to VENICE but it is more scalable and it can run at higher frequencies. The authors reported estimated average cycle count speedup of 116x with 64 ALUs and up to 918x for matrix multiplication while taking a NIOS II/f as reference. But wall clock time speedups drop significantly because the operating frequency degrades from 283 for the NIOS to 122MHz for the biggest MXP on a Stratix IV device. On a similar development platform that we have used during FGPU development [9], MXP could achieve a maximum speedup of 2.07x over the ARM+NEON implementation for similar 32bit applications that we have targeted in the FGPU benchmark.

To parallelize data handling on vector processors, intrinsics or architecture-dependent code have to be inserted into the application code [19] [21]. Automatic vectorization can be performed by the compiler but it usually delivers suboptimal results [26]. On the other side, FGPU as well as GPU programmers distribute the workload for different problem sizes on a configurable number of work-items. They do not need to think about the underlying hardware structure. Scheduling the work-items on the different CUs is done at runtime. Register files of all work-items are stored in hardware and context switching is possible on-the-fly. In addition, FGPU does put and workload on other system components and it manages all data transfers by itself. Vector processors usually share data and instruction caches with a scalar CPU. Many soft vectors use a multi-bank scratchpad for temporal storage of the data under processing. The programmer should manually initiate DMA transfers to get the data from the main memory into the scratchpad while processing other pieces of information [20] [21].

6. CONCLUSION

FGPU is a scalable, portable, flexible and highly customizable SIMT soft processor architecture designed specially for FPGAs. Its platform and execution models as well as its ISA architecture are inspired from the OpenCL standard and it can be programmed through a well defined interface. FGPU includes a multi-bank and direct-mapped cache system which has been optimized to serve many outstanding read and write requests at once. It can drive multiple 32- or 64bit AXI4 interfaces to fetch data from global memory at maximum throughput. By taking the average over the whole presented benchmark and over all FGPU configurations that have been presented in this paper, power savings between 3.2x and 4.5x simultaneously with speedups between 10.6x and 48.5x have been achieved over a MicroBlaze implementation on the same FPGA. The penalty in area overhead was between 3.0x and 17.7x. Compared to an equivalent ARM implementation with the NEON SIMD engine, the smallest FGPU core could achieve the same performance while the biggest one could provide a speedup of 3.5x in average.

7. FUTURE WORK

We intend to extend the ISA of FGPU to cover more benchmarks. Enabling branches at the work-item level would be necessary to implement algorithms like reduction and sorting. A very important milestone is providing a compiler for OpenCL kernels by developing a backend for the LLVM framework. Implementing local memories for the CUs as well as local and global atomics are planned for far future. Integrating the floating point DSPs that are available in some modern FPGAs within the proposed architecture would extend the targeted application domain significantly.

8. REFERENCES

[1] Top500 Consortium: The Top 500 supercomputing sites. http://www.top500.org [Online; accessed 11-Sep-2015].

[2] A. Al-Dujaili, F. Deragisch, A. Hagiescu, and W.-F. Wong. Guppy: A GPU-like soft-core processor. In *Field-Programmable Technology (FPT), 2012 International Conference on*, pages 57–60, Dec 2012.

[3] Altera Corporation. Implementing FPGA Design with the OpenCL Standard. White Paper, 2013.

[4] AMD, Inc. Southern Islands Series Instruction Set Architecture. Reference Guide, 2012.

[5] K. Andryc, M. Merchant, and R. Tessier. FlexGrip: A soft GPGPU for FPGAs. In *Field-Programmable Technology (FPT), 2013 International Conference on*, pages 230–237, Dec 2013.

[6] ARM Limited. Take GPU Processing Power Beyond Graphics with Mali GPU Computing. White Paper, 2014.

[7] R. Balasubramanian, V. Gangadhar, Z. Guo, C.-H. Ho, C. Joseph, J. Menon, M. P. Drumond, R. Paul, S. Prasad, P. Valathol, and K. Sankaralingam. Enabling GPGPU Low-Level Hardware Explorations with MIAOW: An Open-Source RTL Implementation of a GPGPU. *ACM Trans. Archit. Code Optim.*, 12(2):21:21:1–21:21:25, June 2015.

[8] D. Capalija and T. Abdelrahman. Tile-based bottom-up compilation of custom mesh of functional units FPGA overlays. In *Field Programmable Logic and Applications (FPL), 2014 24th International Conference on*, pages 1–8, Sept 2014.

[9] S. J. Jie and N. Kapre. Comparing soft and hard vector processing in FPGA-based embedded systems. In *Field Programmable Logic and Applications (FPL), 2014 24th International Conference on*, pages 1–7, Sept 2014.

[10] Khronos Group. OpenCL 1.2 Specification, 2012.

[11] I. Lebedev, S. Cheng, A. Doupnik, J. Martin, C. Fletcher, D. Burke, M. Lin, and J. Wawrzynek. MARC: A Many-Core Approach to Reconfigurable Computing. In *Reconfigurable Computing and FPGAs (ReConFig), 2010 International Conference on*, pages 7–12, Dec 2010.

[12] S. Ma, M. Huang, and D. Andrews. Developing application-specific multiprocessor platforms on FPGAs. In *Reconfigurable Computing and FPGAs (ReConFig), 2012 International Conference on*, pages 1–6, Dec 2012.

[13] Mathworks, Inc. GPU Programming in MATLAB. Available on mathworks.com/newsletters [Online; accessed 11-Sep-2015].

[14] Nvidia Corporation. Nvidia's Next Generation CUDA Compute Architecture: Fermi. White Paper, 2009.

[15] Nvidia Corporation. Nvidia Jetson TK1 Development Kit: Bringing GPU-accelerated computing to Embedded Systems (Technical Brief, v1.0), 2014.

[16] M. Owaida, N. Bellas, K. Daloukas, and C. Antonopoulos. Synthesis of Platform Architectures from OpenCL Programs. In *Field-Programmable Custom Computing Machines (FCCM), 2011 IEEE 19th Annual International Symposium on*, pages 186–193, May 2011.

[17] A. Papakonstantinou, K. Gururaj, J. Stratton, D. Chen, J. Cong, and W.-M. Hwu. FCUDA: Enabling efficient compilation of CUDA kernels onto FPGAs. In *Application Specific Processors, 2009. SASP '09. IEEE 7th Symposium on*, pages 35–42, July 2009.

[18] R. Rashid, J. Steffan, and V. Betz. Comparing performance, productivity and scalability of the TILT overlay processor to OpenCL HLS. In *Field-Programmable Technology (FPT), 2014 International Conference on*, pages 20–27, Dec 2014.

[19] A. Severance, J. Edwards, H. Omidian, and G. Lemieux. Soft Vector Processors with Streaming Pipelines. In *Proceedings of the 2014 ACM/SIGDA International Symposium on Field-programmable Gate Arrays*, FPGA '14, pages 117–126, New York, NY, USA, 2014. ACM.

[20] A. Severance and G. Lemieux. VENICE: A Compact Vector Processor for FPGA Applications. In *Field-Programmable Custom Computing Machines (FCCM), 2012 IEEE 20th Annual International Symposium on*, pages 245–245, April 2012.

[21] A. Severance and G. Lemieux. Embedded supercomputing in fpgas with the vectorblox mxp matrix processor. In *Hardware/Software Codesign and System Synthesis (CODES+ISSS), 2013 International Conference on*, pages 1–10, Sept 2013.

[22] K. Shagrithaya, K. Kepa, and P. Athanas. Enabling development of opencl applications on fpga platforms. In *Application-Specific Systems, Architectures and Processors (ASAP), 2013 IEEE 24th International Conference on*, pages 26–30, June 2013.

[23] Xilinx, Inc. UltraScale Architecture and Product Overview (v2.2), DS890, 2014.

[24] Xilinx, Inc. Block Memory Generator v8.2, LogiCORE IP Product Guide (PG058), 2015.

[25] P. Yiannacouras, J. Steffan, and J. Rose. Exploration and Customization of FPGA-Based Soft Processors. *Computer-Aided Design of Integrated Circuits and Systems, IEEE Transactions on*, 26(2):266–277, Feb 2007.

[26] P. Yiannacouras, J. Steffan, and J. Rose. Portable, Flexible, and Scalable Soft Vector Processors. *Very Large Scale Integration (VLSI) Systems, IEEE Transactions on*, 20(8):1429–1442, Aug 2012.

A Study of Pointer-Chasing Performance on Shared-Memory Processor-FPGA Systems

Gabriel Weisz[1,2] Joseph Melber[1] Yu Wang[1]
Kermin Fleming[3] Eriko Nurvitadhi[3] and James C. Hoe[1]
[1] Computer Architecture Lab at Carnegie Mellon University, {gweisz,jmelber,yuw,jhoe}@cmu.edu
[2] Information Sciences Institute, University of Southern California, gweisz@isi.edu
[3] Intel Corporation, {kermin.fleming,eriko.nurvitadhi}@intel.com

ABSTRACT

The advent of FPGA acceleration platforms with direct coherent access to processor memory creates an opportunity for accelerating applications with irregular parallelism governed by large in-memory pointer-based data structures. This paper uses the simple reference behavior of a linked-list traversal as a proxy to study the performance potentials of accelerating these applications on shared-memory processor-FPGA systems. The linked-list traversal is parameterized by node layout in memory, per-node data payload size, payload dependence, and traversal concurrency to capture the main performance effects of different pointer-based data structures and algorithms. The paper explores the trade-offs over a wide range of implementation options available on shared-memory processor-FPGA architectures, including using tightly-coupled processor assistance. We make observations of the key effects on currently available systems including the Xilinx Zynq, the Intel QuickAssist QPI FPGA Platform, and the Convey HC-2. The key results show: (1) the FPGA fabric is least efficient when traversing a single list with non-sequential node layout and a small payload size; (2) processor assistance can help alleviate this shortcoming; and (3) when appropriate, a fabric-only approach that interleaves multiple linked list traversals is an effective way to maximize traversal performance.

1. INTRODUCTION

Motivations. There are now a growing number of FPGA-accelerated computing systems that support coherent shared memory between processors and FPGAs, including the ability for the FPGAs to directly read from and write to the processor's cache. Both Xilinx and Altera have this capability in their SoC products, which integrate processor cores and a reconfigurable fabric on the same die [1, 18]. The Convey HC-1 was an early commercial FPGA acceleration system that supported shared memory with the host processor [4]. More recently, Intel and IBM have respectively announced initial server products that integrate cache-coherent shared-

memory processors and FPGAs at the system level [13, 2]. These new platforms promise to enable FPGA acceleration for a new class of applications with irregular parallelism.

Irregular parallel applications, including many data analytic and machine learning kernels in data center workloads, operate on very large, memory-resident, pointer-based data structures (i.e., lists, trees and graphs). For example, databases use tree-like structures to store the indices for fast searches and combining information from different database tables. Similarly, many machine learning algorithms within big data applications rely on graphs, which use pointers to represent the relationships between data items.

The parallelism and memory access patterns of these applications are dictated by the point-to relationships in the data structure, which can be irregular, and sometimes time-varying. This reliance on pointer-chasing imposes stringent requirements on memory latency (in addition to bandwidth) over a large main-memory footprint. As such, these applications are poorly matched for traditional add-on FPGA accelerator cards attached to the I/O bus, which can only operate on a limited window of locally buffered data at a time.

Pointer-Chasing. While the class of irregular parallel applications is broad and varied, a fundamental behavior is pointer-chasing. In pointer chasing, the computation is required to dereference a pointer to retrieve each node from memory, which contains both a data payload to be processed and a pointer (or pointers) to subsequent nodes. The exact computation on the payload and the determination of the next pointer to follow depend on the specific data structure and algorithm in use. In this paper, we ignore these differences and focus on only the basic effects of memory access latency and bandwidth on pointer chasing. It is our contention that the optimization of basic pointer-chasing performance ultimately determines the opportunities for FPGA acceleration of irregular parallel applications.

For this purpose, we fixed a simple reference behavior, namely a linked-list traversal. This reference behavior is parameterized by (1) node layout in memory (best- vs. worst-case in our experiments); (2) per node data payload size; (3) payload dependence (an artificial constraint that payload must be retrieved before following the next pointer); and (4) concurrent traversals (availability of multiple independent traversals). Taken together, these parameters abstractly capture the execution differences of different pointer-based algorithms and data-structures. The two execution requirements are that (1) the linked-list is initialized in DRAM and (2) the data payload must be delivered into the fabric

FPGA'16, February 21-23, 2016, Monterey, CA, USA

© 2016 ACM. ISBN 978-1-4503-3856-1/16/02... $15.00

DOI: http://dx.doi.org/10.1145/2847263.2847269

in order.[1] All other details are open to interpretation and optimization by the implementation.

Implementation Considerations. The shared-memory FPGA computing systems under consideration may have multiple pathways between the fabric and main memory, and between the fabric and the processor. Because of this, the best approach for implementing even simple behaviors, such as linked-list traversals, is not obvious, even before taking into account the data-structure-specific parameters discussed above. In Section 4, we will discuss the range of implementation options and their considerations in the context of an abstract shared-memory processor-FPGA architecture. In Section 5, we will demonstrate concretely the manifestations of these effects on real shared-memory processor-FPGA systems available today including the Xilinx Zynq, the Intel QuickAssist QPI FPGA Platform, and the Convey HC-2. Our key results demonstrate that:

1. A fabric-only approach is least efficient when traversing a single list with non-sequential placement and small payload size.

2. Processor assistance can help alleviate this shortcoming.

3. When appropriate, interleaving multiple list traversals can be very effective in optimizing traversal performance by allowing pipelined memory operations.

A particular point of interest is our incorporation of a tightly-coupled processor in the solution space. Implementing the FPGA's memory subsystem in soft logic can dramatically lower its performance (due to lower frequency and a reduced cache capacity) relative to what can be achieved in hard logic. The processor-FPGA link technology in use and the placement of the FPGA in the system can also have a major impact on its memory access latency. The effects of these design choices are most prominent when using an in-fabric engine to traverse a linked list with non-sequential placement and small payload size. In this paper, we study a range of hybrid approaches that use processors (with an order of magnitude higher clock frequency and cache capacity) to assist in delivering the data payload to the fabric. Processor assistance also has the added benefit of greatly simplifying the implementation of complicated pointer-based data structures and algorithms found in realistic applications by expressing these behaviors in software. Our study points to this hybrid approach as a promising avenue for supporting irregular parallelism on future shared-memory processor-FPGA systems.

Paper Outline. Following this introduction, Section 2 reviews background material on shared-memory processor-FPGA systems and irregular parallel applications. Section 3 defines the reference linked-list traversal behavior. Section 4 discusses general design considerations. Section 5 demonstrates the key effects observed on select shared-memory processor-FPGA systems currently available. Section 6 offers recommendations on the design of future systems with the goal of accelerating irregular parallel applications. Finally, Section 7 concludes.

2. BACKGROUND

Shared-Memory Processor-FPGA Systems. As early as 2010, FPGA vendors have created "System-on-Chip" devices that integrate hard-logic processor cores, a reconfigurable fabric, and shared memory into the same chip [1, 18]. While this approach allows tight integration between the processor cores and reconfigurable fabric, the existing product lines have targeted the embedded market in terms of the included cores, fabric capacity, and DRAM interfaces. The Convey HC-1 was an early server-class FPGA acceleration system that supported shared memory with the host processor [4]. Intel and IBM have recently announced server-class products that integrate FPGAs and processors at the board level using proprietary cache-coherent interconnects [13, 2]. These later systems support best-of-breed processors and FPGAs, but incur latency and bandwidth overheads by using inter-package board-level links and relying on soft logic to implement the memory interfaces on the FPGAs. Because of these overheads, the design choices and performance level of today's commercially available products should not be taken as representative of what future shared-memory processor-FPGA architectures could or should be. Optimistically, these products are indicative of a growing interest in FPGAs as first-class computing substrates, which will hopefully lead to still significant evolution in step with the emergence of "killer" apps.

Irregular Parallel Applications. A major premise of this paper is that shared-memory processor-FPGA systems can be effective for accelerating irregular parallel application kernels common to data center workloads. Machine learning algorithms are at the heart of search and many image- and speech-recognition tasks that make up big data applications. Graphs are the core data structure used by these algorithms [6, 8], and use pointers to represent relationships between information. Databases store information in a number of tables. They use indexing structures to allow fast retrieval of information across these tables. These operations commonly require chasing pointers within a tree-like structure (e.g., for efficient range-based searches [5]).

A common theme in the execution of irregular parallel applications is pointer-chasing over a large in-memory data structure [15]. Traditional add-on FPGA accelerator cards are attached to the I/O bus, and can only efficiently access small amounts of data that has been bulk-copied to the DRAM installed on the card. These cards are thus limited to working on a limited window of locally buffered data. Prior work that accelerated irregular parallel application kernels on add-on FPGA accelerator cards first "regularized" the task into contiguous chunks of data, which were then handed off to the FPGA accelerator one by one for processing. This was achieved either by exploiting next-level batch-processing parallelism between tasks (e.g., [16, 14]) or by pre-processing to create parallelizable task partitions through scheduling and data reorganization (e.g., [12]).

On a shared-memory processor-FPGA system, the fabric can directly access the full data set, in some cases with the benefit of virtual address translation. In prior work, Umuroglu, et al., studied a breadth-first graph traversal using a Xilinx Zynq SoC FPGA that shares memory between

---

[1]For the purposes of this study, we are not concerned with justifying why the data need to be processed in the fabric. Other works have shown FPGAs offer raw performance and power efficiency that make them attractive for these types of applications [3, 10, 7, 16, 14, 9].

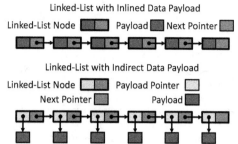

Figure 1: Two possible implementations of the linked-list struct with an inlined data payload and an indirect data payload.

the ARM cores and fabric [17]. Their work assigned different phases of the breadth-first traversal processing to the ARM core and the fabric respectively. Hurkat, et al. studied FPGA acceleration of a machine learning algorithm that took advantage of Convey's special high-throughput interface to a large pool of memory [9].

3. LINKED-LIST TRAVERSAL

Regardless of the exact data structure and algorithm, irregular parallel algorithms repeatedly follow a pointer to the next node in order to find the associated data payload, and then perform the associated computation. In this paper, we ignore the computation, and instead focus on the pointer-chasing backbone of a dynamic execution instance and the fetching of the data payload along the way. This is what we attempt to capture in the simple reference behavior of a linked-list traversal. Establishing a simple reference behavior enables an exploration of the many possible optimizations of pointer-chasing mechanisms on real systems. Despite its simplicity, the parameterizations defined by this reference behavior allow us to capture the most salient execution characteristics of many different pointer-based data structures and algorithms.

Linked Lists. A generic singly linked list is a sequence of nodes. Logically, each node contains a "next" pointer and a data payload; the next pointer points to the next node in the sequence. In this study, a linked-list traversal is parameterized in four dimensions: (1) node layout in memory; (2) per node data payload size; (3) payload dependence; and (4) concurrent traversals.

- **Layout:** In practice, the placement of the nodes in memory depends on the data structure, the algorithm, and the memory allocator. In our study, we consider only the best case and worst case data layouts. For the best case data layouts, the linked-list nodes are laid out sequentially in memory to make optimal use of the spatial locality optimizations in standard memory subsystems. In the best-case studies, sequential prefetching is allowed as an optimization. For the worst case data layouts, the linked-list nodes are laid out in large strides (16 KBytes) to defeat cache block and DRAM row buffer reuse. In the worst-case studies, we explicitly disallow prefetching based on this known stride as an optimization. Real world linked lists would fall somewhere between these two extremes.

- **Payload Size:** We considered data payload size as a parameter (varying from 4 to 1K bytes in our studies). The payload size should correspond to how much of

the payload needs to be examined in the traversal of a real-world pointer-based data structure or algorithm (and not their full declared payload size).

- **Payload Dependence:** This third parameter is an artificial constraint that the payload must be retrieved before the next pointer in the linked list can be followed. This is to model the effect of payload data dependence when traversing a real-world pointer-based data structure. For example, the behavior of traversing a sorted binary tree to produce a sorted sequence would be captured by a linked-list traversal without payload dependence; the behavior of searching a sorted binary tree (requiring examining the value at a node before descending to the next node) would have to be captured by a linked-list traversal with payload dependence.

- **Concurrent Traversals:** The final parameter allows for the possibility of benefiting from concurrency when performing multiple independent traversals. For example, two branches of a sorted binary tree could be traversed concurrently to have their sorted sequences concatenated afterwards. This degree of freedom is extremely helpful in overcoming the effects of high memory access latency.

Design Freedom. We impose no other restrictions on the application developer in order to maximize flexibility in optimizing the reference behavior for the platform. For example, we do not stipulate the pointer size, which presumably should be chosen to be natural to the platform. Furthermore, we do not stipulate that the node struct contains the actual payload field—instead each node struct may contain a pointer to a payload held separately from the node (see inlined vs. indirect payload in Figure 1). For indirect payloads, the nodes and the data payloads are separately laid out sequentially or strided, corresponding to best and worst-case data layout. As will be discussed in the next sections, the implementation for a given platform has full freedom to make use of the available mechanisms to optimize the linked-list traversal performance under different parameterization settings.

Performance Metric. For our study, we require that a sufficiently large linked list (16K nodes in our experiments) is initialized in main memory. We require the data payload to be delivered into the FPGA fabric in order. We are interested in the steady-state rate of traversing this linked list by pointer chasing. In the design of this study, we do not focus on the start-up cost, which could be significant for pointer-based data structures and algorithms that involve only short pointer-chasing sequences. In cases where short sequences need to be serialized, their behavior over repeated traversals effectively matches that of traversing long sequences. In cases where short sequences are independent and can be traversed concurrently, efficient implementations are addressed by the hardware interleaved concurrent traversals that we present later in the paper.

Linked Lists as a Proxy for More Complex Data Structures. Although singly-linked lists are simpler than other pointer-based data structures such as trees and graphs, the linked-list traversals demonstrated in this paper can be used as a proxy for algorithms that traverse trees and graphs. For example, searching for an item in a sorted tree reduces

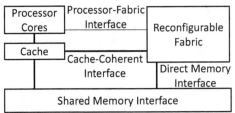

Figure 2: Model of the datapath in a shared-memory processor-FPGA system

to a payload-dependent traversal, as discussed above. Similarly, a graph traversal can be reduced to following the first edge of the current vertex that connects to an unvisited vertex, and intiating a new (possibly parallel) traversal for each additional edge of the current vertex that connects to an unvisited vertex.

4. SYSTEM-LEVEL CONSIDERATIONS

In this section, we discuss at a high-level the range of options and their implications when supporting pointer-chasing on shared-memory processor-FPGA systems. The discussion in this section is not tied to the reference linked-list traversal, but is generalized to a broad range of pointer-based data structures and algorithms. The next section will offer observations from concrete implementations of the parameterized reference linked-list traversal on real platforms.

4.1 Platform Options

Figure 2 shows a generic shared-memory processor-FPGA system architecture, highlighting the major interface options connecting the processor cores, the memory, and the reconfigurable fabric. This figure does not differentiate between die-level and system-level integration of the fabric and processor cores.

The processor cores will typically be connected to the shared main memory through a coherent cache hierarchy.[2] The processor cores can directly interact as masters with the soft-logic blocks on the fabric through a memory-mapped Programmed I/O (PIO) style interface. Not shown in the figures is the option for a programmable DMA copy engine (master) to push or pull data from the fabric (slave) through this interface.

The main feature of a shared-memory processor-FPGA system is of course the ability for the fabric itself to act as the master in reading and writing the shared memory, with some systems even supporting virtual address translation. Through shared memory, it becomes possible for the processor and fabric to interact through unbounded, diverse means. The processor cores and fabric may not have symmetric access to the shared memory, resulting in possibly large differences in their experienced bandwidth and latency. The fabric's access to shared memory may be cache-coherent or non-cache-coherent:

1. The fabric's memory interface feature a cache-coherent link, allowing the processor cores and fabric to automatically see a coherent view of memory. Furthermore,

in some systems, cache-coherent accesses from the fabric may be serviced from the processor cache instead of main memory. Data requests that hit in the processor cache will incur lower latency and achieve higher bandwidth. A cache-coherent shared memory allows the processor cores and fabric to interfere constructively when accessing shared memory. This feature is available on the Xilinx Zynq and the Intel QuickAssist QPI FPGA Platform. On some systems, it is further possible for the fabric to construct its own private coherent cache in soft-logic. This is the case for the Intel QuickAssist QPI FPGA Platform but not for the Xilinx Zynq.

2. The fabric may also have a non-cache-coherent interface to the shared memory in addition to the coherent interface. A possible motivation for offering a non-coherent interface, beside implementation simplicity, is higher bandwidth and lower latency for accessing data residing in main memory. A major downside, especially if the processor cores and the fabric are interacting in a fine-grained fashion, is the cost for the processor core to explicitly ensure coherence through costly cache flushes or through precise discipline in issuing memory address sequences.

In a given system, some variations of all or a subset of the interface options in Figure 2 may be found. The available interface options will offer different tradeoffs in latency, bandwidth, and invocation overhead. Some interface options might be replicated for higher aggregate bandwidth or to allow multiple outstanding transactions. All in all, there are significant complexities in considering all of the interface options and their exact designs to optimize something as simple as linked-list traversal on a real system.

4.2 Performance Model

We offer a simple performance model to assist in reasoning about the pointer-chasing behavior that we are trying to optimize. In general, for a pointer-chasing traversal that touches n nodes of a pointer-based data structure and $s_{payload}$ bytes of data payload per node, ignoring the computation time, the average traversal time per node can be stated as:

$$T_{per-node} = T_{management}/n + (L_{node} + \\ BW_{node}^{-1} \times s_{node} + \\ L_{payload} + \\ BW_{payload}^{-1} \times s_{payload}) \quad (1)$$

In the equation, $T_{management}$ includes all of the time involved in setting up and tearing down a traversal. This time is of lesser concern as it is amortized by n which we assume to be large in the reference behavior (Section 3). L_{node} and $L_{payload}$ represent the latencies in passing data across the interface providing nodes and payload data, respectively. BW_{node}^{-1} and $BW_{payload}^{-1}$ represent the corresponding incremental per-byte times for passing data. Equation 1 separates the time to read the node struct (for the pointer mainly) from the time to read the data payload using different L and BW^{-1} values. This allows for cases where an optimized implementation takes different paths for fetching the node struct vs. the payload. For the case of small inlined data payload fetched together with the pointer, $L_{payload}$ and $BW_{payload}^{-1}$ become 0.

[2]At this level of discussion, the precise organization of L1 vs. L2 and private vs. shared processor core caches is not important. We also omit details such as the possibility of mapping SRAM scratchpads or other memory-mapped devices into the shared address space.

Equation 1 assumes that the path traversed in a data structure depends on the data payload values (e.g., searching a sorted binary tree). In the cases where the traversed path is independent of the data payload values (e.g., depth-first-visit of a binary tree), it becomes possible to decouple the pointer-chasing sequence from the data payload fetch sequence (e.g., where one agent is performing pointer chasing to generate a stream of data payload pointers to be fetched by a second agent). Taking advantage of this decoupling by overlapping the two fetch sequences results in a traversal time is determined by the slower of the two sequences. The average traversal time per node when there is no payload dependence can be approximated as:

$$
\begin{aligned}
T_{per-node} = T_{management}/n + MAX\Big((L_{node} + \\
BW_{node}^{-1} \times s_{node}), \\
(L_{payload} + \\
BW_{payload}^{-1} \times s_{payload})\Big)
\end{aligned}
\tag{2}
$$

The appropriateness of Equation 1 vs. 2 is captured by the payload dependence parameter in the reference linked-list traversal behavior.

Lastly, if the data structure or algorithm permits interleaved traversals of multiple data structures or independent parts of the same data structure, the effective latencies are reduced through latency hiding effects. The degree of the performance improvement will depend on the degree of interleaving and their indirect effects (e.g., increased row buffer conflicts or cache thrashing).

As a final note, the latency and bandwidth in the above first-order models are to be taken as averages. The instantaneous latency and bandwidth of an interface will in general not be constant and will be context specific. For example, both DRAM and caches will exhibit much shorter effective latency during sequential memory references than random or strided references. This effect is exercised by the best-case vs. worst-case node layout parameter of the reference linked-list traversal behavior.

4.3   Implementation Approaches

Software-Only Traversal. Although this work is predicated on delivering the linked-list payload to the fabric, we begin by discussing pointer-chasing in software using processor cores. The most obvious benefit of pointer-chasing from the processor cores is the ease of implementation afforded by software. This is particularly important for complicated algorithms and data structures. Furthermore, hard-logic processor cores benefit from a much higher clock frequency and a more sophisticated and higher capacity memory hierarchy. For example, in the current Intel QuickAssist QPI FPGA Platform, the Xeon processor enjoys a much more powerful and higher-performing memory subsystem than what is achievable from the FPGA. The Xeon processor presents a hard-to-beat design point if we focus only on the pointer chasing aspect of the traversal (ignoring the FPGA's potential advantages in payload memory accesses and payload processing). On the other hand, the disadvantage of a software-only traversal is its inability to customize at the datapath level for performance or efficiency.

Fabric-Only Traversal. The starting points in this study are hardware traversal engines built as soft-logic in the fabric. The optimal design of such traversal engines would include the logic to traverse the pointer-based data structure, and would also include an accompanying co-designed memory interface and subsystem, subjected to an extreme degree of customization. We summarize below the most profitable opportunities we encountered in our study:

1. For data structures with an indirect payload, a hardware traversal engine may separately issue the pointer and the payload memory fetches to the coherent and non-coherent interfaces, respectively, if both are available. This approach reserves the cache capacity for any available (cache-block granularity) spatial and temporal localities in the traversal of the nodes. The non-cache-coherent interface keeps the payload fetches (without temporal locality) from polluting the cache and may even be able to offer higher payload fetch bandwidth.

2. If it is known that the pointer and payload memory fetches exhibit good spatial locality (such as modeled by the best-case sequential layout in the reference behavior), a hardware traversal engine could sequentially prefetch ahead of the current node's memory location in case the following locations are needed soon. If the memory interface operates at a cache block granularity, some degree of spatial prefetching happens unavoidably; the hardware traversal engine need only add logic to recognize when subsequent nodes to be visited fall within the current cache block. In general, a hardware engine should take advantage of specific knowledge of the pointer-based data-structure and the traversal algorithm in speculative run-ahead-type optimizations.

3. When the path traversed through the pointer-based data structure is independent of the data payload values, a hardware traversal engine should decouple and overlap the pointer chasing and the data payload memory access sequences. This concurrency leads to improved behavior modeled by Equation 2 rather than Equation 1.

4. When multiple concurrent traversals are allowed, a hardware traversal engine should be much more able than software to achieve the high degree of interleaving necessary to fully hide the memory latency and saturate the memory bandwidth. When allowed, interleaving multiple traversals is a very powerful optimization technique for overcoming the effects of memory latency, and works well in general over the remaining parameters (layout, payload size, and dependence).

Hybrid Traversal. The most challenging scenario for a fabric-only traversal is traversing a single data structure with a small data payload size and prefetch-unfriendly node layout in memory. This challenge singularly accentuates the impact of memory read latency. Our pointer chasing study on shared-memory FPGAs was in fact motivated by this scenario and by the prospect of incorporating the processor cores in a hybrid solution. A basic approach would be for the processor core to traverse the pointer-based data structure, fetch and prepare the data payload to be streamed into the fabric using any one of the interface options. Though simple, this approach (which we call hybrid-push) is very

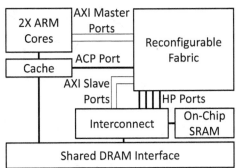

Figure 3: Datapaths between memory, the ARM cores, and the fabric in the Zynq

Table 1: Experimental parameters.

Reference Behavior Parameters	Values
Node Layout	best case (sequential), worst case (16-KByte strided)
Payload Size	2, 4, 8, 16, 32, 64, 128, 256, 512, or 1024 bytes
Payload Dependence	Yes, No
Traversal Concurrency	1, 2, 4, 8, 16, 32, 64, 128 ways

Implementation Options	Values
Payload Location	inlined, indirect
Traversal Approach	software-only, fabric-only, hybrid-push, hybrid-pull
Fabric Memory Path	HP, ACP
Fabric Memory Fetch Size	8, 16, 32 Bytes
Core-to-Fabric Path	PIO, DMA
Core-to-Fabric DMA Staging	in DRAM, in OCM

effective for traversals with small payload sizes. But the inefficiency of multiple movements of the data payload grows with payload size.

When the data structure can be traversed independently of the data payload values (or can be traversed using only a very small portion of the payload and minimal processing), a better approach is for the processor core to traverse the pointer-based data structure and stream pointers to the data payload into the fabric. The fabric in turn fetches the data payload directly from shared memory. This approach (we call hybrid-pull) not only benefits from more efficient use of memory bandwidth but it also benefits from overlapping the pointer-chasing and the data payload memory accesses (Equation 2). An important benefit of both hybrid approaches is the ease of development coming from handling complicated data structures and algorithms in software.

5. REAL SYSTEM EFFECTS

In this section we offer a detailed look at how the high-level considerations discussed in the preceding section play out in real systems that include the Xilinx Zynq, the Intel QuickAssist QPI FPGA Platform, and the Convey HC-2EX. By focusing exclusively on the reference linked-list traversal behavior, we are able to make a very thorough examination of the implementation space. It is important to note that we are not evaluating the suitability of these current systems for supporting pointer chasing; we certainly make no attempt to compare them. Our goal with these studies is to convey to the readers the real effects and complexity that comes from the different mechanisms and implementation options. We devote most of this section to our extensive design study on Xilinx Zynq because it provides the most diverse range of implementation options.

5.1 Xilinx Zynq

5.1.1 Platform Description

For the Xilinx Zynq study, we worked with the ZC706 evaluation board (containing a XC7Z045 SoC FPGA). Figure 3 provides a high-level view of the Zynq datapath, showing 2 ARM cores and a reconfigurable fabric. The Zynq architecture provides the full selection of interface options discussed in Section 4.1.

The reconfigurable fabric on the Zynq supports high bandwidth DRAM accesses through (a) four 64-bit non-cache-coherent "High Performance" (**HP**) ports, and (b) one 64-bit cache coherent "Accelerator Coherency Port" (**ACP**) port. The Zynq fabric can also access on-chip SRAM (referred to

as **OCM**) that is shared with the ARM cores through these ports. The ARM cores interact with the fabric using programmed I/O (**PIO**) through two 32-bit memory-mapped AXI master ports. Included in the ARM system is a built-in 8-channel **DMA** engine that can copy data between any source and destination regions in the global addresss space.

5.1.2 Implementations

We conducted a nearly exhaustive design study of the parameterized reference linked-list traversal behavior over the full combination of implementation options available on the Zynq. Table 1 summarizes the behavior parameters (presented in Section 3) and the Zynq implementation options discussed below.

The in-fabric portion of the traversal engines are developed in Bluespec System Verilog [11]. We tested shared memory accesses from the fabric using both the coherent ACP port and the non-coherent HP ports. The traversal engine supports a compile-time configurable data block size (tested at at 8, 16 and 32 bytes) for fetching linked-list node structs. This is to enable sequential prefetching (allowed by the best-case node layout scenario). The traversal engine supports issuing a new memory request one cycle after a data block is delivered to it, and can interleave multiple traversals at run time, allowing a single engine to support the parallel traversals described below. We used ISE 14.7 to compile the Verilog emitted by Bluespec. The synthesized traversal engines ran at 200 MHz. None of our engines utilized more than 10% of the XC7Z045.

We utilized a single 667 MHz ARM core in "bare-metal" mode for the software components of the implementations. The ARM core sends payload (in hybrid-push) or payload pointers (in hybrid-pull) to the fabric through the AXI master port by either PIO or DMA. When using DMA, we stage data by copying one or more payloads (or pointers) into one of several contiguous buffers in DRAM or OCM. Staging data achieves much higher bandwidth than PIO, and amor-

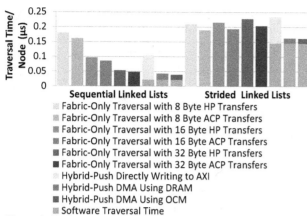

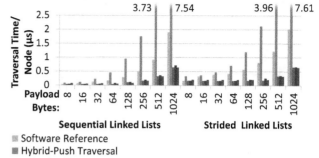

Figure 4: Performance achieved traversing linked-lists with 4 byte payload inlined within the linked-list nodes.

Figure 5: Performance achieved traversing linked-lists containing pointers to a larger data payload.

tizes the cost of initiating DMA transfers.[3] We built the software component with Xilinx SDK 14.7 with gcc -O3.

5.1.3 Observations

Below we present the most illustrative results from our comprehensive design study cases.

Single Linked-List with a 4-Byte Payload. Traversing a single linked-list with small payload (4-Bytes, inlined) presents the most difficult scenario. Figure 4 reports the per-node traversal time achieved under several implementation options. Results for both best-case and worst-case node layouts are reported. The fabric-only traversals reach a steady state for linked list with under 10 nodes. The hybrid-push traversals that use DMA require linked lists with 20 to 30 nodes in order to reach a steady state.

The first 6 bars in the series correspond to the fabric-only traversal engines using the HP or ACP interface to issue 8, 16 and 32 byte transfers. We see that using the ACP interface results in a slightly faster traversal time. For the best-case sequential layout, we see an improvement in traversal time as we increase the transfer size. This is due to spatial prefetching effects; the same is not observed for the worst-case strided layouts. In cases where prefetching is ineffective, the performance of traversing a single linked list with a small payload is entirely dictated by the platform's memory latency performance. What may be counterintuitive is that the Zynq, which does not have the DRAM bandwidth or capacity of the server systems, has the best memory latency performance due to its tight integration and hardwired memory path.

The next 3 bars in the series in Figure 4 correspond to hybrid-push using PIO, DMA with DRAM staging, and DMA with OCM staging. These bars are stacked to show how much time is spent by pointer chasing in the ARM core and how much time is spent in pushing data payload to the fabric. Hybrid-pull is not reported, as it does not make sense in this context since the ARM core would have to send the same size data (4-byte pointer or 4-byte payload per node).

We are encouraged to find a real-life example of the hybrid approach improving over the fabric-only approach on small payload scenarios. DMA from DRAM or OCM performed roughly equally;[4] and hybrid-push PIO performance is much worse because the ARM core actually stalls on each write (for approximately 100ns in our measurements) until it receives the bus response. As should be expected, software pointer-chasing is also much slower for the worst-case node layout, but hybrid-push still did better than the fabric-only implementations.

Single Linked-List with Varying Payload. Figure 5 reports the per-node traversal time of a single linked-list with payload sizes ranging from 8 Bytes to 1 KBytes. Again, the results for both best-case and worst-case layouts are reported. For this set of results, the linked-list nodes contain pointers to the payload (indirect payload). Five bars are shown for each payload size. The first bar, provided as a reference only, is the time of a software-only traversal. This software-only traversal touches all payload data but does not send payload data to the fabric (as required by the reference behavior). In many cases, especially for large payload sizes, the software-only traversal is in fact slower than sending the payload data to the fabric. This serves to provide another justification for delivering the payload into the fabric besides the assumed FPGA acceleration of processing.

The next 4 bars correspond to hybrid-push, hybrid-pull using HP for payload fetch, hybrid-pull using ACP for payload fetch, and a highly optimized fabric-only implementation that uses ACP for fetching the node structs as 32-byte blocks and HP for fetching the indirect payload.

We can see the advantage of hybrid-pull over fabric-only on the smaller payload sizes. Keep in mind that hybrid-pull is only valid for traversals that are independent of the payload values. As the payload size increases, hybrid-pull's advantage over fabric-only diminishes as the traversal time become dominated by the payload fetch time through the HP ports. Both hybrid-pull and fabric-only are able to reach 98% of the peak bandwidth of a 64-bit wide HP interface at 200 MHz.

When payload sizes exceed 4 bytes, hybrid-push is always slower than fabric-only. But for smaller payload sizes and payload dependent traversals, hybrid-push may still be a valid option due to its ease of development.

Interleaved Concurrent Traversals. For this final set of Zynq results, we return to linked lists with small 4-byte

---

[3]DMA initiation costs are high enough that performing a DMA transfer for each linked list node is slower than PIO.

[4]The DMA engine transferred data from the processor cache rather than memory, masking the performance difference between OCM and DRAM.

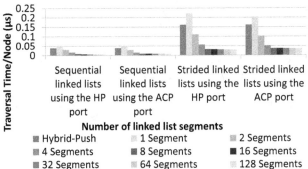

Number of linked list segments

■ Hybrid-Push ■ 1 Segment ■ 2 Segments
■ 4 Segments ■ 8 Segments ■ 16 Segments
■ 32 Segments ■ 64 Segments ■ 128 Segments

Figure 6: Performance achieved through interleaved linked-list traversal, including the best "Hybrid-Push" results from Figure 4 for reference.

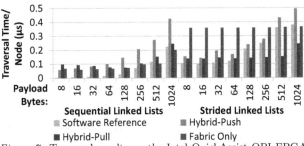

■ Software Reference ■ Hybrid-Push
■ Hybrid-Pull ■ Fabric Only

Figure 7: Traversal results on the Intel QuickAssist QPI FPGA Platform with indirect payload.

inlined payloads, but achieve better performance through parallel memory accesses. We break the 16,384 element linked list into shorter linked list segments. These linked list segments are traversed in a multi-threaded fashion using a single traversal engine, which interleaves the memory requests by the different threads. Figure 6 reports the per-node traversal time when interleaving 1 to 128 concurrent traversals. Results are presented for the best-case and worst-case node layouts, retrieving data using HP and ACP interfaces. The per-node traversal time of DMA hybrid-push from OCM is included as the first bar as a reference.

In all cases, the traversal time improves predictably as the number of concurrent traversals is increased up to 8 (reaching 93% of the HP interface's peak bandwidth). The effect is most dramatic in the worst-case data layout scenarios where all the references have to pay the full latency to DRAM. Issuing multiple outstanding reads from different traversals effectively keeps the traversal engine busy. For more than 16 traversals, the traversal time improves slowly because the HP bandwidth begins to saturate.

5.2 Intel QuickAssist QPI FPGA Platform

The Intel Heterogeneous Architecture Research Platform program has made the Intel QuickAssist QPI FPGA Platform [13] available for academic research use. The currently available Intel QuickAssist QPI FPGA Platform is a pre-production system that pairs a server-class multicore Xeon processor with an Altera Stratix V FPGA using Intel's cache-coherent QPI interconnect. The QPI interface extends shared memory to the FPGA, providing coherent access to DRAM attached to the processor as well as the processor's last-level cache. The Intel-provided soft-logic infrastructural IPs include the QPI interface, a 64-kilobyte cache, and the support for address translation. In our own benchmarking, we have seen the FPGA achieve approximately 6 GByte/sec of read bandwidth and about 350ns read latency over QPI to DRAM. Experimental results on this hardware platform reflect experiments performed at CMU. Results in this publication were generated using pre-production hardware and software, and may not reflect the performance of production or future systems.

Figure 7 reports the per-node traversal time for linked-list traversals with indirect payload of 8-1K bytes. As before, we report the traversal time under both best and worst case node layouts. There are four bars for each payload size in each layout case. The first bar, is a software-only reference traversal by the Xeon processor. This software-only traver-

sal touches all payload data, but does not send payload data to the fabric.

The next two bars are hybrid-push and hybrid-pull results, where the processor and fabric share the traversal effort to provide data to the fabric. Over increasing payload sizes, the traversal times stay about the same until the traversals switch from latency bound to bandwidth bound. As these cases are primarily latency bound, the processor's comparatively low-latency access to DRAM supports a hybrid traversal approach. However, without other interface options between the processor and the FPGA, all processor-FPGA interactions are implemented through shared memory using loads and stores. Thus, for hybrid-push, the processor copies the payload into a circular buffer in shared memory to be read by the FPGA. The hybrid-pull approach copies pointers to the payload into the buffer, and the FPGA fetches the data itself. The hybrid-push approach generally is slower than hybrid-pull, but can perform well with very small sequential payloads, where it can take advantage of the Xeon's superior cache, higher clock speed, and lower memory access latency.

The fourth bar shows fabric-only traversals. Fabric-only traversals were faster for sequential traversals due to spatial prefetching effects (the same observed in Figure 4). Each 64-byte cache line packs 8 sequential linked list nodes into each cache line. Furthermore, minimal latency between the hardware components fetching the linked list nodes and the hardware components fetching the payloads contributed to the speedup in sequential lists, as compared to the hybrid-pull approach. Overall performance in sequential traversals was still latency limited (by the latency of fetching payload data) until the payload size reaches 256 bytes. As before, fabric-only traversals of strided linked lists were the slowest. However, we achieved similar performance improvements to those in Section 5.1 by parallelizing the traversal: breaking up the strided linked lists into up to 8 segments and traversing these segments in parallel yielded linear performance improvements, and surpassed the performance of the hybrid traversals. We believe that future systems could improve the performance of hybrid approaches by providing low-overhead messaging and data transfer channels that reduce the synchronization overheads that applications incur when performing fine-grained communication.

5.3 Convey HC-2EX

Convey's HC-1 FPGA computing system featured shared memory with Intel host processors. The current generation HC-2 system replaces hardware shared memory with an FPGA system on a PCI-E bus containing a large capacity DRAM memory system, emulating a shared memory

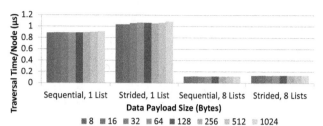

Figure 8: Parallel traversal results on the Convey HC-2EX with indirect payload.

abstraction in software. Due to this hardware implementation, our design study on the HC-2 focuses on the fabric-only approach. Even without shared memory, the HC-2, with its high-performing, high capacity DRAM subsystem, is still relevant to the acceleration of pointer-based irregular parallel applications.

We worked with a Convey HC-2EX [4] that includes proprietary "scatter-gather" memory modules. These unique memory modules allow the Convey machine to achieve peak memory bandwidth even on non-sequential accesses, up to 20GB/sec for each of its 4 user-logic FPGAs. Convey's memory subsystem is implemented in soft-logic using additional dedicated FPGAs. At first glance, Convey's emphasis on supporting irregular memory access patterns should be beneficial to pointer-chasing irregular parallel applications. For parallel traversal experiments on the Convey, we attached a separate Convey-optimized traversal engine to each of the user-visible memory ports. We do not show software or hybrid traversal results on Convey because the processor must go through the PCI-E interconnect to accesses the FPGA-attached DRAM.

Figure 8 reports the per-node traversal time for linked-lists with indirect payloads of 8 to 1K bytes. The left two clusters are for traversing a single linked-list under best-case and worst-case node layout, respectively. In this case, a single traversal engine utilizes 2 of the 16 memory crossbar ports available to one user-logic FPGA, one for fetching the node structs and one for fetching the payload data. The right two clusters are for traversing eight linked-lists concurrently using 8 different traversal engines and all 16 memory crossbar ports, still from one user-logic FPGA.

The Convey's performance is barely sensitive to node layout in memory, due to its unique support for non-sequential memory accesses. The Convey's per node traversal time is also not very sensitive to payload size. This is in part explained by Convey's very high memory bandwidth, but it also points to memory latency as the dominant effect in the single linked list traversal results. It may be surprising that the Convey's traversal time on a single linked-list is rather unexceptional, only on par with the Zynq. Recall that the Convey's memory subsystem stands out for its DRAM bandwidth. Even if Convey did not trade longer latency for better bandwidth optimizations, they would incur an unavoidable latency penalty by implementing their memory subsystem in soft logic. In the latency dominated traversals of a single linked list, the Convey can have no advantage over the hardwired memory subsystem in the Zynq. However, the Convey has plenty of bandwidth to sustain multiple current traversals without interference, as seen in the improvements in the 8-way traversal results. Even the 8-way traversal results do not even come close to saturating the bandwidth available on the Convey platform.

6. DISCUSSIONS

In this section we attempt to extrapolate from our study of pointer chasing.

Irregular Parallel Applications. Irregular parallel applications present an ideal target for shared-memory processor-FPGA acceleration. The demands of more regular applications could largely be satisfied by simpler solutions of memory bandwidth and capacity improvements. It is an irregular parallel application—with the requirement for irregular access over a large memory footprint and the opportunity for tightly coupled processor-FPGA collaboration—that really calls for the full potential of shared-memory processor-FPGA architectures.

Hardwired Memory Subsystem. With the growing use of FPGAs for compute acceleration, it is not inconceivable that an FPGA designed with computing in mind should come with a hardwired memory subsystem. We saw in the Zynq example that a modest commitment of die area to hardwiring the memory subsystem can yield large gains in performance and power efficiency over soft logic. To go one step further, there should be an entire compute-oriented FPGA memory architecture that addresses computing needs, ranging from memory hierarchy and cache-coherence nuts-and-bolts, to memory virtualization and protection, to what is the best presentation of memory to the fabric for use by spatial computing kernels.

Memory Performance. With hardwiring of the memory subsystem, there also needs to be a decision on the level of memory performance desired for FPGAs. With the exception of Convey, FPGAs and FPGA acceleration systems have generally been under-powered in their DRAM bytes-per-second relative to their potential for ops-per-second. Additional memory performance can go toward both unleashing computing performance and increasing application generality. Our study pointed especially to the importance of latency performance for irregular parallel applications. This can be achieved by both direct (faster, shorter links) and indirect (caches and prefetchers) means.

Memory Parallelism. Our study also repeatedly pointed to memory parallelism as a powerful technique to overcome memory latency. Memory parallelism should play an important role in shared-memory processor-FPGA system design. This can manifest at all levels, ranging from memory system design, to accelerator development tools, to algorithms. For our study, a tool that automated the process of creating parallelized traversal engines (possibly with annotations by the application developer indicating valid parallelization opportunities) would have made it much easier to achieve the best possible performance on data structure traversals.

Processor-FPGA Interactions. One motivation of the current work was to show that tightly-coupled processor-FPGA interactions in shared memory architectures can be used to improve performance (hybrid-push, hybrid-pull). Although not demonstrated by this study, there clearly are large dividends in eliciting software assistance to handle complex or non-critical tasks. Both hardware and software infrastructural support to simplify and speed up processor-FPGA interactions warrant increased attention in future shared-memory processor-FPGA systems. Although shared memory is elegant in its generality, there is room for special interfaces such as fast, short messaging FIFOs. The need for performance and efficiency when accellerating in hardware can tilt the balance toward efficiency rather than elegance.

7. CONCLUSION

The conceptual simplicity of linked lists can belie their significance and its complexity. In this paper, we used a reference linked list traversal behavior as a proxy to study the potential of shared-memory processor-FPGA systems in accelerating irregular parallel applications that rely on pointer-based data structures and algorithms. We examined a broad range of implementation considerations and options both at a high level and through concrete implementations on real systems. We point to memory latency as the dominant performance factor when traversing a single linked list, and observe that interleaving multiple concurrent traversals can overcome stalls caused by memory latency. We find that incorporating tightly-coupled processor assistance can also be an effective approach.

8. ACKNOWLEDGEMENTS

CMU authors are supported in part by NSF CCF-1320725 and by Intel. The authors thank Altera, Xilinx, Intel, and Bluespec for tools and hardware donated to CMU.

9. REFERENCES

[1] Altera, Inc. Arria 5 Device Overview, January 2015. AV-51001.

[2] Bruce Wile. Coherent Accelerator Processor Interface(CAPI) for POWER8 Systems, September 2014.

[3] Sai Rahul Chalamalasetti, Kevin Lim, Mitch Wright, Alvin AuYoung, Parthasarathy Ranganathan, and Martin Margala. An FPGA Memcached Appliance. In *Proceedings of the ACM/SIGDA International Symposium on Field Programmable Gate Arrays*, FPGA '13, pages 245–254, 2013.

[4] Convey Computer Corporation. Convey Personality Development Kit Reference Manual, April 2012. Version 5.2.

[5] Thomas H. Cormen, Charles E. Leiserson, Ronald L. Rivest, and Clifford Stein. *Introduction to Algorithms, Third Edition*. The MIT Press, 3rd edition, 2009.

[6] Jia Deng, Wei Dong, Richard Socher, Li-Jia Li, Kai Li, and Fei-Fei Li. ImageNet: A Large-Scale Hierarchical Image Database. In *CVPR09*, 2009.

[7] Christopher Dennl, Daniel Ziener, and Jürgen Teich. On-the-fly Composition of FPGA-Based SQL Query Accelerators Using a Partially Reconfigurable Module Library. *Field-Programmable Custom Computing Machines, Annual IEEE Symposium on*, 0:45–52, 2012.

[8] Geoffrey Hinton, Li Deng, Dong Yu, Abdel rahman Mohamed, Navdeep Jaitly, Andrew Senior, Vincent Vanhoucke, Patrick Nguyen, Tara Sainath George Dahl, and Brian Kingsbury. Deep neural networks for acoustic modeling in speech recognition. *IEEE Signal Processing Magazine*, 29(6):82–97, November 2012.

[9] Skand Hurkat, Jungwook Choi, Eriko Nurvitadhi, José F. Martínez, and Rob A. Rutenbar. Fast

[10] Maysam Lavasani, Hari Angepat, and Derek Chiou. An FPGA-based In-Line Accelerator for Memcached. *Computer Architecture Letters*, 13(2):57–60, July 2014.

[11] Rishiyur Nikhil. Bluespec System Verilog: Efficient, Correct RTL from High Level Specifications. In *Formal Methods and Models for Co-Design, 2004. MEMOCODE '04. Proceedings. Second ACM and IEEE International Conference on*, pages 69–70, June 2004.

[12] Eriko Nurvitadhi, Gabriel Weisz, Yu Wang, Skand Hurkat, Marie Nguyen, James C. Hoe, José F. Martínez, and Carlos Guestrin. GraphGen: An FPGA Framework for Vertex-Centric Graph Computation. In *Field-Programmable Custom Computing Machines (FCCM), 2014 IEEE 22nd Annual International Symposium on*, pages 25–28, May 2014.

[13] N. Oliver, R.R. Sharma, S. Chang, B. Chitlur, E. Garcia, J. Grecco, A. Grier, N. Ijih, Yaping Liu, P. Marolia, H. Mitchel, S. Subhaschandra, A. Sheiman, T. Whisonant, and P. Gupta. A reconfigurable computing system based on a cache-coherent fabric. In *Reconfigurable Computing and FPGAs (ReConFig), 2011 International Conference on*, pages 80–85, Nov 2011.

[14] Kalin Ovtcharov, Olatunji Ruwase, Joo-Young Kim, Jeremy Fowers, Karin Strauss, and Eric S. Chung. Accelerating Deep Convolutional Neural Networks Using Specialized Hardware, February 2015.

[15] Keshav Pingali, Donald Nguyen, Milind Kulkarni, Martin Burtscher, M. Amber Hassaan, Rashid Kaleem, Tsung-Hsien Lee, Andrew Lenharth, Roman Manevich, Mario Méndez-Lojo, Dimitrios Prountzos, and Xin Sui. The Tao of Parallelism in Algorithms. In *Proceedings of the ACM SIGPLAN Conference on Programming Language Design and Implementation*, PLDI '11, pages 12–25, 2011.

[16] Andrew Putnam, Adrian Caulfield, Eric Chung, Derek Chiou, Kypros Constantinides, John Demme, Hadi Esmaeilzadeh, Jeremy Fowers, Gopi Prashanth Gopal, Jan Gray, Michael Haselman, Scott Hauck, Stephen Heil, Amir Hormati, Joo-Young Kim, Sitaram Lanka, Jim Larus, Eric Peterson, Simon Pope, Aaron Smith, Jason Thong, Phillip Yi Xiao, and Doug Burger. A Reconfigurable Fabric for Accelerating Large-Scale Datacenter Services. In *41st Annual International Symposium on Computer Architecture (ISCA)*, June 2014.

[17] Yaman Umuroglu, Donn Morrison, and Magnus Jahre. Hybrid Breadth-First Search on a Single-Chip FPGA-CPU Heterogeneous Platform. In *Proceedings of the 25th International Conference on Field Programmable Logic and Applications*, FPL '15, September 2015.

[18] Xilinx, Inc. Zynq-7000 All Programmable SoC Overview, October 2014. v1.7.

Hierarchical Implementation of Sequential Tree-reweighted Belief Propagation for Probabilistic Inference. In *Proceedings of the 25th International Conference on Field Programmable Logic and Applications*, FPL '15, September 2015.

Poster Session 1

A Low DDR Bandwidth 100FPS 1080p Video 2D Discrete Wavelet Transform Implementation on FPGA

Mohammed Shaaban Ibraheem, Syed Zahid Ahmed, Khalil Hachicha, *Sorbonne Universités, UPMC Paris 06*
Sylvain Hochberg, *CIRA*
Patrick Garda, *Sorbonne Universités, UPMC Paris 06*
Contact: m-shaaban.ibraheem@lip6.fr

DWT plays a vital role in image processing applications. It provides a better image compression quality compared to DCT based compression such as JPEG standard. In this work, we present a novel high-throughput, fixed-point lifting scheme DWT implementation on Altera's StratixIV FPGA that outperforms several published FPGA implementations. Our proposed architecture at just 125MHz and DDR2 running at 250MHz provides throughput of 100fps for full HD 1080p frames for 5 stages of DWT (equivalent of 25fps 4K video). The novelty of our work is unified 2D DWT computation architecture that eliminates the problem of column-wise image pixels access from the DDR. Hence it also eliminates the transpose schemes proposed by some works that only give limited benefit in enhancing DDR access. Our architecture uses only six line buffers and reads and writes linearly just once to and from the DDR for a given stage. We exploited the FPGA's on-chip dual port memories and built four-port line buffers by running the memories at twice the speed of logic allowing reading/writing data at both positive and negative clock edges. Using these four ports we created an optimal pipelined architecture for DMA reading, Horizontal 1D DWT, Vertical 1D DWT and DMA writing. The scalable nature of our architecture is well positioned on the roadway to 4K and upcoming 8K video processing that will be easily possible due to higher bandwidth DDR4 interface equipped latest and upcoming FPGAs.

Keywords: Image compression; Discrete Wavelet Transform; Lifting Scheme; FPGA; Fixed-point arithmetic; DDR access

DOI: http://dx.doi.org/10.1145/2847263.2847321

A Scalable Heterogeneous Dataflow Architecture For Big Data Analytics Using FPGAs

Ehsan Ghasemi, University of Toronto
Paul Chow, University of Toronto
Contact: eghasemi89@gmail.com

Due to rapidly expanding data size, there is increasing need for scalable, high-performance, and low-energy frameworks for large-scale data computation. We build a dataflow architecture that harnesses FPGA resources within a distributed analytics platform creating a heterogeneous data analytics framework. This approach leverages the scalability of existing distributed processing environments and provides easy access to custom hardware

accelerators for large-scale data analysis. We prototype our framework within the Apache Spark analytics tool running on a CPU-FPGA heterogeneous cluster. As a specific application case study, we have chosen the MapReduce paradigm to implement a multi-purpose, scalable, and customizable RTL accelerator inside the FPGA, capable of incorporating custom High-Level Synthesis (HLS) MapReduce kernels. We demonstrate how a typical MapReduce application can be simply adapted to our distributed framework while retaining the scalability of the Spark platform.

Keywords: big data; Apache Spark; MapReduce; FPGA

DOI: http://dx.doi.org/10.1145/2847263.2847294

Accelerating Database Query Processing on OpenCL-based FPGAs

Zeke Wang, Huiyan Cheah, Johns Paul, Bingsheng He, *Nanyang Technological University*
Wei Zhang, *HKUST*

The release of OpenCL support for FPGAs represents a significant improvement in extending database applications to the reconfigurable domain. Taking advantage of the programmability offered by the OpenCL HLS tool, an OpenCL database can be easily ported and re-designed for FPGAs. A single SQL query in these database systems usually consists of multiple operators, and each one of these operators in turn consists of multiple OpenCL kernels. Due to the specific properties of FPGAs, each OpenCL kernel can have different optimization combinations (in terms of **CU** and **SIMD**) which is critical to the overall performance of query processing. In this paper, we propose an efficient method to implement database operators on OpenCL-based FPGAs. We use a cost model to determine the optimum query plan for an input query. Our cost model has two components: *unit cost* and *query plan generation*. The unit cost component generates multiple <unit cost, resource utilization> pairs for each kernel. The query plan generation component employs a dynamic programming approach to generate the optimum query plan which consider the possibilities to use multiple FPGA images. The experiments show that 1) our cost model can accurately predict the performance of each feasible query plan for the input query, and is able to guide the generation of the optimum query plan, 2) our optimized query plan achieves a performance speedup 1.5×--4× times over the state-of-the-art query processing on OpenCL-based FPGAs.

An Improved Global Stereo-Matching on FPGA for Real-Time Applications

Daolu Zha, *University of Science of Technology of China*
Xi Jin, *University of Science of Technology of China*
Tian Xiang, *University of Science of Technology of China*
Contact: ustczdl@mail.ustc.edu.cn

A real-time global stereo matching algorithm is implemented on FPGA. Stereo matching is frequently used in stereo vision systems, e.g. for stereo vision applications like objects detection and autonomous vehicles. Global algorithms perform much more significant than local algorithms, but global algorithms are not implemented on FPGA by reason of rely on the high-end hardware resources. In this implementation the stereo pairs are divided into blocks, the hardware resources are reduced by processing one block once. The hardware implementation is based on a Xilinx®Kintex 7 FPGA. Experiment results show the implementation performances significant and 30 fps@1920x1680 is achieved.

Keywords: Stereo Matching; Real-Time; FPGA; Global Algorithm; Hardware Accelerate

DOI: http://dx.doi.org/10.1145/2847263.2847292

ENFIRE: An Energy-efficient Fine-grained Spatio-temporal Reconfigurable Computing Fabric

Wenchao Qian, Christopher Babecki, Robert Karam, Swarup Bhunia, *Case Western Reserve University*
Contact: wxq18@case.edu

Field Programmable Gate Arrays (FPGAs) are well-established as fine-grained hardware reconfigurable computing platforms. However, FPGA energy usage is dominated by programmable interconnects, which have poor scalability across different technology generations. In this work, we propose ENFIRE, a novel, energy-efficient, fine-grained, spatio-temporal, memory-based reconfigurable computing framework that provides the flexibility of bit-level information processing, which is not available in conventional coarse-grain reconfigurable architectures (CGRAs). A dense two-dimensional memory array is the main computing element in the proposed framework, which stores not only the data to be processed, but also the functional behavior of a mapped application in the form of lookup tables (LUTs) of various input/output sizes. Spatially distributed configurable computing elements (CEs) communicate with each other based on data dependencies using a mesh network, while execution inside each CE occurs in a temporal manner. A custom software framework has also been co-developed which enables application mapping to a set of CEs. By finding the right balance between spatial and temporal computing, it can achieve a highly energy-efficient mapping, significantly reducing the programmable interconnect overhead when compared with FPGA. Simulation results show an improvement of 7.6X in overall energy, 1.6X in energy efficiency, 1.1X in leakage energy, and 5.3X in Unified Energy-Efficiency, a metric that considers energy and area together, compared with comparable FPGA implementations for a set of random logic benchmarks.

Keywords: Fine-grain Reconfigurable Hardware; FPGA; Memory Based Computing; Energy-Efficiency; Spatio-temporal Computing

DOI: http://dx.doi.org/10.1145/2847263.2847325

Floorplanning of Partially Reconfigurable design on Heterogeneous FPGA

Pingakshya Goswami, *University of Texas at Dallas*
Dinesh Bhatia, *University of Texas at Dallas*
Contact: pxg131330@utdallas.edu

The floorplanning problem in FPGA has been a topic of research for more than a decade. Although the floorplanning problem has been thoroughly explored for homogeneous FPGAs, very less work has been done for heterogeneous FPGAs. In this paper, we have designed a floorplanner for partially reconfigurable design in heterogeneous FPGAs which takes into consideration the diversity of resources present inside the FPGA device and their locations. The floorplanner is based on fixed outline simulated annealing algorithm. We proposed a priority based sorting algorithm mimicking Olympic Medal Tally for initial floorplanning which is a preprocessing step for simulated annealing. Also, a White Space detection algorithm is proposed for efficient management of white space inside the FPGA device. We defined a cost function, which consists of weighed sum of wirelength, area and resource wastage, and minimized this cost function using simulated annealing. In this work, we also described a method to calculate two different types of resource wastage and suggested a method to reduce it. The performance of our floorplanner is evaluated using MCNC benchmarks on Xilinx Virtex 5 FPGA architecture. We have compared our proposed floorplanner with other results reported in the literature and observed substantial improvement in the overall wirelength as well as the execution time. Finally, we integrated our floorplanner with Xilinx PlanAhead to automate the floorplanning process. We generate the floorplan of a partially reconfigurable median filter, which consists of seven reconfigurable regions. When a comparison is made between the manually generated floorplan and the automatic floorplan generated by our tool, a significant improvement is observed in terms of parameters like total area occupied by the reconfigurable regions, frequency of the operation and total time required by PlanAhead to place and route the design.

Keywords: Heterogeneous FPGA; Floorplanning; Partial Reconfiguration

DOI: http://dx.doi.org/10.1145/2847263.2847323

Increasing the Utility of Self-Calibration Methods in High-Precision Time Measurement Systems

Matthias Hinkfoth, *University of Rostock, Germany*
Ralf Salomon, *University of Rostock, Germany*
Contact: matthias.hinkfoth2@uni-rostock.de

Asynchronously operating systems, such as tapped delay lines, are the designer's favorite, if high resolution and precision in time are required. Their drawback, however, is that they require extensive calibration, which prohibits, among other things, sporadic recalibration during the mode of operation. Recent research has shown that the tight coupling of two selective high-precision systems inside a single FPGA substantially reduces the required calibration time: it was reduced from several hours to about 30 minutes. But even this method has not solved the problem that human intervention is required for selecting suitable calibration points. The research presented in this poster suggests that a hybrid approach is able to solve this problem: rather than tightly coupling two systems, the present approach employs hybrid elements, called X-BOUNCE, that seamlessly incorporate an X-ORCA element into a BOUNCE element. In the practical experiments, X-BOUNCE has reduced the required calibration time from 30 minutes to one second and has abandoned any human intervention. Furthermore, the proposed X-BOUNCE element can be realized by just one FPGA-LUT, which allows for easy scalability. The results were produced on a Cy- clone II FPGA that has implemented 200 X-BOUNCE elements. Unfortunately, some elements exhibit a calibration inaccuracy that can be as large as 300 ps.

Thanks to Christian Haubelt for the equipment Agilent 81150A. Thanks to Ralf Joost for helpful discussion.

Keywords: Time Measurement; Calibration

DOI: http://dx.doi.org/10.1145/2847263.2847311

Knowledge is Power: Module-level Sensing for Runtime Optimisation

James J. Davis, Eddie Hung, Joshua M. Levine, Edward A. Stott, Peter Y. K. Cheung, George A. Constantinides, *Imperial College London*
Contact: {james.davis06, e.hung, josh.levine05, ed.stott, p.cheung, g.constantinides}@imperial.ac.uk

We propose the compile-time instrumentation of coexisting modules—IP blocks, accelerators, etc.—implemented in FPGAs. The efficient mapping of tasks to execution units can then be achieved, for power and/or timing performance, by tracking dynamic power consumption and/or timing slack online at module-level granularity. Our proposed instrumentation is transparent, thereby not affecting circuit functionality. Power and timing overheads have proven to be small and tend to be outweighed by the exposed runtime benefits.

Dynamic power consumption can be inferred through the measurement of switching activity on indicative, frequently toggling nets. Online analysis is able to derive a live power breakdown by building and updating a model fed with per-module activity counts and system-wide power consumption. Such a model can be continuously refined and its use allows the tracking of unpredictable phenomena, including degradation.

Online measurement of slack in critical (and near-critical) paths facilitates the safe erosion of static timing analysis-derived guardbands. This then enables the co-optimisation of power and timing performance under given external operating constraints, including those which change over time. Assuming functional compatibility, high-priority tasks would suit execution within modules with excess slack. This could be reduced via dynamic frequency scaling, thereby increasing throughput.

Keywords: Power measurement; Timing slack measurement; Instrumentation; Optimisation; Runtime management; Online algorithms; Task mapping

DOI: http://dx.doi.org/10.1145/2847263.2847316

FPGA'16, February 21–23, 2016, Monterey, CA, USA.
ACM 978-1-4503-3856-1/16/02.

Machine-Learning driven Auto-Tuning of High-Level Synthesis for FPGAs

Li Ting, Harri Wijaya, Nachiket Kapre, *Nanyang Technological University*
Contact: nachiket@ieee.org

Modern High-Level Synthesis (HLS) tools allow C descriptions of computation to be compiled to optimized low-level RTL, but expose a range of manual optimization options, compiler directives and tweaks to the developer. In many instances, this results in a tedious iterative development flow to meet resource, timing and power constraints which defeats the purpose of adopting the high-level abstraction in the first place. In this paper, we show how to use Machine Learning routines to predict the impact of HLS compiler optimization on final FPGA utilization metrics. We compile multiple variations of the high-level C code across a range of compiler optimizations and pragmas to generate a large design space of candidate solutions. On the Machsuite benchmarks, we are able to train a linear regression model to predict resources, latency and frequency metrics with high accuracy ($R^2 > 0.75$). We expect such developer-assistance tools to (1) offer insight to drive manual selection of suitable directive combinations, and (2) automate the process of selecting directives in the complex design space of modern HLS design.

Keywords: Machine Learning; FPGA CAD, Timing Closure

DOI: http://dx.doi.org/10.1145/2847263.2847297

Re-targeting Optimization Sequences from Scalar Processors to FPGAs in HLS compilers

Ronak Kogta, Suresh Purini, Ajit Mathew, *IIIT Hyderabad*
Contact: ronak.kogta@research.iiit.ac.in

A high-level synthesis compiler translates a source program written in a high level programming language such as C or SystemC into an equivalent circuit. The performance of the generated circuit in terms of metrics such as area, frequency and clock cycles depends on the compiler optimizations enabled and their order of application. Finding an optimal sequence for a given program is a hard combinatorial optimization problem. In this paper, we propose a practical and search time efficient technique for finding a near-optimal sequence for a given program. The main idea is to strike a balance between the search for a *universally* good sequence (like that of O3) which works for all programs vis-a-vis finding a good sequence on a *per-program* basis. Towards that, we construct a rich downsampled sequence set, which caters to different program classes, from the unbounded optimization sequence space by applying heuristic search algorithms on a set of Microkernel benchmark programs. The optimization metric that we use while constructing the downsampled sequence set is the execution time on a scalar processor. Given a new program, we try all the sequences from the downsampled sequence setand pick the best. Applying this technique in the LegUp high-level synthesis compiler, we are able to obtain 23 % and 40 % improvement on CHStone and Machsuite benchmark programs respectively. We also propose techniques to further reduce the size of the downsampled sequence set to improve the sequence search time.

Keywords: High level synthesis; Optimization; Compilers

DOI: http://dx.doi.org/10.1145/2847263.2847315

Poster Session 2

A High-throughput Architecture for Lossless Decompression on FPGA Designed Using HLS

Jie Lei, *Xidian University & UCLA*
Yuting Chen, *UCLA*
Yunsong Li, *Xidian University*
Jason Cong, *UCLA*
Contact: jielei@mail.xidian.edu.cn

In the field of big data applications, lossless data compression and decompression can play an important role in improving the data center's efficiency in storage and distribution of data. To avoid becoming a performance bottleneck, they must be accelerated to have a capability of high speed data processing. As FPGAs begin to be deployed as compute accelerators in the data centers for its advantages of massive parallel customized processing capability, power efficiency and hardware reconfiguration. It is promising and interesting to use FPGAs for acceleration of data compression and decompression. The conventional development of FPGA accelerators using hardware description language costs much more design efforts than that of CPUs or GPUs. High level synthesis (HLS) can be used to greatly improve the design productivity. In this paper, we present a solution for accelerating lossless data decompression on FPGA by using HLS. With a pipelined data-flow structure, the proposed decompression accelerator can perform static Huffman decoding and LZ77 decompression at a very high throughput rate. According to the experimental results conducted on FPGA with the Calgary Corpus data benchmark, the average data throughput of the proposed decompression core achieves to 4.6 Gbps while running at 200 MHz.

Keywords: Lossless decompression; Accelerator; HLS; FPGA

DOI: http://dx.doi.org/10.1145/2847263.2847305

An Activity Aware Placement Approach For 3D FPGAs

Girish Deshpande, *University of Texas at Dallas*
Dinesh Bhatia, *University of Texas at Dallas*
Contact: girish.deshpande@utdallas.edu

In order to cope with increasing demand for higher logic densities and shrinking feature sizes, there has been a concerted effort by academia and industry towards the design of three dimensional integrated circuits (3D ICs). Various architectural approaches have been investigated over the past few years in order to realize functional 3D ICs. A majority of such research has been focused on devices such as memories, caches and other application specific circuits. Not much work has been done in the FPGA community on the exploration of 3D FPGAs both at the architectural and EDA

levels. This work aims to look at placement methodologies and metrics for island style 3D FPGAs from a thermal perspective. The novelty of our approach lies in the fact that unlike previous related works on 3D FPGA placement which rely solely on wirelength and TSV (Through Silicon Via)-count minimization to evaluate placement, we propose a 3D placer that also takes into consideration, the transition density of each net to ensure a more thermally balanced spatial distribution of nets on the chip. This placement methodology tries to place nets which exhibit higher transition densities on the lower most layer of the FPGA. The lowest layer is typically closest to the heat sink and placing nets with higher switching activity on this layer will aid heat dissipation in a more effective manner and reduce hot spots on the chip. This placer was tested on a four layer 3D FPGA model using MCNC benchmarks and on average, around 40 % of high activity nets were placed on the lowest layer as compared to a placer that did not employ transition density based cost scaling during placement.

Keywords: FPGA; Placement; 3D Integration; EDA

DOI: http://dx.doi.org/10.1145/2847263.2847322

An Extensible Heterogeneous Multi-FPGA Framework for Accelerating N-body Simulation

Tianqi Wang, *University of Science and Technology*
Bo Peng, *University of Science and Technology*
Xi Jin, *University of Science and Technology*
Contact: jinxi@ustc.edu.cn

N-body simulation plays a significant role in scientific research and engineering development. Direct-summation N-body algorithms compute the particle interaction in an exact way, but this algorithm have a computational complexity of $O(N^2)$. To simulate a large system efficiently and flexibly, lots of high performance implementations on FPGA have been developed.

We propose an extensible framework for heterogeneous multi-FPGA based direct-summation N-body simulation and a model to decompose workload among FPGAs. In the framework, we try to use existing FPGA boards rather than design new specialized boards to reduce cost. It can be expanded conveniently with any available FPGA board and only requires quite low communication bandwidth between FPGA boards. The communication protocol is simple and can be implemented with limited hardware/software resource. For the purpose of improving the system's performance, the model divide workload based on the logic resource, memory access bandwidth and communication bandwidth of each FPGA chip. We implemented this framework in a numerical simulation project about MOND (Modified Newtonian dynamics), and achieved two orders of magnitude speedup compared with CPU implementations.

Keywords: Algorithms, Design, Performance

DOI: http://dx.doi.org/10.1145/2847263.2847303

An FPGA-Based Controller for a 77 GHz MEMS Tri-Mode Automotive Radar

Sabrina Zereen, *Invotek Electronics*
Sundeep Lal, *VerifEye Technologies*
Mohammed Khalid, *University of Windsor*
Sazzadur Chowdhury, *University of Windsor*
Contact: mkhalid@uwindsor.ca

This paper presents a Xilinx Virtex 5 FPGA platform based signal processing algorithm that was designed, implemented and experimentally verified for use in a MEMS based tri-mode 77 GHz FMCW automotive radar to determine range and velocity of targets in the vicinity of a host vehicle. It provides short (SRR), medium (MRR), and long-range radar (LRR) coverage using a single FPGA. The MEMS radar comprises of MEMS SP3T RF switches, microfabricated Rotman lens and a microstrip antenna embedded with MEMS SPST switches, in addition to other microelectronic components. A CA-CFAR module has been used to eliminate false targets in a multi-target clutter affected scenario. The developed algorithm enables the MEMS radar to detect 6 targets in a time span of 6.1 ms between a distance of 20 meters to 170 meters with range resolutions of 0.07, 0.11 and 0.19 meters respectively for SRR, MRR and LRR. A maximum relative velocity of 300 km/hour can be determined with a velocity resolution of 6.84 km/hour. The refresh rate is 2.048ms for each mode of radar which is nearly 40 times lower than the commercially available BOSCH LRR3 radar. The developed FPGA based radar signal processing algorithm can be implemented in an ASIC which can be batch fabricated to lower the production cost for high chip volumes. This will enable automotive radars to become a standard item for all the vehicles on the road.

Keywords: MEMS; Radar; FMCW; FPGA; Rotman lens

DOI: http://dx.doi.org/10.1145/2847263.2847288

An FPGA-SOC Based Accelerating Solution for N-body Simulations in MOND

Bo Peng, Tianqi Wang, Xi Jin, *University of Science and Technology of China, Collaborative Innovation Center of IC Design and Manufacturing of Yangtze River Delta*
Chuanjun Wang, *University of Chinese Academy of Sciences*
Contact: jinxi@ustc.edu.cn

Modified Newtonian dynamics (MOND) has shown a great success as a modified-potential theory of gravity. In this paper, we present a highly integrated accelerating solution for *N*-body MOND simulations. By using the FPGA-SoC, which integrates both FPGA and SOC (system on chip) in one chip, our solution exhibits potential for better performance, higher integration, and lower power consumption. To handle the calculation bottleneck of potential summation, on one hand, we develop a strategy to simplify the pipeline, in which the square calculation task is conducted by the DSP48E1 of Xilinx 7 series FPGAs, so as to reduce the logic

resource consumption of each pipeline; on the other hand, advantages of particle-mesh scheme are taken to overcome the bottleneck on bandwidth. Our experiment results show that 2 more pipelines can be integrated in Zynq-7020 FPGA-SoC with the simplified pipeline, and the bandwidth requirement is reduced significantly. Furthermore, our accelerating solution has a full range of advantages over different processors. Compared with GPU, our work is about better in both performance per Watt and performance per cost.

Keywords: FPGA-SOC; Accelerating; N-body; MOND

DOI: http://dx.doi.org/10.1145/2847263.2847307

Automated Verification Code Generation in HLS Using Software Execution Traces

Liwei Yang, *Nanyang Technological University*
Swathi Gurumani, *Advanced Digital Sciences Center*
Suhaib A. Fahmy, *Nanyang Technological University*
Deming Chen, *University of Illinois at Urbana-Champaign*
Kyle Rupnow, *Advanced Digital Sciences Center*
Contact: yangliwei.uestc@gmail.com

Improved quality of results from high level synthesis (HLS) tools has led to their increased adoption. Despite the automated translation from high level descriptions to register-transfer level (RTL) implementations, functional verification remains a major challenge. Verification can take significantly more time than the design process; if there is a functional mismatch, developers must back-trace thousands of signals and cycles to determine underlying cause. The challenge is further exacerbated with HLS-produced RTL, which is often not human readable.

To overcome these challenges, we present a verification technique that uses software-execution traces and automated insertion of verification code into the HLS-generated RTL to assist in debugging. The verification code helps pinpoint the earliest instance of RTL simulation mismatch, either caused by HLS engine bugs or design bugs, and related instructions. We also integrate a watchdog timer to examine the execution of control-flow and perform source-to-source transformation on benchmarks to take advantage of our proposed instrumentation. We also create a framework to insert various types of bugs, e.g. data-flow, control-flow and operational bugs, to evaluate our technique. We use the CHStone [1] benchmark suite and demonstrate that our verification detects over 90% of the inserted bugs, with over 70% of them detected within 10 cycles. In addition, the proposed flow can detect real-life bugs existing in previously released versions of CHStone suite as well.

Keywords: Verification; High-level synthesis; Trace-based

DOI: http://dx.doi.org/10.1145/2847263.2847313

FPGA'16, February 21–23, 2016, Monterey, CA, USA.
ACM 978-1-4503-3856-1/16/02.

DCPUF: Placement and Routing Constraint based Dynamically Configured Physical Unclonable Function on FPGA

Jing Ye, *Institute of Computing Technology, Chinese Academy of Sciences*
Yu Hu, *Institute of Computing Technology, Chinese Academy of Sciences*
Xiaowei Li, *Institute of Computing Technology, Chinese Academy of Sciences*
Contact: yejing@ict.ac.cn

With the development of Integrated Circuit (IC), it is a growing trend that the CPU and the FPGA are integrated into one chip. To improve the security of CPU+FPGA IC, we explore the reconfigurable feature of FPGA to implement a novel Dynamically Configured Physical Unclonable Function (DCPUF). PUF is a hardware security primitive that utilizes unpredictable process variations to produce particular challenge-response pairs, so even the chips with the same design would produce different responses for the same challenge. In the DCPUF, the FPGA configuration bits, which are specifically designed with dedicated placement and routing constraint, constitute the challenge. When a challenge is input to a CPU+FPGA IC, the CPU uses it to configure or partially configure the FPGA, and then waits for the FPGA to reply a response. In comparison with existing PUFs, the DCPUF has three major advantages: (1) different from existing PUFs with fixed designs, the logic of DCPUF is dynamically configured for each challenge, i.e. the circuits for producing different responses are different, leading to higher security; (2) much more electronic parameters affected by process variation are leveraged to make DCPUF more robust against attacks; (3) for CPU+FPGA IC, no extra hardware is needed. The experiments on real CPU+FPGA ICs show the proposed DCPUF keeps good randomness and stability.

Keywords: CPU+FPGA IC; PUF; Reconfiguration; Placement and Routing Constraint

DOI: http://dx.doi.org/10.1145/2847263.2847312

Evaluating the Impact of Environmental Factors on Physically Unclonable Functions

Sebastien Bellon, *ALaRI – USI*
Claudio Favi, *Nagra*
Miroslaw Malek, *ALaRI – USI*
Marco Macchetti, *Nagra*
Francesco Regazzoni, *ALaRI – USI*
Contact: regazzoni@alari.ch

Fabrication process introduces some inherent variability to the attributes of transistors (in particular length, widths, oxide thickness). As a result, every chip is physically unique. Physical uniqueness of microelectronics components can be used for multiple security applications. Physically Unclonable Functions (PUFs) are built to extract the physical uniqueness of microelectronics components and make it usable for secure applications.

However, the microelectronics components used by PUFs designs suffer from external, environmental variations that impact the PUF behavior. Variations of temperature gradients during manufacturing can bias the PUF responses. Variations of temperature or thermal noise during PUF operation change the behavior of the circuit, and can introduce errors in PUF responses. Detailed knowledge of the behavior of PUFs operating over various environmental factors is needed to reliably extract and demonstrate uniqueness of the chips.

In this work, we present a detailed and exhaustive analysis of the behavior of two PUF designs, a ring oscillator PUF and a timing path violation PUF. We have implemented both PUFs using FPGA fabricated by Xilinx, and analyzed their behavior while varying temperature and supply voltage. Our experiments quantify the robustness of each design, demonstrate their sensitivity to temperature and show the impact which supply voltage has on the uniqueness of the analyzed PUFs.

Keywords: Physically Unclonable Functions, PUFs, Security,

DOI: http://dx.doi.org/10.1145/2847263.2847308

Stochastic-Based Spin-Programmable Gate Array with Emerging MTJ Device Technology

Yu Bai, *University of Central Florida*
Mingjie Lin, *University of Central Florida*
Contact: mingjie@eecs.ucf.edu

This paper describes the stochastic-based Spin-Programmable Gate Array (SPGA), an innovative architecture attempting to exploit the stochastic switching behavior newly found in emerging spintronic devices for reconfigurable computing. While many recently studies have investigated using Spin Transfer Torque Memory (STTM) devices to replace configuration memory in FPGAs, our study, for the first time, attempts to use the quantum-induced stochastic property exhibited by spintronic devices directly for reconfiguration and logic computation. Specifically, the SPGA was designed from scratch for high performance, routability, and ease-of-use. It supports variable granularity multiple-input-multiple-output (MIMO) logic blocks and variable-length bypassing interconnects with a symmetrical structure. Due to its unconventional architectural features, the SPGA requires several major modifications to be made in the standard VPR placement/routing CAD flow, which include a new technology mapping algorithm based on computing (k, l)-cut, a new placement algorithm, and a modified delay-based routing procedure. Our mixed mode simulation results have shown that, with FPGA architecture innovations, on average, a SPGA can further achieve more than 10x improvement in logic density, about 5x improvement in average net delay, and about 5x improvement in the critical path delay for the largest 12 MCNC benchmark circuits over an island-style baseline FPGA with spintronic configuration bits.

Keywords: Emerging devices; FPGA; Stochastic

DOI: http://dx.doi.org/10.1145/2847263.2847317

Testing FPGA Local Interconnects Based on Repeatable Configuration Modules

Zhen Yang, *Fudan University*
Jian Wang, *Fudan University*
Meng Yang, *Fudan University*
Jinmei Lai, *Fudan University*
Contact: jmlai@fudan.edu.cn

This paper provides a novel technique for testing FPGA local interconnects based on repeatable configuration modules (RCMs). In order to fully detect all the possible faults, local interconnects together with the adjacent logic blocks in an FPGA are programmed to form a set of RCMs that are repeatable all over the FPGA array. After the RCMs for configurable logic blocks (CLBs) and other types of embedded cores (such as digital signal processor, block random access memory) are constructed, test configurations are generated by connecting the RCMs one by one throughout the whole FPGA array. The number of test configurations depends on the structure of the FPGA and the exact types of hard cores inside the FPGA. Experimental results show that a total of 47 test configurations are sufficient to achieve 96.2% fault coverage for Xilinx XC4VLX200 FPGA local interconnects.

This project is supported by the State Key Laboratory of ASIC and System, Fudan University, No. 2015MS007.

Keywords: FPGA; testing; local interconnects; repeatable configuration modules

DOI: http://dx.doi.org/10.1145/2847263.2847309

FPGA'16, February 21–23, 2016, Monterey, CA, USA.
ACM 978-1-4503-3856-1/16/02.

Poster Session 3

A 1 GSa/s, Reconfigurable Soft-core FPGA ADC

Stefan Visser, *TU Delft*
Harald Homulle, *TU Delft*
Edoardo Charbon, *TU Delft*
Contact: h.a.r.homulle@tudelft.nl

There exist many applications where analog interfacing is abundant, e.g. sensor networks, automotive, industrial control, (quantum) physics etc.

In those fields the use of FPGAs is continuously growing, however a direct link between the analog world and the digital FPGA is still missing (except for the newest generation of FPGAs, where analog-to-digital conversion is present, but limited in performance). External analog-to-digital converters (ADCs) are combined together with the FPGA to form a complete, application-specific system. This system is thus limited in compactness, flexibility, and reconfigurability.

To address those issues we propose an ADC architecture, implemented in a FPGA, that is fully reconfigurable and easy to calibrate. This allows to alter the design, according to the system requirements. Therefore it can be used in a wide range of operating conditions and adjusted to changes in supply voltage and FPGA temperature.

This architecture employs time-to-digital converters (TDCs) and phase interpolation techniques to reach a sampling rate higher than the clock frequency (400 MHz) of up to 1.2 GSa/s. The resulting FPGA ADC can achieve a 6 bit resolution over a 0.6 to 1.9 V input range. The system non-linearities (INL, DNL) are less than 0.45 LSB. The main advantages of this architecture are its scalability and reconfigurability, enabling applications with changing demands, on one single platform.

Keywords: ADC; TDC; FPGA; analog-to-digital converter; time-to-digital converter; calibration; reconfigurable; soft-core

DOI: http://dx.doi.org/10.1145/2847263.2847310

A Full-Capacity Local Routing Architecture for FPGAs

Xifan Tang, *EPFL*
Pierre-Emmanuel Gaillardon, *EPFL*
Giovanni De Micheli, *EPFL*
Contact: xifan.tang@epfl.ch

Reconfigurable systems employ highly-routable local routing architecture to interconnect generic fine-grain logic blocks. Commercial FPGAs employ 50% sparse crossbars rather than fully-connected crossbars in their local routing architecture to trade off between the area and routability of the *Logic Blocks* (LBs). While the input crossbar provides good routability and logic equivalence

for the inputs of the LB, the outputs of the LBs are typically assigned to a physical location. This lack of flexibility brings strong constraints to the global net router. Here, we propose a novel local routing architecture that guarantees full logic equivalence on all input and output pins of the LBs. First, we introduce full-capacity crossbars to interconnect the outputs of the fine-grain *Logic Elements* (LEs) to the output pins of the LBs. Second, in the local routing, we use a combination of fully-connected and full-capacity crossbars. The full-capacity crossbars are used for the feedback connections in place of the standard fully-connected crossbars to ensure a full routability while reducing the area footprint. Fully-connected crossbars are still employed for the input connections to maintain the logic equivalence of the inputs. As a result, the novel local routing architecture enhances the routability of the LB clusters without any area overhead. By granting the outputs with logic equivalence, the proposed local routing architecture unlocks the full optimization potential of FPGA routers. Architectural simulations show that without any modification on *Verilog-to-Routing* (VTR) tool suites, when a commercial FPGA architecture is considered and over a wide set of benchmarks, the novel local routing architecture can reduce 10% channel width and 11% routing area with 10% less area×delay×power on average. Therefore, the novel local routing architecture enhances the routability of FPGA, and brings opportunities in realizing larger implementations on a single FPGA chip.

Keywords: FPGA; Crossbars; Full-capacity; Local routing;

DOI: http://dx.doi.org/10.1145/2847263.2847314

ARAPrototyper: Enabling Rapid Prototyping and Evaluation for Accelerator-Rich Architecture

Yu-Ting Chen, Jason Cong, Zhenman Fang, and Peipei Zhou, *University of California, Los Angeles*
Contact: ytchen@cs.ucla.edu

Compared to conventional general-purpose processors, accelerator-rich architectures (ARAs) can provide orders-of-magnitude performance and energy gains. In this paper we design and implement the ARAPrototyper to enable rapid design space explorations for ARAs in real silicons and reduce the tedious prototyping efforts. First, ARAPrototyper provides a reusable baseline prototype with a highly customizable memory system, including interconnect between accelerators and buffers, interconnect between buffers and last-level cache (LLC) or DRAM, coherency choice at LLC or DRAM, and address translation support. To provide more insights into performance analysis, ARAPrototyper adds several performance counters on the accelerator side and leverages existing performance counters on the CPU side. Second, ARAPrototyper provides a clean interface to quickly integrate a user's own accelerators written in high-level synthesis (HLS) code. Then, an ARA prototype can be automatically generated and mapped to a Xilinx Zynq SoC. To quickly develop applications that run seamlessly on the ARA prototype, ARAPrototyper provides a system software stack and abstracts the accelerators as software libraries for application developers. Our results demonstrate that ARAPrototyper enables a wide range of design space explorations for ARAs at manageable prototyping efforts and 4,000 to 10,000X faster evaluation time than full-system simulations. We believe that ARAPrototyper can be an attractive alternative for ARA design and evaluation.

Keywords: Accelerator-Rich Architecture, FPGA Prototyping, Performance Evaluation, Accelerator Integration, Customized Memory System

DOI: http://dx.doi.org/10.1145/2847263.2847302

Doubling FPGA Throughput via a Soft SerDes Architecture for Full-Bandwidth Serial Pipelining

Aaron Landy, *University of Florida*
Greg Stitt, *University of Florida*
Contact: landy@hcs.ufl.edu

Serial arithmetic has been shown to offer attractive advantages in area, clock frequency, and functional density for FPGA datapaths but suffers from a significant reduction in throughput compared to traditional bit-parallel designs that is prohibitive for many applications. In this work, we present a full-bandwidth SerDes architecture specialized for Xilinx FPGAs that enables serial pipelines to accept inputs and generate outputs at the same rate as bit-parallel pipelines. When combined with the clock improvements from serial pipelines, we show that this approach offers more than $2.1\times$ average increase in throughput compared to bit-parallel pipelines. Although previous work has shown that serial pipelines can achieve similar results for some limited situations, the key contribution of this work is the ability to replace potentially any existing FPGA pipeline with a higher-throughput serialized alternative. We also present a serialized sliding-window architecture that improves throughput up to $4\times$.

Keywords: FPGA, serial arithmetic, SerDes, sliding window

DOI: http://dx.doi.org/10.1145/2847263.2847301

Enhanced TERO-PUF Implementations and Characterization on FPGAs

Cedric Marchand, Lilian Bossuet, *Laboratoire Hubert Curien, University of Lyon, Saint-Etienne, France*
Abdelkarim Cherkaoui, *TIMA Laboratory, Grenoble, France*
Contact: cedric.marchand@univ-st-etienne.fr

Physical unclonable functions (PUF) are a promising approach in design for trust and security. A PUF derives a unique identifier using physical characteristics of different dies containing an identical circuit, so it can be used to authenticate chips and for identification. The transient effect ring oscillator (TERO) PUF is based on the extraction of entropy due to process variations by comparing TERO cells characteristics. The TERO cell is designed

and implemented with a symmetric structure that requires special selection of the gates used and the delays of all connections inside the cell. Implementing this cell in FPGAs is challenging because the structure of FPGAs does not automatically allow designers to choose connections between elements. However, by manually specifying constraints and using specific features of the target FPGA family, the symmetry of the TERO cell can be established and reproduced in larger designs.

In this work, the design of the TERO cell is described for two different FGPA technologies (45nm Xilinx Spartan 6 and 28nm Altera Cyclone V). The statistical characterization of the TERO-PUF with the two targeted FPGAs has resulted in a uniqueness of 48.46% with Spartan 6 and 47.62% with Cyclone V. The result for the steadiness is 2.63% with Spartan 6 and 1.8% with Cyclone V. These results are close to the results obtained by several works that use ring oscillator RO-PUF which are considered the best candidate for PUF implementation on FPGAs. However, TERO-PUF is less sensitive to electromagnetic analysis than RO-PUF. Additionally, unlike RO-PUF, TERO-PUF is able to generate multiple bits per challenge (from one to three) and we have shown during the statistical characterization that the TERO-PUF provides from 0.85 to 1 bits of entropy per response bit.

As a conclusion, our work clearly shows that TERO-PUF is an serious alternative to RO-PUF for PUF implementation on FPGAs with strong statistical characteristics and more security than RO-PUF.

Keywords: Physical unclonable function, PUF design, FPGA, PUF characterization

DOI: http://dx.doi.org/10.1145/

FPGA Power Estimation Using Automatic Feature Selection

Yunxuan Yu, *University of California, Los Angeles*
Lei He, *University of California, Los Angeles*
Contact: yunxuan.yu@hotmail.com

Because layout stage consumes the lion share of FPGA synthesis runtime, pre-layout power estimation can be viewed as an early stage estimation and is needed for power minimization at the early design stage. Consisting two phases of feature selection and model training, data mining is effective for data based modeling, yet it has not been applied in a rigid fashion for FPGA power estimation as the existing algorithms can be viewed as model training using features selected manually. In this paper, we apply machine learning with automatic feature selection to pre- and post- logic synthesis estimations, named pre-synthesis and post-synthesis estimation. Experiments using Lattice Diamond MachXO2 family show that compared to the post-layout power simulation, post-synthesis estimation is 20x faster with 8.62% average error, while pre-synthesis estimation is 600x faster with considerably larger error that still needs further improvement. Furthermore, compared to existing algorithms using manually selected features, our post-synthesis estimation using automatic feature selection reduces error by 2-3 times. Finally, the ranking of features is able to provide insights for power minimization.

Keywords: FPGA; RTL Power Estimation; SVM; Feature Selection

DOI: http://dx.doi.org/10.1145/2847263.2847327

HGum: Messaging Framework for Hardware Accelerators

Sizhuo Zhang, *Massachusetts Institute of Technology*
Hari Angepat, *Microsoft*
Derek Chiou, *Microsoft*
Contact: szzhang@mit.edu

Software messaging frameworks help avoid errors and reduce engineering effort in building distributed systems by (i) providing an interface definition language (IDL) to precisely specify the structure of the message (the message *schema*) and (ii) automatically generating the serialization and deserialization functions that transform user data structures into binary data for sending across the network and vice versa. Similarly, a hardware-accelerated system that consists of host software and multiple FPGAs, could also benefit from a messaging framework to handle messages both between software and FPGA and also between different FPGAs. The key challenge for a hardware messaging framework is that it must be able to support large messages with complex schema while meeting critical constraints such as clock frequency, area, and throughput.

We present HGum, a messaging framework for hardware accelerators that meets all the above requirements. HGum is able to generate high-performance and low-cost hardware logic by employing a novel design that algorithmically parses the message schema to perform serialization and deserialization. Our evaluation of HGum shows that it not only significantly reduces engineering effort but also generates hardware with comparable quality to manual implementation.

Keywords: HGum; Messaging Framework; Hardware Accelerator

DOI: http://dx.doi.org/10.1145/2847263.2847289

Low-Swing Signaling for FPGA Power Reduction

Sayeh Sharifymoghaddam, *University of Toronto, ON, Canada*
Ali Sheikholeslami, *University of Toronto, ON, Canada*
Contact: Sayeh@ece.utoronto.ca

FPGAs are widely used in digital circuits implementation because of their lower non-recurring engineering cost and shorter time-to-market in comparison with ASICs. However, there are still area, performance, and energy efficiency gaps between FPGAs and ASICs. In this work, we propose a new FPGA architecture to narrow the energy efficiency gap. Since more than 62% of FPGA power is consumed in its interconnect, we target power consumption of the interconnect and try to reduce dynamic power consumption of this part using low-swing signaling technique.

To implement low-swing signaling, high-to-low and low-to-high voltage level converters are added to the switch boxes and connection blocks of the basic architecture. Simulation results on 20 largest MCNC circuits and 19 computational benchmarks confirm that the proposed architecture achieves an average of 13.5% total power reduction with the cost of less than 1% area and delay overhead. To the authors' knowledge, the proposed architecture in this work is the first architecture that provides low-swing signaling for single driver unidirectional routing scheme. Moreover, the proposed architecture has the maximum CAD tool flexibility and no extra constraint is required for the placement and routing algorithms.

Keywords: low-swing; FPGA; global interconnect

DOI: http://dx.doi.org/10.1145/2847263.2847319

Stochastic-Based Convolutional Networks with Reconfigurable Logic Fabric

Mohammed Alawad, *University of Central Florida*
Mingjie Lin, *University of Central Florida*
Contact: mingjie@eecs.ucf.edu

Large-scale convolutional neural network (CNN), well-known to be computationally intensive, is a fundamental algorithmic building block in many computer vision and artificial intelligence applications that follow the deep learning principle. This work presents a novel stochastic-based and scalable hardware architecture and circuit design that computes a convolutional neural network with FPGA. The key idea is to implement a multi-dimensional convolution accelerator that leverages the widely-used convolution theorem. Our approach has three advantages. First, it can achieve significantly lower algorithmic complexity for any given accuracy requirement. This computing complexity, when compared with that of conventional multiplier-based and FFT-based architectures, represents a significant performance improvement. Second, this proposed stochastic-based architecture is highly fault-tolerant because the information to be processed is encoded with a large ensemble of random samples. As such, the local perturbations of its computing accuracy will be dissipated globally, thus becoming inconsequential to the final overall results. Overall, being highly scalable and energy efficient, our stochastic-based convolutional neural network architecture is well-suited for a modular vision engine with the goal of performing real-time detection, recognition and segmentation of mega-pixel images, especially those perception-based computing tasks that are inherently fault-tolerant. We also present a performance comparison between FPGA implementations that use deterministic-based and Stochastic-based architectures.

Keywords: Stochastic convolution; FPGA; convolutional neural network.

DOI: http://dx.doi.org/10.1145/2847263.2847318

t-QuadPlace: Timing Driven Quadratic Placement using Quadrisection Partitioning for FPGAs

Nimish Agashiwala, Satya Prakash Upadhyay, Kia Bazargan, *University of Minnesota Twin Cities*
Contact: agash003@umn.edu

Conventional Simulated Annealing (SA) based placement methods for FPGAs generate high quality results in terms of wirelength and critical path delay, but at a high runtime cost. In case of modern multi-million gate FPGAs, SA-based methods for placement take a large portion of runtime in the FPGA CAD flow. In this paper, we propose a fast and efficient timing driven open-source analytical placement engine targeted at global placement for FPGAs followed by low temperature SA for detailed placement. Our global placement engine uses quadratic programming to minimize wirelength and employs dynamic net weights based on timing criticality between the nets to minimize the critical path delay iteratively. Experimental results show, on average, a 30% runtime improvement for our proposed global placer compared to VPR placer while having approximately the same critical path delay at an expense of 3% larger overall wirelength and channel width after routing with 20 largest MCNC benchmark circuits. The runtime improvement is seen despite the fact that our global placement engine is currently implemented in MATLAB. We expect our runtime to improve notably once we port the code to C. On combining the detailed placement runtime, our proposed approach performs faster for almost all the large circuits having more than 250 blocks. The results show that this placer performs faster global placement across all benchmarks, hence it is easily scalable with modern complex FPGA designs.

Keywords: Placement; FPGA; CAD; Timing Driven; EDA

DOI: http://dx.doi.org/10.1145/2847263.2847306

FPGA'16, February 21–23, 2016, Monterey, CA, USA.
ACM 978-1-4503-3856-1/16/02.

Author Index

Abazari, Amin 195
Adaikkala Raj, Chinnakkannu .. 169
Adler, Michael 128
Agashiwala, Nimish 284
Ahmed, Syed Zahid 274
Aklah, Zeyad 173
Al Kadi, Muhammed 254
Alachiotis, Nikolaos 118
Alawad, Mohammed 283
Alkalay, Shlomi 15
Anderson, Jason 90
Andrews, David 173
Angepat, Hari 15, 283
Babecki, Christopher 275
Baeckler, Gregg 2
Bai, Yu 279
Bazargan, Kia 284
Bellon, Sebastien 279
Bhatia, Dinesh 275, 277
Bhunia, Swarup 275
Blair, Zac 195
Boland, David 244
Bossuet, Lilian 282
Burger, Doug 15
Burovskiy, Pavel 179
Cao, Yu 16
Carrillo, Jorge 4
Caulfield, Adrian 15
Chandra, Vikas 16
Charbon, Edoardo 281
Cheah, Huiyan 274
Chen, Deming 5, 224, 278
Chen, Yao 224
Chen, Yuting 277
Chen, Yu-Ting 281
Cherkaoui, Abdelkarim 282
Cheung, Peter Y K 276
Chi, Yuze 105
Chiou, Derek 15, 148, 283
Chiu, Gordon 159
Chobe, Yogesh 4
Chow, Paul 274
Chowdhury, Sazzadur 278
Chromczak, Jeffrey 159
Chung, Eric 15

Cong, Jason 277, 281
Constantinides, George A. 48,
                            234, 276
Dai, Guohao 105
Dasika, Ganesh 16
Davis, James J. 276
De Micheli, Giovanni 281
DeHon, André 100
Deshpande, Girish 277
Draper, Jeffrey 205
Ebeling, Carl 64
Emer, Joel 128
Fahmy, Suhaib A. 278
Fang, Zhenman 281
Favi, Claudio 279
Firestein, Oren 15
Fleming, Kermin 128, 264
Fraisse, Henri 74
Gaillardon, Pierre-Emmanuel 281
Gaitonde, Dinesh 74
Galloway, David 159
Gamsa, Ben 159
Gao, Xitong 234
Garda, Patrick 274
Ghasemi, Ehsan 274
Gojman, Benjamin 100
Goswami, Pingakshya 275
Grigoras, Paul 179
Guo, Kaiyuan 26
Gurumani, Swathi 5, 224, 278
Hachicha, Khalil 274
Haselman, Michael 15
He, Bingsheng 274
He, Lei 282
Heil, Stephen 15
Hinkfoth, Matthias 275
Hochberg, Sylvain 274
Hoe, James C. 264
Holenstein, Thomas 215
Holohan, Kyle 15
Homulle, Harald 281
How, Dana 64
Hu, Yu 279
Huang, Bo-Yi 42
Huda, Safeen 90

Huebner, Michael 254
Humphrey, Matt 15
Hung, Eddie 276
Hung, Shih-Hao 42
Hwang, James 4
Ibraheem, Mohammed Shaaban . 274
Ienne, Paolo 80
Janssen, Benedikt 254
Jin, Xi 274, 277, 278
Joshi, Abhishek 74
Juhasz, Tamas 15
Kapre, Nachiket 169, 185, 276
Karam, Robert 275
Kastner, Ryan 195
Kathail, Vinod 4
Kaur, Puneet 15
Kaviani, Alireza 74
Keller, Andrew M. 205
Khalid, Mohammed 278
Kogta, Ronak 276
Kumar, Akash 149
Lai, Jinmei 280
Lal, Sundeep 278
Landy, Aaron 282
Lanka, Sitaram 15
Lee, Dajung 195
Lee, David 205
Lei, Jie 277
Levine, Joshua M. 276
Lewis, David 64, 159
Li, Bingzhe 36
Li, Boxun 26
Li, Xiaowei 279
Li, Yunsong 277
Lilja, David J. 36
Lin, Mingjie 279, 283
Linscott, Timothy A. 100
Liu, Xinheng 224
Lo, Daniel 15
Lortkipanidze, Manana 80
Luk, Wayne 179
Ma, Sen 173
Ma, Yufei 16
Macchetti, Marco 279
Malek, Miroslaw 279

Manohararajah, Valavan 159

Marchand, Cedric 282

Massengill, Todd 15

Matai, Janarbek 195

Mathew, Ajit 276

McCloskey, Chase 205

Melber, Joseph 264

Milton, Ian 159

Mohanty, Abinash 16

Najafi, M. Hassan 36

Ng, Harnhua 169

Nguyen, Tan 5, 224

Nguyen, Tuan D. A. 149

Novo, David 80

Nurvitadhi, Eriko 264

Oguntebi, Tayo 111

Olukotun, Kunle 111

Ovtcharov, Kalin 15

Owaida, Muhsen 80

Papamichael, Michael 15

Paul, Johns 274

Peng, Bo 277, 278

Purini, Suresh 276

Püschel, Markus 215

Putnam, Andrew 15

Qian, Wenchao 275

Qiu, Jiantao 26

Ramanathan, Nadesh 48

Regazzoni, Francesco 279

Richmond, Dustin 195

Ridd, Parker 205

Rubin, Raphael 100

Rupnow, Kyle 5, 224, 278

Salomon, Ralf 275

Schmit, Herman 64

Seera, Raja 15

Seo, Jae-sun 16

Serre, François 215

Shanker, Pankaj 3

Sharifymoghaddam, Sayeh 283

Sheikholeslami, Ali 283

Shui, Tom 4

So, Hayden Kwok-Hay 1

Song, Sen 26

Srivastava, Ankur 54

Stitt, Greg 282

Stott, Edward A. 276

Su, Jincheng 138

Suda, Naveen 16

Sun, Welson 4

Tadros, Rimon 15

Tang, Tianqi 26

Tang, Xifan 281

Teo, Kirvy 169

Thong, Jason 15

Ting, Li 276

Tsai, Min-Yu 42

Tu, Chia-Heng 42

Upadhyay, Satya Prakash 284

Van Dyken, John 159

Vanderhoek, Tim 159

Visser, Stefan 281

Vrudhula, Sarma 16

Wang, Chuanjun 278

Wang, Jian 280

Wang, Jie 26

Wang, Tianqi 277, 278

Wang, Yu 26, 105, 264

Wang, Zeke 274

Wawrzynek, John 1

Weisz, Gabriel 118, 264

Wickerson, John 48, 234

Wijaya, Harri 276

Winterstein, Felix 48, 128

Wirthlin, Michael J. 205

Woods, Lisa 15

Wu, Qiongzhi 195

Xiang, Tian 274

Xu, Ningyi 26

Yang, Fan 138

Yang, Hsin-Jung 128

Yang, Huazhong 26, 105

Yang, Liwei 278

Yang, Meng 280

Yang, Zhen 280

Yang, Zhiyuan 54

Yanghua, Que 169

Yao, Song 26

Ye, Deheng 185

Ye, Jing 279

Yu, Jincheng 26

Yu, Yunxuan 282

Zeng, Xuan 138

Zereen, Sabrina 278

Zgheib, Grace 80

Zha, Daolu 274

Zhang, Sizhuo 283

Zhang, Wei 274

Zhou, Dian 138

Zhou, Erjin 26

Zhou, Peipei 281

www.ingramcontent.com/pod-product-compliance
Lightning Source LLC
LaVergne TN
LVHW060137070326
832902LV00018B/2826